MW00624603

Captive
University

★

The Soviet-
ization of
East German,
Czech, and
Polish Higher
Education

★

1945–1956

★

CAPTIVE
UNIVERSITY

THE SOVIET-
IZATION OF
★ EAST GERMAN,
★ CZECH, AND
★ POLISH
HIGHER
EDUCATION,

1945–1956

JOHN CONNELLY

THE UNIVERSITY
OF NORTH
CAROLINA
PRESS

CHAPEL HILL AND
LONDON

★

© 2000
The University
of North
Carolina Press

★

All rights
reserved

★

Set in Minion
by Tseng Information
Systems

★

Manufactured
in the
United States
of America

★

The paper in this book
meets the guidelines for
permanence and durability
of the Committee
on Production Guidelines
for Book Longevity
of the Council
on Library Resources.

Library of Congress
Cataloging-in-Publication Data
Connelly, John.
Captive university : the
Sovietization of East German,
Czech, and Polish higher
education, 1945–1956 / by John
Connelly.
    p.   cm.
Includes bibliographical
references and index.
ISBN 0-8078-2555-7
(cloth : alk. paper) —
ISBN 0-8078-4865-4
(pbk. : alk. paper)
1. Higher education and state—
Germany (East)   2. Higher
education and state—Poland.
3. Higher education and state—
Czechoslovakia.   4. Communist
education—Germany (East)
5. Communist education—
Poland.   6. Communist
education—Czechoslovakia.
I. Title.
LC178.G29 C66   2000
379.431—dc21   00-030262

★

Portions of this book
appeared previously,
in somewhat different form,
in "Students, Workers,
and Social Change:
The Limits of Czech Stalinism,"
Slavic Review 56, no. 2 (1997):
307–35, and are reprinted here
with permission of the
American Association for
the Advancement
of Slavic Studies.

★

04 03 02 01 00
5 4 3 2 1

FOR MY PARENTS

CONTENTS

This study has its origins in several seminars in Communist politics and societies taken at the University of Michigan in Ann Arbor some fifteen years ago. At that time the postwar period was the domain of political science, and in centers for Russian and East European Studies the former were pursued almost to the exclusion of the latter. Indeed, if one was interested in the stalinist period,* there seemed practically no reason to study the separate histories of the societies of Eastern Europe, for as we learned from one Sovietologist, if "one knew what was happening in the Soviet Union, one pretty much knew what was happening in Eastern Europe."

I am deeply grateful to two scholars who nevertheless insisted upon the diversity of the region: Professors Zvi Gitelman and Roman Szporluk. It was in a seminar of Professor Szporluk that the present project first took shape. In his office one day in January 1986, Professor Szporluk suggested to me the unusual promise held by comparative studies of stalinist Eastern Europe. Because Moscow attempted to enforce uniform implementation of its models throughout the region, it established a "control" for politics and isolated other explanations for political development. Studies of divergence in the stalinist period would therefore offer fresh perspectives on the societies of Eastern Europe—in particular, how their varying political cultures influenced processes of Sovietization. From personal experience, Professor Szporluk knew that these societies had not been made uniform, even at the height of political terror. The institution we imagined for focused comparison was the university: a staging ground for social and ideological change, and a place that the Communist Parties in question had to dominate. There should have been no important differences in the histories of East European universities under stalinism.

Alas, such a project was too grand for a seminar, and my paper was limited to a review of the sparse literature on Polish higher education. I discovered the following summer in Warsaw that for the time being archival restrictions prevented investigations of postwar Polish history, and the envisioned project therefore seemed undoable.

Several years later, while pursuing doctoral work in German history at Harvard University, I had the good fortune to find the archives of East Germany at least partially open to research on the postwar period. Thanks to

---

* This study abides by Padraic Kenney's suggestion that "stalinist" be written with a small "s" to emphasize system rather than person. See Kenney, *Rebuilding Poland,* 4.

the intercession of Professor Martin Guntau of Rostock, I was permitted to work in the Rostock University as well as the Mecklenburg State Archive in Schwerin in the summer of 1989. The officially approved project title read "The Assistance of the Soviet Military Administration in Denazifying the Universities of the Soviet Zone of Occupation." I would like also to thank the then director of the Rostock archive, Frau Steffen, as well as Frau Kusch and Dr. Rainer Mühle, for generosity shown to an "US-Amerikaner" behind a still intact Berlin Wall.

Soon that wall opened, as did the archives of Eastern Europe. The comparative project became a possibility. I was fortunate to have in Charles S. Maier a *Doktorvater* whose attention was not consumed by the sensations of the moment. Far from discouraging so imprudently broad a topic, he pushed me to expand my questions, along with the time horizon. All of this while encouraging a respect for the limits of historical understanding! I hope that he sees at least some of his own ambition and modesty reflected in this work. As he predicted, the enterprise has taken a decade, almost evenly.

In the summer of 1990 I embarked upon almost two years of research, which would have been impossible without the generous assistance of a number of institutions. In conducting research in Germany in 1990–91 I benefited from funding of the Center for European Studies and the Sheldon Foundation at Harvard University, as well as the International Researches and Exchange Board. Research in Czechoslovakia in the summer and fall of 1991 was supported by a Krupp Foundation Fellowship of the Center for European Studies at Harvard University, and archival stays in Warsaw and Kraków in the 1991–92 academic year by a Fulbright-Hays Fellowship. A writing grant of the American Council of Learned Societies was of tremendous help in bringing the dissertation to a conclusion in 1994.

The staffs of the archives I used were generous beyond description, permitting me to amass enough material for ten dissertations, while themselves suffering cutbacks and having to relocate voluminous collections. In Germany I worked in the university archives in Rostock, Berlin, Greifswald, and Leipzig; the Federal Archive in Potsdam; the former Central Party Archive of the SED (SAPMO-BA), now in the Federal Archive; and the state archives in Weimar and Schwerin. I owe particular thanks to Drs. Klaus Oldenhage and Wolfgang Merker of Potsdam, as well as Volker Lange, Anneliese Mueller, and Solweig Nestler of the SAPMO.

In the Czech lands my work took me first to the former Central Committee Archive, where I benefited from the expertise of Drs. Nosková and Bilimsky. For assistance in gaining admission to this archive I am indebted to Drs. Vilém Prečan and Josef Opatrný of the Institute for Contemporary History of the Czech Academy of Sciences. Thanks also to the staffs of the

Archive of Charles University and the Czech (then Czechoslovak) Academy of Science, two exceedingly pleasant places of research, and especially to Drs. Zdeněk Pousta, Josef Hanzal, Karel Litsch, Miroslav Kunštát, Michal Svatoš, Petr Svobodný, Blanka Zilynská, Radka Edederová, Antonín Kostlán, and Hana Barvíková. Former university archive director Professor Jan Havránek, known to generations of North American historians for his broad erudition, has given of himself so generously and influenced my thinking so deeply that it is impossible for me to conceive of this project without him. He has been an inspiration in every sense of the word.

In the ancient university town of Kraków, Poland, I likewise had tremendous good fortune in the archives of the university and academies of sciences. I am especially thankful to Rita Majkowska, Piotr Milczanowski, Ewa Dziurzyńska, Marta Płatek, Tomasz Filip, Marzena Włodek (Polish Academy of Sciences in Kraków); Leszek Hajdukiewicz, Urszula Perkowska, Wanda Baczkowska, Mieczysław Barcik, Danuta Grodowska-Kulińska, Adam Cieślak, Helena Kręt, Halina Zwolska (Archive of the Jagiellonian University); and Anna Kozłowska, Ewa Malicka, Iwona Bator, Elżbieta Burda, Zbigniew Koziński, Lucyna Nowak, Zdisław Pietrzyk, Anna Sobańska, Ryszard Tatarzyński, Marian Zwierczan, and Teresa Wojciechowska (Jagiellonian University Library). For assistance in the State Archive in Warsaw I would like to thank Edward Kołodziej.

The many contemporaries who shared reminiscences with me are listed in the bibliography, but I would like in particular to thank Professors Stanisław Grodziski, Marian Zgórniak, and Stanisław Grzybowski for taking time to explain to me their milieu. During my first reconnoitering in Poland in 1986 I met Poland's unparalleled authority on scholarship under socialism, Professor Piotr Hübner, now of Toruń University. Professor Hübner has selflessly shared with me the fruits of his many years of labor in state and Party archives, and has enriched my thinking on Polish scholarship in more ways than I can catalog.

Archives are almost as valuable for the people one meets in lunchrooms and cafés as for the folders one receives in reading rooms. In Potsdam and Berlin I learned much from Mitchell G. Ash, David Pike, Kees Gispen, Roland Köhler, and Anna-Sabine Ernst; in Prague from Igor Lukes and Karel Bartošek. For conversations and advice extended beyond archival premises I am also grateful to Timothy Garton Ash, Bärbel Baltes, Stanisław Baranczak, Lewis Bateman, Vladimír Čermak, Ladislav Čerych, Grzegorz Ekiert, Jan Foitzik, Geoffrey Giles, Daniel Jonah Goldhagen, L. E. Gorizontov, Jan T. Gross, Michael Grüttner, William W. Hagen, Anke Huschner, Konrad H. Jarausch, Eva Jonas, Karel Kaplan, Padraic Kenney, Krystyna Kersten, Laurie Koloski, Jeffrey Kopstein, Anthony Levitas, Jan Lewandowski,

Paweł Machcewicz, Pavel Machonin, Carol and Czesław Miłosz, Władysław Miodunka, G. P. Murashko, A. F. Noskova, Derek Paton, Miloslav Petrusek, Adam Podgórecki, Ethan Pollock, Witold Rodkiewicz, Helmut Smith, Justin l'Anson Sparks, Anna Spiss, A. S. Stykalin, Teresa Suleja, Andrzej Zięba, and Jan-Christoph Zoels.

Both before and after I completed the dissertation several institutions invited me to share in their intellectual and social lives. At Harvard I took advantage of the generosity of the Center for European Studies and Lowell House, and am deeply indebted to Abby Collins, Guido Goldman, and Stanley Hoffman as well as Masters Mary Lee and William Bossert for creating ideal conditions for graduate learning. After completing the dissertation I was invited to partake in several joint research projects, for which I am grateful to Gerald D. Feldman, Victoria Bonnell, Manfred Heinemann, Dieter Hoffmann, Kristie Macrakis, Jürgen Kocka, Michael David-Fox, and György Péteri. Thanks as well to Professor Kocka for introducing me to Ralph Jessen, who is in his context what Piotr Hübner and Jan Havránek are in theirs: the leading authority on academia. The reader will see in my notes how great is my debt to all three. I also benefited from research visits to the Institut für Zeithistorische Forschung in Potsdam and the Herder Institut in Marburg, and would like to express appreciation to their directors, respectively Christoph Klessmann and Eduard Mühle.

Generous support of the German Marshall Fund, the American Council of Learned Societies, and the Centers for Studies in Higher Education, Slavic and East European, and German and European Studies, and the Council on Research at the University of California at Berkeley permitted me to expand my original research to include Soviet perspectives, as well as more careful consideration of the development of the professoriates. The Spencer Foundation supported not only leave time for writing, but also several months' research in Poland in the fall of 1998, for which I am profoundly thankful. For research assistance in Moscow I would like to thank Marina Dobronovskaia.

Since joining the history faculty at Berkeley this work has profited immensely from conversations with colleagues, especially Margaret Lavinia Anderson, Andrew Barshay, Gerald D. Feldman, Thomas Brady, Paula Fass, David Frick, Sheldon Rothblatt, Peter Sahlins, and Irvin Scheiner. I am particularly indebted to those colleagues who read the entire manuscript: Reggie Zelnik, Nicholas V. Riasanovsky, and Yuri Slezkine. Norman M. Naimark of Stanford University and Mitchell G. Ash of the University of Vienna read the manuscript for the UNC Press. They encouraged me to make much more of my work than I had intended, and I am deeply grateful to both. I am also obliged to Alexander Vucinich for reading the sections on Russian higher education. Shawn Salmon, Klara Schneider, and Daniel Rolde lent invaluable assistance in the final stages of preparing the manuscript for press.

Special thanks to my wife, Fiona, for the faith and love that make my work possible. My deepest debt of gratitude is alluded to in the dedication.

This book consists of three parts that build upon each other, but also can be read independently, according to individual taste. For example, readers with less interest in administrative history might move directly to part II. I ask indulgence for the many names in the text that may be difficult to pronounce. They are a necessary component of an argument on continuity in three professorial communities; for readers familiar with one of these contexts the mere mention of many names will be highly instructive. References to biographical sources are provided to permit further background reading.

A few terms appear frequently in the text that are not often encountered in the English language. Above all is "higher school," which is used to mean "institution of higher education" and corresponds to the German *Hochschule,* Czech *vysoká škola,* or Russian VUZ. The text also speaks frequently of "philosophical faculties," which correspond to faculties or schools of arts and sciences at North American universities. An attempt has been made to streamline the usage of academic titles. Each of these countries had a similar hierarchy: at the top "ordinary" professors, next "extraordinary" professors, then docents, adjuncts, assistants. I have translated these titles into more English-sounding equivalents: "ordinary" appears as "full" and "extraordinary" as "associate" professors; "adjuncts" are "adjunct professors," and "assistants" are "assistant professors." Full-time faculty members with a second dissertation (habilitation) — *Dozenten, docenci, docenti* — are called docents. In the Central European system, in general only the ordinary and extraordinary professors and docents had what we refer to as tenure. An assistant lived in great dependence upon his or her professor, who was usually a chair holder or institute director. The Polish *zastępca profesora* is translated as "acting professor." Occasionally the words "college" or "campus" are inserted in their American senses in order to diversify usage, though strictly speaking they have no Central European equivalents. When the word "science" appears alone, it has the narrower English connotation of hard sciences. The broader Central and East European *Wissenschaft, věda,* or *nauka* are rendered as "scholarship."

The term "worker-peasant" is a direct translation from Central European parlance, and indicates the blue-collar labor force — in both city and countryside — and its children. The category may seem crude, but it was clearly distinct from the professional and entrepreneurial classes that had dominated higher education under the old regime. "Workers" and "peasants" thus denote the underprivileged. Courses set up to give people of this group remedial preparation for university are called "worker-peasant faculties," or "worker courses." These terms are used interchangeably, to indicate the comparable institution in each country. Similarly "worker student" is often used as a synonym for "worker-peasant student.".

Over the course of research, I have faced two opposing forms of criticism, one deriving from the comparative nature of the project, the other from its modest revisionist claims. Before the conclusion of archival work, I was routinely informed by experts in the field that no significant differences existed between the cases studied, and therefore comparison would be fruitless. "Das war damals doch alles ganz gleich!" (Everything back then was precisely the same) were the words with which an esteemed German expert in Czech history dismissed the project in 1993. Then, ironically, after publication of my findings, a criticism emerged that I was creating a "straw man" of uniformity! Whatever their judgment on this score, I hope readers will agree that there is much to be learned by investigating images of uniformity—illusory or not.

The following abbreviations are used in the text. For additional abbreviations used in the notes, see pages 293–95.

ABF	Worker-Peasant Faculty (East Germany)
ADK	graduate of worker course (Czech lands)
AZWM	Academic Union of Fighting Youth (Poland)
CC	Central Committee
CDU	Christian Democratic Union (Germany)
CPSU	Communist Party of the Soviet Union
ČSM	Union of Czechoslovak Socialist Youth
ČSR	Czechoslovak Republic
ČSSR	Czechoslovak Socialist Republic
DK	worker course (Czech lands)
DVV	German Central Education Administration
FDGB	Free German Trade Union
FDJ	Free German Youth
GDR	German Democratic Republic
IKKN	Institute for Training Scientific Cadres (Poland)
INS	Institute of Social Sciences (Poland)
KPD	Communist Party of Germany
KSČ	Communist Party of Czechoslovakia
KUL	Catholic University of Lublin
LDP	Liberal Democratic Party of Germany
mgr.	MA (Master of Arts, Poland)
Narkompros	People's Commissariat of Enlightenment (Soviet Union)
NEP	New Economic Policy (Soviet Union)
NKVD	People's Commissariat of Internal Affairs (Soviet Union)
NSDAP	National Socialist German Workers' Party
PPR	Polish Workers' Party
PPS	Polish Socialist Party
PSL	Polish Peasant Party
PZPR	Polish United Workers' Party
rabfak	workers' faculty (Russia)
RIAS	Radio in the American Sector (Berlin)
ROH	Revolutionary Trade Unions (Czechoslovakia)
SBZ	Soviet Zone of Occupation (Germany)
SD	Security Service of the Nazi Party

SED	Socialist Unity Party of Germany
SPD	Social Democratic Party of Germany
St.B.	State Security (Czechoslovakia)
Stasi	Ministry for State Security (East Germany)
SVA	Soviet Military Administration
SVAG	Soviet Military Administration in Germany
UB	Security Office (Poland)
UJ	Jagiellonian University (Kraków)
UMCS	Marie Curie-Sklodowska University, Lublin
ÚPV	Office of the President (Czechoslovakia)
UZZ	University of the Western Lands (Poland)
VOKS	All-Union Society for Cultural Relations with Foreign Countries (Soviet Union)
VTUZ	institution of technical higher education (Soviet Union)
VUZ	institution of higher education (Soviet Union)
Wici	Peasant Youth Movement (Poland)
ZAMP	Union of Polish Students
ZMP	Union of Polish Youth

In the fall of 1948, the Communist Party of the Soviet Union proclaimed its lessons of history universally valid and began to impose its system of political organization upon the ruling Communist Parties of Eastern Europe.[1] A process of duplication commenced that was unprecedented; within a few years, a once multifarious scenery of cultures and histories between Elbe and Bug resembled a belt of miniature Soviet Unions, each with collectivized agriculture, steel and coal industries, broad alleyways of socialist-realist communal housing, marching columns of uniformed youths, omnipresent banners of little Stalins like Walter Ulbricht, Klement Gottwald, or Bolesław Bierut. Western observers were stunned at the apparent totality and uniformity of transformation. In 1959 Zbigniew K. Brzezinski wrote that "the repetition of the Soviet experience of the thirties would be bound to create an environment essentially like the Soviet environment."[2] A central role in bringing Soviet models to Eastern Europe was attributed to Soviet advisers, to whom, in the words of Joseph Rothschild, East European Communists owed "absolute obedience."[3]

Such visions of an unimpeded and complete Sovietization of Eastern Europe continue to shape the historical imagination.[4] Scholars have long recognized a relative openness in the early postwar period, but the stalinist years (1948–54) are still treated as an "ice age," akin to a natural catastrophe, when the Party/state shaped dormant societies as it saw fit, without regard for their separate histories and cultures.[5] A partial exception has been recognized for Poland, with its relatively mild antichurch policies and inner-Party purges, and sluggish collectivization drive.[6] Yet a leading scholar has recently described Polish society as having "nothing to place in the way of constructing . . . the Soviet model of a totalitarian state . . . in all spheres of state, public, and national life."[7]

In their depictions of social reality in stalinist Eastern Europe, historians have largely reproduced perspectives of the 1950s. To contemporaries, the region indeed appeared uniform. In the spring of 1952, after visiting construction sites, department stores, universities, and other public spaces in Warsaw, Gdańsk, and Wrocław, Victor Klemperer, specialist in Romance literature at Halle University in East Germany, and a diary writer of unusual discernment, felt moved to coin the term "uniformitas sowjetica postbellica." After sitting for three hours on the podium of Warsaw's May Day parade, the septuagenarian noted: "this was the dreariest, most uniform, most orchestrated part of our trip to Poland. I survived it. But what did I get out of it? The most complete sense of *uniformitas* imaginable."[8]

1

Historians have had little occasion or reason to question such images. On the one hand, they have lacked competing perspectives; and, on the other, they, like inhabitants of the region, remain dazzled by the enormity of state terror in the early 1950s, which claimed victims even among the Party's truest supporters. Regimes capable of such extreme violence appeared unrestricted in their powers, and even if the Soviet system was not duplicated to the last detail, there seemed to be no task of substance that East European Communist Parties could not accomplish in the same way.

This book questions such received wisdom, and attempts to show that behind a facade of uniformity separate national traditions continued through the stalinist period in much of the "northern tier" of East Central Europe, creating different contexts for politics and for societal experience. It explores policies adopted toward a single, central institution, the university, and portrays those years as an episode in the histories of three peoples — the Czechs, East Germans, and Poles. Universities were key to making the states in which these peoples lived socialist because they reproduced not only national histories and ideologies, but also elites, or, in the words of East German ideological chief Kurt Hager, "commanders."[9]

More important, however, than contesting inherited notions of uniformity is learning from differences — differences in the application of Soviet models in East Central Europe. The primary goal of this book is to reveal aspects of historical development that would not be apparent if these three societies were examined separately. In their slavish duplication of Soviet experience, East European stalinists unwittingly created a veritable laboratory for such comparative study: the tremendous pressures for uniformity in effect "controlled" for politics, helping isolate certain "variables" that have suffered neglect in studies of political development — in particular, social structure and political culture.[10] As we shall see, the institutions and programs created in these years in East European higher education were nearly identical; what varied were the people who operated within them. Depending on national environment and sociocultural milieu, they had differing attitudes about the value of education, and about central organizing concepts of this period — the state, in particular, but also Soviet-style socialism.

The diverse experiences of stalinism that are the focus of this book in many ways prefigured the widely divergent paths East European societies took in the post-stalinist era. Higher-education policies of the stalinist years created preconditions for the behavior of intelligentsias in the Czech lands, East Germany, and Poland during the crises that periodically shook the region after 1956. This view challenges the recent interpretation of the post-stalinist period by Grzegorz Ekiert, which stipulates that "cross-national differences in the region and distinct characteristics of different state-socialist regimes were the result of successive political crises and complex responses of the party-states, regional power, and actors within society to these crises." The view suggested here is the opposite: namely, that the propensity to crisis grew out of conditions created in the early postwar years, which themselves grew out of specific national circumstances. The soundness of the socialist edifice depended upon its foundations.[11]

The lessons of Soviet history in regard to university education were clear. Leading representatives of "bourgeois" ideology, especially in the social sciences, humanities, and law, had to be denied contact with students. After the Bolshevik Revolution law faculties in Russia were closed, a number of professors dismissed, and in their place "social science faculties" opened, with "a strong dose of Red Professors."[12] In 1922 some 100 to 150 "anti-Soviet lawyers, literati, and professors" were deported from the Soviet Union.[13] The breaks in the social sciences were deepened in the Stalin revolution of the late 1920s and early 1930s, when the very existence of universities was called into question.

After universities had been emptied of enemies, they had to be filled with ostensible supporters: students from underprivileged social strata who would reward the regime with loyalty for upward social mobility. During the early breakthrough periods in Soviet history, preference was given to students of "worker and peasant background." Special courses—called *rabfaki* (worker faculties)—were set up to give such students remedial instruction for universities, and their numbers rose from a small fraction to over half the student body. They were schooled in Marxism-Leninism, which supposedly channeled the energies of class consciousness. Central direction of all these policies was placed in the Communist Party's Central Committee.[14]

To contemporaries, the higher-education systems that emerged by 1953 in the Czech lands, East Germany, and Poland appeared to be faithful reproductions of Soviet models. In each case the Communist Party Central Committee supervised university operations through a Soviet-style Ministry of Higher Education; at universities Soviet-style "prorectors" were implanted to coordinate "schooling" in Marxism-Leninism; students, who had previously been able to choose the lectures they would attend, were now subjected to planned curricula and obligatory classroom attendance. They prepared for batteries of Soviet-style compulsory examinations from textbooks translated from the Russian—in practically every field. In order to create a socialist intelligentsia, student admissions favored "worker-peasant" students and courses were established to help prepare workers for higher education who had not finished high school: "preparation courses" (*kursy przygotowawcze*) in Poland, "worker courses" (*dělnické kursy*) in the Czech lands, and worker-peasant faculties (*Arbeiter- und Bauernfakultäten*) in East Germany. The teaching staffs had changed too: in each place prominent representatives of "bourgeois" disciplines such as sociology or modern philosophy had been removed, and colleagues that remained behind were made to lecture and teach according to detailed, state-approved study programs. Universities increasingly became teaching colleges, as research facilities were shifted to Soviet-style academies of science. Dozens of Soviet professors toured the region, helping turn theory into practice.

Yet when one uses sources that have become available since 1989 to examine how these systems actually functioned, one notices unexpected divergences — before, during, and after the stalinist period. In East Germany wartime migrations and a radical denazification caused an unparalleled break of the professoriate in 1945. Over 80 percent of the teaching staff active at the war's conclusion did not continue, and only in the mid-1960s did the professoriates of the six universities in East Germany again reach full strength. In the Czech lands and Poland, by contrast, the old professoriates freely reconstituted themselves after the war and reached prewar strength within a few years. Yet in 1948 their paths diverged. After the February coup in Prague revolutionary action committees, led by Communist students, purged the Czech professoriate of alleged reactionaries. Especially hard hit were the social sciences; of several dozen professors teaching law in 1948 in Brno and Prague, only six remained by 1951. In Poland, by contrast, no such purge occurred, and though some professors were retired early and several others were limited in their teaching, practically none were dismissed. Even in philosophy, law, and history, fields central to propagating the new ideology, old, non-Communist professors continued teaching through the stalinist period.

In student policies the Communist Parties under study also achieved differing results. Though each proclaimed the need to recast the student body in more proletarian forms, only in Poland and East Germany did the numbers of working-class and peasant students approach the proportion of their classes in society as a whole. The three parties had faced similar challenges. People of working-class or peasant background were drastically underrepresented in the upper tiers of the educational system throughout the region. In 1935–36, 9.9 percent of freshmen at Polish universities were of worker background, and 11.7 percent of peasant background.[15] As late as 1948, only 7 percent of Czech university students were of working-class origin.[16] In 1932, 3 percent of Germany's students came from workers' families.[17] The three societies under discussion had comparable proportions of manual workers, as well as comparable proportions of university students per age cohort. The major difference among them was the large rural sector in Poland.[18] Yet in the Czech lands, at the moment of greatest success in student admissions policies, working-class and peasant students constituted 42 percent of the student body, in contrast to almost 60 percent in Poland and East Germany.

The Polish and Czech Communist Parties thus diverged in major ways from the minimal expectations upon Soviet-type societies, and they did so in a time when Communists were losing their lives for minor disagreements with Soviet policy. In terms of the ultimate aim of creating loyal and competent elites, these divergences had important consequences: Poland's Communist Party relied on "bourgeois" professors to transmit important ideological messages to the younger generation, and universities therefore proved unfit to carry through an ideological transformation of that country's elites. Czech elites continued to be drawn predominantly from the middle classes and were never made grateful to the Party for their stations in life. They saw their incomes decline relative to those of the working class and were a perennially dissatisfied social stratum. In both Poland and the Czech lands the university-trained intelligentsias, and especially students, acted as destabilizing forces throughout the post-stalinist era, much in contrast to their counterparts in East Germany. In Warsaw of 1968 or 1980–81, and in Prague of 1968 or 1989, students played pivotal roles in movements for reform and revolution. If students filled the streets of East Germany, it was to display support for the regime, even as late as October 1989, when other East Germans were chiseling at the foundations of power.[19]

An investigation of these divergences probes the limits of totalitarian rule in Eastern Europe and helps elucidate the factors that enabled Czechs, Poles, and East Germans to define and maintain their identities in differing ways. Each of the three parts of this study explores one sort of limitation to the Sovietization of higher education in East Central Europe: first, inefficiencies and contradictions in the mechanisms of imperial rule; second, political and intellectual culture, especially in Poland; and third, social structure, especially in the Czech lands.

The book's first part describes Central European and Soviet systems of higher education and tells how the structures of the latter replaced the structures of the former in the late 1940s and early 1950s. To what extent did Soviet officials actually supervise the transfer of their system to Eastern Europe? How may the distrust and mismanagement of an overly centralized system have impeded the duplication of Soviet models in Eastern Europe? It is hoped that this discussion will lend greater precision to the term "Sovietization," which is commonly used to describe the general processes leading to the emergence of Soviet-type societies, with little attention to the exact relations between native and Soviet Communists, or to the exact extent of duplication.

The second and third parts of the book examine how Czech, East German, and Polish societies shaped the power of would-be totalitarian states.

Part II shows how a relatively cohesive milieu of Polish professors, united by political and intellectual culture, restricted the abilities of the state to transform it and thus also the university. Milieu is understood as a self-reproducing social unit, with its own values, habits, and demands for loyalty.[20] This section of the book pays special attention to questions of legitimacy and moral capital, and how these quantities shifted according to professors' behavior under the rule of German National Socialism.[21] Collusion with the Nazi regime had robbed the German professoriate of sources of inner strength with which to oppose the Socialist Unity Party of Germany (SED). In the Czech case, not collaboration with Nazi occupiers but rather wartime passivity left professors lacking the will to oppose communism. The war had acted to shift hierarchies at Czech universities and transferred legitimacy to students, who had been at the forefront of anti-German resistance. In Poland, professors were recognized to have accrued moral capital during the war. They had organized underground cultural resistance to the Nazi occupiers and, like Czech students, had paid for their activities with concentration camp sentences. At a deeper level, this section argues that national political culture placed the Polish professoriate in natural opposition to the new regime: for Polish professors, unlike Czech or German colleagues, a socialist state imported from Russia seemed profoundly threatening to national identity.[22]

Part III examines how inherited social structures shaped Communists' abilities to transform student bodies, and thus make future elites. In the Polish case, social structure aided political program. The leadership desperately needed well-trained managerial and technical elites and found a natural constituency in the country dwellers who were drawn into the cities in the early 1950s. Taking students of working-class or peasant background into an expanding educational system was therefore not an insuperable challenge. Its Czech counterpart, by contrast, inherited a modern society with large and differentiated elites, as well as an extensive system of higher education. There was no need to expand universities, but the Party faced the challenge of forcing downward mobility among the middle-class clients of higher education in order to fill universities with children of working-class background. The problem was that workers lived in highly intact and self-confident milieus and hesitated to enter the foreign environments of university campuses.[23] In this case East Germany serves as a foil: it was likewise a highly developed society, but the leadership nevertheless managed to persuade workers to enter the unaccustomed setting of higher education.

Limitations to stalinism in Eastern Europe have received relatively little attention from social scientists.[24] The decisive role of Soviet advisers was considered axiomatic in early studies of Sovietization; because of lack of sources, however, it was not possible to examine ways in which native Communists were entrusted with "Sovietizing" their own societies. In recent years a breakthrough has been achieved by Norman Naimark in his *The Russians in Germany,* which stresses the initial openness and the complex evolution of Soviet policies in Germany.[25] A careful study of the following period has been completed for Czechoslovakia by the leading Czech expert Karel Kaplan; it demonstrates the presence of a multitude of Soviet advisers throughout the Czech government and Party, especially in the police and army, but also in various ministries, including the Ministry of Education. Kaplan does not actually study the outcome of these advisers' work, however. Russian historians who have dealt with this topic have cast doubt on the extent of their influence in cultural affairs.[26] In particular, Russian historian A. S. Stykalin has shown the practical difficulties encountered by Soviet agents of the All-Union Society for Cultural Relations with Foreign Countries (VOKS) in their endeavors to spread Soviet culture abroad, deriving from indecision, fear, lack of translators and other experts, and bureaucratic infighting. It proved safer to leave matters as sensitive as culture in the hands of trusted native Communists.[27]

The issue of cultural or structural resistance to stalinism in Eastern Europe has likewise been little investigated. One rare attempt to expose the diversities of East European stalinism — especially in rates of industrialization — seeks explanations exclusively in the "reluctance" or "resistance" of native Communist elites to adopt Soviet-style socialism.[28] Leading experts on higher education in the region have concentrated on official declarations and duplication of institutions and conclude that Sovietization was practically unimpeded.[29] The few historians who have investigated limitations to Sovietization emanating from society have focused on workers' resistance, a topic that is well developed in the parallel historiographies of Soviet and Nazi totalitarianisms.[30] Jiří Pernes and Andrew Port have rescued from obscurity workers' demonstrations that took place in Brno and in the Wismut mines in 1951,[31] and Padraic Kenney and Jeffrey Kopstein have shown how workers in Poland and East Germany forced their respective regimes to withdraw from confrontation, and thus placed early limitations on wage policies.[32] Within the massive research devoted to the GDR in the past decade a number of important studies have emerged on opposition and resistance, partly of workers, but also of farmers, physicians, and engineers.[33]

These single-country inquiries have helped chip away at the monolith of East European stalinism, but much remains to be learned about the region as a whole. Far more is known about East Germany than about Poland or Czechoslovakia, not to mention the lands farther south and east. Why did the countries of the region take separate paths? Why was Poland regularly shaken by upheaval and East Germany relatively stable? Why was East Germany more permeated by Communist ideology than Poland? Why were Czech students perennially at the forefront of antiregime protest, while Czech workers remained relatively quiescent?

Comparative study shows not only that societies in East Central Europe differed markedly and continued to differ markedly through the stalinist period, but also that the states in the region—which had grown out of local contexts—diverged in their approaches to society. The role of the state as a sovereign agency is often underplayed in social history, as stories are told from previously neglected perspectives. But just as society proved capable of reacting to challenges from above, so did the state often anticipate and react to challenges from below. This fact is readily visible at universities, places where both students and professors, but also state functionaries, had clear interests and competing agendas.

The university is therefore an opportune place not only to explore the diversity of a region thought to be uniform, but also to consider unexplored continuities and discontinuities in the dynamic of state-society relations, and thus to suggest modifications in the periodization of postwar history. The general tendency in describing postwar Eastern Europe has been to connect single-country histories to the timeline of international events. After the relatively open immediate postwar years, the Tito-Stalin split of 1948 caused a renunciation of "national" roads to socialism throughout the East European countries dominated by the Soviet Union, accompanied by purgings of the Party apparatus. The following four to five years witnessed the apparently identical social, economic, and cultural policies of high stalinism. Stalin's death in 1953 initiated a "thaw" in Eastern Europe, with greater room for internal criticism, and the gradual emergence of more liberal groupings in the Communist Parties, as Soviet and East European leaderships sought new bearings within a Marxist-Leninist framework. Khrushchev's secret speech three years later shook the faith of the Party cadre to its core and seemed to presage a return to national roads to socialism. Such hopes were shattered with the crushing of the Hungarian Revolution in November 1956, and the system as a whole found temporary stability as local "neo-stalinist" apparatuses asserted dominance over "revisionists"—that is, proponents of a more flexible Marxism.[34]

Viewed from the perspective of university education, all three cases confirm the general accuracy of this received account but also reveal important continuities through the stalinist years, according to local dynamics. As early as 1946–47 certain enduring features of higher-education policy were visible in each place. In Poland the leadership had already proclaimed its intention to engage in broadly based cooperation with the professoriate, regardless of field. The tasks of rebuilding Poland simply seemed too huge to permit the sacrifice of experts, even in the humanities. This strategy of compromise accumulated momentum, and was maintained, despite changing laws and institutional forms.

In East Germany, by contrast, both Soviet occupation authorities and German Communists recognized early the potential of higher education for creating politically loyal elites. In the social sciences, eschewing compromise, they embarked on a program of purging and student selection as early as 1946, through the twin tools of denazification and "democratization," that is, preferences for social background in student admissions. The SED inducted worker-peasant students into its ranks, and no other Party so skillfully combined the discipline of organizational membership with the incentives of upward social mobility. In contrast to comrades in Poland or the Czech lands, East German Communists insisted from the start on holding government offices relevant to education, whether in the *Land* (state) ministries or in the central administration in Berlin.

In the Czech lands the Communist Party achieved an impressive election victory in May 1946, but chose to forfeit influence in educational policy by ceding the Education Ministry to the rival National Socialists.[35] KSČ intelligentsia policy became one of neglect, always lagging behind the policies of fraternal parties in such areas as worker training courses or political indoctrination; and, despite pervasive organizational presence, the KSČ never achieved a decisive breakthrough toward the creation of loyal elites. Surprisingly, Czech Communists did not purge the state education bureaucracy until 1950–51 or assert central Party control at universities until after 1953. They behaved much like the spoiler state described by Jan T. Gross—skilled at denying, inept in creating power.[36]

Because of the Polish Party's long-range strategy of compromise, and the relative intactness of the professoriate, Polish universities were poised to take advantage of the opportunities that emerged in the uncertain time after Stalin's death in 1953. Several "excesses"—for example, in the discrimination against "bourgeois" students, in the overloading of lesson plans, in the banishment of "reactionary" scholars to universities many hours from their homes—were now quietly reversed. Although journals in the social sciences and humanities still presented a predominantly Marxist point of view, room now opened within and without Marxism for critical perspectives. Forces from above and below melted the stalinist ice and came together in 1956, a year in which the political constellation in Poland irrevocably changed. Certain intellectual freedoms were reclaimed that the state no longer challenged. Professors of philosophy and sociology returned to teaching, contacts reopened to the West, and ideological pressures were relaxed in scholarly publications.

The years 1953 and 1956 had differing meanings in the East German and Czech contexts. In the former place, the Party leadership proclaimed the "building of socialism" in 1952 and, with it, an intensified hunt for enemies at universities, especially in the Protestant churches' Student Fellowships (Junge Gemeinden). The crisis of 17 June 1953 encouraged the pursuit of a purportedly more liberal "New Course," in which a reconfirmed Ulbricht leadership managed to realize the same goals as before at universities, if less noisily, and with greater attention to the need of using the carrot as well as the stick. Ideological indoctrination continued, as did intensive recruitment of workers for university and attempts to "plan" graduate studies. Valued specialists, particularly in the technical and medical sciences, were offered salaries many times those received by East German workers—or by colleagues in the Czech lands and Poland. The professoriate in East Germany had been purged and recreated; now it was bought off.

The challenges of 1956 sorely tested the East German regime, which was baffled by events in the Soviet Union and troubled by murmurings in its own population. Yet after the Hungarian Revolution, Walter Ulbricht moved quickly to squash ostensible opponents, many of them university teachers and students. Policies of worker-peasant recruitment and indoctrination continued. What stands out about East Germany in comparative context is the unbroken construction of state socialism despite repeated challenges. The next crisis of 1961 was again resolved to the Ulbricht regime's favor, as a wall was constructed through the city of Berlin.

The decisive moment of postwar Czech history was February 1948. In that month a relatively liberal regime, which by and large respected the civil rights of Czechs and Slovaks, was replaced by a Communist regime. At universities power fell in the hands of Communist students in "action committees." Yet because the central Party leadership took little interest in the work of these committees, more or less trusting in the force of intergenerational animosity, there was little coordinated state policy in the early years of Communist rule. The only common currency was radicalism: in the humiliation and removal of professors, in the interrogations and expulsions of students, in the penetration of university curricula with stalinist thought. For a few years, top specialists in medicine and the sciences were paid so little that they became dependent on relatives in the countryside for provisions. The confusion of this period at universities was tied to successive rounds of bloodletting among the Party elite: the man in charge of universities in the Central Committee during this period, Gustav Bareš, was Jewish and feared for his life.[37] Only after Stalin's and Gottwald's deaths in early 1953 did some calculability enter higher-education affairs, as gray Leninists like Ladislav Štoll and František Kahuda became ministers. Rather than spell liberalization, the year 1953 marked an assertion of central power. In 1956 there were student demonstrations in Prague and Bratislava, and several months of heavy criticism by basic Party organizations of the barrenness of everyday life.[38] Yet, like its East German counterpart, the KSČ reasserted control after the Hungarian Revolution and, indeed, purged university faculties once more in 1958. Only in the early 1960s did economic crisis force a discussion of reform.

In part, these stories of postwar intellectual and university policy have been told in a diverse spread of books, dissertations, and articles that have appeared over the past fifty years. A few brief outlines of higher-education transformation have appeared in larger surveys of East European history, but otherwise research has focused on separate cases.[39]

Best known by far is the East German story, because many veterans of the early postwar university struggles emigrated to the West, where they published or contributed basic accounts of day-to-day Communist policy, which have since been supplemented by work appearing after 1989, though not substantially revised.[40] Several first-class histories appeared at anniversaries of the Free University of Berlin, which was founded by East German students.[41] From the East German side a number of university histories, documentary collections, dissertations, and memoirs that can still be used with profit were produced.[42] Initial work on universities after 1989 frequently dealt with their martyrology,[43] yet more recently scholars have turned attention to specific aspects of East German higher-education policy: denazification, construction of individual faculties and disciplines, early postwar reforms, student opposition, and the role of the Soviet Military Administration.[44] Several general studies appeared on East German cultural policy.[45] These are supplemented by memoirs and parts of university history.[46] In a richly documented monograph, Berlin historian Ralph Jessen has investigated the emergence of a distinctly East German academia, while arguing for the continuity of certain scholarly milieus largely beyond Party penetration, especially in the sciences and medicine. In these findings he has been seconded by Anne-Sabine Ernst in her work on physicians.[47]

After the East German story, the record of Polish universities has been most fully illuminated by historical research. The earliest general account was produced in the Federal Republic of Germany, but subsequently valuable works appeared within People's Poland on specific issues: worker-peasant education, early state policy, general policies toward culture, and the histories of single universities.[48] In the 1970s and 1980s several illuminating volumes of memoirs and interviews appeared.[49] Because of his critical evaluations of the Polish United Workers Party, the leading expert on Polish scholarship in the postwar period, Toruń sociologist Piotr Hübner, was limited in publishing, and not until 1992 could the full extent of his efforts become known.[50] The post-Communist period has also seen publication of other more specialized studies — on student admissions, the development of historical sciences, the history of Wrocław University under stalinism,[51] as well as new memoirs.[52]

Postwar university history in the Czech lands remains relatively unexplored, having benefited neither from the close scrutiny of a Western neighbor, nor the relatively open political constellation of post-1956 Poland. Two early studies of Czechoslovak higher education based on fragmentary materials were produced in the Federal Republic of Germany.[53] This situation improved briefly during the late 1960s, when a number of important studies appeared on state intelligentsia policies, focusing above all on the phenomenon of "leveling" but also on previously taboo topics such as the university purges in the 1940s.[54] A highly valuable history of the University of Brno was issued just before "normalization" struck universities — that is, the purge of all who sympathized with the Prague Spring.[55] Yet after this, with few exceptions, there was silence until after 1989, when repressed and purged members of Charles University's Institute on University History could again attend to their duties.[56] The fruit of its labors has been a massive and highly valuable four-volume history,[57] which has been supplemented by a number of noteworthy memoirs.[58]

If there has been relatively little scholarship on universities in most of the region until recently, there also has been relatively little clash among historians on issues associated with universities. The goal has been to get out basic facts — for example, the precise method by which certain universities, like Jena, were reopened; the exact extent of discontinuity in certain areas of science; or the Party affiliations of new historians in the 1950s. On a more general level there have been the predictable accusations of a "treason of the clerks" in each country, with such academics as Václav Klaus, Jens Hacker, and Jacek Trznadel leading the attack. Occasions for thoughtful consideration of the intellectual's role under communism have been rare.[59] Relatively little scholarship has emerged in the post-1989 era by which to evaluate the precise extent of the intelligentsia's support for stalinist socialism.[60]

The general view in Poland, where the issue has been most vigorously discussed, is that the intelligentsia was supportive of the Communist regime. Critics have focused above all on the behavior of leading writers, but former dissident Jacek Kuroń has wondered, "How was it possible that the Polish intelligentsia, especially young people, so massively joined the system?"[61] As before 1989, explanations fall roughly into two categories: those that highlight the seductions of ideology, and those that emphasize opportunism.

The most penetrating analysis of the first sort remains the 1951 essay of poet Czesław Miłosz, *The Captive Mind,* which traces the self-delusion and fatalism that gripped several writers of the author's acquaintance who became Communists in the late 1940s. Memorable are the notions of "Ketman," who masks true belief behind a variety of disguises (professional Ketman, aesthetic Ketman, Ketman of revolutionary purity, etc.), and the Pill of Murti-Bing, which, willingly swallowed, promises intellectuals complete knowledge and a feeling of social usefulness. Murti-Bing was the dialectical thinking of the "New Faith." Fear and opportunism were secondary in this process: "The pressure of the state machine is nothing compared with the pressure of a convincing argument."[62] The most eloquent response to this approach has emerged from Poland's other great contemporary poet, Zbigniew Herbert, who, unlike Miłosz, stayed in stalinist Poland, where he took great pains to avoid compromise. His rejection of Murti-Bing was not the end point of some tortured journey of the soul, however, but "fundamentally a question of taste." For him, the regime's self-portrayal was nauseating. In interviews he has accused writers who published in the early 1950s of acting out of "fear and bad faith," and for "base material motives."[63]

To a large extent both writers' views derive from indirect observation, however; Miłosz left Poland in 1951 and had spent most of the late 1940s as a diplomat in Washington; Herbert lived in Poland, but in a sort of internal emigration, a place where "no force on earth" could make him read Stalin's *Short Course on the History of the CPSU.*[64] He did not know the daily concerns and motivations of the writers of that period. How did leading intellectuals actually receive the regime? How precisely did they subordinate themselves, and what were their reasons for doing so? The present study attempts to respond to such questions through analysis of part of the intellectual elite, university professors and students, less well known than leading writers perhaps but in their didactic functions equally crucial for reproducing a nation's self-understanding. Perhaps Miłosz's account exaggerates the deceptive allures of stalinism, but Herbert's dichotomous view cannot do justice to a complex reality. Ironically his principled condemnations emerged in a conversation with literary historian Jacek Trznadel (b. 1930), who as a young adult was an enthusiastic stalinist and at Wrocław University did his best to disturb the lectures of the "idealist" literature professor Kolbuszewski.[65] Either Trznadel's new anticommunism is an acquired taste, or the story was more complicated. In general, onetime Communist scholars who later identified themselves with the opposition, regardless of country, tend to pass over these years in silence, with little information about what they did or why.[66]

The younger generation of intellectuals, particularly in Czechoslovakia, has not been so reticent about its reasons for entering the Communist movement. Several figures who achieved fame in the Prague Spring—Jiří Pelikán, Čestmír Císař, Zdeněk Mlynář, Jiří Hájek, and Alexander Dubček—have left records of their experiences as young Communists in the early postwar years. Yet more persuasive and affecting is the autobiography of a lesser-known figure, Heda Margolius-Kovály, a gifted translator and the widow of a victim of the Slánský trial, Rudolf Margolius.[67] Her decision to join the Party was dictated in part by national circumstances—the betrayal of the West in 1938 and liberation from the East in 1945—but also by the apparent moral superiority of Communists, many of whom, like Kovály and her husband, had been inmates of concentration camps: they "behaved like beings of a higher order. Their idealism and Party discipline gave them a strength and an endurance that the rest of us could not match."[68]

In the case of postwar Germany, Jeffrey Herf has spoken of a divided memory, separating the western and eastern halves of the country; for the Czech generation that matured politically after 1945, memory has also been divided, but the Communists' opponents, who resisted the logics so compellingly presented by Kovály, have been denied a voice. After the upheaval of February 1948, non-Communists were systematically removed from all spheres of cultural production, most significantly, the university. In purges of January and February 1949, young Communists expelled one-fourth of their fellow students; in some faculties, like law, the total was half. The purged were driven into manual work, from which they never emerged.

Central contentions of the Communist side of this generation have therefore gone uncontested. Above all is the myth of a better Czechoslovak way to socialism. Heda Kovály has written that no one "doubted that we would be able to run our own show, in a way that was quite different from the Russian totalitarian model. A 'national road to socialism' was basic to our thinking, even to the thought of Klement Gottwald, the secretary general of the Czechoslovak Communist Party, who was encouraged to believe in it by Stalin himself. Marshall Tito, who had introduced a special brand of communism in Yugoslavia, was still a hero at the time, and following his example in our own country seemed a real possibility."[69]

With these words, Kovály has unwittingly revealed a truth about Czechoslovak communism: in the years of which she speaks Tito was building stalinism. This indeed was the program of Gottwald and his Party. Well before their 1948 coup and the onset of high stalinism, KSČ functionaries repeatedly alluded to the stalinist methods they would employ after achieving full power, including the elimination of political opposition through coercive means, and the degradation of intellectual and cultural life. Their road to socialism always involved terror. What they did not promise, and of course did not anticipate, was how that terror would go beyond their class enemies—for example, the "bourgeois" Czech women's advocate, Milada Horáková, who had spent the war in Nazi prisons, and was executed by the KSČ in 1950—and turn against the Party itself.[70] In the recollections of Czech Communists, stalinism deformed only after it had hurt them personally.

Contrary to the view propagated by the victors of 1948 in Czechoslovakia, the choice for communism did not represent a majority option for the generation of 1945: repeatedly the young intelligentsia throughout East Central Europe rejected communism in the early postwar years in student council elections. They did so not out of some atavistic attachment to the old order, or because they wanted to cover the tracks of collaborators, but rather out of a clear sense of the dangers posed by the revolutionary left to civil rights and intellectual culture. In East Germany students several times elected liberal and Christian Democratic leaders with records of opposition to German National Socialism. They opposed communism as another form of totalitarianism.[71]

What none of the Czechoslovak Communist memoirists has explained is how they, as sensitive and thoughtful young people, could attach themselves to a movement whose cultural and intellectual policies were formulated by dilettantes such as Gustav Bareš and Ladislav Štoll, and whose "information minister" was a man with boundless contempt for the life of the mind: Václav Kopecký.

This work does not exhaustively compare universities and general higher-education policies but rather concentrates on striking differences in Communist approaches to universities in order to bring forth fresh perspectives on the three cases. By focusing on professorial staffing in the social sciences and student admissions policies, it attempts to envision the university as the Party envisioned it: as an instrument of ideological and social transformation.[72] From the early postwar years, Communists made clear distinctions between natural and technical sciences on the one hand and social sciences on the other. For example, on 30 July 1947 a staff member at the German Central Education Administration (DVV) in East Berlin made the following note regarding admission for graduate studies:

> The candidates for medical and mathematical-technical subjects must in every case have sufficient academic [*fachlich*] preparation. Besides this we need to demand that they have a positive political outlook in our sense. For candidates in social scientific faculties political dependability is to be the primary condition. In these fields candidates can be accepted who have not had the prescribed course of development, as long as they can prove that they have established the prerequisites for successful training in private studies.[73]

Relatively little attention is devoted in the pages that follow to medical or natural sciences, which in all three cases preserved significant continuities, whether of personnel or milieu.[74]

Of the university's dual functions to create knowledge and to create elites, this work concentrates on the latter, though continuities in the professoriate did of course have significant bearing on the shape of scholarly disciplines. The continued existence in Poland, for example, of several prewar schools in history, philosophy, and sociology contributed to the relatively advanced standing of Polish social sciences in the East bloc. One need only think of the international reputation of such figures as Leszek Kołakowski, Zygmunt Bauman, Andrzej Walicki, Witold Kula, or Bronisław Geremek, all of whom had studied with prewar professors and published important scholarly work in People's Poland. But they did so after the period under study. Between the years 1949 and 1955 the differences in application of stalinist orthodoxy in Polish, Czech, or East German social science publications were subtle at best. Furthermore, the purgings of the early 1950s did nothing to preclude a reawakening of the Czech social sciences in the early 1960s, a time during which sociologists in Prague and Brno produced world-class studies of social stratification, and Czech historians investigated the past critically. A sort of amalgamation of gifted younger Party scholars, like Pavel Machonin, took place with the recognized experts of the older generation who were still alive, like Josef Král. These promising developments were cut short by the crushing of the Prague Spring. Perhaps in East Germany the liberalization of the early 1960s could have produced social science scholarship of international renown, although the peculiar need in that half country to provide "socialist" alternatives to western scholarship would have complicated participation in international scholarly life.[75] The point is that the policies explored in this study formed a context for but did not determine later developments in the social sciences or other disciplines.

This study limits itself to three societies partly for the sake of manageability, but partly because they constitute a natural context within the region. Universities in East Germany, Poland, and the Czech lands all based themselves on Austro-German models of higher education, and the professoriates emerged from almost identical professional socialization, including doctorate and habilitation under the direction of nearly omnipotent chair holders. Before World War I, professors and graduate students moved freely between the universities in Prague (German and Czech), Leipzig, or Kraków. Like the uniform political logic of Sovietization, the similarities in academic regime across state boundaries help isolate matters of specifically Czech, Polish, and German political culture.

The three societies also formed a natural unit in the views of Communist policy makers, who, somewhat at odds with classical notions of Moscow-centric international relations, traveled to neighboring states in the early 1950s in search of ideas on how to implement Soviet models. And the Czech, East German, and Polish populations took each other to be points of reference as well.[76] The ease of communication strengthened cross-border contacts: Czech and Polish academics simply wrote and spoke with each other in their native tongues, and Germans communicated with functionaries and academics from Poland or the Czech lands in German. Contacts with Hungary, not to mention lands further southeast, were not as easy or intensive.[77]

Slovakia does not quite fit into this context, as no independent Slovak academic elite existed before World War I. An elite emerged only in the first Czechoslovak Republic with the aid of Czech academics, who were decisive in the creation of a university in Bratislava. Within Czechoslovakia, Slovak academic affairs were administered separately from the Slovak capital Bratislava, thus permitting Slovakia to be treated as a separate entity. Still, occasional reference is made to Czechoslovakia when policies were pursued in both halves of the republic.

Historians of Eastern Europe have taken an ambivalent approach to East Germany. Most have considered it outside the East European context, partly for the specificity of German history, partly because of the singularity of a socialist state consisting of half of a country, and partly because of its disappearance after 1989. Joseph Rothschild wrote that his "decision to omit in-depth coverage of East Germany [from *Return to Diversity*] has been vindicated by history, as that *soi-disant* state has now vanished from the map of Europe."[78] Historians of East Germany have for the most part agreed on the specificity of that country and left countries further east outside their consideration.

Whether or not one considers East Germany part of East Europe, a study that considers East Germany part of the Soviet bloc tells things about East Germany and Eastern Europe that would otherwise not be apparent. Above all, it helps explain the relative stability of East German communism. What stands out in East German history from the perspective of higher education are four things: the unparalleled delegitimization of the old elites; the strong hand and interest of the Soviet Military Administration in East German development; the continued massive migration of people through an open border, the only open border in the Soviet bloc; and, finally, a relatively cohesive and determined leadership stratum. A comparative perspective points above all to a need to understand East Germany sociologically; perhaps more than any other socialist society, East German society was a postwar creation, formed in part through highly conscious interventions, with instruments fashioned by an unusually resolute Party elite.

One last factor favoring the comparability of Communist higher-education policies in these three societies concerns the archives that were amassed during the stalinist years in the Communist central committees in East Berlin, Prague, and Warsaw. They reflect almost identical organizational principles, with the same divisions and subdivisions and Soviet-style nomenklatura; all that seems to vary are the languages and archival numbering systems. The same is true of the archives of the former ministries of higher education in these three cities. The historian exploring those archives has the initial impression of being in a single, separate world.

PART ONE.

SOVIETIZATION

Before World War II, the basic goal of Soviet and East Central European universities was the same: to train specialists who would be useful in economic, political, and cultural life. Yet beneath this surface similarity they were as different as their societies. Universities in Eastern and Central Europe were public institutions with important powers of self-rule: faculty councils elected deans, made professorial appointments, and decided what would be taught. Universities in the Soviet Union were appendages of the state apparatus, and line items in the state plan; the ministerial and Party bureaucracy selected deans, controlled professorial appointments, and dictated the content of textbooks and lectures. In East Central Europe, though universities produced legions of bureaucrats, they also provided space for liberal education and the cultivation of critical thought. Soviet universities attempted to constrict and direct thought systematically, as students were forced into subjects of study that were narrow in the extreme, and made to memorize the principles of a single worldview: Marxism-Leninism.

Making East Central European universities Soviet was thus a revolutionary act that would require compulsion. Opposition to Sovietization was likely to be greater in Poland, the Czech lands, and Germany than it had been in Russia, because traditions of academic self-governance were well established in East Central Europe and supported by legends going back generations, whereas in Russia universities had learned to run their own affairs only very recently. As state agencies in an underdeveloped society, their mission had been more clearly utilitarian than that of their East Central European counterparts, which were pervaded by vague commitments to "value-free" scholarship. Professors in Eastern and Central Europe were politically conservative, and thus less open to reform than the more liberal Russian professoriate. Finally, there was a sense in parts of that region, especially Poland, that the Soviet system was alien and threatening to national culture.

Transfer of this system to Eastern and Central Europe also encountered more prosaic difficulties. East European Communists were dedicated Sovietizers, but they had to procure information on Soviet higher education, translate it, and then comprehend it. Each of these steps was more complicated than it appeared at first glance. After 1949, requests for detailed information on Soviet cultural institutions poured into Moscow from all over the world, and the responsible Soviet agencies—the Soviet Ministry of Higher Education and the All-Union Society for Cultural Relations with Foreign Countries (VOKS)—suffered systemic overload. The Communists in the countries under study never received a guide to Soviet higher education; rather, they had to try to make sense of a complicated array of laws, decrees, ordinances, speeches of great leaders, and a few historical works. And these were always in short supply. The most important questions were unanswered. Would the East Europeans go through stages as the Soviets had, or simply attempt to copy the end result? Were there things in Soviet history that did not warrant repeating? Could the structures of a superpower really be adapted to small countries?

As we shall see in detail in chapter 3, there was nevertheless much agreement on what constituted the basic features of the Soviet model in higher education. But the countries of East Central Europe came at it from different directions, because the political regimes of the early postwar period had differed markedly. In 1945, East German Social Democrats and Communists (forcibly united in April 1946 in the Socialist Unity Party of Germany, SED) took control of the state higher-education machinery and consulted with Soviet functionaries on a day-to-day basis. The SED felt relatively secure in its knowledge of the Soviet system and achieved important organizational breakthroughs in such things as worker studies as early as the fall of 1946. Unpopularity and weakness in cadres discouraged Polish comrades from taking bold initiatives, however, and a long-term trend of compromise had already become discernible in the summer of 1945.

In the Czech lands, Communists neglected higher-education policy in the immediate postwar period, but after they seized power in February 1948, changes were swift and radical. Communist students with scanty knowledge of the Soviet Union now became the decisive voice in Czech university politics. They carried out a revolution of their own with little direction from the Party leadership—let alone from Moscow—and, having expelled dozens of professors and students, faced the problem of what to do next. In the weeks and months of the spring and summer of 1948 student "action committees" met and planned everything that seemed integral to Soviet-style higher education: worker-peasant studies, ideological education, stipends, extensive curricular reforms. But still they were plagued by fears of having failed to capture the spirit of the Bolshevik experience.

And so KSČ student functionary Jiří Pelikán jumped at the chance to be included on a coveted trip to Moscow for celebrations of the October revolution in November 1948. Expecting serious conversations with Soviet counterparts, he packed his suitcases full with materials on Czech higher-education reform. After three days journey by air and rail, Pelikán finally arrived in Moscow, where he and his compatriots were hustled onto a sight-seeing program, which culminated in the 7 November parade on Red Square, where he caught a glimpse of Stalin. Yet, with the end of the trip quickly approaching, Pelikán became impatient to fulfill the "real purpose" of his journey. A meeting was thus hastily arranged in the Central Committee of the Soviet youth organization Komsomol:

> The comrade listened to my report without great interest. He was much older than me, perhaps forty, and looked more like a grade school teacher than a Komsomol leader. Nothing lay on his desk but a pencil and paper. Our offices in Prague were a complete mess, overflowing with file-folders; this empty, spotless desk was for me a model of organization. To my great surprise he did not take notes. I attempted to describe our situation and wanted to hand over to him the files we had assembled in Prague, but he interrupted me.
>
> "I see you are doing good work," he said. "Changes of this sort take time; even here things are not as they should be. There is too much formalism and bureaucracy; this delays our work."
>
> He wished me a pleasant journey. Our discussion had lasted twenty minutes.

Pelikán, later director of Czechoslovak television and a popular figure of the Prague Spring, managed to enthuse his comrades in Prague and, for the time being, suppressed the many doubts this trip had awakened.[1] He had learned the fundamental lesson of Sovietization: that basic ideas on the implementation of Soviet models would have to be formed locally. This was a lesson that East German functionaries were learning in day-to-day contact with Soviet military officials, and that a number of Polish functionaries had brought with them from years spent in the Soviet Union.

★

CHAPTER ONE

SOVIET AND CENTRAL EUROPEAN SYSTEMS OF HIGHER EDUCATION

The difference between Soviet and Central European universities was easiest to see in their respective relations to the state. The former were part of the state hierarchy, with no recognized autonomy, whereas the latter, though regulated by law, possessed a large measure of self-rule. Soviet universities had to justify their activities according to the needs of the centralized economy, and by the late 1920s a theory had emerged whereby only intense, narrowly focused training could produce needed specialists. Less "practical" subjects, like the humanities, suffered neglect. Central European universities also met the needs of the state, by graduating administrators, officials, and the professional classes. The professoriate was politically loyal and could be trusted to administer state examinations faithfully.[1] Indeed Central European universities were state institutions,[2] with budgets controlled by ministries of education.[3] The ministry created and restructured universities, and regulated procedures of academic qualification and length and schedule of the academic year.[4] But despite state intervention, in the 1930s the humanities and the social sciences continued to dominate the university curriculum.[5] In this same period over 60 percent of Soviet higher-education capacity was devoted to the technical sciences, and for a time the existence of universities seemed in doubt.

These differing traditions can be traced back to the nineteenth century, when universities throughout Central Europe came under the influence of the ideas of Wilhelm von Humboldt.[6] They were supposed to be devoted to research and teaching, neither of which was to be placed in direct service of the state or any other cause; only as ends in themselves might they serve other ends. Despite the growth of natural sciences and the central presence of medical and law faculties in the latter decades of the nineteenth century, universities did not consider themselves training institutions but rather places where scholarship could be pursued for its own sake; philosophical faculties continued to predominate.[7] Although the ideals of interest-free scholarship were never realized, they strongly influenced professors' sense of purpose.

Academic freedoms were safeguarded by academic autonomy. The basic unit of university governance was the faculty, whose affairs were run by the professors. Faculties decided who should join the academic community, for they controlled both student admissions and the granting of advanced degrees (the doctorate and habilitation). Professors enjoyed lifetime tenure, determined what and how they would teach, and enforced discipline at the university, both for themselves and for their students. In ways that varied slightly across the region, the faculties elected their deans as well as the university's first representative, the rector.[8] Rector and deans presided over university affairs in regular meetings of the academic senate, which was the university's main representative organ. Despite requirements for ministry approval of appointments, before the 1930s the state in practice rubber-stamped universities' choices.[9]

Such traditions of university self-rule were hardly known in tsarist Russia. Until 1905 Russian professors enjoyed no corporate autonomy and were state servants enrolled on the table of ranks, not permitted to elect their own representatives. Concessions promised by the government in that revolutionary year were not granted. The Russian state continued to interfere in university operations through censorship and policing to a degree unknown in lands ruled from Vienna or Berlin.[10] The relatively limited demands of Russian professors for autonomy — supported by students — met with consistent repression. In 1911 alone tsarist authorities dismissed or refused teaching privileges to over 130 professors of Moscow University, and expelled some six thousand students.[11] They also pressed thousands of students into military service. Such events seemed fantastic by Central European standards.

Because of the dominant ethos of the period when German university models were transferred to Russia, Russian universities' sense of purpose differed from that of Central European universities. German higher-education reform embodied the ideals of the early nineteenth century: education was primarily to serve the cultivation of the individual. The Russian academic community came into being in the "positivistic and even scientistic intellectual atmosphere" of the mid-nineteenth century, and Russian ideas of scholarship (nauka) became dominated by natural sciences in a way that was not known in Central or Western Europe.[12] The Russian university understood itself more as an instrument of "social progress than of individual cultivation."[13] This more utilitarian approach to higher education was reflected in the proliferation of single-subject institutions, which had no parallels in Central Europe.[14]

Utilitarian tendencies in Russian higher education were reinforced by the dire need of Russian society for education. Although universities throughout Central and Eastern Europe were also elitist institutions, the gap between them and the rest of society was not nearly as wide as in Russia, and they never felt the same pressure to contribute to a relief of social disparities. To be sure, education acted to reproduce inequality throughout European higher education. In the 1920s and 1930s the laboring classes were strongly under-represented, even in relatively enlightened places like Czechoslovakia. In the extreme German case only 425 students (1.3 percent) enrolled in 1925 were of working-class background.[15] Yet those inequalities were not as extreme as in Russia. Early in the twentieth century, when literacy in Germany and the Czech lands approached 100 percent, half of Russia's school-age children attended no school at all. When long-delayed reforms finally came due, education would have a crucial role in creating a more humane society.

Bolshevik Higher-Education Policies and the "Great Break"

Early Bolshevik higher-education policy was a radical response to the dis-parities in Russian society and intensified the utilitarianism of the previous regime. Initial reforms must have seemed shocking to Central European ob-servers: in the summer of 1918 the Russian Commissariat of Enlightenment (Narkompros) abolished any university admissions requirements other than age.[16] All titles and distinctions of rank were abolished, so that in some places recent university graduates achieved the same standing as senior professors.[17] The state no longer stipulated or recognized requirements for teaching per-sonnel.[18] Now Narkompros arrogated to itself the power to appoint profes-sors, which had for a short time been the prerogative of faculties.[19]

Narkompros simply closed down faculties believed to be uncooperative; law faculties were replaced by entirely new structures called "social science faculties," which were staffed by people loyal to the Communist Party, about half of whom did not have academic qualifications. Because of continuing shortages of loyal social scientists, in 1922 the Central Committee decided to close all social science schools except those in Moscow, Petrograd, Saratov, and Rostov.[20] In the early 1920s it deported a group of 100 to 150 "anti-Soviet lawyers, *literati* and professors." The aim was not only to remove danger-ous ideological influences but to intimidate those professors who remained behind.[21]

There were certain practical limitations to these measures. Students with-out qualifications could not succeed, and therefore the Commissariat sup-ported the creation of "worker faculties" (*rabfaki*), which gave workers high school equivalency in three to four years' time. In 1919 the *rabfaki* were made full-fledged departments of higher-education institutions, and their students came to enjoy the same rights as other students. Those desiring ad-mission had to present a note from a factory committee or a Communist cell certifying endorsement of the Soviet regime. In 1920–21 there were 54 *rabfaki,* and by 1923–24 a total of 130 *rabfaki* enrolled 46,000 students.[22]

The NEP period marked a temporary retreat from early radicalism: the *rabfaki* were scaled back, and in 1923 the government reintroduced student admission requirements, including an examination in the Russian language, mathematics, physics, and social sciences.[23] Students of "bourgeois background" again became a majority. Yet the political pressures on universities were not entirely relaxed—for example, students of unwanted social or political background were purged in 1924, and in 1925 the government introduced centralized admissions standards.[24] The NEP period was a time of contradictions, and debates raged on how Soviet Russia should develop.

With the ascendancy of Stalin, those debates were decided in favor of rapid industrial growth, and the First Five-Year Plan increased the capacities of higher education in a way that was unprecedented in history. The number of higher-education institutes grew from 152 in 1929–30 to 701 in 1931–32.[25] Because of the need for engineers, the growth was slanted toward technical education: from 1928 to 1929 the Party increased expenditures for industrial and technical institutes threefold.[26] In 1928–29, 41 percent of students trained for industry; three years later, that figure had increased to 70 percent.[27] The supremacy of technical education was also reflected in the introduction of "production practice," narrow specialization, and "brigade" methods of group learning to universities.[28]

This "Great Break" proved the nadir of university education in the Soviet Union. In 1929 the official student newspaper asked "Are Universities Necessary?" The answer was predictably negative: as "monstrous conglomerates" holding to "medieval" notions of "pure science," universities hindered the progress of modern, specialized knowledge.[29] The logical thing was to break faculties off universities and transfer them to the competent production ministries.[30] This scheme supposedly rationalized planning, because production ministries could coordinate the needs of their sectors with the output of the schools under their charge. Universities thus sacrificed medical faculties, chemistry and physics laboratories, and language training, all of which became independent institutes. In 1930 provincial universities were dissolved, and remaining universities were pared down to a core of pure sciences.[31] Yet even these withered in the utilitarian climate. At Leningrad University's mathematics department it became impossible to specialize in mathematics, for the professional designation "mathematician" seemed to smack of the past.[32]

Students' lives changed drastically. They studied at such new schools as the Moscow Machine Tools Institute, Gorky Institute for Water Transport Engineers, and Odessa Technological Institute of Cereals and Flours, and, not surprisingly, their majors were highly specialized.[33] Because of projected undersupplies of engineers, student vacations were cut back to almost nothing, and times of study reduced. Yet the impatient government did not wait for graduation to make use of students' labor: during the First Five-Year Plan technical higher schools were required to attach themselves to industrial enterprises, and students were made to work at partner factories throughout the school year. At first the ratio between time spent in production practice and academic study was 1:2, but it was gradually increased to 1:1.[34] Because technical higher schools were matched with inappropriate factories, production practice often hindered productivity. Schools might be matched to any kind of enterprise — for example, a sausage factory.[35] There was also an evolution away from traditional forms of teaching: the lecture system, supposedly symbolic of professorial power, was increasingly replaced by seminars and "brigade methods." [36]

The Great Break also witnessed dramatic increases in numbers of students of proletarian background. In July 1928 the Soviet Central Committee decided to embark on large-scale recruiting of workers and Communists, especially for engineering studies.[37] It allotted high stipends in order to attract a university freshman class in which 65 percent of the students would be from the working class.[38] The *rabfaki* were revived, and by 1932 enrolled over a third of a million students.[39]

The influx of new students was matched by renewed purging of politically undesirable elements. "Spontaneous" purges removed offspring of clergymen and nobles in the student body.[40] Teachers who failed to be "reelected" to their posts by Communist-controlled committees were dismissed. In this way, 219 of 1,062 professors were forced out of their positions in 1929–30, although given the tremendous need it seems likely that many found their way back to teaching at a different institute of higher education. Those professors who survived the purging often had to submit themselves to public self-criticism, orchestrated by Communist students in what Michael David-Fox calls a "proletarian student movement." [41]

Because of its radicalism and amateurishness, the Great Break proved counterproductive. "Brigade methods" of learning, the abolition of lectures, and the persecution of professors all hindered the production of specialists. In the summer of 1931 Stalin formally rehabilitated the "bourgeois intelligentsia," and the recruitment of workers to full-time courses at higher schools was quietly abandoned.[42] Now workers would be encouraged to add to their qualifications at evening schools. By the autumn of 1932, only national minority students retained special preference in university admissions. In 1940, *rabfaki* were closed. An end was also put to some of the experimental forms of learning: lectures were reintroduced and students were examined individually rather than in groups. Production practice was reduced and professors' salaries differentiated according to academic status and seniority.[43]

This partial restoration of conventional higher education was accompanied by a partial recovery of universities. Those that had been closed were reopened in 1931–32, though they now taught almost nothing but science; humanities and social sciences were studied only in a few specialized institutes in Moscow and Leningrad. Not until 1934 did the Central Committee reestablish the historical faculties at Moscow and Leningrad universities. "Responsible" Soviet spokesmen less frequently expressed "vulgarly utilitarian" attitudes toward higher education, and a Central Committee resolution of 1936 declared that the country needed "cultured cadres with an all-round education . . . who have mastered the knowledge of all the riches which mankind has fashioned."[44]

Soviet Models in Higher Education

The essentially functional approach to university education did not change, however: history faculties reemerged in order to facilitate the writing of history textbooks.[45] The "Great Retreat" was not so much an abandonment of the measures adopted in the early 1930s as an attempt at pragmatic synthesis. Never would a detailed Soviet model emerge out of what Michael David-Fox has termed a "cyclical dynamic of upheaval and retrenchment," but by the mid-1930s certain basic contours of the Soviet higher-education system had become apparent.[46] It was characterized by central direction, subordination to state planning for the needs of cadre training, thorough politicization, and promotion of upward social mobility (*vydvizhenie*).[47] Its spirit was anti-intellectual and utilitarian.

Central direction lay with a Union Committee for Higher Education at the Council of People's Commissars of the USSR, which in 1946 was converted into a Ministry of Higher Education of the USSR.[48] The ministry was divided into departments whose directors met regularly in a *collegium,* which carried out day-to-day business and was advised by leading professors of the State Academic Council. The ministry's work was supervised by the Communist Party Central Committee, from which all important initiatives emerged. Although universities had lost autonomy after the Bolshevik Revolution, the principle of one-man management (*edinonachalie*) by the rector was confirmed only after the confusion of the Great Break, during which students had enjoyed substantial powers. Now, rather than students having an upper hand over the old intelligentsia, university directors could apply pressure upon students who did not perform, for example, by withholding their stipends. The rector was assisted by prorectors for teaching, research, part-time study, and administration.[49]

This central direction served above all to subordinate higher education to the needs of the planned economy. Down to the smallest detail, university operations were entered into the central plan. The First Five-Year Plan's preference for technical education and narrow specializations was modified but never abandoned. By the time of Stalin's death, Soviet institutions of higher education (VUZy) offered some 900 specializations, mostly vocational in orientation.[50] Soon, attempts were made at reform. A decree of August 1954 stipulated that "specialists of broad profile" were needed, and the following month 274 broader specializations were announced, grouped into 5 general branches and 22 categories. But the pressure toward specialization proved irresistible and by 1979 there were 449 subjects. Almost all of the growth had taken place in the applied sciences.[51]

In keeping with the principles of the planned economy, higher-education activity was standardized. Higher schools were uniformly divided into faculties, directed by deans, and then into departments (*kafedry*), directed by senior professors. A system of ranks was established in 1937 for VUZ staff, consisting of rector, prorector, dean; professor (head of department) and ordinary professor; and docent and assistant.[52] Rectors and prorectors were appointed at ministerial level; heads of department were nominated at the VUZ, but required approval of the ministry.[53]

A VUZ might or might not have graduate students, but their training was centrally controlled. The system of graduate training (*aspirantura*) was formalized in the mid-1930s and revised in November 1950. People under forty with a VUZ diploma could apply for admission to *aspirantura,* which lasted three to four years, and led to a degree of candidate of sciences (*kandidat nauk*). Applicants had to pass entrance examinations in the fundamentals of Marxism-Leninism, a foreign language, and their specialization. The first part of *aspirantura* lasted two years (the "candidate's minimum"), after which graduate students (*aspiranty*) were examined in dialectical and historical materialism, a foreign language, and a topic basic to their field of study. The remaining year was devoted to writing a dissertation on a theme approved by the rector and the VUZ academic council.[54] After thesis defense, the *aspirant*'s papers were sent to a central attestation commission that could annul decisions.

Compared with Central European universities, Soviet VUZy seemed like exalted grammar schools. In Central Europe, students appeared for examinations in their field of study every few years and, in the meantime, could attend lectures that interested them, with no supervision. Professors gave lectures as they chose, usually in their specialty. The high school diploma — called *Matura* in formerly Austrian areas, *Abitur* in German lands — signified intellectual adulthood. By contrast, Soviet students could not choose subjects of study and were forced to adhere to fixed lesson plans and examination schedules that were standardized throughout the country. From the early 1940s attendance was made mandatory and, like factory workers, students spent lots of time at their "shop floor": up to thirty-five hours weekly, in semesters that lasted from early September to late January and from early February to late June.[55] Clusters of official sociopolitical organizations existed at VUZy to supervise rules of conduct that applied equally to students and staff.[56]

"Production practice" and close relations to industry were not abandoned; rather, ways were sought of making them more effective. Students of practical disciplines spent much of their time, including their brief vacations, learning the skills of their future professions. Nikita Khrushchev took special interest in the challenges of matching students with appropriate workplaces. Himself a former proletarian student, the Soviet leader strove to minimize distinctions between student and worker, and between full- and part-time education.[57]

Centrally directed planning made Soviet institutions of higher education uniform in organization but not equal. In general, universities trained all kinds of specialists, but in the main theoretical disciplines they also produced research workers and teachers.[58] After the Great Break a few universities, especially those in Moscow and Leningrad, were made into showcases. The former was to become the "largest factory in the world for studying and researching natural science."[59] Such great universities had the most faculties and a privileged claim on resources. They were the first places where humanities reemerged in the late 1930s. Throughout Soviet history a number of specializations could be studied only at major universities. Higher-education "institutes" — a term never adopted in East Central Europe — by contrast specialized in single fields of learning, and tended to provide practical training.

While the rector was responsible for executing state policy, the university's Communist Party organization supervised political training. This organization was subordinated to the Party's Central Committee and was technically responsible for the supervision of Party policy. In practice, the Party first secretary at universities could become the most powerful man at a VUZ. The operations of VUZy were thoroughly politicized. Regardless of specialty, students were made to take course work in two ideological subjects for the duration of their studies: Marxist-Leninist philosophy and political economy.[60] Because of a shortage of Marxist professors, a special Institute of Red Professors was created in 1921 to train teachers for the social sciences.[61] At the time of Khrushchev's ascent to power, work in these subjects consumed 8 to 11 percent of students' course time. Subjected to the most direct control in the remaining curricula were political economy and philosophy, both of which were available as basic specializations. Economics and planning, on the other hand, were broken down into a large number of subspecializations—thirty-one in 1954 and forty-three by 1975.[62]

Finally, Soviet higher education attempted to fashion a new intelligentsia, though admissions policies fluctuated over the decades. In June 1931 Stalin proclaimed that the "*the working class must create its own productive-technical intelligentsia, capable of standing up for its own interests in production, as the interests of the ruling class.*"[63] Yet apparently that task was thought to be mostly completed, for, as mentioned, organized recruitment of workers to VTUZy was soon abandoned.[64] The major requirements for admission became once more the school-leaving and the entrance examinations.[65] As mentioned, the *rabfak* itself was phased out by 1940. Yet this was not the final word: in 1955 Khrushchev again attempted to encourage the socially underprivileged to get a university education, in order to reduce the distinction between "student and honest toiler." The challenge of doing so was as great as ever, however: in 1958 only 30 to 40 percent of students in Moscow came from workers' households.[66]

Czech expert Otakar Kádner noted in the early 1930s that Soviet primary and secondary schooling, despite all of the changes that had taken place, still retained their original "character and purpose" and remained comparable with Central European variants. But "Russian universities have changed so much in inner and outer structure under the Soviet regime that a new type of institution of higher education has emerged." He had a remarkably clear view of what had taken place. Prominent among the changes Kádner recorded were student admissions favoring peasant and working-class children, and transfer of research facilities from universities to special institutes—especially at the Academy of Sciences. "Of course," wrote Kádner, "dictatorship could not tolerate academic autonomy," and academic senates were replaced by administrative boards whose members were appointed by the state. Marxist ideology penetrated all university subjects, and law "in our sense" had disappeared, as had philosophical faculties. Their major component, philosophy, had been narrowed to a dogmatic form of Marxism, which all students were made to learn.[67] Some limited correction took place after 1931 but did not alter the aim of subjugating education to the needs of the state—a goal that directly contradicted the ideals of the Central European university.

★

CHAPTER TWO

DYNAMICS
AND
AVENUES
OF
SOVIET-
IZATION

During the Solidarity period (1980–81), Poles experienced freedoms that had been unknown in the postwar period. But while most looked ahead, the young journalist Teresa Torańska used the new openness to explore the past. Perhaps inspired by the heroine of Andrzej Wajda's film *Man of Marble* (1976), she chose to investigate the stalinist period. Little was known about these years in Poland, including when they began. This indeed was the first question posed in Torańska's interview with Edward Ochab, the Central Committee secretary in charge of culture and education from 1950 to 1956. But it was asked of her and not by her. Upon receiving a schoolbook answer, namely the years 1948 to 1955, Ochab objected that such a periodization was "without foundation and even illogical": "I reject the division 'stalinist and before,' because that would imply that in the earlier period, when the germs of people's democracy were being created, the influence of stalinist methods, or of the stalinist apparatus, or Stalin personally was weaker." For justification, he pointed to the terror of the early postwar period, in which thousands of Poles had been arrested and deported.[1]

While Ochab's understanding may be specific to Poland, it holds a truth for the region as a whole: namely that the process of constructing the stalinist system, with its extremes of police terror, economic irrationality, and ideological crudity, did not begin neatly in 1948 but was built on foundations that had been created earlier.[2] This fact is most evident in the economy, where most of the nationalizing and expropriating had occurred before 1948. But it was also true of higher education: the more that Communists could dismantle of the old system's conservative canons and structures in 1945 or 1946, the less they would need to do later.

Because of the constraints of the early postwar period, Communists had to share power and could not simply decree radical change. Fortunately for them, however, the atmosphere favored social reform, and if they cared to take initiatives for increasing the numbers of worker students at universities, or exposing students to Marxist views of history, they found many allies, especially among Social Democrats. As the Czech case suggests, much indeed depended on whether the Communists cared — that is, much depended upon the culture of the Party leadership. Yet each Party also operated in more and less propitious contexts for change: in terms of its own strength in membership, and in terms of the outside aid it would receive from "allied" forces. In East Germany, the "allied" forces included the Soviet Military Administration in Germany (SVAG).

An argument can be made that the SVAG created a unique situation in East Germany as far as Sovietization was concerned. As a source of authority and resources, the SVAG was crucial for creating preconditions for Soviet-style socialism; however, even in 1946 the relation between Germans and Soviets was cooperative, based on common agreement about the need to move forward carefully and on the fact that the Soviets had neither the manpower nor competence to micromanage education in their zone of occupation. Once the threshold to high stalinism was crossed sometime in 1948, East German Communists found their situation not so different from that of their Polish and Czech comrades: they had to make important decisions on how to build socialism, on whatever foundations they had fashioned for themselves since 1945. Therefore their experience of Sovietization has relevance beyond the Soviet zone.

Early Higher-Education Policies

Of the three Parties under study, the Czechoslovak showed the least interest in educational matters in the early postwar period. To be sure, the KSČ held the Ministry of Education in the person of Professor Zdeněk Nejedlý in the first postwar Czechoslovak government. Yet after its May 1946 election victory, the KSČ leadership chose to abandon that ministry in favor of the Ministry of Domestic Trade, and left education to the Czech National Socialists. After the coup of February 1948 Nejedlý once again laid claim to the education portfolio, but until then the Czechoslovak Communists limited themselves to two minor structural adjustments that had been agreed upon in April 1945 as a part of the Košice accords.[3]

The first change was to add pedagogical faculties to the universities in Prague, Brno, and Bratislava. This relatively uncontroversial change had been demanded by progressive educators in the First Republic, who objected to the practice of giving university education to high school teachers but not to teachers at lower levels. Yet because the staffs of pedagogical faculties tended to support the KSČ, the Czech National Socialists did little to aid their development after claiming the ministry in May 1946.[4] This partisan political opposition was reinforced by the university community, which doubted whether pedagogical faculties gave university-level education; in Prague two of the professors of pedagogy did not possess the usually obligatory second dissertation (habilitation).

The second change also worried those concerned about academic standards: three new chairs—in Soviet law, Soviet literature, and Soviet history—were introduced at Charles University and then staffed by individuals without the habilitation.[5] The chair in Soviet literature was taken by Bohumil Mathesius, a well-known translator and popularizer of Soviet literature from the interwar period.[6] Vladimír Procházka, the new professor of Soviet law and economics, had likewise been an engaged left-wing publicist and translator.[7] The most influential addition was Arnošt Kolman, professor of Soviet philosophy and history. Though a native of Prague, Kolman was an old Bolshevik. After falling into Russian captivity in World War I, he had participated in the October revolution, and reputedly knew Lenin. He then survived the succeeding decades, while becoming a leading Soviet authority in the philosophy of science. The Kolman that surfaced in Prague in 1945 retained Soviet citizenship and spoke a Czech full of Russicisms, attributes that if anything enhanced his popularity among leftist students, for whom he became an inspiration.[8] There was some question as to the equivalency of his Soviet training, but the philosophical faculty, "still in the glow of the Soviet victory" as one member put it, voted him full professor anyway.[9]

Otherwise the Czech Communist leadership did not promote higher-education reform in this early period, and left university politics to Kolman's student enthusiasts, who struggled over power in student councils and dormitory committees, and advocated curricular reform, especially of legal studies. In February 1948 the Party leadership permitted these students to form "action committees" and purge the professoriate and student body. Both before and after 1948 Czech Communist students had a political significance that was unique in the region, reminiscent of the "proletarian student movement" of the Soviet Union in the late 1920s. Not until 1953 did the Party leadership assemble the will to break student power in basic Party organizations and introduce more coordinated, if not liberal, higher-education policies.

Like their Czech comrades, Poland's Communists relinquished hold of the Ministry of Education for almost two years, from June 1945 to February 1947. In this period responsibility for education fell to the Polish Peasant Party (PSL), under Minister Czesław Wycech.[10] But the Communist Polish Workers' Party (PPR) managed to hold onto the ministry's Higher-Education Department through later dissident Władysław Bieńkowski and Belorussian fellow traveler Eugenia Krassowska.[11] In this early period the PPR concentrated on one issue in higher education: student admissions. During first meetings with the professors of Jagiellonian University in January 1945

Communist minister of education Stanisław Skrzeszewski demanded space at universities for students from underprivileged backgrounds.[12] In May, his ministry released a decree creating an "introductory year" (*rok wstępny*) for students not having sufficient educational background for university. The decree did not specify the social groups that were to be recruited, however, and the courses that emerged that fall were undersubscribed and contained people of ambiguous social background. Therefore leftist students of the organization ZWM "Życie" got involved, and created their own network of courses, the "preparatory courses" (*kursy przygotowawcze*), which attempted to prepare "worker and peasant" students for the "introductory year." Because of the thinness of Party presence in admissions' committees, student admissions policies did not begin to register successes until the end of the decade, however.

In the fall of 1947 the PPR attempted a less successful initiative, namely a higher-education decree that aimed at increasing the ministry's rights to promote and transfer professors and to appoint deans and rectors. As will be shown in detail, mere rumor of the proposal unleashed a fury of protest among Polish professors, and out of fear of alienating otherwise loyal scholars, the Party backed off, passing a decree more limited than originally intended.[13]

In the first postwar year, East German Communists took charge of education throughout the state administration—a control they never relinquished. The single non-SED official in a *Land* education ministry had been removed by late 1946.[14] In April 1947 functionary Alfons Kauffeldt summarized what the Party's "fundamental demands" had been up to that point: "promotion of worker and peasant studies, eliminating fascist teachers and students, political schooling of students."[15] Much more will be said about each of these policies, but what they boiled down to at this stage were, first, general admissions' guidelines expressly favoring children of the "working classes," complemented by a dozen or so courses (*Vorstudienanstalten*) that gave hundreds of underprivileged young people high school diplomas and preferred admission to university; second, the deepest purges of faculty in the region, costing four in five academics their positions; and third, attempts to introduce Marxism into university curricula, in the form of innocuous-sounding courses called "Political and Social Problems of the Contemporary World."

All of these initiatives had borne fruit by 1947 and pushed the SED to think a step further. In response to the Party's first "fundamental demand," universities had increased the numbers of students of working-class and peasant background to more than 30 percent, far higher than in Poland or the Czech lands at that point. Now the SED could go on to make the new student body not only proletarian but also politically loyal. Indeed, political demands were now made of student applicants—for example, membership in a "democratic organization" — that were not paralleled in the Czech lands or in Poland. Similarly, having removed hundreds of faculty members, the SED could move on to "training" a new generation of academics. At Soviet urging, the Central Education Administration (DVV) began recruiting students for graduate study as early as 1947. Previously, graduate training outside the direct control of university faculties was unheard of — and still was in Prague or Warsaw. And finally, the need to train people who could teach "Political and Social Problems of the Contemporary World" now gave rise to special faculties for the "social sciences," which were appended directly to universities in 1947. Along with these, other new faculties were added to universities as bases of Marxist influence, including pedagogical faculties, as in the Czech lands, but also the worker preparation courses, which had been meeting in such places as high schools. Czech Communists never attached worker-peasant faculties to universities, and Polish Communists did so only in 1951.

That such things were achieved so quickly is all the more impressive when one considers a unique handicap suffered by the SED: according to German tradition, the state administration through which it acted was decentralized. In Poland or Czechoslovakia, responsibility for universities lay with a central ministry; however, in East Germany, it lay with the *Land* governments — for example, in Schwerin for the universities of Rostock and Greifswald. It was therefore impossible at the outset to orchestrate reforms in higher education from East Berlin. Centralization of educational affairs in the zone was additionally complicated by the Soviets' attempt to maintain influence in all of Germany. Because they did not want to be accused of taking steps to divide the country, they did not grant the DVV in East Berlin the right to intervene in the provinces until 1949, after political division had become an evident fact.[16]

But the fact that all zonal ministries were staffed by the SED meant that central direction of zonal education policy could gradually be realized through Party discipline. In late 1946 DVV president Paul Wandel decided to coordinate the activities of educational authorities throughout East Germany by convening monthly conferences for the education ministers. The first conference agreed to work out uniform drafts for scholarship regulations, disciplinary matters, medical examinations, graduate training, and doctoral examinations.[17] The universities reviewed the drafts that issued from these meetings, and ministers took them home for enactment by their provincial governments.[18]

It later proved of great benefit to the SED that it began serious work in higher education so early, because years could be absorbed by the most fundamental tasks. Nothing, for example, was more central to the new social science curricula than economics, but simply producing a plan of studies in that subject required five years. In June 1946 the DVV charged Professor Bruno Gleitze of Berlin with drafting such a plan. By October he and colleagues Kuczynski and Rogowski had made up a new plan, which was in essence the old plan minus its anti-Semitic provisions. This was rejected in December by Professor Ludshuveit of SVAG, who insisted that economic training receive a "practical" component. The ministers' conference of March 1947 created a commission that was to put together a new draft. Suggestions were collected and redistributed, and the DVV did its best to construct consensus. By August 1948 it finally had a plan of studies that could be used in Berlin. In the meantime Professor Gleitze, a former Social Democratic Party (SPD) member, had fled the zone. But attempts to arrive at a central plan of studies continued. In November and December 1949 Otto Halle, a former Buchenwald inmate in charge of higher education in the Ministry of Education of the GDR, was working on a series of drafts to the SED Education Department. Ultimately these were not used. Efforts continued after Halle was relieved of duties in 1950.[19] In the winter semester of 1950–51, Professor H. Gehring of Halle University submitted a plan of lectures in economics based largely on texts of A. Weber, W. Sombart, and G. Schmoller.[20] Not until the early 1950s was a study plan devised that guaranteed some general implementation of Marxist-Leninist teaching in economics.[21] For all this lag time, the SED was still ahead of the game, however; in the early 1950s Czechoslovak Communists were just beginning to design central study programs.

Explaining Differences in Early Higher-Education Policies

The reasons for the SED's relative success in transformation find deeper exploration later in this book, but at this stage three key factors seem apparent: the determination of the leadership to control and use education, the availability of a large stock of motivated cadres, and the support of the Soviet Military Administration.

The most compelling evidence for the first factor has been suggested — namely, the measures taken right after the war to establish Party hegemony among students and the "next generation" of professors. The central leadership's determination is also reflected in policies adopted toward its own apparatus, whose activities in higher education it began coordinating in 1946. Leading functionaries were jolted into action by the presumption of the Party cell of the University of Halle, which organized a "central" higher-education conference in November 1946, with comrades from every university in the zone. Representatives of the Central Secretariat, however, had not been consulted, let alone invited.[22] Such "unauthorized" behavior seemed problematic because local Party offices supposedly used "inappropriate means," that "harmed the development of universities."[23] In May 1947 the Central Secretariat created a Higher-Education Council, with Anton Ackermann, the leading Communist voice on cultural matters in the early postwar period, as chair. The participants of the ministers' conferences were a subset of this body, which also included the first secretaries of the university Party cells, and a number of SED professors.[24]

But the local organizations were not renegades: the participants of the November meeting had voted for greater supervision by the SED *Land* orga-

TABLE 2-1

PPR Membership among First-Year Students at Polish Universities,
    1947–48

Place	Number of First-Year Students	Number of Party Members	Percentage
Warsaw Polytechnic	939	28	3.0
Jagiellonian University	2,988	46	1.5
Poznań University	1,440	32	2.2
Toruń University	620	35	5.6
University and Polytechnic, Wrocław	709	56	7.9

Source: AAN, KC PPR 295/XVII/61.

nizations.[25] If anything, they were simply impatient for action. The presence of a larger and more impulsive set of base organizations in East Germany was the second reason for the SED's success. Thanks to the early attention to worker-peasant faculties, over one-quarter of all East German students belonged to the SED as early as 1946–47; at two of the largest universities in the zone, Halle and Leipzig, the total exceeded one-third.[26] In February 1947, 29 percent of the members of the teaching staff in Rostock, 23 percent in Jena, and 20 percent in Leipzig belonged to the SED.[27]

The Polish Workers' Party, by contrast, was so weak among the professoriate that it usually could not appoint its own adherents to important positions in university administration and needed to rely upon the cooperation of "progressive" scholars.[28] Small handfuls of academics felt personal allegiance to the PPR or its successor, the Polish United Workers' Party (PZPR): in May 1948, only 82 (3.7 percent) of 2,188 professors, and 109 (2.9 percent) of 3,762 assistant professors were PPR members.[29] The Communists' luck among students was hardly better: in early 1948, the overall strength of the PPR among Polish students did not exceed 4 percent (see Table 2-1).

Such weakness provoked feelings of inferiority. Stefan Jędrychowski, director of the Economics Department of the PPR Central Committee, told a meeting of leftist university teachers in June 1947 that next to the church and schools, universities were one of the "centers of regeneration and perpetuation of the ideological remnants of reaction" in Poland. The isolation of professors from the rest of society had become a "tragic dilemma, since it clashes with the reigning official reality. Universities are hotbeds of intellectual opposition . . . [and] we are confronted with a paradox: Marxism, which is the effective weapon of the laboring masses, comes in at last place at our universities; Marxist theory is condemned *ex cathedra* at universities, with no one even bothering for a scholarly justification. A few Marxists are even ashamed of their Marxism, and they play dumb in order not to embarrass themselves in front of their colleagues [*usiłują stosować mimikę, żeby nie razić w otoczeniu*]." [30]

Even for Jędrychowski official reality was far from real. At the same meeting Poland's master ideologue Adam Schaff explained the low esteem of Marxism at universities through the machinations of "bourgeois" professors who conducted "open political agitation expressly directed against the government." Marxists at Polish universities often felt "embarrassed because we represent such an unpopular view." [31] Indeed, some PPR members were so embarrassed that they hid the fact of their membership when enrolling at university. [32] The Party had yet to become a visible presence at universities: many PPR leaders still held to the conspiratorial practices of Nazi occupation. [33]

The Party leadership's impulse to organize Communists in Polish higher education derived not so much from a desire to regulate activity at the base as to stimulate it. At the suggestion of Adam Schaff, in 1947 the Party leadership created a system of "cells of six" (*szóstki*) at universities consisting in equal proportions of representatives of the PPR and the Polish Socialist Party (PPS) among the professoriate. A central cell of six in Warsaw with leaders from both parties was supposed to supervise the work of these cells. Often there was little to supervise, however: at some places the PPR did not have even three members in the teaching staff. [34] For the time being the *szóstki* were too small to have a noticeable impact on teaching and research. [35]

Because of the dearth of specialized cadres, the Central Committee's knowledge of higher-education matters remained superficial; the cells of six were supervised by educational officers of the PPR district (voivodeship) committees, who usually had little interest in universities. [36] This contrasted to the situation in East Germany, where a set of interlocking hierarchies had emerged in university affairs, with dozens of functionaries in district committees, university and faculty organizations, and the provincial ministries. There was an advantage to the decentralized situation: many Communists in East Germany were called upon to practice using the state apparatus in the five provincial ministries. A number of KPD/SED officials who began working on higher education in the provinces in 1946 became available for work in Berlin when the central government was created in 1949.[37] They were trustworthy, had a multitude of personal contacts at universities, and when they arrived in Berlin came under the influence of individuals who had very specific plans for universities, like Paul Wandel, Kurt Hager, and, not least, Walter Ulbricht.

Polish and East German universities fit well into their respective political contexts: the Party was popular in neither case, but managed to create a significant cadre in the latter. Because of Polish Communists' historical and contemporary associations with Russia, however, the PPR had perennial difficulties establishing itself in Polish society, a fact reflected in low membership. Poles entered the Communist movement at a far lower rate than the citizens of neighboring states. For example, in February 1948, 4.3 percent of the Polish population belonged to the Communist Party, compared with 9.2 percent of the East German and 25.3 percent of the Czech populations.[38]

Like the PPR, the SED was handicapped by popular perceptions of its close association with the Soviet occupiers and fared poorly in the relatively open 1946 Berlin elections.[39] Nevertheless, such an association was not as irreconcilable with national identity in East Germany as it was in Poland, and opportunists could join the SED without being labeled traitors. The SED also benefited from a stronger prewar Communist apparatus, especially in Saxony, as well as an early influx of thousands of Social Democrats. Communist and Social Democratic Parties were united throughout Eastern Europe in the early postwar period, but in Poland and Czechoslovakia the process occurred late in 1948, whereas in East Germany the "unification Party Congress" had been held in April 1946. It is true that many former SPD members were later purged from the SED, but for the time being they helped promote a reformist agenda in education, which after 1948 proved an excellent platform from which to launch revolutionary change.[40]

The KSČ was by far the most popular Communist Party in East Central Europe, and also the most successful political organization in the Czech lands: in 1945, over one million people streamed into its ranks, and in May of the following year, it won more than 40 percent of the vote in free elections.[41] Like the German Party, the KSČ inherited some significant areas of organizational strength, but it could also take advantage of the First Czechoslovak Republic's legacy of failure and the trauma of Munich, as well as its close association with the Soviet liberators.

But Czech higher education does not fit very neatly into this picture. As we shall see, there were a number of passionate Communists among Czech students, who, unlike their Polish counterparts, were proud to wear their Party pins on campus, and wielded considerable powers in 1945, and then again in 1948. Yet, as a whole, Czech universities refused to embrace communism in the early postwar period. In Prague and Brno the KSČ did not make inroads into the professoriate until the spring of 1948, when in fear for their jobs dozens of professors joined the Party. But before that point Communists were at best a self-assured minority, constituting slightly under 9 percent of the faculty at Masaryk University in Brno, and just 7.5 percent of the law and 5.4 percent of the medical faculties of Charles University.[42] Between 7 and 9 percent of the students in Prague, and 5 and 6 percent in Brno belonged to the KSČ in the year before the Communist seizure of power.[43]

Czech universities were out of step not only with most of Czech society, but also with much of the Czech intelligentsia. As is well known, many highly regarded authors and cultural critics agitated for the KSČ.[44] Professors' and students' conspicuous rejection of communism singled them out for a series of polemical attacks by top functionaries in the latter half of 1947, and for special attention by the "action committees" which the Party called into existence in February 1948. Such committees were formed to purge every institution in Czechoslovak public life, but they "worked" longest at universities, dissolving only in the fall. Even then, the Party leadership failed to formulate a coordinated policy toward higher education and until after Stalin's death left Communist students in control of university Party organizations, with minimal interference from the Central Committee. These years of "revolution from below," driven by intergenerational animosities, were the closest thing to cultural revolution seen in the region under study. The Czech expression for this form of university administration was *studentokracie.*

Soviets in East German Higher Education

The final factor favoring the SED's unusually quick start in transforming higher education was the presence in East Germany of the Soviet Military Administration and, in particular, the Soviets' twin agendas of denazification and democratization, which gave German Communists unique opportunities to create foundations for socialism. The relations between SED and SVAG were extraordinarily complex, suggesting a sort of creative symbiosis. Neither could rule in Germany without the other, but each thought it knew what was best for Germany, and was determined to prove it. The East Germans took Soviet models—especially the *rabfak*—and improved on them; however, the Soviets insisted that the East Germans were lagging far behind not only the Soviet Union, but also other people's democracies. The SED's later insecurity in the international realm, its constant hunger for recognition, perhaps had roots in this early postwar tutelage.[45]

Soviet influence on East German higher education was perhaps more profound than on any other system of higher education. East Germany was the only place in the emerging socialist world, including the countries of Southeast and East Asia, where Soviet officials felt a direct responsibility for the creation of a cultural and educational system.[46] The SVAG Education Department in Karlshorst possessed a unique network of control, extending through Soviet education departments in the five *Land* capitals, down to a Soviet officer at each East German university.[47] Precisely because of the Soviets' great potential leverage, this case has broader significance for understanding the general dynamics of Sovietization. Even in the place where, technically speaking, they could do as they liked, the Soviets chose to place as much executive power as possible in the hands of native Communists, almost from the start.

Before the East German administration had fully come into being, Soviet officers were already registering impatience about German officials who hesitated to take action — especially in issues of denazification.[48] If one views these early years as a time of creating preconditions for socialism, denazification appears as a unique building tool, because it permitted immediate remolding of student bodies and faculty according to political considerations. In the first postwar semester, East German authorities received Soviet sanction to prefer candidates for studies who could present evidence of "antifascist, democratic" convictions. Before long the only unimpeachable evidence of such convictions was membership in the SED or an affiliated organization, and "fascist" became a shorthand for "anti-Soviet" or "reactionary."[49]

Denazification also permitted early shaping of curricula and libraries. In June 1947 the chief of the SVAG Education Department, Professor Zolotukhin, complained to DVV president Wandel that a number of former Nazis had been permitted to teach. He demanded "real control of scholarly activity," including study plans presenting a Soviet point of view.[50] Early the following year the Soviets ordered a purge of libraries in their zone, in order to remove "Nazi and militaristic literature, as well as literature hostile to the Soviet regime or anti-Communist and anti-Soviet." But writings of "white émigrés" were also on the hit list.[51] In October Soviet functionary Artiukhin complained to Wandel that his employees were "unscrupulous" in approving lesson plans — for example, a plan about race theory at Halle University. He demanded that the Germans give the Soviets more time to inspect lesson plans, and more detail.[52]

For the Soviets, democracy was not realized through "free" elections but rather through the empowerment of the largest group in society, the working class, and "its" party, the SED. Local and central Soviet agencies paid close attention to changes in the percentage of working-class students at East German universities and occasionally intervened to support the equipping of worker-peasant faculties. They measured support for the SED through student council elections. When the Communists fared poorly, or were publicly criticized, Soviet security organs became involved, and ordered expulsions and arrests of dozens of students.[53] The logic of "democratization" also applied to administration, where the combination of Soviet pressure and German ambition made for a state bureaucracy supportive of socialism. The Soviets exerted extraordinary ideological pressure on the central adminis-tration, noting even the party affiliations of janitors and typists.[54] In neither Poland nor the Czech lands would such lofty demands be made of employees of the central bureaucracy, even in the early 1950s.

An agency as exalted as the SVAG did not get its hands dirty in the nitty-gritty of day-to-day administration, and contented itself with sporadic inter-ventions. Only in the immediate postwar months does one read of regu-lar visits by Karlshorst staff members to provincial universities, inspecting above all denazification.[55] Thereafter, interference was limited to issues of central importance, in particular the technical sciences, planned learning, and ideologically sensitive matters like social science instruction and stu-dent council elections. The Soviets were also concerned that budgets be bal-anced. In a 1947 ministers' conference DVV president Wandel described the value of these interventions: "pressure from the SVAG is very useful, since it often happens that we who stand in daily life have a tendency to make compromises that are not good in the long run."[56]

The Soviets did not have the resources for detailed administration of higher education in their zone, even had they possessed the will to achieve it. The Soviet Ministry of Education neglected the cadre requests of the SVAG Education Department for years, which as a result had neither sufficient nor competent staff. Most officials did not speak German, let alone under-stand German education, and communications to the Germans took place either in Russian or rudimentary German.[57] In a characteristic pronounce-ment Zolotukhin told the Germans in 1946 that universities "have to act as fathers to the children and concentrate on the upbringing of this youth."[58] For reasons of competence and manpower alone, Germans and Soviets had no choice but to cooperate in higher education policy. The Soviets approved study plans, but the Germans wrote them.[59] Likewise, the German Commu-nists wrote opinions on professors and selected university rectors, and the Soviets gave approval after the fact.[60] From an early point the Germans not only executed, but also drafted Soviet orders.[61] We are accustomed to think-ing of "Soviet advisers" in East Central Europe, but in East Germany the Germans were the advisers.[62]

Even former Leningrad Rector Zolotukhin poorly understood German university traditions, as became clear in his 1946 suggestion to the Germans that a "socialist university" be created in the Soviet zone, to educate "highly qualified cadres for work in state, Party, and trade-union functions" in two-year courses of studies. Proposed subjects included "history of the USSR, incl. CPSU, program and statute of the SED, history of German law, constitutions of the democratic states, history of German and Russian culture, political economy." The German functionaries Otto Meier, Otto Grotewohl, and Paul Wandel concurred that this proposal was unsuitable, because Germany was not yet a socialist state, and because this "university" lacked even the basic prerequisites for a law faculty, let alone the many disciplines of a university. A consensus emerged to create social science faculties at Rostock, Jena, and Leipzig,[63] as well as administrative seminars "for the training of a new generation of administrators."[64]

German functionaries learned to treat Soviet perceptions of German reality with some bemusement. In March 1947 the SVAG released Order No. 55 on the "training of the next generation of academics." The DVV was told to recommend "200 active antifascists" within ten days of this order. In late November of that year, at the second meeting of the SED Higher-Education Council, DVV representative Hans-Joachim Lichtenstein emphasized how impracticable this order had been: "It has become terribly clear to us that, if we use the word in its strict sense, we cannot in all of Germany get hold of 200 active antifascists who are also academically qualified. For that reason we have interpreted the order to mean people who are politically open-minded and have worked at least since 1945 in building democracy." Despite this revised understanding, only 75 candidates were identified, and 32 of these were found unsuitable: "Comrades! One of the gentlemen of the SVAG has suggested to us forty gentlemen for university teaching posts. But I can only imagine that the gentlemen from the SVAG have given us erroneous information, because 75 percent of the people were over 50 years old, and eight even over 70 [laughter], so that after consultation with the officials in the departments concerned only 3 of these 40 gentlemen are left."[65]

If the Soviet role in German higher education was not one of micromanagement, it was nonetheless crucial. The contribution of the DVV (and by extension SED) to educational transformation was competence and human resources, that of the SVAG was physical resources and political backing. Political backing included terror, and because the Soviet secret police routinely arrested critics of Communist policy, German Communists could feign innocence of the repression that undergirded their power. For example, in 1950 the rector of the University of Leipzig warned his students not to "disturb" student council elections, for fear of "possible effects on the behavior of the Soviet Control Commission."[66]

Though early initiatives in worker education emerged from German quarters, the Soviets were particularly forceful in their support of worker courses, for which they helped procure space, facilities, and funding. An April 1946 Soviet "investigation" of Berlin University had discovered a number of "shortcomings," especially in "preparation [of students] from the broad democratic masses of the laborers." The German Central Education Administration was told to implement courses for workers within three weeks, "at the latest." In Saxony too the Soviets pushed worker education, requiring, for example, that the government spend more money on worker courses,[67] and in 1949 contributing building space and deliveries from reparations to the worker-peasant faculties in Leipzig and Dresden. They also offered advice: worker-peasant pupils should live together in dormitories and form "learning collectives." In their experience "young people, when they rent private rooms, are all too easily exposed to harmful influences." According to a German report, the Soviets took deep interest in the curricula and "in every single applicant."[68]

Sometimes advice included warnings not to repeat the mistakes of Soviet experience. In 1946 Communist officials in Leipzig had wanted to do away with prerequisites for university admission, as the young Soviet regime had in 1918. Soviet officers forbade this. In Poland, by contrast, Communists went ahead with a plan to accept up to 20 percent of new classes with no entrance examination. The result was massive failure and a further discrediting of Communist higher-education policy. Arguably, a more direct Soviet presence may have saved the Polish Communists from this, and an even worse blunder in higher education — namely, the two-step studies, which reduced most students' university education to three years. There was no direct Soviet model for this reform, but it seemed a repetition of some of the extreme experiments of the early 1930s, which had engendered the "Great Retreat."

Despite their limited numbers and understanding, the Soviets also motivated much activity in East Germany through sheer impatience for visible changes. The problem for German functionaries was that one Soviet agency frequently contradicted another; indeed, education authorities sometimes contradicted themselves. Interpreting Soviet intentions became an art: slightly varying a popular propaganda slogan, SED functionaries of the perestroika period joked, "Von der Sowjetunion lernen will gelernt werden."[69] Although the SVAG Education Department consistently supported worker education, refusal of its financial arm to permit payment of salaries in 1947 almost brought the operations of the Berlin worker-peasant course to a standstill. President Wandel intervened in mid-January with Marshal Sokolovskii, but funds were not allocated until April.[70] As mentioned, the SVAG refused to grant the DVV competences beyond Berlin, yet Professor Zolotukhin frequently inquired why Paul Wandel was not doing more to supervise the implementation of denazification provisions throughout the zone, or the uniform application of the study plans that had been proposed at ministers' conferences.[71] Experience in the Soviet bureaucracy perhaps had made Zolotukhin and other SVAG officials as incapable of imagining decentralized administration as they were of imagining Western-style democracy.[72]

Despite its frequent irrationality, the unpredictable Soviet style achieved results. For example, Zolotukhin may not have gotten his "socialist university," but the institutions that did emerge from his initiative had lasting importance. A dynamic of gradual escalation developed: the Germans would be criticized in any case, but penalized only if they seemed to tolerate anti-Soviet behavior. In anticipation of Soviet impatience, they therefore went beyond what the Soviets had explicitly sanctioned. No methods, for example, were too extreme to guarantee SED election success. SED officials with the fewest scruples, like old Communists Otto Halle and Gottfried Grünberg, or the former *Wehrmacht* officer Franz X. Wohlgemuth, thrived under these conditions and, while advancing their careers, created the solidest foundations in the region for Soviet-style higher education.[73]

The Transfer of Soviet Models

German scholar Manfred Heinemann has employed the term "self-Sovietization" to describe the political transformation in East Germany. The analysis here concurs with this description: precisely at the point that East European Communists were called on to imitate Soviet patterns, the Soviet Military Administration was turning over formal power to German agencies, like the Ministry of Education of the GDR. German Communists had no choice but to Sovietize higher education themselves, and they did so almost automatically. When, for example, in June 1951 education functionaries had to decide on a division between the medieval and modern eras, they took for granted that Soviet texts would supply an answer.[74]

The term "self-Sovietization" applies even better to the Czech lands, where there were no Soviet officers to begin with, and never long-term Soviet advisers in education.[75] From 1948, KSČ education functionaries obsessively attempted to duplicate the lessons of Soviet experience. No matter was too insignificant. When writing recommendations for the construction of a new mining school in Ostrava in 1951, leading Czechoslovak functionary Luděk Holubec wrote that "lesson plans and organizational structures must be worked out according to Soviet models."[76] There was also a reflexive resort to Soviet models for higher schools of chemical engineering and economics established the following year.[77] The political directives of the Ministry of Education for 1953 included a prolongation of studies "according to the Soviet model," publication of new university textbooks translated from Russian, regular meetings at faculty councils to discuss Stalin's teachings, cooperative agreements with industry "on the Soviet model," and yearly work norms for teachers "on the Soviet model."[78]

Despite complicated historical relations with Russia and the Soviet Party, Polish Communist functionaries also became compulsive Sovietizers. In June 1949 the rector of conservative Jagiellonian University opened direct communication with the Soviet Ministry of Higher Education for lesson plans.[79] Because of a shortage of politically reliable academics, many functionaries believed that training a new generation of Polish social scientists would be impossible without Soviet professors.[80] In some places, this attitude extended far beyond the social sciences: the first secretary at Wrocław's Medical Academy wrote in 1950 that the chair of neurology had been vacant for a year, and no replacement could be found: "considering the complete lack of neurosurgeons in Poland we ask the science department of the Central Committee to consider the possibility of inviting to Wrocław a Soviet specialist in neurosurgery."[81] The following year the Polish Ministry of Higher Education was having lesson plans translated from Russian in all fields, though a shortage of translators delayed the preparation of plans in the technical sciences.[82]

As will be shown in chapter 3, the results of this massive effort in duplication were impressive. By 1953 higher-education institutions of East Central Europe bore all the hallmarks of the Soviet variant. But why was the direct Soviet role in this transfer so limited? Was there no concern that it be done properly? The weak Soviet presence in education contrasts with other realms, like internal security, foreign policy, military affairs, and various branches of industry; here, many dozens of Soviet advisers lived and worked in Eastern Europe for years, directly supervising implementation of Soviet models.[83] Why was this not the case in higher education?

Answers have to do both with the inefficiencies of an overtaxed imperial mechanism, and with stalinism's genuine obsession about security and hierarchy. It seems that the top Soviet leadership preferred to keep channels of information limited in order to avoid ideological contamination. They trusted local Communists, within their own stalinist hierarchies, to oversee the import of Soviet ideas. Moreover, foreign cultures seemed too delicate to be entrusted to Soviet cadres, often poorly versed in East European complexities.[84] The results of resolute interference were difficult to calculate, but little would be lost from a passive posture and occasional interventions, because education did not have an immediate effect on Soviet imperial power. And there was reason to be optimistic: reports of delegations and embassy officials on East European universities reached the Soviet Central Committee apparatus a few times a year, and not surprisingly their tenor was overwhelmingly positive—on the one hand East European Communists were indeed doing everything in their power to imitate Soviet experience, and on the other lower-level Soviet functionaries had little incentive to draw attention to themselves through criticisms that were not stimulated from above.[85]

Information about Soviet higher education was therefore transferred to Eastern Europe above all through native Communists who knew the Soviet system intimately from lengthy stays in the Soviet Union. Almost all East European functionaries in education and culture had proved their devotion to the Soviet Union on Soviet territory. Paul Wandel and Arnošt Kolman had belonged to the Soviet Communist Party, and Polish minister Skrzeszewski and his deputy Eugenia Krassowska had spent part of the war in the Soviet Union, as had the Central Committee functionaries Edward Ochab and Jakub Berman. The "gray eminence" of Polish Communist ideology and science, Adam Schaff, was awarded a *kandidat* degree in philosophy from Moscow State University in 1944, and claimed equal fluency in Polish and Soviet scholarship. Likewise East German State Secretary Harig, and his chief deputies Wohlgemuth and Gossens had lived and worked for years in the Soviet Union, the latter two as prisoners of war and members of the National Committee for a Free Germany.

The Czech case diverges somewhat, in that direct knowledge of the Soviet Union was concentrated at the top. Czech Central Committee functionary Gustav Bareš as well as ministers Zdeněk Nejedlý and Ladislav Štoll had spent the war years in the Soviet Union. Nejedlý considered himself a Slav as much as a Czech, and signed correspondence to the Soviet Union with a patronymic.[86] In late 1951 "comrade Soviet doctors" found Nejedlý too ill to carry out the functions of minister, and his duties were assumed by Information Minister Václav Kopecký, who had likewise spent the war in the Soviet Union. Yet the physicist Miloslav Valouch, who directed the Higher-Education Department of the Ministry of Education from 1949 to 1952, had no personal knowledge of the Soviet Union and had entered the Communist movement only in 1945. Likewise, young functionaries in the Central Committee apparatus, like recent university graduates Luděk Holubec and Čestmír Císař, did not possess firsthand knowledge of the Soviet Union.

Regardless of the degree of their direct experience, all of these functionaries were thoroughly dedicated to the proposition that East European education should become as Soviet as possible. But their knowledge of Soviet education was frequently dated, and not sufficiently detailed to serve as a guide for duplication of Soviet models. Therefore they, and Communists in other people's democracies, began to approach Soviet agencies for study programs, textbooks, examination schedules, and the like. Requests were usually forwarded via the VOKS representatives in Soviet embassies to the responsible agency in Moscow, in this case the Ministry of Higher Education. What began as a trickle in 1947 soon became a flood: in 1950 the ministry sent 100,000 study programs and 2,000 lesson plans to institutes of higher education around the world, at a cost of 95,000 rubles.[87] Given the backlog at VOKS and the ministry, East European universities began attempting direct contacts with Soviet universities—increasing the central Soviet bureaucracy's concern for security. On 28 April 1950 the Ministry of Higher Education requested permission to "establish the exchange of scholarly and educational literature between higher-education institutions of the

Soviet Union and the countries of people's democracy." In this letter reference was made to

> a number of educational and scientific institutions of the countries
> of people's democracy (Rumania, Bulgaria, China, etc.) [which] have
> turned to VUZy of the USSR with a suggestion of regulating exchange
> of scholarly publications and educational-methodological materials.
>
> The Ministry of Higher Education considers it expedient to assist
> VUZy of the countries of people's democracy by way of establishing a
> systematic exchange of scholarly and educational-methodological ma-
> terials. By a decision of the Council of Ministers of the USSR of 11 July
> 1949, No. 2985-1239c, the establishment of such an exchange was per-
> mitted between the VUZy of the USSR and Poland.
>
> The regularization of exchange of literature with the VUZy of only
> one of the countries of people's democracy could give rise to undesir-
> able attitudes in other countries of people's democracy.[88]

Thenceforth the Institute of Eastern Studies [Institut Vostokovedeniia] in
Moscow[89] collected study plans of all institutes of higher education in the
Soviet Union, which were forwarded through various channels to the countries of Eastern Europe and elsewhere.[90] A full regularization of exchange of
scholarly materials to Eastern Europe did not take place until January 1951.[91]
In addition there was a Soviet-Polish Commission for Scientific-Techno-
logical Cooperation between the USSR and Poland that helped coordinate
"technical assistance" for Poland in the early 1950s.[92]

The outcome of all of this effort was disappointing: the Parties under
study never received the information they considered necessary for duplication of the Soviet educational system — though often they received an abun-
dance of things they had not requested. For example, in 1948 officials of the
House of Soviet Culture in Berlin complained about receiving from VOKS
such works as *The Origin of Christian Literature* and *Epigraphy of the East*.[93]
Yet later that year a delegation of Soviet historians to Poland learned that
leading Polish Communist Władysław Wolski could receive the complete
works of Lenin only through an English publisher.[94] By 1950 it was impossible to receive Western literature in provincial Poland, but Soviet literature
was also not available.[95] In 1951, there was only one copy of the 1950 Soviet
constitution in all of Kraków, and only two copies of a recent Soviet textbook
on constitutional law.[96] A Soviet delegation to Poland in November 1952 reported that even the Central Committee's elite Institute for the Training of
Scientific Cadres was undersupplied with Soviet literature on philosophy,
history, and economics.[97]

A Soviet delegation attended the opening of the Czechoslovak Academy
of Sciences that same month and "complained of the difficulty of receiving

Soviet scientific works." Academician Vinogradov explained: "There is no doubt that the distribution of our specialized scientific works to the scientific centers of the countries of people's democracy is rather accidental, and that orders and requests from scholars who are friendly toward us are not always filled exactly and accurately. There is also no doubt that it is far from a regular occurrence that works sent to Soviet scholars by scholars from the countries of people's democracy reach their addressees."[98] In 1954 Czech functionaries were still using a guide to Soviet higher education published in 1947 by a functionary who had since been purged for wartime collaboration. Ministerial agencies in Czechoslovakia became so desperate for information on the system that they were trying to replicate that they engaged Czechoslovak students studying in the Soviet Union to obtain it for them. After reaching Moscow these students contacted Soviet ministries with requests for information. In September 1955 chief of government Viliam Široký demanded that this practice be stopped, for fear that information so procured might fall into the wrong hands.[99]

A number of East European scholarly delegations traveled to the Soviet Union in hopes of attaining information more directly. Here too, the results were disappointing. A large Polish delegation under Minister of Education Stanisław Skrzeszewski visited Moscow and Leningrad for several weeks in early 1949. Due to security concerns, the agenda was carefully circumscribed, however. The Polish functionaries spent many hours sight-seeing, and at the theater and ballet. Even the visit to Leningrad University was like a holiday tour, with a full description of its history, including the great people in its past, and basic facts and figures, rounded off with a stop in the library, a laboratory for brain research, and Mendeleev's workplace. Because of visa complications, the delegation had not included any leading figures in higher education.[100]

One of Skrzeszewski's goals was to meet with President Vavilov of the Soviet Academy. This wish was expressed soon after arrival, on 24 February, and approval was sought with the director of the European Department in the Ministry of Foreign Affairs, A. M. Aleksandrov. He approved the meeting as such but insisted that the topics of discussion be cleared with Deputy Minister Zorin. Perhaps anticipating the difficulties, Sovietizer Skrzeszewski suggested innocuous themes: "the principles of Soviet science" and "the structure of scientific institutions in the USSR."[101]

The greatest success of the trip was the acquisition of books and pamphlets weighing 1,500 kilograms.[102] But even this transfer was not simple: though led by a minister with years of Soviet training, the Polish delegation required special permission to take these materials out of the Soviet Union.[103] Concerns for security delayed transfer of the most apolitical of information. In September 1948 the top Soviet functionary with responsibility for universities, Iu. Zhdanov, requested that M. A. Suslov permit Soviet mathematicians to read lectures in Poland that had already been published in the Soviet Union.[104]

Despite later claims that the Skrzeszewski trip had placed Poland's educational system on a new track,[105] internal documents give no evidence that its findings were used in a coordinated way.[106] Because of similar bureaucratic difficulties, and perhaps also fear of foreign contacts, East German and Czech missions to the Soviet Union did not take place until 1951 and 1953, respectively.[107] The Czech trip had been delayed for over three years[108] and included no professors, a fact in keeping with the extreme low regard for academia in the Czech Party.[109] After it returned, complaints emerged that this first Czechoslovak mission to the Soviet Union was insufficiently popularized.[110]

Soviet Experts in Eastern Europe

A final conduit of information comprised Soviet professors who came to lecture at East European universities from the 1949–50 school year onward. They had a twofold mission: to help create or restructure central ministries and higher-education institutions, and to help train specialists in fields that seemed poorly developed. At the beginning, the need was greatest in philosophy, economics, and Soviet history and literature; but in subsequent years the East Europeans requested Soviet experts above all in the natural and technical sciences.[111] Between 1946 and 1955 some sixty-one Soviet professors gave instruction at Polish higher schools. They aided in the drafting of lesson plans for pedagogy and economics of rail transport, and in organizing departments of zoological technology, mechanical engineering, and agricultural mechanization.[112] In the early 1950s East German Communists were especially keen on gaining lecturers in chemistry, astronomy, mathematics, physics, engineering, agriculture, veterinary medicine, economics, and Slavic languages and literatures.[113] Professors visiting Czechoslovakia in 1951 taught Marxism-Leninism, history, Soviet economics, biology, pedagogy, planning, veterinary medicine, mining, and electrical, mechanical, chemical, and agricultural engineering.[114]

The impact of these professors on higher education seems to have been moderate. They did not advise doctoral dissertations from start to finish, nor did they stay long enough to influence more than a few classes of undergraduates.[115] Strong personalities, such as Major G. I. Patent or Soviet citizen Arnošt Kolman had attracted and influenced dozens of students in Jena, Rostock, or Prague in the early postwar years, yet there are no reports of charismatic or influential Soviet professors in the early 1950s.[116] Instead we read that students were obliged to attend the Soviets' lectures, and that the guests were often not as qualified as the Soviet side claimed.[117] They lectured as a rule in Russian, a language known by few in Eastern Europe — even the students majoring in Russian at Warsaw University in 1951 did not "command the Russian language."[118] A Soviet law professor reported that the students in Kraków "understand Russian poorly and after three lectures they raised the question of the necessity of a translator. I read the last four lectures with a translator, which entailed a significant abridgment of the material. The translations were not always entirely felicitous. Not all of the teachers at the faculty sufficiently understand the Russian language."[119] The reception of Soviet lecturers at Czech universities was relatively cool, and their talks were plagued by poor attendance. One of them said that she had felt at home everywhere in Czechoslovakia, except at universities.[120]

The Soviet visitors also exercised limited influence on policy implementation. Occasionally Soviet scholars were strongly supportive or strongly critical of their hosts, but the rule was neutrality to indifference. Soviet scholars tended to cooperate and maintain a low profile, because they had little incentive to go beyond the limited goals of their stays.

The outstanding case of a supportive Soviet scholar was the medievalist B. D. Grekov, who visited Poland repeatedly and sent back to Moscow optimistic reports about the development of Polish historiography. His supportive role culminated in a 1952 meeting with the Polish Party leadership urging the appointment of non-Party professor Tadeusz Manteuffel as head of the Institute of History of the Polish Academy of Sciences.[121] For Grekov and his colleague E. A. Kosminskii, sympathy for the historical establishment in Poland dated back to their own training at Warsaw University before World War I.[122] Similarly, in June 1954 a delegation of Soviet archaeologists reported to have "encountered a positive attitude everywhere toward Soviet science. Polish scholars follow our literature very carefully."[123] Soviet professors who lectured in Czechoslovakia in 1953 urged moderation of the anti-intellectual course of Czechoslovak leaders.[124]

Yet just a few years previously, Soviet scholars came to Prague and Warsaw with different sorts of advice. The historian P. G. Sofinov visited Charles University in early 1949 and noted that a "serious battle awaits Czechoslovak universities . . . even among the better part of the professors one observes a feeling of self-satisfaction and placidity."[125] Often, low-ranking Soviet visitors felt vastly superior to their most distinguished East European counterparts. Sofinov, a rather insignificant figure who taught at the Military Institute of the Soviet Ministry of Internal Affairs (MVD), noted that

> University professors who have joined the Communist Party believe themselves to be consummate Marxists. Professor of literature Mathesius seriously assured me that he and his colleagues had completely mastered Marxism-Leninism and had already propagated it in the

period of the first bourgeois Czechoslovak Republic. It is completely obvious that there are no bases for such statement. Even the best representatives among the older scholars — like the rector of Charles University Mukařovský or the dean of the philosophical faculty Havránek — are far from able to apply Marxism to their daily scholarly work.[126]

At the very time Grekov and a cultural (VOKS) delegation were visiting Poland in late 1949, a delegation of Soviet physiologists led by L. N. Fedorov attended celebrations in Warsaw of the hundredth birthday of I. P. Pavlov. A particular focus of their attention was the Polish scientist Jerzy Konorski of Łódź University, who had just published a book critical of Pavlov in England.[127] The Soviets expressed their concerns about this book in meetings with top Party leader J. Berman and educational functionaries Petrusewicz and Krassowska, and then finally with Konorski himself, in what degenerated into an interrogation with the goal of "unmasking the double-dealing of the author and his obsequiousness to American reactionaries." Konorski, as well as Krassowska and Petrusewicz, argued that the book had been nonpolitical.[128] At the conclusion of their stay the delegation was given a reception at the PZPR Central Committee. During a toast to "science" spoken to Polish premier Józef Cyrankiewicz, Fedorov "directed attention" to "the necessity for the utmost coordination in the system of educating scientific cadres and the scientific activity of scholars in all branches of science in one center, working under the direct leadership of the Central Committee of the PZPR."[129]

Whether supportive, critical, or disinterested, Soviet experts were not decisive in the construction of East European higher education, however. Konorski, the most dangerous "double-dealer" identified by Soviet scholars in Poland, remained a professor and continued teaching, researching, and publishing throughout the stalinist years.[130] Jakub Berman had promised the Soviet delegation that "leading Party organs would immediately concern themselves and draw appropriate conclusions," but in early 1951 a Soviet delegation to Poland discovered that Konorski's views were still popular. The Soviet Central Committee functionary in charge of higher education recommended a broad campaign in the Soviet scientific press against Konorski.[131] He recognized the difficulty of steering cultural and scientific developments in Poland.

Other attempted interventions in East European cultural and educational affairs by Soviet visitors failed because the Soviet leadership would not permit them.[132] In August 1950 a delegation of Soviet physiologists stopped in Poland at the invitation of the PZPR Central Committee on their way back from a conference in Copenhagen, in order to give lectures on Pavlov. The delegation wrote that Polish colleagues were passing through stages that they had gone through "long ago." Their reputation as titans of science seems to have preceded them. In Kraków, after lectures by E. A. Astratian, V. N. Chernigovskii, and V. V. Zakugov, not a single question was asked. "The chair, as if by a prearranged plan, after 15 to 20 seconds thanked the Soviet delegation and quickly closed the meeting . . . the meetings, especially in Kraków, showed that a significant part of the old scholars of Poland do not wish to change their . . . worldview, and do not want to exchange opinions and cooperate with Soviet scholars. They are *masked enemies of everything new* and progressive." The denunciation came to embrace the representatives of the Polish Ministry of Health, including department director Grinberg, who "sanctioned this behavior through their silence." Several "leading employees of the Ministry of Health display a 'policy of nonintervention' toward reactionary scholars, i.e., they essentially approve of their reactionary activity."[133]

In the late summer of 1952 the Soviet medical professor A. V. Snezhnevskii likewise complained about the Ministry of Health, because "almost all the leading positions are held by Jews." The Soviet third secretary took notes during a "discussion at the embassy": "Grinberg (whose sister is married to the member of the Politburo J. Berman), Tausmanowa, and others, select the delegations of doctors, students, and *aspiranty* to visit the Soviet Union, of whom half are Jews. Professor Snezhnevskii asserted the danger, which in our view is real, that this situation in the Polish Ministry of Health does not contribute to the strengthening of Poland." Supposedly Jewish doctors tended to have "connections" with America.[134]

To respond to such denunciations, the Soviet leadership would have had to take over the Medical Academy in Kraków as well as the Ministry of Health in Warsaw, and begun to assume direct responsibility for Polish medicine. Even in East Germany, a country under military occupation, the Soviets never contemplated going this far. To unseat Grinberg would have been to topple Berman, and that would have destabilized Polish intellectual policy. Both Soviet and Polish Communists had more pressing tasks. And so such reports were filed away.

After Stalin's death the Polish leadership made little pretense of taking the Soviet side in scholarly disputes. In July 1954 it sent home the Soviet philosopher Sudakov who had proved unable to work with colleagues at Warsaw University. In his view, that university was a seedbed of reaction that could be salvaged only after some radical thinning. He was disturbed in particular by the presence of robed priests in a building housing the department of Marxism-Leninism.[135]

In October 1954 meetings took place between Soviet and Polish historians in Gdańsk and Warsaw. Polish historians wanted to delay the translation of a Soviet history of Poland because of a number of serious "defects." At a final meeting with Polish leaders Ochab and Berman, the former would only "very softly and delicately repudiate the objections of the Polish historians." According to the Soviet report, the Polish historians "spoke of defects in the most general sense. Comrade Ochab expressed his wish that Polish scholars help Soviet scholars remove the basic gross errors and distortions in the first volume of the history of Poland, that an editorial board be created at the press consisting of qualified scholars who could determine the character of the desired changes. Comrades Ochab and Berman directed the attention of the Polish scholars to the need to criticize this book honestly in the Polish as well as the Soviet press." [136]

The volume was never translated into Polish.[137] Yet such conflicts were uncommon. Usually contacts between East European functionaries or scholars with Soviet counterparts served to help fine-tune grander policies already under implementation — for example, drafting lesson plans in the economics of rail transport or critiquing a Soviet-style thesis defense.

In the years of high stalinism, Soviet scholars were rarely permitted to reciprocate the hospitality of East European colleagues by extending invitations to visit the Soviet Union. Long-term stays in the Soviet Union were limited to students, whose youth supposedly made them able to interpret Soviet reality in an unbiased way. It was an expression of faith in the power of Soviet training that these students — and students from around the globe — were sent to Soviet universities not for one or two semesters, but for full five-year programs of studies.[138] Between 1951 and 1956 the East German leadership sent between 150 and 200 students each year, and by March 1957 887 undergraduates and 58 graduate students from the GDR were studying in the Soviet Union.[139] As early as the summer of 1947 there were over 300 Czech students in the Soviet Union, and a few dozen Poles.[140] Even under Edvard Beneš, the Czechoslovak government was taking better advantage than the Polish Communists of the opportunities to "strengthen and deepen the contacts with fraternal Slavic peoples." [141] In March 1948 46 Polish students were studying in the Soviet Union,[142] but by August 1954 the number had increased to 1,655 undergraduates and 113 graduate students, and by April 1955 to approximately 2,000 students.[143] In February 1956 there were 1,211 Czechoslovak students in the Soviet Union.[144] In all three cases, students were enrolled overwhelmingly in technical, natural, and medical sciences.[145]

Scholarly exchange improved somewhat in the post-Stalin period, with the regularization of contact through academies of science and bilateral cultural agreements. Individual sections of the Soviet Academy of Sciences calculated how exchanges with East European scholars stood to benefit them, and there were first attempts at reciprocity of learning.[146] But even after 1956, arranging stays of East European scholars in the Soviet Union remained a tortuous process, and the tension between a desire to supplant Western influence in the people's democracies, and a fear of ideological contamination issuing from them, hardly abated.[147]

A number of Central European observers have objected to the term "self-Sovietization," because of the implication that East Europeans chose the Soviet system freely.[148] That was certainly not the case; even in the Czech lands, when a majority of voters chose the KSČ in 1946, they were not opting for Soviet-style socialism, let alone the subordination of their wealthy society to the needs of an emerging superpower. Rather, they were expressing a popular desire to break with an embarrassing past, and move gradually to a more egalitarian, if vaguely defined system, taking advantage of their society's comparative advantages, without the extreme dislocations and terror of stalinism. Similarly, there were strong sentiments in favor of thorough social reform in Poland and East Germany, and leading figures in the respective Party leaderships pleaded for national roads to socialism.

. The comments of Edward Ochab notwithstanding, all of this had changed by 1948, and Communists in East Central Europe were made to understand that the duplication of Soviet models was a condition not only for staying in power but for staying alive. Under these conditions, it is not surprising that they became obsessively interested in duplicating these models. The term "self-Sovietization" is fully appropriate, because Soviet security concerns kept the channels of information to Eastern Europe narrow, and left Communists there no choice but to discover and implement the Soviet system themselves. Neither were there advisers to tell Polish, Czech, or East German functionaries what to do, nor were there even dependable supplies of basic information like lesson plans and textbooks. As we have seen, the demand for information about the Soviet Union from Czechoslovakia became so intense by 1954 that ministries in Prague began contacting their Soviet counterparts via Czech students studying in Moscow.

Such desperation was extreme in Czechoslovakia, because the terror there was extreme. For reasons that have never been entirely illuminated, neither the Polish nor the East German parties ever generated as much violence toward themselves, and, unlike Rudolf Slánský, purge victims like Władysław Gomułka or Paul Merker managed to survive the early 1950s.[149] If the degree of terror grew out of local circumstances, that was even more true of the dynamics of higher-education transformation.

In each of the societies under study, specific long-term dynamics had emerged out of local conditions even before the imposition of Soviet norms in Eastern Europe: in the Czech case, a curious absence of concern in the Party apparatus for higher education; in the East German Party, by contrast, a steady and pervasive attention to higher education as part of a general strategy of grounding power. The difference was expressed in such East German innovations as the worker preparation courses (*Vorstudienanstalten*) (1946), or the social science faculties (*gesellschaftswissenschaftliche Fakultäten*) (1947), both of which had specific roles in creating a new intelligentsia. The former were supposed to make workers' and peasants' children into students, the latter students into cadres.

Each leadership could express its own style in the relatively open early postwar period but also had to adapt to the contours of the society it attempted to rule and to more and less favorable conjunctures. This lesson seemed especially acute in Poland: although PPR leaders possessed ambitions similar to those of East German counterparts, they were forced to limit themselves because of the hostility of their society and their own weakness in cadres. If they moved too quickly, they might be burned—for example, in the effort to enact sweeping changes through a decree in higher education in 1947.[150]

The story of the failed Polish decree suggests a lesson to keep in mind as we consider the impressive changes to academic laws and structures in the following chapter: namely, that these did not always coincide with changing power relations. For example, unlike the Polish Party the KSČ did not attempt a new higher education law until 1950. Before that point, Czech higher education was governed by a confusing array of ordinances dating back to the first half of the nineteenth century. Yet because KSČ functionaries possessed majorities in all important organs of university "autonomy," they could use existing laws for their own purposes—for example, measures enacted to discipline students in 1849 still worked quite well a century later.[151]

Emphasizing formal changes—like alterations in constitutions, or official designations of states—a number of observers, beginning with Soviet Colonel Tiul'panov of SVAG, have supposed a more protracted development toward socialism in the GDR than in other East European countries.[152] The case of higher education suggests, however, the greater importance of actual, informal changes in Party strength (the percentage of Communists in faculty councils, or the percentage of workers' and peasants' children in the student body) as against the outward survival of old structures (the faculties, traditional degrees, and academic senates; or the refusal to use Russian nomenclature to describe them). Although it lagged behind in such obvious structural changes, the SED had been making quiet progress in creating its own cadres in higher education from 1946 onward.

When the SED leadership finally decided to introduce a socialist constitution and a general reform of higher education in 1968, it was building on ground that had been prepared for decades; the *Sektionen* (not *katedry*) that replaced faculties quickly took root, because they reflected existing realities—rather than anticipating or encouraging their emergence. These *Sektionen* were unusually adaptable organizational units, and became the envy of socialist educational planners throughout Eastern Europe, including Po-land.[153] There, a number of organizational changes enacted in the early 1950s had to be retracted after the upheaval of 1956 — precisely because they were not supported in Polish society. The lesson of East German experience was that administrative change had to follow changes in power relations, and that the several elements of higher-education policy — student admissions, graduate training, restructuring of the professoriate — had to be pursued in a coordinated way.

★

CHAPTER THREE

SOVIET
MODELS
IN EAST
CENTRAL
EUROPEAN
HIGHER
EDUCATION

For all that has been said about the complications of transferring Soviet models to Eastern Europe, a visitor in late 1953 would have hardly noticed differences in higher-education systems across the region. As in the Soviet Union, university affairs were managed by a Ministry of Higher Education divided into departments for social sciences, *aspirantura,* worker education, teaching methods, evening education, and the individual academic disciplines. In East Germany that ministry (called State Secretariat) was created in 1951 as part of a series of reforms known as the "second higher-education reform." The state secretary was the Soviet-trained philosopher of science Gerhard Harig.[1] The following year the ministries in individual *Länder* were abolished. In Poland, a Ministry of Higher Education was created under the direction of former socialist Adam Rapacki in April 1950.[2] And in Czechoslovakia a Ministry of Higher Education emerged early in 1953 under the direction of Ladislav Štoll, a Soviet-trained publicist.[3]

In each case the minister presided over a Soviet-style *collegium* consisting of his department chiefs, which met weekly to discuss business. There were also Soviet-style councils of experts to advise the minister, called in Czechoslovakia the State Council for Higher Education and in Poland the Main Council of Higher Education. In each case the members were appointed by the minister himself.[4] These advisory boards helped plan the development of higher education, and supervised academic standards, both of students and teachers.[5] The councils had the right to give "opinions," but the minister was responsible only to the Party's Central Committee. For example, in Poland the minister appointed the rectors, as well as prorectors, deans, vice-deans, and university administrative directors; yet all of these positions had entered the Party nomenklatura and had to be cleared by the Central Committee or the Politburo. The minister also had the right to determine lesson plans and schedules of studies, to create and liquidate faculties and *katedry,* and to transfer or dismiss academic employees.[6]

Going down to the universities a visitor to stalinist Eastern Europe would have found a system of "one-person rule" (*edinonachalie*) entrusted to the rector. Rather than primus inter pares, he was now a manager of state policy. According to Czechoslovak law the rector "directs and manages the higher school and is responsible for its ideological and educational activity. He represents the higher school in public." He was appointed by the president of the republic for three years and would "as a rule" be a professor. New laws also created a rector's office, and an administrative director (called secretary) subordinate to the rector.[7] One Polish professor summarized the new system as follows: university personnel consisted either of officials who administered or officials who lectured. The rector was simply the chief administrator.[8]

Sometimes the chief administrator belonged to the Party, but—in the Czech and East German cases—his assistants, the "prorectors" for social sciences, student affairs, and graduate studies (called everywhere *aspirantura*), almost always did. The institution of prorector was thus altered to fit the Soviet model: traditionally the Central European prorector was simply the equivalent of a vice-rector. In East Germany prorectors were generally not from the university teaching staff, but imposed upon universities by the State Secretariat. The prorector for student affairs was supposed to guarantee a "consistent socialist cadre policy."[9] In Poland prorectors were introduced after 1951; for example, in 1952 Warsaw Polytechnic had two prorectors for teaching, one for science, and one for youth matters.[10]

In all three cases faculties remained, but in Poland and Czechoslovakia the department (*katedra*) became the basic unit of research and teaching, as had the *kafedra* in the Soviet Union. It was supposed to supplant the power of faculties and institutes, and by uniting several related subjects, to ensure efficiency in planning. Before 1933 the *katedra* in Poland had simply been a professorial chair, but now as the "basic organizational unit in higher education" it could employ professors and assistant professors. The government encouraged universities to combine departments in related fields into "collective departments" (*katedry zespołowe*). Departments from several institutions, for example the departments of mathematics at Kraków's Academy of Mining and Metallurgy and at Jagiellonian University, could become a collective department. In Czechoslovakia, the departments were supposed to unite "teachers of the same academic or artistic subject, or of closely related subjects."[11] Because of concern not to undermine the rhetoric of national unity, East German stalinists waited until 1968 to create such units (*Sektionen*).

Beyond the mission of training highly qualified experts for the state, universities also contributed to the formation of a socialist intelligentsia. A "main goal" of the Five-Year Plan announced in July 1950 by SED Party leader Walter Ulbricht was "to raise the niveau of science and scholarship." This would be achieved in part through emphasis on worker-peasant studies, making use of the "rich experience of the Soviet Union in this area."[12] That same month, the Fifth Plenum of the PZPR Central Committee proclaimed the objectives of the Six-Year Plan, among which figured the expeditious creation of a new intelligentsia: "With a goal of the more rapid formation of an intelligentsia with roots in the laboring people, and above all in the working class, it is necessary to confront the task of serious change in the social complexion of the growing army of students through a planned selection to higher schools."[13]

In each case special courses styled on the Soviet *rabfaki* were set up to help prepare people for higher education who had traditionally been excluded, and the numbers of students of working-class and peasant background rose rapidly. The true elite, however, was to consist of the several hundred students chosen each year for studies in the Soviet Union.[14]

Fragmenting and Technicalizing Higher Education

Higher education figured prominently in the central state plan and was planned to the last detail. Narrow specializations and narrowly specialized institutions proliferated as higher education surrendered functions unrelated to the training of experts for the socialist economy. Law, medical, theology, and agriculture faculties were detached from universities and converted to separate higher schools. Research facilities went to Soviet-style academies of science. New institutes of higher education were almost exclusively of a technical character, and in order to shatter barriers between higher education and "life" — East European Communists employed Soviet jargon — they were located close to related industrial production and placed under the ministry that best knew their place in the plan.[15]

Perhaps because of the strength of the old professoriate there, the breaking down of universities went furthest in Poland. This was change that could be decreed. In 1949–50 medical and pharmaceutical faculties became medical academies, subordinate to the Ministry of Health. From 1951 to 1953 agricultural and theological faculties likewise became higher schools in their own right.[16] Economics departments were removed from their traditional homes at law faculties, and new higher schools for economics were set up in Kraków, Poznań, Wrocław, Stalinogród (Katowice), Szczecin, Sopot, Częstochowa, and Łódź. In Warsaw, the Central School of Economics became the Central School for Planning and Statistics.[17] Finally, physical education faculties were also removed from universities and established as separate higher schools.

Restructuring shifted academic resources away from the humanities and social sciences. Previously, one could study philosophy at any university in Poland, save the state university (UMCS) in Lublin. Now, studies in philosophy, psychology, or pedagogy were possible only in Warsaw. Traditional master's studies in finance law, international law, and the theory of law and state were available only in Warsaw; criminal and civil law only in Warsaw, Kraków, and Wrocław. One could still study law or history at every university, but most offered only abbreviated three-year courses for low-level administrators or teachers.[18] After 1951 the law faculty in Toruń could no longer accept students. In order to circumvent the remaining conservative law faculties, the Ministry of Justice supported several nonuniversity law schools, in particular the Teodor Duracz Central Law School in Warsaw.[19] The impact of the changes was reflected in enrollment figures: from 1949 to 1969 numbers of students in engineering increased tenfold, whereas in the humanities student enrollment increased only by four times.[20]

The Czechoslovak higher-education law of 1950 separated theological faculties from the universities in Prague and Olomouc and placed them under the administration of the State Office for Church Affairs.[21] This office was supposed to ensure that "the education of theologians is conducted in a people's democratic spirit and in accord with church principles." A July ordinance concentrated training of Catholic theologians at the theological faculty in Prague. Protestant theological training was likewise centered in Prague at two separate faculties for the two major strains in Czech Protestantism.[22]

A diminished need for lawyers and pharmacists coincided with a heightened need for engineers. An ordinance of late June opened higher engineering schools in Plzeň and Ostrava, and a higher chemical school in Pardubice, but closed the pharmaceutical section of the medical faculty in Prague, as well as the law faculty in Brno.[23] Even after the events of 1948, law faculties were said to suffer shortages of "ideologically mature specialists," and students of pharmaceutical sciences were judged "very bad, because they are mostly recruited from the entrepreneurial sector and from bourgeois families (especially the girls)."[24] Students in remaining law faculties would be trained "solely for the needs of the judiciary and the legislative offices of central agencies. The facilities of Brno's closed law faculty were made available to the city's Technical University.[25]

The restructuring rapidly shifted the balance of student majors. Of the freshman class in 1949–50, 32.8 percent embarked on technical studies; the following year that figure increased to half.[26] The trends of specialization and compartmentalization continued. In 1951 the Edvard Beneš Technical University in Brno was taken over by the army, and a Higher School for Civil Engineering was opened with the remaining facilities. In July 1952 the agricultural and forestry faculty of the Czech Technical University in Prague was split into a Higher Agricultural School and a new faculty of forestry. One month later the chemical faculty at Prague's Technical University became a Higher Chemical School. In 1953 a Higher School of the Russian Language and a Higher Party School of the Central Committee of the KSČ were opened in Prague. As in Poland, larger faculties were split; for example, the philosophical faculty in Prague was divided into philosophical-historical and philological faculties, and the natural sciences faculty was separated into mathematical-physical and biological faculties.[27]

Universities in East Germany were better able to maintain their inherited structures, yet here too new institutions were narrowly focused, like the Higher School for Transportation in Dresden, or the medical academies in Erfurt and Magdeburg. A unique East German creation was the social science faculties opened in Jena, Leipzig, and Rostock in 1947; by 1949 they had obviated the need for university economics, and the economics components of the law faculties at these places were discontinued.[28] Institutions were formed outside universities that gave advanced training in politically sensitive areas. In 1946 the SED leadership created a Party Higher School in Zella-Mehlis, and in 1948 a "Walter Ulbricht Administration Academy" at Forst-Zinna; in 1952 this academy was moved to Potsdam, and joined with other institutions to become the "Walter Ulbricht Academy for Legal and Political Science." In 1949 a Higher School for Economic Planning was created in Berlin-Karlshorst; it merged with several other schools three years later to become a "Higher School for Economics."[29] An Institute for Social Sciences at the SED Central Committee was modeled on the Academy of Social Sciences at the Central Committee of the CPSU.[30]

East Germany too witnessed a promotion of the technical and natural sciences at the expense of the humanities. For example, the plan for 1953 allotted the Technical University in Dresden almost one-third the total state budget for higher education. It received more than twice as much as Humboldt University in Berlin, and as much as the universities of Leipzig, Jena, and Rostock combined.[31] Worker-peasant faculties in East Germany heavily favored technical subjects. From 1951 to 1955 the number of students in technical sciences rose 463 percent, while in philosophy, languages, and the arts only 112 percent.[32]

Controlled Learning

The shift to planned education dramatically altered the unstructured, "anarcholiberal" existence of East Central European students. In addition to tightly scheduled classes in their narrowly defined majors, they now attended exercises in military training and physical education, as well as lectures and seminars in social sciences (political economy, historical and dialectical materialism). For the length of their studies students had no electives and spent upward of thirty-five hours a week in the classroom with the same group of twenty to thirty fellow students, similar to the Soviet *kruzhok,* which translated as *kroužek, Seminargruppe, grupa* (study group). These groups, assisted by the local equivalent of the Soviet youth organization Komsomol (ČSM, FDJ, ZMP), encouraged "collective" learning and "socialist competition." Supervised by a faculty member, they were supposed to carry out control functions in the widest sense of the word.

In Czechoslovakia limited reforms of studies had been attempted in 1948, with the goal of bringing universities "closer to production and practical life."[33] But changes were not felt in full measure for several years. In the summer of 1951 teams of experts finally completed detailed programs of studies and examination schedules, and "production practice" became an obligatory part of studies.[34] Numbers of classes were set high because functionaries felt that students should spend as much time at school as workers spent on the factory floor. Due to the general uproar incited by these measures, weekly hours were reduced to thirty-six in 1954, but this standard was not maintained everywhere. In the brief thaw of 1956 the youth organization magazine revealed that students in Olomouc were spending forty-two hours a week at lectures.[35]

The overloaded schedules were not efficiently organized. There were no central campuses, and often students spent much of the day traveling from and to faculties located at opposite ends of the city. Yet functionaries contrived to keep a watchful eye over the student population. In the first year of studies one student was selected as study group leader and was supposed to check on class attendance and organize "help" for weaker students.

Quantitative growth was achieved at the expense of quality. In 1937 there were 17.9 students for every university teacher, but by fall 1952 the ratio had shifted to 37.4 to 1; and by 1956, to 48 to 1.[36] Dismissals of professors forced increasing reliance on teachers without traditional qualifications, especially at law and philosophy faculties: in the fall of 1948 five professors and eight lecturers were teaching in Prague's philosophy faculty who did not have the habilitation.[37] At the law faculty, one full professor and twelve lecturers did not have the habilitation. This trend did not, however, extend to the medical and natural sciences faculties. Though three times as large as law, the medical faculty at Charles University had only one teacher without the traditional qualification in the fall of 1948.[38] In order to make up for the lack of qualified teachers, advanced graduate students took over much of the teaching, but often they simply read instructional materials aloud, which students busily copied into their notebooks.

Students performed poorly in these straitened circumstances. In 1954, 34 percent of the first-year students in Prague's medical faculty failed their examinations, and in technical faculties the figure approached 50 percent.[39] Universities now often impeded intellectual growth. One student of Brno's philosophical faculty complained to the ČSM daily *Mladá fronta* in May 1956: "To study independently—this was the wish of us all. But this wish has not been fulfilled, and, until now, it could not be fulfilled. We have to apologize to our teachers for not being able to keep up with professional journals and for not taking part in important premieres and lectures outside the faculty. We had only one wish—to get a good night's sleep, in order to have enough energy to put up with the next day's sitting and note taking. In our faculty we do nothing but write things down."[40]

If students did not have time for studies, they also did not have time for politics; Central Committee functionaries agreed in a 1954 meeting that the excessive demands at universities created an "atmosphere of indifference and passivity in relation to questions of political life."[41]

Students' lives in East Germany and Poland were constricted in similar ways. The SED did not need well-rounded scholars, but "specialists who functioned according to plan discipline." By 1953 students attended 28 to 32 obligatory hours of lectures weekly and had to work 12 to 14 hours daily to keep up. FDJ groups were charged with making sure they adhered to study plans after classes.[42] In 1951, the German seven-month academic year was extended to ten months. Technically, students still had two months vacation, yet the FDJ encroached upon this time as well, by sending students to get practical experience in their appointed lines of work.[43] In Poland, advanced graduate students were forced to spend a fixed number of hours in their offices, whether they had work there or not, in the name of "labor discipline."[44]

The strains of the plan likewise caused a decline in teaching quality. The number of students per full professor in East Germany went from 54.5 in 1948 to 74.5 in 1952, and the percentage of university teachers without a doctorate from 18 to 28 percent. At Leipzig the number of nonacademics in the teaching staff rose steadily from 9 percent in the winter semester of 1946–47 to 29 percent in the fall semester of 1951–52.[45]

The major organizational change in Polish students' lives involved the "two-step" studies introduced in the 1949–50 school year. Normal five-year courses of study were broken into two "steps." There was no Soviet precedent for this arrangement, but its goal of quickly producing experts for the economy was arguably in the Soviet spirit.[46] The majority of students now completed studies in three years and were assigned jobs according to state needs. A smaller number of more gifted students—smallest in the humanities and social sciences—continued studies in a second "step," and after two more years received master's degrees.[47] To give a sense of the proportions: at Jagiellonian University there were 246 first-year law students of the first "step" in the 1951–52 academic year, but only 28 law students in the first year of the second "step."[48] Studies of medicine were not affected.[49] As in neighboring countries students' obligations increased many times, and the full schedules left little time for study, let alone pursuit of special interests.[50]

In each case the higher-education systems were given neither the resources nor the time to realize planners' ambitions, and the result was, in György Péteri's phrase, "systemic overstretch": "Thousands of students, lacking appropriate secondary education, were enrolled and rushed through universities in which neither competent teaching staff nor the equipment and general conditions necessary for up-to-date professional and scientific training could possibly be secured."[51] The Polish institution of two-step studies caused a severe syndrome of the more general condition; three years were simply not enough time to produce an engineer, or any kind of specialist who could be useful to the economy. Fear that the Six-Year Plan would not be fulfilled because of the poor training of specialists moved the Polish government to abolish two-step studies in 1954, and return to traditional master's studies.[52] The problem could not be undone so quickly, however. In 1956, difficulties in getting competent specialists became so great that the Polish government appealed to the Polish émigré community *in the West* for engineers to work on a state project to construct rail lines in Transjordania.[53] In the Czech lands industry similarly lamented universities' failure to graduate properly trained specialists.[54]

Determination to follow Soviet ways did not stop at undergraduate education. In the early 1950s the Polish, Czech, and to a lesser extent East German leaderships replicated Soviet-style graduate training, with its two-step doctorate, detached from the process of qualifying for university teaching, and subject to central approval. In Poland and the Czech lands, degrees of *kandidat* and "doctor of science" now replaced the traditional Central European doctorate and habilitation. As in the Soviet Union, the new degrees could also be earned outside the university, for example, in the Academy of Sciences. The abolishment of the old system caused much pain; hundreds of Polish doctoral candidates hurried to defend their dissertations before the new measures took effect in April 1952; similarly, when it became clear in 1956 that the government would revert to the old practice, many hundreds waited to defend until the Soviet-style degrees were abolished two years later. In the meantime, in an act of massive structural resistance, Poles simply stopped getting scientific degrees.[55]

In the Czech lands it was not so much the new advanced degrees as the abolishment of the traditional professional degree of "doctor" that caused distress, particularly among law and medical students. In late 1953, medical students about to graduate without the age-old "dignities" agitated all over Czechoslovakia in defense of tradition. One group from Bratislava visited every university town hoping to arrange an all-state conference on the subject.[56] Another group of worker students addressed their concerns to former minister Zdeněk Nejedlý: "In hospitals we will be footmen for the gentlemen doctors, and in courts and law offices we shall be mere scribes, because people will always want to deal with the blacksmith and not with his lackey. Here we see that centuries of tradition are more powerful in our country than the forced experiments of a few individuals who want to be famous reformers."[57]

In all three countries measures were taken to direct centrally the awarding of advanced degrees, as well as the appointment of new faculty. Between 1951 and 1953, the three states began enlisting significant numbers of candidates for the first degree in a centrally coordinated *aspirantura*.[58] Full-time *aspiranty* were generally given a three-year stipend, without teaching responsibilities, in order to produce their first dissertation, and receive the *kandidat* degree. They were supposed to be new kinds of graduate students, who abided by detailed, centrally approved timetables for completion of requirements; took batteries of examinations in numerous subjects, including Russian and Marxism-Leninism; passed through several stages of qualification, at faculty, university, and ministry level; and then accepted three years' work at a place designated by the state.[59] Their academic advisers were selected from a small group of professors whom the regime considered suitable for the training of socialist cadres. However, much graduate training still occurred through the old institution of "assistantship," in which professors chose their successors, subject, of course, to official approval. But here too graduate students had to defend new-style degrees and complete examinations in Russian and Marxism-Leninism. And, as mentioned, the degree itself was no longer awarded by the faculty but rather by central state commissions in which scholars loyal to the Party had decisive say.[60]

East German Communists showed their characteristic mixture of vigor and restraint in graduate studies. For the sake of their national unity rhetoric, they maintained the traditional doctorate and habilitation until 1968, and until the late 1950s hardly touched the relationship between full professor and assistant professor in the sciences and in medicine.[61] Yet they had begun planning graduate studies from 1947 — far earlier than in neighboring countries[62] — and in some places, eager Party functionaries referred to planned graduate studies as *Aspirantur* as early as 1948, though it was not officially called that until 1951.[63] From the early 1950s the SED was routinely placing its candidates in graduate studies in history, the social sciences, and agricultural sciences — fields that had been purged of "bourgeois" specialists.[64] Unlike the PZPR or KSČ, it was also systematically recruiting not only Communists, but also people of worker and peasant background: in the fields just listed 69.5 percent of the students were SED members and 50.9 percent worker-peasant candidates.[65]

The Role of the Party

Less obvious to someone visiting East Central Europe in the 1950s would have been the role of the Communist Party in orchestrating university affairs. In each country there were twin state and Party hierarchies, with offices of the latter supposed to supervise offices of the former, though in practice supervision often amounted to direct rule.[66] Major initiatives in educational affairs—for example, the creation of new schools, or changes in student admission policies, or the releasing of a new law—invariably originated in the upper reaches of the Party hierarchy, but these initiatives, often expressed in very general terms, were translated into the specifics of the state plan by top ministry officials.[67] The Party then "controlled" the realization of the plan through mechanisms extending downward to the universities. Basic Party organizations monitored plan fulfillment at universities, and Central Committee functionaries monitored their work, intervening personally when they sensed trouble: for example, discrimination of worker-peasant students, unusually high failure rates during examinations, or any ideological "distortion."

The connection between university Party organizations and the Central Committee was closest in East Germany, where, as has been mentioned, the Central Committee became directly involved in local university affairs in 1946. In 1946 and 1947 departments for culture and education had come into being in the central committees of all three Communist Parties, and by the early 1950s they had expanded and subdivided. In East Germany, the department's Division for Higher-Education Issues became a Department for Science and Higher Education in 1952. The first director, Alfons Kaufeldt, was succeeded by Herbert Busse in 1948, who was followed by Ernst Hoffmann in 1950 and Kurt Hager in 1952.[68] Hager lasted at this position until 1989,[69] thus incorporating the unparalleled continuity of SED cultural policy through challenges that had shattered leaderships elsewhere. Directly after the formation of the PZPR in late 1948 a Department of Science was created in its Central Committee. Its first director was biologist Kazimierz Petrusewicz, who was replaced in April 1952 by Zofia Zemankowa.[70] Their work was supervised by Central Committee secretaries Jakub Berman and Edward Ochab.

The Czech case diverges from the first two in the strength of local Party organizations. Though a "Culture-Propaganda" Department had existed in the Czech Central Committee from 1946, the loci of Party higher-education policy until 1953 were the student-run "higher-education committees of the

KSČ" in Prague and Brno.[71] Until that point major issues could be decided locally. At universities, too, the party committees were in the hands of students. The Central Committee began building a department devoted to education and science in the early 1950s, directed first by Gustav Bareš — a man paralyzed by fear during the arrests of that time — and after 1953 by B. Mucha. This department had four sectors, one of which was devoted to higher education (director: Luděk Holubec), and one to science (director: V. Pelíšek).[72]

This section has tried to suggest new ways of thinking about the Sovietization of East Central Europe. In higher education, there was no blueprint for the transfer of the Soviet system to Czechoslovakia, East Germany, or Poland. Occasionally Soviet experts and professors toured the region, but their advice was of a highly limited, technical character. Not they but rather local Communists Sovietized East European higher education, according to local constellations. We have seen how this was true for the early postwar years, when each leadership had considerable freedom in cultural and educational policy. In the succeeding period, stalinist facades of uniformity made continued diversity more difficult to perceive.

Viewed close-up, these facades reveal small inconsistencies. Take the case of the worker courses, modeled on the Soviet *rabfak*. As we shall see in greater detail in chapters 12 and 13 there were any number of variations. East German worker courses lasted three years and were attached to universities, whereas Polish counterparts lasted two years and were not. Czech worker courses lasted less than a year and were not even in university towns, let alone on university premises. When one looks closer, one sees even more differences: Czech and East German courses enrolled higher percentages of Party members; Polish authorities began recruitment for courses somewhat later in the year than East German; stipends were somewhat higher in the East German case; the Czech courses were abandoned in 1952, the Polish in 1954, and the East German not until the mid-1960s. All three differed from the purported model: the Soviet *rabfak* had been used intensively only in the early and late 1920s, and enrolled even higher percentages of Party members than the Czech or East German variants. If one were to look even closer one would note more differences — for example, in hours spent on individual subjects, in the organization of free time, in reading lists for Marxism-Leninism.

These variations in a single institution suggest a deeper lesson about Sovietization: that Soviet failure to provide the East Europeans with sufficient information about their system derived not only from systemic overload, or obsessions about security, but also from the impossibility of deriving unambiguous lessons from Soviet history, which was a series of improvisations. Soviet history did not tell East Europeans how much energy to devote to specific elements of higher-education reform, in what order to tackle them, or in what relation to each other. It also provided no formulas on how to transfer the organizational structures of a superpower to a small Central European nation — if indeed that was at all possible. A man of unquestioned loyalty to the Soviet Union, Zdeněk Nejedlý, had severe doubts in this regard, and in 1951, as terror began to breed hysteria in Czechoslovakia, he even told comrades in the KSČ Central Committee that they should not "transfer Soviet experiences mechanically."[73] Ironically, a stronger presence of Soviet advisers may have strengthened his hand; for example, members of the Soviet Military Administration in Germany occasionally argued against blanket adaptation of Soviet norms. Yet how Soviet advisers might have behaved in Prague is by no means certain, for they too drew differing lessons from Soviet history.

Still, these variations did nothing to alter perceptions of the most pressing tasks at universities: to change consciousness through political control of social science faculties, and to create socialist elites by admitting students of worker-peasant background. Only students drawn from underprivileged backgrounds would owe loyalty for professional success to the Party; and only students educated in transformed environments would cultivate new consciousness. Each Party should have carried through comparable purges of the professoriate, and enrolled similar — if not identical — contingents of worker-peasant students at universities. Yet the relative success of Communist Parties in fulfilling each of these missions depended on the limitations and opportunities of local contexts.

The shapes of these contexts became apparent in the immediate postwar years, when Communists in the Czech lands and in Poland left responsibility for the education ministry to their opponents, the Czech National Socialists on the one hand, and the Polish Peasant Party on the other. Yet the PPR nevertheless attempted to change the social composition of the student body and, upon regaining the ministry in 1947, to enact a new higher education decree. The KSČ by contrast did very little. In this same period East Germany's Communists both held onto power in the state education administration and carried through some important early initiatives, in purging the professoriate, enrolling worker-peasant students, and introducing Marxism to curricula.

To some extent these differences can be explained by leadership preferences: as the most popular Party in the Czech lands the KSČ clearly had the power to become involved in higher education if it wanted to. It chose to do other things. However, the Polish case suggests that the societies within which each Party ruled set certain limitations to their ambitions: the higher-education decree failed because the Party simply had no cadre to enforce it at universities. East Germany's Communists were perhaps not more beloved than the PPR, but they enjoyed important advantages in a society that had lost a war: above all the presence of a military occupation authority that demanded the replacement of old elites with worker cadres. Yet the East German case brings us back to the question of leadership preferences; clearly the SED leaders invested more personal energy in issues of education and culture than did their Czech counterparts. Although the social structures of the Czech lands and East Germany were similar, East Germany's Communists had emerged from a different set of sociocultural milieus.

Despite all of the formal powers each Party amassed after the beginning of high stalinism in 1948, none freed itself from the contextual advantages and limitations that became visible in the early postwar years, and these largely account for the major variations in the Sovietization of universities that are the subject of the remainder of this book.

PART TWO.
THE LEGACY OF THE
OLD PROFESSORIATE

University institutions of self-rule stood in the way of Communist desires to subordinate higher education to state planning. But these institutions could be destroyed with relative ease. From 1947 to 1951 governments throughout East Central Europe issued injunctions transferring essential powers from senates and faculty councils to ministries of education. A more serious hindrance to plan fulfillment was presented by the old professors, with their unpredictable ways of thinking and acting. When they formed a majority in faculties, milieus of belief and habit persisted which transmitted traditional values to young people, along with the knowledge deemed necessary by the Party. Even within the new lesson plans, most old professors taught that scholarship should pursue its answers independent of momentary political logic.

Party functionaries faced a dilemma: on the one hand they could not rely upon old scholars to inculcate young people with the values of socialism, yet on the other they needed their expertise to establish the material foundations for socialism. A full purge of the professoriate would make impossible the training of the architects, engineers, and healers of the new society. A high degree of continuity was therefore maintained in the technical, natural, and medical sciences. Even the most ideologically rigorous party, the SED, had to make substantial compromises with professors of medicine, for example, by agreeing to their choices of successors.[1]

Yet a different logic applied in the social sciences and humanities. The sudden disappearance of "bourgeois" law professors or historians did not seem to jeopardize the building of socialism. As top cultural functionary Anton Ackermann told SED officials and academics in May 1949, "When a reactionary philosopher or historian leaves [for West Germany], we smile. But the situation is different with physicians, mathematicians, or technicians, whom we need and cannot replace."[2] After 1947 repressive measures

71

drove the philosophers and social scientists who had survived denazification into the Western zones. Thenceforth strict political standards applied in graduate admissions in the social sciences and humanities.[3] In the Czech lands, the purges of 1948 were severe in history, law, and the social sciences, but left professors in technical and medical sciences relatively untouched. There were Soviet precedents for such distinctions: dismissals of professors in the first years of the revolution had concentrated on social scientists. It was thought that they, unlike physicians, could be easily replaced; in both the Soviet Union and Eastern Europe experts in Marxist-Leninist philosophy or history were trained in crash courses, often lasting less than a year.[4]

Poland's Communists did not recognize these distinct logics, however. "Bourgeois" professors of law or history continued lecturing and holding seminars through the stalinist period, and though a number of philosophers and sociologists were forbidden to teach, they retained their status as professors. How to account for this Polish peculiarity has been the subject of a subterranean debate among Polish scholars. Once prominent Party social scientists, like Adam Schaff or the Oxford economist Włodzimierz Brus, portray postwar Poland as an oasis of cultural and intellectual pluralism, and attribute this state of affairs to the Party elite's supposedly limited agenda, of reassembling the Polish world of scholarship and — at most — adding Marxism to it. They were supposedly Polish patriots, who modernized their country, while shielding it from the designs of a rapacious neighbor — whose influence is correspondingly emphasized.[5] Opponents, including most experts on science and scholarship, as well as the mainstream Polish intellectual community, highlight the willful damage Poland's Communists did to scholarship, by closing departments and scientific societies, firing assistant professors, banning or censoring publications, and massively propagating falsehoods — all of this shortly after World War II, which, relatively speaking, had caused more devastation in Poland than in any other country.

Recently opened archives support the latter view. Behind closed doors, leading exponents of Polish Communist cultural policy spoke like colleagues in other people's democracies, repeatedly enunciating their wish to transform higher education radically. In a February 1945 memorandum Jakub Berman's adviser on the "academic front," Professor Ludwik Sawicki, wrote that the Party program would not be "reformist moves, but a thorough reconstruction of the structure and attitudes of the world of learning."[6] At a conference of the Education/Cultural Commission of the PPR Central Committee in June 1947 Stanisław Skrzeszewski proposed "the same model realized in other people's democracies, namely removal of the 'reactionary head' [główka] of every university."[7] Several months later, at a meeting of Poland's rectors, Skrzeszewski demanded the "removal of all careerist, profiteer, and other elements from the university."[8] A 1950 meeting of the "Marxist historians" connected to the PZPR Central Committee, including Celina Bobiń-ska, Nina Assorodobraj, and Stanisław Arnold, agreed to "personally attack [Professors] Górski and Konopczyński."[9] That same year, top cultural functionary Stefan Żółkiewski submitted a plan for the step-by-step dismissal of senior and junior faculty in Polish philology departments.[10]

What made the Polish case special was not Polish Communist intentions; the top leadership desired the same sorts of radical changes in the social sciences and humanities that had occurred elsewhere. What was special in the Polish case was the professoriate. Compared with colleagues in the Czech lands or East Germany, Polish professors, even in the social sciences, stood united in opposition to communism. Their cohesiveness derived from the culture of the Polish university milieu (*środowisko*), with its strong and exclusive sense of identity. It kept Poland's Communists from doing the harm to universities that they had intended.

Of most obvious political relevance in this milieu was the shared adherence to the Polish brand of Roman Catholicism, with its definite codes of behavior. Ironically, the judgment of Czesław Miłosz that religion had lost its power in Europe after the war was accurate almost everywhere except in his own land.[11] More than ever, the church was considered the bulwark of national culture in Poland. The destruction of its old leadership during the war, and the widespread involvement of priests in the decentralized structures of the underground, had loosened the nexus of church and state, and linked the perceptions and values of the clergy and the people more firmly than ever.[12] A new generation of progressive Catholic intellectuals had emerged who were steeped in the ideas of Jacques Maritain and François Mauriac, and easily matched Communist polemicists in their dedication to social reforms. These intellectuals could also counter the quasi-religious attractions of communism, because they represented a fresh approach to questions of faith, while remaining well grounded in traditional theology.[13] Czesław Miłosz later recalled his resistance to the allures of Vladimir Mayakovsky: "one syllogism from Thomas Aquinas annihilated him."[14]

All of this gave Polish Catholicism legitimacy, and that legitimacy translated into organizational strength: the church was an aggressive force that pervaded Polish university life in a way that had no parallel in the Czech lands or East Germany. Communist professors celebrated church weddings, robed monks wandered the halls of Marxism-Leninism departments, and hundreds of students learned philosophy, politics, and theology from priests during hiking trips in the mountains, or in sodalities and institutes of "religious knowledge." The major figure in Polish literature at Jagiellonian University, Stanisław Pigoń, was a card-carrying member of Maximillian Kolbe's Immaculate Medal Society, an organization devoted to the conversion of "sinners, heretics, and schismatics."[15] He and other major figures at the university had close ties to Karol Cardinal Wojtyła, who had once studied Polish literature in Kraków.[16] When Pigoń died in 1968, Wojtyła gave the homily. A few years later the future pope celebrated the funeral Mass of Pigoń's junior colleague Kazimierz Wyka—the most serious proponent of Marxism at Jagiellonian University.

In encounters with Poland in the 1940s and 1950s, Soviet officials and scholars continued to be "amazed" by "the strength and influence of the Catholic Church, both in educating children and in scholarship."[17] In 1950 the Polish state publishing house printed 150,000 copies of a Russian grammar for the tenth grade. The authors were three Polish professors. Two years later one of these texts fell into the hands of the Soviet embassy, which noted the first example of a noun with some surprise: *bog* (God).[18] An embassy report from the summer of 1958 still registered a pervasive presence of Roman Catholicism at Polish universities: "with the agreement of the [university] administration, a Friday fast from meat was strictly observed" in cafeterias in Poznań; priests visited dormitories and helped students in material need—in Toruń the church had a fund for this purpose amounting to 180,000 złotys. Cardinal Wyszyński made frequent personal appearances in university towns, and declared in a sermon to more than 3,000 students in Warsaw that "Christ is the only salvation for the Polish people."[19]

Even institutions of higher education that the Party could mold from the start, like the Medical Academy of Silesia, seemed permeated by religion. A November 1953 report for Jakub Berman on worker students' academic problems lamented that "the teaching staff and school administration are people completely foreign, if not hostile, to us. They are strongly linked to the local clergy and have a bad influence on young people. Professor Chorążek, the rector of the academy, is a friend of the local parish priest, spends lots of time with him, and is undoubtedly inspired by him in many cases. . . . A mood of religiosity reigns at the academy; in the dormitories there are religious pictures above almost every bed and there are little altars."[20] Chorążek's predecessor had initiated the 1948–49 school year with the demand that a Roman Catholic chaplain be appointed for the academy.[21]

At Toruń University, another institution of higher education opened after the war, the first postwar rector (1945–49), historian Ludwik Kolankowski, had been a personal friend of Pius XI. His replacement, professor of law Karol Koranyi (1949–51), was also unlikely to help gain students for socialism: he had recently converted to Roman Catholicism.[22]

For historical reasons, the Catholic Church did not possess comparable legitimacy in the Czech lands; indeed, for many it was, like historic Russia in Poland, an enemy of the nation.[23] The mainstream opponents of communism were decidedly anticlerical and failed to enunciate—let alone organize—an ideological alternative; in fact they shared key concepts with the

Communists: Slavism and socialism.[24] In the words of one leading Catholic critic, all that remained to counter Communist ideology was a "wishy-washy philosophy [*Philosophem*], a vague ideology of solid middle-class decency, of 'all people being basically good.'" Opportunism and conviction merged in this gray zone; many intellectuals became propagators of Marxism-Leninism not because "they were forced to, but because their own beliefs were no match for the attraction of communism."[25] Given the trauma of Munich, the failures of Western-style democracy, and the apparent inevitability of "socialism," many professors behaved as if history stood against them.[26] Communist Arnošt Kolman later recalled wiping the floor with his opponents in the early postwar years, even before the KSČ possessed the state machine: "I had to scuffle with the most resolute and skilled polemicists, with the journalist Slavik of the National Socialists, with my colleague the philosophy professor Kozák, with Pavel Tigrid and the right Social Democrat Bělehrádek. I will not pretend to be modest: I emerged victorious from all these battles of words and felt like a matador."

These are memories not of a man relishing triumph, but of an aged émigré from Brezhnev's Russia considering the reasons why his life had "gone wrong."[27] One of his opponents, Prague philosopher Josef Král, has verified the accuracy of Kolman's account, in a memoir written by hand in the late 1960s and kept safe until 1989 by the archivists of the Czechoslovak Academy of Sciences. Looking back on the early postwar years, he recalled Kolman's great "rhetorical gifts," "self-confidence bordering on arrogance," and his strange attraction for wavering colleagues. Though they knew that Kolman was not qualified, Král and his colleagues voted him a full professor in 1945. "The enemy was then in the castle," and began probing and exploiting the personal and political loyalties of the faculty—a process that culminated in the purge of February 1948, carried out by students inspired by Kolman.[28] Under such circumstances, students who were not swayed by Kolman's rhetoric defended university autonomy. Their core consisted of the Catholic Popular Democrats, who crushed the KSČ in several student council elections before February 1948 and were especially strong in Moravia. Their alternative visions were obliterated from public memory after this point, however, and the religious life of Czech students became a purely private affair—not even revealed in church.

Likewise for historical reasons the churches in East Germany could not confront the state either as vehicles of popular opposition or as clear ideological alternatives. Neither Catholic nor Protestant churches had done much to oppose National Socialism; indeed, much of the clergy had supported the Nazi regime—in particular its rapacious foreign policy—with little reservation.[29] They were poorly positioned to take a stand of principle against Communist totalitarianism. The SED easily produced com-

promising documents on its most determined opponent, the Berlin Protestant bishop Otto Dibelius, who had a mixed record in the Third Reich.[30]
Those few with moral legitimacy derived from activities in the "Confessing
Church"—like Martin Niemöller or Heinrich Grüber—could not find unambiguous words of censure for the Communist regime because they understood the SED as the representative of the working classes, which had long
been neglected by the churches.[31]

They also felt remorse for the crimes of their country, and never dreamed
of addressing the state with the sort of language chosen by Cardinal Sapieha
of Kraków and Polish Primate Wyszyński in February 1950. During intensified harassment of Caritas, a charitable organization strong at universities,
they accused Bolesław Bierut of conducting a "battle with God": "Our letter
is the voice of the conscience of the Polish nation, and this voice appeals to
you, as president of the republic, and is compelled to consider you [the informal "Ciebie"], Mr. President, and your government responsible to God
and to history for the battle with religion and with the Church in Poland."[32]
The Polish church may not have had "legions," but it had the power of its
own language.

The cohesion of Poland's professors ran deeper than Roman Catholicism,
however. Major figures of the Polish professoriate—philosophers Tadeusz
Kotarbiński and Kazimierz Ajdukiewicz, historian Tadeusz Manteuffel, or
the sociologist Józef Chałasiński—had no attachment to organized faith, yet
sided with their colleagues against the state. As members of the Polish intelligentsia they possessed an elite identity that had no parallel in the Czech lands
or in East Germany. Derivation from this group was far more important than
professional "habitus" in determining Polish professors' attitudes toward the
state. After all, they shared with Czech and German colleagues a sense of
professional exclusivity and an exalted role in forming national elites. The
attitudes toward scholarship of Berlin theology professor Hans Lietzmann
(1875–1942) could have stood as ideals in Prague or Kraków: "dedication
to science, clean methodological work, full and objective exhaustion of the
source base, and a readiness to permit the results to be determined by these
sources."[33] Yet such a "habitus" was formed only after professors reached the
university.

Professors' primary socialization occurred earlier: in the Czech and German cases, in the small but heterogeneous middle classes of complex modern societies; in the Polish case, in a smaller and far more cohesive group
situated at the pinnacle of a society that was overwhelmingly agrarian.[34] Historically the Polish intelligentsia had emerged from the *szlachta* (gentry),
and so while German or Austrian professors may have aspired to the life-
style of the local gentry, Polish professors believed they were the gentry.[35]
They were formed in milieus that reproduced such premodern values as hos-

pitality, military prowess, and "honor." Young people of other social backgrounds were slowly absorbed into these milieus through marriage — and the university. The intelligentsia grew as Poland became more modern, but its self-awareness was reinforced by public institutions: before World War II, two groups in Polish society were legally considered worthy of "satisfying" honor, those who could produce evidence of gentry (*szlachta*) heritage, and those with a high school diploma (*matura*).[36] As an elite within this elite, professors felt an even stronger sense of duty to its codes of behavior. When formulating policy, Communist officials took into account professors' "collective feeling of the obligation to behave with honor." In the words of one PPR functionary, concern for honor translated into a "fetish" for academic freedom.[37]

Even after the trauma of World War II, the Polish intelligentsia continued to believe in its supposedly natural right to lead.[38] If anything, the war had enhanced its self-confidence. Teachers, writers, and students published hundreds of underground journals and organized plays and poetry readings, as well as a complete network of conspiratorial education.[39] They were continuing traditions dating back to the nineteenth century, when complex networks of conspiratorial activities had emerged in defense of "Polishness."[40] Many professors simply returned to organizational forms and idioms they had practiced before World War I. As a student in Warsaw in 1905, philosopher Tadeusz Kotarbiński had taken part in school strikes protesting Russification of Polish education. He and his friends taught younger students and employed the same vocabulary to describe conspiratorial learning (*nauka w tajnych kompletach*) that would be used during World War II.[41]

Such experiences left Polish professors, along with much of the Polish population, with negative attitudes toward Soviet-style socialism, because it seemed to represent a renewed attempt to suppress Polish identity. The socialist state appeared at best a necessary evil of Poland's geographic situation, something to be opposed or circumvented, and many Polish Communists grew to describe themselves as pragmatic, Yalta Communists.[42] In any case, they had to justify their behavior in light of Poland's history.

In neither the Czech lands nor East Germany was the socialist state necessarily seen as a threat to national identity.[43] Czech intellectuals may have defined themselves against German culture, but historically they achieved their ends through accommodation with an Austrian German state, culminating in the foundation of Czech faculties at Prague's university in 1882. German professors likewise knew no tradition of organizing education and culture beyond, let alone against, state authority. They stood at the center of a *Bildungsbürgertum* that idealized the state and was pervaded by antiliberal and authoritarian sentiment.[44] Professors opposed the Weimar Republic and its constitution, but felt obligated to support the "state" as the "incorporation of their own mighty nation." "State" was a "metapolitical value," which help explain professors' "apolitical" behavior from the *Kaiserreich* into the years following World War II.[45] In the "half nation" of East Germany, respect for the state bordered on reverence and was reflected in the general pride taken in wearing official uniforms as well as in the regime's own self-description: the first worker and peasant state on German soil. This new state also possessed security services that awakened behavior patterns — like the *deutsche Blick* (the German glance) — learned under a previous German regime.[46]

Many German professors refused to embrace socialism, but few understood it as a movement at odds with their national interests. For those who felt remorse for Germany's past, the SED skillfully merged Marxist doctrine with an ideology of antifascism, which had an unusual force in eliciting loyalty for the socialist state. There was also a sense of obligation toward Russia that tended to blunt historical antipathies toward Slavdom.[47] Those who did not like this vision of the nation could seek a different vision beyond the intra-German frontier.

In the Czech lands a vaguely defined "socialism" inspired general enthusiasm, even among the anti-Communist intellectual mainstream. Associations with Russia were positive; indeed leading non-Communist intellectuals like Václav Černý or Zdeněk Kalista imagined Czechoslovakia as synthesis of West and East, fulfilling the legacies of both the French and Russian revolutions.[48] For most Polish intellectuals, by contrast, the Bolshevik Revolution and its aftermath had represented an existential danger.

The following chapters consider how the three professoriates operated in such differing political cultures. These cultures were not immutable, and initial consideration is given to ways in which events of the interwar and war years solidified the Polish professorial community on the one hand, and split and eroded the legitimacy of German and Czech professoriates on the other. Despite unparalleled losses in personnel, war did much to reinforce the sense of mission and solidarity among professors in Poland and bound the university milieu more tightly together. By contrast the war left moral ruin in the physically intact Czech environment, as elites emerged with identity and sense of purpose profoundly shaken. The crisis of identity among East German professors was even more severe, and the delegitimization so extensive as to cost them a role in shaping their own future. East German universities recommenced life with two-thirds of the staff cut, and subsequent additions, both in structure and personnel, carefully controlled. This was especially true of the faculties that lie at the heart of this study: humanities and social sciences. In Poland and the Czech lands, by contrast, universities could largely reconstitute themselves.

None of the university communities in question willingly acceded to

Communist rule; in each place student opposition emerged in the early post-war years. In the Czech lands and in Poland students staged public demonstrations, while East German students elected liberals and Christian Democrats as their student council representatives. In each case the increasingly unitary states responded by arresting dozens of opponents. Yet the response of professoriate differed according to context: enforced silence in East Germany, freely chosen distance in the Czech lands, and active solidarity in the Polish case. Only Polish professors joined with students in defense of university autonomy. The February coup of 1948 was the culminating act of political passivity among Czech professors, as Communist students purged universities, and many dozens of professors streamed into the KSČ, hoping for benevolence.

It was the force of community—of the *środowisko*—that protected Polish professors from such a fate. Concluding chapters show how their attachment to the values described here maneuvered the Polish state into a series of compromises, allowing professors to maintain control of the basic university relation: that between teacher and student. In East Germany and the Czech lands a new milieu emerged at the university, claiming a monopoly on symbols of authority and means of coercion. In both cases this milieu centered around Communist organizations, yet in the former it was relatively well subordinated to the Central Party apparatus, whereas in the latter for several years student-run Party cells retained considerable latitude. This new milieu soon dominated the social sciences and much of the humanities.

★

CHAPTER FOUR

SOURCES OF
LEGITIMACY
AND
COHESION
IN THE
INTERWAR
AND
WAR YEARS

The political cultures of Polish, Czech, and East German academia were exemplified as well as refined in the decades preceding the introduction of Soviet models. During the 1920s and 1930s Polish professors opposed the authoritarian Sanacja regime, with its camps for political prisoners and restrictions on academic autonomy. Czech and German professors by contrast proved quite loyal to their respective states. In the former case, several figures who would play key roles in the anti-Communist opposition of the post–World War II period welcomed state intervention in university affairs as a way of combating dangers from the right. In the latter, a positive ideology of a totalizing state was enunciated within the academy, and many professors greeted the Nazi regime as a realization of their hopes. German universities embraced National Socialism more warmly than any other segment of society.

World War II set contexts for the early postwar years, but it did so in ways that defy expectations. The war is often treated as a phenomenon that simply removed the Polish intelligentsia from the political stage, because of the deculturation policies of two occupying regimes, realized at such places as Auschwitz and Katyn. Polish writer Stefan Kisielewski depicted this cataclysm as a Polish White Mountain, alluding to the battle of 1620 that destroyed the Czech nobility, leaving Czech society without national leadership. Indeed the physical losses sustained by Polish universities were staggering: more than one in three academics perished.[1] Yet the extreme barbarity of Nazi policies provoked a broad societal resistance, including underground education. The war was experienced as a heroic struggle for culture. Within a few years of its conclusion, professors had filled in the gaps in their numbers and faced the regime in a relatively defiant front. Though Czech universities also suffered policies of deculturation, a legacy of resignation pursued Czech professors into the postwar years, as they had not organized opposition. The war split the Czech university community apart, because many Czech students had vigorously opposed the Nazi occupiers and felt that they deserved new powers in the postwar era. With the exception of a courageous but tiny student resistance movement, German universities had supported National Socialism to the end, and entered the postwar years with depleted reserves of moral capital.

Challenges to Academic Autonomy: The Interwar Years

The creation of an independent Poland after World War I brought vast improvements to Polish-language education, but professors found themselves aligned against the new state. Conflict had begun in earnest in 1924, when universities protested the government's tendency to take action without prior consultation — discontinuing positions, for example, ostensibly for financial reasons. In addition, universities resented being bombarded with injunctions and punished by delayed appointments.[2] Tensions grew with the seizure of power by Marshall Piłsudski in 1926 and peaked with his Sanacja regime's resort to political terrorism several years later. In 1930 over 320 professors (60 percent) signed resolutions condemning the internment of political prisoners at Brześć. Professors were the most vocal and best-organized opponents of these arrests in Polish society.[3]

The state attempted to penalize the professors with a law limiting academic autonomy, but drafts of this law aroused a still more vociferous protest, even among the regime's supporters. For example, the prominent Sanacja deputy, Kraków economist Adam Krzyżanowski, abandoned his parliamentary seat and sided with National Democrats at his university, people he otherwise would not speak to. As part of the pacification campaign, in 1933 the government liquidated some fifty-three positions, but professors created new positions for their colleagues. At the inauguration of the 1934–35 academic year, Poznań's rector Stanisław Runge registered "with regret the great losses our university has suffered in the past year among its professors." Although the minister's right-hand man (B. Żongołłowicz) was sitting beside him on the stage, he then proceeded to explain how the university had found new positions for all of the professors who had been dismissed! It did not matter that they were National Democrats and Runge was the strongest Sanacja supporter at the university.[4] Universities throughout Poland found ways of keeping "retired" colleagues: in some cases they were transferred to other chairs, in others employed as docents. Both procedures were entirely legal, because the minister could not deny a professor his right to teach, the *venia legendi*. In the end the ministry attempted to come to terms with the professoriate by modifying the law to permit liquidation of a chair only at the request of the faculty council.[5]

A more serious challenge to the integrity of the university came from the

activities of right radical students, who in the late 1930s organized persecution and beatings of Jews and, most notoriously, "ghetto benches," a section
of the classroom "reserved" for Jewish students. Here the professoriate failed
to take a courageous stance. In some cases this was due to sympathy for
the student radicals, especially in strong National Democratic *środowiska*,
like Lwów or certain faculties in Warsaw. These were places where professors conspired to exclude Jews from studies through a range of unofficial
devices, most frequently by posing questions at entrance examinations that
were impossible to answer. The number of Jewish students at Polish universities progressively declined in the interwar period from 20.4 percent in
the 1928–29 academic year to 9.9 percent in 1937–38.[6] Many went abroad to
study; especially popular was Berlin and, after 1933, the German university
in Prague.

Those professors who disapproved of the thuggery of National Democratic students often feared physical violence for open sympathy with Jewish
students. For example, an assassination attempt was carried out against the
Polonist Konrad Górski of Wilno, who had taken a public stance in favor
of Jewish students.[7] Nevertheless, professors continued voicing disapproval;
best known was the philosopher Tadeusz Kotarbiński, who refused to be
seated during his lectures in solidarity with students who stood in protest of
the ghetto benches. Some fifty-six scholars of Warsaw, Poznań, and Wilno
universities signed a protest against the ghetto benches in December 1937.
The total number of professors signing protests at Polish universities was
nearly 100 — about one in six.[8]

Viewing these events from a teaching position at Berkeley, economist
Oskar Lange called the signatories the "elite of Polish scholarship."[9] The list
included scholars who would play important roles in the postwar period:
philosopher Tadeusz Kotarbiński, sociologists Józef Chałasiński, Stanisław
and Maria Ossowski, and Jan Stanisław Bystroń, biologists Stanisław Kulczyński and Jan Dembowski, psychologist Władysław Witwicki, physicist
Konstanty Zakrzewski, and historians Seweryn Wysłouch, Tadeusz Manteuffel, and Natalia Gąsiorowska. The extreme social inequalities of the late 1930s
and the experiences of the war tended to anchor these scholars on the left,
though few were Communists.

An especially horrific "bonding" experience for the students of historian
Marceli Handelsman was the denunciation of their teacher as well as their
colleague Ludwik Widerszal to the Gestapo by the radical right in 1944. Both
historians were Jews living on "Aryan" papers, and both now perished. This
experience freed T. Manteuffel or A. Gieysztor of any nostalgia whatsoever
for prewar Poland.[10] These scholars entered the postwar period with prestige;
they were academically "solid" and politically "clean." By contrast scholars
known as active supporters of measures designed to limit Jewish presence at

Polish universities often felt compromised in the postwar period and lacked the authority for a stand of principle.[11]

After the war the group that protested the ghetto benches was augmented by a number of recognized scholars who sympathized with the left, but had not taken strong political stances in the interwar period: physician L. Hirszfeld, philosopher K. Ajdukiewicz, legal scholars K. Grzybowski and B. Leśnodorski, Polonists K. Wyka and T. Mikulski, and historians W. Kula and A. Gieysztor. As a whole, this stratum of "progressives" played an important role in the postwar period as mediators between the mostly conservative professoriate and representatives of the Communist Party.

Like Polish institutions of higher education, Czech universities were threatened in the 1930s by a ministry intent upon limiting the autonomy of higher schools. The major component of change was to be in the method of appointing professors. Faculties were still supposed to nominate professors, but only after the ministry had announced competition for a job opening. The proposal would regulate professors' work and explicitly subordinate them to ministry supervision. If they seemed unable to complete their tasks, they could be transferred to other branches of state service. The argument for these changes was efficiency. In comparison to Polish counterparts, Czech professors formulated an equivocal response, however. Though rejected by most of the academic community as infringements of university autonomy, the proposals did attract the support of several leading authorities, including two post–World War II rectors of Charles University, Jan Bělehrádek and Karel Engliš. The former claimed that higher schools were already influenced by politics and hoped that a change in law would limit the influence of reactionaries. The latter criticized the tendency of university faculties to become inward-looking cliques, resistant to new ideas and new people. His colleague and friend František Weyr of Brno argued that a modern state needed to control its subjects, precisely to limit political abuse. He wanted the state to guarantee the freedom of research.[12]

As Jerry Z. Muller has written, *Gleichschaltung* was accomplished from above, below, and within the German university.[13] National Socialists had dominated student politics from early 1930, before the Nazi Party made its breakthrough on the national scene, and they continued thereafter to scrutinize professors' speeches and writings for remarks deemed incompatible with their ideology. Before 1933 relatively few professors had actively supported the Nazis, yet many had sympathized with the enemies of Weimar.[14] After 1933, administrative changes dictating the dismissal of Jewish, liberal, and left-leaning colleagues were absorbed without protest by German universities. Professors streamed into the NSDAP.[15] Their opportunism was too obvious for this to become a comfortable home base, however, and, again reminiscent of later Czech experience, they were constantly chided by radicalized younger colleagues and students for lacking enthusiasm.[16] Such harassment encouraged processes of "self-*Gleichschaltung*" in teaching, writing, and academic affairs.

There could be no question of German professors assembling and reinitiating university life in 1945; they were seen by Soviet occupiers as a major source of legitimation for the Nazi regime and had to forfeit their sovereignty. After they had "opened universities anew" in 1946, Communist functionaries maintained powers in recruitment of faculty and students. A break both in personal and institutional continuity thus took place in the East German professoriate that had no parallel in Poland or the Czech lands, either then or later.

War and the Professoriate

At first glance, Nazi occupation seems to have treated Polish and Czech universities in similar ways. In both places the Germans had concentrated their repressive measures on the intelligentsia, hoping to weaken national resistance, and in both places intellectual elites suffered more than the general population. In November 1939 Polish and Czech universities were closed after massive arrests. On 6 November 1939 the faculty of Jagiellonian University was summoned for a lecture on the "scientific policies" of the Third Reich. Yet, rather than holding a lecture, the Nazis sealed off the exits to the lecture hall and transported the professors to Sachsenhausen.[17] The following week, in the early morning hours of 17 November, German police and army units surrounded dormitories in Prague and Brno and apprehended some 1,850 students—more than 1 in 8 of all Czech students. Nine students and one teacher were shot and two days later 1,185 students were sent to Sachsenhausen, where they met the Polish professors.[18] Ostensibly these arrests were a reaction to students' attempts to disturb "peace and order." [19] Most of the Polish professors and the Czech students were gradually released over the coming years, but at least twenty professors, and many dozens of students, never returned home.[20] The Nazis kept Polish and Czech universities closed throughout the occupation.

One might expect that Czech professors, as outstanding representatives of the one successful democracy in Eastern Europe, would rally to the defense of academic freedom after the war. Yet it was Poland's professors, many of whom had been associated with Sanacja, who attempted to defend scholarly autonomy in 1946 and 1947. The differing patterns of behavior are tied to the legacies of Nazi occupation: Polish professors had responded to anti-educational policies with resistance, Czech colleagues had not. To be sure, several Czech professors took leading roles in the anti-Nazi opposition—for example, professor of Romance literature Václav Černý and biologist Vladimír Krajina—but they conceived of their work in military and political terms, and neither they nor their colleagues coordinated an educational response to Nazi policies. A few professors conducted instruction in philology and, since hospitals remained open, in medicine. There was also the botanist Karel Domin, who actively sought out and taught students. In the chemical research laboratories of the Bat'a firm in Zlín, docent Stanislav Landa attempted to organize regular university courses; for his troubles he was accused after the war of collaboration by personal enemies and "bullied out" of Zlín.[21] But these were exceptions.

Pressures for conspiratorial instruction began building shortly after the Nazi conquest of Poland. Older students wanted to complete examinations, and high school graduates wanted to begin university studies.[22] They contacted teachers, and teaching soon began, mostly in small groups in private apartments. Underground universities quickly built momentum, because both teachers and students welcomed the opportunity to escape a few times a week from the demoralizing world of Nazi occupation. They were also motivated by a concern for Polish culture: beyond killing thousands of intellectuals, the Nazis tried to pollute the minds of young people with gambling and pornography. The centrality of Polish culture to the enterprise is reflected in the subjects of the first courses: Polish literature, philology, and history.[23]

These courses were taught in Warsaw from the late winter of 1940. By the fall, a full range of subjects was being taught in the Polish capital by the staffs of Warsaw and Poznań universities as well as Warsaw Polytechnic.[24] Throughout the occupation Warsaw was the center of conspiratorial universities, because it concentrated the greatest number of higher schools and of intellectuals, including many expellees from parts of western Poland that were annexed by Germany. Enough former staff amassed from Poznań to permit the "reopening" of that city's university in Warsaw: in order to symbolize the commitment to regaining territories in Poznania and Pomerania, it called itself "University of the Western Lands" (UZZ).[25] In part because of the arrests of professors, instruction at Jagiellonian University in Kraków did not get going until early 1942.[26]

The greatest practical problem for the underground universities was to secure facilities, since libraries, classrooms, and laboratories were off limits. In some of the technical disciplines, and in medicine, Poles conspired to make unofficial use of institutions the Germans permitted to maintain operations—hospitals, for example, where medical students received disguised instruction while performing practical work. Beginning in March 1941, first- and second-year medical students also received technical training in a "school for first-aid personnel," which had been opened under German auspices. Similarly, students of physics and chemistry took camouflaged university courses at a state technical high school, at the former institute for experimental physics of Warsaw University—now a "workplace of physical measurements"—and at two officially sanctioned high schools for chemistry.[27] The Germans also permitted a first-aid course to emerge in the Warsaw Ghetto, at which professors of Warsaw's medical faculty conspired to teach university-level courses to 500 students from 1940 to 1942.[28] For the most part courses used prewar texts and curricula, though there was also some printing of new lecture notes (*skripta*) and even an occasional book.[29] Reading material was procured either by the Polish staff of closed libraries or from professors' collections.[30]

Technically speaking, these activities were governed by the underground state. In late 1940, a Department of Education and Culture was created under the historian Czesław Wycech, and from the fall of 1940 that department's commission for higher education was directed by the first postwar rector of Warsaw University, physicist Stefan Pieńkowski. There was also a planning commission that drafted projects for postwar education.[31] Yet the role of the underground government was limited mostly to coordination of instruction and dispersing of funds. Because of their conspiratorial nature, universities were decentralized and understood themselves to be sovereign corporations, as did each seminar or lecture group (*komplet*).

Leading experts count 6,300 students as having participated in university-level conspiratorial courses during the war. This amounts to more than 13 percent of the students enrolled in 1938. Over 4,000 of these students studied in Warsaw, and only about 500 in the next largest city, Kraków. About 48.4 percent studied humanities and social sciences, 33.3 percent medicine, 10.3 percent technical and natural sciences, and 8 percent agriculture and forestry. Over 700 teachers worked with these students, of whom 34.9 percent were professors, and 18.3 percent docents. About half of the prewar professoriate thus took part in secret education.[32] Approximately 700 master's degrees were granted.[33] Some 34 percent of the diplomas issued between 1944 and 1946 were in the social sciences and humanities, and 28 percent in medicine.[34] Many academic careers began in the underground.[35]

Discovery of a conspiratorial group could lead to torture and death, and therefore universities carefully concealed themselves from the surrounding world.[36] Professors were known only by pseudonym, and students admitted only after screening.[37] They had to take oaths of loyalty and keep their participation secret.[38] Remarkably, the force of this oath was enough to protect the conspiracy; despite vague knowledge of the existence of underground education, the Gestapo did not succeed in penetrating the conspiratorial structures.[39] Neither students nor teachers tended to dwell on risks, however, because no one could calculate survival in occupied Poland. In "manhunts" (*łapanki*) the Germans routinely arrested hundreds of people who happened to be on a street, or in a train or trolley car at a given moment.

Going to underground lectures was a risk, but so was going out to buy a bottle of milk.

Only by chance did the Germans once uncover and destroy a class in operation. During a street search on 5 January 1944 the Gestapo apprehended the student Hanka Czaki who was carrying lecture notes and other conspiratorial materials. She was subsequently tortured to death. Her materials implicated fellow student Ewa Pohoska, who likewise died in prison.[40] When the Gestapo broke into Czaki's apartment they found a sociology class in progress. Six of the male participants and the teacher, docent Dr. Władysław Okiński, were shot, along with the owners of the apartment. But this terror was not directed primarily against education. Information was found in Czaki's apartment pointing to her involvement with the Home Army. Whether the Gestapo could fathom that underground education was taking place, or that students would risk death for the sake of learning sociology, are matters open to dispute; in this case, students' protests that they had *only* been studying sociology were not accepted.[41]

The risks seemed greatest for professors and staff. The former were constantly on the move from one conspiratorial meeting to another, heightening the danger that they might fall into a *łapanka*. Administrators had to carry written records including students' names and addresses. In 1943, while on her way to a class, the secretary of Poznań University's Maritime Institute suddenly found herself surrounded by six German policemen. She had ten names of the institute's first class in her purse. The police did not recognize them and let her pass.[42] Underground universities found imaginative ways of dealing with danger. In Lwów examination lists were written in Arabic between verses of the Koran.[43] One class in Roman law in Warsaw once discovered that the apartment building in which they were studying had been surrounded by German soldiers and police. The Germans began searching, probably for underground soldiers, floor by floor. How to explain the presence of over a dozen young people in one apartment? "We used our heads," one student later recalled, "the host began taking dishes out of the cabinet. Someone made something resembling sandwiches. Someone else put on a record, and a few couples started dancing. . . . The intruders were informed that a 'Geburtstag' was being celebrated." In a similar case the students were quickly spread among the apartments of the house.[44]

Despite growing terror from late 1943, numbers of students in conspiratorial education continued to multiply. No course was interrupted for more than a few days. After the evacuation and systematic dynamiting of Warsaw in the fall of 1944, courses reemerged in the places where faculty and students took shelter: Kielce, Częstochowa, Jędrzejów, Radomsko, Milanówko, Ostrowiec Świętokrzyski, Pruszków, Grodzisk.[45] Poznań University survived its second evacuation.

Universities were only a prominent part of something larger—namely, Polish society, which, like the universities, had compulsively self-organized after the destruction of public institutions. This was civil society. And the underground university was a university, not to be confused with buildings, infrastructure, and administration; it was a community of scholars and masters, who would seek refuge for their purposes in the last small, unendangered spaces of the Polish capital and, after its obliteration, then of Poland itself. It persisted even in prisoner-of-war and concentration camps, where lectures were organized on the history of art, history of Germany, idealist philosophy, forensic medicine, principles of feeding. One account recalls: "classes and lectures were held at any spot available: in the baths, in lavatories, in the barracks, or when prisoners were 'taking a walk.'" [46] As Jan T. Gross has written in regard to the underground movement in general, such activity was not primarily directed *against* the Germans, but rather *toward* maintenance of collective life. [47] Indeed, the Poles, unlike the Czechs, French, or Yugoslavs, did not call their underground activity "resistance." Rather they referred to it as "conspiracy," "organization," or simply "underground." [48]

The question emerges as to why conspiratorial education was not organized in the Czech lands. After all, the Germans closed universities there, too. The answer is complex, but the context within Poland gives some hints. Much depended on the traditions inherited from the empires that once ruled East Central Europe. Underground education began much earlier and developed more fully in former Russian and German areas of Poland than in the former Austrian lands. Although most professors returned during 1940, courses in Kraków did not begin until 1942, whereas students and faculty in Warsaw or Lublin began conspiring in 1939–40. It was more natural for them. As mentioned, many of the professors had themselves taken part in conspiratorial education under the tsar. Likewise, in Prussian Poland there had been struggles for Polish culture at the turn of the century, culminating in a school strike by more than 30,000 students. The idea of continuing education unofficially was therefore a familiar one to most Polish scholars, but did not occur to Czech counterparts. [49] Furthermore, even in the regions that had belonged to the Habsburg Empire, Poles had never coexisted with a German population as Czechs had, and therefore did not have the same experience in accommodation. [50]

More important were the differing characters of Nazi occupation in Poland and in the Czech lands. As a rule, the Germans allowed only rudimentary education in Poland. In the words of Heinrich Himmler, Poles were meant to become a people "capable of counting to 500, writing their name, and recognizing that to be obedient to the Germans is a divine commandment." [51] In the western areas of Poland that had been attached to Germany, schooling was permitted only up to grade four, two hours daily, and in German. At age twelve Polish children were registered for labor service. Later in the war some exceptions were made for the sake of trade schooling, which could be held in Polish. In Central Poland Polish children received seven years' schooling and were registered for obligatory labor at age sixteen.[52] Schools were overcrowded and remained closed for extended periods, due to lack of heating material, arrested teachers, or use of school facilities for military purposes.[53] If Poles were not to become a nation of half-literates a massive response was necessary. And indeed conspiratorial education embraced all forms, from the first grade upward.

The Germans' strategy was far more differentiated in the Czech lands. Here they did not close schools but tried to corrode them from within. If schools taught the history of Bohemia, or European philosophy, it was from a chauvinistic German perspective. Prewar textbooks were filtered through a censor and many hundreds prohibited. Weekly hours in German were gradually increased, in the end embracing even subjects like mathematics and geography. The high schools that prepared for university, the *gymnázia,* were kept open, but the total number of students attending them fell from 95,184 in 1938–39 to 42,838 in 1943–44. In their place the Germans promoted practical education: numbers of students in technical schools rose in the same period from 21,707 to 37,540, and in apprenticeship programs from 91,984 to 152,023.[54]

Why should students and teachers go into the underground when they could continue in legality? The Germans carefully manipulated Czech fears of losing education. When it seemed that students or teachers were not behaving, top Nazi officials would summon functionaries of the Czech Protectorate government and threaten dire consequences; what had happened to universities, after all, could also happen to high schools. These Czechs in turn would summon school directors and inform them of the need to avoid all semblance of ill will toward the Germans.[55]

University professors also had much to lose. Though universities were closed, the Germans permitted a complete world of research and publishing to continue. Unlike Polish colleagues, Czech professors remained on salary, though several were retired prematurely. Libraries and professional associations remained open. Whereas the Germans had stopped publication of all Polish professional journals in 1939, a number of Czech medical, scientific, and even historical and legal journals continued.[56] The journal of the Prague linguistic circle, *Slovo a slovesnost* (Word and literature), appeared until 1943 and printed work by leading members.[57] The major Czech legal journal *Právník* (The lawyer) has appeared without interruption since 1861.[58] Under these conditions, members of Prague's and Brno's law faculties added significantly to their curricula vitae: for example, Karel Maiwald and

Karel Kizlink each wrote sixteen articles, and in 1944 the latter published two books; their colleague Bohuš Tomsa wrote thirteen articles; Karel Engliš published an economics text for high school students; and so on.[59] Publications for the popular market were even more impressive: in 1943 alone 3 million copies of Czech-language fiction, scientific, religious, and school texts appeared in the Protectorate.[60] Institutions continued that supported research: the Czech Academy of Arts and Letters remained open, conducting scholarly meetings, and dispersing moneys to researchers. In 1942 the Germans permitted the founding of a Czech Sociological Society, which offered weekly lectures at Café Savarin in Prague.[61]

Gradually the Czechs became ever more involved in the German world, a fact that made charges of collaboration difficult to withstand in the postwar period. It was the Czech government that began censoring textbooks and discriminating against Jews even before the Germans marched into Prague in March 1939; it was Czech teachers who began classes with right arms raised to the "German salute," celebrated Hitler's birthday, damned the émigré government, and joined the "League against Bolshevism."[62] They were also entrusted with communicating the Germans' view of history: the Nazis set up a special pedagogical institute in Rankenheim near Berlin which indoctrinated Czech teachers in Nazi views of history, geography, German literature, and biology. Several teachers adjudged "resistant" were recommended for forced labor and the "best" teachers were assigned as group leaders.[63] Polish academics and teachers were never subjected to such humiliation.

In this rather demoralized atmosphere, small disagreements were exacerbated and drove professors further apart. Czech philosophers, who might have been a model of unity in a time of trial, carried their personal differences onto the pages of two competing journals subsidized by the Protectorate government: *Ruch filozofický* (Philosophy in action) and *Česká mysl* (The Czech spirit). In 1941 the former had published an unsigned review of Josef Král's history of philosophy, which had appeared in Prague that same year: "even those who are financially dependent upon Král cannot claim that his rendering of this subject is an improvement over older Czech works. He has been lecturing on these things for almost two decades, but hardly anyone could envy students this feast for the soul. Pseudopositivistic straw remains straw in this or any other form. The most painful thing is that the genius of the Czech language writhes in agony on every other page."[64] In a letter of 15 June 1942 Král explained to economist Karel Engliš why he was pressing a libel suit through the Protectorate courts against *Ruch filozofický*:

> Recently *Ruch filozofický* has attacked me as well as [Prague professor of pedagogy Josef] Hendrich, and [Prague philosophy professor J. B.] Kozák, and printed signed and unsigned pieces of its editor and other

writers (from among my personal enemies [Brno sociologist Professor Emanuel] Chalupný). These are far from objective criticisms of my person and my work, but rather scandalous personal affronts. This scandalous behavior is a disgrace to our university as well as academic community and detracts from our scholarly life; this at a time when our universities are closed and when any other defense besides a legal one is impossible or very difficult. Thus they have brought dishonor to our academic world, not only at home but elsewhere as well.[65]

The ambiguity of wartime experience left a legacy of distrust and suspicion in the Czech lands.[66]

The War and Postwar Behavior

Besides a legacy of resistance, the war left Polish professors with important assets of experience: firsthand knowledge of the Soviet system. Dozens of professors and students witnessed the Sovietization of education in Soviet Vilnius or L'viv between 1939 and 1941. After the Nazi occupation of all of Poland in mid-1941, Poles from the east could share their impressions of Soviet and Nazi occupation with colleagues living further to the west—for example, musicologist Adolf Chybiński, professor in Lwów, with his friend Jerzy Lande, professor of law in Kraków. In December 1941 he informed Lande that the Nazi invasion had saved him from being deported by the Soviets to Central Asia with hundreds of thousands of other Poles:

> Recently I discovered that I was supposed to be deported to the East on 24 June "in order to protect a leading authority from the results of bourgeois influences" (no joke!). The reasons? I refused to attend meetings and seminars in Marxism and Leninism, I rejected scholarly cooperation with the East, I did not respond to official and private letters from beyond the Zbrucz [Poland's prewar eastern boundary] asking me to sign this and that statement, I did not fulfill the duties of the "director of a *katedra*," I refused to surrender my decorations and awards, I refused to receive official guides [*opiekunom*] who wanted to visit me at home, I did not show proper respect for the "great musicologists" of Kiev and Moscow, who wanted to "collect information" on scholarly affairs, and showered me with compliments. And they did not succeed, those pettifoggers [*prachwostom*], those rascals. One of them attempted to intimidate me with accusations of "scholarly sabotage," to which I responded in front of witnesses that I never have been, am not, and have no intention of being afraid of anyone or anything.

Whether Chybiński actually lived up to these standards of patriotism is not at issue; what is important is that such standards existed and acted to constrict perceived collaboration with the "Bolsheviks." After leaving Lwów in 1945 Chybiński accepted a chair at Poznań University. In January 1947 he wrote Lande asking for help in resolving a dilemma: whether to have his history of Polish music published by the Soviet Academy of Sciences: "What would you do in such a case? I am interested in the principle. I am leaning toward accepting the offer. What concerns me is whether and how the so-called public [ogół] will accept the fact that first I publish something in a foreign language which only later can appear in our language. For the time being there is no other option." Lande's response was delayed, and in the meantime Chybiński accepted. Yet he felt a need to justify himself: "I agreed, and whether you believe it or not, not for the honorarium, but rather in order to make propaganda, honest propaganda. But I can already hear the voices of my 'friends': that scoundrel of the deepest dye has betrayed Polish science for 'Soviet rubles,' and is publishing with the Moscovites rather than in his fatherland." [67]

Intimate knowledge of the Soviet world triggered a sense of caution among Polish professors. Postwar authorities even considered such knowledge dangerous and staged the severest purge of junior faculty in Toruń, a place with a high concentration of former Wilno residents. They could not purge all of the Polish professors who had lost friends and relatives at Katyn, however. Tadeusz Manteuffel, the key figure in Polish historical studies of the 1950s, was told in a "conclusive manner" by painter Józef Czapski during a 1948 visit to Paris the identity of the perpetrators of the Katyn massacre and the likely fate of his own brother Edward.[68] In the Czech lands and East Germany, by contrast, those professors who knew the Soviet system firsthand—like Zdeněk Nejedlý or Gerhard Harig—became dedicated to popularizing it.

The blending and confusing of Soviet and Nazi totalitarianisms had thus begun during the war in Poland; inhabitants of Lwów like Chybiński referred to troops of the two armies as "guests from the East and West." [69] Though few took part in armed insurgency against the "guests" when they returned from the East in 1944–45, the heroic context—one might also say "discourse"— of opposition continued, which had been bequeathed by the romantics and immeasurably strengthened by the Nazi occupation. Philosopher Władysław Tatarkiewicz had worked on his O szczęściu (On happiness) during the occupation. The manuscript was one of the few things he was able to rescue during the evacuation of Warsaw:

> During the Warsaw Uprising in August 1944 I managed to take the manuscript from our burned-out house. On the road to the camp at Pruszków a German officer examined my baggage. "A scholarly work? That is no longer needed!" he screamed. "There is no such thing as

Polish culture any more: *Es gibt keine polnische Kultur mehr.*" Saying
that he threw the manuscript into the gutter. I decided to take the risk
and I picked it up. And that is how the manuscript was saved.[70]

When they censored, arrested, or shut down schools, Polish Communists
entered spaces in popular memory occupied by the Nazis and called forth
responses bordering on the conspiratorial — especially the "protection" that
permeated postwar Poland. Polish professors had taken great risks for the
sake of teaching and research and were determined to protect those quantities under the new and endlessly more subtle assault.

What is more, the occupation had delegitimized central state intervention. Poles enjoyed freedoms during the Nazi occupation that they had not
known in over a century, for, as Jan T. Gross has written, "within Polish
society proper, no single authority could effectively curtail, limit, or repress
the free articulation of all possible shades of political opinion."[71] Tadeusz
Kotarbiński recalled after many years that the low point of occupation, the
winter spent in Radom after evacuation from burning Warsaw, was for him
a high point: "the most productive and perhaps didactically most intensive
year in my many years as a professor was this academic year, when officially
universities in Poland were silent."[72] Responsible to no one but himself and
his students, he taught things for which there had been no room in university
curricula, like the philosophy of culture.[73]

One leading intellectual wrote after the war that "the entire structure of
our psyche collapsed as if struck by a bomb," yet, as Piotr Hübner has argued,
such characterizations do not apply to the Polish academic community.[74]
Rather than break professors' "faith in established values," the war created
a sense of urgency about the need to protect the university.[75]

Czech professors entered the postwar period with much self-doubt after
years of passivity. They were out of place in the radical moment of 1945,
with its calls for democracy, socialism, and national revolution, and many attempted to ingratiate themselves with those who seemed to have authority —
the students and the left. In August 1945, Professor Václav Hora (b. 1873),
who had been retired in September 1939 against his will, requested reinstate-
ment. In the letter to his dean he emphasized the positive reputation he enjoyed among students: "The Union of University Students has expressed its
regret that I have not been invited to work in the professorial council, and
tells me that 'the entire student body of the law faculty, which knows me as a
democratic and progressive scholar, will welcome with joy my participation
in rebuilding the law faculty.'"[76]

The fact that few professors had offered resistance required explanation
in a time when the Czech people were portrayed as united in opposition
to the German occupiers who had recently escaped across the border. Pro-

fessor Josef Tureček, expert in canon law at Charles University, painfully admitted on a questionnaire that he had not belonged to any "illegal movement"; "however," he detailed on a separate sheet of paper, in a number of other ways he had frustrated the Germans' policies in the Czech lands:

1. I dauntlessly protected a number of students from arrest, when a number of Gestapo agents came to my final lecture on 17 November 1939 in order to arrest Czech students.
2. I rejected invitations to attend lectures by Czech fascists [vlajkařů].
3. I refused to subscribe to the [Prague German daily] Der neue Tag.
4. I refused to receive a purely German telephone book.
5. I sabotaged the civilian air raid shelter.
6. I perseverantly and systematically sabotaged the removal of every kind of waste product [veškerých odpadků] from house no. 792 in Prague-Dejvice, although someone threatened to inform the Gestapo.
7. I hid skis and ski poles when we were told to surrender them to the German army for use in the campaign against Russia, although someone in my house threatened to inform the Gestapo.
8. I listened to foreign radio stations, and regularly took part in secret debates about these broadcasts in various places.
9. I cheered up the Czech people living in my area.[77]

As was often the case in postwar Prague, the absurd was not merely farcical. Tureček joined the Communist Party in 1945, one of only three law professors to do so, and as dean in 1948 supervised the purging of his faculty.[78] A similar case of a scholar with great need to compensate in the postwar period for perceived shortcomings during the war was the physicist Miloslav Valouch, who joined the KSČ "immediately" after the occupation, and busied himself with explanations for failing to separate earlier from his wife—who was of Czech-German heritage.[79] In 1948 Valouch was the department chief in the Ministry of Education who signed the dismissals that had been demanded by student-led "action committees." If he and Tureček could no longer strike out at the enemy occupier, they would strike out at new enemies—their colleagues.

★

CHAPTER FIVE

THE
FOUNDA-
TIONS
OF THE
EARLY
POSTWAR
YEARS

After the war Polish professors, who had never lost a grip on university teaching, felt it was their natural right to reopen universities. Survivors simply returned to the buildings from which the Germans had banished them six years earlier and set up the new academic year. This continuity was perhaps the most important legacy of conspiratorial instruction.[1] In East Germany, the Soviet occupation regime did not permit universities to reopen until early 1946, after all former Nazis had been removed.[2] As a result of denazification, the ongoing deportations of specialists, and other unaccounted-for attritions, including war casualties, teaching staff active in the winter semester of 1944–45 declined from 1,630 to 286 (17.5 percent) by the summer semester 1947. The number of full professors fell from 461 to 123 (28 percent).[3] Professors lost their sovereignty in university affairs, because Soviet and East German agencies had to approve every action they took, including appointments of staff.[4] In the Czech lands "revolutionary" organs, with students playing a strong role, got universities up and running in May 1945, and professors were at first relatively passive. These divergent beginnings foreshadowed divergent experiences of stalinism at universities: vigorous, informal self-organization of Polish scholars, a gradually expanding role for central state organs in East Germany, and the hardly checked rule of students at Czech universities.

Denazification of the East German Professoriate

The formation of Communist power was gradual throughout the region, and even in East Germany the creation of coordinated central rule took several years. In 1945 the authority of the center was more negative than positive, better at forbidding and removing than creating, and active only sporadically. The major activity of the first postwar years was denazification: dissolving fascist influences in the curricula, faculty, and student body. This agenda placed the occupiers and their German helpers in opposition to the traditionally apolitical professoriate. Even non-Nazi rectors of 1945 assumed the existence of only a small core of active Nazis among their colleagues and felt no need for deep transformations. They wanted simply to reconnect to "German university tradition." Thus a group that formed in Berlin in May 1945 to discuss the future of German universities included the classicist Wolfgang Schadewalt, who had entered the NSDAP in 1932 and the following year pushed his mentor Ernst Fraenkel out of the university as a "non-Aryan."[5]

Such independent activity alarmed the Soviets. In October they ousted Berlin rector Eduard Spranger, who had wanted independently to "negotiate" the university's interests with the Communist city magistrate. In the Soviets' eyes Spranger "combined a reactionary philosophical worldview with equally reactionary political views."[6] He was replaced by a more compliant colleague, classical philologist Johannes Stroux.[7] In the wake of a controversy over denazification, the Soviets closed Greifswald University and forced the appointment of a loyal university *Kurator,* who carried out the traditional task of monitoring university activity for the state. The Academic Senate had reduced faculty from 162 to 84, but resisted going further, though 55 remaining faculty members had belonged to the NSDAP or one of its subdivisions. Under the leadership of Rector Ernst Lohmeyer, a theologian who had been punished by the Nazis for membership in the Confessing Church, it also resisted standardizing the curricula.[8] Lohmeyer tried to appease the Soviet Military Administration (SVA) by appointing a Communist as professor of Marxism-Leninism, though he had no university degree, and by enlarging the department of Slavic languages and converting it into an East European Institute. In the German context, "Eastern Europe" included Russia.

Like Greifswald, Leipzig University tried to conduct its own denazification, but did so under duress, because the Americans had taken forty-three professors westward when they cleared the Soviet zone in July.[9] Only four would ever return. Thereafter the Soviets helped themselves to a few of the remaining experts, for example Professor Robert Döpel, the only professor remaining at the Institute of Physics, who left for the Soviet Union that summer.[10] In early September the university worked out a formula with the Soviets that stipulated the retention of former Nazis "who were under pressure of the NSDAP and did not act as active National Socialists." Yet by 15 November, only 49 of 252 professors remained, including 9 of 83 at the medical faculty, and 7 of 57 in the natural sciences. The university senate resisted pressures for deeper cuts and made multiple appeals for relief.

With the American evacuation westward the university town of Jena likewise lost valued scholars, including the directors of almost all natural science institutes and several of the medical institutes. Only one of these, chemist Franz Hein, would return.[11] In October Jena became the first university the Soviets permitted to reopen. Yet further university openings were delayed, because authorities in Moscow rejected Marshall Zhukov's request to conclude denazification in the zone. The Soviet Foreign Ministry demanded further purging of public institutions, especially universities.[12] On 11 November a further sixty professors were dismissed that Leipzig university had wanted to protect, and two weeks later fifty more teachers were released at Jena.[13]

The precise causes of this radicalization are uncertain, but it seems that a number of political incidents heightened Soviet skepticism of universities, and local German Communists, like Saxony's Kurt Fischer or Paul Wandel of the DVV, took advantage of such incidents for their own political ambitions. Despite the self-purgation launched in the summer, the Soviets discovered in early October that a former Nazi still directed Leipzig's university library.[14] In Jena, the university had to be closed again after students mocked a Soviet officer's claim that his country's living standards outstripped those of prewar Western Europe.[15] The Soviets likewise grew suspicious of Leipzig university authorities who argued that their "scholarly reputation was sealed" if they had to release an additional six professors.[16] According to later statements of Paul Wandel, at this point both Soviet and German Communists had begun to wonder whether universities were at all suited to training a new intelligentsia.[17] A decision was made to begin more or less from scratch: before universities could reopen, all remaining Nazis had to be removed from teaching positions.[18]

Indeed East German historians did not refer to the inauguration of the winter semester in January and February 1946 at Berlin, Leipzig, Halle, Greifswald, or Rostock as a "reopening" but as a "new opening." Not only were numbers of teaching staff reduced by more than three-quarters, but the traditional organs of self-governance became a pale semblance of their pre-Nazi selves. Official approval, which had been an occasional formality limited to appointments and curricula, now became a constant necessity. In the immediate postwar period Soviet officers watched universities' every movement, scrutinizing faculty promotions or appointments and spot-checking student admissions. They determined upward limits for student body growth, reviewed university budgets, and censored teaching in ways that were unprecedented in Germany. They hindered appointments and, in cooperation with the Communist-controlled *Land* governments, occasionally imposed their own choices of students and teachers.[19] As has been mentioned in chapter 2, the Soviets paid particular attention to ideologically sensitive subjects, for a time completely banning teaching in philosophy and history, and restricting the teaching of law.

Of course, universities had some say in these issues. Neither Soviet nor

German Communist agencies could control every aspect of their operations, especially in these early years, and were reliant upon professors' cooperation. Faculty councils and senates had to lure professors from elsewhere in Germany to fill vacant positions. And until the early 1950s Soviet ambitions to control course content were not fully realized, even in economics. Yet the codetermination universities retained in these matters would be successively curtailed, as the central East German authorities grew in competence and power. The break with the past in East German university development was the earliest and most decisive in the region, and is dramatically reflected in the discontinuities of the professoriate (see Table 5-1).

TABLE 5-1

Continuity of the East German Professoriate
(including emeriti and docents)

Type of Faculty	Active, Winter 1944	Still Active, Summer 1947	Percentage
Philosophical	343	71	20.7
Mathematics/natural sciences	380	60	15.8
Agriculture/veterinary medicine	115	25	21.7
Theological	74	29	39.2
Medical	569	90	15.8
Law	152	11	7.2
Total	1,633	286	17.5

Source: Jessen, "Akademische Elite," 320–22.

Neither Allied nor Soviet decrees had necessitated such a purge.[20] In the social sciences and much of the humanities, the break was permanent, because at the point in 1947 when former Nazis began returning to the natural sciences and medicine, a second round of purges began against "bourgeois" scholars in the human sciences.[21] No other institution in the Soviet zone was more thoroughly depleted of staff; even in the police forces, justice administration, and schools, room remained for at least some former Nazis.[22] The decision to single out universities reflects both Soviet ambition and distrust. On the one hand, Soviet officers wanted universities to begin training an intelligentsia that would be true to democratic principles — as they understood them.[23] On the other they recognized the potential dangers of losing control over universities. They did not want to repeat the experiences of 1945, and when a university threatened to go out of control, they intervened decisively.[24]

A break was also visible in administration. Traditionally, the *Kurator* functioned as mediator between state and university, and all correspondence to the state authorities had to clear his desk. In 1945 the Soviets appointed reliable *Kuratoren* in Halle, Rostock, and Greifswald, all of whom took major roles in politicizing their respective universities.[25] In December 1945 and January 1946 the Soviets also imposed more pliable rectors on the universities of Rostock, Leipzig, and Greifswald. In Rostock the socialist chemist Rienäcker replaced conservative physician Wachholder, and in Leipzig the philosopher Gadamer took the place of the archaeologist Schweitzer, whom the SVA had identified as a "fanatic opponent of the Communist worldview."[26] The most spectacular change of rectorship occurred in Greifswald. The day before the university was to "open anew," Rector Lohmeyer was apprehended by Soviet secret police, supposedly for crimes committed during the war by troops under his command. He is thought to have died in a Soviet camp in Germany in 1947. Yet to his family and colleagues, Lohmeyer's fate remained a mystery. As was typical in such cases, they were told neither the fact of nor the reason for his arrest. Thus, on the morning of 15 February 1946, a shocked faculty of thirty-four professors attended the "new opening" of Ernst-Moritz-Arndt University in Greifswald. The freshly appointed rector, physicist Seeliger, had been entreated to accept his office the previous evening by a representative of the Central Education Administration, his colleague Robert Rompe.[27]

Reopening Czech Universities

University activity in the Czech lands recommenced with student activity. In the early months of 1945 leftist students formed illegal groups and planned a new academic year. As Soviet troops closed upon Prague in early May, these student cells emerged from hiding and claimed an important role in the "National Uprising" against the Germans. Students formed armed legions, and arrogated key powers to themselves, such as the disbursal of stipend moneys, the management of dormitories, and the right to purge their own numbers without judicial appeal. Widespread sympathy for their wartime sufferings made student leaders unusually self-confident.[28]

Professors remained comparatively docile. They seemed an integral part of a failed establishment, having figured among the founders of the First Republic and acted as ministers of finance, foreign affairs, education, and justice. Several had also served in the Protectorate government. In the immediate postwar period Czech professors for the most part accepted limitations to their freedoms, even when opposition was possible. For example, they recognized the nomination of deans and rectors by revolutionary committees rather than insist upon customary election.[29]

In 1945 professors of Charles University voted the appointment of several new colleagues for the chairs in Soviet studies that have been mentioned in

chapter 2, despite their lack of standard qualifications. A law faculty committee unanimously recommended Vladimír Procházka, though of his writings
only "a few were written using the proper scholarly method." There was not
even a suggestion that his teaching qualifications be tested in the conventional habilitation lecture.[30] Fully aware that he "was really only a candidate
of science," Josef Král voted for Arnošt Kolman's professorship, because "still
in the glow of the Soviet contribution to our liberation, we wanted to have
an expert in Soviet philosophy. I hesitated, I pointed out that according to
his scientific qualifications he belonged in the natural sciences faculty . . . but
since I was of the opinion that Marxism-Leninism had continued to develop
in the Soviet Union and I felt a need to add foreign philosophical influences
to our thinking . . . I suggested his specialty be called exact sciences and
Soviet philosophy." Kolman encountered a willingness to please bordering
on servility among his new colleagues, who in Král's words suffered from a
"complete lack of self-respect." [31] In 1948 he repaid the debt to his colleagues
by supervising the action committees that purged their faculty.[32]

The case of Brno shows that such submissiveness was not necessary: the
Košice accords mandated the creation of chairs in Soviet studies, but they
did not require that professors disregard the formal procedures for appointment.[33] When several Communist lawyers in Brno demanded professorial
appointments for themselves in 1946, the faculties concerned simply refused.
Dean J. L. Fischer of the philosophical faculty wrote that "in view of the
qualifications of the self-appointed candidates, the faculty notes that universities are not the most suitable terrain for political agitation, and the faculty
will defend this position in all cases, to the last consequence." [34]

On 10 May 1945, Dean Jan Rypka of Prague's philosophical faculty had
returned to his offices on the banks of the Vltava River, but found student
legions in control of the buildings, busily planning the new semester.[35] In the
words of Communist student functionary Jan Kazimour, they were doing
so "not on the basis of a decree, but by their own strength, and with their
own weapons." [36] This was no time to be concerned with legal formalities;
students cleared away the debris, repaired shattered windows, transported
books, and got a schedule of classes printed. An "action committee" inaugu-
rated an "extraordinary semester" in early June.[37] According to historian
Josef Polišenský, a young lecturer at the time, Dean Rypka cooperated fully
with the students.[38] A Union of University Students was formed which came
under the sway of well-organized Communists and demanded a "purge of
professorial bodies and central education authorities not only of collaborators and traitors but of incompetent people and people who do not understand the needs of the day." [39] Such a statement by students was unimaginable
in Germany or Poland at that time.[40] The union even began approaching
professors with offers of teaching positions.[41]

The reopening of the other institutions of higher education in the Czech lands proceeded with less drama. Soviet troops liberated Masaryk University in Brno several days before Prague. Most of its buildings had been held by the German occupiers; for example, the law faculty served as Gestapo headquarters and the largest dormitory had been a prison, where over 1,200 people were executed. Brno's conquest left more destruction than Prague's, but instruction recommenced by mid-May. The following month a student union emerged as well as faculty trade union organizations.[42] In February 1947 the Czechoslovak government reestablished a university in Olomouc that had been closed by the Austrians in 1867, which, counting the technical universities in Prague and Brno, brought the total of higher-education institutions in the Czech lands to five.

From the fall of 1945, a semblance of normalcy entered Czech university life, and indeed political life in general in the Czech lands. Professors now reclaimed their right to elect their own representatives—at Charles University they confirmed all but one of those chosen by "revolutionary organs" in the summer—and a less convulsive student life emerged as young people enrolled by the thousands and attempted to make up for time lost during the war. The mood in the student union gradually shifted toward the political center. As will be shown in greater detail, students, especially of the medical and law faculties, tended to be more clear-sighted than their elders as to the dangers posed by Communists to intellectual and political freedoms, and handed the Communists a series of election defeats in student union elections of 1946 and 1947.[43] The KSČ could not be completely eliminated from the union's governing board, however, because it had anchored the principle of "proportional representation" in the union statutes when it enjoyed greatest power in the revolutionary days of 1945.

The Reawakening of Academic Life in Poland

The first university to reopen in "People's Poland" was the Catholic University of Lublin (KUL). Faculty members reassembled on 23 August 1944, shortly after the town had been swept of German troops, and the university recommenced operations on 12 November. Though fourteen professors had been lost during Nazi occupation, the prewar total of twenty-four professors (full, associate, assistant) was reached in the 1944–45 school year after the addition of eight professors from Lwów, three from Wilno, and four from Central Poland.[44] Having suffered no war damage, KUL could immediately commence instruction and expansion. No state university save Kraków was able to reach prewar strength until 1948.[45]

As a counterbalance to KUL, the government founded a state university (UMCS) in Lublin in October 1944. Under PPS activist rector Henryk Raabe four faculties opened that same month: medical, natural sciences, agricultural, and veterinary.[46] This arrangement guaranteed that the universities in Lublin would not duplicate each other's offerings, but it also kept ideologically sensitive studies outside the state-controlled institution.[47]

A true reawakening of Polish academia was heralded by the reopening of Jagiellonian University in Kraków on 18 January 1945. Due to skillful Soviet maneuvers, the city was taken intact from the Germans, and it gave refuge to dozens of professors from lost and destroyed academic centers: Poznań, which had been appended to the Reich and devastated as a "fortress city"; Warsaw, which even in 1948 was still a sea of ruins; and the eastern cities of Lwów and Wilno, which had been consumed by the Soviet Union. Kraków absorbed their intellectual energies, and in subsequent years radiated them back into Poland, especially to the new universities in Toruń, Łódź, and Wrocław. Indeed, the rectors of these places came frequently to Kraków looking to supplement their own faculties.[48] They also mended networks of contacts.[49]

Although it had lost about one-third its professorship, Jagiellonian University surpassed its prewar numbers of teaching personnel in 1945–46.[50] Together the two conservative universities of Kraków and KUL graduated 57.2 percent of Poland's new lawyers that first postwar academic year, and were responsible for 51 percent of the master's degrees granted in 1946.[51]

Because of its near obliteration, Warsaw's reemergence as capital seemed in doubt in 1945, and so did the reopening of Warsaw University. Just as plans existed to transfer the capital to Łódź, so did the Ministry of Education begin planning the relocation of Warsaw University and Polytechnic to Łódź. But these plans came to naught when Warsaw's professors returned to the rubble of their university and began rebuilding. Without waiting for ministry permission, faculty councils prepared for a new semester.[52] They argued that even in 1945, Warsaw's population more than justified a university: if one included the undestroyed right-bank districts, the city counted 300,000 inhabitants.[53] A group of representatives of the university met on 14 April with the vice-minister of education, Communist Władysław Bieńkowski, and a three-member commission of Tadeusz Kotarbiński, Stefan Pieńkowski, and Bogdan Nawroczyński began preparations for the reopening of their university. Thanks in part to Pieńkowski's wartime connections to Minister of Education Czesław Wycech, permission was secured in mid-July for conducting classes in the fall.[54] But rebuilding in Warsaw proceeded slowly: not until the 1947–48 academic year would the city reach its prewar capacities in students and personnel.[55]

Denied the energies of nearby Warsaw, the new university in Łódź became among the weakest in Poland. This was particularly unfortunate for the small Polish Workers' Party, because Łódź was the strongest working-class center in Poland, and the only place a socialist university was conceivable. Łódź indeed was a magnet for leftist intellectuals. It became home to the two leading journals of the left, *Kuźnica* (The forge) and *Myśl Współczesna* (Contemporary thought), and of the "Democratic Club," a group of about thirty intellectuals, with Adam Schaff as a cofounder.[56] The university's first rector was the reformist educator and freethinking philosopher Tadeusz Kotarbiński. He was joined by the renowned left-leaning sociologists Józef Chałasiński, Stanisław and Maria Ossowski, Nina Assorodobraj, and Jan Szczepański, as well as historians Witold Kula and Natalia Gąsiorowska.[57] Yet precisely because of its leftist reputation and lack of academic traditions Łódź was not taken seriously by other universities. They shunned the university there, refusing to help it onto its feet.[58] To make matters worse, much of the early faculty came from Warsaw, Lwów, and Wilno, and as those milieus reemerged Łódź lost teachers.[59]

The reputation of leftism was somewhat inflated, however. The PPR never controlled Łódź's university, just as it never controlled Łódź's workers.[60] All of the leading thinkers there, save perhaps Schaff, had a standing independent of the Party, and many suffered harassment after 1948. Scholars of a dogmatic Marxist-Leninist persuasion felt isolated in Łódź as they felt isolated elsewhere in Poland. In late 1945 professor of law Stanisław Ehrlich lamented his lot as the unusual Leninist at Łódź University. He did not trust Kotarbiński, and suspected that permission from him to hold lectures in "Soviet Law" was merely a "gesture supposed to testify to the democratization of the university." In fact a Roman Catholic priest who was professor of canon law could reduce the hours of that lecture if he chose. Ehrlich attracted young Marxist lecturers to Łódź, but they eventually went to Warsaw. So did he.[61] Shortage of faculty jeopardized even undergraduate education. In 1951, of fifteen assistant professors in chemistry, nine had not yet received their first degree (*diplom*). Łódź suffered an unusually high dropout rate, and other universities became hesitant to recognize degrees granted there.[62]

Besides Łódź two other new universities emerged in Poland in 1945: Wrocław and Toruń. As time would show, however, they were not entirely new.

The former was established in the ruins of a university destroyed in the war's closing battles. The German city Breslau had been declared a fortress in January 1945 but had not surrendered until after Berlin, four months later. Due to the scale of destruction, it was decided to establish a combined University and Polytechnic in Wrocław, with common senate, rector, administration, and dormitories. The new institution's faculty came overwhelmingly from Lwów University and Lwów Polytechnic; its first rector, S. Kulczyński, had been rector of Lwów University and was a cofounder of the new Democratic Party, which was allied with the PPR. But he had his own agenda. At the university's opening ceremony on 9 June 1946 he told listeners that they were "the material heirs of the ruins of the German university and polytechnic in Breslau, but the spiritual heirs of the borderland culture of Lwów."[63] The polytechnic side of the institution developed so poorly that in 1947 ministry officials considered transferring its capacities to Gdańsk or Gliwice. But the university grew steadily, advancing from 64 faculty members in 1945–46 to 138 in 1948–49. In 1945–46 half the professors in the humanities and over 60 percent of the law faculty came from Lwów.[64]

Toruń had survived the war largely intact. It could not claim an institution of higher education on which to build, although the local citizenry had been pushing for the creation of a Pomeranian university since 1918. Now they were aided by professors from Wilno. In early April ten faculty members from that city gathered in Łódź, and asked the Ministry of Education that the "teaching staff from Stefan Batory University (of Wilno) in its composition of 1 September 1939 be used in its entirety for the creation of a university in Pomerania." After receiving permission from Warsaw in late April, Toruń's National Council founded the Nicolaus Copernicus University. By July the new university had a senate, and ministerial decrees called into being faculties of humanities, mathematics and natural sciences, law and economics, and fine arts.[65] Toruń's faculty remained constant at about sixty from 1945 to 1948, though numbers of students doubled to three thousand. It was dominated by professors from Wilno, with colleagues from Lwów a strong minority.[66]

By permitting academic communities from Lwów and Wilno to reemerge in Wrocław and Toruń, the ministry not only missed an opportunity to create something new, it also tolerated the reconstitution of particularly anti-Soviet professorships.[67] At a conference of PPR academics in June 1947 a Comrade Sztefek from Wrocław complained that "the majority of professors are Lwówians with a pronounced complex of Sovietophobia." He found that transferring personnel away from Wrocław would be "difficult," however, because of the group cohesion.[68] The following year a report described the "harmful role" of teachers in social studies in Wrocław who lectured on such things as "Lwów—historical injustice to Poland."[69] For many Poles, supporting the imported regime was a denial of national identity, but for these Poles it was also an affront to personal biography.

The war had established differing contexts for the reconstitution of professoriates in East Germany, the Czech lands, and Poland. East German professors were heavily implicated in the Nazi past, and most lost their positions in the denazification of 1945–46. Those that were able to continue teaching had to recognize that they no longer possessed rights they had enjoyed before 1933: to name their successors, to determine curricula, or to preside over the admission of new students. Because of the war, initiative in these affairs had shifted permanently to the state.

In the Czech lands, initiative in university affairs fell first to students—mostly of the left—who organized the armed legions that occupied university property in May 1945 and founded a Union of University Students. By the late summer of 1945, the swells of revolutionary enthusiasm had subsided, however, and the faculties were once again dominated by mostly centrist and conservative forces, both among students and the professoriate. Yet certain precedents were established of extralegal organization—like action committees and honor courts—and many young Communists experienced a thrill of telling professors what to do that they never forgot. In some ways February 1948 was a reprise of that first "National Revolution," with the difference that nothing now could brake the play of intergenerational animosities.

In Poland, professors had never surrendered their initiative in university affairs, and no one contested their right to get universities up and running again in 1945. Though heavily decimated, they were strong enough to cover teaching vacancies and, aided by quick promotions, returned to full strength in a few years. The strongest of the reemergent milieus was the conservative Kraków, a city fully intact, and it was here that dozens of professors from all of Poland converged repeatedly in the early postwar years, seeking new colleagues and building informal structures of interest articulation—that is, networks of patronage and influence. The relatively weak Polish state could do little to impede the constitution of these hardly visible networks, and they came into play when that state attempted to assert influence over academia in 1947.

★

CHAPTER SIX

STRUGGLES
FOR THE
UNIVERSITY

The early postwar years are known as a time of relative openness in East European politics. Communist Parties were made to restrain their ambitions for immediate seizure of power, and they attempted cooperation with "progressive bourgeois" elements in parliaments that, to the naked eye, seemed democratic institutions. In Czechoslovakia and East Germany there were elections with some real choices in 1946, and in all three countries non-Communists participated in government. A limited debate on politics could occur in the press and at public meetings. Therefore opportunities remained to protest growing infringements of democratic practice in these emerging "people's" democracies.

Most sensitive to such infringements were students. Like counterparts the world over, Czech, East German, and Polish students spoke out boldly and acted impulsively. Many of them shared the fate of students who protest repressive regimes: Polish, Czech, East German, and Soviet security forces arrested hundreds of young people for remarks deemed reactionary or anti-Soviet in the early postwar years. Like academics the world over, professors urged restraint. Yet they did so in ways consistent with the patterns that have been suggested: with acts of solidarity in the Polish case, enforced reticence in the German case, and in the Czech lands with occasional haughty condemnation of student "frivolity" but in general with indifference. Only in Poland did professors understand attacks on students as attacks on the university and organize accordingly.

The organizations through which students staged protest differed according to context. In Poland, the traditional student associations of "fraternal help" reemerged in 1945 with a strong conservative and nationalist presence. In the Czech lands, unions of university students had been formed in the summer of 1945 with majority representation of leftist students. In the fall of 1945, central education authorities of East Germany permitted the creation of "student working groups" with representatives of the four sanctioned political parties (KPD, SPD, LDP, CDU). The respective student organizations were set up at faculty and then university levels, and accorded responsibility for issues of student welfare and advocacy. The student unions were citywide in Prague and Brno and had the unusual right of controlling dormitories and stipend moneys. In Poland larger student organizations existed in the form of the socialist (ZWM) and peasant student (Wici) clubs. Not until 1948–49 would Communist-controlled youth organizations modeled on the Soviet Komsomol (FDJ, ČSM, ZMP) co-opt organized student life throughout East Central Europe.

The most important function of student organizations was to provide a platform for the enunciation of political preferences. Students felt an especial need to take political stands, because in each place the work of national parliamentary institutions had been constricted to suit the needs of Soviet foreign policy. Even in Czechoslovakia, the place with the widest tolerated spectrum of political opinion, the initial postwar years were a time of mind-numbing appeals to "national unity." Only four parties were permitted to operate in the Czech lands (Communists, Social Democrats, National Socialists, Catholic Popular Democrats), and political opposition was seen as illegitimate. Students were sensitive to the growing Communist strength behind the facades of unity: in the trade unions and socialist parties, but also in the interior, defense, and information ministries.[1] They objected to the increasingly uniform opinions received from above, and frequent outbursts of anti-intellectualism on the part of Communist officials.

In all three places, Communist popularity suffered as students encountered the Communists' practice: use of the police to intimidate opponents, manipulation of the wartime legacy through control of information ministries, and, in general, a violent propaganda suggesting that opposition to communism was treason. Student protest represented a liberal alternative to the extent that it insisted upon procedural guarantees for freedom of expression and assembly, though only in East Germany did an explicitly liberal discourse emerge, most impressively under the leaders of the Rostock and Leipzig student councils, Arno Esch and Wolfgang Natonek.[2] In East Germany and Poland many students in addition were motivated by an anticommunism mingled with contempt for the Soviet Union.

The Czech Lands and Poland: Student Demonstrations

The first demonstrations in the region occurred in December 1945 when students of Prague's Technical University were told that restrictions had been imposed on the number of university textbooks that could be printed. They decided to protest at the Communist-held Ministry of Information, which regulated paper distribution, because they could see that many tons of paper were being expended for political propaganda. Self-important Minister Václav Kopecký happened to be in his office when the demonstrators arrived, chanting "fewer newspapers, more books!" and "Dear Minister, what are you doing? We're out of school, and you're still in bed." He told a students' delegation that they were "reactionaries," and vowed to have them arrested.[3]

Kopecký and his comrades then made this at-worst sophomoric protest into a political scandal. "Revolutionary" union cells from all over Czechoslovakia showered the university deans' offices with protest resolutions: the working class was not making its extraordinary sacrifices to build a new Czechoslovakia so that a few spoiled students could disrupt "national harmony." Miners from Ostrava alleged that the students had supported Czech wartime collaborators.[4] The trade-union committee of the Krušná Hora mine demanded that "the incident, which disturbed the calm of our workers' hands and spirits, be investigated as soon as possible and those who bear guilt for these demonstrations be compelled to take responsibility."[5]

Rather than defend their students, a number of professors joined in the criticism. In a letter to several factories, and to Minister Nejedlý, Rector Zdeněk Bažant of Prague's Technical University condemned the "student attacks upon several members of the government and exclamations with an anti-worker tendency. . . . under no circumstances may our student body allow reactionary elements to jeopardize the unity of university students by driving a wedge into the ranks of the National Front, and by striving to undermine the faith of the broad masses in the government." He urged students to behave "properly."[6] The faculty committee of the Department of Mechanical and Electrical Engineering, though it had not a single Communist representative, voted to reprimand the students for their demonstration.[7]

Even more disruptive of the decreed unity of intelligentsia and workers were the "Brno events" of February 1946. A Major Šoffer of the Czechoslovak Army's General Staff gave lectures at Brno's Technical University in military studies. Šoffer had a reputation for anti-Communist insinuations. During a 30 January lecture he told his listeners that they were not "simpleminded workers, who had saved up Reichsmark after Reichsmark, voluntarily worked overtime, and discovered the meaning of life in black market trading. . . . the intelligentsia is the center of the atom, everything else must keep an honest distance."[8] The following day Brno's Communist daily *Rovnost* denounced the major, and, probably because of Communist influence at the Ministry of Defense, he was soon recalled from teaching duties.[9] On the morning of 6 February, upon discovering Šoffer's lectures canceled, some 200 students went to protest at *Rovnost* headquarters. In the early afternoon, the trade-union cell at the Brno armaments plant—a plant that had been praised by Adolf Hitler for its contribution to the German war effort—

received a call that "fascist" students had attacked *Rovnost*. At the union leadership's instructions the plant emptied and workers marched upon the Technical University, where they chanted "Close down the universities!" "Professors to the mines!" "Expel the fascist students!" Windows were broken. The demonstration's leaders demanded that the university's administration punish the student demonstrators. At least thirteen were arrested.[10]

In Prague the "Brno events" were debated in Parliament, but non-Communist politicians failed to defend students' right to protest, or the major's right to teach as he saw fit. Once again, trade-union cells from all over the republic littered universities with statements of condemnation. The trade-union committee at the Brno-Slatina steelworks demanded in a letter of 6 February to Zdeněk Nejedlý that Major Šoffer be "immediately arrested and punished" for his "lectures, conducted in reactionary style." Two days later the trade unionists at the clothing manufacturer J. Enes in Chrudim urged that the "organizers of the putschist demonstration be identified and punished exemplarily."[11]

Student demonstrations of the same year in Poland lacked these appearances of class conflict. Major Šoffer's tactlessness notwithstanding, the war had indeed driven workers and intelligentsia further apart in the Czech lands, because the Nazis had persecuted the latter while coddling the former. The rations allotted to Czech workers were on a par with those of German workers, and Czech workers increased earnings due to wartime demand.[12] By contrast, the Czech intelligentsia, and in particular students, had been singled out for repression. In Poland Nazi occupation left a simpler legacy, because no social group had been allotted favorable treatment. As noted, the terror had been random, and whether workers, peasants, or intellectuals, most Poles viewed the new regime as a suspicious import. It refused to allow free elections, knowing that unlike Czechs, Poles would not show a mandate for communism, and would vote Mikołajczyk's PSL (Polish Peasant Party) into power. Polish Communists were fearful of spontaneous public expression and reacted brutally when young people throughout the country celebrated the traditional national holiday, Constitution Day, on 3 May 1946. In the eyes of Poland's Communists, in May there could be only one holiday, 1 May, the feast of labor.

This "first confrontation" (Wojciech Mazowiecki) of the new Polish regime with Polish society was especially serious in conservative Kraków. After morning Mass at the Church of Our Lady, thousands of young people streamed out onto the central square, chanting "long live Mikołajczyk!" and "no more propaganda!" Bystanders cheered. But the demonstrators were kept by security police from leaving the square, and scuffles ensued. One student was shot in the face. Crowds eventually did manage to escape the square and regathered at other points in the city, where manifestations of discontent lasted for hours. Several hundred persons were arrested.[13] The protests were not limited to Kraków; high school and university students as well as boy and girl scouts staged marches in cities and towns all over Poland that day.[14]

Polish Communists were less successful than their Czech comrades in bringing workers into the streets against students, though they did try to organize anti-intellectualism in very similar ways. In May 1946 the PPR press reported workers leaving their mines in Gliwice and Sośnice and, "without washing themselves," going out to demonstrate for the "closing down" of the Gliwice Polytechnic. Yet reports from the underground organization Freedom and Independence drew a different picture: "workers were agitated by PPR provocateurs to thrash the students, and break into and loot the stores and property of those living in Victory St. who had cast flowers to students on the second and third of May. But these workers, although escorted by force, and guarded by Soviet troops, stood motionless with heads bowed."[15]

Polish society proved more cohesive than Czech society. This greater cohesion translated into joint action at universities, and between universities. Polish students and professors organized locally, but also nationally in defense of their interests, and, as in the wartime conspiracy, they did so without central direction, let alone permission. In the weeks after the 3 May arrests in Kraków, students in all major university towns struck for the sake of colleagues who had been arrested. The issue, *in their words,* was "solidarity."[16] These actions led to new arrests, for example, in Poznań of 633 students.[17] Most of the students were released in the course of the year, but these would be the last street demonstrations by students in Poland for a decade. Student organizations came under increasing political pressure, and by 1950 "fraternal assistance societies" had disappeared, and the final "enemies" been eliminated from the leadership of the student "academic clubs" (*koła naukowe*).[18]

Poland: First Challenges to Academic Autonomy

Polish professors not only tolerated, but encouraged, the striking, for example, by canceling classes. Yet the student strikes exposed them, and the university community as a whole, to intensified repression; the regime used the strikes as an excuse for curbing university autonomy. Universities were said to harbor "reactionary forces." As Wojciech Mazowiecki notes, plans to limit university autonomy were not new. There had been a number of attempts by the Education Ministry in 1945 to interfere in academic appointments.[19] But the student strikes were a welcome pretext for renewed efforts. Official newspapers printed statements that were precisely like those released by the Czech and East German Parties: the working class sustained universities and would not permit them to educate students who were hostile to its interests. But the pretext proved of limited use, because the Party had unwittingly mobilized the professoriate.

On 12 May 1946, the rectors of Polish institutions of higher education came together at Warsaw University to draft a response to rumored plans for a central "council" to supervise universities and work camps for wayward students. They expressed "amazement" that this council was supposed to work independently of the Ministry of Education; and the ministry's plans to punish students with forced labor seemed "reminiscent of practices that are most alien to the sense of decency and justice that has been created in our people during the painful experiences of the years of heroism." In a speech to the PPR Central Committee of 2 June Władysław Gomułka claimed not to be bothered by the historical precedents: "Hitler made work camps and so you think this is a fascist idea. But Hitler made the idea fascist, we can make it proletarian." The Kielce voivode, Eugeniusz Wiślicz, put a finer point on the matter: "It is a great thing to have a model, if the results are good. Like Hitler we can organize work camps, but with a democratic ideology." [20]

In practice the PPR was indeed concerned about appearances and momentarily backed down from this project. Yet a year later plans reemerged in a supposedly more moderate form from the pen of former Sanacja legal scholar Maurycy Jaroszyński, who proposed organizing higher education beneath a "Main Council," which could decide habilitations, transfers of faculty, creation and dissolution of institutes, admission of students, and curricula — that is, almost every issue of importance to universities. Each university would receive a "director of administrative matters" to watch over the work of the rector. The qualifications of those sitting on the Main Council were not made clear. Only the Polish Parliament would have the power to alter its decisions. [21] The project unleashed a "storm" of outrage in academic circles and once again mobilized the rectors. [22]

As in East Germany, and later in the Czech lands, the new regime's plans to reduce university sovereignty were not offered to the public as attacks on academic freedom. Rather, they were packaged as necessary steps to join the university to the modern world and break down ancient privileges that hindered productivity. The "spirit of the age" was centralized planning, and a higher-education system not "incorporated" into the central plan was portrayed as a medieval relic. [23] The issue was also supposedly one of justice: how could universities remain immune to change, when the rest of Poland was being turned upside down? Students were again targeted for criticism. They were accused of studying according to whim and with little regard for the interests of the "people," and of living out their "golden years." Supposedly only 5 percent of students in prewar Poland finished their studies on time. Because of the continuing underrepresentation of the working class, universities remained "breeding grounds" for reactionary views and anti-

Semitism.[24] Beyond changes in the student admissions process, proposals emerged to divide students into professional and academic tracks and to monitor carefully their course of studies.[25]

In fact, professors were not opposed to changes that would make universities more effective.[26] Demands made by Skrzeszewski in 1945 for courses preparing underprivileged youths for college met with eager acceptance, and agreement on the need for reorganization and greater funding was widespread.[27] During discussions in the summer of 1945 Tadeusz Kotarbiński championed a complete centralization of research as the most rational method of organization. But he assumed that direction would naturally go into the hands of the Polish Academy of Arts in Kraków, the only general scientific society in Poland. He urged huge monetary allocations for scientific research. At a meeting of the Rectors' Council in 1946 Professor Warcholski likewise advocated increased funding and proposed seeking a loan from the United States.[28]

This broad agreement on the necessity of reorganization revealed the core of the dispute between state and universities: academic freedom. The issue was not modernizing science and education; it was who would do it. The state failed to persuade the academic community of its greater competence, and the PPR's pursuit of power increasingly seemed an end in itself.[29] Archival documents support this perception. Ministry official Marowski wrote in a May 1946 memorandum that there would be no "order on the university youth front" until faculty councils lost power over admissions decisions.[30] During a discussion of admissions policies in the fall of that year, Central Committee higher-education chief Trojanowski told Stanisław Arnold of the Ministry of Education to "prepare materials limiting the autonomy of higher schools."[31] The results of rectoral and dean elections in late 1946, and not backward structures, caused á joint meeting of PPR and PPS academics to talk about the "medieval" university system in Poland.[32]

University senates quickly drafted replies to Jaroszyński's "project." Jagiellonian University attempted to be conciliatory, recognizing the need for some state body to coordinate higher education, and recommended the creation of a separate ministry for education and science. But the faculty was deeply disturbed at the proposed monopoly over higher education for fifteen individuals, of uncertain qualifications. What about academic standards? The Polish discourse permitted professors to invoke their status as caretakers of national culture in a way that German or Czech colleagues did not: "No temporary directive is justified as a basis for such sweeping administrative jurisdiction, especially when Poland suffers a catastrophic lack of qualified scientific specialists. No incidental consideration can warrant this incapacitation of the professorial world, given its honest services for the

Fatherland."[33] The professors of Warsaw University went back deeper into history:

> Universities best understand the needs of science and higher educa-
> tion. Handing dictatorial authority over these areas of culture to fifteen
> nominees, with as yet undetermined qualification, can only, at the ruin
> of science and higher education, open the gates to incompetence, pro-
> tectionism, political pressures, and administrative arbitrariness. . . . To
> call such a project democratic is difficult. It is not Polish in spirit, for in
> Poland the university has enjoyed autonomy since the end of the four-
> teenth century. If during times of bondage dark reactionary forces took
> autonomy away from our universities, or attempted its limitation, they
> did this under pressure of the invading powers, or directly as a result
> of their actions. The Nowosilny Senate, for example, carried out such
> an assault on Wilno University in 1823.[34]

The inheritors of Wilno's traditions at Toruń University also reached into Poland's history and, like their Warsaw colleagues, suggested unfavor-able parallels. Similar collegial bodies had advised governments on higher-education affairs — the memorial uses the German *Oberschulkollegium* to de-scribe them — in eighteenth-century Sweden, Austria, Russia, and Prussia. Not coincidentally, these were the countries that had once destroyed Poland. But the plan also violated the regime's own progressive rhetoric: "the very fact of regressing in an era of democracy to models from eighteenth-century absolutism leads to undesirable reflections." But the Torunians could conjure even less flattering analogues: "The fascist Germans in the time of reorga-nizing higher education introduced in the law of 21 January 1935 in para-graph three the transferability of professors." Such a provision in a Polish higher-education law was "simply not acceptable" now that the Nazis' plans to eliminate the Polish intelligentsia were well known.[35]

A meeting of Polish rectors of 8–9 March 1947 conceded the need for re-forms, but rejected the government proposal. It claimed that present laws were sufficient to guarantee the government a role in academic matters, be-cause the minister had to approve habilitations, professorial appointments, and changes of statute. Every rector consented to the proposal, except Pro-fessor Kuczewski of the Silesian Polytechnic in Gliwice. He was the sole Communist in the group. But so strong was the pull of the academic com-munity — of the *środowisko* — that he changed his mind. On 11 March 1947 he wrote to Rector Pieńkowski of Warsaw University: "Since, besides me, every rector without exception decidedly condemned Professor Jaroszyń-ski's preliminary project, I have revised my position and in the end signed the resolution passed in this matter by the Rectors' Council."[36] The leading

PPR member among Kraków's professors, agronomist Teodor Marchlew-ski, likewise refused to support the project, and wrote that Jaroszyński did not "understand science" and suffered from a "complex": "Certain formula-tions in the project—for example, that the rector or dean should watch over scholarship—these are stories for well-behaved children." [37]

Anticipating such negative echoes, top PPR officials tried to distance themselves from Jaroszyński's initiative, which, in a reflection of this period's relative chaos, had not been cleared with them ahead of time. [38] Eugenia Kras-sowska, vice-minister of education, complained that Jaroszyński's project created a natural conflict between the ministry and the proposed Main Council. For example, the minister would have no power to determine the staffing of university chairs. She wrote that "the minister as a political agent must have a decisive voice in basic matters." Though she was by no means a defender of university autonomy, Jaroszyński's project had temporarily driven Krassowska onto the side of the professoriate. [39] Other leading officials likewise had mixed feelings about the proposals. [40]

The decree on higher education of 28 October 1947 was thus a measure of compromise and indecision, and it remained valid only to 1951, one year shorter than planned. Its provisions were quite distant from the totalistic notions of Maurycy Jaroszyński, and, for the time being, universities were not significantly limited in their powers to promote new teachers. The Main Council's most important power was negative: it had to confirm habilita-tions carried out by the faculty councils. University senates and faculty coun-cils remained but were expanded to embrace assistant professors. A new general university council came into existence that included six students, but its functions were purely advisory. Administrative directors were now appointed for universities, but they were supervised by the rector. The Main Council suggested candidates for rector, deputy rector, deans, and assistant deans from candidates selected by universities. The rector, for example, was chosen from three professors and then appointed by the president. [41] The de-cree divided power in higher-education administration because the minis-ter had to ask the approval of the Main Council before creating new higher schools, faculties, and chairs. Higher schools, which desired to be left alone, benefited from this institutionalized rivalry above them. [42]

Assaults of Rhetoric upon Czech Universities

The year 1947 also witnessed an assault by Czech Communists on univer-sities. Unlike their Polish colleagues, Czech professors did not organize a response. The immediate pretext for the attacks was the election by Charles University in June 1947 of former finance minister Karel Engliš as its rector. Engliš was a well-known critic of planned economies, and the professors of

Charles University knew that by choosing him they would aggravate Communist leaders. Government premier and Party chairman Klement Gottwald called the election "a further example of the penetration of the influence of the reaction into several parties of the National Front."[43] On 9 July, the Communist press launched a series of attacks against university professors with a polemic in KSČ daily *Rudé právo* by its editor Gustav Bareš. Suggesting a touch of sore conscience, Bareš dwelt upon Engliš's depiction of the Czechoslovak economy as "a regime of unfreedom."[44] Other articles alluded in threatening tones to Brno law professor Jaroslav Stránský as the "present" minister of education.

As the planned 1948 general elections drew closer the campaign against Engliš and Stránský intensified. The KSČ daily told its readers in October that "it is, of course, a mistake that this Dr. Engliš is still rector of Charles University."[45] In a speech to Communist students on 3 December Václav Kopecký admitted that it would be very "embarrassing for us to see the 600th anniversary of Charles University take place behind such dubious representation." He continued:

> On more than one occasion we have had to restrain Prague's workers from taking action against [Czech] National Socialist students. The causes of the reactionary spirit [at universities] lie in the present course of the education administration. . . .
>
> After the revolution we made the mistake of admitting practically everybody to universities. Now we have to enroll people who have a positive attitude to the government and to the new order.
>
> . . . For the sake of progress it is necessary that the worldview of dialectical materialism take first place at universities. . . . Our universities often give less education than a worker receives from reading Communist newspapers. You are welcome to your opinion but do not oppose us, for anticommunism is high treason.[46]

Kopecký contended that a "purge of the professoriate is necessary" and threatened the leader of the National Socialist students, Emil Ransdorf, with arrest.[47] Other KSČ leaders joined the anti-intellectual chorus. Trade-union chief Antonín Zápotocký proclaimed a war against the culture in which students had been raised:

> Their caste upbringing was perhaps not as noticeable in schools as it was in social education. Student dance hours, student soirées, student balls, etc. All of this neatly limited to the caste, only for the invited, and for their guests "coming out" into society. All of this so that venerable bourgeois matrons will have a guaranteed selection of the men who are supposed to fertilize their ripening seedlings [*oplodňovat jejich*

dozrávající sazenice]. And for that reason this selection, before its own ripening to real life, has to receive its own registered trade marks: JUC, PhC, MUG, IngC, etc.[48]

Amazing in retrospect is how openly the Communists described what they intended to do. No one who read newspapers in 1947 could have illusions about a gentler Czechoslovak road to socialism: if the KSČ came to power, universities would become "shop floors" and both students and teachers made to "work." In a meeting in April 1947 at the rector's office of Charles University, KSČ student leader Vladimír Pilát complained that "some professors do not comprehend the development of the time and do not understand that their teaching contradicts people's democratic rules. These professors should be given guidelines, according to which they will teach." To this his opponent the Czech National Socialist Emil Ransdorf replied that "either universities are free in their work, or they are church-bound theological faculties."[49]

Communist students fully exemplified their political culture before the February 1948 seizure of power, labeling opponents "traitors," demanding the arrest of alleged "enemies of the republic," and calling for deeper purges of supposed collaborators in the student body.[50] As in the textbook "scandal," Communists did their best to stir hatred. Their great opportunity came in the spring of 1947, after the expiration of an early postwar compromise that had permitted law students to take their state examinations separately.[51] Most students wanted this system of "separate examinations" to continue, because it was easier to spread out examinations than take them on three consecutive days. Professors, naturally perhaps, wanted the return of the old system. The Communists called for a boycott, and *Mladá fronta,* the Communist youth daily, proclaimed that "all Czech youth" supported it. All Czech youth except for four students, who took their examination on schedule: "Every student's face radiates joy for unity against outdated regulations, and contempt for those who, hoping to have an easy examination, betrayed the student ranks. All around the law faculty announcements are posted with black-framed pictures of the four who violated solidarity. Every student in the faculty is convinced that these uncollegial colleagues will be expelled from the Student Union."[52] The contempt reserved in other places for war criminals was vented upon violators of "student unity": "All young people in our country now know how bravely the students of the law faculty of Charles University behaved in pushing through the reform of studies, above all the modern system of separate examinations."[53] One is reminded of Zbigniew Herbert's contention that it was not so much character that caused him to reject the allures of the New Faith; rather it was "fundamentally a question of taste."[54]

The sober-minded rector of Charles University, Karel Engliš, saw quite clearly what lay ahead. He used the reception of an honorary doctorate in April 1947 to stage a warning:

> At issue here is the elimination of individualism, of the individual's free will, of individual responsibility and individual merit, the elimination of competition and selectivity in scholarly and artistic work; such work is to be collectivized and managed, and in the end administered, standardized, and dogmatized as if it were a purely economic matter. But this is the road away from free thought toward dogmatism, when everything depends upon what is the current state need. The spirit of the nation is to be chained and administered.
>
> What is especially dismaying is the haste with which this is happening, which does not even allow time to consider consequences, for at issue here are the very foundations of the nation's cultural creation. Mistakes in the economic realm can be measured in billions, but this is not the case in the cultural-political realm, where mistakes are far more momentous.[55]

Despite such clear visions, no front emerged among professors in defense of the university. The senate of Charles University issued a statement defending its rector from Gottwald's and Kopecký's attacks, but the senate of Prague's second higher educational institution, the Czech Technical University, could not find a majority to condemn Kopecký's attacks.[56] On 16 December, several professors of Masaryk University in Brno expressed support for Engliš, a former faculty member of theirs, but the university failed to approve a statement of protest because a resolution could not achieve unanimity.[57] Czech professors as a group were not, in contrast to popular stereotype, left-leaning; like East German and Polish colleagues, they were overwhelmingly conservative. Czech professors did not accept communism; they capitulated to it.

Yet Czech universities did not capitulate to communism. In late 1947 students at both Masaryk and Charles universities elected non-Communist majorities to their student unions. These results alarmed the KSČ leadership, who feared that the country as a whole was moving to the political center. The student union in Prague decisively condemned Kopecký's attacks on Karel Engliš.[58] But students were puzzled at the behavior of the older generation. Why did the government not dissociate itself from Kopecký's words? "The impression has been created," a resolution read, "that the government identifies itself with these statements, which are starkly inconsistent with the democracy of our constitution, the Košice Program, and with the basic thoughts of the president of the Republic."[59] Yet the president, professor of sociology Edvard Beneš, made no public protest.

The student union of Brno found even tougher language to respond to the information minister's insinuations: "University students have always fought against Nazism and fascism and will continue to stand up against every kind of totalitarianism, no matter in what form. Our patriotism is not identical with membership in a political party. Similarly we do not consider opposition to any political party to be high treason. . . . Students will decide their worldview for themselves. Are we no longer living in a democratic state?"[60] Notable is the use of history to make political argument. Unlike Polish professors, these students reached only into recent memory, and acted as both less, and more, than the university community. They upheld academic ideals, but spoke only as students, and not in the name of corporate integrity and tradition.

But they were also more than students: like the earlier generation that took to the streets of Prague in November 1939, they thought of themselves as the nation's conscience.[61] In February 1948 students in Prague were the only Czechs who protested the Communist seizure of power. Making explicit references to the "spirit of 17 November (1939)" and "centuries of tradition," twice several thousand gathered in the old town of Prague, and marched across the Vltava, and through the streets of Malá Strana. Despite appeals to bystanders to join the march, they remained alone as they surged upward toward the Castle, in order to demonstrate their "loyalty and devotion" to the president, and to Czechoslovak democracy. Beneš indeed received a small delegation on 23 February—to whom he assured he would "be at pains to preserve the National Front and parliamentary democracy"—but the second attempt to reach him two days later was blocked by police. During clashes one student was shot in the leg, and scores were arrested.[62] These students were isolated from their professors, from their Communist colleagues, and from Czech society. Elsewhere in Prague, hundreds of thousands of factory workers attended mass rallies celebrating Klement Gottwald and the victory of "people's democracy."

East German Student Opposition

East German student politics partly resembled the Czech constellation. Students composed the core of anti-Communist sentiment both at universities and in society at large, and they voted against Communist candidates in the student council elections. But the general conditions under which they operated were quite different. Students were admitted to university in East Germany by toleration of the occupation authorities and could be dismissed for mere suspicion of "reactionary" activities. Worse, from 1946 onward Soviet authorities made a regular practice of arresting the leaders of the anti-Communist students. Political opposition triggered mechanisms of terror in East Germany that were unknown in Poland or the Czech lands.

But Communists in East Germany did not merely react with repression; they also began enrolling large numbers of putative supporters from the working classes. The preferences in admission given to these students, along with students belonging to the SED, brought the tensions between workers and students that had been instigated in the streets of Brno or Prague directly onto East German university campuses.

Student councils had been created in late 1945 in the Soviet zone, but they were not permitted to elect their own leaders until the summer of 1946. In contrast to the East German local elections of the fall of 1946, where it had emerged with close to absolute majorities, the SED suffered defeats in the student council elections of late 1946 and early 1947. A number of issues caused the students to vote down the Communists. Foremost was the behavior of the occupying power, whose soldiers continued to brutalize the German population — especially women — well into 1947, when efforts were made to limit contacts between Soviets and Germans.[63] But students had specific problems with the new regime. In meetings before the 1946 elections Berlin medical students protested the DVV's imposition of a student statute, and objected to the first signs of political education in their curriculum. One speaker said that "Communism, with its demands for total commitment [*Totalitätsansprüchen*], does not belong in a university." Another objected to the conversion of the university to a "Party school."[64]

Like their Czech comrades, East German Communists had also alarmed students with expressions of hostility toward intellectual enterprise. Repeatedly, they told students to "work" and serve the "people." Such anti-intellectualism was pervasive in the Party apparatus, particularly among the predominant "worker cadres," but it was not unknown among intellectuals.[65] Marie Torhorst, minister of culture and education in Thuringia after 1947 and the first female minister in Germany, came from a pastor's family and had received a doctorate in mathematics from Bonn University in 1918.[66] In early 1948 she wrote that "the new state, in which power emanates from the people, cannot allow students who are not aware of their responsibility toward the people ever to have a leading position. Such students are an intolerable burden for the university. It would be nonsensical for the new state to carry the enormous costs which every student incurs, even if he receives no stipend or tuition waiver. Students cannot forget for a moment that their education is paid for by the tax contributions of working people."[67]

More typical of the SED apparatus was Torhorst's Mecklenburg counterpart, Gottfried Grünberg. Grünberg, by profession a coal miner, had taken part in the Spanish Civil War and spent years in the Soviet Union as a Communist functionary. According to his own account, he responded with surprise to news that the Party had chosen him to be minister of education: "Education? . . . I have only been to a one-room village school. . . . And of

culture I know nothing at all." To this his superior is supposed to have responded: "That's great. You know how not to do things, do it better." [68] What
he lacked in formal education he compensated for in understanding of the
"masses." In March 1947 a conference of Communist education officials was
convened to discuss recent political "incidents" at Berlin University, namely
political gatherings of students. Mecklenburg's minister told his comrades
that "the people are against this artificially instigated hubbub. . . . the university is an institution of the people, and the students have an obligation
to serve the people. They are servants of the people. They do not study for
the sake of studying, but rather in order to carry out important functions in
the life of the people." [69]

There was also a component of social anxiety to anti-Communist students' dissatisfaction: they were of middle-class background and felt increasingly marginalized by the SED's admissions policies. In a 1947 speech
Leipzig student leader Wolfgang Natonek captured the fears of many with
a memorable comparison to Nazi admissions practices: "There was a time
when a person with a non-Aryan grandmother was prevented from studying. We do not want a time when a person without a prolet-Aryan grandmother is prevented from studying." [70] Non-Communist students made their
objections in terms not of class but of political fairness. In an article printed
in West Berlin in March 1948, East Berlin student leaders suggested that the
new admissions criteria were dominated entirely by political desiderata: "We
hear that the SED is preparing a recruitment campaign for Berlin University,
whose goal is to exhaust available reserves of high school graduates, holders
of wartime graduation certificates [*Reifevermerksinhaber*], comrades who
have graduated from worker courses — and if necessary even some 'progressive applicants with Party leanings' [*Parteicharakteristik*] — and bring them
to university by using the admissions process with which we are sufficiently
well acquainted." [71]

Mixed into such polemics were allegations that the new students were not
up to par academically. Before the 1946 elections, one SPD representative
told a meeting of medical students that "workers should be admitted not
because they are workers, but because they are able." [72] Though most East
German worker students performed adequately or better, they were projected as congenitally unfit for studies. [73] Students who had taken the traditional road to university, via *Gymnasium* and *Abitur,* suggested that the
new students had achieved admission purely on the basis of political favoritism. To underscore their own traditional education, they made casual use
of untranslated Latin phrases in public statements. [74] Indeed, suspicions and
hostilities of students from middle-class backgrounds may have contributed
to worker students' sense of group identity and support for the SED. Ger-

many in 1948 was splitting not only at the boundaries separating western and eastern zones but also along lines of sociocultural milieu.

The reasons for most students' dissatisfaction with the new regime were complex, but their choice of leaders was simple. They elected the small minority of their number who had opposed National Socialism and had the moral capital with which to oppose the Communists.[75] As in the case of Polish professors and Czech students who had been concentration camp inmates, these East German antifascists acted with special authority. Ironically, the Soviets had initially placed faith in them, believing that opponents of the old regime would naturally support the regime they were establishing. For example, they stationed one of the conspirators of the 20 July 1944 plot to kill Hitler, Georg Wrazidlo (CDU), at the helm of the Berlin student council in the fall of 1945.[76] The first public act of this council came as an unpleasant surprise to the Soviet Military Administration: it protested the decorating of Berlin University in red banners on May Day 1946. Twenty-seven students, all recognized "victims of fascism," signed a statement comparing this event to the Nazi politicization of higher education. They admonished university rector Johannes Stroux that a university "serves scholarship and education and is not a Party institution."[77] For this Wrazidlo was demoted and replaced by an SED member.

In the first student council elections of the summer of 1946, Berlin students chose as council chair Otto Hess, whom the Nazis had categorized as a "half Jew" and assigned to an Organisation Todt penal battalion. When the SPD and KPD were forcibly merged into the SED in April 1946, he insisted on remaining in the SPD, which could operate in Berlin because of the city's four-power status. Students in Greifswald also chose as their leader an SPD member who refused to join the SED: the Jewish dental student Erich Londe.[78] In Leipzig, students elected the liberal antifascist Wolfgang Natonek, and their colleagues in Jena voted for the liberal law student Erich Weber. Weber had been expelled from high school in 1944 for remarks deemed critical of the Nazi regime.[79] Many of the students who led the Berlin student council of 1948 that created the Free University had similar credentials. Joachim Schwarz had been associated with Munich's White Rose movement, and his collaborator Otto Stolz was a recognized "victim of fascism." Horst Hartwich and Helmut Coper were "half Jews" who had survived Organisation Todt. Stanisław Kubicki, a cofounder who designed the student admissions forms for the Free University in 1948, had a Polish father who died at the hands of the Gestapo.

In 1945 the KPD was as confident of support from victims of fascism as were the Soviets, yet by 1947 Communist functionaries in the DVV interpreted such status as a sign of trouble.[80] In February one scribbled next to the name of a newly elected student council leader in Berlin: "close to the SPD, racial mongrel, first degree" (*Mischling 1. Grades*). The internal DVV records also list one student council member as a "Jew" and another as a former concentration camp inmate. Claus Reuber, chair of the council, was recorded as a racial "mongrel" — again the Nazi expression *Mischling* is used without further commentary — who had spent two years in prison.[81] Like Polish comrades, East German Communists had few scruples about using categories invented by the Nazis, even if the purpose was to discriminate against those who had been victimized by the Nazis.

Later that year, the SED decided to weaken provisions that had favored victims of fascism in student admissions guidelines. DVV official Professor Wilhelm Hauser (SPD/SED) explained the rationale at meetings of the SED Higher-Education Council in late 1947 and early 1948: the SED had been giving preference in admissions to people "who were racially persecuted, or for some other reasons that often had political causes, but nothing to do with our cause. As a result in the course of the last two years . . . a number of people have come to university who really don't belong to us, even if they are not exactly our enemies."[82] But now the situation would change: "In a purely political sense, we were not able to be as selective about people who were politically and racially persecuted last year. But this will gradually improve. Now we have refused about 50 percent of the applications."[83]

In the German context, anticommunism is often understood as a postwar ideological shroud, concealing the discomforting legacy of National Socialism. But as Hauser's remarks suggest, for many East German student leaders anticommunism was a continuation of opposition to National Socialism. The leader of Leipzig's student council, Wolfgang Natonek, recalled the postwar period from forty years' distance: "If I drew any conclusion from the horrible time of National Socialism — in which I, son of émigré writer Hans Natonek, was classified as 'stateless' and had to suffer bitter destitution with my mother — it was to show civil courage so that such a thing was not repeated."[84]

Many of these student leaders did not initially intend to become involved in politics. In 1945 they conformed well to the apolitical cliché of the times: they wanted to rebuild the conditions for material prosperity. It was the new regime and its insistence that nothing could be "apolitical" that politicized these students. Natonek recalled how he became a candidate for student representative in the philosophical faculty:

> A fellow student, of whom it was said that she had lost father and brothers in the 20 July conspiracy against Hitler, knew me from a seminar in German literature. She asked if I did not want to run for a position in the philosophical faculty. I hesitated, though she made me feel

obliged to accept. What finally caused me to say yes was an eye-opening experience that vividly reminded me of the Nazi dictatorship. After a lecture of Professor Korff ("The Spirit of the Age of Goethe") that was held for students of all faculties and always overcrowded, a young man came up to me whom I did not know. Clearly he had confused me with someone else. He asked, "Is it your turn or mine to deliver notes to the tower today?" Back then the SED headquarters was in the Kroch tower on Augustplatz. Could it be, I wondered, that something we thought was behind us is happening all over again, namely a state in which one person spies on the next, and in which everyone is afraid to say what he thinks? And so I let them put my name on the ballot.[85]

The measures advocated by Hauser to attract more compliant students took time to show effect. In the short run Soviet and German Communists subdued their opponents with political terror. In March 1947 Soviet secret police agents arrested six students of Berlin University, including Wrazidlo and student council member Manfred Klein (CDU). Their families were not even informed that the arrests had taken place. Wrazidlo was subsequently sentenced to twenty-five years at hard labor. The next wave of arrests swelled over Leipzig in the late summer of 1947. Among the arrested was the admissions delegate of the Leipzig student council, CDU member Wolfgang Weinoldt. He was condemned to twenty-five years in a work camp. It was later claimed that he and his fellow victims had worked for the *Ostbüro* of the SPD.[86] Wolfgang Natonek was arrested in November 1948 and his Rostock counterpart Arno Esch was abducted a year later and condemned to death.[87] Over 400 students were arrested in East Germany between 1945 and mid-1953.[88]

Despite the arrests, students continued to speak out against the new regime. Hans-Adolf Hilgenfeld, a member of Jena's student council, proclaimed in early February 1948: "We're interested in democracy—and not in the oriental people's democracy that's practiced here in Eastzonesia."[89] His colleague Erich Weber (LDP) asserted at a meeting of the student branch of the Free German Trade Union on 10 December 1947 that "these days Nazism gets blamed for everything. It is guilty of a lot of things, but not everything!" Informants passed these statements on to Soviet authorities, who soon ordered a shake-up of the university, including expulsions, the unseating of student council representatives, a review of students receiving scholarships, the appointment of new professors, a change of rectors, and further arrests. The senate was given an SED majority by adding representatives of the Thuringian Ministry, as well as the director of the SED-dominated social sciences and worker preparation (*Vorstudienanstalt*) faculties. The faculty councils were expanded to include teaching assistants and people who "per-

form especially valuable services for the educational and scientific obligations of the faculty," that is, Communists.[90] This was probably the deepest
direct Soviet intervention ever into the workings of a university outside the
Soviet Union.[91]

Weber stayed a step ahead of the Soviet secret police, slipping away to
West Berlin in the spring of 1948, where he joined several dozen students
from Berlin's student council in founding the Free University.[92] These students were aided by West Berlin politicians and the public, as well as officials
of the American occupation forces, who provided facilities in the south-
western district of Dahlem. The more conservative British had been skeptical.[93] So had Germany's professors. West Berlin's major daily *Der Tagesspiegel* claimed that with few exceptions, professors of the Humboldt University had "bowed to tyranny," because so few had openly supported the
initiative to found the Free University.[94] Professors defended their inactivity
by highlighting the dangers for German unity. Botany professor Elisabeth
Schiemann wrote in June 1948 that "a university in the West would mean a
final splitting apart of Berlin. This is the main reason why many professors
are against it."[95] But professors—whether in East or West Germany—were
also not as sensitive as students to violations of academic autonomy. Despite
the evidence of an increasingly restrictive regime, Schiemann, for example,
argued that students should concentrate on "reforming" the existing university rather than creating a new one. When DVV president Paul Wandel had
the Berlin student leaders Stolz, Hess, and Schwarz expelled from the university, the university senate announced that the expulsions had taken place
beyond its jurisdiction. It would not permit the posting of a student council statement condemning the recent violation of "the principle of academic
autonomy."[96] The rector of Munich University likewise refused to support a
resolution against the expulsion of Stolz, Hess, and Schwarz "on the grounds
that all the facts pertaining to the expulsions were not available."[97]

How can one explain such professorial passivity? Undoubtedly, East German professors were operating under tighter limitations than colleagues in
Poland or the Czech lands. An attempt in 1948 by the faculties of Jena University to protest some rather crude allegations by Paul Wandel that they
were not "working" only hastened fulfillment of the measures just described.
Yet whether in East or West, German professors could not imagine academic
activities beyond the blessings of the state. A Free University was too "political" for them. The rectors of both halves of Germany heavily criticized the
founding of the Free University in their Würzburg meeting of November
1948; the representative of Göttingen claimed it had a "propagandistic character . . . which had been possible to avoid even in the Third Reich."[98]

Under both dictatorships, German professors attempted to keep peace
with the authorities. Therefore, the authorities did not need to do all the

dirty work themselves. In Berlin, the SED could count on two highly respected "bourgeois" scholars, the rector Johannes Stroux and DVV vice-
president and internist Theodor Brugsch, to help discipline the student
body. In 1947, these men initiated proceedings against the organizers of
an election meeting of Berlin's medical students that had harshly criticized
the SED. The students were charged with "violation of trust" and support of "profascistic" elements.[99] Stroux and Brugsch unwaveringly supported the SED, in part because of deeply felt and blinding "antifascism," in
part because of unusual professional opportunities, but also from a lack of
imagination that went deep into the ranks of the non-Communist professoriate. When in 1947 the SED in Leipzig demanded the expulsion of a
student (Plätzsch) who was said to have insulted the honor of worker students, only one professor, Theodor Litt, would support that student's right
to a trial. The rector, Hans-Georg Gadamer, claimed that "only the expulsion of Plätzsch could make good the political harm that he has caused."[100]
Gadamer's basically loyal attitude toward the education authorities of that
time comes through in a memoir written decades later: Paul Wandel and
Robert Rompe, functionaries who orchestrated the successive diminution of
academic integrity in the Soviet zone, are described by Gadamer as "intelligent" men with whom one could reason, in contrast to the less cultivated
provincial bureaucrats.[101]

In 1948, with increased repressiveness heralding the onset of high stalinism,
initiative in higher-education affairs in Poland and East Germany passed to
the central state apparatus. After this point there are few reports of student
or professorial meetings protesting state policy. Opposition moved into hidden spaces, into channels among and between professors, and was expressed
in coded language with minimal aims — for example, achieving the entrance
of individual, gifted students. Such structural resistance was more successful
in Poland: because of the persistence of the old professoriate, more academic
space lay beyond the reach of the state.

★

CHAPTER SEVEN

BREAKING
THE
PROFES-
SORIATE

After 1948 breaks became visible in the political development of East Central Europe. In Hugh Seton-Watson's terminology, actual and "bogus" coalitions were replaced by one-party regimes, as Communist Parties swallowed their socialist rivals and purged themselves of leaders who advocated "national" roads to socialism.[1] In higher education too, breaks became visible both in structural development and in personnel. Communists asserted control over administration, appointed rectors, converted courses of general education into courses in Marxism-Leninism, and openly proclaimed their intention to copy Soviet models. Fields of study considered incompatible with Marxist scholarship, like sociology, classical economics, or "bourgeois" philosophy, were discontinued, and replaced by Marxism-Leninism. Law faculties in Brno, Toruń, and Rostock were closed. And in somewhat different ways, Communists isolated and frequently removed university teachers considered hostile to Marxism, most insistently in the social sciences.

Yet these similar programs were implemented within the differing contexts that emerged in the early postwar period. In East Germany, an open border to the West combined with the institutional and personal rupture of 1945 to permit the most complete break in professorial continuity. Faced with increasing restrictions to their teaching and research, the few "bourgeois" professors in the social sciences who had survived denazification began to accept positions in West Germany. Whereas in Poland or the Czech lands professors "escaped" into less ideologically sensitive topics to avoid compromise, East German professors literally escaped to other universities in their own land.[2] At the same time, former Nazis began making their way back into the East German professoriate, especially in the natural and technical sciences and in medicine.

In the Czech lands, the Communist Party leadership placed power over university affairs in the hands of Communist students, who purged the professoriate and then the student body. As in 1945, revolutionary action committees emerged, but this time there would be no complaints of a failure to complete their tasks. The Party leadership retroactively modified some of these committees' more extreme decisions.

In Poland, professors found themselves in an uneasy stand-off against the Party. In the months following the expulsion of the German army from Polish territory, survivors had patched together prewar networks of professorial influence and "protection." When in 1946 and 1947 the fledgling totalitarian state attempted to curtail professorial control over universities, professors organized protest as they had in the 1930s and forced the government into momentary retreat. After 1948 these "conspiratorial" gatherings of professors ceased, however; even if not Party members, newly appointed rectors and deans were "loyal." No longer were public manifestations of dissent possible. Yet beneath the level of Party committees and university administration, old professors remained, as did innumerable personal contacts between them, and, as we shall see in greater detail in chapters 8 and 9, that meant that ministry and Party officials still had to negotiate their ambitions at universities, even in the social sciences.

"Victorious February"

The break of 1948 was particularly spectacular in the Czech lands. Given their hostility to communism, it came as no surprise that universities stood high on the list of places to be purged in February of that year. As in every institution in the country, "action committees" were set up in order to remove supposed collaborators and other "reactionaries." Communist students, including a number of later dissidents, were the leading force in higher-education action committees, both in faculties and citywide coordinating committees.[3] Prague's Central Action Committee for Higher Schools consisted of more than a dozen students, several workers, and five Communist professors: Julius Dolanský, Radim Foustka, Arnošt Kolman, Miloslav Valouch, and Josef Tureček.[4] It grew into a KSČ Higher-Education Committee that regulated Party policy toward universities in Prague until the early 1950s.

By 25 February this committee had removed the most "objectionable" members of Charles University, all from the law faculty: the rector Professor Karel Engliš and his colleagues Jan Matějka, Ladislav Vošta, Vratislav Bušek, Jiří Cvetler, and docent Dr. Novotný. At the same time it expelled the student council leaders and replaced them with Communists. The action committee of the philosophical faculty was particularly vigilant, because the students had come under the spell of Arnošt Kolman.[5] The new dean of the faculty, Professor J. B. Kozák, was not a KSČ member, but did nothing without the Communists' approval.[6] By 27 February the following members of the philosophical faculty had lost their positions: professors Miloslav

Hýsek, Josef Hutter, Josef Král, and Otakar Machotka, the docents Zdeněk Kalista, Cyril Stejskal, Ladislav Heger, Zdeněk Ullrich, Jan Patočka, Josef Hendrich, Václav Chaloupecký, Hubert Ripka (former minister of foreign trade), and František Kovárna, as well as two lecturers and two assistant professors. They were called "collaborators or active agents of enemies of the republic."[7]

The new minister of education Zdeněk Nejedlý vowed to protect students from interruptions in teaching,[8] but now that the faculties were officially understood to be "shop floors," academic standards had to be secondary for him as well. The law faculty's action committee scrambled to cover the gaping vacancies by appointing Communist officials from the ministries who had no experience in university teaching—for example, Otto Fischl (Ministry of Finances), Pavel Levit (Ministry of the Interior), Karel Rotter (Ministry of Foreign Affairs), Bedřich Spáčil (Ministry of Finances), Václav Vlk (director of Scrap Materials), Vladimír Kadlec (director of the Economic Department of the Presidential Chancellery).[9] The professor of international law Antonín Hobza (KSČ) was called back from retirement. A dozen new lecturers were appointed in the philosophical faculty who did not have the normally obligatory habilitation. Three of these, Jaroslav Charvát, Václav Husa, and Oldřich Říha, became the core of the new history department. Although they had no experience in teaching, they were soon made into full professors.[10]

Professor Engliš gave Minister Nejedlý twenty-four hours to reconsider the decision of the students and express confidence in him as rector. Probably delighted, Nejedlý let the deadline pass, and Engliš had no choice but to resign. His predecessor Professor Bohumil Bydžovský was then "elected" to replace him. But the Communist leadership regretted this change in rectors—Klement Gottwald even accused Communist student leader Jiří Pelikán of "thinking with his arse"—because delegations from England, France, and Switzerland protested by withdrawing from the 600th anniversary celebrations of Charles University in April 1948, which were meant to show Czechoslovakia going about business as usual.

A history of the University in Brno written during the Prague Spring depicts February 1948 as a time when "Communists showed that they were ready for action above all by rapidly finding solutions to basic questions in faculties where they were a decided minority."[11] On 25 February a Central Action Committee of the National Front for Higher Schools was created in Brno with Professor František Trávníček of the university's pedagogical faculty at its head. Two days later each faculty had its own action committee.

Initially the action committee of the law faculty hesitated to act, but was quickly replaced by a committee consisting entirely of students and employees. As in Prague it carried out the most thorough purges.[12] Seven of thirteen professors were let go immediately: Ministers Jaroslav Stránský (education) and Adolf Procházka (health), and Professors V. Kubeš, F. Weyr, B. Kučera, Fr. Kop, and Z. Neubauer.[13] Kubeš was then arrested attempting to flee abroad. In April the new dean and assistant dean of this faculty signed a letter to the *Times* of London claiming that their colleagues had been wartime collaborators who had "enticed" students to break laws.[14] In the pedagogical faculty ten external teachers were forbidden to teach.[15] This "phase" of the purges also witnessed the liquidation of the anti-Communist student leadership: its leader, Catholic Rudolf Osička, was arrested and forty-one students expelled.[16]

In both Prague and Brno the forces of intergenerational animosity quickly broke through the academic structures that had consolidated since 1945. Neither rectors nor deans, nor even the Ministry of Education had the power to overturn the decisions of the action committees.[17] Still, the problem emerged of retroactively "legalizing" what the action committees had done. On 15 March 1948 the ministry sent universities instructions on how to treat measures passed by the action committees. Most important as far as professors were concerned was a Ministry of Interior decree of 27 February stipulating that professors and other "employees" who by law could not be dismissed should be placed on "leave" (*na dovolenou s čekatelným*).[18] That was precisely the measure used by the Nazis in 1940 to "resolve" the situation of professors who were not working despite their status as "active."[19] This meant that a number of professors who had been summarily dismissed were permitted back to the faculties, and then placed on leave, usually forfeiting their rights to teach or examine. Others, considered neither "harmful" nor "dependable," were limited in their teaching, examining, and evaluating of students' work.[20]

In the view of many young Party functionaries, the purging of 1948 had not caused a sufficiently clean break from the past, however. They were disturbed that a number of unrepentantly "bourgeois" professors, including Karel Engliš and Václav Černý, now were taken back onto university payrolls.[21] Some sort of permanent solution had to be found. On 21 September 1951, the Presidium of the State Council for Higher Education drew up a list of professors in Prague and Brno to be released because they "had neither the political nor the ideological prerequisites for further activity at higher schools." By 1 October a group of eleven professors in law, philosophy, history, Romance languages, civil engineering, architecture, mathematics, and economic geography were retired; and twelve professors in law, archaeology, English, Romance languages (Černý), philosophy, and economics fired outright.[22] A further three professors of law were given three months' notice, and eight professors of natural sciences forcibly retired. Finally, eight professors of geography, phonetics, classical philology, hydrobiology, theoretical physics, and inorganic chemistry were pensioned after replacements had been found.[23] Václav Černý recalled how he was gradually edged out of academia:

> After 1 February 1950 the ministry gave me "sabbatical" leave I had not requested for the remainder of the academic year. There was a deceptive suggestion in all this that I would return from "sabbatical" in October 1950, but on 16 October the dean's office instructed me to wait and refrain from teaching. As of 1 May 1951 this waiting continued at half pay. Then in the first days of May Rector Mukařovský informed me in the presence of Dean Havránek that the ministry was terminating my employment *because I was not attending to my job,* and requested that I find work outside of higher education before June.

The letter informing Černý of this measure was not signed.[24]

Structural changes exacerbated the discontinuities caused by such dismissals. In 1949, sociology and philosophy were abolished as university subjects, and in 1950 the law faculty in Brno was closed. Although legal studies in Rostock and Toruń would likewise be discontinued, Czech jurisprudence sustained particular damage because it had been taught at only two faculties. Brno's faculty had importance beyond the Czech lands, however, because it was home to a legal tradition known throughout Central Europe: František Weyr's school of normative theory.[25] In Poland the Communist Party would have had to close four faculties, including that of Jagiellonian University, and fire dozens of professors, to achieve a comparable effect. In fact, it closed only one of seven faculties and kept most of the professors of that faculty employed at other universities.

Brno's faculty had proved unreformable, despite the replacement of its professors with Communists, like the journalist Blažke (civil law), assistant professor Pošvář, and former Social Democrat Bohuslav Ečer (international law); and, in the words of F. Weyr, "some lawyer named Dr. Hochman" (economics) as well as "some Dr. Chyba" (constitutional law), "a young man who just got his doctorate."[26] Though loyal, these newcomers lacked "ideological maturity." But, as one internal government report mused, perhaps socialist Czechoslovakia did not require so many lawyers: "In today's social order the need for lawyers will be smaller than it once was. Graduates of the law faculty will be trained solely for the needs of the judiciary and the legislative offices of central agencies."[27] The facilities of Brno's law faculty were made available to Brno's Technical University, which, as mentioned, was soon seized by the army.[28] Brno's law students were transferred to Prague or Bratislava, but only one teacher, the newly minted Professor Blažke, was allowed to continue.[29]

Though the law faculty in Prague remained open, few professors survived the early Communist era. By 1951 only six of twenty-four professors from the pre-1948 period remained: Tureček (canon law), Wenig (trade law), Solnař (criminal law), Štajgr (civil law), Vaněček (legal history), and Andres (civil procedure). Their positions had been greatly weakened due to the influx of nonacademics. In May 1949, half the "professorial council" were non-professors, and by the winter semester of 1950–51 most of the teaching at the law faculty was carried out by nonprofessors. Individuals without even a doctorate gave lectures in the history of the Communist Party of the Soviet Union and political economy. Teaching of administrative law, legal history, and criminal law was entrusted to officials from the ministries or the KSČ Central Committee.[30] In 1951, deanship of the faculty was transferred from Tureček to Jan Bartuška, a former judge who had sat in Parliament for the KSČ since 1946, but first gained teaching experience in 1949. He remained dean until 1954, when he became minister of justice. In 1968 he lost all state functions due to his role in the legal crimes of the early 1950s.[31]

Sociology and most branches of philosophy were discontinued as sup-posedly "bourgeois" sciences in 1949 and 1950. Again Brno suffered a stun-ning loss. The leading Czech school had emerged there during the interwar period under the direction of Professor Arnošt I. Bláha, a student of T. G. Masaryk.[32] In early 1949 Bláha and his colleague E. Chalupný pleaded with the Central Committee to spare Brno's sociology. Chalupný argued that he had been teaching the "scientific aspects of Marxism along with sociology" all his life, and even risked imprisonment under the Austrians.[33] These ap-peals availed nothing, and both Bláha and Chalupný were retired the follow-ing year. Students of sociology were transferred to other fields, but the fact that they had majored in this "bourgeois" discipline was noted negatively in their personnel folders.[34]

Prague's leading professor of sociology and philosophy, Josef Král, was among those forcibly retired in 1951.[35] Docent Jan Patočka, perhaps the most important Czech voice in philosophy in this century, was also forbid-den to teach. During the reorganization of 1950–51, departments (*katedry*) were introduced at Czech universities, and seminars for philosophy trans-formed into departments of Marxism-Leninism. In Prague the department was placed in the hands of the high school teacher Ludvík Svoboda (not be confused with the general of the same name), and in Brno the depart-ment came under the direction of a man who had advanced from student to professor in a single year: Gustav Riedel. Riedel had not succeeded in com-pleting his studies before February 1948, but after the Communist seizure of power his doctoral dissertation was accepted by Professor Bláha. Reminis-cent of Arnošt Kolman in Prague, Riedel then repaid the debt by making it impossible for Bláha to teach. The Department of Marxism-Leninism also took charge of the seminar for social sciences as well as the teaching of philosophy. Thus the philosophy faculty no longer had its own Department of Philosophy.[36]

From 1950 to 1952 Riedel was the dean of Brno's philosophy faculty and presided over its Marxism-Leninism Department until his death in 1960. Within Brno's faculty the losses were above all in sociology (Bláha, Chalupný, Trapl, Obrdlík) but also history (Dřímal, Friedl, Hájek, Horák, Urbánek) and philosophy (Konečný, Zbořil). It is important to note that Riedel disabled not only conservatives but also towering figures on the academic left, like his teacher Bláha and J. L. Fischer.[37] He also helped liquidate a promising working group in logic led by Konečný. Brno's losses were sometimes Prague's gains: in 1954 the Brno philosophy faculty refused the application for graduate studies (*aspirantura*) of Konečný's student Karel Berka, who was to become Czechoslovakia's leading historian of logic. Mirko Novák, a historian of philosophy, left for Charles University in 1954. A few younger students of philosophy took positions in 1950 and 1951, but they were so overburdened with teaching duties that they scarcely had time to become educated.[38]

At the philological faculties the discontinuities were less jarring. All of the professors teaching in Prague in 1953 had been professors before 1948, though two of the twenty-six were appointed after February. In 1948 there had been thirty-eight professors teaching these fields (linguistics, literature, philology). More serious breaks occurred at the level beneath the professoriate. Eleven of thirteen docents were dismissed, and of the ten teaching in 1953, only one had the habilitation.[39] Medicine and the natural sciences were hardly touched at the level of professor. Of fifty-six professors and forty-nine docents at Prague's medical faculty, one professor and three docents were removed in 1948, and four professors and two docents were restricted in their teaching.[40] In Brno the trends were comparable at the level of professor: twenty-six of twenty-nine medical professors survived at least until 1951, as did twenty-one of thirty professors of the philosophy faculty. Yet teachers beneath the level of professor were vulnerable regardless of faculty: three of eighteen docents survived until 1951 in the philosophy faculty, and four of forty-two in medicine.[41] In 1948–49, one-fifth of Brno's medical students and one-third of its teaching and research assistants were released. The places of docents were taken by external teachers who could be hired on a yearly basis.[42] Though the number of docents declined, the total number of teachers increased.[43]

Brain Drain from East Germany

After 1948, the SED likewise consummated breaks in philosophy, history, sociology, and law. These subjects had hardly recovered from denazification when they were either abolished or transformed into handmaidens of the new ideology. Increasingly out of place, the social scientists who survived denazification began to accept positions in West Germany. The drain was especially marked among professors of philosophy, whom the Soviets had required to fill out questionnaires in order to elicit their philosophical creeds. Almost all, it turned out, were "idealists and eclectics." The internal Soviet report emphasized that "only people who had started teaching in 1946–47 would be able to restructure the mentioned disciplines on a democratic basis."[44] By 1950 practically all the philosophers active at East German universities in the early postwar years had left for the West, including Nicolai Hartmann, Eduard Spranger, Erich Hochstetter, and Hermann Wein (Berlin); Theodor Litt, Hans-Georg Gadamer, and Alfred Petzeld (Leipzig); Hans Leisegang and Max Bense (Jena); Walter Bröcker, Karl-Heinz Volkmann-Schluck, and Johannes Erich Heyde (Rostock); and Rudolf Schottlaender (Dresden).[45] As in the Czech lands, sociology was subsumed by Marxism-Leninism, but unlike Czech colleagues, East German sociologists could move to positions in the West.[46] If, as Anton Ackermann suggested, the regime hoped to get rid of "reactionary" social scientists, then its wishes were fulfilled.

The case of Leisegang, a student of Husserl and Dilthey, and once a prisoner of the Nazis, suggests the moral authority lost with this exodus. He provoked authorities during a May 1948 student assembly by remarking that the university may not become a "seminary or school for functionaries."[47] The meeting had been called to consider a vote of confidence against Leisegang; despite increasingly open terror, three-fourths of the 1,500 students voted in his favor. In October the Thuringian ministry under Marie Torhorst (SED), herself a former inmate of Buchenwald, and Thomas Mann's guide to Weimar the following year, dismissed Leisegang for his "hostile attitude toward the new democracy." Like many other critical thinkers from the East, Leisegang then made his way to the Free University in West Berlin.[48]

Leisegang's colleague from Halle, Paul Menzer, also a student of Dilthey, likewise came under attack in 1948 when SED students denounced his lecture as a "stronghold of reaction and fascism." Menzer, who had been dismissed by the Nazis in 1933 for showing solidarity with a Jewish colleague, was now forcibly retired. Remaining full professors accused Halle's rector Eduard Winter of having "liquidated the old university" because of his failure to protect Menzer from the student attacks. Winter was one of the few old professors of history to remain in East Germany, but because of his collaboration with the SD and SS during the war, he did not have the moral stature to resist the SED.[49] An atmosphere of disrespect for more independent old professors, in part encouraged by the SED leadership, also led to the departure or resignation of historians Hugo Preller, Friedrich Baethgen, Friedrich Meinecke, Johannes Kühn, Fritz Hartung, Hans Haussherr, and Eugen Meyer.[50]

A glance at a few faculties suggests the severity of the breaks in law and history: of thirteen professors teaching history at Jena, Leipzig, and Rostock in the 1944–45 semester, only two remained in 1953, and one of those had switched places.[51] Of seventeen professors teaching in the law faculties of Jena and Leipzig in that last wartime semester, none was left by 1953.[52] Capacities were contracted, and a relatively small cadre of loyal historians and lawyers, many without academic credentials, began training a large cohort of young Communists. Borrowing on the work of Ilko-Sascha Kowalczuk, who has studied the process among historians, one might call these the first two generations of GDR academics.[53] Graduate training for historians was concentrated in Leipzig, Berlin, and Jena, and Marxists like Jürgen Kuczynski, Ernst Engelberg, or Walter Markov supervised dozens of dissertations. A very small number of "progressive bourgeois" historians assisted, but only two (Eduard Winter and Martin Lintzel) had been full professors before 1945.[54] After 1958, Winter was the only "bourgeois" historian of repute left in the GDR.[55]

From 1948 the SED proved willing to readmit former NSDAP members to the teaching faculties, but strictly differentiated between natural, technical, and medical sciences on the one hand, and humanities and social sciences on the other. In 1954, only 11 percent of the professors in philosophical faculties, and 16.7 percent of the social scientists had belonged to the NSDAP, compared with 45 percent in the medical and 42 percent in the technical disciplines.[56] The influx of former NSDAP members does not, however, imply a mending of broken continuities, for most had not been university professors. Of 248 professors teaching at three universities (Berlin, Rostock, Leipzig) in 1953, only 27 (10.9 percent) had been employed as university teachers before 1945.[57] Such a break, across fields, has no parallel in the Czech lands, let alone in Poland. The SED also faced a challenge in building new faculty that did not exist in either of the neighboring countries: namely a double labor market, which forced it to compete with West German universities, and West German industry, for talented academics. Not until the late 1960s were East German universities able to compensate numerically for the personnel losses sustained in 1945–46.[58] By contrast, Polish and Czech universities made up wartime losses by 1948.[59]

Officially, the East German administration was charged with luring West German professors into the GDR, but, though willing to offer competitive salaries, its success was marginal. The root of the problem was the all-powerful state's insecurity. On the one hand, fear of Western infiltration caused unacceptable delays in securing central approval for appointments.[60] On the other, unceasing harassment by the GDR state apparatus tended to drive scholars out of rather than into the GDR. Education authorities were well informed about this harassment, because universities forwarded letters from scholars who had escaped to the Federal Republic. These scholars, often feeling some remorse about abandoning their institutes and laboratories without notice, wrote back to former colleagues explaining their step once safely in the West. Before fleeing, they usually divulged their intentions only to closest friends. Occasionally, however, a highly valued and thus self-confidant scholar might tell SED functionaries to their faces why he or she was considering leaving the GDR. In 1953 Humboldt University's most respected chemist, Erich Thilo, seriously considered an offer from Heidelberg. Alarmed, two leading functionaries of the State Secretariat met with Thilo to hear what disturbed him about life in the GDR:

> He is not in agreement with the methods of struggle used against the [Protestant] student fellowships at schools and universities. As an example he named the high school that his son attends (Graues Kloster). He can no longer accept responsibility for educating his children at our high schools. He is "outraged and appalled" by the actions taken against private retail trade and gave several examples of acquaintances who had gone bankrupt due to taxes. He can no longer square these "barbaric" tactics with his conscience. He objects to the prohibition on West Berliners' shopping in the Democratic Sector [East Berlin]. He is "appalled" to see Germans in "Russian uniforms" (he means the Barracked People's Police). He rejects the methods of our agitation and propaganda and wishes to see free travel between East and West Germany immediately, without Interzonal passports. . . .
>
> We asked which changes were needed to strengthen his decision to stay here. Professor Thilo answered that it would be necessary to take back all measures that were alien to a "normal Central European" and to which he will never grow accustomed. But in this regard we could not help him, because such measures were part of "the system."[61]

Indeed, officials in the State Secretariat were part of the system, charged as much with controlling as with attracting scholars. Thus the protocol of a February 1953 meeting of state and Party functionaries spoke in the same paragraph of the need for "planned recruiting of scholars from West Germany" and for "stronger control of the [Protestant] student fellowships."[62] Education functionaries acted as though harassment and incentives affected two different groups of people. Two months later the State Secretariat received a letter from the Central Committee demanding to know, "Which directive has been issued in relation to communications between universities and institutes of the GDR and West Germany? How has the relevant order of Comrade Walter Ulbricht been realized, prohibiting individual correspondence?"[63]

Such realities of East German life did not remain concealed from potential Western recruits, for scholars of East and West Germany saw each other frequently at conferences. Chemist Hans Bode from Hamburg refused a generous offer to teach at Humboldt University in 1953, and explained to Thilo that he feared he would not be able to work "exclusively on scientific problems, and matters connected with them (institute, etc.), independent of the [political] circumstances."[64] The migration westward was a steady stream, with periodic gushes matching periods of intense repression: the accelerated building of socialism in 1952 or the forced conversion to a "socialist university" in 1958.[65] It stopped only with the construction of the Berlin Wall in August 1961. By that point, the SED had already created its own professorial cadre in the social sciences and much of the humanities and, with the border safely closed, could begin insisting on its choices in medicine and the natural sciences as well.[66]

Purges of the Polish Professoriate

The Polish government also enacted a series of measures after 1948 to limit the influence of "reactionary" professors in the social sciences, with the following justification: "our students are not receiving a cohesive Marxist worldview, but rather remain under the influence of uncrystallized or directly idealistic influences."[67] As in Czechoslovakia and East Germany, teaching in sociology, classical economics, and most fields of philosophy was seriously curtailed. Major representatives of the Lwów-Warsaw school of philosophy Kazimierz Ajdukiewicz, Tadeusz Czeżowski, Maria Kokoszyńska, and Tadeusz Kotarbiński were limited to teaching logic.[68] Philosopher Władysław Tatarkiewicz and ethnographer Jan Bystroń were given paid "vacations" in 1949 and could not teach at all. Husserl's reputedly favorite student Roman Ingarden was made "inactive" in 1949[69] and philosophers Janina Kotarbińska and Henryk Elzenberg were forbidden to teach.[70] Leading sociologists Stanisław and Maria Ossowski could neither teach nor publish throughout the stalinist period. Economist Wacław Fabierkiewicz in Łódź was at first made "inactive" and then transferred to the Łódź Textile Institute, where he worked as a consultant.[71]

In fields that continued authorities limited several "reactionary" scholars' access to students. Toruń philologist Konrad Górski was given "unlimited sabbatical for the purpose of carrying out scholarly studies."[72] Classical philologist Tadeusz Sinko lost his chair, and Sergiusz Hessen (pedagogy), Jan Czekanowski (anthropology), Edward Taylor (economics), Stefan Kuczyński (history), and Wincenty Styś (law) were all restricted in their teaching.[73] Historian Ludwik Kolankowski received unsolicited "academic sabbatical" in 1952.[74] Legal scholar Władysław Wolter was forbidden to lecture for several semesters.[75] In 1951, Professors Kazimierz Suchecki and Aleksander Kozikowski of the Agricultural University in Poznań were limited in research and teaching because of "serious ideological-political errors."[76] Other scholars were retired against their will, despite the shortage of teaching staff—for example, archaeologist Józef Kostrzewski (Poznań), professor of administrative law Stanisław Kasznica (Poznań), historian Władysław Konopczyński (Kraków), Polonist Stanisław Adamczewski (Łódź), psychologist Władysław Heinrich (Kraków), and art historian Reverend Szczęsny Dettloff (Poznań).[77] A number of politically objectionable docents, like philosopher Izydora Dąmbska or legal scholar Andrzej Mycielski in Wrocław, were dropped from university payrolls and had to seek employment elsewhere.[78]

Finally, several professors were transferred from their universities and made to teach in foreign environments; for example, historians Henryk Barycz, Henryk Wereszycki, and Kazimierz Piwarski and legal scholars Jan Gwiazdomorski and Marian Zygmunt Jedlicki, all of Kraków, were sent to western universities in Wrocław and Poznań, in order to weaken one "reactionary" milieu and strengthen Poland's claims to the new western territories. These transfers were understood to be a punishment. Also understood was that the punishment could be intensified.

As a whole these measures cannot be equated with the purges that depleted the East German professoriate in 1945–46 and the Czech from 1948 to 1951, however. The scholars transferred to other universities could after all continue teaching. More important, no professors in the core social and human sciences of history, law, and Polish philology were dismissed outright. And even those in philosophy and sociology who were restricted in their teaching retained their status as professors throughout the stalinist years, and continued receiving salaries and conducting research. They could still examine students and review doctoral dissertations and habilitations.[79] Members of the Lwów-Warsaw school of philosophy managed to train a number of logicians and philosophers of science. Kazimierz Ajdukiewicz even acted as rector in Poznań from 1948 to 1952.[80] The fact that certain disciplines had not achieved full independence in Poland meant, in addition, that they could be taught in faculties that continued, especially the law faculty. For example, Jerzy Lande of Jagiellonian University taught sociology as part of a course on legal theory.

Continuity was the rule even in universities transplanted from the East. Between 1939 and 1945 the university communities of Wilno and Lwów had been devastated by two occupations and dispersed all over the maps of Europe and Asia. Yet by 1947 these communities, reconstituted in Toruń and

Wrocław, had begun to fend off a new series of blows. Toruń's law faculty with its fourteen institutes was closed entirely, and the following institutes were closed in the humanities and social sciences: Romance languages, German, English, sociology, psychology, ethnography, and philosophy. Still, because of the predominance of the old professoriate, the Party could not secure hold of the fields that remained, Polish philology and history. By the end of the stalinist period only one Marxist taught in the history faculty, later rector Witold Łukaszewicz.[81] Toruń's professors of law continued teaching at other universities.[82]

Beyond a few junior scholars (see Table 7-1), there was little influx into Toruń's History Department during the early 1950s. Docent Dr. Jan Gerlach came from the liquidated law faculty in 1952, and Stanisław Staszyński joined Hoszowski's institute in 1953. By 1955 Witold Łukaszewicz had assembled a half-dozen left-leaning students in institutes of modern and world history. The natural sciences in Toruń maintained almost complete continuity through the stalinist period. Of nineteen ordinary and extraordinary professors who founded the institutes of mathematics, physics, astronomy, biology, geology, mineralogy, and geography between 1945 and 1947, seventeen were active without interruption up to and beyond 1956.[83]

The second university transplanted from the East, from Lwów to Wrocław, likewise continued relatively unimpeded during the stalinist period. Of the thirteen professors teaching in the philological-historical faculty in 1955–56, only four had come after the self-constitution of the faculty in the years from 1945 to 1947. One of these was Maria Kokoszyńska of the Lwów-Warsaw school of philosophy, and another the "reactionary" historian of antiquity Józef Wolski, who had been moved out of Łódź for political reasons.[84] In the law faculty only two of eleven professors had come after 1947, one was the political exile from Kraków Jan Gwiazdomorski, and the other was Michał Wyszyński, a Roman Catholic priest who came from Toruń after the law faculty there was closed.[85]

If the Party could not shatter milieus transplanted from Eastern Galicia and Lithuania, its chances against places like Poznań or Kraków were slim. Even for Polish standards, measures taken against Kraków were moderate. As mentioned, one historian was forcibly retired,[86] and several professors were transferred to other universities. Yet beyond this, there were no breaks in law, history, or Polish philology, not to mention the natural sciences. Jagiellonian University was united against attempted interventions from Warsaw, even under Rector Teodor Marchlewski (PZPR), who had been professor at the university since 1925, or law faculty dean Konstanty Grzybowski, a socialist who had taught at the university since 1929.[87]

In Warsaw a core of professors that constituted itself after the war remained through the following decade, but the university grew rapidly and

TABLE 7-1

Continuities of the History Faculty of Toruń University

Directors of Institutes (*Katedry*) of History

Professor	Specialty	Time at Toruń	Notes
B. Włodarski	*Medieval Poland*	1945–66	
L. Kolankowski	*Modern Poland*	1945–52	Placed on academic leave
S. Hoszowski	*Social and economic history*	1945–56	Moved to Kraków
R. Mienicki	*Eastern Europe*	1945–55	Placed on academic leave, d. 1956
Karol Górski	*History of Pomerania*	1945–73	
K. Hartleb	*History of culture*	1945–51 (d.)	Succeeded by Doc. Dr. Jadwiga Lechicka, with faculty from 1946 until her death in 1965
Doc. Dr. B. Pawłowski	*Modern history*	1946–60	
W. Łukaszewicz	*Modern history*	1951–75	
W. Hejnosz	*Archival studies*	1945–65	Came from closed Law Department in 1951

Continuity of the Younger Generation in History (as of 1956)

Adviser/Institute Director	Student/Junior Colleague	Position Begins (begins studies in Toruń)
B. Włodarski	*Doc. M. Gumowski*	1945
	Dr. T. Grudziński	1949 (1946–47)
L. Kolankowski	*Dr. A. Dygdala*	1945
	Mgr. J. Serczyk	1949 (1946)
S. Hoszowski	*Mgr. J. Wojtowicz*	1949 (1947)
R. Mienicki	*Dr. Leonid Żytkowicz*	1945 (not permitted to teach 1951–54)
Karol Górski	*Mgr. Józek Mossakowski*	1946
Doc. Dr. B. Pawłowski	*Dr. Mateusz Puciata*	1946
W. Hejnosz	*Dr. K. Jasiński*	1947

Sources: Kalembka, Pracownicy nauki; Tomczak, Wspomnienia pracowników.

added many new faces. All of seven professors teaching history in 1947–48 were still on the faculty in 1955–56, with the exception of medievalist Stanisław Kętrzyński, who had died. Yet by 1955–56 the faculty had grown to twenty-eight full and associate professors, as well as seven acting professors. Of the former group, sixteen had belonged to the university faculty in 1947–48, yet many of the newcomers were imposed upon the faculty. In the words of Tadeusz Manteuffel, "the university became a dumping ground for people who for various reasons could not maintain their positions elsewhere."[88] Still, Handelsman students Gieysztor and Małowist controlled two of four chairs, and Gieysztor was institute director and the devout Catholic Stanisław Herbst associate dean. They dominated the faculty through intellectual power and personal integrity, and they were loyal to one another. In contrast to historical institutes at universities in Berlin, Leipzig, or Prague, this was far from a Party domain. Of the twenty-eight full and associate professors, eleven belonged to the Party, and they were separated by sharp divides. The most important figure, Stanisław Arnold, was Handelsman's first student, and the two other senior Party scholars, Natalia Gąsiorowska and Żanna Kormanowa, despised one another. Kormanowa was the one professor who behaved disloyally toward the group. In Warsaw's law faculty the situation was similar: of thirteen professors teaching in 1947–48, ten remained in 1955–56 (one had died), but the faculty had expanded to twenty-six.[89]

The most remarkable example of the Party's failure to shatter a self-constituted milieu was the Catholic University of Lublin. The Catholic University did suffer repression: in 1949 state authorities transferred KUL's law and economics faculty to the state university in Lublin (UMCS), and in 1954 they closed down KUL's pedagogical faculty. But they did not shut down KUL's humanities faculty.[90] Demands from Party activists that KUL be closed completely or students taking part in retreats be "punished" were denounced by upper-level Party officials as "leftist excesses."[91] According to non-Catholic observers like the Polonist Maria Rzeuska or the philosopher Izydora Dąmbska, KUL was an island of academic freedom. In 1952 Rzeuska reported to Kraków's doyen Stanisław Pigoń on a lecture series she had given at KUL: "I am moved by what I saw at KUL. The students are immensely intelligent, savvy, well read. You can see at once that they do not waste time on superfluous things; they learn what one should learn. And there are a lot of them. In Warsaw we have 150 students [in Polish philology], and they have 280. I believe that in the present conditions they are playing the role of pioneers."[92] After holding three lectures at KUL in 1955 Dąmbska wrote to a friend: "Please no ironic smiles, but old religions are less malicious than new ones. Going to a seminar at KUL after all those meetings at other scholarly institutes was like breathing the air of the Tatras after inhaling the stink of a mass march in a coal basin."[93] Because the Party did not dare to close KUL, the humanities in Lublin remained beyond state control.

The differing postwar contexts of the Czech lands, East Germany, and Poland produced different stories. In the first case, the record shows interruption and upheaval, limited mostly to the social sciences and segments of the humanities. Yet throughout Czech academia a new force emerged after the 1948 coup: Communist students, both undergraduate and graduate, relatively uncontrolled, idealistic, resentful, and ruthless. In East Germany the Party achieved a more complete break in the professoriate through a revolution from above, orchestrated by Soviet and German Communist agencies. Finally, in Poland, one discerns massive challenges and massive changes, but at the center of it all, throughout the academic disciplines, a solid core of old practices and values. What remains to be explored is how professors in Poland managed to hold onto their positions, and what effects their continuance had for the central university relation of student and teacher. What remains is an exploration of the power and the meaning of milieu.

★

CHAPTER EIGHT

THE
POWER
OF
SOCIETY
AND THE
POWER
OF
MILIEU

Unsettling signs of the early postwar years, like the unexplained disappearance of opposition politicians or the increasingly strident anti-Western rhetoric, heralded approaching calamity. These years were like the moments before a storm. In 1948 stalinism broke upon Eastern Europe in full force, and state harassment poured down on universities, in a continuous hail of decrees, pronouncements, and public threats, all eroding freedoms of teaching and research. Students and professors received instructions for every minute of the day: what books to read and write, which classes to attend and teach, and "invitations" to after-school "production discussions" or rallies that lasted deep into the night. University premises, like all public places, were awash in the colors and emblems of the new regime: peace doves, caricatures of Western statesmen, quotations from the "classics" of Marxism-Leninism-Stalinism, and of course, serenely menacing portraits of the leaders.[1] New acronyms filled the air, "Stasi," "St.B." and "UB," all the local equivalents of the Soviet NKVD, all promising violence for anyone opposing the state's intention to regulate human activity to the smallest detail.

Universities were supposed to become places of material production, and students and teachers were kept "on the job" for upward of forty-eight hours a week. Stalinism exhausted, and left little time for recovery. Instead of vacation, summers were "production practice" or labor "brigades." As "academic administrators," professors were expected to deliver almost daily reports on their departments' activities — reports that they did not have time to write, and the centralized bureaucracy did not have time to read. The result was mountains of useless paper,[2] and dozens of delayed or frustrated careers.[3]

More disturbing, the stalinist years were a time when foremost humanists and social scientists were prevented from research and hampered in their publishing; and when many dozens of their students either had to seek non-academic employment or bide their time in activities foreign to their interests. This was true of all three societies under study. Jan T. Gross has written that stalinism was the number of books not written; at universities stalinism was this, but it was also the number of courses not taught, ideas not discussed, degrees not granted. The damage caused to culture during stalinism is immeasurable.

The state enforced its will through staggered intimidation, ranging from student activists who would make loud noises during lectures, to anonymous phone calls late in the night, to random short-term arrests.[4] Students and teachers knew that saying the wrong thing could cost them their positions or their freedom. Fear in turn made opportunism a virtue and corroded human relations, as increasingly politics encroached upon private spheres. Polish Communists' particular way of disciplining academic thought involved frequent "scientific congresses," in philology, linguistics, art, and biology, all leading to the massive First Congress of Polish Science in the summer of 1951 with over 1,000 "guests" and dozens of "scientific sections," all meant to communicate the new ideological messages to the academic community and to ostracize outsiders.[5] In the formulation of Communist historian Żanna Kormanowa, the Congress of Science was "an instrument of struggle," for "attacking National Democrat and Catholic" scholars.[6] Even socialists, like Henryk Wereszycki, were forced to engage in self-criticism. Yet after absolving the ritual at the conference of Polish historians in Otwock in 1951, he was still accused by ideologue Roman Werfel of having "confessed only to a cold, when he was actually in the final stages of consumption."[7]

East European academics endured the deprivations of this time cut off from the rest of the world; for over five years even the most trusted scholars were routinely denied permission to travel to conferences abroad. Private correspondence with Western publishers and colleagues was censored and an object of suspicion. Indeed, any intimation of independently attained knowledge of the outside world could draw one into a vortex of recrimination. Students in the Czech lands and East Germany were interrogated by youth functionaries to detect information gained through Western news broadcasts. The guilty were denied stipends or the right to study. Persons with relations in the West, or who had traveled to the West, attracted the wrath of functionaries who felt insecure behind their unlimited powers. One chemist returned after two years in England to a post in Lublin, only to be publicly denounced as a "deserter" by Eugenia Krassowska, Polish vice-minister of education. He shot himself.[8]

Each university community lasted out the storm of stalinism under differing kinds of shelter, shelter provided by the old professoriate. In East Germany its presence was thinnest, and a relatively large and disciplined Party cadre took directives to the heart of the university, to the relation between teacher and student. In the Czech case a strong and popular Party leadership had empowered Communist students to subvert the teacher-student relationship, and for several years these students dominated university operations through control of Party organizations. Yet in Poland, old professors remained at their posts teaching and influencing students, and staffing various university committees. Their students and students' students were likewise situated throughout Polish academia. The university continued as a community of tradition and value, bound together by a thick web of personal intimacies and professional friendships that extended several generations into the past.

Such premodern interrelations had been weaker in East German and Czech academic life because from the late nineteenth century German and Czech universities had behaved increasingly according to the formalized procedures of state institutions. In Poland, such procedures were a dressing upon decisions made by the professors. Characteristically, in the three countries studied, only in Poland does a native expression denote a mesh of traditional ties like the university: *środowisko,* which translates into a word borrowed in English, German, or Czech from the French: *milieu.*[9] At the major universities in Poland the *środowisko* remained intact from top to bottom, and across faculties. In East Germany and the Czech lands, any remaining networks of "private" interest articulation, beyond channels legitimated by the state, were successively marginalized after 1948 as a new milieu emerged at the center of the university: the Communist Party, with its separate idioms, values, and regulated hierarchies. It attempted to supplant existing dependencies and loyalties, including those of the family. At Polish universities, by contrast, the Communist Party led a marginal existence, and its activities were marked by an indolence suggesting that central ideological messages had failed to reach much of the Party cadre.

As has been argued for the pre-1948 period, none of these three cases can be understood outside the larger national contexts. Professors and students breathed the same air as their conationals, an air filled in each case with differing beliefs about the political. Most Poles thought of state socialism as a continuation of forces that intended the annihilation of the Polish church, rural community, and family—in short, of Poland. If anything, this feeling intensified after 1948. To many in the older generation, Party membership appeared a betrayal of national and academic culture, explicable in a few cases by the seductions of Marxism, especially to the young, but in the overwhelming majority of cases by opportunism. In the Czech lands and East Germany Party membership was not viewed as an essential compromise of national interest. Indeed, given the absence of strong religious alternatives, and the recent traumas of Munich on one hand and National Socialism on the other, many came to see Soviet-style socialism as salvation, and not, as it was in the Polish context, a necessary evil.

Evidence of the enduring strength of these attitudes among professors in the three contexts was the varying willingness to join the Communist Party. The institutional logic was close to identical, and the respective Parties started from similarly small bases in each professoriate. After 1948, increasingly the three Parties controlled remuneration and avenues of professional advancement, giving professors, especially in the social sciences, compelling incentives to sign into the ranks of the Communist movement. Failure to do so could delay careers for many years — or frustrate them entirely. Polish professors were perhaps best acquainted with the logic that applied after 1948, because many of them had experienced it once before, at the Soviet University in L'viv from 1939 to 1941.

Professors in the Czech lands and East Germany behaved according to the rules of the new game. Intimidated by the violence used against universities in February 1948, Czech professors massively sought refuge in the Communist Party. Communist student and later sociologist Pavel Machonin was entrusted with organizing the recruiting drive. He presented a plan on 16 March that provided for every faculty doubling its KSČ membership within a month.[10] Less than two months later, the number of KSČ members at institutions of higher education in Brno had increased by eight times, and the character of KSČ university organizations went from sectarian to "broadly mass-based."[11] By November 1949 the percentage of university faculty belonging to the KSČ exceeded half at the four most important higher educational institutions in Bohemia and Moravia (Charles University in Prague, Masaryk University in Brno, and the Technical Universities of Prague and Brno; see Table 8-1).[12] Even at such a conservative place as the civil and geodetic engineering faculties in Brno, 80 percent of the scholars joined the KSČ; a functionary reporting on these events the following year spoke of a "post-February psychosis."[13]

In East Germany the movement into the Party was more gradual: by 1954, 28.8 percent of professors belonged to the SED, and by the end of the decade Party members exceeded one-third of the total.[14] In contrast to the situation in the Czech lands, there were significant differences per field, however, in approximately inverse relation to numbers of former NSDAP members in that field. In 1954, only 15 percent of professors in medical and 21 percent of those in technical faculties belonged to the SED, whereas 37 percent of the professors in philosophical faculties and 74 percent of the professors in the social sciences were SED members.[15] By 1961, approximately 90 percent of the historians teaching at East German universities belonged to the SED. Among economists and legal scholars, that figure was even higher.[16]

Despite similar professional incentives, Polish professors did not join the Communist Party (see Table 8-2) in significant numbers. Moreover, the PZPR failed to introduce a large number of its adherents into academia, even as numbers of university faculty grew, from 2,665 (1949) to 5,687 (1953), to 12,840 (1958).

TABLE 8-1

Communist Party Membership in the Czech Professoriate, October 1949 (in percentage)

Faculty	Joined before February 1948	Joined after February 1948
Masaryk University, Brno		
Law	18.2	27.3
Medicine	12.1	54.6
Philosophical	9.3	39.5
Natural sciences	6.7	56.7
Pedagogical	38.9	43.9
Total	19.0	47.2
Charles University, Prague		
Medical	18.5	15.0
Total	21.1	21.4
Czech Technical University, Prague		
Civil engineering	29.6	29.6
Electrical engineering	33.0	26.4
Chemical engineering	11.1	5.5
Special sciences	46.8	27.7
Economics	16.7	0
Total	27.1	21.5

Source: SÚA, AÚV KSČ, f. 19/7, a.j. 311, 313/5, 314.

Low membership meant that the PZPR was denied access to the relation between teacher and student. In East Germany, Communist professors were the lowest link in a chain of command, and afforded the Party leadership direct influence in the faculties, because the rules of democratic centralism obligated Party members to fulfill decisions of supposedly elected superior organs. While medical and veterinary medical faculties presented problems to the SED throughout the 1950s, the social sciences and humanities became saturated with cadres.

Polish professors as state employees were bound to carry out the duties specified by state authorities—for example, to respect procedures of appointment or to submit regular reports on academic tasks—but when the door closed to the classroom, or to many informal meetings between colleagues, the Party was usually left outside. For that reason, Party leaders desperately wanted professors to join, especially those enjoying respect. In June 1948, Education Minister Stanisław Skrzeszewski told a meeting of PPR and PPS academics that "we have to devote effort to getting first-class scholars into our ranks, professors of renown, of high moral character, who enjoy

TABLE 8-2

The PZPR in the Polish Academic Community (in percentage)

	1949	1953	1958
Professors	7.8	10.7	11.4
Junior faculty	7.3	12.5	16.1

Source: Hübner, *Nauka polska,* 174, 210.

Note: Professors include full (ordinary), associate (extraordinary), and docents; junior faculty are adjunct professors, advanced assistant professors, and assistant professors (*adiunkci, starsi asystenci, asystenci*).

authority in their *środowisko.* That's the sort of person we have to get into the Party. There's no trick in signing up a freshman—the trick is getting first-class professors."[17]

The Logic of PZPR Higher-Education Policy

Why did the Polish Party leadership resign itself to its weakness in academia? Perhaps it made sense to assent to compromise in the rather ambiguous immediate postwar period, yet such a strategy made little apparent sense after 1948, when the political agenda narrowed, and throughout the Soviet bloc "bourgeois" scholars were viewed as inherently unfit for contact with students. Would the Party's ability to form a new intelligentsia have suffered irreparable damage from the dismissals of a few more "hostile" jurists, historians, or experts in Polish literature? Or, perhaps more important, from the influx of large numbers of PZPR members into the junior faculty? We know that Communist Polonist Stefan Żółkiewski desired the retirement of Stanisław Pigoń. Stanisław Ehrlich, baron of legal sciences in the Party, called Kraków's senior scholar Jerzy Lande a heretic in private correspondence, and considered his colleagues Adam Vetulani and Jan Gwiazdomorski unredeemable. Surely placing ten or fifteen such figures on extended sabbatical would not have endangered the construction of socialism.

To portray matters in such a way is to lose sight of the constraints under which Polish Communists operated. They thought in terms of Polish society, and not simply the professoriate; and as the work of Padraic Kenney and others has shown, this society had not been robbed of inner strength and co-hesion by Nazi and Soviet occupation. It reacted to injustice through armed insurgency, boycotts, and strikes, or through simple failure to cooperate. Even after 1948, Poles continued to join the Communist Party at about half the rate of the populations in neighboring countries, and thus the Polish Communist Party was more thinly staffed than the Czechoslovak or German Communist Parties.[18] After open opposition was finally subdued in 1948, the Polish regime's opponents organized in the underground, and historians estimate that tens of thousands of young people took part in conspiracies into the early 1950s.[19]

When Poland's most stalinist rector, Józef Parnas of UMCS in Lublin, had thirty students of his university expelled in 1949, he received a threat from an organization calling itself "death to Stalin." Parnas felt isolated and afraid: "Is this kind of distinction good for me and UMCS? The organization 'Death to Stalin' has condemned me to death. In this light [i.e., of the expulsions] it even seems justified. But is no one at the Ministry of Education interested in the personal safety of the citizen rector of UMCS? . . . Perhaps the min-istry believes that Parnas as a former Soviet partisan will defend himself?" He had wanted to "chuck out" (*wywalać*) almost 300 students.

Ministry and other central agencies were more wary than Parnas and tended to advise against mass expulsions or other actions that might en-gender opposition.[20] They knew that conspiratorial instincts remained very much alive in academia. In 1952 authorities uncovered stores of weapons and ammunition belonging to "enemy organizations" at the universities in Kraków and Warsaw.[21]

Despite an open border to the West, East German Communists did not feel such constraints in dealings with "hostile" professors or students. On 30 May 1952 the Secretariat of the SED Central Committee decided to purge the university in Halle of "criminal and hostile elements." State secretary and former Buchenwald inmate Professor Gerhard Harig traveled to Halle and personally carried out an expulsion of eighty students. Though a profes-sor of philosophy at Leipzig University, and an integral part of the vaunted "Leipzig milieu" of those years, Harig carefully fulfilled the demands of his Party. He targeted students who "systematically speak out against our state and the measures of the government, carry out anti-Soviet rabble-rousing propaganda, have connections to West Germany and West Berlin, or who for moral and academic reasons are not suited for studies. . . . Students of the upper bourgeoisie were given special attention. Students who were in West-ern prisoner-of-war camps, and partially attended courses there, likewise received special attention."

Harig and his subordinates made use of results from courses in social sci-ences and Russian to identify targets. They also talked to teachers and to some of the "most dependable comrades." Harig wrote in his report for Walter Ulbricht that students received a written notification of the expulsion, but that "no reason is given in this communication; rather the student is asked to appear in the office of the prorector in order to settle his case (e.g., for surrendering his study book). During this consultation the reason for his removal is communicated orally. The student receives nothing in writing about this."[22] For all their haughty orthodoxy, East German Communists were no more eager than Communists in Poland or the Czech lands to affix their signatures to evidence of their misdeeds.

In the Czech lands the Party leadership exploited youthful idealism and achieved an even more impressive purgation of the student body. The instruments were "academic evaluations." In early 1949, several dozen groups of three to four student Communists sat in judgment over all students enrolled in the Czech lands and, in the end, refused permission to continue to over one-fourth of their peers. They were a force of fear. One protocol of an "evaluation" held in Prague recorded that the student in question "would say anything and everything to save himself."[23]

In neither the Czech lands nor East Germany did central state authorities operate in fear of their societies, yet Polish Communists could never ignore their own weakness and, for fear of being outflanked, hesitated to push society too forcefully on any single "front": the church, the peasantry, industrial workers, universities. From the beginning, the top leadership took care not to alienate potentially supportive elements of the intelligentsia, and attempted to enlist cooperation for the massive task of rebuilding Poland. Władysław Gomułka explained the Party's strategy in an address to delegates at the first PPR congress of December 1945:

> It is true that professors are reactionary, but we cannot train new professors overnight. Professors spend years gaining qualifications, long years, and we have been in power only a few months. We still have to educate our professors and educate them we will, yet this will take years — as many as one needs to educate a professor. We have to work to help the professors we have, since we cannot close down the universities.
>
> There are hundreds and thousands of ways to exert our influence and to hinder reactionary activity. One of the main and most important ways is the development of our work among young people at school and university. If we have strong support among them, they will exert influence upon professors.[24]

Instead of replacing the professors inherited from bourgeois Poland, the Party and its agencies would attempt to make use of them to train a new elite.[25] Not foreseeing the watersheds of 1953 and 1956, Poland's Communists thought they had plenty of time, and did not want to make unnecessary enemies by alienating potential short-term allies, like socialists or other "progressive" forces.[26] Well aware of the Party's dilemma, professors came to appreciate their own worth, even in times of the greatest persecution. In October 1951 conservative Polonist Roman Pollak of Poznań University wrote to his equally conservative friend Stanisław Pigoń in Kraków: "You write about passing the retirement age. But I also passed that boundary in July 1951. I do not believe that we are so unnecessary that they will be able to get rid of us. The sword hangs above us, but I do not believe the danger is too great."[27]

The self-confidence of professors who had made significant compromises with the state was even greater, because of the embarrassment that would be caused by the sudden withdrawal of their cooperation. The renowned philologist Tadeusz Lehr-Spławiński, former rector in Kraków, was a loyal scholar par excellence, who signed all required condemnations of American foreign policy, lent his name and reputation to several nonacademic publications, and sat in the presidia of the new Soviet-style Polish Academy of Sciences. A staunch Roman Catholic, he never considered joining the PZPR, however. In 1954 he threatened complete withdrawal from the activities of the academy, with all the "undesirable repercussions such a step would provoke, not only in Poland," if an institute for Slavic studies were not created, with him as director.[28] In 1952 he refused to abide by the customary practice in Soviet-type societies of submitting a conference paper for approval before he gave it, contending that "as a full member of the academy I should enjoy enough confidence in official circles that such demands would not be made of me."[29] This of course was a game that could be played only by the elite of scholarship, and not in every issue.

The PPR/PZPR's strategy of a gradual transition to socialism was called "mild revolution." Party leaders imagined that the war had weakened professors' resistance, and would make them more likely to cooperate. In a 1946 memorandum Dr. Jerzy Marowski (PPR), vice-director for higher education in the Education Ministry, suggested luring professors out of their reserves through an appeal to their "fetish" for academic freedom:

> Professors are generally old, with health and nerves destroyed by war, and poorly paid. . . . This state of affairs does not incline them toward opposing the government, but rather makes them favor compromise. They do, however, have a collective feeling of obligation to behave with honor and apparently they are prepared to stage a decisive defense of academic freedom, often going so far as to expose themselves personally to unpleasantries.
>
> This freedom is a fiction; nevertheless it has assumed the charac-

ter of a sort of fetish. In defense of this fetish — and this is a fact very favorable for us — professors are prepared to make many far-reaching concessions.[30]

Offering professors academic freedoms in return for cooperation — this was a bargain that neither Czech nor East German Communists ever felt forced to contemplate. In the Czech case it was the professors who hoped that by making small compromises — for example, enrolling in the Party — they would be left in peace. The strategy of mild revolution was revised after 1948 but not abandoned.[31] Minister of Education Stanisław Skrzeszewski explained his Party's predicament in a June 1948 speech to Communist and socialist university teachers: "Dear comrades, I am not afraid of taking harsh measures. And it seems to me that the Ministry of Education must adopt harsh measures at universities. It must deliver accurate, mortal blows that strike right to the heart. But for us to carry out these blows we have to know the universities, and our arms are still too short to reach them." [32]

Chains of Influence

That was the point: Poland's Communists wanted radical change, but they were too weak to achieve it quickly. In order to reach the professoriate, and their own worker-peasant students, leading PZPR academic functionaries Stefan Żółkiewski, Adam Schaff, and Celina Bobińska had to approach "loyal" and "cooperative" non-Party scholars — like Kazimierz Wyka, Józef Chałasiński, or Tadeusz Manteuffel — and use them as intermediaries. From the standpoint of long-term Party policy, this dynamic proved ruinous, however; because rather than effect Party directives, these functionaries were drawn into unending rounds of bargaining, aware that to loose the trust of their "friends" meant to loose contact with the universities. This role gradually wore away at their self-understanding as Party functionaries; especially after Stalin's death, they came to see themselves as intermediaries, as the "protectors" of the academic community, proud of their ability to limit the damage of a system that they themselves grew to call stalinist.

Stefan Żółkiewski had completed undergraduate training in Polish literature in 1934 at Warsaw University, and joined the PPR in 1942. During the war he took part in underground conspiratorial teaching and edited PPR literary journals. After the war he was a leading voice in the campaigns against romanticism in literature and rose quickly in the Party hierarchy, directing the Department of Culture in the PPR/PZPR Central Committee (1947–49) and editing the important leftist monthly *Kuźnica* (The forge).[33] In December 1950 Żółkiewski gave the Central Committee a complete plan of "personnel reform" in Polish studies for the following five years, which would "remove reactionaries from positions of influence on young people."

The plan specified the professors to be terminated and gave precise dates for the employment of Marxist assistant professors. It also provided for the closing of Polish departments in Łódź, Toruń, and Poznań until 1955, when sufficient Marxist staff would be available to reopen them. *Almost none of this plan was realized.* Professors S. Pigoń and J. Kleiner of Kraków, S. Kolbuszewski of Wrocław ("ideologically foreign"), S. Skwarczyńska of Łódź, Adjunct Professor J. Spytkowski of Kraków ("hostile"), Docent Z. Szmydtowa ("fideist"), and Assistant Professor J. Pelc of Warsaw were all scheduled to be "removed from university work," but they taught through the stalinist period. Pigoń and Kleiner were kept on even after reaching mandatory retirement age. The departments to be closed stayed open, and Professors R. Pollak ("routinist") and Z. Szweykowski ("fideist") led Poznań's Polish department through these years. The one person identified for removal who actually was removed was Warsaw Adjunct Professor Maria Rzeuska ("formalist"), who had to stop teaching in the summer of 1954. Yet the following year her supporters in the department—including Professor Z. Libera, a person chosen by Żółkiewski—succeeded in having Rzeuska promoted to docent. Strangely, Żółkiewski himself supported this promotion.[34]

How can one explain such a miserably underfulfilled plan? One possibility is that Party leaders did not approve the entire scheme, because it ran against the general policy of "mild revolution" and might have provoked more resistance than was manageable. This was a time when the Organizational Bureau of the PZPR Central Committee was intervening almost weekly to correct excesses of lower-level functionaries in the countryside.[35] Also possible is that Żółkiewski himself, having spent the war years in Poland and therefore endangered as a "home Communist" in the late 1940s, presented an unrealistically radical plan in order to forestall criticism. In January 1949 he had been removed from the Central Committee apparatus and made to concern himself exclusively with Polish studies, precisely because of supposed opportunism in dealings with "bourgeois" intellectuals at *Kuźnica*.[36]

Yet as we have seen, the PZPR was not completely adverse to removing professors from teaching, and the question remains as to why there was no greater shake-up in Polish studies. It seems that Żółkiewski grew to understand that more dismissals would incite the opposition of "progressive" scholars, without whom he could not reach universities. Although he had finished master's studies before the war, in 1950 Żółkiewski was still an outsider to the academic community. He did not yet have a doctorate. Unless he wanted to reform Polish studies by himself with the help of a few other students, he needed the assistance of people with authority and reputation. Moreover, this was a time of dramatic teaching shortages, and more important than Żółkiewski's plan to produce Marxist faculty was the ministry's plan to train new students.

Crucial to Żółkiewski's quest to exert influence in Polish studies was Kazimierz Wyka of Kraków, a pioneer of Marxist methodology in Polish literary studies who never joined the Party. He had joined the Department of the History of Polish Literature of Jagiellonian University in 1934 and received both the doctorate (1937) and habilitation (1946) there, before advancing to associate professor in 1948.[37] Żółkiewski could not take forceful measures against professors in Kraków without the consent of Wyka.

Wyka for his part behaved loyally toward his teachers and colleagues and would not consent to their removal. When possible, he interceded, for example pushing for the long overdue advance of Franciszek Bielak in 1957.[38] For their part his teachers kept him informed of their needs. In 1956 Juliusz Kleiner requested Wyka's intervention for Feliks Araszkiewicz of KUL, who had recently been denied the title of professor: "Would you, dear colleague, as the major caretaker of Polish studies in the [State Central Qualification Commission] please effect a reassessment of this judgment? I beg you. Let it be a present for my fiftieth anniversary as a scholar, and for my seventieth birthday."[39] The academic world of Bielak, Kleiner, and Wyka was extremely sensitive to state harassment. To fire and arrest professors in Kraków immediately triggered associations of the Gestapo and the morning of 6 November 1939. Indeed, Wyka's own *Doktorvater,* Stefan Kołaczkowski, had returned fatally ill from the camp at Oranienburg and died a week later.[40]

Wyka had his own interest in maintaining this position of mediator. On the one hand he derived professional legitimacy from the continued respect of the milieu that had formed him, but on the other his close relation with Żółkiewski permitted fullest use of the best years of his academic life, as teacher, researcher, and knowledge broker. Wyka's world extended beyond Kraków; he was on cordial or better terms with the major figures in Polish studies at Wrocław University (T. Mikulski), the Catholic University of Lublin (C. Zgorzelski), and Toruń University (K. Górski and A. Hutnikiewicz). In the extended period of uncertainty after Stalin's death Wyka's position on the overlap between traditional and Marxist scholarship became one of outstanding importance, as the two worlds moved closer toward each other, and possibilities emerged to heal the wounds of stalinism and fuse academia more solidly.

In 1955 Żółkiewski returned to an exalted position in the PZPR Central Committee, and Wyka began to approach him about undoing some of the injustices perpetrated upon the humanities in Kraków.[41] Żółkiewski was an enthusiastic supporter of the "thaw" in Polish literature, and sought the aid of Wyka to found a critical monthly in Kraków.[42] By this point the former saw himself not so much as the executor of the Party's will, but as a middleman, as someone who would "defend" the reasonable interests of "loyal" and "progressive" colleagues, as well as of his comrades. There had always been a dissonance between his rhetoric and his practice, and even his 1949 program of reorganization is laced with inconsistencies and suggests a certain ideological softness. For example, both T. Ulewicz (Kraków) and W. Floryan (Wrocław) were described as "ideologically foreign," yet "loyal."[43]

In order to qualify for Żółkiewski's support, one did not need to enter the Party, but only to show a general openness toward Marxist methodology.[44] Dr. Bogdan Zakrzewski of Poznań was given credit for his "goodwill," and when he was threatened with dismissal for family associations with the Polish London Government, Żółkiewski arranged for his transfer to Wrocław.[45] And as mentioned, in 1955 Żółkiewski supported the advance of Maria Rzeuska ("formalist") to docent. He too was drawn into the orbit of the środowisko. In 1968 Żółkiewski was removed from all positions at Warsaw University and in the Party after defending students who had been arrested during the March events.

In the field of history the boundaries separating Party and non-Party were vaguer than in Polish studies; in the central milieu of Warsaw, the division ran through a web of friendship and personal respect of the interwar seminar of the renowned Marceli Handelsman.[46] Handelsman's first student, Stanisław Arnold (Ph.D., 1920), was the preeminent Communist historian of the early postwar era, and he and other students of Handelsman's school —T. Manteuffel, S. Kieniewicz, M. Małowist, A. Gieysztor, H. Jabłoński— formed the core of Warsaw's history faculty. The bonds uniting them had been strengthened through joint activity in the Home Army; Handelsman, Gieysztor, Kieniewicz, and Manteuffel had worked along with W. Kula in the Bureau of Information and Propaganda.[47] Though they embraced Marxism with differing degrees of interest after 1945, these historians remained loyal to each other personally, even in the tense years of stalinism. Arnold and the openly Marxist Kula (married to PZPR member Nina Assorodobraj) did not join in attacks on "bourgeois" historians. Indeed, Arnold acted to protect non-Party historians even outside this circle of old colleagues and teachers.[48]

The decisive moment for Polish historical studies came in late 1951, at the Otwock conference, attended by historians from all of Poland, and Soviet historians Grekov, Kosminskii, and Tretiakov. Here a number of doctrinaire Communist historians, like Ż. Kormanowa, T. Daniszewski, and R. Werfel, launched a rhetorical assault on the historical establishment. Like Żółkiewski, they often lacked advanced academic training. Yet the wretchedness of their scholarship could scarcely be concealed—even from the Central Committee apparatus, much less the Soviet guests, two of whom had studied in Warsaw before World War I. In a private audience they urged Polish Party leader Bierut to spare Polish historiography the devastations of these untrained revolutionaries—perhaps having some parallels in mind from home—especially in light of the "progress" the mainstream of Polish historians was making toward Marxist thought. They were frequent visitors to Poland and could, for example, compare the presentations at Otwock to those of the Wrocław historians' conference in 1948.[49]

Indeed, a massive shift had been taking place toward social and economic history, areas in which Polish historians were weak. Directly after this meeting Prime Minister J. Cyrankiewicz announced that an Institute of History would be formed at the Polish Academy of Sciences under the distinguished non-Party medievalist Tadeusz Manteuffel.[50] Thus the most important historical organization in People's Poland fell into the hands of a man dedicated to limiting the damage of the totalitarian state.[51] A relaxation of tensions ensued, especially in the fields of medieval and early modern history.[52] Stefan Kieniewicz later recalled early 1952 as a time when one could "breathe more easily."[53] On the basis of the work accomplished in social history in these years, fruitful contacts were established after 1956 with the Annales school. Stalinism lasted relatively briefly in historical studies.

The second major Polish school of history in Kraków was even less touched by the perturbations of stalinism. Unlike Warsaw, it showed practically no sympathies for the left, and not a single professor and only one junior professor entered the ranks of the PZPR during the early 1950s. The Party's one rather bashful attempt at injecting Marxism into this środowisko was embodied by the young Communist Celina Bobińska. Though Soviet-trained, she would not seem a suitable candidate for "stalinizing" the Krakovian historical milieu, however. Her father, Communist Party of Poland leader Stanisław Bobiński, had been murdered in the great purges, and her husband, Central Committee member Władysław Wolski, spent years in the gulags and was expelled from the PZPR for deviations in 1950, then transferred in punishment to Kraków's public library. For resisting pressures to disown Wolski, Bobińska was forbidden to hold Party functions and made to join him in Galician exile.[54] The Party leadership thus removed one of its most promising historians from the center of power.[55]

Bobińska had done everything short of divorcing Wolski to avoid being sent to Kraków. In an appeal to the PZPR Central Committee she described Kraków as a "reactionary, National Democrat środowisko," where she would feel tempted to "represent the Party in various institutions"; however, the Party penalty forced her into "passivity, which means approbation or solidarity."[56] These appeals availed nothing, and in the fall of 1950 Bobińska indeed arrived in Kraków, where she was received with a mixture of suspicion and bemusement. She took the place of a man of legendary memory, productivity, and academic authority, W. Konopczyński, who had been forced to retire in 1948. Despite her *kandidat* degree gained in Moscow, Bobińska did not command the basic literature on her subject and spoke a Polish full of Russicisms.

To sober observers she soon revealed a sharp intellect and independent will, however. In seminars Bobińska did not treat Marxism as an orthodoxy delivering ready answers but rather encouraged students to think critically. Like Żółkiewski, she came to desire the respect of the *środowisko*, and found herself "protecting" the interests of younger scholars outside the Party who were occasionally threatened by denunciations, like Anna Owsińska, Emanuel Rostworowski, or Marian Zgórniak.[57] In 1951 she came to the aid of medievalist Professor Roman Grodecki, who had been denounced by the student Tadeusz Nowak (PZPR) for supposedly discriminating against Marxists. Indeed, Grodecki had stated publicly that he would not "clutter" his seminar with "Marxist literature." Along with Bogdan Kędziorek, the first secretary of the PZPR at Jagiellonian University, Bobińska acted to defuse these charges, demonstrating that Marxist literature did indeed exist in the institute library. Nowak and his wife were then transferred to Warsaw.[58] Unlike young Communists in the Czech Republic, she was dedicated to the proposition that one had to make use of older scholars, and she imagined the transition to socialism in Poland as very gradual.[59]

Most important in attempts to convert Polish social sciences and humanities to Marxism was Adam Schaff, who like Bobińska had received an advanced degree in Moscow, yet like Żółkiewski had completed a first degree at a Polish university, the University of Lwów. Schaff therefore had feet in both academic worlds. Less impulsive than Żółkiewski, Schaff from the start anticipated the many years required to transform philosophy and the social sciences, but also recognized that non-Party professors were not suited to training Marxist scholars. In 1950 Schaff was permitted by the Party leadership to scour the Party's ranks for talent in the social sciences, and later that year he formed an elite Institute for Training Scientific Cadres (IKKN) in Warsaw (renamed in 1953 the Institute of Social Sciences [INS]), which was supposed to produce a first generation of Marxist philosophers, economists, historians, and legal scholars.[60]

The institute exemplified the heterodox credentials of its founder. Its staff was schooled at the Moscow Academy of Social Sciences, and Soviet professors were a presence at IKKN throughout its existence. Yet as a man of two worlds, Schaff also hoped to introduce an intensive, seminar style of instruction, as he imagined existed at English colleges. He attracted a talented group of tutors and professors, including Tadeusz Kroński, Leszek Kołakowski, Bronisław Baczko, Adam Kersten, Włodzimierz Brus, Seweryn Bialer, Henryk Holland, Maria Turlejska, Roman Zimand, Czesław Madajczyk, and Jerzy Holzer. Perhaps hoping to impress non-Party professors, Schaff cultivated a relatively liberal atmosphere at his institute. Students took advantage of a full range of reading materials, including Western journals available at the library of the Secret Police. For a project on "themes of industry" young economist Tadeusz Kowalik could read the Polish émigré journal *Kultura*. Claiming to want to write papers critical of the thought of Trotsky, Bukharin, and Rykov, other students requested the writings of these men in the original.[61]

Some of the younger historians and social scientists at IKKN, like Maria Turlejska, began murmuring in 1950 about the "camp system" they had to endure at the institute and poking fun at the self-important Schaff.[62] After Stalin's death in 1953, liberally informed and gifted IKKN students were poised to test the limited freedoms of the thaw. In a meeting at INS in February 1954 Turlejska refuted accusations of hard-liner Roman Werfel ("scholastic approach, blurring of Marxism"), telling him that "the history of peoples has been confined, not so much to the history of the working class as to the history of a single party, forgetting everything else, including the peasantry."[63] INS students shared in the outrage that permeated Polish intellectual circles after revelations of Secret Police abuses. During the Third Central Committee Plenum of January 1955 institute members voiced "great criticism."[64] In discussions in the offices of Party theoretical journal *Nowe Drogi,* they emphasized the necessity of "finding the courage to take up difficult, irritating social problems."[65] Such sentiments spilled over into the pages of popular journals of the thaw like *Nowa Kultura* (New culture) and *Przegląd Kulturalny* (Cultural review), in which INS students took prominent roles in debates on culture and science. Scholarly controversy and discussion had been forced into one narrow groove of Marxist interpretation in 1948–49, and five years later it was from there that they reemerged.

After the reinvigoration of Polish humanities and social sciences in 1954–55, INS gradually lost its separate and elite role within the Party and had increasing troubles attracting students. It was quietly closed in 1956. Its famous graduates took positions at universities and at institutes of the Academy of Sciences, where they represented a variety of approaches to scholarship— Marxist and otherwise.[66] The stalinist elite became a revisionist elite. What was unusual about Poland was not so much the absence of Marxism, as its existence in a broad context, which forced a certain diversity in Marxism as well.

Besides the IKKN/INS, no significant rifts had emerged in the Polish university community during the stalinist period. It was a relatively cohesive formation, held together from top to bottom in Polish studies by personal relations extending from people like Żółkiewski and Wyka, to Wyka's conservative teachers Stanisław Pigoń and Juliusz Kleiner; in law from a stalinist like Stanisław Ehrlich to socialist Bogusław Leśnodorski and then to Leśnodorski's staunchly Catholic teacher Adam Vetulani; or in history from PZPR historians Arnold and Bobińska to the non-Party Marxist Witold Kula, to "progressives" Tadeusz Manteuffel and Stefan Kieniewicz, to the Catholic

Stanisław Herbst. Each of these chains was linked by the respect of student and teacher, or the friendship of colleague to colleague.

The Political Geology of Polish and East German Academia

In terms of political function, one can imagine the Polish professoriate as consisting of three strata. At the top were PZPR members charged with fulfilling Party policy, in the middle left-leaning or "progressive" scholars, and at the bottom a bedrock of non-Party scholars, for the most part conservative and Roman Catholic. A key ingredient in lending solidity to this formation was nationalism; after the war many dozens of conservative or nationalist scholars, like legal scholar Ludwik Ehrlich, linguists Tadeusz Lehr-Spławiński and Witold Taszycki, historian Zygmunt Wojciechowski (director of the Western Institute in Poznań, and onetime friend of National Democratic leader Roman Dmowski), archaeologists Józef Kostrzewski and Włodzimierz Antoniewicz, or anthropologist Jan Czekanowski, served People's Poland by endeavoring to prove the ancient presence of Slavs in Silesia and Pomerania, which had recently been severed from Germany. Many of this latter group were Roman Catholics who had been alienated by Pius XII's 1948 letter apparently siding with Germany in the dispute over these territories. Some of them, like Lehr-Spławiński, became active in the state-supported group of "patriotic" Catholics called PAX.[67]

When one compares the Polish and East German professoriates of the 1950s, two differences quickly become apparent: the absence in the latter of an independent "progressive" stratum that might have mediated between the Party and the non-Party professoriate; and the absence in the former of a large group compromised by the past. The Nazi regime had demanded explicit support from the German professoriate, and therefore a massive group existed with records of membership in a host of compromised organizations: SA and SS, "supporting members" of the SS, the National Socialist Teacher's Union, and of course the NSDAP itself. With the conclusion of denazification in 1948, the number of former Nazis began to grow, reaching over one-quarter of the whole by 1954. Often, former Nazis had waited for years under conditions of great material uncertainty for reentry to the university, and once readmitted they proved, as Robert Havemann would later write, the East German stalinists' "most submissive servants."[68] Within the geology of East German academia, former NSDAP members merged with SED cadres and reinforced the position of the state. The thin sliver of "bourgeois" social scientists and humanists with records of opposing National Socialism had largely disappeared by 1948. Numbers of rehabilitated victims of the Nazis among East German professors had been minuscule to begin with.[69]

The few compromised nationalists in the Polish professoriate are also instructive of the usefulness of the politically tainted to a socialist state. In an intimate place like Kraków it was impossible for a professor to conceal his past. One aspiring and well-recommended docent of history, Kazimierz Lepszy, was known as a once enthusiastic National Democrat, who person-ally took part in some of the "actions" against Jewish students in the 1930s. After the war he did all he could to drive a wedge between himself and his mentor, the former National Democratic deputy Władysław Konopczyński, and proved a loyal executor of the state's wishes at Jagiellonian University, as institute director, prorector, and then rector.[70] It should be noted that the regime itself limited the delegitimization of former National Democrats, be-cause it held the national card in reserve, a fact that became fully evident in the anti-Semitic campaign of the late 1960s.[71]

In 1948 the East German regime created a special organization to exploit the political energies of former National Socialists: the National Democratic Party of Germany. A cofounder of this party in the university town of Greifs-wald was the chemist Hans Beyer. As an SA man at Berlin University in the 1930s Beyer had made sure that colleagues in his institute raised their arms to "Heil Hitler" — the "German" salute. His former director in the chemical institute, Professor Erich Thilo, described Beyer's past in letters of 1946 and 1947. Beyer had "kept the technical and scientific staff in constant fear and terror and left nothing untried that might give everyone a feeling of inse-curity. He acted as a watchman of the German salute and participation in marches and manifestations and noted and registered every ill-considered or careless remark." During the war, Beyer had been taken prisoner at Stalin-grad and become a supporter of the Soviet system. This made his former director no less wary: "The present full-scale renunciation of the beliefs that he once endorsed with the greatest energy — he joined the National Commit-tee for a Free Germany after surrendering in Stalingrad and now endorses the ideas of socialism of the eastern sort with the same energy — does not change anything, if anything it strengthens the feelings of personal mistrust toward him."[72] But by 1949 Beyer's past had become an advantage. In mid-1949, Franz X. Wohlgemuth of the Ministry of Education in Schwerin, and also a former *Wehrmacht* officer, recommended Beyer for the rectorship in Greifswald: "Professor Beyer, presently dean of the philosophical faculty, district chair of the National Democratic Party, also a man of understand-ing and agility. With his exhaustive academic training he certainly offers few points for attack. Politically Beyer works well (formerly member of the NSDAP, proved himself well in Soviet imprisonment)."[73] Beyer served the SED throughout the 1950s, standing on its side during student unrest in 1955, when Greifswald's medical faculty was converted into a military medical faculty.[74]

Borrowing on the work of Ivan Szelényi and George Konrád, Ralph Jessen has referred to East German scholars with credentials both in the Party and in academia as "double citizens," with the ability to deal in both worlds, and often act as mediators. Beyer was not a double citizen, however, but rather a man who had exchanged one sort of citizenship for another. And he was by no means exceptional; in the period from 1954 to 1962, over 60 percent of the rectors of East German institutions of higher education were former NSDAP members—almost twice the percentage of former NSDAP members in the professoriate as a whole![75]

Scholars who might act as "double citizens" in the East German social sciences and humanities were relatively few, however. A handful of leading figures had enjoyed some academic training before the war—historians Jürgen Kuczynski, Walter Markov, or Ernst Engelberg earned doctoral degrees—but they had not held university positions. They came from the Party to the university, and, as will be argued in greater detail, their primary loyalty was to the former. Indeed, in the East German context, it was the former that dispensed legitimacy. The Party in East Germany rarely had to negotiate central issues of research, staffing, or teaching with social scientists; rather it used members of its own cadre to communicate or execute decisions directly at universities.

In Poland most scholars who belonged to the Party had first belonged to their respective university faculty, toward which they felt primary loyalty. Many of the younger scholars who made their way into the ranks of the PZPR, like Bogusław Leśnodorski, Juliusz Bardach, Henryk Markiewicz, or Kazimierz Opałek, retained bonds to their teachers. If East German professors enjoyed "dual citizenship," these Polish professor Communists were at best bilingual—that is, fluent in the language of historical and dialectical materialism, but also of other more widely accepted methodologies. They remained citizens of the university.

If Polish universities escaped the ravages of stalinism relatively unscathed, that was because of the basic rejection by teachers and students, and indeed most of Polish society, of the values of the new regime. A Soviet-style socialist state was something profoundly threatening to Polish identity, and the support it elicited was mostly of a pragmatic nature. In neither the Czech lands nor East Germany did the populations confront the new state with an underlying attitude of opposition. In the former, intellectuals had essentially positive attitudes toward socialism and toward the Soviet Union. University professors, like the mainstream intelligentsia, failed to enunciate a cohesive alternative to the program of the Communist Party. In 1948 they and their students stood divided, and, with the exception of several students' demonstrations, accepted the new regime without resistance. Many East Germans felt a deep resentment toward the Soviet Union, and had mixed feelings about "socialism," but shared an attitude of respect toward the state, whether they felt it to be theirs or not. What remains to be explored in the next two chapters is what concretely the Polish professoriate achieved through its opposition, and to what degree new milieus emerged at East German and Czech universities.

CHAPTER NINE

THE
MEANING
OF
MILIEU

Polish scholars do not compare their history with the histories of surrounding countries. In their eyes, the stalinist years were a time of hardly mitigated destruction. Polonist Artur Hutnikiewicz has written that Poland's Communists "wanted to rebuild and create something supposedly perfect, but in their blind self-absorption they liquidated and destroyed everything in their midst. 'Reforming' they got rid of people, often the best, the most gifted, the most self-sacrificing. Wanting to educate in a 'progressive' and 'revolutionary' spirit, they created ideal, hothouse conditions for the training of conformists, opportunists, and careerists."[1] Looking back upon the dismissals of junior faculty that took place in 1949–50, historian of literature Irena Sławińska writes that "the injuries caused by this purge of the humanities have proved lasting and in certain areas the wounds have yet to heal. One—actually several—generations have suffered great harm, by being denied lectures and contact with outstanding personalities, scholars of the first rank with uncommon erudition and general cultivation."[2]

That Communist historian Celina Bobińska was "relatively" tolerant for her time seems of little relevance in Kraków today. There the scholarly community judges her not so much for what she did as for what she did not do. For three decades she dominated what for many is the most compelling chapter of Polish history, the time of the partitions, yet students avoided her Russian-accented lectures. In her research she hardly moved beyond narrowly framed studies of Galician peasants and produced little of lasting value. She became a full professor in the 1950s, yet the better-qualified Henryk Wereszycki never received a professorship and the perquisites that go with it, though—or perhaps because—he produced one of the few political histories of modern Poland taken seriously in the West. His lectures and seminars had almost cult appeal, partly for a broad, problematizing approach to history, partly for the beauty of his language.[3] No one can calculate the damage of neglect accomplished by an unqualified scholar like Bobińska, at a chair once held by such celebrated figures as Józef Szujski and Michał Bobrzyński.

In Warsaw, sociologist Antonina Kłoskowska contemplates the damage done by the socialist state to sociology. She achieved an international reputation in this field, yet at best admits that "things could have been worse." It is true that her time was not entirely wasted during the early 1950s. Sociology had officially ceased to exist, but she could work in Józef Chałasiński's Institute for Studies of the Press. Yet for Kłoskowska this was a postponement, not a satisfaction, of intellectual passions. She took part in small conspiratorial seminars in the Warsaw apartment of Stanisław and Maria Ossowski during these years, but these were moments full of dread, and students left the seminar two at a time in order not to attract attention, just as they had under the Nazis. Kłoskowska looks back upon everything she published in socialist Poland and wonders how it might be rewritten.

The Realities of Compromise

When one surveys the most visible signs of intellectual production of the stalinist years—journals and books, study programs, public declarations by academics—the assessments of Hutnikiewicz or Kłoskowska indeed seem compelling. To the extent that they could exist at all, Polish historical or philosophical journals were laden with articles written according to a simplified Marxist scheme, and with "reports" of the most recent decisions of Party congresses or plenums on science, completely ignoring a wide range of issues. Even the most "bourgeois" professors cast their scholarship in the terms of the new era. One is surprised to find the conservative medievalist Roman Grodecki writing on the "Class Wars in Polish Artisanry and Mining," or the supposedly uncompromising legal scholar Jan Gwiazdomorski demanding that students writing seminar papers "consistently apply the methods of historical materialism."[4] His colleagues in the Department of Civil Law in Wrocław, though also trained in prewar faculties, likewise claimed to base their teaching on the "classics of Marxism-Leninism."[5]

Polish professors wrote glowing reports of trips to the Soviet Union, published statements condemning American and lauding Soviet foreign policy, disowned their prewar scholarship, and sat on state commissions that centrally decided issues that had once been key elements of university autonomy, like habilitations.[6] They praised the wisdom of Stalin, and adapted to new trends: socialist realism, dialectical materialism, political opportunism. Rarely did they openly criticize the regime.[7] We find individuals later viewed as beacons of moral perfection, like historian Henryk Wereszycki, obediently marching at the head of manifestations for "peace" in his Wrocław exile; or Kraków linguist Tadeusz Lehr-Spławiński and the persecuted Wrocław legal scholar Andrzej Mycielski cooperating with former fascist Bolesław Piasecki in usurping power at the Catholic weekly *Tygodnik Powszechny* in 1953.[8] The examples of public compromise are innumerable; even the rector of the Catholic University of Lublin, Father Iwanicki, is considered by many to have gone too far in his dealings with representatives of People's Poland. Important voices in Polish public opinion now discuss the "betrayal of the clerks" and make blanket reference to intellectuals' "services to People's Poland."[9] Professors are easily portrayed as integral parts of an evil regime.

Such points of view may be widespread in the post-Communist period, but they existed in the 1950s as well, and not necessarily on the right. Dr. Maria Rzeuska, to this day the unsurpassed interpreter of Nobel Prize–winning novelist Władysław Reymont, had belonged to a group of left-leaning intellectuals in interwar Wilno, including S. Jędrychowski, H. Dembiński, J. Putrament, and later Vice-Minister of Education E. Krassowska. But she was an independent leftist. After being released from teaching in 1954, she ignored the advice of the conservative Stanisław Pigoń to get things published through channels provided by the state. For example, Adam Schaff and Stefan Żółkiewski had created opportunities at their respective institutes for ostracized scholars to translate and edit classical texts.[10] Thus Władysław Tatarkiewicz edited and his wife translated Hume, and Izydora Dąmbska translated and edited a volume on Leibniz.[11] Rather than accept the mercy of Żółkiewski or Schaff, however, Rzeuska preferred to sell her library book by book, in order to have time to write "critical" works, even if they could not be published. In a letter of 6 February 1955, sent through the mails of socialist Poland, she described her decision to Pigoń, who was taking full advantage of the opportunities provided by the regime:

> Why do I sell my books when I could be earning money working on textbooks at the Institute of Literary Research, or by editing texts? After all, as you write, I could do this without detriment to my "scholarly personality."
>
> I will try to explain this to you, and if here and there you feel hurt, I ask your forgiveness. You have brought up something that is important and hurtful, and not only in a moral sense.
>
> As is generally known, all segments of scholarship in Poland have suffered terribly and reduced their standards. In part this is a result of the war, but perhaps even more, of current policy, and in general, of the situation that has existed for the last ten years in Poland. In every branch of scholarship things are bad, but *literary studies lie in ruins*. Literary studies have been a particular victim of a concealed policy of destruction, even more than philosophy, which has been liquidated.

> Literary sciences *have been destroyed* through the elimination of any scholarly problematic and by their conversion into a trumpet of vulgar propaganda. Perhaps in order to camouflage this effort texts, textbooks, and various kinds of dictionaries are published en masse. One cannot claim that accurate publication of texts and dictionaries has no value. It is useful if it develops along with a scholarly problematic in the strict sense. But it cannot replace such a problematic, and in the current situation even presents a number of dangers: the deception and anesthetization of the scholarly conscience, the exhaustion of scholars' creative imaginations, the restriction of intellectual curiosity and intellectual restlessness. The situation is horrible. Outstanding professors of the older generation, many of them trained during the greatest flowering of Polish philology, cling to this massive publishing enterprise like a baby to a mother's breast.[12]

There was something to this criticism: in 1956 philosopher Henryk Elzenberg complained to his rector when the faculty applied to the ministry for his reactivation. He had always considered teaching a burden.[13] Rzeuska never returned to teaching; perhaps she considered the compromises too great. In 1957, during the greatest freedoms of destalinization, she published a full-scale attack on Polish studies, suggesting that a number of scholars had been driven to their death by stalinist functionaries. Toward the end of her life in 1982, plagued by an enduring nervous illness, she broke off contact with many close friends whom she had come to see as "venal."[14]

Yet for those who taught at universities in People's Poland, completely avoiding compromise was impossible, especially in the social sciences. "Uncompromising" scholars such as Adam Vetulani or Stanisław Pigoń worked with central state commissions that passed judgments on colleagues or teaching programs. By implication they therefore recognized the legitimacy of structures that had usurped functions of universities.[15] The small gestures of conformity of Jan Gwiazdomorski or Henryk Wereszycki have been mentioned. Each of these scholars, exiled to Wrocław but living in Kraków, had been pushed to the boundaries of the endurable. They could witness their potential fate by looking at sociologist Stanisław Ossowski or philosopher Władysław Tatarkiewicz, denied contact with students and marginalized in the scholarly world. Yet even these had not entirely rejected cooperation with the state, the former, for example, by sitting on the editorial board of Adam Schaff's *Myśl Filozoficzna* (Philosophical thought), the latter by lending his name to Schaff's editions of the classics of philosophy and, in a sense, legitimizing them.

Even Maria Rzeuska, for whom the Communist state came to represent the historical embodiment of evil, owed her position to that state. She received work as adjunct professor at Warsaw University in 1948 not by standard academic procedures—that is, by the request of her department—but as an appointee of the Ministry of Education. The staff of the department, unlike Rzeuska mostly conservative and Roman Catholic, feared her, a personal friend of Vice-Minister Krassowska, as a "political plant." The department director, Professor Borowy, instructed other young lecturers to have the "most proper relations" with Rzeuska, in order to "preserve possibilities of normal work." That is, they were instructed to make compromises with the uncompromising. One of Borowy's students commented that Rzeuska's critique of 1957 was popular in a time when "a condition for success is a good memory of other people's past, and forgetfulness of one's own."[16] This student's abiding mistrust of Rzeuska shows how the fear endemic to stalinism assumed a dynamic of its own and successively poisoned human relations; those outside the Catholic *środowisko* surrounding Borowy were not only foreign but potential enemies.

Protekcja: *Professors Protect Each Other*

The question for university professors was therefore not whether but how to compromise. A range of possibilities existed: from those who supervised cooperation with the state, like Stefan Żółkiewski, Żanna Kormanowa, or Adam Schaff; to older scholars who appeared to embrace the new faith, and brokered compromises, like Kazimierz Wyka, Tadeusz Manteuffel, and Józef Chałasiński; to the highly differentiated majority of non-Party professors, each of whom struck small bargains and hoped for better times. A partial alignment of scholars' interests with those of the state, especially in the rapid training of experts to rebuild Poland, or in propagating the Polishness of the new Western territories, helped ease this cooperation. What the regime hoped to get from this arrangement is clear. To have renowned scholars like philosopher Tadeusz Kotarbiński or the physiologist Ludwik Hirszfeld take part in state-sponsored conferences and congresses, teach at state universities, or accept state awards, created the image of a professoriate that endorsed People's Poland. More important, as has been mentioned, the regime hoped to use these scholars' knowledge to train a new generation. But memoirs and interviews reveal that many scholars also hoped to gain something in return for their willingness to cooperate. If so, what?

In a most general sense, willingness to compromise meant that professors remained in control of the university and could use their positions to protect one another. The Party failed to sever long-standing networks of professional influence and friendship, connecting students, teachers, and colleagues all over the map of Poland, throughout the academic disciplines. When professors had problems with authorities, or with each other, they contacted friends, and friends of friends. These connections extended upward into the state apparatus, to which the university belonged. Practices of this sort were less crucial to the more modern lands of Bohemia and East Germany, neither of which knew traditions of antistate conspiracy, let alone insurrection. With the purges of 1945 and the subsequent streams of emigration to West Germany, academic networks in the social sciences and humanities were largely dissolved in East Germany, and the source of authority, influence, and legitimacy soon became the Party. Throughout the 1950s mechanisms evolved that made imperfect controls work better. Continuities in the Czech lands were greater, especially in medicine and the natural sciences, but old networks of influence running through Czech social science faculties all but ceased to exist.

"Interventions" seeking "protection" went from Polish professors directly to top ministry and Party functionaries. Not surprisingly such opportunities were especially frequent in the faculties that staffed the state apparatus: the law faculties. Most impressive was the protection enjoyed by Kraków's legal historian, the Catholic scholar Adam Vetulani. When Vetulani was threatened by transfer in 1949, his former student Prime Minister Józef Cyrankiewicz intervened.[17] During the late 1940s Vetulani's colleague Jerzy Lande remained in almost weekly contact with two students of his seminar who had advanced to positions of vice-minister and state secretary, Czesław Nowiński and Leon Kurowski, in order to arrange for such things as leaves of absence, teaching appointments, and official approval of habilitations. This network extended to the law faculties in Toruń and Łódź, where other of Lande's students taught.[18] It stretched to Warsaw University and Professor Henryk Piętka, who had studied with Lande under the direction of Leon Petrażycki in St. Petersburg. Petrażycki had inspired loyalty bordering on devotion among his students; his liberalism and tolerance were reproduced in Lande's seminars in Wilno and in Kraków, mixing Marxists like Nowiński or Kazimierz Opałek with the anti-Communist sociologist Adam Podgórecki.[19] Perhaps because Marxism had always belonged to his world, Lande was fearless in dealings with the high and mighty in Warsaw, for example, the lord of legal studies, Professor Stefan Rozmaryn: "Marx and Engels undoubtedly had valuable, though inadequate, things to say about law and the state, but one cannot formulate a complete theory from these theses. . . . perhaps it would be more reasonable to supplement their work with more up-to-date theories?"[20]

As Lande was devoted to Petrażycki, so his students were devoted to him; they wrote to him, their *mistrz* (master), with the mixture of reverence and intimacy characteristic of Old World paternalism. When he entered the PZPR in 1951, Kazimierz Opałek brushed aside charges of doing little to "influence" Lande ideologically, telling his interrogators that Lande was of an "advanced age" and should be left in peace.[21]

Professors in the humanities likewise made use of contacts in the Party and state apparatus. For example, both Tadeusz Manteuffel and Kazimierz Wyka, "cooperative" scholars par excellence, used their influence with Party authorities to help undo the transfers of colleagues from one university to another against their will. These two scholars believed that they had given something to the regime and deserved something in return. In January 1955 Manteuffel wrote fellow historian Kazimierz Piwarski, who had been commuting to Poznań from Kraków since 1950, that the time was ripe to "make use of Krauze" (Bronisław Krauze, the Central Committee functionary responsible for history) in "efforts to return you to Kraków." For his part, Manteuffel had attempted to "predispose" Krauze "favorably."[22] The following year Kazimierz Wyka was intervening with Stefan Żółkiewski to have both Piwarski and Henryk Wereszycki returned to Kraków. On 7 July Żółkiewski wrote that "as far as Piwarski and Wereszycki are concerned I will very gladly support your suggestions. . . . I will initiate appropriate steps, and work over [Vice-Minister of Higher Education Eugenia] Krassowska and plead your case [będę urabiał Krassowską i bronił sprawy]."[23] On 11 August 1956 — and thus before the great changes of October — the Ministry of Higher Education transferred Henryk Wereszycki back to Kraków. Piwarski followed a month later.[24]

Protekcja: *Professors Protect Scholarship*

But these transfers of professors were only the most visible injustices perpetrated on universities. A more massive challenge was directed against the vulnerable junior faculty. In July 1950 Minister of Higher Education Adam Rapacki complained at a meeting organized by the PZPR Central Committee that the "political stance of the assistant professors [kadra asystencka] is worse than that of the professors." The regime adopted a two-pronged approach to improving this situation. On the one hand it created mechanisms to attempt to ensure that only politically correct scholars entered the professoriate. Professors still recommended assistant professors, and faculties still conducted habilitations, but actual appointment depended on recommendations of local Party organizations, and professional advancement on approval of tiny handfuls of professors in the "Central Qualification Commission for Scientific Workers" in Warsaw. On the other hand authorities attempted to purge the ranks of assistant and adjunct professors.

Because of its failure to conduct purges among tenured professors, the state had to negotiate its ambitions, however. In this early period conflicts occurred almost exclusively in the social sciences and humanities.[25] A number of underqualified scholars entered universities, but because of the insistence on academic standards by certain old professors, the Party was forced to push its candidates, for example, in Marxism-Leninism, onto less respected sidetracks, especially positions as "acting professor" (*zastępca professora*). Neither Party nor professoriate could force its will, and a certain give-and-take applied; for example, in 1955 one left-leaning (though non-Party) historian was taken into the Kraków history faculty as a "balance" for Emanuel Rostworowski, who came from the Austrian nobility.[26]

The Central Commission meant to insure that no politically hostile candidates advanced into the professoriate, and it continued to fulfill this function; only after the incipient destalinization in 1955–56 could people like Stanisław Stomma or Irena Sławińska finally get the titles they deserved. But the presence of professors who knew each other, and shared standards of scholarship transcending ideology, made the Central Commission also into a form of "quality control," limiting the ability of any single faculty to push through its own political protégés. Professors in and outside the Party cooperated in gatekeeping, because, as a Central Committee reporter ruefully noted, Party members "did not wish to incur the disfavor" of their colleagues. Progress in getting PZPR members into academia was therefore miserably slow: of 302 promotions to university docent or professor approved by the Central Commission between 1951 and 1954, 42 were Party members.[27]

Academic standards obtained in the heavily politicized law faculties even at the height of Polish stalinism in 1953–54, a time when, in the words of senior legal historian Adam Vetulani, "the demands made on candidates for scholarly titles markedly diminished." For example, in 1954 the Central Commission frustrated two political promotions of the Law Department of Wrocław University: Dr. Jerzy Falenciak (Roman law) and Dr. Karol Cincio (criminal procedure). Professors S. Sliwiński, W. Osuchowski, and K. Kolańczyk checked the advance of Falenciak (PZPR) and frustrated attempts by the Ministry of Higher Education and the Wrocław Party organization to promote Cincio (PZPR) to docent. The former's work tended to be polemical and could not be considered a "creative scholarly achievement."[28] The latter's would-be habilitation (*praca kandydacka*) was 113 pages in length, including notes and sources. Three opinions were produced of this work by March 1955, two positive (from Wrocław) and one negative. Professor Sliwiński of the Central Qualification Commission determined that these were too brief to form a judgment, however. He and two other experts (L. Schaff and W. Wolter) produced decidedly negative opinions of Cincio's work, because it neither added to knowledge nor introduced "anything new from the standpoint of theory." Wolter wrote that the "author treats his scholarly work as a lecture for undergraduates, and not as a critical study." A renewed attempt by the ministry to promote Cincio in November 1956 failed.[29]

Protekcja: *Professors Protect Students*

The other component of the Party's strategy was a purge of assistant and adjunct professors who were judged to be undesirable by local Party organizations.[30] In 1948 Stefan Żółkiewski had requested lists from Party representatives at universities of "those assistant professors (esp. at humanities faculties) who should be dismissed in view of their political position and negligible value as scholars."[31] This was part of an ideological offensive known as "Action N."[32] Action N triggered networks of influence among senior professors in protection of junior faculty. And, as was the case with practically every other Party "offensive," limited enthusiasm and the mixed loyalties of state and Party functionaries mitigated the effects of anonymously issued central decrees.

The ostensibly delicate transplant from Wilno, Nicolaus Copernicus University in Toruń, suffered the greatest devastation of Action N. As mentioned earlier, it was the one university to lose its law faculty (with fourteen institutes), and by 1956 its humanities faculty had been stripped of everything but history and Polish.[33] In the fall of 1949 an unsigned letter arrived at Toruń University from the Ministry of Education announcing that eleven assistant professors were to be dismissed, presumably for "bourgeois" inclinations, though the letter gave no reason. But here the local professoriate became involved. Arrangements were made for six of the released to go on as assistant professors, with no breaks in their training at all, three of these in Toruń. Though unpublicized, the purge became news throughout Poland, and in 1950 invitations arrived for three of its victims to continue teaching at the Catholic University of Lublin. All but two of the eleven made academic careers.[34]

The strike against Toruń appears to have had no parallel, but it was not isolated. In other places the ministry performed its harassment by refusing dozens of requests for habilitation, for example, five in Kraków's law faculty alone by May 1949.[35] There were many other sporadic attempts to discontinue undesirable individuals at the level of assistant professor, yet in general professors managed to protect their students, especially those with excellent qualifications. Poland's extensive academic community, the tremendous need for teachers, and the perennial lack of qualified "progressives" all played into the hands of professors willing to exploit their networks of acquaintances and friends. Indeed, professors' networks functioned as an information market: a scholar who was irredeemable in one place might prove irreplaceable in another.[36]

The case of Toruń shows how such networks worked, and how non-Party professors kept vulnerable junior colleagues employed, and dogmatic Marxism at the margins of Polish academic life. Waldemar Voisé, victim of

Action N, was a legal historian of outstanding promise and unusual tenacity, but given his negative cadre reports and the closed law faculty, he had no future in Toruń. The university gave Voisé a position in the library while his professor, Toruń rector Karol Koranyi, looked elsewhere. In 1951 he wrote a letter of recommendation for Voisé to the University of Warsaw, which, if the Polish bureaucracy had functioned even half efficiently, should have been a hopeless venture. But the professor of legal history at Warsaw University, Juliusz Bardach, knew and respected Koranyi; Koranyi moreover was close to Bardach's *Doktorvater,* Kraków's Adam Vetulani.[37] And so class enemy Dr. Voisé was taken on to complete his legal training at the height of stalinism, and none of the indolent and faceless bureaucrats who had checked his career in Toruń seemed to mind that he would teach and research directly beneath their windows in Warsaw.[38]

Now that Voisé was part of the network, he could use his influence to help other scholars who stood outside the Party. In the spring of 1953 he was engaged by Bardach as secretary for the exhibition "Renaissance in Poland," and was able to intervene with a number of publishers in order to accelerate the printing of several works by his former teacher from Lwów, Ludwik Ehrlich, now in Kraków. He used his position to produce a letter of support for Ehrlich by Stefan Żółkiewski, a member of the executive committee for staging the exhibition.[39]

The PZPR seemed to possess every advantage in transforming Toruń's Polish Studies Department. With Action N two leading non-Marxists from Wilno, I. Sławińska and C. Zgorzelski, had been forced out of the university—they found refuge at KUL—and then one by one three of four professors in the department died away between 1950 and 1952. The fourth, Professor Konrad Górski, was placed on indefinite leave in 1950.[40] This left Dr. Artur Hutnikiewicz, a decidedly non-Marxist interpreter of novelist Stefan Żeromski, with non-Party assistant professor dr. Bożena Osmólska, Professor Bronisław Nadolski (PZPR), and mgr. Sławomir Rogowski (PZPR), whom even Stefan Żółkiewski described as "weak as a scholar [and] an intriguer and careerist." The local Party committee wanted to be rid of Hutnikiewicz, and the local press proclaimed that "the comrades of Toruń University are counting on the ministry to stand by them in this fierce ideological struggle."[41] Small bands of students organized disruptions of lectures, though the majority remained loyal and followed Hutnikiewicz's recommendations during their studies, methodological and otherwise.[42]

But precisely because of the shortage of teaching staff, his unusual talents as teacher and scholar, and support among the old professoriate, Hutnikiewicz proved immovable, and remains in Toruń to this day.[43] He may have been isolated among the remaining Polonists in Toruń, but he was not isolated in academia. His dean, Professor Hoszowski—like Hutnikiewicz, formerly of Lwów University—and several other historians who remained after 1950 (Karol Górski, Jadwiga Lechicka) interceded for him, as did his former adviser from Lwów, Professor Floryan, teaching at Wrocław University. In 1954, Floryan told his colleague Kazimierz Wyka in Kraków about Hutnikiewicz's talents and about his plight, and Wyka invited Hutnikiewicz to a meeting at the Institute of Literary Research in Warsaw, at the outset of the thaw. The scholars in attendance assessed Hutnikiewicz's work (*Żeromski and Naturalism*) as original scholarship of outstanding merit. A seven-person ministry commission traveled to Toruń to instruct Party members there to coexist with Hutnikiewicz. In February 1956 the Central Qualification Commission in Warsaw finally approved his appointment to docent,[44] and after the Polish October Konrad Górski returned to teaching duties. Together Hutnikiewicz and Górski formed the next generation of specialists in Polish literature at Toruń.[45]

As the case of Voisé suggests, networks including non-Party scholars were of special use in keeping ideologically "alien" professors in print during the stalinist years. Tadeusz Mikulski, a "progressive" professor of Polish literature at Wrocław University, held the key position of editor of *Pamiętnik Literacki* (Literary journal), and maintained social and professional contacts with such diverse figures as Stefan Żółkiewski and Jan Kott on the one hand, and his teachers Stanisław Pigoń and Juliusz Kleiner on the other. Like Kazimierz Wyka, Mikulski was a major force in Marxist literary criticism, and like Wyka he valued his independence and remained outside the Party. He also valued, and perhaps even continued to need, his teacher's affirmation, and wrote Pigoń on an average of two to three times a month until his early death in 1958.[46] Mikulski mediated between Pigoń and the censors, in one case, for example, removing the word "meritorious" (*zasłużony*) that Pigoń had used to describe the Jesuit Order, but otherwise keeping the piece intact. Pigoń was likewise assisted in publishing by Poznań's Roman Pollak, an intimate friend since student days in Kraków before World War I, who possessed contacts to Poznań's Western Institute.[47]

The possibilities for non-Party and even ostracized professors to publish during these years were—relatively speaking—remarkable. Konrad Górski and Tadeusz Czeżowski were kept from teaching, yet each published over twenty articles, chapters, and reviews between 1949 and 1955. Both Czeżowski and Henryk Elzenberg managed to publish abroad in the early 1950s.[48] It is true that Schaff's journal *Myśl Filozoficzna* published attacks on non-Party philosophers Tadeusz Kotarbiński and Kazimierz Ajdukiewicz, but it also gave them the opportunity for rebuttals that were not blatant "self-criticism."[49] Although Hutnikiewicz was attacked by a former worker student in the local Toruń press, there was also room there for positive discussions of his work, for example by poet Zbigniew Herbert, who under a pseudonym described Hutnikiewicz as an "outstanding scholar." Again one encounters the indolence of the Polish bureaucracy. Hutnikiewicz himself was able to write for local newspapers and the PAX-sponsored *Dziś i Jutro* (Today and tomorrow), from 1949 to 1955 publishing over twenty pieces.[50]

The Professorial Family

The scholarly world was about more than professional advancement and publishing, however. In Poland modern state structures, and indeed modern infrastructure in general — like railways or travel offices — were relatively poorly developed, and personal connections were burdened with tasks that could be settled through less intimate means in countries further west. The era of socialism made personal connections a necessity throughout East Central Europe, but this was especially true in Poland, the place where socialism was taken least seriously, and functioned worst in its own terms. The scholarly community thus became a mixture of old boys' network, guild, and extended family, and settled such things as provisions of food, vacation accommodations, care of emeriti and widows,[51] housing, foreign travel,[52] and even matchmaking. While at the pension "Anna Maria" near the winter resort of Zakopane in 1951, thanks to the connections of Stanisław Pigoń, Roman Pollak had made the acquaintance of Basia, Pigoń's niece:

> Basia has stirred my admiration with her good sense and self-control. What a solid character and resolute demeanor! I must confess to you that I am already prepared to enter negotiations with you in the name of my Jędruś with the purpose of contracting matrimony, because I do not wish that anyone else should get a head start in this matter. Before taking the first cautious steps toward negotiation with her grandmother and then with her mother, I would first like to be assured of your benevolence and request your succor in things to come. But for the time being let this stay between us.[53]

The stuff that gave Polish academia coherence was primarily personal; the separate fields were held together by student-teacher relations bordering on the reverential. Pollak and Pigoń had both been students of Jagiellonian University's Stanisław Windakiewicz (1863–1943), as had the major figures of Polish literature in Warsaw W. Borowy, J. Krzyżanowski, and M. Brahmer. Pollak's colleague in Polish studies at Poznań Zygmunt Szweykowski was a student of Pigoń's Kraków colleague Juliusz Kleiner, as was Toruń's leading figure Konrad Górski and the outstanding young Kraków Marxist literary historian Henryk Markiewicz. All of the senior figures in Polish studies in the 1940s and 1950s had either been students or students of students of Stanisław Tarnowski (1837–1917), who was professor at Jagiellonian University from 1871.[54]

Similarly, Professor Kazimierz Twardowski (1866–1938) of Lwów University, a charismatic figure of "uncompromising integrity," was the progenitor of contemporary Polish philosophy. In the words of Z. A. Jordan, Twardowski "taught as much by example as by his lectures and seminars. He left an inheritance which is not measurable in purely intellectual values, an invisible power which, once generated, pervades the minds of those who have been affected by it and who in turn pass it on to growing numbers. Twardowski was one of those men who, though little known outside the walls of colleges and universities, yet exercise a wide and powerful influence on the life of the nation to which they belong."[55]

These student-teacher relations were supplemented and complicated by actual family ties. Pollak had already married his daughter off to the protégé of his historian colleague Kazimierz Tymieniecki, Tadeusz Cieślak. In lists of seminars and institutes of Poznań University one regularly encounters the same names: the brothers Alfons and Zenon Klafkowski were both assistant professors in public law; the director of the Institute of Ethnology, Professor E. Frankowski, was married to his adjunct Maria; and the director of the Institute of Prehistory, J. Kostrzewski, was father and *Doktorvater* to the assistant professor at the institute, Bogdan. Zygmunt Szweykowski held a chair in Polish literature, his son Jerzy one in botany. In the law faculty Edward Taylor taught economics, and his son Leon was adjunct professor for civil law. Marian Wojciechowski worked as assistant professor in the historical seminar, and his father Zygmunt taught the history of law. Zygmunt's father in turn had been professor of Polish literature in Lwów. Universities in postwar Poland tended to be self-reproducing, primarily in the academic but also in the biological sense.

Kraków was even more "interrelated." The organization of the city forced university staff into constant professional and personal interaction. They lived and worked in an extraordinarily compressed space; from the main university buildings in the center of town one reaches every spot on the perimeters of the pre-1914 city in a 15- to 20-minute walk. When the municipality expanded in the 1920s, the university came into possession of a number of apartment buildings on the ring road that borders the old city, thus keeping the staff in the university's orbit, even after hours. Dozens of senior and junior faculty live in these apartments to this day. For example, the present rector, Aleksander Koj, lives in the same apartment as his predecessor of the stalinist years, Teodor Marchlewski.[56] Yet he assumed this apartment not as rector, but as husband of the daughter of Marchlewski, Professor Anna Marchlewska-Koj. Marchlewski himself was the son of Leon Marchlewski, rector during the 1930s. The Jagiellonian University calendar of 1947–48 indicates over eighty relatives of the first degree as employees, and many dozens of more distant relatives.[57] Among the present academic community of Kraków one is constantly bumping into offspring of earlier generations: Kazimierz Wyka's daughter Marta also teaches in the Department of Polish studies; Adam Vetulani's son is professor of pharmacology; Jan Gwiazdomorski's nephew Henryk Szarski is professor of anatomy at Jagiellonian University, emeritus. Konstanty Grzybowski's son Stanisław teaches history in the Higher School for Pedagogy, and his cousin Stefan is professor of law and rector emeritus. Grzybowski had married into the influential Estreicher family, which supplied professors to Jagiellonian University for generations.[58] The medical faculty remains a place almost impenetrable to those standing outside the "family."

This thick web of interrelations made it impossible to separate the personal from the academic. Polish professors had as many disagreements as any academic community, but widespread expectations of loyalty toward costudents (one's "brethren") and teachers (one's "fathers" and "uncles") acted to limit the damage academics would do to each other. Acts of disloyalty were instant news throughout the community. As in a family, a set of norms applied even among those who grew to detest one another. The powerful linguist Tadeusz Lehr-Spławiński was greatly irritated by a critique of his work on Polish Slavic studies from the pen of docent Henryk Batowski, and in November 1949 requested to be removed from any position in which he might have to write an opinion on Batowski, who was under consideration for a professorship. He did not want to behave in a way that might bring disapprobation from his community.[59]

The hostile political surroundings strengthened this solidarity. When in 1955 irritations over a review he published caused Stanisław Pigoń to suggest to Konrad Górski of Toruń that they break off their acquaintance, the latter objected that their "responsibility toward society" precluded such a move.

> Of course, if this had happened in the prewar years, no one would care, but now, when we both belong to a small handful of the Catholic intellectual elite, which is under pressure of the enemies of religion and church, a break between us may also be a scandal for Catholic society and a delight for the atheist camp. . . .
>
> We are somewhat like married people who do not love one another and cannot stand living with each other, but do not divorce in order not to give rise to a public scandal.[60]

When in 1952 Adam Schaff's journal *Myśl Filozoficzna* published a withering review of the work of Kazimierz Twardowski, one of Twardowski's students, Poznań rector Kazimierz Ajdukiewicz, asked Schaff how he would "react, if someone wrote about your esteemed Father, in the way that [Henryk]

Holland wrote about Professor Twardowski." The question was not entirely academic, for Ajdukiewicz was also Twardowski's son-in-law.[61]

Denunciations are known to have emerged in this period from students and assistant professors, but few from the professoriate itself. In the brief period of liberalization after October 1956 faculties suddenly found themselves in possession of confidential Party documents. One professor of Warsaw University's History Department, counting some thirty professors, was discovered to have issued reports compromising colleagues: Żanna Kormanowa, who had been re-formed in the Soviet Union. She was publicly humiliated in 1956 by legal historian Bogusław Leśnodorski (PZPR).[62] Many hundreds of state and Party files, as well as weeks of interviews, reveal one other political denunciation among the professoriate: by Professor B. Skarżyński of Kraków against his colleague biologist J. Konorski of Łódź in 1949. But the denunciation was spoken in Moscow, to Soviet hosts at Pavlov festivities. Skarżyński could imagine that he would not be held accountable in his community.[63] At home in Poland professors at worst acted neutrally — for example, by failing to protest politically based discrimination — but, as mentioned, often socialists like Celina Bobińska, Teodor Marchlewski, or Konstanty Grzybowski did what they could to preserve their communities, within the narrow boundaries that existed.[64]

Old Professors as Teachers

The professoriate thus managed to maintain minimal conditions for survival and reproduction. But to return to the question posed earlier: what did the continuity of the professoriate mean for the substance of the university, the relation between teacher and student? The simple answer is that within the new guidelines, old professors could continue teaching and evaluating students' work much as they always had, even in the social sciences, and even in discontinued fields, like sociology. In the early 1950s sociologists, anthropologists, and legal scholars, such as J. Chałasiński, K. Dobrowolski, T. Szczurkiewicz, and J. Lande, were able to discuss the work of sociologists in courses on related subjects. In the lecture course "History of Precapitalist Formations" at Łódź University, Chałasiński introduced students to the work of Montesquieu, Locke, and Malinowski.[65] In 1950–51 Lande still taught and examined in sociology, including the works of Vico, Durkheim, G. Tarde, Simmel, Guizot, Comte, P. Lilienfeld, and Spencer; though he taught Marx, he advised his students not to treat Marxism as a "dogma." In a seminar on legal philosophy offered in 1951–52, Lande contrasted Marxist approaches to those of his teacher Petrażycki, for example, on the origins of law. Not a single work of Marx, Engels, or Lenin figured on the reading list, and there was no mention whatsoever of Soviet authors.[66]

Various standard courses on the law in Kraków were equally liberal. Lande's colleague Ludwik Ehrlich gave a two-semester course on the history of international law in the academic year 1951–52 and mentioned Soviet approaches only in his twenty-eighth lecture of 13 November, which he introduced as follows: "today, in keeping with a decision of the law faculty council, I will discuss Soviet scholarship on international law." The following day he returned to his schedule, and for the rest of the academic year neither Marxist nor Soviet theories were a subject of discussion; the October Revolution was not mentioned let alone accorded special relevance to human history. Ehrlich had identified his preferred methodology at the outset: "neopositivism." [67] Professor Tadeusz Silnicki taught canon law at Jagiellonian University in the early 1950s. He dwelt at length on the threats to "freedom of conscience" in the new constitution, and concluded that "when the state did battle with the church, it usually came to regret it." [68] Typed lecture notes on West European law still in use in Kraków in 1949 included the following passage: "In 1923 Soviet Russia attempted to create a federal state of Soviet Socialist republics united by a common constitution. Yet because of Soviet terror this constitution remains an illusion." [69]

In the lectures and evaluations of many old professors Marxist methodology appears as a thin veneer overlaying rather straightforward social and political history. Ironically, it was those who took Marx most seriously, like historians Witold Kula, Marian Małowist, or Stefan Kieniewicz, who proved most resistant to treating Marxism as an orthodoxy. Evaluations of students' work by "progressive" scholars such as Kazimierz Wyka, Kazimierz Lepszy, or the "loyal" non-Party historian Tadeusz Manteuffel show the barest traces of official doctrine.

As mentioned earlier, Lepszy had become "progressive" in order to cover the tracks of his past enthusiasm for National Democracy. And though he dissociated himself from one of his teachers, Lepszy remained a product of the Kraków school in which he continued to operate. Today, his "progressive" stance would appear as mainstream social history. In judgments of master's theses there is no mention of Soviet literature, and only very rarely of Marxist "classics." In one case he recommended the work of Karl Kautsky. Lepszy did not discriminate against more traditional history writing—for example, of Anna Owsińska, whom he praised for "source-based, independent, and creative" discussions of German policies in Poland during World War I, and the Polish question at Versailles.[70] Other important categories of judgment are "mastery of historical method, precision . . . Benedictine working habits, and intimate knowledge of the epoch." [71] Having recognized the need to account for politics in spheres beyond the political, he could argue for a more compelling narrative history, for example, by the young Warsaw historian Janusz Tazbir in his work on the "Reformation in Poland": "His book is too difficult, not sufficiently vivid or dramatic. Perhaps he should introduce more stories, more dramatic images, more living people. I understand that a Marxist analysis of the Reformation demands above all a new interpretation of social ideology, but in this form the book does not excite the reader's interest [*nie porywa*]. For example, one could introduce fantastic scenes of the Gdańsk revolt of 1523–26, which was carried out under Reformation slogans."[72]

Students had simple choices when looking for role models; they could identify with scholars of outstanding erudition and professional and personal self-confidence, like Adam Vetulani or Stanisław Pigoń, or with the half-educated and outnumbered representatives of Marxist-Leninist scholarship. The latter lived ghettoized existences in institutes of political economy or Marxism-Leninism, invariably places where the teaching staff did not have academic qualifications. To give some sense of the perspective from below: in 1953 law students in Kraków had eighteen hours of lecture in their first semester, of which thirteen were with old, non-Party professors Vetulani (history of Polish state and law), Lande (theory of state and law), Patkaniowski (general history of state and law), and Wolter (logic). The five remaining hours were in Marxism-Leninism and political economy, and taught by individuals holding only master's or doctor's degrees. In the course of their studies, these law students had 60 percent of their lectures with full and associate professors.[73] In history, a faculty that had lost five major figures to emigration, death, and retirement, the total was 35.8 percent.[74]

If one shifts attention to Prague, one finds a different situation quantitatively and qualitatively. Many professors there had joined the Party and were painfully aware that cadre evaluations were being written by the student Communists sitting in front of them. A number of professors had been kept on the faculty in 1948 subject to good behavior, and some of these were dropped in the following three years.[75] Those that remained adjusted, for example, by disparaging their own "learnedness" in favor of the "basic common sense of our working people" in the course of teaching.[76] In order to survive as university teachers in these years, many Czech professors felt they had to deny their identities as intellectuals.[77]

Only a few old professors remained in the social sciences and were heavily outnumbered by the underqualified. In the 1954–55 academic year, professors offered only 16.3 percent of the lectures in history taught at Charles University.[78] In the law faculty, some thirty "external teachers" took the place of almost twenty professors who could no longer teach.[79] The few professors who remained, like V. Vaněček, J. Tureček, and V. Procházka, as a rule already belonged to the Party and hardly cut a distinct profile from the newcomers: their evaluations of students and colleagues were at least in part political, and they poured heavy doses of Marxism-Leninism into lectures to their "comrade students." [80]

The story of Polish intellectual life under stalinism reads differently at universities than in classic accounts or in recent polemics. Surely there were "captive minds," especially in the younger generation, but the majority of academics perceived the new regime without illusions, and public compromises were carefully calibrated. Few needed to play "Ketman," because few needed to appear as adherents of the "New Faith." On the other hand, there are few signs of "betrayal of the clerks," or of the heroic resistance so dear to the national idiom. University life involved constant bargaining and compromising, extending deep into the Party and the state apparatus. In the broad gray zone between the non-Party professoriate and the state apparatus, the boundaries separating "collaborators" and those quietly, pragmatically salvaging scholarship, are nearly unrecognizable. Indeed, the distinction between Party and non-Party appears to have limited meaning, as we encounter dozens of PZPR members "protecting" professors and friends outside the Party. The difficulty of distinguishing sensibly between Party and non-Party is a symptom of the Party's lack of legitimacy.

A consideration of Czech and East German universities shows that in these countries as well, Party membership was at best a rough measure of the Party's power, for in these two places the Party's legitimacy extended beyond the boundaries of Party membership.

★

CHAPTER TEN

THE
MILIEU
OF THE
PARTY

If one conceives of milieu as a self-reproducing social unit, with its own values, habits, and demands for loyalty, then one is impressed by the emergence of new milieus at East German and Czech universities in the 1950s, namely the Socialist Unity Party of Germany and the Communist Party of Czechoslovakia. Because large numbers of East German and Czech academics at all levels became attached to the Communist Party, that Party could take its presence deep into university operations, to a degree that the social science and humanities faculties became pervaded by demands for *partiinost'*—that is, that teachers and students give primary consideration of the interests of the Party in their work. Professors and students became "comrades," with common Party socialization, language, and experiences of ritual. Party members had to attend courses in Marxism-Leninism, weekly organizational meetings, and political manifestations and were technically permitted no recourse to personal or professional interests. Even the behavior of their children was exposed to Party scrutiny.

The totality of the Party's demands was most visible in banalities. One recognized Party members through Party lapel pins and other kinds of emblems, like youth organization patches. In East Germany the Free German Youth wore loud blue shirts with open collars. Whatever Party members had to say to each other—especially in this period—was embroidered with ritualistic forms of greeting. "Hello" became "honor to labor!" (*práci čest!*) in Czechoslovakia and "friendship!" (*Freundschaft!*) in East Germany.[1] Letters were concluded with "socialist greetings." In the Czech lands state agencies made out their form letters to "esteemed comrade" (*vážený soudruhu!*), whether the addressee was known to belong to the Party or not. Anyone worthy of the state's attention was likely to be a Party member. This practice was also applied in correspondence from Czechoslovak agencies to Polish professors, where it seemed distinctly out of place.

Most important, the Party united people through common informality. Especially in the Czech lands, students and assistant professors now could, and did, address full professors as "ty." Professors for their part called students their "comrades."[2] It is impossible to exaggerate the loss of prestige symbolized by this new practice. Professors who were primarily Party members were no longer professors in the old sense of the word. An admonition in March 1950 to comrade students by the dean of Prague's law faculty, Josef Tureček, gives some idea of the change in atmosphere: "We have people at this faculty to whom your fathers would have bowed their heads, and you act improperly toward them. . . . We do not want to impose upon you, but I think that when a lecturer enters the room, you could stand, and not continue smoking until the lecturer asks you to stand."[3]

In East Germany the Party leadership never permitted such erasing of status at universities; within and without the Party the formal "Sie" continued to draw distinctions between the more and less powerful, though the threshold to "Du" was lower than in the West among people of similar rank. In the wake of cultural revolution titular distinctions among professors were abolished in the Czech lands, but in East Germany a hierarchy remained of professors with chair, with full contract, with contract.[4] Each degree was associated with a different level of teaching responsibility and salary. In Poland, too, the old distinctions of full and associate professor remained.

One can of course exaggerate the importance of apparent superficialities, but the case of Poland suggests that where there was no appearance of Party control, there was also no reality of Party control. Here the new forms of address had largely failed to penetrate the professoriate — even when professors belonged to the Party. In the correspondence of Stanisław Arnold, Bogusław Leśnodorski, Juliusz Bardach, or the Soviet-trained Celina Bobińska there was next to no attention to "socialist" forms of greeting. "Dear Comrade" was all but unknown, and none of these people closed with "socialist greetings." Even ministers and state secretaries preferred being referred to by their official titles.[5] The Polish Party did not make the informal "ty" its chosen form of address; rather it attempted to supplant what seemed an archaic form of address, "Pan" and "Pani," which mean "Lord" and "Lady," with the second-person plural "Wy," used as singular. As it happens, "Wy" is also the polite singular and plural in Russian, like the French "Vous," and when used as a singular in Polish sounds like a Russianism. This form was all but unknown in the Polish professoriate. Polish professors continued — and continue — to be addressed not simply by "Pan," but by "Pan Professor." The closest equivalent in current American English are the forms used to address a rare dignitary: Your Eminence, Your Excellency. Party members among the professoriate addressed one another as "ty" when they were friends, and

"Pan" or "Pani" when they were not. In other words, they camouflaged any Party identity that they may have possessed.[6] The Polish Party simply did not offer the prestige that they desired.[7]

Party Work at Universities

The differing positions of the Party in these three university systems become more palpable through an examination of the everyday activities of the respective university Party committees. Available data allow a close comparison of the work of university Party organizations in Kraków and Leipzig, the second universities of their respective countries, both with reputations of harboring vibrant intellectual milieus.

In Poland, the Party organization existed at the margins of the university. In December 1949 there were but two PZPR members among the twenty-six full professors of the humanities faculty of Jagiellonian University, and one among the associate (extraordinary) professors. There were no Communist Party members among the nine docents, and only one among the six acting professors. The following year, in the wake of a general Party purge, two of the four PZPR members were removed from the Party, history professor Kazimierz Piwarski, and the university's foremost expert on Marxism-Leninism, Józef Sieradzki.[8] In January 1951, of several hundred faculty members at Jagiellonian University, only sixteen belonged to the Party.[9]

In February 1948 fourteen of seventy-four (18.9 percent) university professors in Leipzig were SED members. This measurement was taken after the latest hemorrhage of professors westward — four full professors, including Rector Hans-Georg Gadamer, left in 1947 — and during the slow trickle of persecuted or exiled Communist intellectuals to East Germany, including sociologist Wieland Herzfelde, historian Walter Markov, and journalist Hermann Budzislawski, all of whom taught in Leipzig. There were five SED members among fourteen associate professors and twenty-nine (31.2 percent) among ninety-three assistant professors.[10] In the early 1950s the Leipzig Party leadership consisted of several leading professors, like historian Ernst Engelberg or economist Fritz Behrens, and revealed ambitions to transform the university as a whole.

In 1952 the Leipzig organization was planning a year of "Party schooling" for "bourgeois professors," assigning "tasks" to the rector and the "comrades" of the law faculty, and reporting on political work among mathematicians, chemists, and physicists.[11] The Kraków organization consisted almost entirely of students, and its work hardly transcended inner-Party trivialities, such as procuring banners and flags for the May Day parade, counting how many comrades did not come to meetings, or deciding what to do with those who had lost their Party membership cards.[12] Such concerns tended to reinforce their ghetto existence. More substantively, Communists in Kraków were discussing how to begin influencing the law faculty, where they were still a small minority. As the law faculty in Leipzig was a Party domain, with practically every teacher a Party member, the Leipzig organization could move on to considering how natural scientists might subordinate their work to planning. Given their meager numbers, Kraków Communists avoided such concrete issues and spent hours in discussion of generalities, with little in the way of effective resolutions. In October 1950 the results of one "discussion" were summarized as follows:

> There was little consideration of class war in the countryside. . . . It was evident that the rector's office, which is responsible for the work of the entire university, does not examine the fulfillment of its own recommendations. There was also too little talk of ideological schooling and how to plan it. . . . the Party organization has to fight against bureaucratism at Jagiellonian University and revolutionize its style of work. The realization of the Six-Year Plan requires an improvement of work at Jagiellonian University, for which the rector is responsible. The Party should assist him every step of the way.

And so on. In a resolution of February 1955, the organization decided to "assist the university authorities in organizing a general conference of the faculty members of Jagiellonian University on issues of scholarship and teaching." [13]

The Leipzig University Party organization was part of a larger and more effective apparatus. Beneath it were sizable faculty organizations, which gave regular reports on their activities and it reported directly to the Central Committee. Top functionaries thus held their fingers on the pulse of university life, and could react quickly to perceived changes. Despite their greater numbers, East German Communists hardly felt more secure in power than Polish comrades, however. Open opposition had disappeared several years before, and now they were plagued by doubts that students and teachers were not revealing their true opinions. [14]

Communist leaders at Jagiellonian University had similar doubts, yet in 1952 they had more pressing concerns than the political opinions of non-Party youths—for example, they had yet to organize the work of their own faculty organizations. The university committee was only loosely connected to higher Party strata, including the district committees and Central Committee. [15] When Zofia Zemankowa, the Central Committee functionary in charge of higher education, inspected the Jagiellonian University Party organization on 12 November 1951, she was treated almost as an intruder. Zemankowa had criticized the Krakovians for "superficial" and undisciplined work that ignored real problems, such as high dropout rates, and for failing to censure a Comrade Karas who had recently been married in a church—though he often emphasized his "materialist worldview." After these remarks she was told by the student Józef Kijowski that her remarks were "boring and incorrect, as well as un-Marxist."[16] Kijowski, a student of history whose parents worked a small farm, nevertheless finished his studies on time, and Karas later became rector.[17]

Such words, let alone the fact that they went unpunished, would have seemed surreal at East German Party organizations, with their very different sense of hierarchy and discipline. Indeed, the Polish students who went to East Germany for studies simply confounded their SED observers. Though handpicked by their Party, the Poles behaved as if unaware of the existence of a state, or, perhaps more accurately, they viewed state agencies as things to be circumvented. According to reports from Thuringia, they refused cooperation with SED "guides"; traveled about the country to meet friends, without permission; and asked to be excused from Marxism-Leninism lessons, supposedly due to "poor knowledge of German." To this last point an SED Central Committee functionary had scribbled "impossible!" (*unmöglich!*). They kept "hostile radio stations," like RIAS (Radio in the American Sector of Berlin) and Radio Free Europe, "on constantly." Several of the Poles set up contacts to local Protestant student groups, and attempted to influence Korean students, "to act against the rules [*Ordnung*] of the university and to refuse cooperation with the FDJ and Party." The behavior of the Polish students stood in contrast to that of "the remainder of students from socialist countries." The female Polish students were considered especially dangerous, and both local and Central Committee functionaries urged that they be sent home.[18] In April 1957 the East German Politburo decided to recall the East German students studying in Poland.[19]

Given the experiences of the wartime underground state, it is absurd to claim, as Polish Communists often did, that the Polish population somehow lacked a sense of organization and discipline, however.[20] The true origin of the halfhearted performance of Kraków's Party organization was a failure of the leadership to inject a sense of belief and seriousness — of legitimacy — into the Party cadre. Indeed, Party work in Kraków had an almost farcical quality to it. In a meeting of 14 March 1951 one ZMP activist attempted to join the Party but attention was drawn to the fact that he listened to broadcasts from London. He explained that he could do so without danger of contamination because of his "advanced worldview" (*wyrobiony światopogląd*), though he freely admitted to having read nothing by Stalin.[21] There were constant complaints of things said at Party meetings leaking out into the public. On 14 September 1951 a Comrade Oworowski lamented a "lack of aggressiveness and revolutionary vigilance" in the Party organization: the lack of "vigilance [was] reflected among other things in the failure to check who has been entering the auditorium at today's closed election meeting."[22] Not quite two years later one of the few PZPR members in the Kraków medical faculty was recorded as having participated in a "libation with guitar and song" organized "at news of the death of comrade Stalin."[23]

Unseriousness on the part of Comrades Kijowski and Karas in Kraków might be explained through the extraordinary speed at which the Party grew. Insufficient time had elapsed to sever links with the church and to create new attitudes toward authority. But what about the top Party leadership? Here too we have evidence of a halfhearted practice of Marxism-Leninism. In March 1952 Central Committee functionary Zemankowa was called upon by the Politburo to assemble a delegation to travel to the Soviet Union to receive original manuscripts from the time of Copernicus. She wrote that a natural candidate would be Professor Wilhelmina Iwanowska, who taught astronomy in Copernicus's hometown of Toruń, except that Iwanowska was a "person completely foreign to us, perhaps even with an anti-Soviet complex, though honest and reserved." It is hard to imagine an East German Communist having something positive to say about someone suspected of being anti-Soviet, yet Zemankowa recommended sending Iwanowska to represent Poland in the Soviet Union![24]

The Polish Party and Polish Political Culture

Striking among Poles was the peculiar attitude not only toward the state but also toward conationals. To be sure, the Party elite—Jakub Berman, Adam Schaff, Edward Ochab—looked upon Polish society as something foreign and hostile. In a characteristic statement, Berman described late 1944 to Piotr Hübner as a time when "*we* conquered Poland." Adam Schaff has complained of the difficulties of establishing Marxism in Poland, but admits: "this was the only Poland *we* had." But further down, Communists could not afford to alienate themselves from the world around them. Lublin rector Parnas had received death threats for attempts to expel students[25] and the major PPR representative at Lublin University, Witold Reiss, was removed after professors he had alienated discovered that his academic work had been plagiarized. In a letter to the Party, Reiss complained of a "witchhunt" against him and wondered how it had been possible that these professors had "mysteriously found out about the political opinions" that Reiss had written for the Ministry of Education.[26]

This was possible because much of the apparatus had not internalized the basic Leninist dichotomy between enemy and friend, and remained susceptible to requests for unofficial assistance. The word "enemy" nevertheless served frequently as an explanation for something that could not be explained directly: the unpopularity of the PZPR. Hostility toward the Party was so pervasive in Polish society that "enemy" became a rhetorical device to justify inactivity.[27] It appears frequently in the reports of functionaries, but has a comparatively abstract quality, for example, as the unidentifiable source of dangerous rumors—that Polish students graduating from Soviet universities would be sent to work for five years in Siberia, or that the level of scholarship at these universities was "impossibly high" for Polish students, and so on.[28]

In East Germany the equivalent expression was also used frequently, both inside and outside the SED. The urgency to conjure enemies was even greater than in Poland, because the open border to the West gave the population constant, visual evidence of the failings of socialism, and unusual pressures forced "enemies" to materialize as living and breathing agents.[29] A personal enemy was needed to explain why apparently satisfied colleagues suddenly left for the West, why "hostile" students appeared to have irrefutable arguments, why ration cards were necessary to obtain products in East Berlin but not in West Berlin, why piles of rubble had yet to be cleared from Eastern German cities. The enemy behaved according to an odd dialectic: when one forbade students to spend vacations in the West in 1956, "he" enticed them all the more, so that finally one had to build a wall. The enemy became more popular than ever.

The SED placed several pithy words in circulation that conveniently fused hostile intention, deed, and agent: *parteifeindlich* (hostile to the Party), *staatsfeindlich* (hostile to the state), and *republikfeindlich* (hostile to the Republic). The latter two were of concern to more than just the Party cadre, and entered the discourse of loyal citizens of the GDR, like professor of French in Halle Victor Klemperer or Leipzig philosophy professor Ernst Bloch. In an effort to deflect attacks against his own supposed "revisionism" in 1957, Bloch composed a declaration beginning with the words: "I have heard that a number of statements hostile to the republic [*republikfeindliche Äusserungen*] have been printed in the West German press and make reference to me. Recently an especially scandalous article was written by [Bloch's student Gerhard] Zwerenz."[30] That the expression "staatsfeindlich" could sneak its way into philologist Klemperer's vocabulary is all the more noteworthy, as he kept careful record of deformations of language under the Nazis and Soviets. No equivalent usage seeped into the speech of non-Party members in Poland; indeed institutions like universities and the Catholic Church insisted in addressing the state in their own idioms.[31]

The failure of the Polish Party to internalize the requirements of Leninist hierarchy extended to dealings with the Soviets, even during Stalin's lifetime. At a meeting concluding their 1949 visit to the Soviet Union, the Polish team was asked by Minister of Education Voznesenskii for "critical remarks." Unexpectedly perhaps, the team responded: Professor Biernawski of Kraków's Academy of Mining and Metallurgy, while praising the rich provisions for science in the Soviet Union, also noted the "overcrowding" of facilities; and Minister Skrzeszewski worried about the danger of "verbalism" in the Soviets' lesson plans, especially in history and literature.[32]

Reports on East European students in the Soviet Union rarely mention the behavior of East German students, but Polish students appear constantly. In late 1951 a complaint emerged from the Ural Polytechnic Institute at Rostov on the Don about the "self-segregation" of Polish students. After watching the movie "Bogdan Khmel'nitskii," they "falsely interpreted historical facts, and pointed out the supposed incorrectness of the plot of the film."[33] According to a Polish report of August 1954, one student had taken a stack of religious pictures with him to Odessa "from a priest by way of his grandmother for distribution in the USSR." There were cases of listening to the Voice of America, and one student in Kharkov quit the Party because in his view there was a "basic contradiction between the masses and the Party; the masses had no trust in the Party."[34]

Studentocracy

In the late 1940s and early 1950s, the Party was even more present at Czech than at East German universities and for a time went beyond the customary limitations of "political supervision" to actually running day-to-day operations.[35] In meetings of March 1948 student Communists at the Central Action Committee of the National Front in Prague began planning political indoctrination, the preparation of workers for university, student admissions, and the deployment of university graduates in the economy. These were things that neither the KSČ Central Committee nor the Czechoslovak Ministry of Education had thought about up to this point. The students also delegated to themselves supervision of the 600th anniversary celebrations of Charles University, the oldest university in Central Europe, the following month.[36]

In subsequent years Communist students produced reform plans for university curricula, purged their own numbers, and wrote political letters of recommendation for professors. They retained control over university affairs because the top Party leadership did not act to restrain their powers, and because they far outnumbered professors in Communist organizations.[37] In February 1949, there were 6,410 KSČ members at Prague's higher schools. Of these, 5,489 were students, and 394 "teachers and professors." At the law faculty 296 students faced 8 "teachers and professors," and in the philosophical faculty 731 students shared the organization with 27 teachers and professors.[38] In 1950, the important position of university secretary was held by recent university graduates at Brno University, Prague's Technical University, the Academy for the Performing Arts, and the University of Politics and Economics.[39] Central Committee functionaries in charge of culture and higher education, like Luděk Holubec and Čestmír Císař, were likewise recent university graduates.[40] The average age of political directors of worker preparation courses in 1951 was thirty-three.

Fatalism gripped Czech professors after the Prague coup, and, as we have seen, by 1949 most belonged to the KSČ. Brno classicist Ferdinand Stiebitz told students that they should join the Communist Party in order to avoid difficulties. This is what he had done.[41] Professor J. L. Fischer, rector at Palacký University in Olomouc, who as dean in Brno had stood firm in 1947 against attempts to nominate professors from outside the university, submitted entirely to the student-run action committees. In February 1948 he joined the presidium of the district action committee as its representative for "culture," explaining to his deans that he hoped to use his influence "to protect the interests of Palacký University."[42] Before addressing a deans' meeting in April, Fischer praised the work of students sent to monitor the meeting.[43]

Private correspondence between two of Czechoslovakia's leading "bourgeois" legal scholars, Karel Engliš and František Weyr, gives some notion of the climate of those months. Weyr, in odd agreement with the Party, wrote that the increases in membership could not be attributed to force. He described the case of "renegade" Assistant Professor Pošvář, "who has supposedly also gone over to the Communists. But how compulsion, which everyone points to in such cases, was involved here is not entirely clear to me, given his absolutely apolitical behavior and his absolute passivity." In Weyr's view people joined more for promise of reward than out of fear of losing their jobs. The lowly Pošvář now became dean. Yet even professors who had been discontinued did not seem above reproach to Weyr. After being placed on enforced vacation, they were offered sick leave, which provided better benefits:

> It was given me to understand that I am to file an application for sick leave and the whole thing can be taken care of more smoothly. But this is precisely what I will not do until I receive some sort of explanation that my removal from the faculty will be redressed or that it was illegitimate. Every decent person at our age has, it seems to me, primary concern for the memory he leaves behind after death and this he will not jeopardize recklessly for the sake of some financial advantage (merit bonus, etc.). But it seems that there are not many such people among us and that people don't give a damn what will be written about them in history books fifty years from now. But it matters to me and I suspect it does to you, too.[44]

Perhaps unknown to his friend, Engliš was himself on sick leave and went along with the charade until forcibly retired in 1950. In February 1949 he wrote his dean that he had announced lectures though the action committee of his faculty "did not desire that I teach, but indicated that merely announcing the lectures suffices in order to get full pay."[45] Weyr was retired in 1949. When he died tragically in June 1951, Engliš was permitted to write the obituary.

By joining an organization dominated by students, professors placed their lives under constant scrutiny and exposed themselves to humiliation. This was especially true in Brno organizations, where the Party Center could not react quickly to student "excesses." During the fifth district conference of Communists at Brno higher schools in early 1951 professors were not shown "the least respect." The student Communists coolly received visitors from Prague, including top cultural functionary and later minister Ladislav Štoll, and failed to accord university rectors a special welcome. These were treated as subordinate Party members and did their best to distract attention from themselves. One rector simply read off a statement the students had prepared for him, and not a single professor was nominated for the district higher-education committee, despite the urging of the central Party and state apparatus.[46]

According to reports written in 1952, student-dominated Party organizations "interfered with university administration and frequently tried to replace it."[47] In particular, the basic Party organization at the faculty of chemical engineering in Brno made several "serious political errors":

> It sent the State Council for Higher Education [in Prague] a telegram saying that it had discussed the question of appointing a certain professor and decided to turn him down. It concluded the telegram with the strict order: "immediately cancel further action."
>
> Giving orders in this way to the organs of educational administration is not acceptable. The organizational committee of the Party can invite the dean or other representative of educational administration to its meetings; it may demand a report from him, or present its suggestions. But the responsible functionary of school administration decides about measures to be taken. The basic Party organization may not order the dean about or replace him.[48]

Despite a decision of the Political Secretariat, students refused to share Party organizations with professors.[49] In 1952 basic Party committees were elected in the pedagogical and medical faculties in Brno without a single representative of the teaching staffs.[50] If the students would not respect decisions of top echelons of the Party hierarchy, they were not at all impressed by orders from the Ministry of Education, which retained much of its pre-1948 staff until purges of 1950–51. Fearing accusations of "opportunism," ministry officials hesitated to reverse the excesses of studentocracy, by, for example, letting some of the students purged in 1949 return to studies after they had "proved themselves."[51]

In the general atmosphere of terror of these years, students established their own reign of fear. Lower-level Party organizations did not merely dismiss professors and docents, they sent them to factory work, usually after several semesters of "schooling" in Marxism-Leninism. For example, the Party organization at Prague's law faculty sent docents to work in the metal industry.[52] "Leading functionaries" were "fearful" to defend professors when attacked by students and "submit[ed] themselves to the decisions of Party organizations out of fear that they will be accused of opportunism."[53] At a joint meeting of professors from Olomouc and Brno in September 1953 a young Communist from the latter city, historian and later Prague Spring supporter František Jordán, "induced" Brno University rector Trávníček (b. 1888) to declare renowned sociologist and former Olomouc rector J. L. Fischer "intolerable as a teacher at any kind of school."[54] Communist students at Prague's medical faculty "victimized" old professors—for example, by holding back publication of a work by Professor František Studnička for over a year, although this work had been awarded a state prize. The students did not "understand that teachers, members of the Party, had gone through a complicated political development, and had to battle against many remnants of old education": "Instead of helping teachers in these battles Party organizations have brought uncertainty and fear into their ranks, through constant disciplinary measures, often for trifles."[55]

The most spectacular event in studentocracy was the First Ideological Conference of Higher Schools in Brno of February 1952. Its exalted purpose of pointing "the way for the subsequent development of Czechoslovak scholarship," and the uniformly hard-line speeches made outside observers mistake the conference for a major event in top-down Sovietization of universities.[56] In fact, it was organized without input from the Central Committee apparatus. Youthful functionaries of Brno's Military Technical Academy decided who would be invited and neglected the "strongest schools" in Prague and Slovakia. The central apparatus was not consulted on the content of speeches, nor were the ideological directives that emerged from the conference "agreed upon or collectively discussed. Except for the address of Comrade Kopecký the speeches were the private matter of the speakers." Kopecký, one of the most powerful and ruthless men in the KSČ leadership, endeavored to persuade his young comrades in Brno that "concern for ideology is one of the most important tasks of the [central] Party apparatus . . . the concern of the Party ought to be felt everywhere." But at this conference, "spontaneity and improvisation dominated."[57] A low point was the attempt of classicist Ferdinand Stiebitz—who had urged his students to join the Party—to express his "admiration for Soviet science." For this his comrades accused him of "ideological immaturity."[58]

Even before Stalin's death, Soviet visitors to Czechoslovakia increasingly complained of the "bad results of studentocracy, especially when it comes to criticism of professors by students." In the Soviet Union such criticism issued only from highly placed functionaries: "experience shows that when students criticize professors, professors become fed up with the regime." It was Czech Communists' "obligation to attract to scientific work and train even those teachers who have reservations toward our regime."[59]

The criticism intensified with the thaw in 1953. In the summer of that year a first Czechoslovak delegation of higher-education functionaries brought rather strong advice back from Moscow: "Again and again the leading figures in the ministry warned us about improper, sectarian behavior toward the old technical intelligentsia. They showed us how, thanks to a proper and patient policy of the Soviet government, that intelligentsia has moved to the side of socialism. . . . ideological and intellectual transformation is a complex, sometimes excruciating process. 'Ideas are not old clothes that one can simply take off and change,' were the exact words of the deputy minister of culture comrade Stoletov." The Czech delegation was also told of the important role teachers had in Soviet university Party organizations, in contrast to their own, where "the leading functionaries have been almost exclusively students."[60]

In November, a yearly Soviet delegation of "Czechoslovak-Soviet Friendship" toured Czechoslovakia and lambasted the official anti-intellectualism. One delegation member, professor of pedagogy N. K. Goncharov, spoke at universities to overflowing audiences and met with hundreds of teachers, students, and functionaries. He was impressed by the Czechoslovaks' achievements, such as the unified education system, the political training of teachers, and the improvements in the "social composition" of students. But there were also many "serious distortions that are passed off as Soviet experience. Our mistakes and distortions, which took place during the construction of schools in the past, are passed off as a necessary historical stage. Supposedly Czechoslovak schools need to pass through this 'stage.'" Among the mistakes mentioned were the "overloading" of teachers with political work, "crude forms" used in the "battle against religion," the constant interference of "youth organizations" in pedagogical work, and the presence of unqualified worker cadres in leadership positions at school basic Party organizations.[61]

Although this advice directly contradicted what they had been hearing from Soviet visitors a few years earlier, the KSČ leadership responded promptly.[62] It is difficult to say whether the post-Gottwald Politburo had become so inured to following Soviet patterns as to be incapable of doing otherwise, or whether, like the post-Stalin leadership in the Soviet Union, it genuinely desired greater stability. In any case, Central Committee functionaries were sent to investigate the work of university Party organizations, and after they relayed back more alarming reports of "anarchic-Trotskyite" and "sectarian-nihilistic" attitudes of students toward old professors, the leadership revised Party statutes to emphasize "democratic centralism."[63] At Charles University, the Party committee was finally placed under the direction of the rector and made to include several professors; measures were also taken to improve professors' salaries.[64] After 1953 there were no more complaints of "studentocracy," and during the short-lived liberalization of 1956 a new generation of students voiced criticism about decisions made over their heads.

Professors vs. Professors

Studentocracy scarred professors' sense of identity. Perhaps the most demoralizing experience of these years was the frequent practice of taking action against one's colleagues. The fact that most professors belonged to the Party made such behavior a matter of Party discipline. Through their collaboration in action committees in 1948, professors like Tureček and Vaněček helped remove colleagues of several decades. Ministerial letters requiring involuntary leave, retirement, or dismissal were signed by Zdeněk Nejedlý, professor at Charles University since 1909. In the early 1950s suggestions for discontinuing some of the professors that remained went from the dean's office to the ministry rather than the other way around.[65] Academic senates voided the teaching qualifications of professors who had demonstrated a "hostile attitude toward the People's Democratic regime," by, for example, fleeing westward.[66] Likewise professors in the action committee of the Czech Academy of Arts and Letters voted to exclude fellow members who had been identified as politically untrustworthy.[67] In June 1948 renowned linguist Jan Mukařovský failed to lend his support to colleague Josef Král, who was to be removed from the editorship of *Česká mysl* for publishing an article critical of dialectical materialism. He wrote that "in a period of building socialism one cannot imagine a philosophical journal on a basis other than scientific socialism."[68]

Several professors composed books and pamphlets condemning the work of their colleagues. In November 1949 Václav Vaněček of Prague's law faculty earned the gratitude of the "law council" of the KSČ for agreeing to write the article "Legal History in the Hands of Idealists and Eclectics," targeting Professors Boháček, Čáda, Saturník, and Bušek—men with whom he had taught for decades.[69] In 1951 the dean and assistant dean of Prague's philosophical faculty wrote that the "faculty had not used the departure of representatives of bourgeois pseudoscholarship, like Černý, Vočadlo, Král, Stloukal, and others, for an instructive analysis of the nonscholarly and untruthful nature of their work." [70]

In a number of cases professors used new opportunities to settle old scores. The dean of Prague's law faculty after 1948, Josef Tureček, expert in canon law, got back at several colleagues who had opposed his appointment in the 1930s. In late February 1948 Docent Dr. František Kovárna was dismissed from teaching duties at the philosophical faculty in Prague; expecting further retribution from his colleague and competitor, Professor Jan Mukařovský, who later became rector, Kovárna fled the country. [71] Masaryk biographer Zdeněk Nejedlý found a number of collaborators willing to help decimate Czech scholarship among professors and docents who had taught at Prague or Brno University from the 1930s and earlier: František Trávníček, Julius Dolanský-Heidenreich, František Oberpfalzer-Jílek, Ladislav Rieger, Bohuslav Havránek. [72] Trávníček got even with his enemies, Professors František Novotný and Antonín Beer, making it impossible for them to teach and keeping Beer from the office of rector to which he had been elected. Trávníček himself became rector, a post he held until 1959. [73] At the Edvard Beneš Technical University in Brno the new rector Jiří Kroha used his influence to remove fellow professors Babánek, Uher, Rozehnal, and Fuchs. [74]

The practice of voting against one's colleagues was also widespread in East Germany. In 1958 the senate of the University of Jena voted to dismiss the assistant professor of medicine Dr. Rücker because he had signed a resolution against West German atomic weapons with a false name. [75] That same year a meeting of the trade union at Leipzig University's medical faculty voted to "deliver" the assistant professor "Fiedler" (no first name is noted) to the organs of state security for remarks critical of "distinguished leaders of the working class." [76] It was also standard practice to have Free German Youth (FDJ) seminar groups vote for expulsion of their own members. [77] In 1954 the "young friends" of an FDJ group in Rostock "requested" the direction of their faculty to expel a fellow student who had revealed himself an "enemy of the worker-peasant state" through careless remarks. [78] After reports had been confirmed of students or professors escaping West, those left behind had to attend endless meetings (*Aussprachen*) in an attempt to discern ideological shortcomings after the fact. In order to prevent further escapes, students considered not sufficiently "transparent" were subjected to special scrutiny. [79] Again one sees the peculiar situation of the divided country. East German students were encouraged to develop "walls in their minds" (*Mauern im Kopf*) long before a wall went up in Berlin.

Poland knew only weak echoes of such discussions, and Polish professors and students outside the Party were not forced to vote on expulsions. The state appointed rectors and deans, and did not make professors go through the charade of elections. Retirements or transfers of professors were decided at the level of the ministry and simply communicated to universities — usually anonymously. There was no need for senates or faculty councils to ratify these measures; as state agencies they were simply required to recognize their validity. Academic senates in the GDR existed through the 1950s, and cast unanimous or near-unanimous votes for rectors who had been approved in the SED Central Committee.

Whether or not East German rectors themselves belonged to the Party, they owed their appointments as rector, and often as professor, to the Party/state, which consequently became the locus of their loyalty.[80] When the professors of Rostock University protested the restructuring of higher education in 1952, they found their rector pitted against them.[81] Rectors at this time in Warsaw, Kraków, and Wrocław (Wasilkowski, Marchlewski, and Kulczyński) had belonged to their respective higher-education communities from the 1920s and were primarily representatives of these milieus, whether or not they belonged to the Party. In the Czech case the cohesion of university milieus was weaker: rectors Mukařovský (Prague) and Trávníček (Brno) had belonged to their universities for decades but actively helped disassemble their faculties along political lines.

It should be emphasized that the overwhelming majority of Czech and East German professors did their best to avoid situations that called for questionable behavior, and several even took the risk of speaking out against injustice. At a meeting of the reconstituted professorial council of the philosophical faculty in March 1948, Professor Růžena Vácková, an art historian, told her colleagues, as well as the Communist students who now attended, that "every society lays foundations for a moral order; I judge the character of a moral order by specific criteria. I would be interested in knowing the criteria used in the dismissal of professors and students. But especially of students. Insofar as I was a witness and insofar as I myself took part, I know that moral issues were involved in the students' demonstrations [of 25 February]. And if a criterion for dismissing students was participation in these demonstrations, then I would like to share their fate." [82] Not every professor polled voted for the resignation of Josef Král. Biologist and former rector Jan Bělehrádek wrote that he had not read Král's article, but wanted to make a "statement of principle": "A person who wrote an article that had no scholarly value would not be fit to serve as chief editor of a philosophical journal. But it is an infringement of scholarly freedom to remove someone from such a position only because of the subjective disagreement of one or another readers of the journal. Such a dispute should be settled according to the rules of science, above all through scientifically objective polemics." [83]

The words of Vácková would have been rare anywhere in East Central Europe and, perhaps because the memory of democracy was real and fresh, they were considered especially threatening in Czechoslovakia. Vácková, who had spent two years in Nazi prisons, was arrested again in 1951 and remained incarcerated until 1967. She became a signatory of Charter 77. Bělehrádek failed to return from a 1949 visit to Paris and stayed in the West until his death in 1980.

In East Germany, the existence of an open border to the West, and the dramatic shortage of specialists, permitted professors of medicine unusual freedoms when addressing SED functionaries—when they chose to use them. In 1960, the son and daughter of Professor Peter Matzen, director of the orthopedic clinic in Leipzig, were taken off a train to Berlin for interrogation by the railroad police—a routine measure in those years to discourage attempted escape. Matzen complained to his rector G. Mayer (SED) that "experience shows that such controls are completely senseless, because they have not lessened the stream of refugees in the least, and on the contrary only strengthen the determination of those affected to remove themselves from the zone of *Bevormundung*." In a discussion in his faculty the previous year, Matzen argued that the government should open the borders completely and "give up its policy of pressure and harassment"—then the flight would stop. Two of his colleagues took the opportunity to refute Matzen's words "energetically," however. Even in the medical profession, his civil courage was rare.[84]

But in the Czech case such public statements are difficult to imagine from a professor in any discipline during the 1950s. Especially in the humanities and social sciences, the maintenance of intellectual values required unusual intelligence, tact, and good fortune. Occasionally, the absence of coordinated central academic policy created opportunities for gifted and flexible young Marxists, however. A number of highly talented individuals taught history at Charles University in the stalinist times but kept low political profiles: Jan Havránek, František Kavka, Koloman Gajan, Josef Polišenský.

That Polišenský, perhaps Czechoslovakia's foremost historian in the postwar period, could teach without interruption from 1945 to the late 1960s seems somewhat of a mystery today. He had internalized the advice of one of his mentors, renowned medievalist Josef Šusta, who told him in April 1945: "You know, ours is a lost generation. Yours may be too, but you should try to hold on to your position, so that the historical profession will always be worth something here [*aby ta historie vždycky k něčemu vypadala*]." Several weeks later Professor Šusta, accused of collaboration for acting as president of the Czech Academy of Arts and Letters during the war, committed suicide. To some degree Polišenský had learned to behave tactfully during the war, as a school inspector and high school teacher who had taken part in the courses at Rankenheim. And he was lucky; in 1948 he did not have to join the Communist Party because, as a Social Democrat, he was simply absorbed into it. Because he taught simultaneously at Olomouc and Charles University during the stalinist years, he could arrange to be at one place when trouble was anticipated at the other.[85]

A Socialist Professoriate

In contrast to Polish and Czech counterparts, the East German Party milieu was cohesive within a Leninist hierarchy, and those SED members who took an independent line felt painfully isolated. Notions of strong base organizations, such as those that existed at universities in Prague and Brno, were completely foreign; the last attempt of a local SED university organization to arrange a conference without clearance of the Central Committee occurred in November 1946.[86] If among Czech Communists the operative principle was "cultural revolution," among East German counterparts it was anticipatory compliance (vorauseilender Gehorsam).

It is perhaps ironic but not illogical that a number of the best-known critical thinkers of a later age began their careers advocating heightened repression of colleagues and students. Professor Walter Markov, historian of the French Revolution, was for many years an inmate of a Nazi concentration camp. In 1951 he would have severe difficulties with the SED for supposed "Titoism," which led to expulsion from the Party. In 1948, when student representatives of the CDU and LDP were disappearing from the streets of his city, Markov had this to say to the SED Higher-Education Council: "Then to another very important point. One of the comrades has said that we must establish connections above all to the consistently [konsequent] democratic forces inside the block parties. This is a case of faulty speculation. There is no such thing as a consistent democrat who is a member of a block party [laughter]."[87]

Economist Fritz Behrens became one of the best-known victims of the "antirevisionist" campaign of the late 1950s. A decade earlier, as dean of Leipzig's social science faculty, he spoke out for "systematically limiting competition [in academia] and creating for ourselves a temporary monopoly. Later, when positions have been occupied by our people we can, for all I care, reintroduce free competition, if it should still be necessary [laughter]."[88]

When the mechanisms of destruction caught up with Markov and Behrens, no one remained to help them: one by one potential defenders of academic freedoms in their faculties had moved out of their profession or out of East Germany altogether, with their blessings. Absence of solidarity is a theme that pervades the stories of Walter Ulbricht's would-be opponents. In 1950 Markov's colleague Ernst Engelberg was endangered by accusations of "objectivism," and went on the offensive, using this very epithet to brand other possible dissenters, and thus distract attention from himself.[89] When he fell into disfavor in 1953, philosophy student Gerhard Zwerenz recalled that "in the great city of Leipzig hardly a human being attempted to speak to him." [90] Sociologist Wieland Herzfelde dared to defend Zwerenz in a meeting of January 1957, but after a leading functionary called Zwerenz an enemy of the Party, Herzfelde, a man with an international reputation, rushed to declare that he had "not wanted to ally himself with enemies of the Party!" [91]

In the way that the non-Party professoriate in Poland drew PZPR members into its wake, so in East Germany the Party attracted the allegiance of "progressive" non-Party intellectuals—like Bertolt Brecht or philosopher Ernst Bloch. According to Fritz Behrens, Bloch described himself in 1953 as a "Communist outside the Party . . . who would submit himself to every decision of the Party." [92] Indeed he would later proclaim that "it is the German Democratic Republic on whose ground I stand. . . . criticism can be objective only if it takes place on the ground of the republic." [93] During the next general crisis in 1956 Bloch again insisted on his loyalty to the SED, writing Karl-Marx-University rector G. Mayer that when "the Horthy-regime was on the rise in Hungary, I told the head of the institute: 'It's high time now. When will the Red Army finally march in?' " He further wrote of his "deep differences" with the arrested philosopher Wolfgang Harich and emphasized the care he had taken to hire only graduate students who belonged to the SED, "this in distinct contrast to other institutes at the Karl-Marx-University." [94] He denied students in the coterie that had formed around him and told SED functionaries that he could not be held "responsible for their thinking." [95]

Even during the crisis of stalinism in early 1956, Party intellectuals treated Lenin's interdiction of faction formation as holy writ. They knew of the Party's strictly hierarchical character through many years' work in the apparatus, yet refused to consider common cause with Walter Ulbricht's opponents in the Party leadership, let alone with forces outside the Party. [96] Perhaps the most important meeting of would-be opponents—the November 1956 gathering of editors Walter Janka, Gustav Just, and Heinz Zöger with Wolfgang Harich and Paul Merker in Klein-Machnow near Berlin—agreed to do nothing in order not to "endanger the unity of the Party." [97] Because they were not a "faction," they ignored basic rules of conspiracy. Harich confided his plans to the Soviet ambassador and to Ulbricht himself, and failed to consult his associates before undertaking a spectacular trip to Der Spiegel in Hamburg. [98]

After the crushing of the Hungarian Revolution, philosophy professor Harich became the first victim of Ulbricht's antirevisionism campaign. He was accused of "relations to the reactionary Petöfi circle in Hungary." [99] After thanking the Stasi for arresting him, Harich cooperated in the destruction of mentors and friends. He reported that Bloch "throughout the year 1956 worked himself into a position of hostility toward the SED leadership."[100] The major "revisionist" in Halle, a Slavicist from the university, likewise proved willing to reveal every detail of the "conspiracy."[101] People closest to the arrested refused to help their families.[102] The only "comrades" in East Central Europe to protest the arrest of Wolfgang Harich were Poles. In December 1956, twenty-six members of Warsaw's philosophy and sociology departments—all members of the PZPR—signed the following letter to the editorial board of the *Deutsche Zeitschrift für Philosophie* (German journal for philosophy) in East Berlin:

> The news that our friend, Dr. Wolfgang Harich, member of the SED, one of the most outstanding Marxist intellectuals of the young generation, has been arrested in Berlin, has deeply disturbed us. The circumstances surrounding his arrest and the character of the accusations against him have filled us with indignation. Dr. Harich has been accused of contacts with foreign espionage agencies and attempts to restore capitalism in the GDR, yet we, who know well Dr. Harich's political and scholarly activity, as well as his political opinions, will never believe such outrageous insinuations. We demand that this matter be clarified immediately, and that Dr. Harich be given the opportunity for a free and public defense.[103]

Prominent among Ulbricht's victims in the swelling waves of repression were Party historians, although their enthusiasm for revisionism had been restrained.[104] In 1957 the Party leadership ordered a purge at the editorial board of the major historical journal *Zeitschrift für Geschichtswissenschaft* and disciplined the GDR's foremost economic historian, Jürgen Kuczynski. Kuczynski later noted that all the leading East German historians (except Walter Markov) made a "united front" against him.[105] The attack was led by Fritz Köhler, a historian embarrassed by poorly timed expressions of support for destalinization.[106] Perhaps feeling obliged to compensate,[107] Köhler concocted a conspiracy that included Kuczynski, economist Fritz Behrens, and historian Joachim Streisand, with supposed links to West Berlin.[108] Despite reservations as to Köhler's motives, the SED leadership used him to keep Kuczynski fending off pseudoacademic attacks for years.[109] Such a strategy was not limited to the historical community: simultaneously, second-rate philosophers and economists like Rugard Otto Gropp and Herbert Prauss were mobilized against Ernst Bloch, Fritz Behrens, and Arne Benary. As Kuczynski has lamented: "Real Marxists like Fritz Behrens, Walter Markov, and myself, real progressive scholars like Hans Mayer and Ernst Bloch, were forced to debate with primitive scholarly figures who were promoted and encouraged by the Party. And the Party supported them, indeed directed them against us, especially in the person of Kurt Hager."[110]

In early 1957 a younger colleague at the Institute for Economics in Berlin supplied the SED Central Committee with detailed reports of private conversations between Behrens and Benary, in which the former praised the Leninist period of Soviet history as a time of socialist democracy, when "people could speak their opinions freely." Soon these leading "revisionists" were forced to recognize a higher ideal: Party unity. In February Benary wrote that "it has always been clear to me that the power of the working class stands and falls with the unity of the Party. Yet the discussions we had undoubtedly did nothing to promote the unity [*Einheit und Geschlossenheit*] of the Party, and therefore our political practice did not live up to this correct principle." [111]

Though he rejected demands for self-criticism, Kuczynski fell in line, and many years later prided himself for preventing a school of his own from developing. In 1961 Ernst Bloch, having endured years of harassment, decided not to return from vacation in the West, and Kuczynski denounced him in an open letter, signing "hatefully yours" (*Verachtungsvoll*).[112]

The East German intelligentsia was unusually subservient to the Party because it was the Party's creation. Beyond the elite-creating institutions that are the subject of chapter 12, the SED made use of the sectoral frontier to West Berlin—supposedly the edge of the antifascist world. For left-leaning intellectuals, the step westward became impossible to contemplate: they shared the great unexplored assumption in the political discourse of these years, namely that the GDR had made a clean break with the past. Whatever it was, it was not fascist.[113] Even Western media admitted to large numbers of former Nazis in the West German government, and so to abandon the GDR seemed to abandon hope for a better future.[114] Of the younger generation of dissenters, Erich Loest preferred to await arrest by the Stasi rather than enter a land where "the *Blutrichter* [blood judges] of Freisler still meted out justice." [115] We also have the story of Gerhard Zwerenz, who, despite threat of imminent arrest, spent the summer of 1957 camping at lakes around East Berlin rather than simply take the S-Bahn into West Berlin. Only the coaxing of Karola Bloch, after he had made a daring return to Leipzig, moved him out of the GDR for good.

Antifascism bound the older generation even more tightly to the GDR, because the dangers of fascism seemed more personal. Whether they had been liberated from concentration camps or not, many German Communists and Jews viewed the Red Army as protection from the German people —including workers. That is why Bertolt Brecht and Ernst Bloch welcomed the intervention of Soviet tanks in June 1953, and why Leipzig literary critic Hans Mayer likened striking workers in Leipzig to a fascist mob.[116] Such sentiments have been expressed most trenchantly by professor of French literature in Halle, Victor Klemperer, who had barely survived anti-Semitic

persecution during the Nazi years. In a diary entry of 22 June, he called Soviet
tanks "doves of peace": "I will feel safe in my skin and in my position exactly
as long as Soviet domination lasts here. When it ends, then good night."
Klemperer, a self-described liberal, had joined the KPD in 1945. His attachment to communism grew with each passing year—precisely as the mood
around him turned more anti-Communist and anti-Russian. The passengers
who complained of Soviet rule in the crowded trains he took from Halle
to Berlin seemed the same sort of people he had encountered two decades
earlier. Now, instead of damning the Weimar Republic, they were disputing
the existence of concentration camps, gas chambers, and Germany's responsibility for the most recent war. Any rumors emanating from such quarters
about Soviet camps in East Germany were not taken seriously by Klemperer.
He considered talk of "abducted and arrested students" to be "partly idle
chatter, and partly the clearing away [Aufräumung] of elements hostile to
the state," and fully supported the 1952 purge of students at his university,
though he knew it violated normal university regulations. To his wife's objections that such measures paved the way to "a new concentration camp,"
he responded: "The Nazis were permitted to speak freely, right up to the
point that they carried out their crimes." [117]

With each year an intellectual stayed in the GDR, the heavier became his
or her biography, and the less pleasant the thought of having to unload it
for the West Berlin press and the Western allies. [118] Personal biography gave
East German intellectuals a unique stake in state socialism: of all Communist intellectuals in Europe, only they had chosen it in full knowledge of
East and West. Their subsequent lives had to justify this choice, and that lent
their commitment to socialism a rare fanaticism. French intellectuals could
become stalinists in blissful ignorance of stalinist practice, while Russian or
Rumanian intellectuals could become stalinists in blissful ignorance of the
West. To put it another way: if one conceives of anti-Western ideology as a
form of blindness, many stalinists in Poland or Russia had been born blind,
whereas East German stalinists had blinded themselves. A scar remained,
and it began to throb when someone presumed to tell them how the West
"really" was. Take the case of East Germany's most famous dissident, Robert
Havemann, who flew into a rage in 1957 when a student criticized East German democracy. In response Havemann "said that in comparison to West
Germany we have practically ideal democratic conditions. He explained this
thoroughly and well. It came down to the difference between a prison cell
and a good life in which one occasionally gets angry about the refrigerator
that keeps going on the blink. Then Comrade Havemann got very sharp and
said that students who had not understood this after all these years should
go work in a factory so that they would understand it." [119]

Eventually Robert Havemann renounced such stalinist methods, but only after having them directed against himself in full force. One younger East German Communist, former Leipzig student Günter Zehm, had stalinism — and his blindness — literally beaten out of him. Like Havemann, he knew the West intimately, yet chose the GDR. During semester vacations, he had attended the seminars of Merleau-Ponty in Paris, discussed existentialism in West Germany, and toured Italy. All this made him only more desperate to realize socialism within the GDR. Though naive, Zehm was not uncritical, and he was arrested in 1957 along with other "revisionists." In the moments after arrest

> [I] looked upon the cops, who pressed me into the car and sat to my right and left holding a pillow over my hands so that no one from the street could see the hand-cuffs, in a certain sense as allies. In the weeks [leading up to the arrest] I had been expelled from the Party, had been forced to leave the university, denied all possibilities of bourgeois existence, so that I had to work as a peon for a writer. All this injustice had not sufficiently opened my eyes. Only in prison would communism literally be thrashed out of me. I wanted to debate with the interrogating commissars, and they answered with their fists. What a lesson I learned! . . . How my eyes now were opened to the real quality of the German Democratic Republic. How much did I learn in the following years, when murderers and executioners, whom the regime had hired as guards, spied on me, when I was watched over by threatening machine guns and ferocious dogs, and had nothing to read throughout my captivity except *Neues Deutschland,* the central organ of the SED![120]

Zehm subsequently became an editor at the conservative *Die Welt* in Hamburg.

Whether they fully opened their eyes to it or not, East Germans could never ignore the West, especially in the 1950s. It was present through family visits, radio broadcasts, or an inadvertent glance toward West Berlin, and in a sense the choice for the East was a daily procedure, constantly reinforced. Young academics in the GDR faced special pressure to refute the Western argumentation they knew by heart and may even have embraced, and to deny the evidence of their senses as well as their own wishes — for example, to travel.[121] The open border pushed the SED — and the Stasi — ever deeper into the private lives of GDR citizens, because of the danger that they might join, or be influenced by, relatives living in the West, and because they might fail to denounce friends thinking of escaping.[122]

A Material Stake in Socialism

The freedom to move westward until 1961 created not only an unusual ideological but also material constellation for East German professors, who could take advantage of what Ralph Jessen has called a "double labor market." Throughout the 1950s West German universities and firms routinely filled vacancies with staff and graduates of East German universities. Unlike counterparts in Warsaw or Prague, the East German regime had to accommodate its intelligentsia through a range of incentives, and therefore the East German professorship gradually gained a material stake in socialism, with salaries and rewards far outstripping those of colleagues in the Czech lands or in Poland.[123] In 1951, the government instituted "individual contracts" to keep scholars it wanted from moving West; and thus some institute directors in the Academy of Sciences were able to amass salaries of 12,000 to 15,000 marks (monthly). In the early 1950s the average salary in the GDR was 308 marks. By January 1952 approximately 14,780 contracts had been signed and covered some 20 percent of all professors and docents.[124] In 1960, some 64 percent of professors in the natural and technical sciences, 86 percent in medicine, and 22 percent in the social sciences had individual contacts.[125]

This calculus shifted with the closing of the border to the West in 1961, which permitted the SED to pursue its agenda of "debourgoisifying" the scholarly community free of all pressures from the West German job market. Recruitment into academia was "removed from the gray zone of patriarchal, weakly formalized individual relations," where full professors had shaped junior colleagues not only in an academic but also in a social and cultural sense.[126] Increasingly, worker-peasant cadres came to form a new academic elite, even in the technical and natural sciences.

In Poland, low salaries meant that professors as a rule worked two and more jobs, to the detriment of their teaching. Despite successive increases, by 1957 the monthly salary of a docent barely sufficed to buy a suit. About 60 percent of the professors and docents at Warsaw Polytechnic had one or more additional positions.[127] Humanists endeavored to supplement income through work in scholarly institutes of the Academy of Sciences. In June 1951 Jagiellonian University's Cadre Department reported to the ministry that professors in the agricultural faculty devoted "very little time to the university and have their main occupations elsewhere." Professor Chodzicki received pay for extra lectures, acted as director of two sections at the State Institute for Forestry Studies, but was a "guest" at the university on whom students waited from "morning until late evening."[128]

Academics in the Czech lands were not forced to work two jobs and in general lived better than their colleagues in Poland. But they also lived in a richer society and compared their lot not with that of Poles but with that of other Czechs. The experience of Czech professors, and other members of the intelligentsia, had been one of eroding status since the years of Nazi occupation. The salaries of full professors were relatively high, but starting salaries for academics were lower than the wages of unskilled laborers. Universities could not compete with industry or the state health system for highly skilled graduates; in 1954 professors of medicine had only slightly higher salaries than doctors in state clinics.[129] Specialists in the electrotechnology industry could get close to twice the salary offered in higher education. Czech functionaries noted a more balanced situation in the GDR, where university laboratories were well equipped with instruments and support staff.[130] Especially young Czech workers would not consider entering university, because their pay would drop significantly.[131] Because of these shortsighted policies of leveling, the KSČ would encounter enduring difficulties in transforming the Czech intelligentsia.

The preceding chapters have attempted to account for and show the importance of the Polish peculiarity in academic life, namely the persistence of the old professoriate across disciplines. Explanations have concentrated on the factors that created and reinforced a sense of identity among Poland's professors. Basic was their common heritage in the Polish intelligentsia, with its unusual beliefs about the state and about the Soviet Union, as well as attachment to premodern values such as "honor." A sense of the need to behave with primary loyalty toward the group pervaded the Polish professoriate, especially during the existential challenges of stalinism.

For different reasons, Czech and East German professors lacked the sense of mission, group cohesion, and opposition to state socialism that characterized the Polish professoriate. Czech professors had been relatively inactive in the corporate sense during the war, when they limited their activities either to private scholarship or to publishing and research in German-sanctioned structures. At the war's conclusion they found that the hierarchy at universities had shifted, and students claimed legitimacy based on a greater role in wartime resistance.

The German professoriate suffered crushing losses in moral capital because of its complicity with the Nazi regime. The concrete expression of these losses was an unparalleled decline in personnel. Over 85 percent of the professors active at East German universities in 1944–45 would never return to their positions; the break in the social sciences was so complete as to create a "tabula rasa." [132] In these disciplines scholarship was "redefined," [133] and individuals were employed who felt primary loyalty toward the new center of authority at East German campuses, the Socialist Unity Party of Germany. Among social scientists, this was true even of the handful who had enjoyed academic training under previous regimes, and among those, even among non-Party members. In the Czech lands, purging was also heaviest in the social sciences, but changed the face of academia as a whole. Many thousands of unqualified individuals began teaching, and the number of professors and docents declined from 1,253 (1948–49) to 906 (1953–54).[134]

Professors revealed their differing loci of loyalty in the first challenges to university autonomy of the early postwar years. In all three places majorities within the student body supported political alternatives to communism, yet only in Poland did the professoriate unequivocally side with the students, and only in Poland did professors organize politically in defense of their interests. The absence of an organized self-defense among Czech professors cannot be explained by state repression, which was hardly a factor in Czechoslovakia before the Prague coup of February 1948. Rather, the explanation lies in the political divisions within the Czech university.

The most visible political success of Polish academic senates and rectors in the early postwar years was a compromise in the higher-education decree of 1947. Yet even in the years of stalinism Polish professors continued to force compromise on their regime by behaving with relative solidarity toward one another and refusing to go beyond certain boundaries in their collaboration with the state. Most noticeable was their unwillingness to enter the Communist Party. One might explain this opposition through the incongruity between external and internal incentive structures, to borrow a term from political science. The Polish government, like Czech, East German, and Soviet counterparts, lavished rewards upon scholars willing to associate themselves with the Party: weekend houses, higher salaries, passports. In material terms these things had even greater value in impoverished Poland than in East Germany or the Czech lands. Yet in terms of the values that made the Polish professoriate a community, the step into the Party was difficult to contemplate because it threatened a reduction in prestige.

Yet Party membership was only a rough indicator of Party strength. In Poland the leadership was least successful in accomplishing a basic task that Kenneth Jowitt has identified for Leninist regimes: divorcing the Party cadre from native culture. The PZPR remained suffused with people who justified their behavior in national terms. At Czech and East German universities, by contrast, scholars in the social sciences and humanities, in or outside of the Party, accepted the Party's terms. Thus Ernst Bloch and Hans Mayer felt compelled to make statements of loyalty to the socialist state. As a supposed bulwark of "antifascism," it seemed to possess legitimacy.

Administratively speaking, the shattering of the professoriate that occurred in East Germany and the Czech lands had been a simple operation, involving decrees passed over a few years and directed at a small group of people. More complicated was the Party's other major task, the creation of new elites. Here the Party apparatuses had to reach out across the lands they ruled and attempt to recruit tens of thousands of young people who had neither the inclination nor the preparation for university studies. And the effort had to be sustained at least for a decade to make a difference, that is, past the crises and uncertainty felt throughout the region after Stalin's death.

PART THREE.
THE NEW STUDENT

Communists focused their ambitions in higher education on students. All other measures were futile unless they helped produce a new consciousness in students, who in turn could change consciousness in society as a whole. The new student had to be drawn from groups whose experience made them natural allies in the class struggle — the working class and the peasantry. Universities could teach many things, but they could not teach class hatred, nor could they impart "healthy class instincts." That did not mean that no students could be drawn from the middle classes, but they could not be a majority in the student body. Once at university, worker-peasant students would be given specialized knowledge and the instrument with which to employ that knowledge properly: Marxism-Leninism.

The common effort by Communists in the Czech lands, East Germany, and Poland to make new students took place in the contexts of more and less modern societies. The former two places had significant manufacturing sectors, and large, differentiated, and well-educated elites; but Poland was a predominantly rural society, with some pockets of illiteracy. A huge reservoir of young people in the Polish countryside hoped to move into cities and improve their status. Their agendas intersected with those of a state building socialism; it needed thousands of highly skilled experts and, in particular, engineers.

In Czech society mass advancement from agricultural to factory work occurred generations earlier, and a certain stratification set in after World War I. After half a century of steady growth, the Czech administrative class stagnated in the interwar period, and universities no longer promised upward mobility for children of the working class. Their numbers in the student body dropped from over 40 to less than 10 percent.[1] Increasingly, universities came to seem foreign environments to workers, and because of their relatively high wages, they had little incentive to consider higher education.

In Poland the social discrepancies were far greater. The native middle class was relatively insignificant — indeed, much of it had been Jewish and was destroyed — and a large peasantry faced a small intelligentsia that felt secure in a position of national leadership. Peasants' children who managed to enter this stratum had little doubt that they had moved upward in life.

Universities' value in the eyes of workers and peasants was also influenced by their potential to focus national sentiment. In 1945 Czech universities, once the premier achievement of the Czech national renascence, lost their role in the drive to displace German influence, because the German University in Prague and the German Technical University in Brno were closed, and the Germans expelled from Czechoslovakia. A blow by the Communists to higher education was therefore not felt to be an act against an embattled Czech institution. In Poland, however, Soviet-style socialism was considered the most recent manifestation of an age-old threat to Polish culture, and damage incurred by universities in the building of socialism was likely to arouse the national passions of Poles, regardless of social class.

East Germany serves as a foil for these two more extreme cases. Like the Czech lands, this was a highly industrialized society, with a complex class structure. In contrast to the Czech case, the national issue was not entirely irrelevant here, because animosities against the Soviet occupiers simmered just beneath the surface. Yet precisely because of military occupation, nationalism as a political factor was suspended. Despite these similar circumstances, East German Communists increased the percentage of worker-peasant students at universities to one-quarter by 1946, and in succeeding years that figure increased to over half. How did the SED succeed where the Czech Party had failed?

Regardless of local political and socioeconomic contexts, Communists did not anticipate the difficulties they would encounter in getting underprivileged young people to graduate from universities and enter a new elite. They vaguely imagined the existence of hidden pools of working-class and rural autodidacts, waiting for trade-union functionaries to tap and redirect. Few anticipated the many years and significant resources needed to identify promising high school students of working-class and peasant origin, get them prepared for, accepted at, and then graduated from universities. Organizations would have to go to factories and villages and convince often suspicious parents of the value of university education. Professors and university establishments needed to be persuaded that worker students could sit in the same benches as elite high school graduates. Because the old regime had tracked working-class and peasant students away from higher education at an early age, remedial courses were needed to give them high school equivalency, and because factory work was relatively well paid, incentives were needed to keep them in the classroom.

Likewise, few anticipated the multiple difficulties in teaching Marxism-Leninism: neither qualified staff nor textbooks existed, and students, no matter of what social background or nationality, resisted the teachings of scientific socialism, deriding it as a new "religion" and cutting classes where possible. Communists had thought that workers and peasants of goodwill would readily embrace the new teachings. In Poland they faced an additional challenge: the Roman Catholic Church, which cared as much about politics as they did.

★

CHAPTER ELEVEN

THE
DIFFICULTIES
OF CREATING
MARXIST-
LENINIST
CONSCIOUSNESS

Functionaries in the Czech lands, East Germany, and Poland used higher education to increase students' support for Communist ideology. They imagined that consistent propagation of the Marxist-Leninist worldview would gradually change students' ideas about politics and reinforce shifts in class-consciousness. Because of the ideological "openness" of the early postwar period, however, they were forced to tread lightly with their ambitions at first, and the earliest courses in political education bore innocuous titles like "Political and Social Problems of the Contemporary World" or "Studies of Poland and the Contemporary World." Nevertheless, they were revolutionary additions to conservative Central European universities, because the information they imparted was pro-Soviet and weighted toward the history of workers' movements.

In East Germany and Poland courses in Marxist social science were introduced in 1946 and 1947, but Czech Communists did not get started until after their February 1948 seizure of power. The courses seemed urgently necessary in all three places, because students consistently supported the Communists' opponents in the early postwar years. In free student council elections of the fall of 1947 in both East Germany and the Czech lands Communist student representatives were decisively defeated by liberal, Christian democrat, Catholic, and Czech National Socialist students. In Poland, student council elections were not permitted, but students took a leading role in antiregime demonstrations of 1946.[1] In Poland and the Czech lands students belonging to the Communist Party or Communist youth organizations were minorities, in the former case a tiny minority.

The Shortcomings of Political Indoctrination

The earliest Polish courses promoting the ideology of the new regime ("Poland and the Contemporary World") were introduced in October 1947 and offered lectures totaling sixty hours a year in political economy, economic geography, politics, and history. Examination topics that year included such things as "the Western policies of the Piast dynasty," "the catastrophe of the eastern policies of Polish magnates in the seventeenth century," and "the attitude of Polish society toward the German question from the end of the nineteenth century."[2] By 1949 the ideological climate had changed, and though the courses' name and structure remained the same, students had to study such questions as the "essence of Soviet democracy," "Poland in the camp of freedom," or "characteristics of imperialism — the decadent phase of capitalism."

The effects of the courses seemed questionable, however. In 1949 over 400 of 1,247 students in Kraków failed examinations on "Poland and the Contemporary World." Perhaps even more troubling, success in the exams did not necessarily reflect acceptance of the new ideology. The courses' director wrote that "the prevalent characteristic is superficiality and a tendency toward rhetoric and rant, done most obviously for opportunistic reasons."[3] The "most hardworking participants" in the courses had been students of theology.[4]

In 1950 the courses were renamed "Foundations of Marxism-Leninism,"[5] and the following year instruction became more systematic as the courses were extended to two years.[6] Reading lists for examinations narrowed considerably, from forty or more titles to just a handful. For questions on the subject "Marxism" there was but one book, Adam Schaff's *Introduction to the Theory of Marxism*. Most questions on the "history of the working class" could be answered by using the standard history of the CPSU, or a modern history by the Soviet scholar Efimov. To prepare for questions on current issues, such as "the collaboration and venality of the bourgeoisie as politics of national betrayal" or "the battle of Anglo-American imperialists for Iranian oil," students were advised to read the daily press.[7]

Lack of teaching staff meant that in many places the courses existed on paper only. In 1951–52 the Ministry of Education canceled lectures in dialectical and historical materialism for third-year students in the humanities due to "lack of cadres."[8] A perennial shortage of teachers was apparent, yet neither the Party nor the ministry had begun training faculty in Marxism-Leninism.[9] Recognizing the academic weakness of the subject, students cut their "compulsory" lectures in this subject. In Wrocław not more than one of six students in the second and third years of medical faculties attended. At natural sciences faculties attendance was close to 40 percent, about half the norm.[10] Students who did come to lectures did not always show proper respect. Some read "belles-lettres" and newspapers. One "enemy" at Wrocław's Higher School of Economics had started a rumor that "a new religion has been introduced to the school . . . Marxism." Students in Toruń were overheard joking before entering examination rooms: "I'm going to take my test in religion." [11]

By 1953–54, a high-water mark of stalinism in Poland, students' preparation in Marxism-Leninism had not substantially improved. A report from Łódź noted with relief that "neither the lecturers nor the assistants made serious political-ideological mistakes," yet "at exercises on materialism there have been manifestations of a religious nature. After lectures in the fourth part of 'History of the CPSU' students asked: why do leaders of the working class, and not learned specialists, concern themselves with the essence of matter? How can it be that distinguished natural scientists are religious? There is no doubt that such questions find their way to young people from the expected ideological centers of fideism." [12]

Party functionaries never ceased worrying that students were not taking Marxism-Leninism seriously. At fault was not so much the material as the protracted staffing difficulties. The teachers in Poznań were referred to as "autodidacts." One was a Soviet-educated candidate of science, one had a doctorate, and seventeen had master's degrees, but forty-nine were still third- and fourth-year students. A "certain portion" of the student-teachers treated their appointments only as a "temporary way of earning money." [13] Gliwice Polytechnic, a place with a strong leftist presence, reported frankly that "the Marxism-Leninism Department does not provide instruction at university level." In 1954 it lost its only professor, Bolesław Towarnicki, who wanted to return to teaching mathematics. Eighteen of twenty teachers were either undergraduate or graduate students. The department "had a very weak ideological influence, not only on students but on the entire academic cadre." [14]

Even Warsaw's teaching staff was feeble. Only two "comrades" without academic credentials and Soviet visiting professor Sudakov were available to guide the instruction of fifty-one master's students. Lectures and exercises for undergraduates left much to be desired: "among the students at the university there are a number of complaints about the low level of the lectures. An inspection showed that many are too general, and overloaded with subjects that the lecturer, who limits himself to dry little formulas, is unable to explain. For example, in a lecture about the May theses Comrade Bogacz, when talking about the necessity of the socialist revolution in Russia, limited himself to the claim that it was caused by the law of the necessary concordance of production forces and the character of production relations." Only two of eleven lecturers possessed full academic credentials. The others had learned their Marxism-Leninism in nine-month courses at Adam Schaff's Institute of Social Sciences (INS); their language was "impoverished, dry, full of formulas, and hardly comprehensible for the students."

Throughout Poland, Marxism-Leninism departments hired their staffs "according to chance"[15] and could not insist on political reliability. In Wrocław two teachers had belonged to the Home Army, two were former Zionists, one had been a prewar Polish army officer, one had a father who was arrested for withholding compulsory grain deliveries, and one was "of bourgeois background and poorly prepared." The former army officer was sent back to the law faculty to teach civil law. One of the former Zionist activists was likewise transferred to the law faculty, where he assumed directorship of the department of the Soviet constitution. But the others stayed. In Poland, cadre shortages were such that the Party could not afford to take its own definitions of a correct past very seriously.[16]

Despite this overtaxing of resources, the ministry once again increased the obligatory hours of Marxist-Leninist instruction in 1954. This meant that two leading younger scholars—Marek Waldenberg of Jagiellonian University and Ryszard Frackiewicz, director of the Marxism-Leninism Department of Warsaw's Higher Agricultural School—had to interrupt graduate work at the Institute of Social Sciences and go back to teaching.[17] The Party leadership hoped to buttress Marxism-Leninism departments with other "delegates" from INS. One such supposed member of the new Party elite was delegated to become director of Warsaw's Marxism-Leninism Department, but he "decidedly" refused to go. Even an urgent "request" from leading Party official Edward Ochab could not change his mind! None of the other proposed "delegations" had succeeded by fall 1954.[18] The Central Committee Science Department asked Ochab to procure two to three specialists from the Soviet Union to assist at the largest centers of instruction, but because the stay of the Soviet expert Sudakov had ended in controversy, this solution was also not adopted.[19]

In 1946, a year earlier than Polish counterparts, the East German leadership attempted to institute courses with a similarly inoffensive title: "Political and Social Problems of the Contemporary World." Yet due to lack of staff, by mid-1947 only Greifswald, Berlin, and Halle had managed to hold "satisfactory" lectures. Leipzig rector Gadamer wrote that "it is technically impossible to hold this lecture at present due to lack of appropriate classroom space."[20] He opposed the introduction of courses in political indoctrination because German universities were a "critically ill organism," and any "experiments might be their end."[21] He and others resented new social science, pedagogical, or worker faculties because universities were still denied many traditional functions, like the free election of deans and rectors or, something close to Gadamer's heart, the teaching of philosophy.[22]

In the immediate postwar years zonal authorities hesitated to make courses in Marxist ideology obligatory, fearing that students might have an additional excuse for "cheap martyrdom."[23] Central guidelines existed, but they changed so frequently, and were filtered through so many channels, that each university's course had a different thrust. Also, the DVV did not technically have the competence to enforce uniformity. In August 1948 Major Essin of SVAG complained that teaching plans in dialectical and historical materialism and political economy were too general, so that "each lecturer can do something completely different." [24] By the fall of 1948 every university was offering courses on "Political and Social Problems of the Contemporary World," but not every university required examinations in this subject. [25]

By 1950 officials began planning compulsory instruction in Marxism-Leninism because of continued, uncontrollable student protest. Anonymous "reactionaries" were scribbling critical remarks on bathroom walls and circulating leaflets condemning the sham student council elections. Officials carefully noted the messages written on purposely invalidated ballots: "Down with dictatorship!" "Liberty!" "Disgraceful," "Isaiah 41:24" ("He that hath chosen you is an abomination"). [26] Despite arrests of their leaders, students also continued to defy the Party in public. On 6 June 1950 a meeting was called between department director Otto Halle of the Ministry of Education and the students and professors of the politically troublesome veterinary medical faculty in Berlin. According to scant notes taken of the meeting, the students turned all of the accusations — of failing to support the "democratization" of universities, for instance — back upon Halle: "The attitude of all speakers in the discussion was clearly negative toward the GDR, prejudiced, and in part malicious." [27]

Examinations in social studies would supposedly help identify and remove these enemies. In July 1950 Halle wrote to Walter Ulbricht: "Now we are able to test every student taking final exams in 'Political and Social Problems of the Contemporary World' and thereby achieve a removal of those students who are reactionary-minded." [28] Studies in social sciences were to become "part of the normal course of studies," divided into three parts: first, "political economy," "dialectical and historical materialism," "modern history esp. history of the workers' movement," "political science [*Staatslehre*]," and "political and social problems of the contemporary age"; second, "literature of social scientific basic knowledge," including titles from Marx, Engels, Lenin, Stalin, Plekhanov, Norden, and Ulbricht; third, special lectures on contemporary issues in one's own field. Examinations were divided into written and oral segments and, as in Poland, became a prerequisite for moving forward in studies. [29] Topics for first-year students' written examinations in Leipzig in 1951 included:

1. Explain using the example of West Germany the essence and the characteristics of imperialism.
2. The principle of the right to self-determination and its use — what are the consequences for the present age?

3. What does Marxist-Leninist theory of the national question teach us about the struggle of the German people for its reunification?

Students of the fourth year had the following choice of written topics:

1. Why is the foundation of the GDR a turning point in the history of Germany?
2. Discuss the principle of the right to self-determination and its use by the Soviet Union toward Germany.[30]

As in Poland, wide gaps separated theory from practice. Far from a method of unmasking enemies, the new courses could not even help Party functionaries identify opportunists. Halle's successor Gerhard Harig had been forced to recognize this fact in 1949, when he was attacked at a Party conference for giving a CDU student a grade of one (A) in an essay on "classes and class conflict," though this student made clear that he was not writing his own opinion. The future state secretary promised relief, but first gave vent to his frustrations: "it is not easy to fail a student who can answer every question with ease [amusement]. But means and ways will be found. This case shows that devotion to the Party [*Parteilichkeit*] has not yet been consequently or finally realized in our teaching."[31]

A discussion in the Leipzig SED leadership five years later focused on the same problem. A Comrade Rohland had attended examinations and "noticed that students who don't exactly have a positive view of the GDR nevertheless got a grade of one. They consciously disguised themselves and then rushed through material they had learned by heart."[32]

During the period under study, students never came to view Marxism-Leninism as worthy of their effort, because it failed to achieve academic respectability. Especially those in the sciences came to "M-L" lectures only a few times a semester, in order to get the signatures of attendance required for taking examinations.[33] Until 1954 there was no thought of training Marxist-Leninists in a specialty—for example, philosophy or political economy—and the lectures were atrocious.[34] In October 1956 the student pastor of Leipzig University paid a visit to a class in Marxism-Leninism for the agricultural faculty. For ninety minutes the teacher did not look up from his manuscript; the lecture was "frightfully shallow," and students behaved accordingly: writing letters, finishing homework, playing cards (*Skat*).[35]

At first, the East German professoriate refused to accept such courses as normal parts of the curricula. The dean of Humboldt University's philosophical faculty, Professor Wolfgang Steinitz, informed his rector in November 1950 that—despite the new regulations—the faculty refused to administer examinations in social sciences, because almost all students had taken an examination on political questions at some earlier point. The economists wrote a similar letter. The mathematics and natural sciences faculty "instructed" its dean "to register protest. . . . Making this examination part of the final examinations would, in the unanimous opinion of the faculty members, result in a migration [to West Berlin] of about 90 percent of the students."[36]

Disciplinary problems were most aggravating among the upper-class students. In November 1951 the prorector for student affairs in Leipzig, Robert Schulz, reported that third-year students in the medical faculty, even members of the SED, were cutting classes in political economy.[37] In January only three students of the third semester in the mathematics and natural sciences faculty attended the final lecture in political economy.[38] But first-year students were better behaved. In Berlin and Leipzig between 90 and 95 percent attended lectures, and 95 to 100 percent participated in seminars. In Halle over 90 percent of first-year students regularly attended lectures, but of third-year students in the philosophical faculty the figure was 20 to 35 percent. Even in the pedagogical faculty, usually an SED stronghold, attendance averaged 40 to 55 percent among third-year students. In Jena lecture attendance for the entire university fluctuated between 75 and 80 percent. Medical students came least often (65 to 70 percent), and, as in Poland, the theology students were the most diligent, with 100 percent attendance.[39]

The courses in Marxism-Leninism were understaffed in East Germany, but not as badly as in Poland, because teacher training had started in 1947 at Leipzig University's social science faculty. The SED did not need to make such extensive use of graduate students. There were 66 lecturers and 33 graduate students teaching the "Foundations of Marxism-Leninism" in 1952–53. This meant 350 students per lecturer.[40] Still, there were not enough teachers to devote more than ten minutes per student in oral examinations. In Greifswald examiners complained that they could not really judge students' performance. To alleviate shortages, the State Secretariat decided to train 100 of the best students in "short courses" in Berlin and Leipzig.[41]

Although Czech Communists were forced suddenly in February 1948 to catch up with their northern neighbors, the evolution of their efforts in ideological training did not differ substantially. By early 1950 KSČ leaders had approved a program in the social sciences that mandated a two-hour lecture weekly for all students. First-year students would receive instruction in dialectical and historical materialism, second-year and higher classes on "our people's democracy on the road to socialism."[42] Successful examinations became a prerequisite for advance.

From the beginning, reports were filed complaining of the courses' abysmal quality and of the difficulty of getting students to attend. As in Poland and East Germany, finding qualified teachers proved next to impossible. The few who existed were worked to the breaking point. Later Czech National

Assembly president Čestmír Císař taught the history of the workers' movement at Charles University in the winter semester of 1948–49, and personally examined the oral and written work of 624 students.[43] As in neighboring states, reports proliferated of teachers' inability to teach. The lecturer at Prague's medical faculty had "not mastered the material sufficiently to explain it. He skims the surface, gets lost in phrases, and his delivery is so imperfect in the formal sense that one cannot follow him. He is not able to stimulate interest in the social sciences, encourage students or persuade them." Attendance in his class dropped "constantly."[44] A KSČ reporter drew a rather sobering sketch of the ideological maturity of one study group (*kroužek*) comprising about 20 students in the second year of medical studies: "With a couple of exceptions it was obvious that the students do not keep up with the daily press and cannot understand the interrelations of world events. They skim the surface and command a quantum of knowledge, which they acquired probably shortly before the exams. Their expressive abilities are substandard. Comrades cannot grasp basic facts, and they memorize materials on the CPSU without giving them any deeper thought."[45]

Similar to Polish and East German counterparts, Czech students read other things during lectures, and most stopped coming in the upper classes. In the first to third years attendance varied from 80 to 82 percent, in the fourth year from 65 to 70 percent.[46] In the natural sciences faculty 91.6 percent of first-year students attended lectures, but only 7.4 percent of the fourth- and fifth-year students.[47]

Late in March 1951 the KSČ Central Committee Secretariat decided to devote "special care" to the "schooling" of lecturers in the social sciences. They would take a crash course in the history of the CPSU, history of the KSČ, political economy, and dialectical and historical materialism and live together in dormitories, so that their progress could be "controlled."[48] In the end, the Party judged the effort to have been worthwhile, though several of the lecturers proved politically problematic. One, for example, did not know what "cosmopolitanism" was, and another "comrade recently returned from the sanitarium for treatment of a nervous illness, and still acts in an irritating way." Several "comrades" from Brno had not comprehended the necessity of purging that city's Party daily.[49] These difficulties were compounded by a prolonged staffing crisis in the Czechoslovak Education Ministry. In September Císař, now a Central Committee functionary, wrote that the ministry had not yet carried out the "important decision on creating departments of Marxism-Leninism. Formally the departments were set up, but they were not staffed."[50]

In November the KSČ leadership decided to drop the name "social sciences" and introduce obligatory "studies of the foundations of Marxism-

Leninism" at all higher schools.[51] The following month Luděk Holubec, Central Committee functionary in charge of higher education, made a tour of Marxism-Leninism programs in the provinces. Plzeň and Olomouc seemed barely satisfactory, but in Brno the leading candidate for dean had yet to secure his first degree. Even Holubec had to admit that a student who had failed to graduate could not "suddenly" become chair of a department.[52]

By early 1953 Czechoslovakia had thirty-one departments of the foundations of Marxism-Leninism, philosophy, and political economy, with 372 teachers. But the level of instruction remained unsatisfactory. Only two of this group were professors and seven were docents. A report prepared in the Central Committee spelled out the difficulties: "Instruction is not of a high standard. Marxism-Leninism is not really cultivated as a science at universities, because almost none of the teachers concern themselves deeply and scientifically with any concrete area of scholarship (history, law, philosophy, biology, etc.), and almost all remain on a level of merely superficial, entirely encyclopedic, and sometimes even sketchy knowledge of various scientific areas."[53]

The teachers were themselves usually students. At the Technical University in Prague 173 students of the University of Politics and Economics had been hired simply to guarantee the staffing of seminars. "Massive use of the help of students to conduct seminars is reflected in a low level of Marxist-Leninist instruction."[54] For doctoral candidates (*aspiranti*) the ratio was 30 students per professor, "which makes any personal care at all impossible."[55]

Courses in Marxist-Leninist ideology proved perennially flawed in all three countries. They were understaffed, and the staff was underqualified. Such courses could not gain academic respectability during the period under study. Neither could the Party get its message across adequately, nor could it register changes in students' ideological commitments. Of what value were examinations if theologians got the best scores? At best they were tests of knowledge, at worst evidence of opportunism.

"Unknowable" Students

Ironically, it was precisely as the Party became more "powerful" that it understood ever less about students. By 1949 practically all open opposition among students had been smothered, yet Party functionaries, especially in East Germany, were becoming obsessed with their inability to "know" students and, in particular, to recognize enemies in the student body. They found that despite — or perhaps because of — the new pressures, students no longer revealed their thoughts in the classroom or in youth organization meetings. In 1954 a Leipzig Communist lamented that "students do not tell us what they think." But he also waxed nostalgic for the more open early postwar period: "remember the discussions we had years ago in the student council meetings?"[56] At a September 1952 Party activist conference in Leipzig a Comrade Schuster reported on the difficulties of "evaluating" recent purging at Leipzig University, despite the apparent willingness of students in his faculty to support it. The very unanimity of approval made him suspicious:

> In our faculty the student Schmidt was expelled. He did not recognize the expulsion as valid and requested that his seminar group give its commentary on the matter. The commentary showed that the expulsion was just and all but two friends cast their votes for the expulsion. . . . [Yet] the discussion showed that strongly individualistic tendencies prevail in this seminar. The Party did not know how to care for these students. . . .
>
> I would recommend that the expulsions be discussed to the last detail, so that nothing remains unresolved, so that the opinion does not surface that someone may have been expelled unjustly. Every friend must feel responsible for every other friend in the seminar. If we create this kind of seminar collective as soon as possible, we will be able immediately to recognize all RIAS [Radio in the American Sector of Berlin] slogans that appear there, and unmask RIAS agents, who will be sent where they belong.[57]

Occasionally someone had the nerve and self-confidence to explain to functionaries why this strategy was not working. In October 1955 Dr. Ölsner of Leipzig's medical faculty told the following to an SED functionary of his acquaintance: "People have become cunning [*gewitzigt*] after twelve years of the Nazi regime and if they suspect that a certain person has anything to do with state power—and this applies to members of the Party as well—they shut their mouths."[58] Opinions not uttered could not be corrected. The dilemmas of Marxist-Leninist "persuasion" become fully evident in the record of a discussion at Leipzig University's SED Secretariat from November 1954:

> *Sämich:* Basic problems are not dealt with, discussions are superficial. Sometimes when we lure friends out of their reserve, comrades immediately get carried away, and frighten them back into their reserves. The point is to discuss in a friendly [*kameradschaftlich*] way. People must feel that we are helping them.
> *Hösel:* It depends how. We are ruthless toward enemies.
> *Rohland:* There are a number of non-Party members who are unclear about the politics of the Party and the government and fear being arrested. One must discuss with them in a friendly way.
> *Sämich:* It is difficult to say that it is our fault. I have the impression when I'm with the physicists that everything is talked to pieces. We

allow too much scope [*Spielraum*] for opinions. Discussions that are too long are also not right.[59]

In January 1951 these Leipzig Communists had received a lecture from Central Committee functionary Ernst Hoffmann on how to do battle with agents who "do not appear out in the open, but hide themselves": "As you know there is a tendency in the political organization to conduct this battle via the Stasi. That is not the decisive way. The decisive way is to unmask them ideologically, to summon them for ideological discussions, in a friendly way, on a normal basis. It is an old lesson in the history of the workers' movement that agents of the enemy can be unmasked as soon as we have a discussion with them."[60]

Students drew the appropriate conclusions. In one "discussion" they used "the disappearance of [their] fellow student Rossberg to explain why it is better to say nothing at all, for one cannot change anything anyway, and one would personally reap only sorrow."[61]

Partly because they did not live so directly in the shadow of the West, Polish and Czech functionaries were not as obsessed with thought control as SED counterparts, but complaints also emerged at Polish and Czech universities that "discussions" among students no longer revealed very much. In June 1954 the secretary of the PZPR Voivodeship Committee in Lublin, Comrade Romaniuk, noted that "students wither in an atmosphere" in which "incorrect statements are immediately branded as hostile." While warning against "caving in to liberalism," he advocated an "uncramped warm atmosphere" and "free exchange of opinions."[62] As early as October 1949 a functionary in the medical faculty in Prague complained that most students were "indifferent and reactionary due to their class origin, but today they do not ever expose themselves."[63]

Marxism-Leninism vs. the Churches

Students in Poland were not as persistently subjected to the ideological pressures of the Party apparatus, because it was much weaker. But they were exposed to an ideological force all but irrelevant at Czech or East German universities: the Roman Catholic Church. We have seen its pervasive influence in the professoriate, but it was likewise strongly present in the lives of students. Polish functionaries did not even attempt to keep track of students' attendance at religious services and worried instead about church-sponsored instruction in politics, economics, history, and philosophy.

In April 1953, a time of intense antichurch persecution, about a thousand students of Warsaw University were cutting classes in Marxism-Leninism to attend a "retreat" dealing in part with questions of economics. Among first-year biology majors and second- and third-year geography majors atten-

dance in Marxism-Leninism fell to 40 to 60 percent of normal. They heard
Polish primate Wyszyński lecture in the "student church" on "Catholic ethics
and economic questions." He told his listeners that religion had nothing
to do with capitalism, but that "thinkers of narrow minds claim that existence determines consciousness. But the church has the view that morality
determines existence. . . . Hitler oppressed free countries and his state fell to
pieces. Presently there are countries that force their politics on free countries,
but they will fall apart as well." Wyszyński's audience included youth organization (ZMP) activists who had graduated from a summer indoctrination
camp. Also well represented were the worker-peasant students. One son of
small peasants, the history student Józef Dutek, organized a 300-person lane
for Wyszyński's exit. The primate's influence extended to the university. One
student who belonged to the ZMP stood up during a Marxism-Leninism
lecture that same week and asked the teacher not to insult students' religious
feelings, since "freedom of conscience is guaranteed by the constitution." No
one tried to contradict her.[64]

The Party had attempted to counter the primate before retreats scheduled
for Poznań and Szczecin in late 1952. Poznań officials hurriedly organized a
"mass potato lifting" to keep students far from church. Yet upon returning
from the potato fields Party activists discovered that posters had been hung
in churches announcing a full retreat schedule with Wyszyński, described as
a "friend of students." The Party's efforts to stifle the retreats only exposed
it to ridicule. On short notice the Szczecin Voivodeship Committee scheduled compulsory lectures in military training for Sunday morning, so that
only 150 students could attend the retreat, while 1,700 students sat in poorly
heated lecture halls. These lectures were so clearly contrived that the colonel
holding them at the Medical Academy ran out of things to say. Around
1:00 P.M. students began "grumbling about being tired and cold." After returning from a two-hour lunch break, they clapped their hands hoping to
get the officer to give up. Party activists had to intervene to "master the
situation."[65]

Church-organized ideological training did not cease after the departure of
the primate from a given city. In Toruń, for example, the Jesuits ran an Institute for Religious Knowledge. In 1953 the institute scheduled a lively series of
lectures, discussions, and retreats which the Party discovered only after the
fact. A Reverend Janczak lectured on Stalin's *Economic Problems of Socialism
in the USSR,* telling students that this book contradicted the Soviet claim
of two years earlier that nature could be transformed. Janczak averred that
Stalin was now recognizing the church's view, namely that there were immutable "laws of nature." PZPR officials analyzed the Institute for Religious
Knowledge as if it were symmetrical to their own departments of Marxism-
Leninism: its most frequent participants were called "activists" and "agita-

tors." A Napoleon Pankowski, with "mother in England or America, agitates students to go to church every morning."

The Party feared that churchgoers might be driving its own faithful into a corner:

> Lidia Kędzierska, one of the students of the Institute for Religious Knowledge, posed a question to a larger group of students: "What do you Marxists really disapprove of, is it only religion or is it also the underground activities of priests?" She has spoken out publicly on other occasions as well. . . . As it turns out, the goal of these incidents is to expose ZMP activists and then isolate them from the broader masses of students. Students of the Institute for Religious Knowledge spread all sorts of rumors about ZMP activists, thereby slandering the organization's work.[66]

The ZMP was indeed unpopular. In 1952 Professor Drozdowski, academic adviser to third-year students of dental medicine in Kraków, advised his students not to abide by official examination schedules and to take examinations when they felt they were prepared. In the view of many professors, new study programs forced students to learn too much in too short a time. A representative of the Main Council of the ZMP from Warsaw was also present at this meeting, but when he attempted to defend state policy, he was met by boos and whistling and could not make himself heard. The secretary of the Party organization "took fright and left the meeting."[67]

The climate for nonreligious students was even worse outside the university. Especially in the countryside, where almost half the population lived, parish priests intimidated students who wanted to join the Party or study in the Soviet Union. In one case (March 1953) parents were told during a sermon that their "son has not learned anything in school and has renounced God. Now he is going to the USSR in order to close churches when he returns." In another parents were told that their "son is going the wrong way. He does not believe in God and is turning others away from the faith. He will receive a just punishment from God."[68]

The most threatening place in higher education for the PZPR was the Catholic University of Lublin (KUL). To be sure, KUL suffered state repression during the stalinist era. As has been mentioned, in 1949 its law faculty was transferred to the state university, and in 1954 it had to close its pedagogical faculty. But the core of the university, the humanities faculty, remained intact. Elsewhere in Poland independent student clubs were banned, yet in 1951 students of philosophy at KUL organized their own academic club (*koło naukowe*).[69] KUL was the one place in Poland where students might hear lectures on cubism, or discuss existentialism and the work of Marc Bloch in seminars. Young professors who had been dismissed at state universities in Toruń or Warsaw made the liberal "formation" of young people at KUL into a mission. Irena Sławińska, a particularly resourceful and attractive young professor of Polish philology and theatrology, took small cadres of students on excursions into the mountains where they discussed recent works of theology and philosophy.[70] In mountains further to the West the future pope John Paul II was likewise helping "form" students on hiking excursions. Throughout the 1950s KUL continued to challenge PZPR ideological agendas. According to internal Party reports, "hoards" of young people attended a 1954 lecture on the question: "did God create man or man God?"[71] At all times KUL recruited successfully in the Party's would-be constituency, namely the worker-peasant students.[72]

Unlike its competitor in Lublin, the state university UMCS, KUL had a solid financial foundation, drawn largely from donations collected by the "society of friends of KUL," and remained better equipped in these years. From the 10 million złotys collected yearly, it supported generous scholarships as well as "excellent" dormitories. Its wealth did not entirely depend on money, however, for priests could appeal to parishioners "from the pulpit" for student accommodations. Indeed, in many towns priests reportedly "preyed" on students who could not get space in state dormitories, and put them up either in the quarters "of the faithful" or in their own "well-run" hostels.[73] UMCS lacked sufficient housing even for faculty—many of whom commuted from elsewhere throughout this period. As late as 1954 UMCS lacked lecture halls, a "serious library," and laboratory facilities. Often students starting at KUL did not even know that a state university in Lublin existed.[74]

The "enemy" in Poland was too pervasive to subdue with the intimidation and surgical terror that gained results in East Germany; in Poland such practices endangered short-term state objectives, like successfully graduating students after only three years' study. As has been argued, the "enemy" gradually assumed a somewhat abstract character in Poland; all that was certain was that "he" enjoyed the support of organized religion. Party functionaries laid blame for the smallest infractions at the door of the church. Thus when students sat in Marxism-Leninism lectures knitting, reading fiction, or doing physics homework, this was attributed to the church's "decided battle for the ideological domination of students." The "enemy" served Communist functionaries as a convenient excuse for passivity. A 1952 report from the Central Committee's science department noted that

> The enemy [wróg] demoralizes youth also through drunkenness and debauchery, into which he lures even members of the ZMP. . . .

During the carnival, herring parties [śledziki] enjoyed particular popularity. The symbolic taking of ashes was preceded by festivities that ceased punctually at midnight. The climate at these parties was not the kind that should characterize the amusements of our young people. The most blatant example of perverted kinds of amusement organized with knowledge of the Party basic cell and the school organization of the ZMP was the St. Barbara's day [4 December] party at the Academy of Mining and Metallurgy and the Academy of Fine Arts in Kraków, which degenerated into a typical bourgeois orgy. Proof of how far the enemy has demoralized youth are the words of one participant of this party, a ZMP member, to whom attention was directed at the frivolity of her outfit and behavior. She exclaimed, "I've had enough of your slogans and sermons, for once let me have a good time."[75]

In Poland, religious ritual could shield people from unwanted sermons.

Neighboring lands knew no parallels to this public presence of religion. In Leipzig there was a university church, but never did thousands of students attend services there that challenged state doctrine. In 1968 the SED ordered this church, one of three original Gothic churches in Leipzig, dynamited, along with the main university building. Some 10,000 East Germans witnessed the collapse of these buildings in silent protest. This destruction at the heart of a bomb-ravaged city made way for a "socialist university" with a skyscraper at the center.

In East Germany, there were small Protestant student fellowships (junge Gemeinden), and they became major objects of state harassment during the accelerated course to socialism of 1952–53. The fellowships attracted students with engaging lecture programs and space for mutual support in a time of trouble. They were tenacious. In 1952 the fellowship in Leipzig managed to send information about its meetings to all newly enrolled students and post announcements on university bulletin boards. These were "attached so firmly that they couldn't be torn off."[76] An informer's report recorded about 350 students at the regular "bible evening" of the fellowship in Leipzig on 23 April 1953.[77] The SED responded to these "criminal" activities by expelling hundreds of students from high schools and universities. One woman in Leipzig had revealed herself as an "element hostile to the state" by admitting under questioning that religious faith was more important for her than friendship with the Soviet Union.[78] The academic senate of Humboldt University, including Prorector Robert Havemann, voted on 28 May 1953 that "further membership in the 'student fellowship' is incompatible with the democratic principles according to which students in the GDR are educated during the creation of the foundations for socialism." About 400 students were identified as members, of whom "only" twenty had been expelled by that point.[79]

Under Soviet pressure, the SED announced a "New Course" in June 1953 and some of these expulsions were reversed. Yet soon SED functionaries returned to their strategy of harassment and made student fellowships ever more isolated in the university community.[80] Where Polish Communists feared church forays into political territory, East German church officials came to witness the opposite: SED advances into symbolic and institutional spaces traditionally occupied by religion. In 1954 the SED introduced an atheistic confirmation ritual called "Jugendweihe" and insisted that all young people participate. Because at first the churches refused to permit participation in two confirmations, East German Christians were forced at a young age to make a decision for church or state that affected the rest of their lives. Those who denied the SED-state evidence of their loyalty were usually considered unfit for university studies. Hoping to spare young people existential crises, church leaders finally relented. Gradually, the atheistic eclipsed the Christian in social significance, and is celebrated by many to this day.[81]

Unlike Polish comrades East German Communists also extended their ideological umbrella over theological faculties, which were kept at universities. Here budding pastors could be exposed directly to political pressures, for example, to engage in "social" activities in return for stipends. During the 1950s, "progressive" professors and students became substantial components of GDR theological faculties, and university theologians largely abandoned "intellectual engagement" (*Auseinandersetzung*) with Marxist-Leninist ideology.[82] The large "progressive" blocs in faculties squelched efforts from the base to discuss structural reforms.

Yet pressures from below for change became almost unbearable after Khrushchev's revelations in 1956, and even Walter Ulbricht called university reform a "necessity."[83] As a result, students of the Leipzig fellowship began discussing ways of improving their education; soon, however, they were suspected of activities "hostile to the state" and placed under surveillance by the Stasi. Leipzig pastor Schmutzler sought a declaration of support for these students at a pastors' conference in Berlin in November 1956. But he was disappointed. A colleague from Dresden pointed to the potential dangers of the students' activities, especially in light of the events in Hungary, and the student pastor from Halle even offered thanks to God for Walter Ulbricht—whose leadership had "spared" East Germany the bloodshed of the sort Hungary had suffered.[84] Schmutzler was arrested the following March and kept in prison for four years. When plans emerged later that year to hold a service for him in Berlin's Marienkirche, the State Secretariat for

Church Affairs was tipped off by the theological faculty of Humboldt University in time to arrange disturbances.[85] A church order prohibited Protestant pastors from escaping to West Germany, but much of the flock moved westward, in order to avoid the pressures that had produced theologians who were almost as true to the state as the Party's own cadre.[86]

Organized religion was all but invisible at Czech universities. The Czech lands knew no equivalent of the student fellowships; and only one ostensibly religious incident seems to have disturbed the top leadership. In 1950 a shocking rumor surfaced from the provinces that went all the way to the Secretariat of the Central Committee: several students of a worker course had been spotted at a church service. Subsequent investigations found little cause for alarm, however: these students had been assembling arguments against religion for a class assignment.[87] A few other reports stressed the need for more aggressive atheistic propaganda, especially in Moravia, where Roman Catholicism was relatively strong.[88] One notation from late 1955 criticized the youth organization ČSM for not devoting sufficient energy to "materialistic antireligious propaganda, though some of the students are still in the thrall of religious superstitions."[89] But few students dared practice religion openly: by March 1954 the number of churchgoers at Charles University had shrunk to 273 students, 3.2 percent of 8,418 students enrolled. Still, Party officials were not satisfied.[90]

Consistent with recent historical experience, religion had thus served to strengthen national bonds in Poland, remained a marginal factor in the Czech lands, and was placed in the service of the state in East Germany.

Clear in retrospect is that ideological schooling could have only a limited impact in the short run. The failure of official ideology to win adherents in this period is most compellingly reflected in the inability of all three Parties to meet quotas for university majors in the social sciences, including philosophy and law. Students voted with their feet, enrolling in courses of study least touched by state ideology. Although the capacities in the technical sciences rose massively in these years, none of these Parties had difficulty fulfilling the plan in these subjects.[91] Awareness of a shifting, though supposedly unfailing, Party line was too widespread to permit greater ideological penetration. At best tiny minorities — estimated in each case between 5 and 10 percent — of fanatical and idealistic young people accepted the Party's teachings wholeheartedly. Particularly in East Germany the dual realities of East and West made for a persistent "lack of clarity" among the majority, which was resolved only as the nation, and individual consciousness, divided.

Far more useful in making students "the Party's own" was to attach them to the Party as an organization of professional advancement. Whether they fully and consciously accepted the ideological line of the moment would be secondary; a policy of taking students from humble backgrounds and gradually letting them climb the social ladder—with a price in loyalty for each rung—would bind students to the Party for life, for the Party would make their lives.

★

CHAPTER TWELVE

POLISH
AND
EAST
GERMAN
STUDENT
ADMISSIONS

The Polish and East German leaderships understood the usefulness of universities as tools for social and professional advancement, and by the mid-1950s they increased the numbers of students from working-class and peasant background to slightly less than their proportion in the population as a whole. This impressive outcome was not achieved easily. Many workers needed to be convinced that higher education was worth their while, and many others had to be given necessary preparation. For these, special courses were created, lasting first one, then two, and in East Germany after 1949, three years. Finally, Communists had to overcome resistance to worker education from university communities, which felt the new students were academically inferior and beneficiaries of political preference.

Breakthroughs in Student Admissions: East Germany

East Germany's Communists had an advantage over Polish comrades: they could begin shaping their new student body from the moment universities reopened, because the Soviets' larger agendas of denazification and democratization immediately politicized student admissions. Former Nazi Party members and those who had actively served the Nazi Party, or were officers in the German armed forces, were forbidden to study, and authorities tried to attract individuals who had been held back in education for "racial and political reasons."[1] The group of bona fide "antifascists" was very small, however, and, to the Communists' displeasure, tended to support their opponents. Therefore, as we shall see in greater detail, the definition of antifascist activity was soon augmented to include postwar behavior and, in particular, support for the only "consistently antifascist" organization in German politics: the SED.[2] In general, denazification permitted East German officials to curtail student admissions severely, and the rejection rate for new applicants was high (see Table 13-2). They were heeding Soviet professor Zolotukhin's directive that universities begin small, but "properly."[3] Polish and Czech officials could not justify limitations on student enrollment, however, because Nazi occupiers had kept Polish and Czech universities closed for the duration of the war, and the demand for higher education was irresistible.

Of greater long-term importance was the second component of Soviet policy at East German universities: democratization. In Soviet and German Communist understanding, democratization meant guaranteeing proportionate representation of the laboring strata in all institutions. If 70 percent of society belonged to the working class, then 70 percent of students and professors should come from the working class. This figure was achieved nowhere, but the effect of striving for it was revolutionary change.

In hopes of maintaining leverage in all of Germany, the Soviets hesitated to support zonal-wide initiatives in higher education. A specifically East German student admissions policy would have seemed to split German education.[4] The first initiatives to organize university preparation outside the conventional channels were therefore tacitly encouraged, but not organized, from East Berlin. Rather, they grew out of the enthusiasm and energy of rank-and-file trade unionists, Social Democrats, and Communists, in particular in the South.[5] By the spring of 1946 worker preparation courses (*Vorstudienanstalten*) had sprouted up in the Silesian and Saxon working-class towns of Chemnitz, Görlitz, Plauen, and Zwickau, in addition to the traditional centers of higher education in Dresden, Freiberg, and Leipzig. Because of the heavy concentration of industry there, Saxony was destined to become the reservoir for the East German elite.[6] After a slight delay, socialists further north and west established worker courses in Halle, Jena, and Berlin. Less resolute functionaries in Mecklenburg had to be nudged by comrades in Berlin into setting up their courses in the fall of 1946.[7]

Urged onward by several determined Saxon socialists, improvements to worker preparation courses continued to emanate from the South. Most impressive was the enterprise of Helmut Holtzhauer (KPD/SED), a bookseller who had been incarcerated by the Nazis, and now directed the Leipzig education office.[8] Technically he had no right to intervene in higher-education affairs, but he used his position as the city's representative in university admissions as a springboard for power at the university. In 1948 the energetic Holtzhauer advanced to Saxon minister of education.[9]

Faced with difficulties in finding workers who were willing to sacrifice paid employment, in March 1946 Saxon Communists and Social Democrats set up a Committee for the Promotion of Worker Studies to coordinate recruitment in working-class areas, but also to guarantee some uniformity of structure throughout the *Land*. It was staffed by trade-union officials and charged with "promoting worker studies, examining the political dependability of applicants, and examining their aptitude for studies." It also co-

ordinated scholarship funds for worker-peasant students.[10] In April, district
(*Kreis*) level committees were formed, which operated according to directives received from the Saxon Education Ministry in Dresden and aided in
the political training of worker students, agitated for the courses in factories, and helped collect donations.[11] In 1947 similar committees were set up
in Saxony-Anhalt, Thuringia, and Mecklenburg.[12]

The target groups of the courses were clear from the outset. The Saxon
directive of 1 March 1946 stated plainly — in contrast to the less precise initial
Polish decree — that "admitted to the courses will be participants from the
laboring strata, who are recommended by the democratic parties, the trade
unions, and youth and women's committees."[13] The SED also attempted
to guarantee the loyalty of the socially underprivileged. All over East Germany candidates had to submit information on their own and their parents'
"political activity" and to submit "political character references of democratic organizations."[14] In February 1948 the Central Secretariat of the SED
specified that "selection must be carried out in a far more critical way than
has been the case until now. The candidates for these institutions must be
chosen by way of personal-political examinations."[15]

Suggestions for admission could come from the committees for the promotion of worker studies, which drew on information from factories, or
from the Union of Victims of the Nazi Regime.[16] The courses' guidelines
were proclaimed to be the "formation of the next generation of academics
from such strata of the people (workers, peasants, victims of fascism, and
victims of National Socialism) as have been excluded from high school for
social or political reasons."[17] Such precise elucidation of worker courses' ultimate goals was never attained in Poland or the Czech lands. As we shall see,
neither Polish nor Czech Communists were as certain of what they desired
from the new student, or how to achieve it.

The East German worker courses gradually developed into the most impressive tools of elite engineering seen in the area under study. Yet more
important for the transformations of the student body in these early years
was the SED's domination of committees that decided admission to regular courses of studies. The Party was well represented in the main university
committees and entirely controlled the preadmissions committees, which
"sorted" applications before they went to universities, eliminating hundreds
of candidates.[18] The following priority for university admission was established by the Soviet zone education ministers in July 1947:

1. Applicants of worker and peasant background, so long as they did not
   belong to the NSDAP; graduates of college preparatory courses and
   applicants who were discriminated against under the Nazi regime for
   social, political, or racial reasons.

2. Persons who were not members or candidates for membership in the NSDAP or in any of its subdivisions.

3. Persons, who were members only of the Hitler Youth or the Union of German Girls.[19]

In the politically more innovative southern regions authorities attempted relatively precise definitions of the targeted social groups. In August 1947 a ministry official wrote Leipzig's Rector Gadamer that the committees were to note the occupation of the candidate's father before and after 8 May 1945. They were instructed to include as "peasant" only people whose parents had less than twenty hectares land. The preadmissions committees checked on the information given by applicants.[20] Selectivity remained high because the Soviets kept universities running below capacity: for example, Leipzig University could have accommodated one-third more students in 1947. In the previous two years, some 1,200 candidates were refused for medical studies alone.[21]

A political component entered the selection process in 1946, as authorities began to record students' "antifascist" activities in the *postwar* period. The first attempt by the Saxon government to establish students' "antifascist democratic convictions" through an essay on a current political topic failed over university opposition.[22] Nevertheless, because they were well aware of the political complexion of admissions committees, applicants for studies began to submit evidence from their hometowns attesting to such convictions. The best possible evidence was, of course, a position within an "antifascist democratic" organization, above all the SED. Given the competitiveness of the admissions process, student membership in the parties — especially the SED — rose dramatically. In the words of Hans-Georg Gadamer, by 1947 most students could prove they were "party functionaries."[23]

Beginning in 1947, applicants had to fill out forms requesting precise information on parents' income, size of their holdings in land (if any), and political affiliation. These data were double-checked by hometown organizations of the political parties. The final requirement reminded some of the Nazi concept of *Sippenhaft:* namely, that students were held accountable for their parents' behavior. In the long run, such a requirement had the effect of politically disciplining parents, who became afraid to do anything that might jeopardize their children's education.

Under such pressures the student body underwent rapid transformations (see Tables 12-1, 12-2, and 12-3). There was of course some tension between the importance the Party assigned to political involvement as opposed to social origin. Given initially imprecise understandings of "worker" and "peasant," local SED commissions gave priority to candidates' political affiliation, assuming it went hand in hand with working-class origins. For ex-

TABLE 12-1

Worker-Peasant Students in East Germany as a Percentage of Total Students

	1945–46	1946–47	1947–48
Berlin	14.2 ss	9.7 ws (7.7)	17.0 ws (14.9)
Jena	12.9 ws	30.2 ws (27.3)	33.5 ws (29.5)
Leipzig	13.3 ws	24.4 ws (21.8)	40.3 ws (36.3)
Halle	7.5 ws	10.7 ws (7.0)	31.6 ws (27.1)
Greifswald	8.5 ws	14.6	26.6 ws (20.5)
Rostock	13.8 ss	13.9	27.0 ws (18.3)

Sources: BAAP, R2/865, Bl. 7, 35–37; R2/1060, Bl. 23–26, 32–34;
Kasper, "Der Kampf," 273–75.
Note: Worker students in parentheses. ss = summer semester;
ws = winter semester.

TABLE 12-2

Student Party Affiliations in East Germany in 1946–47 (in percentage)

	SED	SPD	LDP	CDU	No Party
Berlin	9.8	3.7	1.0	1.7	83.8
Jena	30.7	Forbidden	12.3	7.3	49.6
Leipzig	41.4	Forbidden	15.8	14.0	28.8
Halle	34.8	Forbidden	15.2	9.7	40.3
Greifswald	17.8	Forbidden	7.4	12.7	62.1
Rostock	21.0	Forbidden	7.4	8.0	63.7

Sources: BAAP, R2/1060, Bl. 46; Kasper, "Der Kampf," 272.

TABLE 12-3

Worker Students and Communists in the Student Body
of Leipzig University (3 November 1948)

	Total	Worker Students	Percentage	SED	Percentage
ws 46–47	1,330	363	27.3	689	51.8
ss 47	2,411	663	27.5	921	38.2
ws 47–48	3,483	1,062	30.5	1,549	44.5
ss 48	3,270	1,002	30.6	1,475	45.1
ws 48–49	4,082	1,444	35.4	1,859	45.5

Source: "Soziale Struktur der Studierenden an den wissenschaftlichen
Hochschulen des Landes Sachsen seit dem Wintersemester 1946–47,"
3 November 1948, SAPMO-BA, ZPA, IV 2/9.04/465.
Note: ws = winter semester; ss = summer semester.

ample, in early 1946 the KPD cell at the Saxon State Administration directed that at least 40 percent of the worker course participants be KPD-members in order to make the university "a true people's university."[24] In Berlin "special importance [was] attached to certificates and recommendations demonstrating participation in democratic organizations that proves the candidate's worth (the parties, trade union, Culture Union, FDJ, etc.)."[25] Soviet officers likewise promoted the political over the social in student admissions. Though keen on increasing numbers of working-class students, they were primarily concerned that universities remain politically placid, and fostered the enrollment of party members because they could be supervised by their organizations.[26] As we shall see, the understanding of "worker-peasant" in East Germany was as much political as it was socioeconomic, and these two aspects of admissions policies gradually merged.

Breakthroughs in Student Admissions: Poland

A breakthrough in student admissions was also achieved in Poland, but it took several years longer and related almost entirely to students' social background. The issue of worker studies, of central importance to the new regime, was broached in the first meetings of Minister Stanisław Skrzeszewski (PPR) with Kraków's professors in January and May 1945. He proclaimed the government's desire that "sons of workers and peasants" be admitted to studies.[27] His ministry released a decree on 24 May that created "qualifying commissions" to decide on the suitability of candidates for university education. Either they would be admitted directly to higher education, or, if their preparation was lacking, they would be enrolled in one-year courses called "introductory year."

At first, "sons of workers and peasants" were given little incentive to enroll in the new courses, however. On the one hand, there was no attempt to attract them with scholarships; and, on the other, almost all applicants for normal university studies were accepted that first year. Because much documentation had been destroyed during the war, universities usually overlooked the requirement for high school diplomas, and thus any workers interested in university education could simply enroll. In their inadequate preparation for higher education they did not differ greatly from Poles of other social strata, because the Germans had closed high schools to all Poles, and only a minority had benefited from underground education. For several years, therefore, standard university instruction assumed the character of remedial education.[28] Universities did cooperate in setting up "introductory year" courses, but enrollment was quite low, exceeding one hundred only at a few technical colleges and at Warsaw University. At Jagiellonian University—a place very suspicious of such alien implants—only fifteen students signed up.[29] And because the decree had not made the minister's intent explicit, most of these students were not of working-class or peasant background.[30]

Early in 1946 the initiative in worker studies was seized by students in the PPR youth organization, Academic Union of Fighting Youth—"Life" (ZWM Życie). They realized that it was not enough simply to open the gates of universities to workers' and peasants' children, but that efforts had to be expended to attract them. At its second national congress in Łódź in January Życie decided to search for ways to increase numbers of worker-peasant students at universities. After several months, the student Communists introduced a new type of course, the so-called preparatory course, to nine cities. Because one year was too little to supply high school equivalency, this course was intended to prepare students for the "introductory year" courses. Only in 1949 were the two joined into a two-year "preparatory study" (*studium przygotowawczy*). The prime consideration for admission was social background. Candidates were required to have completed at least seven classes of grammar school, but they were not supposed to have advanced in secondary school. Too much high school under the old regime seemed suspicious.

The "first cycle" of the preparatory course lasted from May 1946 until early 1947. Curricula and logistics were taken care of locally, and funding came from youth organizations, local government organs, and regional industry. The driving force in all cases was ZWM Życie, whose members went to factories and rural communities, propagating the courses and seeking desirable candidates.[31] Local representatives of the parties and "social organizations" also sifted candidates. The poor control exercised by the Party over state qualifying commissions meant that their efficiency varied greatly, however.[32] Equally important, ways were sought to mitigate financial hardship, through stipends, cafeteria meals, dormitories, ration coupons for clothing, and travel discounts.

The first class initially amounted to 2,300 students, of whom 45.2 percent came from the working class, and 26.2 percent from the peasantry. Three-fourths belonged to leftist youth groups.[33] A total of 1,500 made it through the three-week selection courses, and of these, 973 finished successfully and began the "introductory year." Their preparation was strongest in mathematics and physics, but many had an inadequate command of written Polish.[34] Łódź had the highest enrollment with 519, followed by Warsaw (395), Kraków (350), Gliwice (248), and Wrocław (127). As in East Germany course participants came under pressure to demonstrate conformity: in Kraków 115 of the 350 participants were listed as "fresh" members of the Fighting Youth Union.[35]

In the meantime, the first graduates of "introductory year" had enrolled in regular university courses, but their performance was disappointing. Of nineteen students from the first "introductory year" at Warsaw's humanities faculty, only six successfully completed the 1946–47 academic year. Four "did not appear to explain the status of their studies, though they were summoned to do so"; one had leave of absence, and another was working and did not go to lectures. Of thirty-one students at the law faculty, only nineteen took their yearly examinations on time. Two of these failed outright, one did well, two satisfactorily, and the rest had to make up one or more parts of the exam. In the natural sciences faculty not one of five students appeared for scheduled exams. Reports from Toruń and Łódź were similar.[36] Officials at Jagiellonian University were not even bothering to keep records on graduates of "introductory year" in their student body.[37]

After their complete seizure of the state apparatus in early 1947, PPR officials began to doubt the efficacy of preparatory courses and "introductory year." Reports from June of that year exposed these courses' questionable impact on the social composition of the student body: of 848 "introductory year" students, 16 percent were of working-class and 24 percent of peasant background, 31 percent intellectual workers, and 29 percent middle class. The figures for workers and peasants were said to be inflated.[38] A significant number of participants in the "introductory year" already possessed a regular high school diploma (*matura*), but had hidden this fact, because course graduates entered university without the now customary entrance examination. A report from Wrocław maintained that 80 percent of the students admitted from the "introductory year" course were "eminently reactionary."[39] Selection to "introductory year" courses in Katowice and the Academy of Mining and Metallurgy in Kraków was supposedly better, because participants came directly from factories.[40]

As in East Germany, initial breakthroughs in student admissions had to be accomplished by other means. In 1947 competition for university admission increased sharply, and the ministry created commissions at the faculties to determine who would be accepted. These consisted of the dean, a representative of the ministry, a member of the faculty council, a representative of the regional trade-union council, and a representative of the regional peasants' self-help association.[41] As in East Germany, applicants took an entrance examination in their chosen subject as well as a political test (called here "Contemporary Poland"). Special state qualifying commissions could exempt up to 20 percent of the candidates from the examination if they had taken part in wartime conspiracy, postwar "rebuilding," or in so-called work for society (i.e., belonged to a political organization).[42] These regulations then subverted the order's intent by stipulating that the commission's director—that is, the dean—would determine the examination's outcome. The dean was almost never a representative of the Party.[43]

Although the Party now managed to force upon universities those candidates it absolutely desired, and keep away those it wanted under no circumstances, selection was still quite haphazard in 1947.[44] The commissions were assembled hastily and usually had only a few days to examine hundreds of files, leaving little time for double-checking applications. They relied on recommendations of the veterans' associations, but these were not controlled by the PPR. In Łódź, a place with relatively strong Party presence, the veterans' organization did not "differentiate activity in the Home Army from activity in the [Communist] People's Army."[45] Documents submitted in support of candidates were phrased so vaguely that even politically vigilant commissions could hardly make use of them.[46] There were also cases of bribes and "protectionism."[47] And, worst of all, students belonging to the PPR often did not admit to membership, because they were embarrassed or feared that it would be held against them in the conservative university establishment. The Party representative in Warsaw was thus unable to determine how many applicants were his comrades.[48]

To prevent a repetition of such mistakes in 1948–49, the recruitment drive was put directly into the hands of the Central Committee's education department. A letter to the voivodeship committees proclaimed that "in 1948 recruitment for the first year of higher studies, for the introductory year, and for the preparatory course remains a Party task of the first order. It will be fulfilled in such a way as to reach at least 30 percent worker and 20 percent peasant youth in the first year of studies." The Central Committee itself would supervise the Ministry of Education, and guarantee "proper composition of examining commissions." Party, youth, trade-union, and peasant organizations were "obligated" to direct to higher schools "the most gifted and socialized [uspołeczniona] worker-peasant youth," and supervise the issuance of certifications to candidates for studies.[49] Notable in comparison with the situation in East Germany was the absence of an intent to transform the student body politically.

The new admissions guidelines required successful completion of an entrance examination, with exceptions only for graduates of the "introductory year." Admission again was decided at the faculty level, by commissions consisting of the dean as chair, a ministry delegate, a member of the faculty council, a representative of the local peasants' association, and a representative of a ministry interested in the faculty's choice of students. Entrance tests again included a written examination in the planned field of study, and the oral examination on "contemporary Poland." The latter encouraged opportunism: for example, one former Home Army soldier in Wrocław was asked: "Was the theory of the Home Army correct, that enemy number one is Germany, enemy number two Russia?" The answer is not recorded, but the student failed.[50] Beyond this, faculties of technical and natural sciences could administer written tests in mathematics, physics, or biology. The recruitment drive of 1948–49 scored small gains over the previous year, with the number of students of working-class background advancing from 22 to 27.5 percent, and of peasant background from 19.7 to 21.9 percent.[51] In reality the improvements were supposedly even better because statistics had become "far more exact."

The following year the PPR registered its breakthrough, when numbers of worker-peasant students in the entering class rose from 49.4 to 54.5 percent.[52] Central to the success of 1949 was stronger involvement of Party youth organizations (ZAMP and ZMP), and the introduction to deans' offices of "technical secretaries," usually ZAMP functionaries who took special care to "control" the admissions process.[53] In the 1948–49 drive important administrative details had been left to the deans' secretaries, who separated applicant folders according to category of preference. Now ZAMP technical secretaries took over these tasks and "through self-sacrificing work contributed significantly to the improvement of the action."[54] The technical secretaries also cut down on corruption in the admissions process by personally presenting admissions folders to examining commissions.[55]

Youth functionaries also guaranteed a radical pursuit of PZPR policy when they sat in the examination commissions, because they did not have the inhibitions of the older generation. Adult trade- or peasant-union representatives who lacked education tended to defer to university experts, and those with education tended to feel solidarity with former teachers. The previous year a functionary had criticized the tendency "to choose [as delegates] only physicians in the medical, dental, and pharmaceutical faculties. This was, of course, entirely disadvantageous. It contributed to a weakening of class vigilance."[56] The work of ZAMP secretaries was local evidence of a more general phenomenon: that the most enthusiastic functionaries were young.

High school graduates of 1949 had to submit certifications of social origin issued by their schools, as well as certifications of "social work" issued by local ZMP headquarters and confirmed by the ZMP district (*powiat*) committees. "Social work" usually meant little more than holding a titular position (like "treasurer") in a "mass" organization. Candidates also had to present a certificate from their school on academic "aptitude." Poland's education authorities were trying to get a sense of academic promise among the entering class, because they wanted to recognize as few reasons as possible to exclude worker-peasant children.[57]

Through this new system top functionaries hoped to pinpoint agencies that were issuing inaccurate certifications. Włodzimierz Michajłów, director of the Higher-Education Department in the Ministry of Education, complained that several years earlier he had not been able to find the person in the peasants union who issued a certification to the daughter of Count Potocki, but now, if a similar situation occurred, "having an address" he could go directly to the responsible school director "and hit him full force." [58] The Party had crafted an organizational network that could be reactivated according to need. For example, at a discussion of the executive of the Warsaw PZPR Committee on 16 August 1949 a Comrade Perelmutter mentioned an impending "inspection" of Warsaw's schools in connection with "reservations regarding the truthfulness of school certifications." [59]

The admissions guidelines also contained a number of improvements, above all a system of ranking, with strict limits on unwanted applicants. Three categories were introduced: Group I consisted of "children of workers, small and medium peasants"; and Group II of "working intelligentsia" who themselves had participated in "social work" or were orphans of people who died in the war or at the hands of the anti-Communist underground (though no specific guidelines were given, "small" peasants were understood to have less than five hectares, and "medium" between five and ten hectares of land);[60] Group III included anyone else and could not exceed 15 percent of the total. Within each group candidates were ranked according to results on the entrance examination. All applicants from the first two categories with satisfactory results had to be admitted before those of the third could be considered. Central authorities hesitated to give strict rules on how small the last category could become, and warned only against eliminating it completely. That would be a "leftist distortion."

On 23 August 1949 Michajłów told a meeting of PZPR members of Warsaw examining commissions "it is necessary to use tactics that expressly privilege this group [Group I]. Their academic preparation can be somewhat weaker. This group will be examined separately, before all others. We will use different criteria for it than for the other groups, so that in principle every candidate with satisfactory scores belonging to this group should wind up in the freshman class." Applicants from the third group had to be exceptional: "if we permit a certain percentage of youth from this group to attend university, then they must be academically first-class and you have to examine them very carefully." Michajłów instructed the examination commission members to mix the applicant files, so that non-Communists could not tell when a certain group was being examined: "I believe that hiding these things from the outside world should be relatively easy." [61] Yet a Comrade Bermanowa objected to this secretive process, because "our professors have access to our files." After professors had decoded the manipulation, "embitterment among youth" would result.

Kazimierz Petrusewicz, the Central Committee functionary in charge of higher education, anticipated problems as well: "There will be ferment, dissatisfaction, etc. That's tough [*trudno*]. This is an expression of class war at the university." One of the "most delicate issues" was the need to use examinations in order not only to conduct class war, but also to make sure that students not oversubscribe politically less desirable subjects: "Comrades, now I would like to move on to one of the most delicate issues. . . . [We have] one hundred candidates for English, one hundred for history of art and three for Russian . . . with a maximum of 15 percent for Group III. This means that if there is more than 15 percent in Group III for English, then they will be dropped. Your task will be to 'flunk' them. . . . We do need people who know English, but we do not need our enemy to know English." The Party had to insure admittance of strong supporters and rejection of strong opponents:

> What do you need to watch out for in the course of the exam? You are going to have to take care of those students recommended by the Party. You cannot allow the sort of situation that we had last year, when someone on the commission held up a piece of paper and said: "No, the Secret Police [UB] won't let him in." That's not the way to do it. You cannot let him in, but you cannot say anything about it. You also cannot demonstratively take out recommendations written by the Party. This does not mean that you cannot have various pieces of paper lying in front of you. But you may not say: "Excuse me, there's no reason to examine him because he's recommended by the Party and he's in." Instead you have to do it like this: you have to remember who these people are, and if they are really deserving and meet expectations, then you have to force them through.[62]

Three faculties were accorded special consideration in admissions: the foreign trade and diplomatic faculties of the Academy of Political Sciences in Warsaw, and the aeronautics faculties at the technical higher schools. Petrusewicz told his comrades of the heightened vigilance needed when selecting applicants for these faculties: "We are well aware what the graduates of these schools will do when they're finished. They will be flying; their profession will be to fly to other countries. They will have the possibility of escaping by airplane. Their work, their service will take place abroad. Here no candidate who has relatives abroad may be accepted and there is absolutely no reason to educate such a person."[63]

Of 33,869 applicants, 39 percent had been assigned to Group I, 27 percent to Group II, and 26 percent to Group III. Of the 22,438 accepted, 57 percent were from Group I, 31 percent Group II, and 12 percent Group III.[64] Of the accepted students, 3,359 (15.0 percent) were graduates of the "introductory year."[65] Despite continuing difficulties with documentation, the Party had improved universities' class composition significantly. In all of Poland 83.1 percent of all Group I applicants gained admission, compared with 68.8 percent of Group II and 34.7 percent of Group III applicants. Accepted were

83.9 percent of the applicants labeled "physical workers" and 78.8 percent of the "small peasants," compared with 59.9 percent of the "intellectual wage earners" and 39.9 percent of the "independents."[66]

Efforts at sifting candidates were matched by a program of early recruitment. At the Party cell level, special three-person commissions (*trójki*) had begun identifying the "most valuable" students in the early summer, as well as those who could be admitted under no circumstances. These commissions did not fully develop their potential that first year, however. Those in Warsaw were judged deficient because they "limited themselves to negative selection" and managed to recommend only several dozen candidates.[67] In the Łódź voivodeship the *trójki* were said to have worked "well enough," though in three areas the recommendations were "superficial."[68] In the city of Lublin the *trójki* hardly developed any independent activity and contented themselves with writing up recommendations based on materials from police files and doorkeepers' hearsay.[69]

The PZPR organizations liberally shared recruiting work with the ZAMP and ZMP. The ZAMP in Gliwice began visits to high schools in April 1949, speaking to more than 3,000 high school students and distributing 1,300 applications for preexamination prep courses. Radio, press, and poster propaganda were used to popularize the action, but this was done "in a dry form, without ideological accents," as a Party reporter ruefully noted. A total of 980 students enrolled in these courses.[70] Reports from a recruiting drive in Lublin several years later cast light on the range of methods used during such "actions":

> A weeklong plan of recruiting was mapped out for the employees of the state railways in Lublin. The basic organization of the ZMP activated 11 agitators, and megaphones were used at the train station and on plant grounds. The area was adorned with slogans and propaganda. As a result of this effort six people signed up. In the Lublin tractor factory recruiting takes place by way of individual conversations, slogans, and fliers. . . .
>
> Most difficult to recruit are young people working in construction. These are village youths with poor academic training, who are interested primarily in making good money.

In general, the recruiting of young people in the villages was "very poor."[71]

Differences and Similarities in East German and Polish Practices

All that remained after the breakthrough of 1949–50 in Poland, it would have seemed, was to improve existing mechanisms. Representatives of the Party now controlled three critical junctions in the university admissions apparatus: the local recruiting commissions, the offices of technical secretaries, and the admissions boards at universities.[72] Non-Party professors felt so powerless at the last institution that they often ostentatiously doodled during proceedings, or purposely agreed with every decision, in order to show that they had no real voice.[73]

Very soon, however, Polish Party officials began to dismantle this constrictive system, fearing it might endanger plan fulfillment. As early as 1950 exceptions were being made for children of the "working intelligentsia," in particular schoolteachers, whose cooperation was considered essential for the state plan. Instructions were given to advance children from such households to Group I if their parents were "important for production and politically valuable."[74] In June 1952 the PZPR leadership decided to "gradually limit the number of students admitted to worker courses."[75] In 1954 Party leaders attributed their failure to fulfill the Six-Year Plan in part to the poor skills of university graduates.[76] Relying heavily on the assessment of the universities, which had always viewed worker education with some suspicion, the Party leadership concluded that high dropout rates and declining performance of students were due to preferences in student admissions based upon social background, and these, as well as worker preparation courses, were now undone.[77] At this point the "two-step" system of studies—probably the main reason for universities' diminishing output—was also abolished, and students returned to the traditional five-year master's degree.

In East Germany the state adhered to its agenda of transforming the student body socially through the 1950s, though it also made some corrections for the sake of plan fulfillment.[78] For example, from 1951–52, children of the "working intelligentsia," as well as children of members of the "intelligentsia who have shown special service," were supposed to be treated favorably in student admissions.[79] A more significant shift in favor of student "performance" occurred in the 1958–59 school year, when the Seven-Year Plan dictated increases in numbers of students across the board. Yet, even then, social origin remained a central consideration in university admissions.[80]

Despite such differing long-term trajectories, the stories of Polish and East German student recruitment show important parallels into the mid-1950s. Each Party leadership had attempted to mobilize its apparatus from top to bottom and involved significant elements of the "transmission belts"—that is, the youth organizations, veterans' organizations, and trade unions. The organizational forms in each case were comparable. Initially both Parties put stock in worker preparation faculties; yet, upon discovering that these faculties required time to make a difference, they concentrated on the committees that decided standard university admissions. These two methods of promoting worker studies reinforced each other: recruiting committees could agitate at factories for both options. In East Germany as well as in Poland there was support from below for the Party's goals, though more exclusively from the youth organization in the Polish case. In both places it proved easier to recruit working-class than peasant youths; and in both places a hierarchy emerged within the group "worker-peasant": at the top people from large factories, and at the bottom small and medium farmers.[81]

In neither place was deeper consideration given to the relation between social class and political consciousness. Functionaries may have interpreted reality through the lens of class, but that lens polarized their vision. The "proletarian family" was seen as a unique school of toughness, obedience, modesty, and hatred. Students of white-collar background, by contrast, were thought at best able to simulate Marxist-Leninist consciousness. They had been reared in intellectual arrogance, and fell easy prey to "doubts" (*Schwankungen*).[82] When there were political difficulties at universities, functionaries reflexively sought explanations in the "bourgeois" background of the students involved. To say the least, these schemata ignored students' personalities. Sociologist Nina Assorodobraj took note of this fact in a 1947 critique of the preparatory courses:

> Although the channels leading to the preparatory course were political and social organizations, and the recruiting bases were factories and village centers, these facts alone do not suffice to classify youth from a social point of view. A worker or peasant background may sociologically imply various processes and various phenomena, not to mention the fact that such a shorthand depiction, in light of the far-reaching differentiation that has occurred among the workers as well as the peasants, is almost devoid of content. Especially after war and occupation, and in a time of deep structural and governmental changes of which we are witnesses in Poland, it is necessary to ascertain that youth of all strata are for us an unknown quantity.[83]

Few functionaries were as thoughtful as Assorodobraj; for them this was a time for achieving measurable results. Anton Ackermann once compared the plan for enrolling worker students to the plan for potatoes, only that, as one SED wit added, "they don't grow as fast."[84]

Physicist Robert Rompe, in charge of the Higher-Education Department of the DVV, unintentionally revealed his inability to scratch the surface of social identity in a speech to functionaries in November 1947. He instructed them that bourgeois influence was "a question of life-style, a pure superficiality [*Ausserlichkeit*], which can become dangerous for many people of the worker and peasant classes who are ideologically not very secure."[85] Ideology meant loyalty and was judged precisely by superficialities: catechismal knowledge of a few "classic" texts, the willingness to wear certain emblems and pins, the forsaking of "Western" styles. Young people who rejected "official reality" became passionate devotees of "superficialities."

Those in Poland who projected their disaffection through slicked-back hair (*mandolina*), tight-fitting trousers, and wide, decorated ties (*krawatto*) were called *bikiniarzy*. One important task of the state admissions committees was to keep such people—referred to simply as "enemies" in Polish Party correspondence—off of university premises, regardless of social class.

East German functionaries' methods of ascertaining loyalty may have been tied to superficialities, but their ideal for students was not simple. They attempted to overcome the tension between demands for political loyalty and particular class background by synthesizing the two. The thinking went as follows: the majority of students would be class conscious because they would be taken from worker and peasant households. Yet in order to make sure that their class consciousness was properly activated in a political sense, worker and peasant students had to be attached to organizations that could "school" them.[86] These organizations, especially the SED, would assume the "leading role" at universities and protect students from remaining "bourgeois" influences. However, worker and peasant students had to demonstrate their potential to be properly schooled long before they arrived at the gates to universities. This was accomplished by an elaborate system of cadre evaluations that began in childhood.

The selection of worker-peasant students therefore had a social *and* a political component. On the one hand the SED endeavored to establish precise understandings of "worker-peasant," and on the other it caused its apparatus to sift candidates for the university as if they were entering the Party itself. Among students there was a small elite consisting of the graduates of worker-peasant faculties (ABFs), who were chosen even more carefully. The ABFs reveal a third component to the SED's ideal student beyond social origin and political allegiance: he or she had to be technically competent. For that reason, ABF instruction was extended to three years in 1949, longer than in any other place, including the Soviet Union. Evidence that East German higher education indeed produced competence was the success of East German engineers in landing jobs in western industry.

Guidelines from 1949 for establishing social background took into account the changes wrought by the German war economy and moved back the cutoff year for membership in the working class. In 1942 the National Socialists had supposedly inducted large numbers of nonworkers into the worker population. As a worker was therefore counted "anyone who was employed as an unskilled, semiskilled, or skilled laborer before 1942; and as a worker's child, those whose father or mother was employed before 1942 as workers." Because of perennial difficulties in attracting people from the countryside, the amount of land one could possess to qualify as a "working peasant" was moved up from ten to fifteen hectares; it would later increase to twenty.[87]

In the case of non-Communists, the enforcement of these guidelines was strict.[88] Children of leading functionaries, however, were considered workers per definition. Political consciousness may have been difficult to teach in schools, but it could be inherited. In the view of SED functionaries, working-class culture reproduced itself through the family. In 1949, Anton Ackermann explained his own situation: "I have been out of the factory since 1929 but still belong to the working class, and if I had a son or daughter old enough for university studies I would demand that my children be counted as workers' children; a Party functionary who has an official position in the Party or administration is a functionary of his class and belongs in the first instance to this class." Similarly, those supporters of the Communist Party who occupied the "transitional occupations" between workers and technical intelligentsia were judged on a case-by-case basis.[89] "Worker" was never apolitical. Those who revealed muddled class consciousness by going to church or criticizing the SED might be retroactively categorized as "nonworkers" or "supposed workers."[90] The point, again in Ackermann's words, was not simply to get workers and peasants, but to get the "right workers and peasants."[91] This was a level of dialectics not reached by Polish or Czech comrades.

From the 1949–50 recruiting drive, no one was accepted to a university in the GDR who was not approved by the district organization of the SED (via the district education office). According to Anton Ackermann, the point was to make sure that "we are dealing with a suitable applicant, with someone who inwardly in his entire worldview and political attitude belongs to us and stands definitely on our side."[92] The district organizations depended upon detailed opinions produced by the Party organizations of the high schools, who supposedly "knew" the candidates best.

The highest category of "worker-peasant" was the graduate of a worker-peasant faculty. In May 1949 Ackermann proclaimed selection to the worker-peasant faculties equivalent to the selection to a Party school. Students of these faculties would constitute a "Party contingent" (*Parteiaufgebot*): "This Party contingent of worker and peasant students, of which we should not speak much or, better, not speak at all in public, but which will have to be pushed even more vigorously, creates a lot of work, and in order to avoid this work people have made things easy for themselves and approved everyone who applied. The result was that last year and this year a very large part of the students who came to universities, whom we had supported and promoted, are not our people . . . and, as is well known, people decide everything."[93]

Because of its weakness in Polish society, the PZPR never developed such ambitions for its worker preparatory students. The Party was no more popular among students than among the population in general; by 1953 barely 9 percent of Polish students were PZPR members, and by 1958 that total declined to 2.5 percent.[94] When PZPR functionaries used the expression "our people," it had a monodimensional political aspect, that is, members of the Party. Students were students. In selection to workers' courses, the emphasis was upon socioeconomic origin, and recruiting committees cast their nets wide, hoping to pull in every applicant from factory and village who was not directly compromised by association with the underground. In East Germany, by contrast, candidates for worker-peasant faculties were "delegated" to the ABF by Party organization or trade-union cell, and then could submit an application.[95] That is, they were taken into the courses by invitation only.

There were no specific definitions of "workers" and "peasants" in Poland. Yet if these categories were less politicized than in East Germany, they were not apolitical. Precisely because Poles were relatively unwilling to give evidence of loyalty through organizational membership, the state attempted to read political consciousness through the lens of class.

The work of a recruiting commission (*trójka*) in the town of Opatów (Kielce) in 1949 gives an idea of how Polish state agencies understood the relation between class and political loyalty. The commission gave positive recommendations to all candidates with less than 4 hectares of farmland who belonged to the ZMP.[96] A girl whose father had 15 hectares was not recommended though she belonged to the ZMP. But a boy with 15 hectares, who was in the ZMP and "positively disposed ideologically" was recommended "with reservations." Two candidates with 9 hectares and not in the ZMP were not approved for studies. They were "negatively disposed to present reality [and] do not deserve consideration for admittance to university." But there were also cases in which passive members of the ZMP were endorsed because of their "classness" (*klasowość*). One such candidate, from a family with 2.8 hectares of land, "does not take active part in social-political work, has a reserved attitude toward the present system, but does not actively show this — he is secretive. May be accepted into a higher school due to his classness."[97]

The more proletarian Polish high school students seemed, the less important were explicit declarations of loyalty. For the less proletarian, however, nominal membership in the youth organization was not enough for admission to university. To succeed, they had to be active in a "politically positive sense." Given the Party's weak presence at Polish universities, the ultimate logic of such a system was to make the upper bourgeoisie the most, and the small peasantry the least politically supportive element of the student population. It was precisely awareness of such a danger that caused the SED to maintain a high political threshold for entering and for graduating from universities, even for the most impoverished workers. In Anton Ackermann's estimation, class betrayal was the greatest potential danger of student admissions policies. If freed from the Party's embrace, "these young people who have gone to university from among us, who come from our ranks, [will] become not our helpers and comrades, but our enemies, whom we will then have to fight." [98]

Like East German counterparts, Polish functionaries projected a vague understanding that both healthy class instincts as well as hostility to socialism could be transmitted from parent to child. As in East Germany, children of Party functionaries were redefined as workers. One recommended "worker" in Opatów was the daughter of an "intellectual worker for the railroad. The father is a member of the PZPR, and carries out the function of secretary of a basic cell." [99] For those who came from households with a "hostile inclination" toward "present reality," considerations of socioeconomic status were likewise all but irrelevant. Most serious were cases of people who were known for, or whose relatives were known for, activity in the antiregime underground.[100] The treatment of such individuals paralleled the SED's early policies toward family members of former Nazis: they were considered to come from contaminated environments.

Opposition to Worker Education

Widespread awareness of political favoritism and inconsistent application of categories of social class combined with middle-class fears of downward social mobility to produce resistance to the new admissions policies, especially in the early postwar years.[101] Yet the contexts for opposition differed markedly in the two societies. The SED was more determined than the PZPR to introduce large numbers of working-class and Communist students into university premises, and the East German political landscape also offered more opportunities for universities to express dissatisfaction with state policy. Until early 1948, free student elections were held that were unknown in Poland, where explicitly political organizations were forbidden at universities. Because of its unpopularity in Polish society and among students in particular, the Polish Party did not attempt a massive introduction of Communists into the university student body. East German conditions therefore both produced more political tensions and offered more occasions for their public manifestation. The background to these differing contexts was ideological: Poland was supposedly foremost among the "people's democracies," while in East Germany considerations of a still-open German question required a multiparty facade.[102]

What most troubled the anti-Communist opposition in East Germany was the way that new admissions procedures seemed to reinforce habits learned under the Nazis—in particular, political opportunism. According to the stipulations of a June 1946 rectors' conference,[103] admissions committees could inquire into students' pre-1945 but also into their post-1945 political involvement. In a meeting of the university senate in the summer of 1946 Leipzig's rector Hans-Georg Gadamer called a proposed written examination on a contemporary political topic a "test of basic convictions" (*Gesinnungsprüfung*), "which offered advantages to students with greater abilities to adapt themselves [*Anpassungsfähigkeit*] but of weaker character."[104] Professor Theodor Litt, of the philosophical faculty, remarked that the authorities were "recommending the same thing that the National Socialists used to demand." Litt had been forced into retirement in 1937 among other things for publicly criticizing Nazi ideologist Alfred Rosenberg.[105] In August 1947 Gadamer claimed that most applicants could present proof that they were "party functionaries." Student representative Wolfgang Natonek agreed: students knew very well which parties gave out certifications, and acted accordingly. The senate voted to condemn "this method of proving basic democratic convictions."[106]

Gadamer, Litt, and other colleagues left that same year for the West, but the embattled student leaders stayed behind. As has been mentioned, they also represented the interests of middle-class students who were fearful of social marginalization, and often insinuated that worker students were unfit for university study. With the founding of a Free University in West Berlin by East German student leaders, and the arrest of their colleagues elsewhere in the Soviet zone, opposition to worker studies was pushed into the underground, however. The arrested liberal students were, perhaps ironically, the last vocal defenders of the traditional German university in the East.

In Poland worker students similarly attracted disbelief: how could people who had completed only grammar school attend university? They were taunted as "double-zeros" (*dwuzerowcy*) and refused the companionship of the more privileged. Students who had reached university via high school drew little sketches on cafeteria tables of the worker students: sitting on a night pot practicing their ABCs, standing in front of the blackboard multiplying $2 \times 2 = 5$; in one place someone had made a drawing of a worker student with an obtuse expression on his face, and a hole in his oversized head.[107] The rector of Warsaw Polytechnic spoke for many of his colleagues when he described worker preparation courses as "completely irrational."[108] Sociologist Józef Chałasiński agreed, arguing that workers could not adapt to traditional styles of learning.[109] As in East Germany, such suspicions may have driven some students closer to the Party: worker course students in Łódź belonged to the Communist Party two to three times more frequently than students in general, though that figure declined in the early 1950s.[110]

Available evidence suggests that worker students performed about average, however, if somewhat worse in the hard sciences. In mid-1947 professors of Leipzig's law faculty told investigators from the DVV that the difference between worker students and students with *Abitur* was not great, because on the one hand worker students were diligent and on the other the *Abitur* had lost value during the Nazi period.[111] By the mid-1950s worker students in Leipzig were outperforming nonworker students in a number of subjects, including medicine.[112] Likewise the performance of Polish worker students did not differ greatly from that of high school graduates.[113] The dropout rates of the two groups were similar (see Table 12-4). The courses themselves had a better success rate than high schools. From 1947 to 1956 an average of 62 per-

TABLE 12-4

Percentage of Freshmen Completing Studies,
Łódź University and Polytechnic, 1947–50

	High School Graduates		Worker-Course Graduates	
	Percentage	*Absolute*	*Percentage*	*Absolute*
Humanities	49.8	561/1,126	48.6	35/72
Law	30.6	515/1,682	40.5	45/111
Medicine	69.0	970/1,407	55.0	55/100
Polytechnic	67.1	698/1,041	50.0	28/56

Source: Wójcik, "Przebieg," 175.

cent of those starting the courses completed them, compared with 56 percent of the students beginning high school in the eighth grade.[114]

Part of the reason for worker students' poorer performance in the hard sciences was a selection mechanism that did not always take account of their aptitude and training.[115] Forcing many years of study into a few months also took a toll on worker students' health: over fifty worker-peasant students at Humboldt University were reported to have suffered nervous breakdowns in early 1950.[116] Such strains were then aggravated by the shortening of vacation time to a few weeks in East Germany, or in Poland by the decrease in study time from five to three years in the wake of the "two-step studies" reform.

Compared with the East German scene, opposition to change in Poland was more implicit and structural. There were no bold pronouncements of university senates or student leaders against the new admissions regulations in the early postwar years, but rather dozens of discreet arrangements in university deans' offices, in local qualifying commissions, and among examiners, which for a time deadened the effects of ministerial instructions. This was a society practiced in conspiracy and in the deception of state officials. Only in Poland do reports surface of universities simply refusing cooperation with worker courses. Professors employed at the courses were "keen on telling [the students] that they won't make it, that they'll fail their examinations, that they should return to their factories." Students of the "intro-

ductory year" courses were not treated with respect by university administration, which believed that "students of the introductory year should be
satisfied that they get any living quarters at all; they may hence receive the
very worst, they may live a dozen and more to a room."[117] The only agency
willing to aid worker studies in Kraków in the early postwar period was the
army. A report filed in 1946 noted the following:

> KRAKÓW: The city is making work difficult. Very tough material con-
> ditions. Lecturers non-Party. No director of education. They received a
> dormitory in awful condition. They are renovating on their own, every-
> one does an hour a day. They are sleeping on the floor — 40 persons in
> one room. The army contributed straw mattresses.
>   Stipends a must. No one can get leave from work.
>   Financial problems, since products have to be bought on the free
> market.
>   In the dorm military discipline. Nothing decent to eat.[118]

Early opposition to new admissions procedures occasionally took the
form of graft and protectionism, affecting even the Party cadre. In 1947
a vice-voivode offered a 100,000-złoty bribe to a comrade on the selection commission, the ministry delegate, so that the daughter of a friend (a
cosmetic factory owner) would be accepted into the chemistry faculty in
Poznań. The bribe did not go off because its intended target had been in a
"state of intoxication." The Party delegate from this place was subjected to
"constant pressure and threats." It seemed that every professor had a list of
candidates he wanted supported.[119] There were also reports in Poland of attempts to falsify social origins, by students taking advantage of the Party's
obsession with superficial signs of allegiance. In 1950 "sons and daughters of
merchants, kulaks, and prewar colonels came to the examinations in dirty
overalls" in order to give the impression that they were workers. Others came
dressed in freshly pressed uniforms of the ZMP, with decorations hanging
from their chests, but gave themselves away by "blessing themselves piously"
before entering the examination.[120]

Such incidents would have seemed surreal in East Germany and highlight
the cultural specificity of Poland, in particular the less serious attitude of
Poles toward the state. But gauging the impact of these incidents on the
social composition of students is difficult. If they are evidence of pervasive
efforts to camouflage social identity, they also suggest that by the late 1940s
the official organizations were finally detecting and frustrating such efforts.
Poland was not somehow condemned to organizational chaos; the wartime
underground state is sufficient evidence of that. The introduction of ideologically committed youths into the admissions process markedly improved

the ability of the central apparatus to direct the work of admissions commit-tees. Indeed, the ZMP and ZAMP constituted important if small submilieus in these years, with many dozens of dedicated functionaries, who unlike the overwhelming majority of Poles took the ideas of state socialism very seri-ously.[121]

Experts who have studied East German and Polish student admissions policies have pointed to a similar unreliability of figures on social back-ground for the early postwar years, perhaps as high as 10 percent in each case.[122] Yet data became more reliable as official channels of information began functioning more effectively, and Polish sociologists and historians routinely make use of statistics produced after 1950.[123] Critics have also pointed to the malleability of the category "worker-peasant," which in each case was heavily weighted toward workers, but also included Party func-tionaries' children. These issues have not been studied closely in the Czech Republic, but there seems little reason to believe that Party statistics there were more or less accurate than in Poland or East Germany; in each place individuals, as well as the state and Party apparatus, had similar incentives to manipulate data and redefine Party functionaries as workers. Therefore gross figures of working-class and peasant students 15 to 20 percent lower than comparable data in Poland and East Germany *at the height of stalinism* invite careful consideration. Somehow the most popular Communist orga-nization in the region failed to make central will felt in admissions commit-tees throughout the land and, as a result, failed to create its own elite.

★

CHAPTER THIRTEEN

CZECH
AND
EAST
GERMAN
PECULIARITIES

One would have expected the most successful transformation of student bodies in the Czech lands, for this was the one place in the region studied where communism was carried to power by native forces. Like its Polish and East German counterparts, the Czechoslovak Communist leadership proclaimed the need to enroll worker students at universities and asserted the universal validity of Soviet experience. At the Ninth KSČ Party Congress, Party boss Klement Gottwald seemed to take his script from Stalin. The Soviet leader had said in June 1931 that "the working class must create its own productive-technical intelligentsia," and eighteen years later his Czech counterpart announced that "the working people must create and educate its own intelligentsia."[1] At the same time KSČ general secretary Rudolf Slánský was championing a strategy for seizing power in higher education that might have inspired any East European Communist leadership: "We will now regulate the selection of students to high schools and especially to universities and higher technical schools. We will mercilessly purge high schools and higher schools of reactionary students and we will be at pains to recruit the majority of students for high and higher schools from workers' families and families of the laboring strata. The working class is the most numerous, and the governing class and the social composition of students must reflect this."[2] In retrospect, KSČ student leader and later reform Communist Jiří Pelikán proclaimed the goals of 1948 "largely correct" because he and his comrades attempted to "democratize universities, which had always lagged behind the development of our country, having admitted only 6 percent working-class children."[3]

The events of the years 1948 and 1949 seemed to reveal a determination to achieve these goals. In February 1948 the Communist leadership unleashed "action committees" to seize power throughout Czech society. At universities the action committees were placed in the hands of Communist students, who had been particularly numerous in the philosophical faculty, and they promptly dismissed dozens of professors.

One year later, verification commissions, again led by young Communists, dismissed thousands of students. These purges were presented to the public as an "academic evaluation" (*studijní provĕrka*) meant to get rid of slackers. Actually the aim was political: during oral examinations conducted by their peers, students were made to comment on "questions of general daily politics . . . as a statement that they are convinced of the rightness of our policies."[4] An internal memorandum explained: "The commissions will expel remaining reactionary elements from the fifth, sixth, and seventh classes of high schools, from the first and second years of advanced vocational schools, and from higher schools. It will further expel students who are unfit because of their social origin and environment."[5]

Who were reactionaries? Later sociologist P. Machonin, a leading figure in the student council, described them as "loafers, golden youth, nihilists, and basic enemies of honest work, incompetents and people socially irresponsible." The strongest force behind the purging was resentment of the wealthy and successful, and thus any adjustment to social origin was at best random. An early report even complained of "frivolous evaluations of students with greater wealth. Sometimes expulsions took place mechanically, even turning against the middle classes."[6] The political interrogations of student by student could eliminate even members of the Party and workers, as occurred in Prague's medical faculty. The "class" hatreds unleashed in this supposedly academic evaluation cut down hundreds of the brightest students: purgers had to contend with the "significant problem in the academic screening of eliminating reactionaries who are satisfactory academically."[7]

Expelled students numbered 8,608 in the Czech lands, or 21.7 percent of those enrolled in the academic year 1948–49.[8] Figures were higher in the law and medical faculties, approaching one-half in the former. Expelled students were subsequently made to "work": "The entire propaganda campaign will present the action to the public as one of freeing up hidden labor reserves from higher schools for the Five-Year Plan."[9] Ex-students were told to report to the ministries of education and social welfare for future employment,[10] chiefly in mining, energy, iron and steel, chemicals, construction, textiles, production of building materials, ceramics, and agriculture. Whoever did not accept these offers was assigned a job according to a decree on forced labor from 1945.[11] Some of the strongest exponents of "reactionary" thinking found "work" in uranium mines near Jáchymov in Northern Bohemia, and many of the male students were inducted into the army.

In a memoir written in the 1970s Pelikán justified the purging of students after February 1948 as an attempt to remove "collaborators": "I need to remind the reader that, after closing Czech universities in 1939, the Nazis arrested thousands of students, shot their leaders and then offered some students the possibility of studying at German universities. Although the Czechoslovak government in exile advised them not to do this, several thousand of them matriculated in Germany, and after the war we were against letting them continue studying in Czechoslovakia."[12] Little of Pelikán's justification — offered in a section of memoir entitled "my own responsibility" — works. The Nazis did not arrest thousands of students, the students shot were not their leaders, the offer to study in Germany was not massively accepted until deep in the war, and at most a few hundred students actually matriculated. Most important, archival documents belie Pelikán's justification for the purges: neither were purging committees of 1949 instructed to ferret out collaborators, nor did they report doing so. As suggested earlier, the issue was supposedly "class struggle."[13] In any case, it is unlikely that many of those who volunteered to study in Germany in 1942 were still studying in the Czech lands in 1949, or that the records were complete enough to identify those that had.[14] With few exceptions, the expelled were not permitted back to higher schools.

Yet if the purging was indeed a reflection of class struggle, one is surprised to find so little mention of social class in assessments of this event two to three years later. A March 1951 report for the KSČ Central Committee recalled that its "purpose was to cleanse higher schools of reactionary, politically unreliable elements among the students and those who abused studies either by not studying at all or by falling behind in studies without important reason."[15] In other words, Communists in Czechoslovakia shared with their comrades in Poland and East Germany an unexamined assumption about the relation between social background and political consciousness: by definition, "reactionaries" originated in the bourgeoisie. Vigilant KSČ officials continued filing reports in the years to come of "sons and daughters of kulaks or the wealthy middle-classes" who had slipped through.[16]

The "academic evaluation" had no parallel in East Germany or Poland. In these countries purges were limited and sporadic.[17] Yet the KSČ failed to devote the same energy to assembling a new elite as it had to disassembling the old: having made students workers, it then neglected to make workers students. The results of this failure became apparent after Khrushchev's destalinization. In April 1957 the cultural journal *Tvorba* wondered how Czech university students could so easily be "swayed" by "hostile" arguments, as they had during antiregime demonstrations that occurred the previous year. The "answer" was not difficult to find. Class composition of students, especially at the ideologically important faculties, had not been fundamentally changed. Only 24 percent of the students of the six arts and science faculties of Charles University were of worker background, and 6 percent were of peasant background. And even these numbers were declining: in the law faculty, for example, 38 percent of sophomores were of working-class background, but only 28 percent of the freshmen.[18] The problem went beyond Charles University: in the Czech Lands, the number of worker and peasant students never approached half the student body (see Table 13-1). In what sociologists later identified as "restratification," numbers of worker-peasant

TABLE 13-1

Worker and Peasant Students at Czech,
East German, and Polish Universities

	Czech Lands (Student Body)	East Germany (Student Body)	Poland (Freshmen)	Poland (Graduates)
1945–46		10.1		
1946–47	18.4			
1947–48	18.0	16.8	41.7	
1949–50		34.0	45.6	
1950–51	36.8	38.6	62.2	
1951–52		41.0	59.9	
1952–53		45.4	59.4	
1953–54	37.3		57.8	58.9
1955–56	37.0	54.8	53.9	56.9
1956–57	38.4	56.6	48.5	56.4
1958–59	41.5	57.7	44.7	54.2
1960–61	37.8	56.0	44.5	53.4

Sources: Stallmann, *Hochschulzugang,* 305–7; *Statistická ročenka Republiky Československé 1957,* 238; *Statistická ročenka Československé Socialistické Republiky 1960, 1962,* 426, 419; SÚA, ÚPV 1110, Č. 211894/48; ÚPV 2481; AÚV KSČ, f. 100/1, a.j. 1155, l. 117; *Statystyka Szkolnictwa* (August 1966): 40; AAN, MO 2869, k. 47–50; MSW 17, k. 91–92.

students declined throughout East Central Europe from the late 1950s, but their representation remained relatively poorest in Czechoslovakia.[19]

What had gone wrong? Why had Rudolf Slánský's pledge not been fulfilled? On the surface, the KSČ did everything that its fraternal parties had done: established preferences for children of working-class background, set up special faculties to give them remedial education, attempted to involve subordinate organizations in vetting and recruiting workers. Yet these measures failed to produce adequate results.

Planning

Czech Communists did not anticipate the problems to come, because they believed in the efficacy of central planning. In fact, the crucial decisions in student admissions policy at the turning point of 1948–49 were made by planners. Between the years 1948 and 1953, officials of the State Planning Office, the Ministry of Education, and the KSČ Central Committee assumed responsibility for coordinating the output of education with the projected needs of the economy. Yet they proved consistently unable to think in the long term across several economic sectors and left themselves almost no

TABLE 13-2

Numbers of Full-Time Students in Higher Education

Year	Total	Per 10,000 of Population
East Germany		
1949	28,500	15.1
1956	85,725	48.9
1966	106,422	62.3
Poland		
1949–50	115,532	46.9
1954–55	143,305	53.1
1957–58	129,045	45.2
Czech Lands		
1949	39,871	44.8
1956	64,016	67.5

Sources: Usko, *Hochschulen*, 32; *Rocznik statystyczny 1958*, 403; *Statistická ročenka Republiky Československé 1957*.

margin for error. They thus put themselves at the mercy of Czech society: if workers did not embrace the new opportunities offered for higher education, the plan for creating a new intelligentsia would not be realized.

Educational planning was not a completely new art; planning offices inherited not only much of the staff, but also many of the concerns of the pre-1948 period. Universities of the first postwar years had seemed overcrowded, and educational planners feared oversupply. Indeed the Czech lands had a high per capita student body, even after the expulsions (see Table 13-2).

State planners projected a glut of university graduates. The Five-Year Plan called for 4,150 physicians, yet there were still 9,722 medical students; it called for 4,436 teachers, and there were 10,503 students at arts, science, and education faculties; it called for 200 veterinarians, and 1,125 students were studying veterinary medicine; it called for 4,535 chemical, mechanical, and electrical engineers, but 8,356 students were preparing for these professions.[20]

After the education reform of 1948, all children attended five years of elementary and four years of middle school. They then chose either to terminate their formal education at a vocational school (*základní odborné školy*) or to continue at a competitive high school, some of which gave the diploma (*maturita*) that qualified for higher education. The schools that could lead directly to higher education (*vyšší střední školy*) were divided into two types: vocational high schools (*vyšší odborné školy*) and classical high schools (*gymnázia*). Both had four-year programs.[21] Planners interested either in increasing the numbers of workers in higher education or in reducing total numbers of postsecondary students had to concentrate on admissions to these schools.

In December 1948 representatives of various ministries agreed unanimously that the numbers of students at competitive high schools far exceeded the need.[22] Therefore admissions to these schools were strictly limited in the 1949–50 school year. Responsible for high school admissions were commissions consisting of high school directors and teachers, the Union of Czechoslovak Socialist Youth (ČSM), and "people's" (i.e., state) administration. However, these commissions were not instructed to sift the applicant pool carefully by social class, and of the 6,522 *gymnázia* freshmen in the 1949–50 school year, 34.3 percent came from workers' and 12.2 percent from small peasants' families, and 34.2 percent from officials' families. KSČ officials expressed satisfaction with these results because "percentagewise in the First Republic the children of workers approached 4 percent, as did the percentage of children of small peasants." [23]

Perhaps this early "success" encouraged complacency, because the KSČ leadership did not introduce strict quotas by social origin. Representation of worker students at high schools changed little in the early 1950s. The entering class of high school students in 1950–51 consisted of 28.5 percent working class and 38.5 percent officials' children. Results were worst in Prague, where school classes consisted of 23.9 percent worker and 52.4 percent officials' children.[24] This was especially bad news, because authorities in the capital had experimented with an admissions scheme that assigned points according to social class. Extra points had been insufficient to offset the poorer academic preparation of workers' children.

Low numbers of workers among high school entrants translated into low numbers of workers among postsecondary students. From the start there was little room for selectivity. In 1949–50 there were 8,188 applications for 7,205 spots at institutions of higher education in the Czech lands. Slightly less than one-fifth (19.8 percent) of the freshmen came from worker families and 9.1 percent came from small- and medium-sized-farm families. The rest were offspring of officials and the independently employed.[25] In Poland and East Germany, by contrast, there were a third to a fourth more applicants than spots — even as the student populations rose.[26] In Poland and East Germany high school admissions had been adjusted, so that high schools produced more working-class and peasant candidates.[27]

The following year selectivity was supposed to improve. Officials were counting on 9,750 high school graduates for about 5,000 spots.[28] Decisions on admission were made by faculty commissions appointed by the minister of education. They evaluated students according to class origin, political consciousness, knowledge of the subject, aptitude, and finally, quotas set by the Ministry of Education. Some steering of applicants to important subjects was attempted via a "day of the open door" at higher schools "according to the Soviet model," where high school students could see for themselves how higher schools worked.[29]

Yet students did not sign up in the requisite numbers. Relatively few candidates applied for law, and many that had "were not socially [třídně] or politically tolerable." By September 1950 the first year in law had been filled only by half.[30] Faculties of mechanical and electrical engineering also encountered severe difficulties in meeting their quotas, partly because teachers had failed to encourage applications to the polytechnic schools. Despite an extended recruiting schedule[31] only one-quarter of the entering class at universities came from workers' families. In technical higher education the figure was one-third.[32]

Failure to coordinate educational planning with other types of planning aggravated recruiting shortfalls. In 1951, planning for labor force development was still taking place on a year-to-year basis. In January the State Planning Office allocated 6,685 students to be accepted to higher schools in the fall, not including graduates of worker faculties. With 10,375 high school seniors, an oversupply of 3,500 applicants should have resulted, which would have enabled careful selection. But the need for army officers had not been considered when this plan was drawn up, and the army suddenly expressed a desire for half the male high school graduates. An emergency meeting was called with representatives of the State Planning Office and the Ministry of Defense, and the army was made to reduce its demands by more than half.[33] Nevertheless, few high school graduates could be rejected; all the planners could do was distribute those who passed the *maturita* among army, advanced teacher training institutes, and universities — all of which supposedly required high ideological maturity and class consciousness. If more than the usual amount failed the *maturita*, even the revised plan would not be met. Rather than universities selecting students, students would select universities.

By July shortfalls had become evident: 850 fewer students than needed had been "recommended" from their high schools.[34] Despite further recruiting, the plan could be fulfilled by only 64 percent in law, 74 percent in veterinary medicine, and 84.7 percent in the philosophical faculties. Results were better in mining and engineering.[35] Like East German and Polish counterparts of the same period, Czech students were "voting with their feet" for less ideologically sensitive subjects.[36] Economics, the University of Politics and Economics, architecture, and traditionally strong law were all undersubscribed.

The most sobering result of the very tight numbers was the low percentage of worker students enrolled. In September 1951, 41.9 percent of the university freshmen were of working-class origin.[37] Nevertheless, Central Committee functionary Luděk Holubec reported in November that recruiting had been a success: "In general" the plan had been fulfilled "quite well," even at technical schools, which had "relatively high numbers." But subsequent wording sounded like damage control: "There is no report yet about qualitative fulfillment, but it seems that the high numbers are not to the detriment of class composition, which will probably be about the same as last year."[38] The outlook for the future was not bright. In 1949 planners had been exercised about what seemed an overproduction of high school students. They were particularly concerned about a bulge of high school students in the fifth and sixth classes: 7,003 students in the fourth, but then 14,585 in the fifth, and 12,531 in the sixth classes.[39] In 1951, however, planners understood that when this bulge of "overproduction" disappeared, the plan would become unrealizable, for the number of high school (*gymnázia*) graduates would sink from 10,375 in 1951, to 5,583 in 1953, and 6,483 in 1954.[40]

The forced expansion of heavy industry along Soviet lines called for steadily higher quotas of postsecondary students, and that in turn called for a shortening of preuniversity education. In desperate imitation of Soviet models, the Czechoslovak school law of April 1953 shortened both middle and high school programs from four to three years, and lengthened university studies from four to five years. This change reduced university preparation from thirteen to eleven years, and was preceded by bitter debates within the leadership, with Żdeněk Nejedlý among the losers.[41] Planners expected an extra burst of university freshmen, because that year's high school juniors would simply skip their senior year right into university. The law nurtured hopes for greater selectivity in postsecondary admissions, and for the first time education authorities scheduled entrance examinations, with a partly political character. Yet, in matter of fact, these entrance examinations served to worsen the social composition of the student body, because examination boards tended to "overemphasize" academic ability.[42] Furthermore, the new graduates were of lower quality than in previous years, because high school seniors had been forced to do the work of an entire year in six-week summer crash courses.[43]

These early mistakes in planning bound Czech Communists' hands for several years. In February 1954 the minister of education Ladislav Štoll wrote chief of government Viliam Široký that

> In planning the training of university-educated experts for the years 1953–54, 1954–55, and 1955–56 the State Planning Office did not suf-ficiently consider the fact that a relatively small number of students would graduate from high schools in those years. As a result it will not be possible to reach the number planned. . . . it will be practically impossible to carry out any kind of selection, especially in the fields in which graduates show declining interest every year. This fact can-not remain without basic influence on the quality of the graduates of higher schools. Of a planned number of 11,390 first-year students in 1954–55, almost 4,000 will not be covered according to preliminary cal-culations.[44]

Selection was especially poor in law, economics, and the social sciences. As this letter shows, top state functionaries had become so concerned with meeting basic quotas that they no longer devoted attention to class composi-tion. At best, they hoped to guarantee that no one "politically objectionable" slipped through.[45]

Resistance of Sociocultural Milieus

A plan with so little room for error required full cooperation of its supposed beneficiaries, as well as of grass-roots Party organizations. Yet middle school students of working-class background continued to shun traditionally alien environments of the *gymnázia,* and KSČ district (*okres*) agencies charged with supervising the recruitment of these children into the new intelligentsia paid only halfhearted attention to high school admissions. Unlike counter-parts in Poland or East Germany, they almost entirely neglected the longer-term challenges of preparing workers for university studies.[46] Neither Party leadership nor ministry intervened decisively to change the local organiza-tions' priorities.[47]

The paths leading to higher education remained in the hands of the former middle classes, though not entirely by default: in keeping with inherited notions of "proper" career tracking, teachers, physicians, and parents sup-ported the choices of middle-class students to continue studies. They for their part continued to believe that the *maturita* gave them a right to attend university and consulted their teachers, and not the plan, about where and what to study.

KSČ *okres* organizations were supposed to determine the composition of examination commissions for competitive high school admissions, but in many places old networks persisted, and teachers still managed to secure places in high schools for preferred students. They acted as if oblivious to official guidelines specifying which students should be promoted. A September 1951 "control" visit by KSČ Central Committee functionaries to Hradec Králové discovered a teacher who "chose girls with the best standing and sent the rest away to more distant schools. She did not care about class relations and refused to accept the daughter of a shock-worker." A high school principal accepted candidates without first "checking on the decisions of the examination commissions." In the town of Trutnov two students were accepted to high school though they had not been officially recommended. The "director had simply arranged things by telephone with the director of the lower school where the students were taking their final examinations, and that director said he had no objections to the girls going to that school." [48]

Reports from Gottwaldov confirm that the Party had not penetrated the relationships between student, teacher, and parent, nor seriously challenged stereotypes about who should attend high school. Children's fate remained in the hands of teachers who claimed not even to know their social origin:

> Teachers think it a success when children resolutely enunciate their desire to go into industry. But they forget that these are children from workers' families, who have always had an inclination toward manual labor. On the other hand children of bourgeois families don't have this healthy instinct and see their objective only in studies at competitive high schools. Even now they make appeals to everyone imaginable if the district or regional examining commission decides they are supposed to go work in factories. The bourgeois disposition of the teachers is revealed above all in their failure to devote themselves persistently to the task of convincing parents and students of workers' background that they ought to go to university. Teachers always have plenty of excuses and apologies for children of bourgeois families, [saying] that they have the best aptitude. . . . some schools, especially in the Gottwaldov district, but also in other districts, did not have sufficient material on the background of the children. [49]

Rather than encourage a shift in traditional patterns of social dominance in higher education, the plan tended to bind Party functionaries' hands. If they acted too forcefully to increase working-class participation, they often jeopardized basic plan fulfillment. In one district people of the "wrong" class background were kept out of high school and the quota for high school freshmen was underfulfilled by half. [50]

Workers' reluctance to pioneer new career paths additionally complicated the KSČ's affirmative action agenda. In the Liberec region workers "had to be persuaded to keep their children in school, because they would have preferred to see their children start earning money right away"[51] In the 1951–52 school year university preparatory schools were the path least chosen by workers' children of the Brno region, but most chosen by officials' children.[52] A Party functionary from the mining town of Jáchymov wrote of a meeting at which parents had proclaimed that "no one is going to tell them where their children ought to go."[53] In Karlovy Vary parents likewise insisted that they "raised the children and will decide what happens to them."[54] Medical doctors contributed to the persistence of prerevolutionary thinking by automatically clearing workers' children for manual trades, while holding back bourgeois children. A doctor in Beroun found 47 percent of the children unsuitable for physical labor because they "can't take the noise."[55]

Because of the persistence of traditional notions about "proper" career choices *gymnázia* remained places where workers were likely to feel alien. Yet the dire need for high school graduates forced KSČ functionaries to make further concessions to children of middle-class background. A proposal passed in January 1952 stated:

> Last year's guidelines for taking students into competitive high schools directed attention to "getting students, who by their social and class origin, and their previous development give reason to believe that they will become an intelligentsia linked by class and ideal with the working class." Some commissions interpreted the selection guidelines poorly and acted mechanistically and formalistically in the examination of social and class origin. For this reason in the new draft the goal of the selection process has been reformulated. The goal is to ensure that "candidates make their way to high schools who have the best prerequisites for studies, and reason to believe that they will become an intelligentsia linked by class and ideal with the working class."[56]

As has been argued, this sort of compromise in the class struggle was not seen in Poland until after Stalin's death, or in East Germany until the late 1950s. And in both cases, measures to recruit workers to university had begun much earlier.

Attracting working-class candidates to competitive high schools remained an abiding problem in the Czech lands. The KSČ never allotted sufficient stipend money to allay workers' fears about loss of income,[57] and the quota for *gymnázia* could be filled only by half, with workers' children strongly underrepresented.[58] As in prerevolutionary times the great majority of *gymnázia* graduates went on to university.

Worker Preparation Faculties

If high schools would not produce enough working-class graduates, the logical step was to seek solutions beyond them. This indeed was the lesson of Soviet experience. The KSČ too set up faculties, known as the *dělnické kursy* (DKs), which were meant to prepare workers for university. Closer examination reveals, however, that here too Czech Communists failed to devote the resources necessary to make these courses work.

In his speech to the Central Committee in fall 1948 Rudolf Slánský vowed that the Party would not wait "many years before high schools and then universities train a new labor force from the working class. We must carry through several temporary and transitional measures in order to get gifted and class-conscious workers to higher schools."[59] By early December the Ministry of Education had drafted a plan to begin preparing one thousand "young workers" for postsecondary studies in early 1949.[60] Yet because of this hasty and late start, Czech Communists labored under misconceptions that counterparts elsewhere had already overcome. They thought it possible to train workers for university in a matter of months. So while their Polish comrades girded for two-year, and the East Germans for three-year courses (*Arbeiter- und Bauernfakultäten*), they were content with ten months of instruction.[61] Regional (*krajské*) KSČ cadre commissions took care of recruitment and selection for the first "run" of workers' courses. In factories they were aided by KSČ cells. The first class consisted of 826 students, of whom 83 percent were factory workers, and all Communist Party members.[62]

Instruction began in January 1949 in five small towns, including such out of the way locales as Velké Losiny u Šumperka and Hořečky u Frenštátu pod Radhoštěm. These places were as remote from university milieus as one could imagine. Instruction for future engineers was slanted heavily toward math and science, but students also received general education in history, Czech, and the social sciences. There were forty hours of instruction plus nineteen hours of exercises weekly. In addition an evaluatory session was held every evening, and four evenings a week were scheduled for cultural-political activities. In September 759 students took the *maturita* and 729 passed; 574 of them (78.7 percent) went into technical fields.

The graduates were appraised as "good" in mathematics and geometry; their skills in Czech orthography were likewise found to be "good," though many had problems with "coherent expression." More serious were the difficulties of a "moral-political" nature. The selection had taken place hurriedly and therefore "it was not possible to instruct factories to conduct a politically mature selection. The best workers were not sent because the factories did not wish to lose them." About 10 percent of the students were adjudged "politically immature,"[63] and many more were lacking in proper class consciousness: "In isolated cases it was clear that the students were not here for gaining knowledge, but rather for bettering their social standing."[64]

The second "run" of the courses in 1949 likewise suffered from a hasty selection process. Now local state administration assumed responsibility for choosing students, but received guidelines too late. This meant that the ministry did not have time to "control" the admissions materials. Courses were plagued by high dropout rates, and 320 (17.3 percent) students were unable to finish.[65] The work ethic of the course participants was described as "exemplary," although several expulsions occurred for stealing, "moral defects," and "Party transgressions." Because of the stresses resulting from squeezing years of preparation into several months, proposals soon emerged for extending the courses to two years: "The students are fighting desperately for time and their state of health is not satisfactory." There were reports of angina and jaundice, and two attempted suicides.[66] Yet because of concern to meet basic quotas for university freshmen, the KSČ Central Committee refused to lengthen the courses until their last "run" of 1953–54.[67]

The poorer political quality of students was attributed to their being "only" 75 percent KSČ members and 70 percent workers.[68] Students' political maturity was recorded as "very uneven." For that reason they had been assigned to "enlightenment seminars and shock-worker groups," which were supposed to be conducted by experienced comrades. There was much talk of the need to live in a collective: "In the second run of the courses collectives of students were successfully created everywhere but not always with equal speed and not in an entirely unified way."[69] Of the close to 1,900 students that began the second "run," 1,527 signed up for higher education.[70]

The selection process for the third "run" of worker courses also started late. Only in March 1950 did the Political Secretariat decide upon detailed guidelines.[71] With the exception of those too young to enter the Party, admission was to be limited to KSČ members. The education offices of District National Councils carried out recruiting and were supported by the Party's regional cadre departments. The fact that different offices were given charge of recruiting each year impeded the formation of efficient organization. The goal for the entering class was 2,000 students[72] and district education offices advertised the courses through leaflets, radio, and press. Local Party agencies were told to supervise this work, intervening where necessary: "[former university] students, or sons and daughters of petty bourgeois families who might have worked in production, may not appear at the courses." The directives did not define "worker."[73]

Although the Ministry of Education also monitored the recruiting drive,[74] control remained inadequate. Top-level functionaries seemed to believe that, set in motion, recruiting mechanisms would function on their own. A report from the following year attempted to explain the failures that ensued:

"The recruiting was not politically secured. . . . The organs of the Party concentrated on selection but not recruitment. The result was a constantly high proportion of non-Party members among the applicants. By 15 July, when the recruitment concluded despite the unsatisfactory process, there were only 1,607 members of the Party among 2,299 applicants."[75]

In one region students of the worker course were themselves enlisted to help recruit in factories. This sort of initiative had worked well in East Germany but did not catch on in the Czech lands, perhaps because worker-course students could not make a convincing case for their schools. DK recruiters had to compete with recruiting drives sponsored by police, army, and Party schools, which promised more immediate paybacks. Moreover, places like Žatec and Šluknov may have offered little to excite the adventurous spirit. In East Germany or Poland the move to worker courses in cities like Berlin, Leipzig, or Warsaw usually signaled the first step in upward social mobility. Also in contrast to the East German case, factories were not made to cooperate in recruitment and persisted in holding back their best workers: "The enterprises did not understand the political meaning of the courses and, for reasons of enterprise patriotism, did not pay attention to recruiting and even less to selection."[76]

The course began to fall behind schedule on account of these recruiting difficulties. Three-month evening review sessions in Czech and arithmetic began a month late. Entrance examinations had to be pushed back to the beginning of August, by which time "with great difficulties the regions put together entrance commissions." The exams were scheduled for the first days of August, but the candidates did not cooperate: 22.7 percent of those summoned did not bother to appear. Only 70 of the 538 no-shows even took the trouble to explain their absence. The reasons given included family, length of studies (especially by females), or previous recruitment to the police or the army.

Of those examined 80.8 percent were recommended for studies. This was about 60 percent of the quota.[77] As in the previous year, the ministry had little time to "verify" candidates' documentation. The planned three months shrank to a few weeks. "But with this the problems do not end," a Party reporter admitted. The plan had called for 2,000 students, but only 1,372 commenced instruction.[78] A report of 13 September 1950 attempted to explain the multiple embarrassments. Its conclusion would have been a useful addition to that year's guidelines: namely that factories should institute year-round recruiting for the courses.[79]

Poor recruitment spelled poor students. The students of the 1950–51 worker courses were on the whole younger than their predecessors. For example, in Hrubá Skála the average age went from twenty-four in 1949–50 to twenty-one the following year. Participants' relative youth also meant a lessening of political maturity and class consciousness, which supposedly resulted in greater passivity and a poorer work ethic. Many of the new students had not been involved in the production process and were not known to their district Party organizations.[80] A reporter observed that "in most courses, even those where selection was better than last year, we are witness to *generally lower political maturity and class consciousness,* and a lack of political practice. . . . In this year's course *once more a significant number of students have little talent.*" Of the 1,354 students enrolled, 230 failed the first "classificatory session" and had to be admonished.[81]

According to all accounts course participants put in full workdays and greatly exerted themselves, even if the results were on average lower than the previous year's. One report claimed the students showed a love of learning typical of workers.[82] They had many activities to keep them busy.[83] Every course had competitions for highest average, best punctuality, and tidiest room. In some courses each student was subjected to fifteen minutes of daily "open criticism."[84] The ČSM was now intimately involved in the courses' operations. It had "become the organizer of studies, cultural and sporting events, and all extracurricular activity." Much of the political schooling occurred in daily newspaper analyses and so-called *20-ti minutovky,* that is, twenty-minute presentations in front of class on themes chosen by the political director. Unlike their East German or Polish counterparts, the DKs could not assist in political agitation at universities because of their distance from the cities. But they did contribute to the political life of the provincial communities where they were located.[85]

In 1950–51 there were thirteen worker courses, and each had a political director. But the political development of these directors had been neglected. Of thirteen directors only five were "worker cadres"; the rest were teachers, professors, and officials. Nine of the thirteen were pre-February 1948 KSČ members and considered satisfactory. A decision was taken that they should all undergo political schooling.[86]

By mid-1951 the DKs had become the major route for workers into the intelligentsia, yet the KSČ leadership had yet to assign them adequate resources, which soon resulted in teacher attrition. Close to one-third of the teaching staff abandoned the DKs in 1950–51. Most prone to leave were gifted teachers, who were recruited by newly established teacher training schools. These had the "advantage" of being located in cities. Replacements were generally of poorer quality, because the district education offices did not seek out the best teachers for worker courses, preferring to keep them in high schools. Even at the height of stalinism, state offices did not "comprehend the importance of this task."[87]

The third "run" of worker courses concluded in the fall of 1951, when 1,179 students took the final examination; of this group 1,101 went on to higher education. Now it was said that this cohort had higher political consciousness and was better prepared academically than the preceding.[88] Yet the situation of worker courses, which each year had been undersubscribed, remained dismal. Interest in the courses was dropping, as demonstrated by "worsened selection, a high dropout rate, worsening class composition, and a poor recruitment drive."[89]

In the 1951–52 school year the number of courses in the Czech lands was supposed to grow to twenty. Initially the plan called for 2,500 participants, but had to be cut back by 500 because of insufficient applicants. Yet even this goal proved too ambitious. Despite a second vigorous recruiting campaign only 1,865 students were enrolled at nineteen courses.[90] The selection was not of high quality. Students of the fourth "run" had a poorer command of Czech than previous groups. They had been out of school several years, and, "besides this, the Ostrava region has never had good Czech speakers." Once again the factories, in many cases supported by the trade union, held back the best workers, offering instead the "expendables." The fourth DK class was in addition the politically poorest to date; most of the new students belonged only to the ČSM and the trade unions.[91] The pool of potential applicants for these courses seemed depleted.

Nevertheless, in 1953 the quota for DKs was doubled to 5,000. The courses were extended by one year to two, but this was to be their final "run," because the recently reformed high schools could supposedly graduate enough worker students.[92] The DKs could be extended by a year since an additional class of high school graduates would supposedly cover the quota for university freshmen in 1953–54. But as we have seen, high schools never overcame their difficulties in attracting workers. Placing faith in them meant surrendering hope of significantly increasing numbers of workers and peasants in higher education.

The goal of 5,000 first-year students at DKs proved unrealistic. Although the ministry had lowered the minimum age to seventeen years, conducted recruitment beyond factories and state farms, and commenced recruiting in November 1952, by April 1953 it had identified only 1,500 students whose acceptance seemed likely. The ČSM was responsible for the campaign, but the ministry was supposed to coordinate the entire action. To meet increased demand, additional teachers were to be lured away from high schools.[93]

Of the approximately 5,000 students who participated in DKs from 1948 to 1950, some 2,600 were attending university in mid-1952.[94] There they became the political "leverage" in higher education. Yet because of their high "cadre value" graduates of worker courses (ADKs) were also terribly overworked, and the results were visible in damaged health: "during the first semester 10 cases of patent tuberculosis were detected . . . (as well as) a significant number of orthopedic and glandular disorders. The resistance to illness is diminished in the graduates of worker courses by the great over-exertion of the nervous system."[95]

Academically the ADKs lagged a bit behind high school graduates, but they struggled to keep up. Like worker-course graduates in Poland or East Germany, they did worse in the hard sciences, better in social sciences and history. Reports from the mechanical and electrical engineering faculty at the Technical University in Prague reflect the impressive exertions made by this first group of worker students: "According to the evaluation of the work of the first semester the ADKs have satisfactory results. On average the ADKs are not far behind the graduates of high schools and industrial schools. They stubbornly work 70 to 80 hours a week. But an entire third of them demonstrated below-average knowledge."[96] Academic quality was said to deteriorate with successive classes of worker-course graduates.[97] Their political leverage also diminished, as ADKs tended to segregate themselves in dormitories and study groups.[98]

The severest limitation on ADK effectiveness was the steady reduction of resources by the KSČ leadership, however. In October 1949 the Political Secretariat of the KSČ Central Committee had promised amenities to the first ADKs. They were to live in dormitories close to the faculties where they studied, receive stipends of 2,000 crowns monthly, and extra money for learning materials. In the Central Committee and the Ministry of Education, specially designated officials would care for their needs. Fifty students were delegated for after-school help.[99] Yet by mid-1952 ADKs at all faculties were complaining that the ministry's fourth department (higher education) did not "concern itself with them at all." The directives of the Political Secretariat had fallen into disuse. ADKs from Brno directed their complaints to the department's chief, physicist Miloslav Valouch:

> In the first year, preparatory students received everything: stipends, books, equipment, etc. From that time the interest and help of the ministry has dropped more and more and has now practically ceased altogether. . . .
>
> The ADKs feel they are going through military service all over again and they never get to see their families. Many have started worrying that they aren't good enough and will have to go back to their factories. Although the ministry knows about this situation, nothing happens.

Under such circumstances normal student problems, like overloaded schedules, seemed many times magnified.[100]

A 1954 educational reform aggravated feelings of worker-course graduates that they were second-class citizens. In order to make Czech higher education approximate the Soviet model, traditional academic degrees were abolished as holdovers of "bourgeois" society. This happened just as the first class of ADKs were to receive university diplomas. Some of them suspected a plot and wrote to Zdeněk Nejedlý, then president of the Czechoslovak Academy of Sciences: "It is difficult to bear this, and more difficult to understand it, for we are being denied a right granted to students of Charles University for centuries. That this was intentionally and purposefully directed against us is indicated by the fact that last year's graduating class from the law faculty, the last purely bourgeois and without worker cadres, was awarded doctoral diplomas."[101] The authors worried that they would not be taken seriously in hospitals and offices without the title of doctor. Evidently there was some truth in the charge raised against this group back in 1949: that they were out for "better social standing."

Explanations

None of the KSČ's affirmative action measures achieved success. Though they made up over 65 percent of society, Czech workers and peasants never composed more than 43 percent of Czech university students. This failure to transform Czech elites proved consequential, because students of the former middle classes would not be as loyal to the worker and peasant state as students drawn from worker and peasant milieus, and an opportunity to achieve far-reaching social change through education would not be repeated. Only in the stalinist years did the Party possess a full range of devices to force change, including the unmitigated enthusiasm of thousands of young cadres, and political terror. To be sure, many Czechs recall this as a time when "bourgeois" families were seriously disadvantaged. Thousands were sent to provincial exile or labor camps for "improper" class origins and the students expelled in 1948 and 1949 were permanently disadvantaged.[102] Those suspected of "reactionary" views were not admitted to university to begin with. Yet despite such measures the KSČ never seriously challenged the old middle classes' hold on higher education.

The most obvious reason for this failure is the broad resistance of Czech society. Comparatively speaking, war had little touched that society's milieus, and traditional notions about social status, supported by traditional educational institutions, like strong vocational schools, remained intact. Working-class milieus in particular exhibited strong continuities through the war: in 1964, close to 80 percent of Czechoslovak industrial workers had been working in industry without interruption since the prewar years.[103] Even the purges of 1948–49 had not been severe enough to shatter the inherited educational world. Into the stalinist period local networks persisted that permitted parents and children to make career choices that thwarted the Party's plans.

Yet the Czechoslovak Communist Party was an equally important hindrance to change. From base to leadership, it simply failed to take an interest

in higher education. Before 1948 there was no agitation for worker preparation courses in the Czech lands, while this issue was becoming an obsession
for East German Communists. These early postwar years had been a time
of relative freedom for local initiatives in education, but KSČ local organizations limited themselves to campaigns for reform of primary and secondary schooling. At the urging of Communist functionaries unified schools
were introduced in September 1945 in Duchcov, Osek u Duchcova, Hrdlo-
vek, Písek, and the Spořilové section of Prague.[104] But neither these KSČ dis-

TABLE 13-3

Women at Institutions of Higher Education (in percentage)

Year	Czech Lands	Poland	East Germany
1945–46	18.4		41.5
1947–48	22.2		36.7
1950	23.1	34.5	30.0
1952	23.8	32.1	24.0
1954	25.1	31.8	28.0

Sources: *Statistická ročenka Republiky Československé 1957,* 232;
Rocznik statystyczny 1958, 402; Stallmann, *Hochschulzugang,* 305, 307.

trict organizations, nor the Communist student clubs, nor the KSČ school
commission, nor leading Communist proponents of university reform, like
Valouch, Tureček, and Nejedlý, became interested in placing workers at universities.[105] There was an extended debate about regulating the entrance of
university students in 1947, but the catalyst was fear of intellectual unemployment and not concern for social transformation.[106] Like Polish comrades of the early postwar period, Czech Communists believed that stipends
and school reform would remove the barriers to university education for
workers, and the disparities would resolve themselves. They were revisionists in an issue that required revolution.

A further index of neglect was policies toward women. In East Germany
and Poland education functionaries attempted to get more women into
higher education as part of their general scheme of educational reform. Here
one encounters not the slightest effort on the part of the KSČ, before or
after 1948, though women were more underrepresented in universities of the
Czech lands than they were in those of Poland or East Germany (Table 13-3).
The efforts to create more opportunity for women were particularly impressive in East Germany, where the first initiatives in student admissions policies of 1946 called for the recruitment of as many "girls and women" as possible.[107] Soviet officers encouraged these measures.[108] SED leaders interpreted

slow progress in increasing numbers of female students as a sign of persistent "petty bourgeois ideology," especially among working-class parents,
who wanted their daughters to have "economically assured marriages."[109] In
Poland, too, functionaries complained of the persistence of outdated attitudes.[110] In both countries Communists attempted to recruit about 40 percent women to worker-peasant courses in the early 1950s, but they never
fully succeeded.[111]

There is not an iota of interest in this matter in the records stored in Czech
archives. In none of the internal Party and ministry reports from the late
1940s and early 1950s is reference made to continued imbalances between
the sexes at universities; neither state, nor Party, nor trade union, ever mentioned the need to get women to universities. Never was an attempt made to
recruit women for worker courses. Moreover, not a single woman worked
at an influential position in Czech higher education. This contrasts to the
Polish case, where the leading higher-education functionaries in both Party
and state apparatuses, as well as the director of worker courses in the early
1950s, were women.[112] It would seem that many Polish Communists aspired
to be modernizers in a developing society, whereas Czech counterparts represented a provincial reaction to an increasingly modern society.

In such highly centralized systems leaders bear clear responsibility for
political shortcomings. Throughout the postwar period KSČ leaders simply
failed to become interested in higher education, and never summoned the
organizational will necessary to shatter tradition. No doubt they labored
under disadvantages: their Party arrived late at socialist revolution in education, and processes that had started as early as 1945 in Poland or East Germany had to be initiated almost overnight in February 1948. In 1949 East
Germany's Communists were putting finishing touches on their worker-
peasant faculties while Czech comrades were still busy improvising. In 1951
the East Germans created a central State Secretariat for Higher Education,
staffed with cadres who had proved themselves in six years of work in the
provinces. At that very moment the Czechoslovak Ministry of Education
was in a protracted crisis of reorganization, only fitfully removing prewar
and pre-February bureaucrats.[113]

These efforts were then complicated by the peculiar self-immolation to
which the Czech Party subjected itself in the early 1950s. Like many other
sectors of the Party/state bureaucracy, the education apparatus became pervaded by denunciations for "hostile behavior," and descended into a state
of panic and chaos in 1950–51. Central Committee secretary Gustav Bareš
was Jewish—like most of the Slánský "coconspirators." This fact was emphasized in visits to the Soviet embassy by Bareš's rival Václav Kopecký, who
portrayed his comrade as belonging to an "entirely alien world, [with] dif-

ferent ways of thinking." [114] Aware of these machinations, Bareš became more concerned with physical survival than with educational policy.[115]

It did not help matters that the minister of education, Zdeněk Nejedlý, took ill, leaving intriguer Kopecký in charge of the ministry.[116] Kopecký was not particularly concerned about educational affairs, however. During his tenure the ministry ceased functioning as a unified whole; its coordinating bodies, the *collegium* and the State Council for Higher Education, did not meet. "Cadre evaluations" decimated the staff, and in this time of uncertainty a sort of "dual power" emerged at the ministry, with one group of administrators following the old deputy Pavlík, and the others his rival Pavlásek, who enjoyed Kopecký's favor. Miloslav Valouch, in charge of higher education, a "poor organizer who wants to please everyone," proved unable to put his department in order.[117] Valouch also suffered from feelings of inferiority, because he did not know the Soviet system firsthand. As a result, issues of basic importance — like worker studies — were neglected. Order did not return to higher-education affairs until the replacement of Valouch, Bareš, Pavlásek, and Pavlík in 1953.

Yet by itself, this self-immolation was not the decisive factor in explaining the KSČ's failure to construct a new elite. After all, that Party's neglect of higher education did not begin or end with the "monster" trials of the early 1950s. And if the Czech Communists awoke only in February 1948 to the need for a student admissions policy, that was a reflection of their other priorities in the early postwar period. It was also a reflection of other priorities if a purge in the Ministry of Education did not occur until 1951 — the leadership neglected the state administration on purpose and promoted the destructive fervor of students.

A more vexing contextual difficulty lay in the socioeconomic structure of the Czech lands, which did not provide Czech Communists with the ready constituencies for social advancement that existed in other parts of East Central Europe. In Poland, Bulgaria, or even Slovakia large numbers of rural dwellers eagerly moved into the growing cities and embarked upon university studies. In the Czech lands social mobility of that sort had occurred generations earlier. Czech Communists inherited large and highly educated technical, administrative, and managerial elites and did not need to create them in the first place. Indeed, they faced the unusual challenge of having to massively shift children of middle-class background from paths leading to higher education to other career paths.

But they never confronted these unusual challenges. In other socialist countries the leadership got involved when elite transformation stalled. Stalin, for example, had personally mandated increases in numbers of workers in the new intelligentsia.[118] In the Czech lands leading functionaries, like

Gottwald, Slánský, or Zápotocký, are noticeable by their inactivity. They might have intervened on any number of issues: for example, they could have obligated factories to delegate the best workers to higher education, or given high schools and universities strict quotas for accepting worker students. Such measures had shown results in Poland and East Germany.[119] Generous scholarships and adequate dormitories would have reduced working-class parents' reluctance to consider higher education for their children.[120] Never did Czech leaders even attempt to define social origin and, worse yet, their admissions guidelines did not explicitly favor workers' and peasants' children.[121] East German guidelines (1950), by contrast, list "origin" next to "participation in societal activity" as a condition for admission, and maintained a hierarchy by social class for admission throughout the 1950s.[122] In the Czech lands, applications for university admission were sent directly to universities from high schools; in East Germany these applications first made their way through local cadre departments of the SED, which prepared "exhaustive" political evaluations, and sent them to district SED cadre departments.[123]

The most striking failure in this long list are the worker courses. Given the resistance to change at the middle and high schools, these would have been the ideal means of quickly providing large contingents of university students from the working classes. That such a policy was feasible is demonstrated by the experiences of neighboring countries, *which Czech functionaries knew about.* In November 1951, a higher-education functionary in Prague had noted that worker-peasant students were dropping out of university at an alarming rate. The reason was not difficult to discern; he had only to look to East Berlin or Warsaw: "The preparation courses for worker cadres are too short. While they are one year long in Czechoslovakia, they last two years in Poland and even three years in Germany. Worker cadres have great difficulties and 300 of them have left the University of Politics and Economics in the course of two years."[124]

Worse than fail to act, the KSČ leadership aggravated its difficulties by continuing a policy of wage-leveling inherited from the Nazis. Through the 1940s and 1950s wages and salaries continued to rise for employees in all areas of the Czechoslovak economy except education and culture.[125] There were simply no material incentives for subjecting oneself to the rigors of higher education. By the mid-1960s a locksmith earned more than a lawyer, and a turner more than a physician.[126] Czechoslovakia gained the distinction of having the lowest income inequality in the world.

In order to guarantee the loyalty of those who now ran the state apparatus, the KSČ set up a series of crash courses *outside the universities* called central workers schools (*Ústřední dělnické školy*) that made factory workers into state bureaucrats, usually in less than a year. The core subject of these courses was the study of Marxism-Leninism, because, as a reporter of the

Ministry of Foreign Affairs wrote in 1950, it "is the most reliable basis for any kind of work."[127] The qualifications of ministerial employees sank during the 1950s as worker cadres came to occupy decisive positions.

The neglect of higher education and university-trained elites was so pervasive as to suggest a cultural explanation for the KSČ's failure: the Party did not attend to higher education because it did not value intellectual enterprise as such. As has been argued, leading "cultural" functionaries like V. Kopecký could scarcely hide their disdain for universities. The anti-intellectualism of the leadership was so intense as to stun even visiting Soviet functionaries. The writer G. D. Guliia, laureate of the Stalin Prize, noted the "special suspicion" of the intelligentsia present among Czechoslovak Party functionaries. From a short meeting with political secretariat member K. Bacílek in 1953, Guliia "gained the impression that Comrade *Bacílek practically does not believe in such a thing as honest intellectuals.*"[128] Economist Peter Wiles has aptly characterized Czechoslovakia as "the only Communist country to be governed by genuine proletarians with genuine feeling that Communists ought to favor directly the manual worker."[129]

Why would "genuine proletarians" in the Czech lands fail to recognize the potential political rewards of higher education? The answer can at best be hypothetical at this stage, but existing data on the development of the Czech working class is highly suggestive. The key factor seems to be the relationship between that working class and the city or, more fundamentally, between industry and cities in the Czech lands. To an unusual degree, Czech industry established itself in the countryside, and attracted labor from nearby villages. Czech village dwellers thus experienced upward social mobility without leaving their traditional milieus, which became what Peter Heumos has called "industrial villages."[130] However, universities are the urban institution par excellence, of questionable value outside the city. Because they were earning good money, Czech villagers — in distinct contrast to Polish counterparts — had negligible incentive to move to the city, and adopt its value structures. One did not need high school, let alone university, to succeed in village milieus. Advanced vocational training was highly regarded, however, because it was useful.

The Czech urban environment also exhibited certain peculiarities that gave workers living there relatively less incentive to attend universities. For the most part, Czech urban classes had emerged from villages and small towns two to three generations earlier. There were no great distinctions of material culture between various segments of urban society; indeed, the wages of factory workers had improved constantly from the beginning of the World War.[131] Therefore city children of working-class background did not feel a distinct advance in status upon entering universities. This contrasted greatly to the situation in Poland, with the enormous social and cultural discrepancies between city and village. Children from Polish villages and small towns who entered universities had no doubt that they were entering a better world.

Failure to pay for university-educated work had political costs for the KSČ. Not only did few workers attend universities, but many positions requiring university education were not adequately staffed. By 1962 there were one-half million such positions in Czechoslovakia, equivalent to 9 percent of the labor force.[132] The crash courses for worker cadres proved inadequate, even for the Ministry of Foreign Affairs.[133] Not coincidentally, 1962 was the year that the Czechoslovak economy registered a negative growth rate — the first time such a thing had happened to a Communist country.[134] The reform movement of the 1960s had its origins in these economic difficulties, and it was driven by an underappreciated intelligentsia. In 1968 it helped topple the stalinist leadership.[135]

The East German Peculiarity

The case of East Germany shows, however, that stalinist leaderships, even of highly industrialized societies, could insulate themselves from such pressures by actively exploiting universities for political gain. The GDR rivaled Czechoslovakia both in economic development and in income equality,[136] yet the SED methodically formed an elite drawn from working-class and peasant milieus, expanding capacity gradually, as worker-peasant students became available. The Soviet occupiers kept the total numbers of students low, and therefore East Germany's Communists did not need to make compromises under an onslaught of students, such as was faced by Polish and Czech universities in the early postwar years.[137]

By pursuing admissions policies favoring worker and peasant students through many academic seasons, the SED transformed the sociocultural complexion of the student body. Yet as we have seen, social background was only one component of that Party's ideal: new students also had to be politically committed. Large applicant pools in the early postwar years permitted the SED to handpick students, and as early as 1946 more than one in three were attached to the SED through Party membership.[138] But webs of dependency, with the Party at the center, were spun to embrace all students, whether they belonged to the Party or not. Any hint of nonconformity could cut one off from resources controlled by the state, beginning with admission to high school and university, then access to dormitories, books, cafeterias, subsidized transport, suitable employment. These webs were taut because East German citizens valued higher education — education was one of the few stable values remaining in German life.[139]

Most impressive in sustaining dependency were the SED's scholarship policies, with their clear hierarchy of groups worthy of support (Table 13-

4). All scholarship students were supposed to be committed to the "people's democratic republic and the thought of socialism," but preference was given to "workers and their children."[140] Polish and Czech leaderships did not attempt to make effective use of scholarship policies. A Polish regulation of 1950 gave equal preference to children of "workers and peasants with small and medium plots," and to children of the working intelligentsia, if they

TABLE 13-4

Percentage of Students Receiving State Stipends

	Czech Lands	ČSSR	Poland	GDR
1951–52:	49.4			88.0
1952–53:	48.7			92.0
1954		46.2		95.2
1955		56.3	71.0	88.4
1956		55.2	65.5	90.7
1957		41.8	60.5	87.8
1958		32.3	55.1	94.0
1959		23.0	51.2	90.6
1960		22.1	53.3	89.2
1961		21.4		88.8
1965		30.3	47.5	84.1
1968		38.7	41.9	90.0
1969		44.8	45.1	

Sources: Historická statistická ročenka ČSSR, 595, 597; SÚA, AÚV KSČ, f. 19/7, a.j. 280, l. 95; Rocznik statystyczny 1960, 357; Rocznik statystyczny 1970, 423, 439; Statistisches Jahrbuch der Deutschen Demokratischen Republik 1960–61, 133; Statistisches Jahrbuch der Deutschen Demokratischen Republik 1970, 386.

required material assistance of the state.[141] As of 1952 the Polish state distributed stipends according to major subject of study.[142] Czech regulations allotted stipends for students according to the *current* income of their parents, independent of social origins.[143] The East German state was not only more careful about how it distributed scholarships; it also devoted more resources to them. They were more effective than student loans, because they could never be repaid.[144]

The centerpiece of SED strategy in higher education were the worker-peasant faculties. As has been argued earlier, these were supposed to create the apotheosis of the new student: class conscious, politically responsible, professionally competent. Unlike other Communists, SED functionaries saw in the ABF not simply a necessity but an opportunity; here was the chance to create a specific group consciousness, very unlike the camaraderie that might emerge in a traditional *Gymnasium*.[145] Unlike Polish and Czech counterparts, the SED maintained the ABF even after high schools had been socially transformed. From 1946 worker courses grew continuously in size and in length, and despite concerns of universities about their strongly leftist character, they were placed directly on university premises in 1948. Brushing aside the concerns of Soviet officers, East German Communists increased the courses' length to three years in 1949, because they feared that less time might jeopardize worker students' attainment of technical proficiency.[146] Worker-preparation-course students assumed rights and obligations equal to those of regularly enrolled students. This was a privilege Czech counterparts never received, and Polish only in 1951.[147] Whoever passed final examinations at a worker course was "to be enrolled immediately and preferentially for regular studies."[148] Like the pedagogical and social science faculties, the worker courses were places from which SED influence could spread to the entire university.

During the 1950s numbers of students at worker-peasant faculties continued to climb, as did competition for space. In 1952 there were 6,634 applications for 4,800 places.[149] Even more young people applied the following year (11,950 applicants for 6,926 spots), and the entering class consisted of 73.6 percent workers' and 13.3 percent peasants' children, compared with 55.5 and 13.5 percent, respectively, the year before. The improvement was due to better coordination between various "mass organizations," particularly the FDJ and Free German Trade Union.[150] By July 1954 there were thirteen worker-peasant faculties with 13,000 students in the GDR. At that moment some 12,500 ABF graduates were enrolled in higher studies.

At the same time that Poland's Communists were phasing out worker preparation courses, the SED was reconfirming its commitment to them. ABF graduates constituted an important segment of the Party functionaries at universities and were received in large numbers into graduate studies. The worker-peasant faculties remained centers of political agitation at higher schools, regularly supplying activists for "country Sundays" and "house agitations." ABF graduates volunteered more often than other students for vacation work details (*Brigaden*) and they assisted at summer camps for young pioneers. The "overwhelming majority" had acted "exemplarily" during the upheaval of 17 June 1953. All that remained to do with worker-peasant faculties was improve them: by enhancing teacher qualification and pushing for "aggressive" instruction.[151]

By the 1960s, enough worker and peasant cadres were available to enact a "debourgeoisification" of university elites. With a new regulation on hiring assistant professors in 1957, the numbers of professors of working-class and peasant background began to rise, from less than 20 percent to 39 percent (1971), and the number of SED members to increase from under 30 percent to 62 percent (1971). From the mid-1960s more than half the new professors hired each year were of worker or peasant background, and after 1970 more than 80 percent of new professors belonged to the SED.[152]

The East German worker-peasant faculties were kept in operation longest and, relatively speaking, recruited the largest classes (see Table 13-5). Persistence was important, because without proper training, worker-peasant students dropped out of university at higher than average rates. Indeed, be-

TABLE 13-5

Worker-Peasant Faculties

Country	Years of Operation	Graduates of Worker-Peasant Faculties as Percentage of Entering University Classes	Length of Course (years)
GDR	1946–66	20	3
Czech Lands	1949–54	10–13	1
Poland	1945–56	8–9	2

Sources: Statistisches Jahrbuch der Deutschen Demokratischen Republik 1960–61, 132–33; SÚA, ÚPV 2481 12/3.81.43/54; AAN, MSW 17, k. 91–92; KC PZPR 237/XVI/120, k. 43; 121, k. 103–5.
* The East German total represents an average figure from 1952 to 1956, and the Czech and Polish numbers are from peak periods of the early 1950s.

cause they attempted to graduate too many worker-peasant students too quickly, Polish functionaries became obsessed with this problem in the early 1950s. Like Czech comrades, they had planned themselves into a corner. Their predicament in turn gave Polish students a sense of power: at a January 1952 meeting of representatives of Poznań University with Vice-Minister of Education Krassowska, Rector Ajdukiewicz told the audience that there had been cases of "improper behavior" among students who felt that the authorities "have no choice but to graduate us, because otherwise they won't fulfill the plan."[153] Functionaries in Warsaw became uniquely sensitive to alienating students, and repeatedly intervened to overturn decisions by local authorities to expel student "enemies." They portrayed the enemy's presence as too pervasive for such measures. In fact, their enemy was Polish society.[154]

The ABF outdid even the Soviet model, the *rabfak,* which was used intensively only in the early postrevolutionary period, and during the Great Break (1928–32). It was scaled down and abandoned altogether in the 1930s.[155] Perhaps awareness that the East Germans were perfecting their model caused the Soviet Military Administration to object to the expansion of the ABF in 1949.

In theory, both the KSČ and PZPR had the same ideal for students as did the SED. But they did less to achieve it. In the former case, the student body was transformed in a political but not in a sociocultural sense. In the latter, the Party embarked upon a more modest, long-term strategy of transformation, concentrating first on the admission of worker-peasant students, and much later on the formation of loyal university-educated cadres. By the early 1950s the changes in the social composition of students appeared quite impressive. Yet this strategy was abandoned midway through the decade, because the Party leadership believed that preferences for the socially disadvantaged were eroding the academic quality of the student body. After 1954, these preferences were broken down, and the worker faculties stopped taking new students. At least, the Polish Party hoped, universities would produce competent experts — as they had before the reforms.

Most compelling evidence of the failure of the KSČ or PZPR to develop the holistic approach to elite formation that the SED took were policies of recruiting new academics, what the Germans called *Nachwuchspolitik*. In neither the Czech lands nor Poland did the Party *even keep records* of the social background of junior faculty.[156]

A number of factors stand out in explaining the SED's relative success in creating new students and a new elite. Several of these are contextual; two have been mentioned in regard to the SED's success in breaking apart the old university elite: the presence of the Soviet Military Administration and the open border to the West. A contextual factor that has not been mentioned is the divide within Germany that cast the GDR in the role of a workers' and peasants' state. But these are not the whole explanation: one also witnesses in the SED a unique concern for higher education and its political uses. This concern seems to reflect a specific Party culture.

The Soviet role is best seen in comparison to the Polish situation. In East Germany one does not read of universities, let alone entire cities, simply refusing cooperation with worker courses.[157] The Soviet Military Administration would not permit such behavior. It reacted swiftly to reports of disrespect for workers, workers' courses, and, most of all, "the" workers' party. Frequently, the Soviets also stepped in with money and helped provide facilities for worker courses. Beyond these courses, Soviet agendas of denazification and democratization permitted rapid politicization of student admissions and gave the SED tools with which to achieve sharp increases in numbers of worker and peasant students after only a few semesters. Part of the motivation behind such measures was ideological: a "democratic" Germany seemed less likely to unleash another war against the Soviet Union.

The open border to the West meant that the SED did not have the same concerns as Czech comrades about middle classes who resisted downward social mobility. For example, many hundreds of East German students who were discriminated against for socioeconomic or political reasons enrolled at the Free University in West Berlin — some commuting from the East.[158] In an indirect fashion this "social safety valve" (James Tent) also reduced resistance to changes in higher education as a whole, by encouraging the departure of the politically most dissatisfied.[159] Increasingly, students came to East German universities from milieus with little knowledge of higher education, and were therefore more likely to accept the SED's version of what the university should be.

The open border also intensified the polarization of capitalism and socialism within Germany. Perhaps like Polish comrades, East German Communists were tempted to make compromises in student admissions policies, but these would have weakened the East German claim to represent the better "German" response to the challenges of education. It is not true to say that the SED did not have the option of a "national" strategy; its "national" strategy sought the realization of a socialist Germany. Indeed, from an East German perspective, only socialism could come to terms with the German legacy. A leading expert on GDR higher education proclaimed in the mid-1960s: "There is no crisis of the university system in the GDR. We have problems at our universities, but no crisis. The deep university crisis that was left by imperialism and fascism was forever removed in the German Democratic Republic by the profound changes after 1945 and, above all, by the construction of socialism. It is not arrogance but rather an understanding of the laws of history when we say that the socialist reforming of the university has fulfilled a task of national dimensions." The major components of this reforming were the removal of "military, fascist, and antihumanistic *Ungeist*" and the "broad access" for workers and peasants to the university "for the first time in German history."[160]

Yet long before all of these contextual pressures began working themselves out in policy, the Communist apparatus in East Germany was demonstrating a concern for worker studies that was simply not matched elsewhere. Just as there was a pervasive disregard for higher education in the Czech Party, so there was pervasive interest in higher education in the German Party. As has been argued earlier, local trade-union and Party cells began working on worker education in 1945, without directives from the center. But the center itself was intensely concerned with issues of education. From the very beginning Walter Ulbricht took a personal interest in educational affairs that was not paralleled in Poland or Czechoslovakia. There are no records of Klement Gottwald, Rudolf Slánský, Władysław Gomułka, or Bolesław Bierut intervening in favor of worker studies at any point.[161] Walter Ulbricht, by contrast, constantly involved himself in the formation of the new elite, whether the issue was Marxist-Leninist schooling, special legal training, stipends, sport instruction, recruiting of women, or, of course, the worker-peasant faculties. In 1950 he personally increased numbers of worker-peasant students to be admitted by threefold.[162] This required an additional investment of 2 million marks, in a year when the investments for the six East German universities totaled less than 15 million marks.[163] A command staff of leading functionaries was formed to visit all local capitals to ensure the realization of this decision.[164]

Anton Ackermann, top Party official in matters of culture in the early postwar years, likewise showed an unparalleled concern for higher education. He personally attended to basic organizational issues, by, for example, involving the leading functionaries of district Party organizations in the work of student selection commissions.[165] In 1949 Ackermann rebuked enterprises on the front page of Party daily *Neues Deutschland* for failing to release their best workers for higher education. He encouraged a search for worker-peasant students among the tens of thousands of graduates of Party schools at all levels: "These people should be the main reservoir . . . for university students." Lower-level bureaucrats throughout Eastern Europe often believed that dependable comrades could not be spared for university education. Yet, unlike Polish or Czech counterparts, Ackermann "obligated" the heads of the Party schooling departments in the *Länder* to go through their files and select "in great number the candidates for universities and higher schools." The recruiting drive was by no means limited to the Communist apparatus, however. Ackermann instructed his deputies "to appeal to the class consciousness of the workers. It is to be made clear to them that they must make temporary sacrifices in order to enable the advancement of worker and peasant children into the new intelligentsia." [166]

To explain this differing attitude toward higher education within the German Party, and within German society, one may again hypothesize about the relation between city and industrialization. Both the German working class, and the leadership of the German workers' movement, tended to a higher degree than Czech counterparts to have emerged from urban environments.[167] They had been socialized into a value system that included secondary and higher education; to aspire to the crowning heights of urban environments, one needed access to the traditionally exclusive institutions of *Gymnasium* and university. The unparalleled inequalities of the educational system in Germany before 1945 also help explain the massive and reflexive embrace of workers' education in East Germany in the first postwar year. One should note, however, that this rush to higher education occurred in a transformed context: this was no longer, even in theory, education for the sake of *Bildung;* this was education for the sake of power.

Just as there was a Polish exception (in policies toward the professoriate) and a Czech exception (in policies toward students), so too was there an East German exception. What was unusual about the East German case is how the leadership unwaveringly merged policies toward professors and students, and then embedded them in a broader set of policies, including not only incentives like stipends and promises of professional reward, but also the construction of Party and youth organizations, the development of courses in Marxism-Leninism, and, most crucially, the calibration of higher education with other levels of education. An expression of loyalty — whether membership in the young pioneers, participation in the atheistic confirmation, or taking a function in a "mass organization" — was required for each advance within the educational system.

Higher education remained highly desirable in East Germany, especially after the building of the Wall, and with time the regime exacted ever greater political prices for its attainment. It was expected that candidates for studies would refrain from contacts with Westerners, and that males would volunteer extra time in the East German army.[168] Indeed, recruiting for the army began in primary school. These mechanisms were perfected: at the end of the GDR all but the most gifted candidates for medical studies were expected to "volunteer" three years of military service — twice the required amount.[169] The SED formed an elite from a "new class" that its own policies had created.

Statistics on worker and peasant students therefore had no meaning as such. A 1958 report from the Soviet embassy in Warsaw on Polish students explains their continuing "open statements against socialism" through the "unsatisfactory social composition of the student body . . . even in 1956, students of working-class and peasant background were not more than 60 percent."[170] A report from the Soviet embassy in Berlin from that same year lists among the accomplishments of the SED in its intelligentsia policy the "extensive system of preparing new cadres of the intelligentsia, especially from workers and peasants. Approximately 60 percent of the students at institutions of higher education in the GDR originate from the working class and the working peasantry."[171] In one case 60 percent was a failure, in the other a success. The difference was the kinds of universities students entered.

Polish worker and peasant students found themselves in university environments that had not been ideologically transformed. Humanists and social scientists like Stanisław Pigoń, Adam Vetulani, or Henryk Wereszycki represented an entirely different world from the Party — with their proud bearing, broad erudition, Old World manners, and harmless eccentricities. Each was an accomplished rhetorician, who could lecture freely in a sort of Polish that was rapidly disappearing from public life, and contrasted sharply to the singsong jargon of Moscow-trained academics. They treated students to the supposed gestures of the high nobility: strict, but fair and self-sacrificing. Pigoń — actually the son of peasants — had received all the medals and honors the Austrian and Polish states could lavish upon a soldier and academic, but he wore only one decoration: an honorary gold pin given him in May 1947 by the embattled independent students' organization Fraternal Aid (*Bratnia Pomoc*).[172] His voluminous correspondence is full of letters from students, whom he continued influencing long after graduation. One, who had become a teacher, wrote in 1953 that "only in very exceptional cases do your bearing and your work not make an impression upon students."[173]

Such professors, and not the half-educated representatives of the Party in academia, provided role models. In these early years, doubts were cast repeatedly upon the credentials of PZPR social scientists, often for plagiarism. The most sensational case was that of prewar Communist and historian Leon Grosfeld, who acted as prorector at the Institute of Social Sciences and deputy director of the Institute of History at the Polish Academy of Sciences until 1956, when extensive excerpts without citation were found in his work from J. Ryng (*Z dziejów kapitalizmu w Polsce,* 1948).[174] The major PPR representative at Lublin University, Witold Reiss, was removed after professors there discovered his plagiarisms of work by R. Taubenszlag. A leading figure in the Poznań University PZPR organization, historian Władysław Rogala, was to conclude work on a doctorate in 1951, but the date of his defense had to be postponed indefinitely, because the dean's office began to suspect that his master's diploma was a forgery.[175] Again and again, the Party's candidates for professorship proved to be academically inadequate. Józef Sieradzki and Celina Bobińska were imposed upon Jagiellonian University despite doubts of the faculty council. S. Rogowski, the major Party figure in Polish studies at Toruń University, did not complete a doctorate until 1961 and never wrote a habilitation. Likewise Jerzy Ziomek, a leading Party representative in Polish studies at Wrocław University until his transfer to Poznań, did not have a doctorate. Shortage of cadres made it difficult even to get competent figures to manage basic organizations. The head of the university committee of the ZMP in Wrocław had to be released in 1952 after declaring at an open Party meeting that "we will win the elections, because there has never been a case in history when a government in power suffered an election defeat."[176]

East German worker and peasant students entered transformed universities in large numbers and found paths to opportunity that had never existed before. The ABF became central to GDR identity, and the mythologizing began early. Bertolt Brecht noted his first encounter with worker students in 1949: "I had a discussion in Hans Mayer's *Kolleg* with worker students about theater. Even the physiognomy of the university has changed. Not only has a new social class been allowed to enter; the old has been practically excluded, so that new students find nothing but their own kind, and cannot be degraded by the example of old-style students [*Kommilitonen*]."[177] With much of the old elite removed, some students—especially in the humanities and social sciences—found new examples to emulate. The writer Christa Wolf, who studied at Leipzig in the 1950s, later recalled the role played by

Communists and antifascists: there "could not be more impressive people for us at that time. Of course they adopted the part of role models, a teacher-student relationship developed in which they were absolutely and in every respect the models, while we were the ones who in every regard were to listen and learn."[178]

Brecht devoted a poem, and SED writer Hermann Kant a novel, to the ABF.[179] But even a writer who turned away from the SED has left testimony to the power of the worker-peasant experience in a context of organized anti-fascism. Gerhard Zwerenz later described first impressions of the lectures of philosopher Ernst Bloch:

> After the first lectures we stood out in the corridor and shook ourselves off like wet dogs. What were we supposed to think of these odd and novel things? These things were novel for us Saxon proletarians and sons of proletarians. We had no clue that what we had encountered was a two- to three-thousand-year-old tradition of philosophy. The West-ern tradition of thought did not count us among its sons. Of course, we had been born in the latitudes of the West, but it had not granted us its goods or its thoughts. We stood naked in this world, and of its culture we had assimilated no more than one needed in order to prose-cute war.[180]

This was the point: to get uncommitted, competent young people, where possible with genuine remorse for fascism, and then form them, in con-trolled environments. Whether a desperately loyal scholar like Ernst Bloch represented an alternative to the values propagated by the SED is debat-able; in any case few worker and peasant students ever encountered a figure remotely like him; most were funneled through technical faculties into a new intelligentsia.[181] Whether they fully embraced the teachings of Marxism-Leninism was secondary, because their life experiences seemed evidence for the most basic tenet of the SED: that this was a state of and for the workers and peasants, and that it was the first such state in German history.[182] Neither their parents nor cousins living under capitalism ever dreamed of graduat-ing from a university. In Poland and the Czech lands, personal history and political canon never mixed in this way, and nowhere would socialism take hold as firmly as in this second generation of the East German intelligentsia.

Universities in East Central Europe did not "return to diversity" after 1956, because they had never ceased being diverse. In Poland a cohesive professoriate remained in place and frustrated Communists' attempts to instill a new consciousness in working-class and peasant students. In the Czech lands, the Party removed politically objectionable humanists and social scientists from universities but failed to mold a student body in which the children of manual laborers formed the decisive element. Cohesive Czech working-class milieus refused to yield young people for university education, and an anti-intellectual Party leadership failed to produce incentives to lure them there. In East Germany, the effects of a lost war permitted the SED to break apart university milieus and to begin forming its own cadres in higher education. Denazification initiated a brain drain to West Germany that continued via the only open frontier in the Soviet bloc: the boundary in Berlin that divided the eastern from western sectors.

As a result of these diverse beginnings, universities occupied different positions on their respective political stages. In Poland and the Czech lands, partially transformed universities produced both significant intellectual dissent as well as popular pressure for change from the 1950s to the 1980s. In particular, Polish and Czech students were among the most active opponents of the ossified Communist regimes in 1956, 1968, 1980, or 1989.[1] East German students were conspicuous by their absence from the turmoil of June 1953 or the radical changes of September–October 1989.[2] The SED was one of the few dictatorships in recent memory that did not have to worry about challenges from students as the foundations of its political and economic power deteriorated. After decades of consistently applied policies — by the remarkably stable Ulbricht-Honecker leadership — universities became the highest stage of an educational system that sifted for conformity at every level. Not only were they places that dependably reproduced official ideology, but they also dispensed gifts and punishments in a way that kept students loyal, for fear of jeopardizing a life's investment in the East German intelligentsia.

The Soviet Union did not take a detailed interest in these matters. At most, small handfuls of Soviet professors and VOKS functionaries helped facilitate desires of East European Communists for specialized knowledge about Soviet higher education. Yet this decentralized Sovietization did not necessitate diversity. Native Communists were dedicated to transferring the Soviet system, and by 1953 they had faithfully replicated its external structures, like the length of the school year and standard curricula in Marxism-Leninism. If they did not succeed in uniformly reproducing the internal life of Soviet universities, that was because they encountered resistance from their societies. History could not be suppressed.

A number of former stalinists in Poland contest this finding. Adam Schaff, the leading Party ideologue of the period, and later a "revisionist" awarded honorary degrees in the West, has argued vigorously that Poland's Communists wanted no more than to preserve Polish science.[3] Yet for most of the academic community, the policies of the stalinist era now seem to be near fulfillment of the radical intentions of Schaff and former comrades Stefan Żółkiewski, Jan Kott, Żanna Kormanowa, or Leszek Kołakowski.[4] Universities were split apart, research agendas dangerously constricted, gifted humanists and social scientists starved of students and material resources. If top Party functionaries did not venture further in their debilitating policies, that was because a deep incursion on one sector of the "cultural front" might leave them exposed elsewhere. They moved carefully, for example, by closing the Catholic University of Lublin one faculty at a time, or by gradually reducing the teaching loads of "idealistic" professors. Such initiatives met with hostility in professorial milieus, and when opportunities arose after Stalin's death in 1953, professors resisted further encroachments on such ideological battlegrounds as editorial boards and student admissions committees.

A discussion of professorial or working-class milieus does not fit easily into existing depictions of East European history, which favor politics and economics over culture.[5] Culture has been neglected in explanations of political development, because it resists "parsimony." It would, of course, be absurd to deny the importance of high politics or economics: the interests of the Soviet Empire imposed severe restrictions on the societies of East Central Europe, and economic backwardness has had noxious implications for political stability to this day. Yet this is far from the complete story. This work has shown that when one exhaustively considers "institutional" history in comparative perspective, political culture not only becomes part of the story but also part of the explanation. National societies at similar distance from the cores of socialism and capitalism nurtured very different attitudes toward the political and had very different experiences of politics.

Poland in particular resists generalizations that derive from the political logic of socialism or the economic logic of capitalism. The regular explosions of opposition that shook that country in the postwar period cannot be explained primarily through class, gender, relations with the Soviet Union, debt crises, or institutional holdovers like the church or universities. After all, East Germany also had workers and peasants exploited by a "new class," women bearing double burdens, a leadership hungry for an independent profile, extensive Protestant and Catholic apparatuses, and a few university faculties with significant autonomies. What was distinctive in Poland was a *national* political culture that united all these factors; Soviet-style socialism was a continuing assault on *Polish* identity, bound to unleash periodic convulsions. A sattled cow indeed.

The study of Polish professors has been part of this larger story. They, like most segments of Polish society, withheld cooperation from Communist authorities despite the blocwide "incentive structures" for career advance. Status requirements specific to the Polish intelligentsia informed their choices. The reasons for Polish professors' particular cohesion have been suggested by M. Rainer Lepsius, who defines milieus as "social units, which are formed by the coincidence of a number of structural dimensions."[6] These dimensions included familial ties extending throughout Poland, a common professional ethos, common interests in reproducing social and economic power, socialization in similar institutions, shared experience of resistance to Sanacja and German National Socialism, and a collective mythology of belonging to a group with a mission of national leadership. The importance of the "familial" ties of the intelligentsia, stretching backward by many generations and creating a nationwide "conscience," can be seen in contrast to the Czech case, where professors had recently emerged from rural and small-town environments with few personal interconnections. Their behavior was largely a private affair.

If Polish professors were united by a strong sense of belonging, they were also united by a sense of who did not belong. Individuals not considered part of the national community — like Jews — were excluded from the full benefits of "heroic" mythology. Though later fearless against the Nazi and Communist regimes, the overwhelming majority of Polish professors were cowed by Polish nationalist students who gravely disturbed academic integrity in the 1930s with the "ghetto benches" they established for Jewish students. Worse yet, very many professors colluded in artificial restrictions to Jewish enrollments, which steadily declined throughout the interwar period. A significant minority of professors — about one-sixth — did attempt to show solidarity with persecuted students, but many hundreds of young Polish Jews found no recourse but to enroll at universities abroad, for example, in Berlin, or, after 1933, at the German and Czech universities in Prague, where anti-Semitic discrimination did not apply.

The Communist Party was also part of the larger story. Kenneth Jowitt has written of the need for ruling Leninist Parties to separate themselves from "native political culture." In none of these societies had sufficient time elapsed for such a separation to occur. Each of the three Party apparatuses, fielded from the societies they attempted to rule, in part reproduced the values of national political cultures. In East Germany, the state remained a cardinal value, and, characteristically, only the GDR was celebrated as a "worker and peasant state." In Poland the Party spoke of "People's Poland" and in the Czech lands it spoke of the "people's democratic regime." SED members may not have taken socialism seriously, but they and the East German population took the state very seriously, whether or not they approved of it. East German universities became an ideal staging ground for administered change, for revolution from above.

The East German bureaucracy performed its duties with a grim enthusiasm, whether in the Berlin ministries and Central Committee, in local capitals, or at the humble desk of the Party secretary in a remote technical school. The typical basic Party organization in the GDR had more meetings that passed more resolutions on more points than a comparable Czech or Polish organization; it also created more complex organizations to achieve more ambitious tasks. Lower-level functionaries constantly hammered away at and harangued their subordinates. If all three Parties had a totalitarian urge, in the GDR that urge was extreme. The difference is reflected in surviving Party documents; words such as "control," "supervise," "unconditional," "every," and "each" figure more often and more prominently in SED correspondence.[7] SED education philosophy was succinctly summarized in a 1950 speech of Central Committee Secretary Ernst Hoffmann: "Es darf nichts unkontrolliert bleiben" (Nothing may escape our control).

The challenges of the early postwar years make the SED's success in organizing a strictly hierarchical apparatus seem all the more impressive. It had inherited the most complex situation in 1945, with conflicting competences of *Land* and center, a presence of the Soviet Military Administration and its local networks, and strong regional KPD and SPD organizations, yet by the early 1950s the Party and state bureaucracy in Berlin were functioning more smoothly than counterparts in Warsaw or Prague. This fact is often lost in recent studies that focus on the "limits" to the East German dictatorship, or on *Eigen-Sinn*. Ironically, totalitarian models assume an ahistorical force in such studies, as East German reality is measured against them, and not against the practiced totalitarianism of neighboring states.[8]

The core of East German communism lay deeper than loyalty to the state, however; it consisted in a set of convictions that crystallized after the trauma of National Socialism, something supposedly caused by the bourgeois capitalist society out of which the Nazi regime had emerged. This core was antifascism. Everyone in the GDR "knew" that the country was based on this principle, even if it was not completely true to socialism. Hadn't leading Party members spent the war in concentration camps? Wasn't the presence of former Nazis in the state apparatus unthinkable in the GDR? Rage born in the Nazi years combined with faith in state intervention and united antifascists with the partially nazified SED apparatus in an attempt to control the thinking of colleagues and students. Characteristic is the case of historian Ernst Engelberg (SED), once an émigré from Nazi Germany, who demanded at a 1954 meeting of the basic SED organization at Leipzig University that "scholars take a clear position in public about current political events."[9] Words spoken at a meeting of November 1953 give some notion of the milieu to which intellectuals like Engelberg attached themselves while pursuing the favor of the antifascist state. First secretary of the Leipzig worker and peasant faculty Reichel told Engelberg and other comrades the following:

> We have ascertained that poor work is a question of consciousness, for there is a great difference between consciousness and ideology. There are many students who write good and very good examinations, and despite this are very bad in terms of consciousness [bewusstseinsmässig]. There are comrades in our faculty who claim the Party wants to destroy them morally [sie moralisch fertig machen]. This is proof that they have poor faith in the Party leadership. In reality they are not concerned about being destroyed morally, but about covering up their mistakes.

The determination to control was aggravated by a special insecurity, rooted in East Germans' intimate knowledge of the West. After Reichel spoke Comrade Heuer from the Chemistry Department, who complained of the "Kalinin Club House": "Recently the Club House has been neglected by the FDJ and the Party. One heard no more of the achievements of Soviet and German science, one heard only woogy-woogy. One should organize many more discussions and lectures there."[10] Antifascism had an even stronger legitimating force for the many young Communists who had idolized Hitler as children. In order to compensate, this "Hitler Youth" generation rejected the supposed recrudescent fascism of West Germany and then, like the heroine in Christa Wolf's *Divided Heaven,* lived to justify this decision after the Wall had closed around them. For many, the present would return to their lives only for a brief moment in 1989 — until a new need for compensation entered through the reopened border.

The open border to the West before 1961 was a unique problem for the SED but also a unique opportunity. Even with a view limited to the university one can see that it helped concentrate certain traditions, attitudes, and beliefs in the GDR. The SED encouraged the migration westward of "bourgeois" scholars, especially in the humanities.[11] Similarly, students of middle-class or religious background who could not be admitted to East German universities could take up studies in the West; the open border fulfilled the function of a "social safety valve," relieving the Party leadership of a need to compensate the once powerful.[12] The SED possessed unique advantages, not only for creating its own elite but also for shaping the society it ruled.

Most Czech and Polish Communists had never seen let alone rejected the West. The core of their convictions lay elsewhere. Unlike East Germans, Czech comrades may not have taken the state very seriously, but they did be-

lieve in their version of socialism, down through the "distortions" of stalinism. Czech Communists had absorbed the attitudes toward ostentatious
wealth of their small town and village milieus and were unequaled in their
desire to erase distinctions between worker and nonworker or student and
professor. What gave the events of 1948 at universities such force was the way
these values were intensified by a would-be cosmopolitan, youthful idealism; this idealism matured and motivated a reform movement twenty years
later. If the fallback position in Party rhetoric in East Germany was "democratic antifascist revolution," here it was "people's democratic revolution,"
and at universities that meant revolution from below.

On this East German and Czech background one sees more clearly the
unusual situation of Poland's Party cadre, which took neither the state nor
socialism very seriously. Especially after 1956, ideology was a thin drap-
ing over a centrally administered system, whose fallback position was the
"nation." The millions of Poles who joined the Communist Party—at about
half the rate of Czechs or East Germans—had to defend their activities in
national terms, and that fact tended to weaken the loyalty of the apparatus toward the Party center. As we have seen, local university functionaries
felt an unusual need to justify themselves to professors, by claiming to "protect" the interests of "their" universities against Warsaw. The power of this
discourse extended to dealings with Soviet functionaries, in which Polish
leaders attempted to plead the exigencies of specific national conditions.
This was hardly a context in which the PZPR might be transformed into the
Leninist ideal of an "organizational weapon."

Students were also part of larger national stories, but at first played a similar role regardless of local context. In the early postwar years, student movements emerged in East Germany, Poland, and the Czech lands that opposed
the violence of Communist rhetoric and behavior. They favored civil liber-
ties and procedural guarantees for democracy. This was a lost opportunity
for liberal politics in Central Europe, all but forgotten behind the dominant narrative created by the "victorious" Communist generation, most elo-
quently represented by such figures as Jiří Pelikán, Jiří Hájek, Christa Wolf,
or Jacek Kuroń.[13] It was not so much the "Hegelian sting" described by
Czesław Miłosz that accounts for the victory of communism among young
intellectuals, as the force of state power, which arrested student leaders, massively expelled suspected opponents, manipulated elections, and terrorized
the student body.

This does not mean that stalinism could get by without social support,
only that to varying degrees the states in question were able to fabricate this
support. One cannot, for example, reduce the stability of the East German
regime to the Stasi, because that only begs the question of how the East Ger-

man state was more successful in creating its police apparatus. This success was predicated upon the unusual contextual advantages that have been mentioned. Having dispensed with old elites, and enjoying the support of the Soviet occupiers as well as an open border to the West, the SED could begin fashioning its own elites from a very early point. It rescued thousands of young people from drab industrial towns of Saxony and Thuringia and propelled them to elite status and modern "comforts" in socialist metropolises like Dresden and East Berlin — all in return for political loyalty and a modicum of professional competence. At universities, people of working-class and peasant background became a significant factor among the professoriate, indeed a majority in the social sciences. The East German elite was the most loyal of the three cases studied, partly because it owed social advance to the Party, and much of the reigning ideology of a "worker-peasant state" seemed to match its own life experiences.

This was a success that eluded the Polish Party, despite the large reservoir of university students from a shrinking peasantry in their country. Because of the continued cultural dominance of the old professoriate, and the Party's ineptitude in reforming university studies, the new students were neither politically loyal nor academically competent, and in 1954 Poland's Communists both weakened preferences for peasant and working-class students and reintroduced the time-honored master's degree in place of "two-step" studies.

In the Czech lands the Party did not succeed in luring workers out of their communities, and middle-class students thus maintained positions at universities and paths leading to them. The point is not so much whether they remained a middle class in the Western sense, because the state took measures to make all employees equal. Indeed, Czech society was characterized by one of the lowest income disparities in the world. The point was rather that individuals of middle-class background considered higher education their birthright and would not repay the socialist state with loyalty in the way that a student of working-class background might.

The opposition of Czech high school students to career tracks different from those of their parents has been referred to as a consequence of social structure, because of the difficulty of readjusting components of a stratified modern society. But it had a cultural aspect as well: the Czech Party failed to change attitudes toward higher education of parents of working-class background because of its own disregard for intellectual enterprise. Besides the egalitarianism that has been mentioned, the Gottwald leadership reproduced a stunning anti-intellectualism that crystallized in outright disdain for universities. In 1947 leading "cultural" functionary Václav Kopecký openly provoked students by proclaiming that workers received more education from reading Party newspapers than students from a university.[14] The neglect of education and culture in stalinist Czechoslovakia was expressed in a pithy formula by functionaries in Brno: "Je jisto, že kultura musí v době nebezpečí ustoupit do pozadí" (In a time of danger, culture gets left behind).[15]

Objections may be raised that political culture is simply what used to be called "national character," yet this study has shown how comparative study challenges national stereotypes. Within Central Europe Germans are famed for organizational talents, yet the most impressive organization encountered in these pages was Polish: the underground state. Despite reputedly strong apolitical and antidemocratic trends within Germany's political culture, some of the most antiauthoritarian individuals encountered in this study were German: East German students of the early postwar years. The most striking thing about the behavior of Polish professors, nurtured in a culture of romanticism, was their ability to seek compromise with the new regime. The reality of 1950s Poland was a spectrum of grays that does not easily fit heroic narratives. Nor does the Czech story fit well into popular antiheroic narratives: perhaps the least "Švejkian" people in this study were the several thousand Czech students—enough to fill a bridge across the Vltava—who, hopelessly outnumbered, marched intrepidly to their defeat beneath Prague's castle. These were not "exceptions to the rule"—they were alternatives.

Objections may likewise be raised about the unity of national political cultures. Within East Germany conflicts emerged in the early postwar years between doctrines supported by authoritarian and nonauthoritarian milieus; neither of these was "German." The national context may have delimited experience, but political attitudes differed and mutated in complex ways according to social class, region, and education.[16] Whatever the sources of antiauthoritarian and professedly liberal beliefs—of people like Wolfgang Natonek and Arno Esch—they were marginalized after 1948–49 and pushed westward. Similar logics applied in the Czech lands: Communists and their opponents shared a certain substratum of beliefs—both, for example, considered the clash of February 1948 almost inevitable—but views on education and politics differed greatly by local and class background, that is, by milieu. One cannot know their "ultimate" sources, but one can see their interplay: precisely a proud middle-class culture built upon education called forth the vicious anti-intellectualism of the half-educated Czech Bolsheviks from Karlín; precisely a strong democracy called forth a strong dictatorship.

The subjective understandings that constitute culture are as historically contingent as the institutions that support them—church hierarchies, faculty councils, editorial boards. These understandings did not make outcomes inevitable, but rather were general conditions that inclined societies in certain directions. The issue of relative Czech passivity in World War II has been mentioned. Yet there is no simple correlation between wartime experience and inherited cultural legacies: had President Beneš decided to resist Nazi Germany, he may well have invited the retribution upon his nation that the Poles suffered.[17] That in turn would have unleashed a far different dynamic of Czech-German relations, and subsequent historians would emphasize the propensity for resistance in the "Czech" or perhaps "Czechoslovak" national character, and imagine roots stretching back to the Hussites and earlier. On the other hand deeper proclivities did nudge, if not force, both societies in familiar directions: it is hard to imagine a Polish statesman behaving like Beneš without risking a coup d'état of the sort suffered by Prince Paul of Yugoslavia in 1941.[18]

Serious difficulties remain in the comparative study of political cultures — for example, that individuals feel pride for the ostensible achievements of "their" nation. More careful consideration shows that, if anything, the relation between the attributes of nation and individual is an inverse one, that the more heroic the context, the more unlikely heroism. Because of the strength of the conservative, Roman Catholic milieu in Kraków, and the pervasiveness of the romantic idiom, it was perhaps simpler for individuals there to oppose rather than embrace communism. One assistant professor at the medical faculty was so embarrassed at having joined the Party in the early 1950s that he whispered the news to his professor, who asked him several times to speak up, and finally replied so that the entire cafeteria could hear: "Joined the Party? That's nothing to be embarrassed about! It's not like having syphilis!"

Such a scene was hardly imaginable in East Germany or the Czech lands, with their very different constellations of political beliefs, and the very different positions of Communist apparatuses in those societies. And so, one might ask, with what justification can an outsider presume to criticize a Professor Stiebitz for his eminently reasonable decision to join the KSČ in 1948, and his encouragement to students to do the same? As Czesław Miłosz has written, people "who understand their place in the world differently cannot be measured by a common standard." Fortunately for us, Professor Karel Engliš did not dispose of the correspondence with his friend František Weyr, and we outsiders, when we write their history fifty years later — as Weyr felt someone would — do not need to inject criticism into that unknowable situation. Criticism was there at the time, and it derived from a local sense of outrage over injustice and unnecessary capitulation.[19] One can debate whether Stiebitz or Weyr was more realistic, for both their paths had costs and benefits. The larger context of East Central Europe — especially

Poland—shows, however, that if Stiebitz, or Pošvář, and dozens of others, became Communists, that was because they *chose* to become Communists, with all the consequences that followed. The point of comparative history is not to impose judgment, but rather to highlight freedom that existed but was not perceived. Occasionally, it may encourage us to cultivate things within ourselves that we first recognize in others.

In addition to the abbreviations used in the text, the following abbreviations are used in the notes.

Archival Sources
AAN: Archiwum Akt Nowych (Archive of Modern Documents), Warsaw
   ANS: Akademia Nauk Społecznych
   BO: Sekretariat Biura Organizacyjnego KC PZPR
   BP: Sekretariat Biura Politycznego KC PZPR
   KC PPR 295: Wydział nauki i oświaty, Komitetu Centralnego, Polskiej Partii Robotniczej (KC PPR)
   KC PZPR 237: Wydział nauki i szkolnictwa wyższego, Komitetu Centralnego, Polskiej Zjednoczonej Partii Robotniczej (KC PZPR)
   KC PZPR 478: Stanisław Skrzeszewski Papers
   MO: Ministerstwo Oświaty
   MSW: Ministerstwo Szkół Wyższych
AČAV: Archív České Akademie Věd (Archive of the Czech Academy of Sciences), Prague
   Josef Král Papers
   Zdeněk Nejedlý Papers
   Miloslav Valouch Papers
   Václav Vaněček Papers
   Arnošt Wenig-Malovský Papers
ANM: Archív Národního Muzea (National Museum Archive), Prague
   Karel Engliš Papers
APAN-K: Archiwum PAN (Archive of the Polish Academy of Sciences), Kraków
   Marian Tyrowicz Papers
APAN-W: Archiwum PAN (Archive of the Polish Academy of Sciences), Warsaw
APKr: Archiwum Państwowy (State Archive), Kraków
   KD PZPR, 62/XV: Podstawowa organizacja Partii przy Uniwersytecie Jagiellońskim
ARAN: Arkhiv Rossiiskoi Akademii Nauk (Archive of the Russian Academy of Sciences), Moscow
AUJ: Archiwum Uniwersytetu Jagiellońskiego (Jagiellonian University), Kraków
   DM: Delegat do spraw młodzieży
   S III: Senat
   Sprzy: Studium przygotowawczy
   WFH: Wydział filozoficzno-historyczny
   Whum: Wydział humanistyczny
   WP III, IV: Wydział prawa
AUK: Archív Univerzity Karlovy (Charles University Archive), Prague
BAAP: Bundesarchiv, Abteilungen Potsdam (Federal German Archive, Potsdam)

C20: Ministerrat der DDR, Teilbestand: Stellvertreter des Vorsitzenden
(Ulbricht)

E1: Staatliche Plankommission der DDR

R2: Deutsche Verwaltung für Volksbildung in der Sowjetischen Besatzungszone
Deutschlands; Ministerium für Volksbildung der DDR

R3: Staatssekretariat für Hochschulwesen der DDR

BPAN-K: Biblioteka PAN Kraków (PAN Library)

GARF: Gosudarstvennyi Arkhiv Rossiiskoi Federatsii (State Archive of the
Russian Federation), Moscow

MLHA: Mecklenburgisches Landeshauptarchiv (Mecklenburg State Archive),
Schwerin

MfVB: Ministerium für Volksbildung

Rkp BJ Przyb: Rękopisy Biblioteka Jagiellońska, Przybytek (Manuscripts,
Jagiellonian University Library), Kraków

Celina Bobińska Papers

RTsKhIDNI: Rossiiskii Tsentr Khraneniia i Izucheniia Dokumentov Noveishei
Istorii (Russian Center for the Protection and Study of Documents in
Modern History), Moscow

SAPMO-BA: Stiftung Archiv der Parteien und Massenorganisationen der DDR
im Bundesarchiv (Archival Foundation for the Parties and Mass
Organizations in the German Federal Archive), Berlin

ZPA: Zentrales Parteiarchiv

IV 2/1: Parteivorstand

IV 2/2: Protokolle des Politbüros des ZK der SED

IV 2/9.04: Abteilung Wissenschaften beim ZK der SED

IV 2/9.08: Institut für Gesellschaftswissenschaften beim ZK der SED

IV 2/10: Abteilung Aussenpolitik und internationale Verbindungen beim
ZK der SED

JIV 2/3: Protokolle des Sekretariats des ZK der SED

NL 90: Otto Grotewohl Papers

NL 182: Walter Ulbricht Papers

SSA: Sächsisches Staatsarchiv (Saxon State Archive), Leipzig

IV 2/9.02: Bezirksleitung Abteilung Wissenschaft, Volksbildung, und Kultur

IV 4.14: Parteileitung der SED der Karl-Marx-Universität Leipzig

SÚA: Státní Ústřední Archív (State Central Archive), Prague

AÚV KSČ: Archív Ústředního Výboru KSČ

f. 02/1: Širší předsednictvo ÚV KSČ

f. 02/2: Politické byro ÚV KSČ, 1954–62

f. 02/4: Politické byro ÚV KSČ

f. 02/5: Politický sekretariát ÚV KSČ

f. 19/7: Kulturní-propagační oddělení ÚV KSČ

f. 19/9: Oddělení stranických orgánů — agendy stranických statistik a
informací

f. 100/1: Generalní sekretariát ÚV KSČ

f. 100/3: Mezinárodní oddělení ÚV KSČ, 1945–62

f. 100/24: Klement Gottwald Papers

f. 100/45: Václav Kopecký Papers

MŠK: Ministerstvo Školství a Kultury

SÚP: Státní Úřad Plánovací
ÚPV: Úřad Předsednictva Vlády
TLHA: Thüringisches Landeshauptarchiv (Thuringian State Archive), Weimar
  MfVB: Ministerium für Volksbildung
UA der HUB: Universitätsarchiv der Humboldt-Universität, Berlin
UAG: Universitätsarchiv, Greifswald
UAL: Universitätsarchiv, Leipzig
UAR: Universitätsarchiv, Rostock

Other
AV: Action Committee (Czech lands)
ČAVU: Czech Academy of Arts and Letters
DDR: German Democratic Republic
KC PZPR: Central Committee of the Polish United Workers Party
MIiP: Ministry of Information and Propaganda (Poland)
NL: Collected papers (Germany)
PAN: Polish Academy of Sciences
PAU: Polish Academy of Arts
POP: Basic Party organization (Poland)
RSFSR: Russian Soviet Federated Socialist Republic
SÚP: State Planning Office (Czech lands)
SVS: Union of University Students (Czech lands)
UMK: Nicolaus Copernicus University, Toruń
ZPA: Central Party Archive (Germany)

INTRODUCTION

1. Brzezinski, *The Soviet Bloc*, 71–72. In this study, "Eastern Europe" is used synony-
   mously with "East Central Europe," both implying the countries of the Soviet
   bloc. "Central Europe" is understood as the area between western Germany
   and Russia, and is used above all for the prewar period.
2. Brzezinski observed that the societies of Eastern Europe "were becoming replicas
   of the Soviet system." Ibid., 85–87, 100–102.
3. Rothschild, *Return to Diversity*, 145.
4. Major syntheses of East European history produced in the past several decades
   have continued to stress the uniformity of East European stalinism, and ana-
   lyze the Soviet bloc under stalinism as a basically undifferentiated whole.
   Robin Okey (1982) described the onset of stalinism in Eastern Europe as "a
   process of uniformization which quickly reduced the East European states
   to slavish models of the Soviet Union." Okey, *Eastern Europe 1740–1980*,
   198. According to Jacques Rupnik (1989), "the Sovietization of East-Central
   Europe meant total control of society by each country's Communist Party,
   but also total Soviet control of the Communist Parties themselves." Rupnik,
   The Other Europe, 109. George Schöpflin (1993) has written that in the stalinist period "an identity of both form and content was imposed on Eastern Europe." Schöpflin, *Politics in Eastern Europe*, 76–77. The major German
   text speaks of the "total *Gleichschaltung* of the lands controlled by the Soviet
   Union," and refers to the period 1947–53 as the "phase of total conformity."
   Hacker, *Der Ostblock*, 413–38. For similar views extending from the 1970s to

the present, see Hoensch, *Sowjetische Osteuropa-Politik,* 44–45; Tomaszewski, *Socialist Regimes,* 165; Simons, *Eastern Europe,* 70–79; Tismaneanu, *Reinventing Politics,* 28; Jowitt, *New World Disorder,* 176; Stokes, *From Stalinism,* 6; Berend, *Central and Eastern Europe,* 39, 43, 48. Surveys that allow more room for diversity in stalinist Eastern Europe include Crampton, *Eastern Europe in the Twentieth Century;* Longworth, *The Making;* and Wandycz, *The Price of Freedom.*

5. The phrase "ice age" is used by Jacques Rupnik, *The Other Europe,* 109–28.

6. Korbonski, "Poland," 265–66; Wandycz, *The Price of Freedom,* 248–50; Davies, *God's Playground,* 2:581–82; Kuroń and Żakowski, *PRL,* 56; Brus, "Stalinism." For an eloquent challenge to the notion of a "helpless" society under stalinism, see Kenney, *Rebuilding Poland.*

7. See the interpretation of an authority on the postwar era, Paczkowski, *Pół wieku,* 238; and the vigorous negations of a milder Polish stalinism in Paczkowski and Karpiński, "Czy PRL była państwem polskim," 64–69. For an interpretation asserting total Party control during stalinism, but also recognizing a Polish peculiarity of a "less extreme" stalinist system, see also Garlicki, *Stalinizm,* 24–25, 73.

8. Klemperer, *So sitze ich,* 2:266–76.

9. In a speech of 12 December 1954 Kurt Hager said that "universities train the leading cadres of our state, economy, and culture; they train the commanders." SAPMO-BA, ZPA, IV 2/9.04/85, Bl. 123–25. See also Seton-Watson, *Eastern Europe,* 229: "In the Eastern European countries the leaders of every generation are those who obtain higher education, the main mechanism by which the ruling class is created."

10. Following Sidney Verba, this work understands political culture as a society's "subjective orientation to politics." Cited in Tucker, "Culture," 176. On the political culture of Communist Eastern Europe, see also Meyer, "Communist Revolutions," 345–70; Jowitt, *New World Disorder,* 50–87; and the contributions in Brown, *Political Culture.*

11. See Ekiert, *The State against Society,* 4. A similar claim has been advanced by Joseph Rothschild: "Only after Stalin . . . could the East Central European periphery's traditional diversities, historical particularities, and sovereign orientations reassert themselves." *Return to Diversity,* 218.

12. On the forced transformation of the law faculty in Moscow to a social science faculty, see Novikov, "Moskovskii Universitet," 173–74; and Stratonov, "Poteria," 196–97.

13. These appear to have been leaders of the liberal intelligentsia. Fitzpatrick, *The Cultural Front,* 51. For a full accounting of the radical break in the Russian social sciences that took place during the 1920s, see the forthcoming dissertation of Stuart Finkel of the history department at Stanford University, "Scholarly Transgressions: The Deportations of Intellectuals and the Politics of Culture in Soviet Russia."

14. See Matthews, *Education in the Soviet Union;* Shumilin, *Soviet Higher Education.*

15. "Skład społeczny studentów I roku szkół wyższych w/g wydziałów w porównaniu ze stanem przedwojennym 1935–36." AAN, MO 2879. Of the Polish population at this time, 29.7 percent was of worker background, 51.5 percent of peasant background. Pilch, *Studencki ruch,* 7–9.

16. In 1947, 3 percent of Brno's students were of working class, 11 percent of agricultural background. Jordán, *Dějiny,* 269. In 1922–23, 16 percent of Czech students were of working-class background, though the working class made up over 60 percent of society. Dąbrowska-Zembrzuska, *Szkolnictwo,* 46.

17. "Zehn-Jahresstatistik des Hochschulbesuchs 1943," Zentralarchiv des FDGB, Bundesvorstand, 11/-/785, cited in Kasper, "Der Kampf," 269.

18. The figures in the Czech lands and East Germany were close to identical: in 1950 "workers and peasants" — that is, manual laborers — amounted to 70.7 percent of the "economically active" population in East Germany, and 70.5 percent of the comparable group in the Czech lands. *Statistisches Jahrbuch der Deutschen Demokratischen Republik 1955,* 26–27; *Vývoj společnosti,* 75. Neither of these calculations breaks down the group "peasants" according to size of holdings, yet these were small after the land reforms of the early postwar years. In 1960 the "gainfully employed" population in Poland (without helping family members) included 27.9 percent peasants and 44.2 percent manual laborers. Lane, "Structural and Social Change," 17. Finding comparable data for Poland in the 1950s is difficult. Approximately 68.4 percent of Poland's employees working in 1949 for salaries or wages in the nonagricultural sector were classified as "physical laborers." *Rocznik statystyczny 1949,* 131. Of Poland's farm population in 1950, including family members, 7.4 percent lived on collective farms, 76.9 percent on farms of less than ten hectares (medium and small peasants), and 39.8 percent on farms of less than five hectares (small peasants). *Rocznik statystyczny 1958,* 31. In 1950, 25.7 percent of the "economically active" population in the Czech lands was involved in agriculture; in East Germany the figure was 25.0 percent, and in Poland, as mentioned, 27.9 percent. *Vývoj společnosti,* 75; *Statistisches Jahrbuch der Deutschen Demokratischen Republik 1955,* 26–27; Lane, "Structural and Social Change," 17. However, if one includes the group "helping members of the family" among the economically active, the Polish total becomes 53.3 percent. *Rocznik statystyczny 1958,* 25. In each society, close to 5 percent of the respective age cohort attended university in the early 1950s. The number of students per cohort was 4.4 percent in the Czech lands, 4.9 percent in East Germany, and 5.0 percent in Poland. This figure is achieved by dividing the average number of daytime students between 1949–50 and 1953–54 (in the East German case, between 1950–51 and 1954–55) by the number of 20 to 24 (in the East German case 21 to 25) year olds. *Statistická ročenka Republiky Československé 1957,* 232; *Historická statistická ročenka,* 428; *Statistisches Jahrbuch der Deutschen Demokratischen Republik 1955,* 23, 113; *Rocznik statystyczny 1959,* 289; *Rocznik statystyczny 1950,* 17. For students per capita, see Table 13-2.

19. On 7 October 1989, the fortieth anniversary of the GDR, thousands of East German students obediently marched in central Berlin at a torch parade, while clashes took place between opponents of the regime and the police in other places in East Berlin, and in Dresden, Plauen, and Magdeburg. See Maier, *Dissolution,* 135–49.

20. This understanding of milieu draws upon M. Rainer Lepsius's classic formulation: "social units, which are formed by the coincidence of a number of structural dimensions, such as religion, regional tradition, economic situation, cultural orientation." See his *Demokratie in Deutschland,* 38.

21. This study follows Max Weber in considering "legitimacy" above all a function of belief. In regard to professors, "legitimacy" implies belief in their authority at and beyond the university, for example among students or in the general public. For a critical discussion of Weber's sociology of legitimacy, see Merquior, *Rousseau and Weber.*

22. For keen insights on the role of the nation's culture in limiting the penetration of the Polish Communist Party, see Korbonski, "Poland," 265–66.

23. On the strength of worker "self-assurance" in the Czech lands, see Myant, *Socialism and Democracy,* 230–31.

24. I find useful Stephen F. Cohen's depiction of stalinism as "excess, extraordinary extremism." In contrast to previous and later Soviet authoritarianism, it "was not merely coercive peasant policy but a virtual civil war against the peasantry; not merely police repression, or even civil-war style terror, but a holocaust by terror that victimized tens of millions of people for twenty-five years; not merely a Thermidorian revival of nationalist tradition, but an almost fascist-like chauvinism; not merely a leader cult, but deification of a despot." *Rethinking the Soviet Experience,* 48.

25. Valuable studies of the Sovietization process include also Birke and Neumann, *Die Sowjetisierung Ost-Mitteleuropas;* Lemberg, *Sowjetisches Modell; Sovětizace východní evropy.*

26. Kaplan, *Sovětští poradci.* Czech and Russian historians have diverged in their interpretations of native initiative versus outside imposition in the Sovietization of institutions in Eastern Europe. For a recent interpretation of a leading Russian expert, see Noskova, "Moskovskie sovetniki."

27. See bibliography for some of Stykalin's publications relevant to this study.

28. Brus, "Stalinism."

29. See Piotr Hübner's detailed study of organizational changes in Polish higher education, *Polityka naukowa;* and Rafał Stobiecki's study of Polish historians, *Historia pod nadzorem,* esp. 40–41, 111–12. See also the early study of the "Sovietization" of East German universities, Müller and Müller, ". . . stürmt die Festung."

30. See Mason, *Nazism, Fascism and the Working Class;* Crew, *Nazism and German Society;* Suny and Siegelbaum, *Making Workers Soviet.*

31. Port, "When Workers Rumbled"; Pernes, "Dělnické demonstrace v Brně."

32. Kopstein, *The Politics of Economic Decline;* Kenney, *Rebuilding Poland.* For the story of political opposition in postwar Poland, see Friszke, *Opozycja polityczna w PRL.*

33. See Bessel and Jessen, *Die Grenzen;* Neubert, *Geschichte der Opposition;* Kaelble, Kocka, and Zwahr, *Sozialgeschichte der DDR;* Poppe, Eckert, and Kowalczuk, *Zwischen Selbstbehauptung und Anpassung.* For an account that highlights the role of state repression, but includes valuable insights on popular opposition, see also Mitter and Wolle, *Untergang.* Several of the studies commissioned by the German Bundestag shed new light on opposition in 1950s East Germany, esp. Hertwig, "Der Umgang." See also the classic study of Fricke, *Opposition und Widerstand.*

34. For general accounts of these processes, see Brzezinski, *The Soviet Bloc;* Rothschild, *Return to Diversity;* Simons, *Eastern Europe;* Crampton, *Eastern Europe in the Twentieth Century.*

35. The Czech National Socialist Party espoused a left liberal platform and had nothing in common with German National Socialism. It was once the party of Edvard Beneš.

36. See Gross, "Social Consequences of War."

37. Eleven of the fourteen defendants of the Slánský trial were Jewish and had been openly accused of "cosmopolite" origin and "Zionist" intrigues. See Taborsky, *Communism in Czechoslovakia*, 106–7.

38. The year 1956 in the Czech lands remains largely unexplored. Intellectual stirrings are dealt with briefly in Kusin, *The Intellectual Origins*, and Rupnik, "Promeškané setkání."

39. See, for example, Féjtö, *A History of the People's Democracies*; Grant, *Schools and Progress*.

40. Foremost in this category are Müller and Müller, ". . . stürmt die Festung," and Richert, "Sozialistische Universität." For a superb overview of SED higher education policies that integrates recent archival findings, see Kowalczuk, *Legitimation*, 83–146.

41. Lönnendonker, *Freie Universität*; Tent, *The Free University*; Rabehl, *Am Ende der Utopie*.

42. Handel and Köhler, *Dokumente der Sowjetischen Militäradministration*; Lammel, *Dokumente*; Klein, *Humboldt-Universität*; Schmidt, *Alma Mater Jenensis*. Valuable dissertations include Kasper, "Der Kampf"; and Merker, "Die Deutschen Zentralverwaltungen."

43. Verband, *Namen und Schicksale*; Kopke, *Mein Vaterland*; Rektor der Friedrich-Schiller-Universität, *Vergangenheitserklärung*.

44. Hoffmann and Macrakis, *Naturwissenschaft und Technik*; Ash, "Verordnete Umbrüche"; Kowalczuk, *Legitimation*, "Anfänge und Grundlinien," and " 'Wo gehobelt wird' "; Feige, "Die Gesellschaftswissenschaftliche Fakultät," and "Zur Entnazifizierung"; Schneider, *Bildung*; Krönig and Müller, *Anpassung*. On the role of the Soviet Military Administration, see Naimark, *The Russians*, 440–64; Haritonow, *Sowjetische Hochschulpolitik*.

45. Pike, *Politics of Culture*; Dietrich, *Politik und Kultur*.

46. Kuczynski, "Ein linientreuer"; Markov, *Zwiesprache*; Mayer, *Der Turm von Babel*; Maeß, *Mögen viele Lehrmeinungen*; Rupieper, "Wiederaufbau."

47. Jessen, "Akademische Elite." This work is now available as *Akademische Elite und kommunistische Diktatur* (Göttingen, 1999). See also Jessen's "Professoren," and "Vom Ordinarius." On student recruitment, see Stallmann, *Hochschulzugang*; and on physicians, Ernst, "Die beste Prophylaxe."

48. See Hartmann, *Hochschulwesen*; Krasiewicz, *Odbudowa*; Chodakowska, *Rozwój*; Fijałkowska, *Polityka i twórcy*; Longchamps, *Uniwersytet Wrocławski*; Kłoskowska, *Uniwersytet Łódzki*; Łuczak, *University of Poznań*.

49. Michałowski, *Wspomnienia*; Tyrowicz, *W poszukiwaniu siebie*; Jarocki, *Widzieć jasno*.

50. Hübner, *Polityka naukowa*. During the perestroika period a valuable abridged edition of his work was permitted to appear. See *Nauka polska*. For a consideration of the transformation of scientific societies in Poland, see his "Last Flight."

51. Lewandowski, *Rodowód*; Stobiecki, *Historia pod nadzorem*; Suleja, *Uniwersytet Wrocławski*.

52. Sławińska, *Szlakami;* Steinhaus, *Wspomnienia;* Ryszka, *Pamiętnik;* Schaff, *Moje spotkania.*

53. Urban, *Die Organisation;* Kratochvil, *Kommunistische Hochschulpolitik.*

54. Hanzal, "Studijní prověrky." See also the studies of Jiří Maňák, "Problematika odměňování české inteligence," and "Sociální aspekty," and the probing studies of Lenka Kalinová, Václav Brabec, and Jana Neumannová in *Revue dějin socialismu* of 1968 and 1969. Shortly before "normalization," the crowning achievement of these studies appeared as Machonin, *Československá společnost.* For an appreciation, see Gellner, "The Pluralist Anti-Levellers."

55. Jordán, *Dějiny.* A shorter but also valuable effort of this period is Kavka, *Universita Karlova.*

56. One useful though heavily biased work to appear during the normalization era is Kráčmarová, *Vysokoškoláci.*

57. See the final volume of the series: Havránek and Pousta, *Dějiny Univerzity Karlovy.*

58. Černý, *Paměti;* Hájek, *Paměti;* Wichterle, *Vzpomínky.*

59. An exception is Reich, *Abschied.*

60. Several studies have emerged on the peripheries of this subject, however. For a judicious survey of Czech intellectuals' political behavior in the prestalinist years, see Abrams, "The Struggle." On Czechoslovak intellectuals throughout the postwar period, see Hruby, *Fools and Heroes.* For critiques of the political behavior of East German universities in June 1953: Kowalczuk, "Volkserhebung"; Huschner, "Der 17. Juni 1953." See also Torpey, *Intellectuals,* which examines the critical intelligentsia in East Germany, and focuses on the 1980s.

61. Kuroń and Żakowski, *PRL,* 42. See also Kuroń, *Wiara i wina.* For further references and discussion, see Kersten, *Między wyzwoleniem,* 100–62; Praszałowicz, "Inteligencja"; Trznadel, *Hańba;* and Słabek, *Intelektualistów.*

62. "People in the West are often inclined to consider the lot of converted countries in terms of might and coercion. That is wrong. There is an internal longing for harmony and happiness that lies deeper than ordinary fear or the desire to escape misery or physical destruction." Miłosz, *Captive Mind,* 6, 12.

63. Trznadel, *Hańba,* 184. An abridged translation can be found in Trznadel, "An Interview."

64. Trznadel, *Hańba,* 183–84. Like all great books, Miłosz's is not without internal contradictions, admitting at times the power of fear over inner conviction, and the inherent weakness of the New Faith, while gloomily musing over its inevitable triumphs. Gobineau's Ketman masked a true religious belief, while belief was surely secondary to the charades practiced in Communist Poland. They were more likely a reflexive and sometimes ritualized form of resistance rather than a surrender of the mind. Like Orwell's *1984,* the book was above all a warning. See also Miłosz's autobiography, *Native Realm,* 120: "Whoever claims that force cannot suffice as an argument overlooks the character of politics, where winner takes all."

65. Trznadel, *Hańba,* 9–38.

66. See Schaff, *Pora;* Kott, *Still Alive;* Knapp, *Proměny;* Havemann, *Warum;* Kuczynski, *"Ein linientreuer."* An exception among memoirists is Kolman, *Die verirrte Generation.* Because of its immediacy, Klemperer's *So sitze ich* affords unparalleled insights into the thinking of a German Communist intellectual.

67. See her *Under a Cruel Star.* See also Pelikán, *Ein Frühling;* Císař, *Člověk;* Mlynář, *Nightfrost;* Hájek, *Paměti;* and Dubček, *Hope.*

68. *Under a Cruel Star,* 59. For accounts of less than heroic Communist behavior in Nazi camps, see Buber-Neumann, *Milena;* Niethammer, *Der gesäuberte Antifaschismus.*

69. *Under a Cruel Star,* 63; Herf, *Divided Memory.*

70. The memoirists cited in note 67 generally do not mention Communist terror against non-Communists with so much as a word, and write very little about the stalinism they helped construct. For example, Alexander Dubček (b. 1921) devotes seven of over three hundred pages to the years 1948 to 1954. See *Hope,* 59–65. Only after the split with Stalin did Yugoslavia begin to espouse a different kind of socialism. For early postwar politics in Yugoslavia, see McClellan, "Postwar Political Evolution," 125–31.

71. For the high number of antifascists among the Communists' opponents in East Germany, see chapter 6 at n. 75; on the results of student council elections in the Czech lands and East Germany, see chapter 5, n. 43; chapter 6, n. 63. A blurb from the *Daily Telegraph* describes Kovály's book as "the portrait of a whole generation, not just in Czechoslovakia, but throughout Eastern Europe." Yet Kovály's portrayals are highly selective. In the debates that took place in her tiny Prague apartment after the war, the task of defending Western democracy falls to Franta, an army officer who had "lived out the war like a hibernating animal" and refused to give Kovály shelter after she escaped from a Nazi death march. His opponent, Zdeněk, "had been accepted into the Communist Party somewhere in the forest, in a tent, by candlelight, with a submachine gun in his hands. . . . Anything he said sounded strong and convincing simply because it was he who said it." She felt "ashamed to be agreeing with his opponent, Franta, who was so rational and prudent and never forgot which side his bread was buttered on." *Under a Cruel Star,* 57–58.

72. See chapter 2 at n. 15 for the SED's "fundamental demands" in higher education.

73. BAAP, R2/1447, Bl. 196–97. See also the remarks attributed to Polish functionary Jakub Berman at a meeting of the scientific council (*rada naukowa*) of the Ministry of Education on 16 July 1945 in AAN, MO 2801, k. 50–51.

74. For a provocative consideration of the issue of continuities in the East German case, see Ash, "Verordnete Umbrüche." On the resistance to ideological penetration of medical faculties, see Ernst, *"Die beste Prophylaxe";* Jessen, "Akademische Elite."

75. See, for example, the story of reform efforts by a group of young scholars (Uwe-Jens Heuer, Klaus Korn, Wolfgang Heise) in the early 1960s at the Humboldt University. Bresch and Noack, " 'Freiheit im Sozialismus.' "

76. Before drafting their own higher-education law in 1950 Czech Communists looked at both Soviet and Polish versions. In November 1951 a Czech functionary complaining of the state of worker studies in his country made explicit references to the situation in East Germany and Poland. SÚA, AÚV KSČ, f. 19/7, a.j. 321, l. 124–25. East German functionaries visited Poland in the early 1950s to study worker education there. BAAP, R3/145, Bl. 374–81.

77. On the history of academia in Hungary in the postwar era, see Péteri, *Academia and State Socialism.*

78. Rothschild, *Return to Diversity*, ix. Okey excludes the GDR, whereas Brzezinski, Simons, and Schöpflin include the GDR in their discussions of East Central Europe.

INTRODUCTION TO PART I
1. Pelikán, *Ein Frühling*, 88.

CHAPTER 1
1. University professors regulated entrance to the state bureaucracies, industry, and the professions. Mitchell G. Ash refers to German universities as "guarantors of elite status" because a range of positions—for example, management in firms—required the doctorate. "Common and Disparate Dilemmas," 40. On the exalted role of professors in the Austrian and Czech traditions, see Havránek, "Nineteenth Century," 12–22. For German universities' support of the pre-Weimar political order, see Ringer, *Fields of Knowledge*, 95–107; Kádner, *Vývoj*, part 2, 610–11.

2. The only private universities in the region studied were the Catholic University of Lublin, and the free university of Warsaw (Wolna Wszechnica), with a branch in Łódź. Kádner, *Vývoj*, part 4, 242. Two of Germany's twenty-three universities were run by their respective cities. Kádner, *Vývoj*, part 2, 617.

3. Lönnendonker, *Freie Universität*, 10.

4. The process of qualifying for university lecturing was the "habilitation," which required a second dissertation, and a colloquium for the faculty. For the Czech habilitation regulations, see Mates, Průcha, and Svatoš, *Vývoj organizace*, 23. For official regulation of the Polish habilitation practice, see Hartmann, *Hochschulwesen*, 471. In many German universities the ministry had a representative directly at the university called the "Kurator," who had the right to review university correspondence with state agencies. Kádner, *Vývoj*, part 2, 601–2.

5. In Poland, the largest major subject in the 1937–38 school year was law, taken by 27.5 percent of all students. In second place were liberal arts and sciences, with 26.2 percent of all students, followed by technical sciences (15.8 percent) and medicine (8.1 percent). Hartmann, *Hochschulwesen*, 8.

6. On the application of Humboldt's ideas in the German tradition, see Bruch, "Slow Farewell." For the absorption of Prussian-Humboldtian models into Austrian—and thus Galician and Bohemian—higher education during the Thun reforms of the 1850s, see Lentze, *Die Universitätsreform*.

7. In the American context, philosophical faculties might be called "faculties of arts and sciences." They included all humanistic and scientific disciplines.

8. In the Czech and Polish cases faculties selected electors of the rector. See Article No. 9 of the Polish higher-education law of 15 March 1933, cited in Hartmann, *Hochschulwesen*, 463; also Kádner, *Vývoj*, part 4, 245. For a discussion of the semiautonomy of higher schools in interwar Czechoslovakia, see Mates, Průcha, and Svatoš, *Vývoj organizace*, 18–21. For descriptions of the Czech, German, and Polish university systems before World War II, see Kádner, *Vývoj*, part 2, 144–57, 599–629; part 4, 242–47. In Germany professors were civil servants, but the state had no right to supervise teaching and research. Jessen, "Akademische Elite," 259.

9. Technically speaking the ministry supervised and did not manage or control universities. See, for example, Article No. 4 of the Polish higher-education law of 15 March 1933, cited in Hartmann, *Hochschulwesen,* 461. All higher-education laws included provisions for frequent consultations between ministry and faculties. In Germany, too, the appointment of a professor without a university's consent was unusual and caused consternation. See, for example, the Adler case in Leipzig (1923), in Muller, *The Other God.* The first case since the founding of a Czech university in 1882 of a professorial appointment not emerging from the faculty occurred on 15 March 1939, when the post-Munich regime of Dr. Hácha named Professor Karel Engliš of Masaryk University in Brno professor at Prague's law faculty. See "Návrh na jmenování profesora Dr Karla Engliše" (undated), in Personnel file Karel Engliš, AUK.

10. There were special university churches as well as university police (*inspektsiia*) to encourage and control the propagation of ideology. Chanbarisov, *Formirovanie,* 15.

11. Some thousand of these were students of Moscow University. Chanbarisov, *Formirovanie,* 20–24; Kádner, *Vývoj,* part 4, 130. Czech expert Kádner described one instance of repression as sounding like a "fairy tale": namely the refusal to permit a bust of Tolstoy to be placed in the main lecture hall of Kiev University. Ibid., 129–30.

12. McClelland, *Autocrats,* 68. For the view that a "pragmatic-utilitarian understanding of higher education" characterized the Russian system from the founding of the Russian Academy of Sciences in 1724, see Mühle, *Die Entsowjetisierung,* 13.

13. McClelland, *Autocrats,* 68–69, 81.

14. Besides a number of independent theological academies, there were independent medical, legal, technical, mining, and historical-philological institutes of higher learning. With the exception of technical subjects, the disciplines at the core of these institutes were taught exclusively at universities in Central Europe. Kádner, *Vývoj,* part 4, 128–29.

15. Ibid., part 2, 613. For more data on inequalities in East European higher education, see introduction at nn. 15, 16.

16. The decree of 2 August 1918 forbade "requesting from the applicants any kind of certificate, except an identification card stating their age." Shumilin, *Soviet Higher Education,* 21. The minimum age was sixteen. The full text appears in Anweiler and Meyer, *Sowjetische Bildungspolitik,* 65–66.

17. Shumilin, *Soviet Higher Education,* 59.

18. Ibid., 64.

19. Fitzpatrick, *Commissariat,* 84.

20. Fitzpatrick, *Education,* 71.

21. Ibid., 76–77.

22. Shumilin, *Soviet Higher Education,* 22.

23. Social sciences were understood as "basic political knowledge." Anweiler and Meyer, *Sowjetische Bildungspolitik,* 33, 124.

24. Fitzpatrick, *Education,* 97; Konecny, "Chaos."

25. Chanbarisov, *Formirovanie,* 193–94, cited in David-Fox, "Assault," 26.

26. David-Fox, "Assault," 12. David-Fox's essay will appear in Michael David-Fox and György Péteri, eds., *Academia in Upheaval: Origins, Transfers, and Trans-*

formations of the Communist Academic Regime in Russia and East Central Europe (Westport, Conn., and London, 2000).

27. Fitzpatrick, *Education,* 198.

28. David-Fox, "Assault," 35–38. The brigade method involved group work on projects under a professor's supervision. Fitzpatrick, *Education,* 191.

29. Fitzpatrick, *Education,* 192; David-Fox, "Assault," 35–38. The assaults of this period on the old intelligentsia and its institutions and norms have been termed a "cultural revolution." See the essays in Fitzpatrick, *Cultural Revolution,* and Fitzpatrick, *The Cultural Front.*

30. David-Fox, "Assault," 24.

31. Fitzpatrick, *Education,* 231.

32. David-Fox, "Assault," 37; Fitzpatrick, *Education,* 189.

33. Fitzpatrick, *Education,* 192–93.

34. David-Fox, "Assault," 36; Fitzpatrick, *Education,* 189.

35. David-Fox, "Assault," 21.

36. Ibid., 20.

37. Fitzpatrick, *Education,* 129, 133.

38. Ibid., 129, 184; David-Fox, "Assault," 12.

39. Matthews, *Education in the Soviet Union,* 98. The total number of students at all Soviet institutions of higher education in 1931–32 was 394,000, of whom 51.4 percent came from the working class. Fitzpatrick, *Education,* 188.

40. David-Fox, "Assault," 14, 23.

41. Ibid., 22–23. These figures are also given in Fitzpatrick, *Education,* 194.

42. Fitzpatrick, *Education,* 209.

43. In January 1932 the Politburo approved better living conditions for "specialists and scholars." David-Fox, "Assault," 50. A decree of 11 November 1937 established a system of ranks and a differentiated scale of salaries. Butiagin and Saltanow, "30 lat," 379; Matthews, *Education in the Soviet Union,* 100.

44. Fitzpatrick, *Education,* 250.

45. Ibid., 232.

46. Gail Lapidus has written that "by the mid-1930s the structure and ethos of the Soviet educational system had assumed a form that would persist for several decades." "Educational Strategies," 396. Anweiler and Meyer write that the system that emerged during the first two Five-Year Plans "was hardly changed in its essential features to the end of the stalinist period." *Sowjetische Bildungspolitik,* 42.

47. This summary derives from categories identified by Russian historian A. P. Nikitin, "Die sowjetische Militäradministration," 406–7.

48. Anweiler and Meyer, *Sowjetische Bildungspolitik,* 220–21. Narkompros was likewise converted into a ministry—of education—in 1946.

49. Matthews, *Education in the Soviet Union,* 108, 114–15.

50. Ibid., 116.

51. Ibid., 117.

52. Butiagin and Saltanow, "30 lat," 379–80.

53. Matthews, *Education in the Soviet Union,* 146.

54. Ibid., 142.

55. Ibid., 118–19, 133.

56. Ibid., 115.

57. By the early 1950s part-time study was well established, on an evening or correspondence basis. Ibid., 127, 135–36.

58. Ibid., 114.

59. David-Fox, "Assault," 53.

60. Matthews, *Education in the Soviet Union*, 123.

61. This institute lasted until 1928. Anweiler and Meyer, *Sowjetische Bildungspolitik*, 32; David-Fox, *Revolution of the Mind*.

62. Matthews, *Education in the Soviet Union*, 117–18.

63. Fitzpatrick, *Education*, 118.

64. Ibid., 209.

65. Matthews, *Education in the Soviet Union*, 130–32.

66. Ibid., 154–56.

67. Kádner, *Vývoj*, part 4, 170–74.

CHAPTER 2

1. Torańska, *Oni*, 26–27.

2. Also true, as Jan T. Gross has suggested, is that the war years created important conditions for the formation of Soviet rule. See his "Social Consequences." This point will be developed in the discussion of professorial communities in chapter 4.

3. In April 1945 representatives of the Czechoslovak London Government met with KSČ representatives in the Slovak town of Košice, and agreed upon the framework of the postwar Czechoslovak political order. For details, see Crampton, *Eastern Europe in the Twentieth Century*, 235–36. Nejedlý had become full professor of musicology at Charles University in 1919, and was known during the interwar years as a supporter of leftist causes, and, strangely, as a biographer of T. G. Masaryk. He spent the war years teaching in the Soviet Union. *Československý biografický slovník*, 482–83. His colleague, the professor of romance literature Václav Černý, wrote that in 1945 Nejedlý finally achieved the power he had "long yearned and prayed for, but now it was given a person long since creatively powerless and of weakened character." *Paměti*, 3:146–47.

4. Major figures in the pedagogical faculties in Prague and Brno—Nejedlý, educator Otakar Chlup, and the linguist František Trávníček—were KSČ members. On the founding of pedagogical faculties, see "Dekret Prezidenta Republiky ze dne 27.10.45 o vzdělaní učitelstva," č. 132/1945, *Sbírka zákonů republiky Československé*, and "Zákon ze dne 9. dubna 1946 kterým se zřizují pedagogické fakulty," č. 100/1946, ibid.

5. Interview with Professor Jan Havránek, 7 July 1993.

6. *Československý biografický slovník*, 445.

7. Procházka had translated the works of Shaw, Feuchtwanger, and Steinbeck into Czech, and was also doctor of law who had spent time in the Soviet Union. Ibid., 572. A committee of the law faculty unanimously recommended him to the Ministry of Education for professorship on 14 November 1945, though among his writings on economics and law only "several were written using the proper scholarly method." His supporter Professor Hobza sought to finesse Procházka's lack of academic qualifications by citing his broad knowledge of

"public administration in Soviet Russia." See the letter of Dean Jan Matějka to Zdeněk Nejedlý of 14 November 1945, AČAV, Nejedlý Papers, č.k. 31.

8. Kolman, *Die verirrte Generation*. Kolman was returned to the Soviet Union in 1948 after criticizing the KSČ leadership for neglecting the class composition of the Party and for its "bourgeois" life-style. He was permitted back to Czechoslovakia in 1960 in order to combat revisionist views but became a supporter of the Prague Spring; interview with Professor Jan Havránek, 7 July 1993.

9. "Vysoké školy — universita," AČAV, Král Papers, i.č. 36.

10. Wycech (1899–1977), a teacher by profession, had been director of education in the wartime underground government loyal to London, and behaved decently toward university communities during his brief postwar tenure. He left office in February 1947 after the PPR victory in elections of the previous month. Mołdawa, *Ludzie władzy,* 443.

11. Bieńkowski (1906–91) left the education administration in September 1946 and was succeeded by Krassowska (1910–86), who had completed studies in Wilno in the 1930s, taught in underground education during the war, and afterward held leading positions in the Democratic Party (Stronnictwo Demokratyczne), which unwaveringly supported the PPR/PZPR. She remained an undersecretary of state responsible for higher education until 1964. Ibid., 337, 379. The staff was rounded out by Professor Stanisław Arnold (PPR), Jerzy Marowski (PPR), Professor Henryk Raabe (PPS), Wiktor Kornatowski (PPR), Eugeniusz Geblewicz, and later Adam Uziembło (PPR).

12. Krasiewicz, *Odbudowa,* 123. For the protocols of Skrzeszewski's meetings, see AUJ, S III 1. Skrzeszewski (1901–78) was a teacher by profession, who graduated from Jagiellonian University in 1924 and joined the Communist Party the same year. He spent the war in the Soviet Union, and served as education minister from December 1944 to June 1945, and then from February 1947 to July 1950. From 1951 to 1956 he was minister of foreign affairs. Mołdawa, *Ludzie władzy,* 422.

13. See chapter 6.

14. The liberal Dr. Emil Mencke-Glückert was responsible for higher education in Saxony until mid-1946, when at the demand of the SVAG he was replaced by Dr. Arthur Simon (SED). Haritonow, *Sowjetische Hochschulpolitik,* 75. Otherwise all leading positions in education in Brandenburg, Mecklenburg, Saxony, Saxony-Anhalt, and Thuringia were held by SPD/SED or KPD/SED members from 1945 onward. This was also true of the central administration in Berlin, except for Professor Theodor Brugsch, who, although not a member of any party, was a close ally of the SED. Broszat and Weber, *SBZ-Handbuch,* 96–99, 118–21, 142–44, 162–63, 183–85, 237–38.

15. 11 April 1947, SAPMO-BA, ZPA, IV 2/9.04/6. Kauffeldt was in charge of higher education in the SED Central Secretariat in 1946 and 1947.

16. The DVV was created by SVAG Order No. 17 of 27 July 1945 and had responsibility for the "administration of schools, kindergartens, educational establishments, and artistic, scientific, cultural institutions." It operated within the Soviet Zone of Occupation but, as the name suggested, was to serve as a basis for a later all-German government. Handel and Köhler, *Dokumente der Sowjetischen Militäradministration,* 14–15. The DVV based its early authority on its informal role of interpreting and communicating Soviet intentions. See, for

example, the DVV letter of 19 November 1946 requiring uniform payment of salaries to professors throughout the Soviet zone, "according to a directive of the SVAG." BAAP, R2/636, Bl. 170. See also the telegram of 30 December 1947 to university rectors and regional ministries of education on the interpretation of Soviet Order No. 56 [13 March 1947] on the payment of salaries to professors in BAAP, R2/638. An agreement of the DVV and *Land* governments of 2 May 1947 specified, among other things, that the DVV had the task of "examining the execution of the orders of the supreme authorities of the SVAG," and "coordinating the work of the *Länder* of the SBZ." Letter of rector to deans, 9 July 1947, UAR, RIII E1-3/1.

17. The DVV's authority was quickly recognized by the Communist-controlled education ministries of the *Länder*. See, for example, the circular of the Mecklenburg ministry of 22 January 1947: "on the direction of the supreme authorities of the SVAG the officers of the DVV have the right to inspect schooling in the Soviet Zone of Occupation." UAR, K1-1005. Paul Wandel (1905–94) was a former Comintern teacher and had not attended college, yet his deputy for university affairs Rompe (1905–93) was a university teacher. Before 1933 Wandel was KPD second secretary in Baden. His former pupil Wolfgang Leonhard described him as the "perfected prototype of the intelligent Stalinist": "when the line changed he was prepared to change his opinion from one day to the next and with crystal clear logic to argue precisely the opposite of that which he had said the day before." Leonhard, *Die Revolution,* 217. Wandel had been recommended by the KPD Central Committee and confirmed by the occupation authorities. GARF, f. 7317, op. 54, d. 4, l. 55. Professor Robert Rompe headed the DVV Higher-Education Department from 1946 to 1949. He had been born of German parents in St. Petersburg in 1905 and before the Nazi seizure of power had received a doctorate in physics and joined the KPD. After 1933 he managed to receive his habilitation from the University of Bonn. This mixture of fluent Russian, academic credentials, and Communist Party membership predestined him for his position. BAAP, R2/934, Bl. 137.

18. This was often not a simple process, because local authorities were suspicious of centralization. Of one attempt to formalize DVV competences in personnel matters, Minister Rücker of Brandenburg exclaimed, "I'll never get that through my parliament!" Meeting of 18 March 1947, BAAP, R2/53, Bl. 108-9.

19. BAAP, R2/1482, R2/1484, R2/1462; SAPMO-BA, ZPA, NL 182/933. By profession a waiter, Halle had been KPD district spokesman in Halle-Merseburg. He spent the years 1935 to 1945 in Buchenwald, and from 1945 to 1949 directed the Higher-Education Department in Saxony-Anhalt. Unable to spell simple German, he was not up to the tasks of director of universities for all the GDR, and was relieved of duties in November 1950. Müller and Müller, "... *stürmt die Festung,*" 396. For examples of his orthography: BAAP, R2/1490, Bl. 15, 53.

20. *Das Kapital* by Marx appeared at the end of the list, an apparent afterthought. Gerhard Harig wrote to the Ministry of Education in Saxony-Anhalt on 7 December 1950 expressing disapproval, because the lectures were not in accordance with the "scientific bases of our economic planning." The semester was already well under way, however. BAAP, R2/1488, Bl. 71, 76.

21. Interview with Professor Johannes Schmidt, Leipzig, 15 June 1991. Coordinating lecture programs in the history of philosophy likewise required years of exer-

tion, with numerous programs rejected as the times changed. BAAP, R2/1422, Bl. 13; R2/1455, Bl. 8.

22. Kauffeldt to the SED *Land* administrations, 24 December 1946. SAPMO-BA, ZPA, IV 2/9.04/6.

23. "Situationsskizze," April 1947. SAPMO-BA, ZPA, IV 2/9.04/6.

24. The professors included Meusel, Kuczynski, Gleitze, Deiters, and Naas from Berlin; Herz from Greifswald; Rienäcker from Rostock; Behrens and Markov from Leipzig; and Henselmann from Weimar. SAPMO-BA, ZPA, IV 2/9.04/6. Ackermann (1905–73), famous as author of the 1946 essay on a "special German road to socialism," by profession a hosiery worker, had been a KPD functionary in Berlin, Spain, Paris, and Moscow, and directed the first Communist "initiative group" in Saxony after the war. He was demoted in 1953 for support of Ulbricht's rivals Herrnstadt and Zaisser. Černý, *Wer war wer,* 10–11.

25. See the "Bericht über die Sitzung der Betriebsgruppenleiter der Universitäten Berlin, Jena, Rostock, Greifswald, Leipzig und Halle am 22. und 23. November 1946 in Halle/Saale." SAPMO-BA, ZPA, IV 2/9.04/456.

26. BAAP, R2/1060. For exact breakdowns, see chapter 12, Table 12-2.

27. Kowalczuk, "Die Durchsetzung," 47. By early 1948 almost one-third (31.2 percent) of the assistant professors in Leipzig were SED members. SAPMO-BA, ZPA, IV 2/9.04/458, Bl. 107–10.

28. A meeting of leading PZPR higher-education functionaries of 19 October 1949 determined that "administrative functions (rector, dean, etc.) should be occupied by our comrades, but deputies do not have to be our comrades, because these are secondary positions, on which we cannot waste our cadres. The rule is to occupy only key positions with our comrades." AAN, KC PZPR 237/XVI/2, k. 2–3. In East Germany, the practice was the opposite: to occupy all but a few positions with SED members, leaving a couple of figurehead spots to "bourgeois" scholars — as supposed evidence of the SED's policy of alliance with progressive forces. These figurehead positions were usually precisely rectors' and deans' offices. Actual authority lay not with the rector, but with the Party first secretary. The implications of low Party membership in Poland are considered in chapters 8 and 9.

29. Fijałkowska, *Polityka i twórcy,* 67.

30. AAN, KC PPR 295/XVII/57, k. 11. Jędrychowski appears as Robespierre in Miłosz's *Native Realm.* He later became minister of finances and foreign affairs. Mołdawa, *Ludzie władzy,* 365–66.

31. AAN, KC PPR 295/XVII/57, k. 20.

32. In November 1947 the PPR delegate for university admissions in Warsaw wrote to the Central Committee that he could not tell them how many candidates for admission were Party members, because "many members have not revealed their affiliation." Rather, if they belonged to another "democratic organization," they often listed it alone and did not mention their membership in the PPR. AAN, KC PPR 295/XVII/61, k. 429, 429a.

33. In 1947 open agitation for communism was still conducted under threat of assassination in many places in Poland. On the continuity of conspiratorial practices, see the protocol of a meeting of PPR and PPS professors of 15 September 1947, which concludes that "an atmosphere of the underground still prevails at universities, and democrats are as if smothered by the sheer quantity of non-

Party members." AAN, KC PPR 295/XVII/58, k. 79. Discussions of November 1947 also concede leftist academics' "inability to emerge from an atmosphere of illegal work" and "the persistence of an atmosphere of illegality in [Communist] activity." AAN, KC PPR 295/XVII/57, k. 38, 46.

34. The PPR had one member among academics in Toruń, two in Lublin. AAN, KC PPR 295/XVII/57, k. 5–6.

35. Basic Party cells (POP) at universities emerged only in 1949. Suleja, *Uniwersytet Wrocławski*, 162–63.

36. See, for example, the comments of Professor Bonder from Gliwice in November 1947, AAN, KC PPR 295/XVII/57, k. 45. Shortly after the PPR took complete control of the Education Ministry in 1947, an "educational and cultural department" was created in its Central Committee for coordination of its policies in these areas. The leader of this department until December 1947 was Stanisław Trojanowski; thereafter, until November 1948, Stefan Żółkiewski. Fijałkowska, *Polityka i twórcy*, 42–43.

37. Provincial staff members who advanced to higher-education work in Berlin included Simon (Saxony), Halle (Saxony-Anhalt), Pätsch (Thuringia), Wohlgemuth and Mamat (Mecklenburg).

38. Grzymala-Busse, "Communist Party Strategies."

39. The SED came in third behind the SPD and CDU, faring poorly even in prewar strongholds of the KPD, like Wedding. Naimark, *The Russians*, 329.

40. Some former SPD members were no less radical stalinists than KPD counterparts. In higher education such figures included Helmut Häntzsche in Saxony, Wilhelm Hauser, Ernst Hoffmann, and Heinrich Deiters in Berlin, and Marie Torhorst in Thuringia. In February 1948, sixty-four officials in the DVV had belonged to the KPD, and twenty-nine to the SPD. BAAP, R2/999, Bl. 50. Two were directors of key departments: Paul Reichwaldt (finances) and Ernst Hadermann (primary and secondary education). The latter had also been a Nazi Party member.

41. *Československé dějiny*, 468.

42. SÚA, AÚV KSČ, f. 19/7, a.j. 104, 313, 314, 316, 328.

43. The figure for Prague is based upon numbers of KSČ members in all Prague higher-education organizations—teachers and staff included—totaling 2,556 in mid-1947, and 2,859 in February 1948, and a student population of about 30,000. Kráčmarová, *Vysokoškoláci*, 91; "Zápis z celostátní odborové konference vysokoškolských pracovníků KSČ a KSS," 3–4 January 1947, in AUK, SVS B35. For statistics on Brno, see Jordán, *Dějiny*, 270.

44. Rupnik, "Intelektuálové."

45. For a discussion of a poor self-image in the SED resulting from this tutelage, see Naimark, *The Russians*, 286.

46. On the difference in attitude toward other places, contrast Soviet reports emanating in 1948 from East Germany, full of concern for directly "hastening the democratization of the Soviet zone," with those coming from Czechoslovakia, where the major concern was to "strengthen cultural ties" or at best "increase Soviet influence." For the former, see the letter from A. F. Kabanov (SVAG) to M. A. Suslov, 24 September 1948, RTsKhIDNI, f. 17, op. 132, d. 65, l. 67; or Tiul'panov to M. A. Suslov, 9 March 1948, RTsKhIDNI, f. 17, op. 128, d. 566, l. 19. For the Czech case, see V. Kemenov (VOKS) to L. A. Slepov, 16 July 1948;

and the report of 13 May 1948 from S. Shundenko, head of the Foreign Department of the Ministry of Higher Education; RTsKhIDNI, f. 17, op. 128, d. 488,
ll. 25–26, 104–12. The Soviets also created a unique technical apparatus in East
Germany for the production of their own teaching materials, for example, the
Soviet printing press in Leipzig. See the report of 11 March 1948 in GARF,
f. 5283, op. 16, d. 138, l. 87.

47. Soviet embassies in Warsaw or Prague did not even have an official in charge
of education, let alone universities. The network in East Germany also extended to Soviet security services, though the precise links are not specified
in East German state and Party documents. The officer at Rostock university, "Comrade Lekutzky," advised the SED Party group how to deal with
challenges of non-Communist students — for example, the "ironic and hidden
allusions" made on their posters — but apparently also passed his information
on to the NKVD, because the LDP at Rostock University was decimated by
arrests. See the SED Party group's report of June 1949, MLHA, MfVB 94, Bl.
59–60. After the founding of the GDR in the fall of 1949, these officers were replaced by education "inspectors." See the "Arbeitsbesprechung der Abteilung
C," 22 November 1949, TLHA, MfVB 3184, Bl. 42.

48. Zolotukhin admonished the Germans on the subject of denazification during
a 29 March 1946 meeting: "The German Central Administration is remote;
even in Berlin where it is close to the university it does not have information."
Soviet officer Nomofinov complained that "not a single representative of the
DVV has been seen in the Province [sic] Mecklenburg–West Pomerania since
October, with one exception, and that gentleman was merely picking up his
personal belongings. Such a bureaucratic understanding of the tasks of leadership is not compatible with today's realities and will not lead to the ideas of
the new Germany." BAAP, R2/1332, Bl. 107, 141.

49. See Connelly, "East German Higher Education Policies."

50. BAAP, R2/1040, Bl. 31. Zolotukhin (1897–1968) had been the editor of *Leningrad-
skaia Pravda* and rector of Leningrad University, and after returning to the
Soviet Union in 1948 he became deputy to the People's Commissar for Education of the RSFSR. Haritonow, *Sowjetische Hochschulpolitik,* 31. He was assisted by N. M. Voronov, a chemist, who headed the higher-education sector
in the SVAG until January 1948, when he was replaced by P. I. Nikitin, a physicist. SAPMO-BA, ZPA, IV 2/9.04/697. Each of the capital cities in the five
newly formed *Länder* had a regional Soviet military headquarters, including
regional education departments.

51. Special attention was to be devoted to the departments of Russian, philosophy,
history, and social and political economy. BAAP, R2/1040, Bl. 19–21.

52. BAAP, R2/1040, Bl. 7–9.

53. Connelly, "East German Higher Education Policies." See the admission of the
director of the Information Agency of the SVAG, Colonel Tiul'panov, in a letter of 9 March 1948 to M. A. Suslov that "security organs of the SVA" had
been involved in "repressing a group of fascist elements among the students of
Berlin University." RTsKhIDNI, f. 17, op. 128, d. 566, l. 19. The Soviets also arrested the leaders of the Rostock and Leipzig university student councils and
dozens of other students. See chapter 6. For the general importance attached
to elections by the SVAG, see Naimark, *The Russians,* 327.

54. In the fall of 1948, 54 percent of the staff of the DVV, at all levels, belonged to the SED (a figure the Soviets believed was low!). Naimark, *The Russians*, 290. The SED held almost all leading positions. In October 1948, twenty-four of twenty-seven officials at the level of *Referent* or higher in the DVV's presidential, personnel, and higher-education departments belonged to the SED. In the personnel department, all five officials were SED members, and of these four came from the KPD. BAAP, R2/999, Bl. 25–29.

55. SVAG orders accorded the local SVA offices the job of checking the personnel suggestions made by the *Land* governments, both for teachers and for students.

56. BAAP, R2/52, Bl. 51.

57. When creating the cadre pool in 1945, the Ministry of Education of the RSFSR had simply assumed that anyone who was university-educated would know German. GARF, f. 7317, op. 54, d. 4, l. 31. Almost none of the Soviet occupation officers had been prepared for administrative work, let alone for such work in Germany. Haritonow, *Sowjetische Hochschulpolitik*, 77. The memoirs of the chief of the Sector for Higher Education in the SVAG from 1948–49, P. I. Nikitin, confirm the view of an understaffed and unprepared Education Department. See his *Zwischen Dogma*.

58. This statement was made at a 29 March 1946 meeting with DVV representatives. BAAP, R2/1332, Bl. 177.

59. See, for example, the work on study plans for social sciences, history, history of philosophy, and economics from 1947, BAAP, R2/1489, Bl. 83; R2/1422, Bl. 13; R2/1485, Bl. 66; R2/1481, Bl. 24. At this stage, the Germans did occasionally make use of Soviet study plans as models, for example, in history. BAAP, R2/1485, Bl. 84. In August 1948 Major Essin of the SVAG stipulated that only top SED functionaries (Anton Ackermann, Fred Oelssner) could write the lecture programs for dialectical and historical materialism and political economy. BAAP, R2/1489, Bl. 106. Oelssner's program had been selected because others left lecturers too much personal choice.

60. Professor Hans-Hermann Schmid (medicine) had been one of the few candidates to emerge from Rostock University after G. Rienäcker's term came to an end late in 1947. The Mecklenburg ministry sought approval from Professor Brugsch of the DVV, yet Brugsch failed to inform Karlshorst until after Schmid's election. Likewise, the SVA in Mecklenburg was not informed until after the fact. This breakdown in communications resulted from the illness of the higher-education expert in the Mecklenburg ministry. Grünberg to the Education Department of the SVA, Land Mecklenburg, 16 December 1947. MLHA, MfVB 2258. As early as June 1946 the SVA in Schwerin was depending upon the opinions produced by the local SED for the hiring of new professors. See the "Aktennotiz" of 8 June 1946 by G. Rienäcker, UAR, RIII I/2, Bd. 1.

61. Haritonow, *Sowjetische Hochschulpolitik*, 78; BAAP, R2/1431, Bl. 25. For examples of such practice in other realms, see Bonwetsch, "Sowjetische Politik," xlvi.

62. Paul Wandel referred to the DVV as "advisers" to the Soviets at a meeting of the SED Party Executive of 14 February 1947. SAPMO-BA, ZPA, IV 2/1/8, Bl. 61–63.

63. The social science faculties were supposed to train Marxist academics. SAPMO-BA, ZPA, NL/90/559, Bl. 1–10. On the role of the Leipzig faculty in changing

the political complexion of the university, see Feige, "Der Aufbau," and Handel, *Chronik*.

64. BAAP, R2/1291, Bl. 44; R2/1431, Bl. 1. Other institutions likewise sought to prepare state and Party functionaries outside the conventional settings. In August 1946 it was decided to create a central academy for training administrators under the auspices of the DVV, the Berlin City Magistrate, and the trade unions. BAAP, R2/1431, Bl. 3.

65. "Stenographische Niederschrift über die Konferenz von Angehörigen der Hochschulen (Hochschulausschuss) am Sonnabend, dem 22. November 1947, und Sonntag, dem 23. November 1947 im Hause des Kulturbundes, Berlin," 71–72. SAPMO-BA, ZPA, IV 2/9.04/6.

66. This was Georg Mayer (SED). BAAP, R2/1897, Bl. 132.

67. Kasper, "Der Kampf," 51, 77.

68. "Bericht über den Stand der Arbeiter- und Bauernfakultäten in Sachsen," 27 August 1949, SAPMO-BA, ZPA, IV 2/9.04/465; and "Monatsbericht für die Monate August und September 1949," 5 October 1949, SAPMO-BA, ZPA, IV 2/9.04/465.

69. This translates roughly as "Learning from the Soviet Union has to be learned." It was a variation on "Von der Sowjetunion lernen heisst siegen lernen" (To learn from the Soviet Union is to learn how to win).

70. BAAP, R2/1454, Bl. 1–12. The concern with money probably stemmed from the economic hardship of that period, following a hard winter, and was aggravated by massive Soviet dismantling. Schneider, *Bildung*, 13.

71. In March 1946 Zolotukhin "demanded" from the DVV that the "curricula that have been confirmed be implemented in all provinces." BAAP, R2/1332, Bl. 143.

72. Another example was political education, in which Major Essin insisted on absolute uniformity in mid-1948 (Note from Glücksmann [DVV] to Lichtenstein [DVV] of 27 August 1948, in BAAP, R2/1489, Bl. 106), yet one year later Otto Halle, in charge of higher education in the GDR Ministry of Education, wrote that "one representative of the SVAG [said that] even in the Soviet Union no one is making the demand that every student take the foundations of Marxism-Leninism to heart." BAAP, R2/1490, Bl. 30.

73. Greifswald Kurator Franz X. Wohlgemuth has left us frank admissions of his election manipulating of early 1947. Having expelled one top vote getter and having "convinced" a second to resign, he wrote: "After succeeding in giving the student council a somewhat clear face, we do not think it would be good to lay claim to the chair and have left it to the CDU. Having fought long and hard for a clear situation, we above all else do not wish to make the students think that party politics is at stake, and for that reason it seems necessary not to demand the student council chair." "Bericht über die endgültige Zusammensetzung des Studentenrates an der Universität Greifswald," 19 May 1947, MLHA, MfVB 2577, Bl. 173. He advanced to the ministry in Schwerin, and then became deputy to the state secretary in Berlin in the 1950s.

74. On the basis of the writings of a number of Soviet historians, as well as information from the Higher Party School of the CPSU, it was decided that the modern era began in 1642. SAPMO-BA, ZPA, IV 2/9.04/103, Bl. 30–31.

75. If any Soviet officials were responsible for keeping an eye on East European educa-

tion, they were the VOKS "plenipotentiaries" in the respective embassies, but their operations were plagued by lack of authority, poor planning, and ignorance. The VOKS delegates to Poland were second or third secretaries in the embassy. For example, the "plenipotentiary" of VOKS in Warsaw in 1950 was the embassy second secretary (Kuznetsov), and the "representative" of VOKS in Warsaw in January 1954 was the embassy third secretary (Lukovnikov). GARF, f. 5283, op. 22, d. 244, l. 483. VOKS Prague representative I. M. Riabov also worked out of the Soviet embassy. In both Poland and Czechoslovakia VOKS was severely understaffed, with one official in charge of monitoring the entire cultural scene, including education. The overwork severely taxed Riabov, who was discovered to have "organized a drinking-party [*p'ianku*] and in a drunken state lost a sum of foreign currency." GARF, f. 5283, op. 22, d. 462, ll. 16-54, 103.

76. SÚA, AÚV KSČ, f. 19/7, a.j. 299, l. 97-100.

77. Government decision of 19 August 1952, SÚA, MŠK, č.k. 314, sig. 3IIa.

78. "Politické směrnice Ministerstva školství, věd a umění na rok 1953." AČAV, Nejedlý Papers, č.k. 73.

79. Letter of 25 June 1949. AUJ, S III 18.

80. Connelly, "Internal Bolshevization."

81. AAN, KC PZPR 237/XVI/117, k. 10. There are no records, however, of a Soviet specialist actually beginning teaching in this area in Wrocław.

82. "Protokół z odprawy dyrektorów i w-dyrektorów departamentów z 13.8. 1951." AAN, MSW 132. The hope was to prepare over 3,000 detailed programs, but Vice-Minister Krassowska complained that delays kept such programs of study from reaching the universities. At this point only pedagogical faculties were able to make "sufficient use of Soviet programs."

83. Kaplan, *Sovětští poradci.*

84. This interpretation was inspired by A. S. Stykalin.

85. Stykalin, "Nauchnaia intelligentsiia stran," 92-104.

86. See the references to "Zdenek Romanovich" in GARF, f. 6646, op. 1, d. 325, l. 8. In a letter to VOKS Moscow of 16 July 1952, Nejedlý signed himself with patronymic. GARF, f. 5283, op. 22, d. 350, l. 146. Nejedlý was utterly dependable. As the president of the Czechoslovak Slavonic Committee, he informed the Soviets of the arrival of a Yugoslav delegation at the Prague Sokol (Gymnastic) Congress in the summer of 1948, and requested the immediate dispatch of Soviet representatives. This was intended to frustrate Yugoslav influence over the international Slavonic Committee. RTsKhIDNI, f. 17, op. 128, d. 1149, l. 52. Kraków's Tadeusz Lehr-Spławiński was addressed by patronymic. See Rkp BJ Przyb 459/73.

87. Costs for 1951 were estimated at 130 to 150 thousand rubles and were slowly becoming prohibitive. GARF, f. 9396, op. 30, d. 282, l. 91.

88. On 15 May the Ministry of Foreign Affairs communicated that it had no objection, and on 11 December the Minister of Higher Education requested permission of the Council of Ministers to proceed. GARF, f. 9396, op. 30, d. 282, ll. 154-55. See n. 91.

89. This institute was subordinated to the Ministry of Higher Education. In 1947 a "special department" (*spetskafedra*) was created at the institute to help organize "educational methodological assistance in higher education for the

people's democratic countries of the East." In March 1951 its work was extended to include the people's democratic countries of the West (that is, Eastern Europe). GARF, f. 9386, op. 30, d. 283, l. 114.

90. According to two communications of the Institute of Eastern Studies of 15 March 1951 to the Foreign Department of the Soviet Ministry of Higher Education, programs of Moscow State University went through the Foreign Department to the Polish embassy; and via the Soviet organization "International Book" as well as through the Soviet Ministry of Foreign Affairs to the GDR Ministry of Education. GARF, f. 9396, op. 30, d. 282, ll. 85–86. The plan of the "special department" of the Institute of Eastern Studies for 1951 included the "creation of a store of study plans and programs for all specialties of higher-education institutes in the USSR," as well as the compilation of "surveys and translations of questions of higher education in foreign countries." Ibid., l. 148. These countries were divided into people's democracies, colonial and dependent states, and the American-English bloc. GARF, f. 9396, op. 30, d. 283, l. 12.

91. A general regulation for exchange with all countries of people's democracy was Order No. 20C of the Ministry of Higher Education of the USSR of 11 January 1951 to its Foreign Department. Reference to the order is made in GARF, f. 9396, op. 30, d. 282, l. 148.

92. This was also a potential channel for the Soviet Ministry of Higher Education to receive information on Poland. See the communication of the president of the Soviet delegation in this commission, A. Mikhailov, to the Soviet Ministry of Higher Education, 21 March 1951, GARF, f. 9396, op. 30, d. 282, l. 134.

93. Letter to VOKS, 13 March 1948. GARF, f. 5283, op. 16, d. 138, l. 87.

94. Iu. A. Zhdanov to M. A. Suslov, 6 December 1948. RTsKhIDNI, f. 17, op. 132, d. 45, l. 100.

95. See the reminiscences of Wrocław mathematician Hugo Steinhaus, *Wspomnienia*, 395.

96. There were sufficient copies of that textbook in Warsaw, but other texts that had already been excluded from the recommended literature in the Soviet Union had been sent "in large quantities" to Poland. Furthermore, the Poles were making their own translations from Soviet legal journals, but the selection was "not always felicitous"; some of these texts had been "exposed to serious criticism" in the Soviet Union. The situation was unfortunate, because in the view of the author, law professor S. S. Kravchuk, "the degree of influence of Soviet juridical science on Polish depends entirely on the quantity and quality of Soviet juridical literature sent to Poland." GARF, f. 9396, op. 30, d. 126, l. 51.

97. They also found very little Soviet scholarly literature in Polish bookstores. GARF, f. 5283, op. 22, d. 431, l. 3.

98. This delegation could not reciprocate gifts of books given by the Czechs because its departure from Russia had been "hurried and unexpected," leaving no time to collect papers and books. RTsKhIDNI, f. 17, op. 133, d. 253, l. 144.

99. Letter in SÚA, SÚP, č.k. 438.

100. A rather secondary figure, Professor Biernawski of Kraków, reported and spoke on higher-education issues. AAN, KC PZPR 478/120.

101. ARAN, f. 579, op. 1 dop., d. 7, ll. 1–5.

102. AAN, KC PZPR 478/121, k. 66.

103. See the telegram of 12 March 1949 to Jakub Berman, AAN, KC PZPR 478/120, k. 64. On 23 March permission was requested by the Soviet Slavonic Committee of the director of the Protocol Department of the Ministry of Foreign Affairs for release of the materials. GARF, f. 6646, op. 1, d. 219, l. 168.

104. RTsKhIDNI, f. 17, op. 132, d. 45, l. 45. The folder contains almost forty pages of mathematical formulas. In 1949, the transfer by the Soviet Slavonic Committee to Czechoslovakia of photographs of Soviet celebrations of the 125th anniversary of the birth of Bedřich Smetana had to be approved by the Chief Administration for Literary and Publishing Affairs (Glavlit). GARF, f. 6646, op. 1, d. 219, l. 163.

105. See in particular the report of the VOKS plenipotentiary in Warsaw, I. S. Kuznetsov, GARF, f. 5283, op. 22, d. 128, ll. 61–65.

106. In a speech later that year even Minister Skrzeszewski stressed that "not everything that is applicable in the Soviet Union can be applied here." AAN, KC PZPR 478/151, k. 149–59.

107. The East German group of ten was led by Gerhard Harig and included the head of the Central Committee's division for higher education, Ernst Hoffmann. SAPMO-BA, ZPA, JIV 2/3/182; IV 2/2/143.

108. Planning for this trip began in 1950. SÚA, AÚV KSČ, f. 19/7, a.j. 259/2, l. 41–57.

109. Czech Communists felt that higher schools did not warrant the trouble of Soviet specialists. In March 1949 the Soviet historian P. G. Sofinov and philosopher P. J. Vyshinskii visited Czechoslovakia, but spent most of their time at Party schools. SÚA, AÚV KSČ, f. 19/7, a.j. 57/1, l. 41. The following year deputy chief of government Fierlinger requested a large contingent of Soviet professors to teach at law faculties, which had been depleted of "bourgeois" professors. His request was rejected with the notation that only "the most pressing need" could be considered. SÚA, AÚV KSČ, f. 19/7, a.j. 58/4, l. 346.

110. See, for example, the report on a meeting of the ministry *collegium* from June 1953, SÚA, AÚV KSČ, f. 19/7, a.j. 240, l. 50; and "Připomínky k vysokoškolskému zákonu," 27 November 1953, SÚA, MŠK, č.k. 315, a.j. 75440.

111. On 24 September 1948, A. F. Kabanov, a deputy head in the SVAG, requested Soviet scholars above all for social-economic, historical, and juridical sciences. RTsKhIDNI, f. 17, op. 132, d. 65, l. 67. On 6 October 1948 the deputy director in the Soviet Ministry of Higher Education wrote to the Soviet Central Committee asking confirmation for four Soviet professors going to Czechoslovakia to read lectures in history, law, economics, and philosophy. RTsKhIDNI, f. 18, op. 128, d. 488, l. 13.

112. From 1953 to 1955 the Polish Academy of Sciences invited 83 Soviet scholars to Poland, while sending 120 Poles in the opposite direction. AAN, KC PZPR 237/XVI/191, k. 52–55.

113. BAAP, R3/152, Bl. 29–35.

114. SÚA, AÚV KSČ, f. 19/7, a.j. 259/2, l. 41–57.

115. For numbers of graduate students trained in the Soviet Union, see nn. 139 and 145.

116. For the work of Patent, see Müller and Müller, ". . . *stürmt die Festung*," 48–49; Schmidt, *Alma Mater Jenensis;* on Kolman, see his *Die verirrte Generation.*

117. For example, five of the fourteen "professors" who came to Czechoslovakia in 1951–52 did not actually possess that title. AČAV, Valouch Papers, sig. IV, i.č.

882. In 1950 Adam Schaff requested Soviet professors in the history of philosophy, aesthetics, history of the USSR, and political economy, but made clear that he did not want to see "people not up to par" (*jakichś słabszych ludzi*). AAN, BP KC PZPR, t. 13, p. 3, k. 271.

118. Report from the spring of 1951 by F. Golovenchenko, lecturer in Russian literature. GARF, f. 9396, op. 30, d. 126, ll. 56–58. One historian of art (Professor A. A. Fedorov-Davydov) lectured to full auditoriums in Poland in 1951, but "part of the audience" did not know Russian at all, and others knew it insufficiently. GARF, f. 9396, op. 30, d. 126, l. 23.

119. Report of Professor S. S. Kravchuk, who visited Poland in the spring of 1951. GARF, f. 9396, op. 30, d. 126, l. 50.

120. After having spoken in factories and in front of Party activists, Professor P. G. Sofinov, a historian at the Soviet Interior Ministry's Military Institute, received a cool reception at Charles University in 1949. The turnout was low, and, in great contrast to factory audiences, the teachers and students did not ask questions. GARF, f. 9396, op. 30, d. 66, l. 90. In April 1951 leading functionaries at the pedagogical faculty in Prague reportedly "did not want to" meet with one of the Soviet lecturers. SÚA, AÚV KSČ, f. 19/7, a.j. 252/1, l. 46–47. See also the report on Soviet docent Cholopovova, who was coolly received in Brno in 1951. Bareš to Pavlík, 18 April 1951, AČAV, Nejedlý Papers, č.k. 14. When four Soviet professors arrived "unexpectedly" in Czechoslovakia on 19 December 1950, they discovered that a program for their stay had yet to be concluded. Mishaps seemed to follow them on their journey; they were not paid on time and students had not been mobilized to hear them. SÚA, AÚV KSČ, f. 19/7, a.j. 300, l. 180; f. 100/24, a.j. 975, l. 39–44; f. 19/7, a.j. 302/2, l. 151–52. See also the reports in SÚA, AÚV KSČ, f. 19/7, a.j. 313, l. 4–7, 8–12, 73–76; f. 19/7, a.j. 272/1, l. 39–43. On failures to host Soviet guests properly in Poland in 1953, see AAN, MSW 20, k. 76–86.

121. For the engagement of Soviet historians after the Otwock conference, see chapter 8. B. D. Grekov also submitted positive reports on Polish historians after a November 1949 trip. GARF, f. 5283, op. 22, d. 244, ll. 15–16. The report by Soviet historians of the Polish historians' conference in Wrocław in September 1948 was also optimistic and criticized Polish Marxists for "leftist attitudes toward the old professoriate." Iu. A. Zhdanov to M. A. Suslov, 6 December 1948, RTsKhIDNI, f. 17, op. 132, d. 45, ll. 96–100.

122. Gorizontov, "Metodologicheskii perevorot," 53; Bardach interview.

123. ARAN, f. 579, op. 2, d. 11, ll. 56–57.

124. See chapter 10 at n. 61.

125. GARF, f. 9396, op. 30, d. 69, ll. 91–92.

126. GARF, f. 9396, op. 30, d. 69, l. 91. For similar attitudes among professors of art history, law, history, and Russian literature visiting Poland in 1951, see GARF, op. 30, d. 126, ll. 23–26, 49–51, 53–55. On East Germany, see the harsh criticisms by the Soviet philosophy professor Vyshinskii of colleagues in Jena in January 1948 in Naimark, *The Russians,* 450.

127. Jerzy Konorski, *Conditioned Reflexes and Neuron Organisation* (Cambridge, 1948).

128. Petrusewicz, a specialist in evolutionary biology, knew of the book but assumed Konorski had made an error "unconsciously." He and Krassowska

tended to see the issue as one of "purely scientific differences." Their colleague Michajłów was more skeptical, however, and agreed with the Soviets' belief in Konorski's "political double-dealing." Konorski was said to be "double-dealing" because, despite his criticism, he claimed to value Pavlov's methodology. GARF, f. 5283, op. 22, d. 244, ll. 35–39.

129. This was the most intrusive statement by a Soviet scholar that I found in the archives used. GARF, f. 5283, op. 22, d. 244, l. 42.

130. He was, however, made to declare a "self-criticism" at a biological conference in Kuźnice in late 1950. Mauersberg, "Nauka," 461. In the early 1950s Konorski worked on his *Chronic Extinction and Restoration of Conditioned Reflexes.* Kita and Pytlas, *Profesorowie,* 98–101.

131. Iu. A. Zhdanov to M. A. Suslov, 19 June 1951. RTsKhIDNI, f. 17, op. 133, d. 180, ll. 97–117.

132. A review in the first issue in 1950 of *Voprosy filosofii* (Questions of philosophy) criticized a book by leading Czech Communist Václav Kopecký on T. G. Masaryk, accusing Kopecký of attempting to make a "progressive figure" out of the former president. As V. Grigor'ian wrote M. A. Suslov on 15 September 1950, this evaluation "caused the dissatisfaction of Kopecký and a number of other leading functionaries of the Communist Party of Czechoslovakia." The authors, D. Sleishek and I. Narskii, were instructed to write a retraction. RTsKhIDNI, f. 17, op. 132, d. 345, ll. 65, 76–77. The historian G. P. Chekanova of Leningrad visited Prague from mid-November 1951 to mid-February 1952 and filed a devastating report on Czech historians, especially leading figure Václav Husa, supposedly of bourgeois background and a graduate of the Sorbonne, who was "extraordinarily weak in questions of Marxist-Leninist theory." She also presumed to pass judgment on the work of Minister of Education Nejedlý, who may have been "popular, but does not attend to practical work." The response of the functionaries receiving this report was to criticize the Academy of Sciences for permitting Chekanova to visit Prague at all. RTsKhIDNI, f. 17, op. 133, d. 221, ll. 18–32. Husa remained at his post and Nejedlý became the first president of the Czechoslovak Academy of Sciences. Cases of direct Soviet "advice" going unheeded are legion. Soviet expert Minin's repeated demands that the Warsaw Polytechnic be split into several schools were never obeyed. AAN, KC PZPR 237/XVI/12, k. 90; Olszewski, *Politechnika,* 137–38. Both the East German and Czech Communists were strongly advised to shorten university preparation to ten years, the former by chief of the Soviet Control Commission in Germany Semenov himself, yet neither fully complied. In addition, the East Germans failed to heed Semenov's advice to separate theological faculties from universities. SAPMO-BA, ZPA, IV 2/9.04/608, Bl. 97–99. The East Germans reduced university preparation to twelve years, and the Czechoslovaks to eleven, but then in the late 1950s the latter raised it again to twelve years. The universities had found such an abbreviated preparation untenable.

133. The Soviet delegation was led by K. M. Bykov. GARF, f. 5287, op. 22, d. 244, ll. 184–86. The report was composed on 27 August 1950 by Iu. Safirov, attaché of the Soviet embassy in Poland, and sent on 16 September by VOKS director Denisov to Grigor'ian at the Central Committee of the Soviet Communist Party.

134. GARF, f. 5283, op. 22, d. 431, l. 56.

135. Sudakov was upset by the Polish side's failure to extend his contract, and be-
     haved boorishly, for example insulting the Russian-language skills of Polish
     physicians who treated him — he said they had German accents — and refusing
     flowers at a dinner given in his honor. In the judgment of the PZPR Central
     Committee, he was not useful because he did not understand Polish "condi-
     tions." AAN, KC PZPR 237/XVI/184, k. 129–30.

136. Report of A. L. Sidorov, director of the Institute of History, Soviet Academy of
     Sciences. ARAN, f. 579, op. 2, d. 11, ll. 112–13.

137. Valkenier, "Stalinizing," 134.

138. In 1957 the East German leadership concluded that this was an extravagant use of
     resources and decided it was better to send primarily upper-division students
     for shorter stays. SAPMO-BA, ZPA, IV 2/9.04/620, Bl. 100–106.

139. SAPMO-BA, ZPA, IV 2/9.04/620, Bl. 77–81, 118–19. By 1960 a total of 919 East
     German students had been trained in the Soviet Union, of whom 74 were
     graduate students (*Aspiranten*). Ibid., Bl. 295–97. In 1956 some 41 graduates
     of Soviet *aspirantura* were active in Czechoslovakia. SÚA, ÚPV, i.č. 2476.

140. AAN, KC PPR 295/VII/3, k. 60.

141. This was a formula used in a 30 June 1947 communication of the Ministry of
     Education to Charles University. AUK, i.č. 718.

142. AAN, MO 3149, k. 33–35.

143. Of the 1954 group, 35.4 percent belonged to the Communist Party, and 15.7 per-
     cent were candidates. AAN, KC PZPR 237/XVI/185, k. 68–84; 191, k. 52–55.

144. Of these, 75 percent were Party members. SÚA, AÚV KSČ, f. 19/7, a.j. 331, l. 36.

145. Of 200 students suggested for studies in the Soviet Union from the GDR in 1952,
     only 34 were in the humanities and history, 10 in art, and 13 in economics.
     SAPMO-BA, ZPA, IV 2/9.04/622, Bl. 6–9. Two-thirds of the Poles (65.7 per-
     cent) selected for studies in the Soviet Union in 1951 were in technical and
     agricultural studies. AAN, KC PZPR 237/XVI/140, k. 34–35. Of the 184 Poles
     who took part in Soviet *aspirantura* from 1949 to 1954, only 36 were in "uni-
     versity" subjects. AAN, KC PZPR 237/XVI/191, k. 52–55. Of the 300 Czecho-
     slovak students scheduled to begin studies in the Soviet Union in 1952–53, 35
     were in the humanities. SÚA, AÚV KSČ, f. 19/7, a.j. 330, l. 39–45.

146. For example, the Soviet academy sent Poland experts in "complex geographical
     research" in 1954 and experts in metallurgy in 1955, in both cases with the clear
     purpose of benefiting Soviet science. ARAN, f. 579, op. 1, d. 288, ll. 10, 22–23.

147. See the complaint of East German scholars on the difficulties of receiving per-
     mission to visit the USSR from early 1958, GARF, f. 9396, op. 30, d. 967, l. 86.
     Even for chemist laureate of the GDR national prize, Professor Treibs (SED),
     it was far easier to attend congresses in the West than in the Soviet Union. For
     the difficulty of arranging scholarly exchange with Poland in 1959, see GARF,
     f. 9396, op. 30, d. 1011, ll. 114–27.

148. See the comments of Jürgen John in "Die Jenaer Universität," 31; and Ingo Bach,
     " 'Selbstsowjetisiert'? War der Einfluss der russischen Behörden auf die Hoch-
     schulen gering?" *Tagesspiegel*, 22 December 1997.

149. The survival of Gomułka has been explained in part by resentment over Stalin's
     liquidation of the Communist Party of Poland, and by fear of leading func-
     tionaries Berman and Minc that the anti-Semitic purges might turn against
     them. Brzezinski, *The Soviet Bloc*, 96.

150. See the discussion in chapter 6.

151. In June 1950 Charles University issued a reprimand to the law student Antonín Knapp for printing lecture notes in the social studies that had not been "authorized." This was done according to section 13, paragraph 2, of the disciplinary order for students of 13 October 1849 (č. 416 ř.z.).

152. Brzezinski, *The Soviet Bloc*, 79; Brus, "Stalinism," 242 n. 7; Lovenduski and Woodall, *Politics and Society*, 57; Bender, *East Europe*, 12. For a portrait of SVAG propaganda chief Tiul'panov, see Naimark, *The Russians*, esp. 318-52.

153. Giles, *The Structure*, 12.

CHAPTER 3

1. Though not technically a minister, Leipzig physicist-philosopher Harig had a vote in the GDR Council of Ministers. Harig (1902-66) had worked as a physicist in the Soviet Union in the 1930s before being sent by the Party back to Germany and the Gestapo. Černý, *Wer war wer*, 168.

2. Rapacki (1909-70), originally from a Lwówian intelligentsia family, had studied economics and was later famous as foreign minister for sponsorship of a plan to free Central Europe from nuclear weapons. He spent the years 1939-45 in a German prisoner-of-war camp, and joined the PPS in 1945. Mołdawa, *Ludzie władzy*, 416.

3. Štoll (1902-81), originally a clerk in a sugar trading company (1922-31), acted in the 1930s as the main Czech Communist critic of surrealism. From 1934 to 1937 he translated the works of Marx and Engels in Moscow. He spent the war as a clerk in a company for corn processing. Afterward Štoll became the major interpreter and enforcer of socialist realism in Czech literature, as well as minister of culture and minister of education. He was made professor in 1949, although he had no doctorate. *Československý biografický slovník*, 717; SÚA, ÚPV, č.k. 517.

4. This provision had existed in the Polish decree of 1947 but was dropped in 1951. Hartmann, *Hochschulwesen*, 65.

5. "Nařízení ministra školství, věd a umění ze dne 1. září 1950 kterým se vydává organisační a jednací řád Statního výboru pro vysoké školy a blíže upravuje jeho působnost," *Sbírka zákonů*, č. 130/1950, 471-74.

6. Hartmann, *Hochschulwesen*, 65-66.

7. "Nařízení ministra školství, věd a umění ze dne 1. září 1950 kterým se vydává organisační a jednací řád Statního výboru pro vysoké školy a blíže upravuje jeho působnost," *Sbírka zákonů*, č. 130/1950, 471-74. In Poland too the rector could be a docent. Hartmann, *Hochschulwesen*, 65.

8. Adolf Chybiński to Jerzy Lande, 16 July 1949. Rkp BJ Przyb 108/74.

9. The prorectors were created by a decree of 21 May 1951. Richert, "Sozialistische Universität," 92-93.

10. Olszewski, *Politechnika*, 138.

11. "Zákon ze dne 18. května 1950 o vysokých školách," *Sbírka zákonů*, č. 58/1950, 115-16.

12. Stallmann, *Hochschulzugang*, 321-22.

13. AAN, KC PZPR 237/XVI/127, k. 14.

14. SED Politburo member Fred Oelssner told East German students in Moscow in a speech of August 1954 that "they are also called upon one day to become

the intellectual leaders of the entire German nation." SAPMO-BA, ZPA, IV 2/9.04/626, Bl. 98. The KSČ Central Committee wrote to its district committees in February 1951 that "the best cadres for our Party and economy will be trained at Soviet universities." SÚA, AÚV KSČ, f. 19/7, a.j. 332, l. 46.

15. For a description of how these imported principles motivated the Czechoslovak higher-education law of 1950, see SÚA, AÚV KSČ, f. 100/1, a.j. 1155, l. 70–98.

16. Hartmann, *Hochschulwesen*, 58–59; Łuczak, *University of Poznań*, 243.

17. Gładysz, *Oświata*, 176.

18. Departament Studiów Uniwersyteckich, Załącznik Nr. 6, "Plan rozmieszczenia I roku studiów jednolitych na r. 1953," 10 April 1953; Załącznik Nr. 5, "Plan rozmieszczenia I roku studiów II-go stopnia w roku 1953," 13 April 1953. AUJ, WP IV 13.

19. The resistance of the academic community to this foreign institution proved so strong that it was "liquidated" in 1951. AAN, KC PZPR 237/XVI/10, k. 4.

20. Lane, "Structural and Social Change," 22.

21. "Zákon ze dne 18. května 1950 o vysokých školách," *Sbírka zákonů*, č. 58/1950, 118.

22. "Vládní nařízení ze dne 14. července 1950 o bohosloveckých fakultách," *Sbírka zákonů*, č. 112/1950, 427.

23. "Vládní nařízení ze dne 27. června 1950 o některých změnách v organisaci vysokých škol," *Sbírka zákonů*, č. 81/1950, 201. The industrial areas of Ostrava and Northern Bohemia had been completely without higher schools until these changes. SÚA, AÚV KSČ, f. 19/7, a.j. 260, l. 50–51.

24. "Zpráva pro Pana Předsedu vlády o osnově vládního nařízení o některých změnách v organisaci vysokých škol," 30 June 1950; "Důvodová zpráva," 22 June 1950. SÚA, ÚPV, č.k. 833, sig. 812/30/10.

25. Letter from Central Committee to regional KSČ secretariats, 24 June 1950. SÚA, AÚV KSČ, f. 19/7, a.j. 104, l. 55.

26. Ibid. SÚA, AÚV KSČ, f. 02/4, a.j. 146/20, l. 3–8.

27. "Vládní nařízení ze dne 2. října 1951 o organisačních změnách na vysokých školách," *Sbírka zákonů*, č. 80/1951, 285–86; "Vládní nařízení ze dne 8. července 1952 o některých změnách v organisaci vysokých škol," ibid., č. 30/1952, 193–94; "Vládní nařízení ze dne 19. srpna 1952 o dalších změnách v organisaci vysokých škol," ibid., č. 40/1952, 211–12; "Vládní nařízení ze dne 4. listopadu 1952 o zřízení vysoké školy ruského jazyka v Praze," ibid., č. 63/1952, 290, "Vládní nařízení ze dne 27. listopadu 1953 o vysoké stranické škole při ÚV KSČ," ibid., č. 97/1953, 372.

28. Müller and Müller, ". . . *stürmt die Festung*," 150. The law faculties were places of the strongest "reactionary" influence. In Rostock, about 40 percent of the law students had cast "invalid" ballots in the student council elections of 1950. "Vertraulicher FDJ Bericht," MLHA, MfVB 2311, Bl. 78. The average for the university was 28.9 percent invalid ballots. BAAP, R2/1903, Bl. 4–7.

29. Richert, *"Sozialistische Universität,"* 70–71.

30. For the trip to this academy of SED functionaries in April–May 1952: "Bericht der Studienreise," SAPMO-BA, ZPA, IV 2/9.08/30, Bl. 178–203.

31. BAAP, E1/17038, Bl. 113.

32. BAAP, E1/9107, Bl. 7.

33. "Prohlášení AV NV Pražských studentů" (undated). AUK, SVS B29.

34. The programs were sent to teachers' vacation addresses so that they could "pre-

pare their lectures during the holidays." SÚA, AÚV KSČ, f. 19/7, a.j. 262, l. 50–51.

35. Urban, *Die Organisation*, 204.

36. SÚA, ÚPV, i.č. 2474, sig. 12/3/38.5; SÚA, AÚV KSČ, f. 19/7, a.j. 284, l. 11.

37. *Seznam osob*, 60–66.

38. Ibid., 11–40; SÚA, ÚPV, č.k. 514, i.č. 2622, sig. 516/1.

39. Urban, *Die Organisation*, 205–6.

40. Cited in ibid., 203–4. For other reports on overworked students, see the documentation from 1954–55, SÚA, AÚV KSČ, f. 19/7, a.j. 272, l. 169, 233. Leading functionaries were apprised of these problems as early as 1952, when Party organizations in Brno noted that "students are overburdened and have no time to grow as humans or for collective life and are becoming narrowly educated specialists." "Stížnosti na s. Valoucha z Brna," AČAV, Valouch Papers, sig. IV, i.č. 852.

41. SÚA, AÚV KSČ, f. 19/7, a.j. 241, l. 76–77.

42. Müller and Müller, "... *stürmt die Festung*," 231–38.

43. Richert, "*Sozialistische Universität*," 84–86.

44. Many protested by reading novels. Steinhaus, *Wspomnienia*, 404.

45. Müller and Müller, "... *stürmt die Festung*," 299–301.

46. Plans for dividing the undergraduate program into professional and academic tracks were first aired in engineering departments during the prewar period. Olszewski, *Politechnika*, 201–2. They became part of the PPR's program in the summer of 1945. Lewandowski, *Rodowód*, 27; Krasiewicz, *Odbudowa*, 323.

47. In 1951 between 25 and 28 percent of the graduates of the first step were supposed to continue on to second-step studies. Żeligowska to rectors, 10 September 1951, AUJ, S III 248.

48. For all fields, the totals were 1,000 and 177 students, respectively. "Zadania planu w zakresie szkolenia na rok 1953 dla Uniwersytetu Jagiellońskiego," AUJ, WP IV 13.

49. Hartmann, *Hochschulwesen*, 58.

50. As early as 1953 leading state functionaries, but also members of the clergy, began to criticize the new schedules as excessively burdensome. AAN, KC PZPR 237/XVI/102, k. 50–52. The apparatus distributed copies of this complaint to high Party functionaries.

51. Péteri, *Academia and State Socialism*, 235–36. On the poor training of high school teachers in Poland, see the article "Złote kadry," *Głos Pracy*, 28 August 1956.

52. Kolankiewicz, "Technical Intelligentsia," 189.

53. A government representative made the appeal to an acquaintance living in Switzerland. He claimed that all important work in industry still had to be carried out by technicians trained in the prewar period, because of the "catastrophic level" of students' education. Radio Free Europe Report, Item No. 6925/56, Press Archive of the Herder Institute, Marburg.

54. SÚA, AÚV KSČ, f. 02/2, a.j. 99, l. 20.

55. In Wrocław the first *kandidat* degree was not awarded until 1955 (in law), and none was ever awarded in Polish literature. Suleja, *Uniwersytet Wrocławski*, 36. In all of Poland, only 35 *kandidat* degrees were awarded in law from 1951 to 1958; by contrast, the law faculty in Poznań alone had granted 76 doctoral degrees between 1945 and 1951. Hartmann, *Hochschulwesen*, 123–24.

56. SÚA, AÚV KSČ, f. 19/7, a.j. 240, l. 122–23.

57. Letter to Nejedlý from "Skupina ADK," 12 June 1954. AČAV, Nejedlý Papers, č.k. 24.

58. Legislation on the *aspirantura* took effect in 1950 in the Czech lands, 1951 in East Germany, and 1952 in Poland. SÚA, MŠK, č.k. 312, MŠVU č. 129 708/50-III/1; Jessen, "Vom Ordinarius," 82–83; Hartmann, *Hochschulwesen,* 121.

59. Suleja, *Uniwersytet Wrocławski,* 35–37.

60. By 1956, some 1,263 individuals had completed *aspirantura* in Czechoslovakia, and about 15 percent of the assistant professors at institutions of higher education were *aspirantura* products. There were at this point 695 daytime and 1,343 part-time *aspiranty*. "Rozbor současného stavu výchovy vědeckých kádrů" (undated [1956]). SÚA, ÚPV, i.č. 3827. In Poland between 1951 and 1958, a total of 784 individuals received a *kandidat* degree, and 83 the doctor of science. In 1956, 1,374 individuals were enrolled in the *aspirantura,* and 12,621 individuals were adjunct and assistant professors—the equivalent of the "tenure track"—at Polish institutions of higher education and other scholarly institutes. Hartmann, *Hochschulwesen,* 112, 122.

61. Opposition to centrally planned graduate studies was heavy in medicine and the natural sciences, and delayed the general adoption of *Aspirantur* until the new assistant professor ordinance (*Assistentenordnung*) of 1957, which gave state functionaries at universities (in Soviet-styled "prorectorates for academic recruitment") decisive say over entrance to academia. Jessen, "Vom Ordinarius," 87–88, and "Zur Sozialgeschichte," 132–34.

62. In 1947 the SVAG released Order No. 55, which called for the training of 200 "active antifascists" in a two-year course of graduate studies. By August 1949 the East German regime had accepted 157 "candidates for scholarly teaching and research" into a program of promotion (*Förderungsverfahren*). Of these, 88 were in the social sciences, humanities, and law; and the rest in medical, natural, or technical sciences; 37 were of working class and 3 of peasant background; 116 belonged to the SED. Jessen, "Vom Ordinarius," 82; BAAP, R2/1906, Bl. 114–17.

63. For example, in Leipzig students taking part in planned graduate studies were referred to as *Aspiranten*. They were mostly Party members, and in contravention of normal procedure, themselves selected academic advisers, with the help of the local SED organization. In July 1950 there were forty-one such *Aspiranten,* of whom thirty-one were in the humanities and social sciences. UA der HUB, 359/2/17, Bl. 138–39.

64. For the situation in Leipzig, see "Analyse über die wissenschaftliche und politische Arbeit an der Karl-Marx-Universität," 9 November 1954, SSA, IV 4.14/53, Bl. 13–14.

65. By April 1953, 1,423 students were in the *Aspirantur,* of whom 60 percent majored in social sciences. "Betr.: Kader-Analyse der wissenschaftlichen Aspirantur," 15 April 1953. BAAP, R3/147, Bl. 132–39.

66. The problem of basic organizations attempting to give orders to university administration was pervasive in the Czech lands in the early 1950s, but not unknown in Poland. For reports from 1952–53 on this problem, especially in Białystok, Szczecin, Łódź, and Gdańsk, see AAN, KC PZPR 237/XVI/4, k. 6, 36, 56, 66–67.

67. For example, on 24 May 1955 Central Committee Secretary Jiří Hendrych directed Prime Minister Viliam Široký to "eliminate deficiencies in the employment of young people," through consultation with several ministers, and with a precise timetable. SÚA, ÚPV, i.č. 2482, sig. 12/3.81.39.

68. Busse (b. 1899) came from an official's family, was a teacher by trade, and joined the KPD in 1930. BAAP, R2/928, Bl. 160. Hoffmann (1909–84) joined the SPD in 1928 and was a blacksmith. He was interned in Brandenburg from 1934 to 1937, and served in a penal battalion from 1942 to 1945. He worked in youth affairs for the SED after the war, and in the SED Central Committee from 1950 to 1954. Broszat and Weber, *SBZ-Handbuch,* 933.

69. In 1954 the Central Committee propaganda and science and higher-education departments were combined to produce the Department of Science and Propaganda, which in 1957 became the Department of Sciences. As of 1955 Hager was the responsible Central Committee secretary, and Johannes Hörnig (b. 1921) became department chief, a position he too retained until 1989. Neuhäusser-Wespy, "Der Parteiapparat," 144. Hager (b. 1912) was involved in higher-education affairs as early as 1950. BAAP, R2/1140, Bl. 95. He came from a worker's family, attended high school, and joined the KPD in 1930. He spent the war in England, returned to Germany in 1946, and was active in propaganda and newspaper work for the SED. Černý, *Wer war wer,* 162–63.

70. The Polish department was relatively understaffed, having only five employees as late as May 1952. AAN, KC PZPR 237/XVI/5, k. 2. Petrusewicz was a biologist from Wilno, and Zemankowa had been recruited from the Propaganda Department of the PZPR Voivodeship Committee in Kraków.

71. Kavka, *Stručné dějiny,* 304. In 1946 the Central Committee's Department of Culture-Propaganda had four subareas, of which one was devoted to culture; one of its subareas was education. The propaganda subarea was directed by Arnošt Kolman.

72. SÚA, AÚV KSČ, f. 19/7, a.j. 234, l. 7. For a brief time in 1950–51, Čestmír Císař also worked in the department. Bareš (1910–79), originally Breitenfeld, from 1926 in the Communist movement, was by profession a journalist, and after the war became editor in chief of Party daily *Rudé právo.* He was a member of the Central Committee until 1952. *Československý biografický slovník,* 25.

73. In this case he was casting doubt on the applicability for Czechoslovakia of correspondence education—which had been developed for a country with huge distances between universities. SÚA, AÚV KSČ, f. 19/7, a.j. 272/1, l. 53–56. Nejedlý likewise vigorously opposed the shortening of college preparation on "Soviet models," finding this unnecessary in a highly developed education system.

INTRODUCTION TO PART II

1. Ernst, *"Die beste Prophylaxe."*

2. "Stenographische Niederschrift des Referats des Genossen Anton Ackermann auf der Arbeitstagung über die Frage der Auswahl und Zulassung zum Hochschulstudium," 9, 6 May 1949, SAPMO-BA, ZPA, IV 2/9.04/464.

3. On the early distinctions made in East German graduate admissions policies between natural and social sciences, see the introduction at n. 73. The different standards can also be seen in the efforts to hire scholars from the West, which

concentrated heavily on natural and technical sciences. For example, in 1953 the East German government had contacted forty-nine West German academics to fill vacancies in the GDR; of these only five were humanists, while eighteen represented the natural sciences and twenty-six medicine. Jessen, "Akademische Elite," 354.

4. Physicist Robert Rompe told the SED Party executive at a meeting of 11 February 1948 that loyal legal experts could be trained in "crash courses" but that biologists or engineers needed at least ten to fifteen years after completing university before they began to work innovatively. Jessen, "Akademische Elite," 326.

5. See Schaff, *Moje spotkania;* Brus, "Stalinism," esp. 243–44; Werblan, *Gomułka;* and reminiscences of former Wrocław Communists in Suleja, *Uniwersytet Wrocławski,* 177; Torańska, *Oni.* For an interpretation by a highly placed functionary emphasizing the role of Moscow, see Bialer, *Wybrałem prawdę.*

6. Quoted in Hübner, *Polityka naukowa,* 120–21. Sawicki was former director of the archaeological museum in Warsaw, and during Nazi occupation had been active in conspiratorial education activities in Warsaw. He joined the Communist Party of Poland in 1934. Lewandowski, *Kierunki,* 132.

7. Cited in Hübner, *Nauka polska,* 39.

8. AAN, MO 2847, k. 394. Józef Sieradzki, the leading PPR figure at Jagiellonian University, demanded a major purge of professors there during a meeting of PPR academics on 5 June 1947. AAN, KC PPR 295/XVII/57, k. 21.

9. AAN, KC PPR 237/XVI/2, k. 37. Medievalist Karol Górski maintained his position through the stalinist years, yet his colleague in Toruń, literary historian Konrad Górski, was forbidden to teach. Władysław Konopczyński, historian in Kraków, was forcibly retired. See chapter 7 at nn. 72 and 77.

10. For the list of Polonists to be dismissed, see Connelly and Suleja, "Projekt." For plans to purge other humanistic disciplines, see Hübner, "Stalinowskie czystki."

11. Miłosz, *Captive Mind,* 7.

12. This is in contrast to neighboring countries, where "state churches" persisted into the postwar period and became easy targets for the new regimes. For the central role of the war in creating a new kind of church in Poland, see the important comparative study of Osa, "Resistance, Persistence, and Change."

13. Jagiełło, *Tygodnik Powszechny,* 12–13.

14. "Whether or not one accepted or rejected that syllogism did not matter; a mind trained on it could not help but be suspicious of words used as an unshackled vital force." Miłosz, *Native Realm,* 123.

15. Thus his membership card, signed 12 August 1947. Rkp BJ Przyb 231/76.

16. Wojtyła refers to Rector Tadeusz Lehr-Spławiński as his "teacher." He also remained in close contact with a professor of legal history, Adam Vetulani, who in Wojtyła's words "very much loved the church, especially our Kraków church." Wojtyła to Vetulani, 22 December 1972, APAN-K, K-III-58, j. 242; Wojtyła to Lehr-Spławiński, 23 January 1964, Rkp BJ Przyb 465/73.

17. From a June 1954 report of a delegation of Soviet archaeologists. ARAN, f. 579, op. 2, d. 11, ll. 56–57.

18. The authors of the book included Professor Tadeusz Lehr-Spławiński of Jagiellonian University. A copy was sent from the VOKS office in Warsaw to the Russian Ministry of Education, and eventually made its way to top ideolo-

gist M. A. Suslov. Officials noted words to be declined: "ugly mug" (*rozha*), "louse" (*vosh'*), "stench" (*von'*); as well as sample phrases from "Russian life": "merchant's wife" (*kupchikha*), "Barbara ran from antique shop to antique shop." I. Kairov, Minister of Education, RSFSR to M. A. Suslov, 22 July 1952, RTsKhIDNI, f. 17, op. 133, d. 297, ll. 1–3. It was decided that in the future Russian texts should be produced in Moscow.

19. GARF, f. 9396, op. 30, d. 968, ll. 9–10.

20. AAN, KC PZPR 237/XVI/12, k. 4.

21. AAN, KC PZPR 237/XVI/77, k. 14.

22. Tomczak, *Wspomnienia pracowników,* 290–93.

23. For many Czechs, the great blow to the Czech nation was the destruction and dispersal of the local nobility that took place after the victory of the Catholic Habsburgs at the Battle of White Mountain in 1620. Jesuits entered the country in droves, reconverting in force and smothering towns in baroque, and German became the lingua franca of the upper classes. For an account of this period from the perspective of a prominent Czech historian of the interwar period, see Krofta, *A Short History,* 75–89.

24. For a vivid discussion of how Czech identity was reconceived to emphasize Slavic and socialist components in the early postwar years, see Abrams, "The Struggle."

25. Lobkowicz, *Marxismus-Leninismus,* xiv–xv. An example from Prague's philosophy faculty is Ladislav Rieger, grandson of famous Czech politician František Ladislav Rieger, who had habilitated in 1931 and long struggled with epistemological problems. After 1945 Rieger, an expert in the natural sciences, found the scientistic "naive realism" in Leninism attractive. Ibid., 22.

26. On the fatalism that took hold of many intellectuals in postwar East Central Europe, see Miłosz, *Captive Mind;* Abrams, "The Struggle."

27. See Kolman, *Die verirrte Generation,* 180. Kolman composed his memoir in Russian while living in emigration in Sweden during the 1970s.

28. "Vysoké školy—universita," AČAV, Král Papers, i.č. 36.

29. Lewy, *The Catholic Church,* esp. 224–57; Denzler and Fabricius, *Die Kirchen.*

30. Besier, *Der SED-Staat,* 66–67.

31. Ibid., 38–46. The Confessing Church was a movement within the Protestant churches of Germany that reasserted Christian revelation, in particular "the word of God," as a guide to Christian action. Many adherents suffered persecution by the Nazis. Denzler and Fabricius, *Die Kirchen,* 61–75.

32. The letter compares Communist attempts to divide the clergy into patriots and traitors with a similar effort by the Nazis: "We would like to remind you that in the years 1941–44 German propaganda also created 'patriot-priests,' and the people of Warsaw still remember this." Raina, *Kościół w PRL,* 223–27.

33. Aland, *Glanz und Niedergang,* 139. For a discussion of "habitus," see Bourdieu, *Homo Academicus,* esp. 149.

34. Of the Heidelberg faculty of the interwar period, 21 percent came from families of independent entrepreneurs and 55.7 percent from families of officials and the free professions. The former group constituted 14.5 percent, the latter 4.7 percent of German society. For further breakdowns, see Jansen, *Vom Gelehrten,* 18. Of the 620 assistant professors teaching at the philosophical and law faculties of Jagiellonian University between 1860 and 1920 on whom data

exist (79 percent of the total), 384 (61.8 percent) came from the intelligentsia, 59 (9.5 percent) from the landed gentry, 87 (14 percent) from the bourgeoisie, 40 (6.5 percent) from the artisanry, 43 (6.9 percent) from the peasantry, and 7 (1.1 percent) from workers' households. The breakdown for docents teaching at the four faculties (theological, law, philosophical, medical) at Jagiellonian University between 1860 and 1920 is nearly the same, excepting a somewhat higher proportion of landed gentry (15.4 percent) and smaller number of artisans (3.7 percent). Perkowska, *Kształtowanie,* 137.

35. Chałasiński, *Przeszłość i przyszłość,* 46–61; Gella, *Development of Class Structure,* 130–64.

36. Chałasiński, *Przeszłość i przyszłość,* 31.

37. See the undated memorandum of Dr. Jerzy Marowski (PPR), vice-director for higher education in the Education Ministry, AAN, MO 2847, k. 104.

38. For a critique of its "inability" to learn from history, see Chałasiński, *Społeczna genealogia.*

39. Half of the Polish underground government's financial assets went toward education and welfare. Gross, *Polish Society,* 256. For nineteenth-century antecedents, see Cywiński, *Rodowody.*

40. In 1901 tsarist police estimated that one-third of the village population in the Congress Kingdom was engaged in illegally learning to read and write Polish. For an excellent overview and references to the literature, see Gella, *Development,* 150–52.

41. Kotarbiński, *Myśli,* 313.

42. For a discussion of attitudes toward the state in Poland by novelist Stanisław Lem and historians Jerzy Jedlicki and Janusz Tazbir, see *Tygodnik Powszechny,* 13 November 1998. On the distinction between life "for show" lived for the state and "real life lived among one's own" during the occupation time, see Wyka, *Życie na niby,* 8; on the unreal aspect of civil marriages in Poland, see Marian Brandys, "Starzy ludzie z Zamościa," *Nowa Kultura,* 1 September 1957, cited in Chałasiński, *Przeszłość,* 166–67.

43. For the differing attitudes toward the state in East Germany and Poland, see also Andrzej Szczypiorski, "Mein Irrtum: Weshalb die Opposition in der DDR nicht mit der polnischen gleichgesetzt werden darf," *Frankfurter Allgemeine Zeitung,* 4 March 1995. Thanks to Margaret Anderson for this reference.

44. Jansen, *Professoren und Politik,* 11. Jessen speaks of the "illiberal German traditions of a profession defined by the state" to describe continuities between the East German and Nazi-era professoriates. "Vom Ordinarius," 99.

45. Vogel, "Anpassung und Widerstand," 28, 64.

46. "Deutscher Blick" refers to the habit of looking over one's shoulder before discussing something political.

47. On the ideological force of antifascism in East German communism, see Meuschel, *Legitimation,* 154; Grunenberg, *Antifaschismus.*

48. This meant a combination of the "Western understanding of freedom and the Eastern requirement of equality." Abrams, "The Struggle," 245–53.

CHAPTER 4

1. Some 38 percent of Polish professors and docents, as well as 32.6 percent of assistant and adjunct professors, did not survive; 660 to 700 academics (includ-

ing 35 percent of all professors) were victims of policies of extermination and hostilities. The percentage losses of academics exceeded those of the general population by over half. Łuczak, "Polnische Wissenschaft," 45; Walczak, *Szkolnictwo*, 188–89; Szarota, "Upowszechnienie," 410–11. In the Czech lands, of a total of 513 professors and 475 docents, 30 professors and 32 docents were killed in prisons and concentration camps. Havránek, "Der 17. November," 200.

2. Jaczewski, "Organizacja," 55–57.

3. In an attempt to quell political opposition, the Piłsudski regime had several thousand opponents arrested in the fall of 1930. See Polonsky in Leslie, Polonsky, Ciechanowski, and Pełczyński, *History of Poland*, 174. There was little echo from other social groups, including writers, of whom only 20 percent joined the protest. Mycielska, "Postawy," 311.

4. Mycielska, "Postawy," 318.

5. Jaczewski, "Organizacja," 196–97.

6. Rothschild, *East Central Europe*, 41.

7. M. Kridl to S. Pigoń, 5 February 1937. Rkp BJ Przyb 257/76.

8. *Robotnik*, 23 December 1937; Żyndul, *Zajścia*, 81. The number of Jewish professors at Polish universities has not been ascertained but is not thought to have been great. Żarnowski, *Struktura społeczna*, 245.

9. See his letter to the *New York Times*, 20 March 1938.

10. For Manteuffel's account of the murder of Widerszal and the arrest of Handelsman, see his unpublished memoir in APAN-W, III-142, j. 119. Other Jewish scholars who survived the war on "Aryan" papers obtained by their colleagues were Marian Małowist, Irena Krońska, Jan Kott, Ludwik Ehrlich, Hugo Steinhaus, and Ludwik Hirszfeld. In the summer of 1944 the right radical underground in Warsaw began circulating lists of suspected "Jews and leftists," many of whom worked for the Home Army's Bureau of Information. Included on the lists were Handelsman, Widerszal, Manteuffel, T. Kotarbiński, and Stanisław and Maria Ossowski.

11. Best known examples on Kraków's faculty in the postwar period were historians Władysław Konopczyński and his student Kazimierz Lepszy. See chapter 8, n. 70.

12. Mates, Průcha, and Svatoš, *Vývoj organizace*, 27–30; Kádner, *Vývoj*, 448; František Weyr, "Právní úprava vysokých škol," *Lidové noviny*, 20 March 1936; Jan Bělehrádek, "Autonomie vysokých škol," *Lidové noviny*, 28 October 1936; Jan Hrabánek, "Stíny autonomie vysokých škol," *Národní osvobození*, 27 February 1936.

13. Muller, *The Other God*, 227–37.

14. Approximately one-quarter of the professors in Hamburg, Tübingen, and Heidelberg belonged to a political party at various points in the 1920s, mostly of the right; their distance to the democratic values of Weimar increased through the decade. Most continued to identify themselves with symbols and feast days of the empire, and neglected those of the republic. Jessen, "Akademische Elite," 22–23; Jansen, *Professoren und Politik*.

15. Of the faculty teaching in Hamburg in 1933, 77.8 percent of the associate, 64.2 percent of the private docents, and 37.9 percent of the full professors joined the NSDAP. The percentage of NSDAP members among new appointees was also high; for example, of 463 professors appointed in 1937–38, 213 (46 percent)

belonged to the NSDAP, and a further 51 (11 percent) to a Nazi organization. Jessen, "Akademische Elite," 25–26. See also Giles, "Professor und Partei."

16. For the case of Leipzig, see Muller, *The Other God,* 278–80.

17. In all, 183 professors were sent to Sachsenhausen from Kraków. Batowski, "Nazi Germany," 216; August, *Sonderaktion Krakau.* Further reprisals followed: on 9 and 11 November 13 professors and docents of the Catholic University of Lublin were arrested; 2 were subsequently shot, and 2 others sent to Sachsenhausen. The rest were released in the course of 1940. Ziółek, "The Imprisonment," 248–49. After occupying the city of Poznań, the Germans took some 30 professors and students of the university hostage, and in November expelled 18 professors with their families to the Generalgouvernement, simply leaving them at the first railway station. Mauersberg, "Nauka," 327. In perhaps the most grisly episode, German troops shot to death 25 professors and docents, as well as over 100 students, after conquering Lwów on 4 July 1941. Several members of the professors' families who happened to be at home, like the sons of Roman Longchamps, Witold Nowicki, Włodzimierz Stożek, and Kasper Weigel, were shot as well. Mauersberg, "Nauka," 328; Łuczak, "Polnische Wissenschaft," 43. The Soviets also had a role in destroying Polish academia: 44 of the reserve officers killed at Katyn were academics. Mauersberg, "Nauka," 332.

18. Ironically, all but one of the students executed had been chosen for leading posts in the student union because of a willingness to cooperate with the Germans. Havránek, "Der 17. November," 196.

19. There had been anti-Nazi manifestations on 28 October and 15 November in which students played a central role. The latter was a funeral for the medical student Jan Opletal, who was mortally wounded at the first demonstration on the occasion of Czechoslovak independence day. Mastny, *The Czechs,* 116–17. Estimates of the number of students involved in the 15 November march range from 3,000 to 4,000. Litsch, "17. listopad," 54, 57; Havránek, "Der 17. November," 187–202.

20. Following intense international protest, including the intervention of Mussolini, the Vatican, and the Swedish and Yugoslav (Ivo Andrič) representatives in Berlin, the professors were gradually released in 1940 and 1941. But some twenty, mostly elderly professors, did not survive. Mauersberg, "Nauka," 327; Buszko, "Solidaritätsaktionen," 67–97. The last professors were released in October 1941. Podradisz, "Bemühungen," 224. Like the professors of Kraków, most of the Czech students were released in 1940, but the last did not return until 1943. According to Litsch, some 400 students did not return at all. "17. listopad," 58.

21. The laboratories had approximately 400 employees, and because of their "cohesion" Landa was not denounced to the Germans. Nevertheless, rumors of activities there did reach the ears of Protectorate strongman K. H. Frank, who announced in a public speech that he would not "tolerate a higher school in Zlín." Wichterle, *Vzpomínky,* 46–47.

22. Krasucki, *Tajne szkolnictwo,* 298–99; Walczak, *Szkolnictwo,* 71–74.

23. Krasucki, *Tajne szkolnictwo,* 299.

24. Kowalenko, *Tajny Uniwersytet,* 25.

25. A self-help committee had emerged in 1940 to aid over fifty families of professors expelled from Poznań to Warsaw. In 1942 a "rector's committee" of the

UZZ was created to solicit donations in the Warsaw region, collecting some 200,000 złotys in two years. Clergy and a farmers' organization helped procure temporary refuge in the countryside for individuals who felt endangered in Warsaw. Kowalenko, *Tajny Uniwersytet*, 144–53.

26. The Catholic University of Lublin as well as the universities in Lwów and Wilno also held secret courses. Hartmann, *Hochschulwesen*, 43–44; Mauersberg, "Nauka," 353.

27. Disguised instruction also took place at a school for mining and geodesy, and at a school for artisanry and crafts that the Germans opened in Kraków. Hartmann, *Hochschulwesen*, 36–37; Mauersberg, "Nauka," 337–38, 352. After having narrowly evaded several searches of apartments in which he was teaching Polish literature, Professor Stefan Krzyżanowski moved classes into a school building under the guise of conducting private vocational training; in case of a visit by the Germans, linguists were told to pretend to be learning German for business; historians, business geography; and the like. He carried lecture notes on the natural resources of China. *Z dziejów*, 130–31. Historian Tadeusz Manteuffel arranged for one first-year class to meet in a convent of the nuns of the Immaculate Conception. *Z dziejów*, 214.

28. Walczak, *Szkolnictwo*, 88.

29. For example, the law faculty of UZZ printed lecture notes on penal law, theory of law, economic geography, history of law in Western Europe, as well as the decrees of the London Government. Kowalenko, *Tajny Uniwersytet*, 52.

30. Hartmann, *Hochschulwesen*, 36; Walczak, *Szkolnictwo*, 78. Trade flourished in used books. Brodowska, "Freie polnische Hochschule," 394.

31. This included Professors Stanisław Ossowski and Bogdan Suchodolski. Mauersberg, "Nauka," 336–37.

32. Ibid., 340. Krasucki estimates the number of participants at 12,000. *Tajne szkolnictwo*, 315.

33. Of these, 200 were at the Warsaw Polytechnic, 130 at the Main School for Agriculture, 120 at Warsaw University, 100 at the UZZ, and 85 at the Main School for Trade. No reliable figures were available from Kraków, Wilno, or Lwów. Mauersberg, "Nauka," 356.

34. Walczak, *Szkolnictwo*, 101.

35. Historian Krzysztof Dunin-Wąsowicz began his historical studies in Warsaw's underground university, as did his fellow docents Andrzej Wyczański, Andrzej Zahorski, Stanisław Kałabiński, and Zbigniew Wójcik. *Z dziejów*, 261.

36. Teachers and students needed an official occupation, which forced them to live double lives. Hartmann, *Hochschulwesen*, 35.

37. Instead of a *matura* they presented a recommendation by a professor or director of a high school. Kowalenko, *Tajny Uniwersytet*, 178; *Z dziejów*, 143–44.

38. Kowalenko, *Tajny Uniwersytet*, 23, 177; Walczak, *Szkolnictwo*, 91–92.

39. Kowalenko, *Tajny Uniwersytet*, 122.

40. Kotarbiński, *Myśli*, 332.

41. One source estimates that up to 90 percent of the students were involved in military activities. Walczak, *Szkolnictwo*, 96.

42. Kowalenko, *Tajny Uniwersytet*, 179.

43. Buszko and Paczyńska, *Universities*, 440.

44. Kowalenko, *Tajny Uniwersytet*, 193.

45. Hartmann, *Hochschulwesen*, 38. Kowalenko estimates that 434 students took courses of the UZZ outside Warsaw. *Tajny Uniwersytet*, 82–87, 113.
46. Dunin-Wąsowicz, "Scholarly and Educational Activity," 383.
47. Gross, *Polish Society*, 202, 238, 256.
48. The Polish word for "resistance" (*opór*) was first used in the 1970s to describe the wartime conspiracy, perhaps in response to the internationalization of the subject. In Germany and the Czech lands the respective words for resistance (*Widerstand, odboj*) were used from the very beginning, and by the participants themselves.
49. See, for example, the wartime memoirs of leading Czech scholars who were involved in the resistance: Krajina, *Vysoká hra;* Černý, *Paměti*, vol. 2.
50. Wandycz, "The Poles," 261–62.
51. This formulation of 1940 is cited in Klessmann, "Die Zerstörung," 178.
52. The Germans produced new texts and made spot checks to see whether Polish teachers were using prewar books. Dobroszycki, *Reptile Journalism*, 110–11.
53. Trade schooling was better developed but adapted to German needs; it lasted two to three years, depending on line of work. Klessmann, "Die Zerstörung," 181–87.
54. Numbers of students in agricultural training schools rose by almost 100 percent. Doležal, *Česká kultura*, 84.
55. This is precisely what happened in October 1941, when the Nazi leadership informed the Protectorate minister of education Kapras that their "patience was running out." He in turn called a conference of school directors and student representatives to warn of impending dangers. The following month President Hácha of the Protectorate demanded that Kapras intervene at any sign of "lack of goodwill" toward the Germans. Ibid., 75.
56. The Germans published twenty-two of their own practical-professional journals in the Generalgouvernement, like *Pszczelarz* (The beekeeper), *Wiadomości Aptekarskie* (Druggist news), *Weterynaryjne Wiadomości* (Veterinarian news), *Ogrodnictwo* (Gardening); in addition to nine dailies and eight weekly or monthly magazines. Dobroszycki, *Reptile Journalism*, 66–76. For a detailed inventory of the many hundreds of newspapers and journals published in the Protectorate, see Pasák, *Soupis*.
57. Pasák, *Soupis*, 194. Prominent resistance member Václav Černý officially published his *Kritický měsíčník* (Critical monthly) until 1942. Pedagogical journals like *Komenský, Střední škola* (High school), and *Věstník pedagogický* (Pedagogical bulletin) appeared until 1943. Somr, *Dějiny*, 252.
58. Pasák, *Soupis*, 278.
59. From personnel files, AUK.
60. Doležal, *Česká kultura*, 151.
61. "Výroční zpráva České společnosti sociologické," 28 June 1943. AČAV, Král Papers, i.č. 654.
62. Doležal, *Česká kultura*, 81.
63. Somr, *Dějiny*, 252; Doležal, *Česká kultura*, 74–80.
64. *Ruch filozofický* 13:2–3 (1941): 93–97. Thanks to Justin Sparks for assistance in translating the title. The previous issue had appeared with a large red "V" on the cover, symbolizing victory for Germany. Page 7 of that issue featured

a statement in bold relief: "Germany's victorious arms protect the liberty of Europe from the encroachment of Bolshevism."

65. AČAV, Král Papers, i.č. 71. The libel case was dealt with by the district criminal court in Prague-Pankrac, and appears to have failed in 1943. Král was especially hurt by allegations that he had received his position improperly. Ibid., i.č. 410.

66. Kovály, *Under a Cruel Star*, 43, 52–55; Zilynská, "Poválečná obnova," 238.

67. His history could not appear in Poland because a competing history was being published by Z. Jachmiecki. Letters of 5 December 1941, 27 January 1947, 18 February 1947; Rkp BJ Przyb 108/74.

68. From Manteuffel's unpublished memoirs in APAN-W, III-192, j. 119.

69. He wrote that Lwówians had begun to rename streets: one street leading eastward, through which "our guests from the East left without saying good-bye," was called "Ulica Dawaj-nazad" (Give-It-Back Street). A street leading in the opposite direction might be called "Strada Tutto-Perduto" when the guests from the West, with their "complexions blue" from the cold, finally left. Letter of 5 December 1941, Rkp BJ Przyb 108/74.

70. Karpiński, *Nie być w myśleniu posłusznym*, 85.

71. Gross, *Polish Society*, 240.

72. Kotarbiński, *Myśli*, 331.

73. Ibid., 329–30.

74. Hübner, *Polityka naukowa*, 6.

75. For an argument on the collapse of established values among Poles, see Kersten, *Narodziny*, 150.

76. The occupation-era dismissal was declared invalid the following month. Personnel file, AUK. Hora had been professor since 1911. See also the report of Professor Jan Matějka of the law faculty to the action committee of the Czech Academy of Arts and Letters of 15 April 1948, stressing his "warm" relations with student Communists as dean, and his unquestioning willingness to accept a Communist professor into the faculty without habilitation. In 1945 Deputy Foreign Minister Vladimír Clementis requested that Matějka secure an honorary doctorate for the Soviet prosecutor of the Moscow purge trials, A. Vyshinskii. Within a day Matějka achieved the approval of his faculty and the university senate. AČAV, f. ČAVU, i.č. 243. In the end the doctorate was not granted, because the Soviet side claimed that high dignitaries could not accept such honors from foreign universities.

77. The house referred to was Tureček's own. One hopes for the sake of his neighbors that the "waste products" referred to were scrap metal, paper, and the like. This questionnaire was filled out by all professors and docents of Charles University in June 1945; Tureček completed his on 8 June. Of the two dozen professors teaching law, two could legitimately claim to have taken part in the work of illegal organizations: Professors Jan Matějka and Arnošt Wenig-Malovský, both of whom were imprisoned. AUK, právnická fakulta, i.č. 558.

78. The other KSČ members among the old professors at this point were the legal historian Václav Vaněček and an expert in international law, Antonín Hobza.

79. In a protracted explanation of his past addressed to Rudolf Slánský in 1951 Valouch blamed his "family relations," that is, a mother-in-law in the NSDAP,

and a brother-in-law in the *Wehrmacht,* for his failing to find "contact" to "illegal activity." His "wife at the time vacillated, because she was very fond of her mother. She herself did not sin in any direct way, but did keep in touch with her family. I myself was not yet politically mature enough to resolve the situation in an uncompromising way, and thus only after liberation did it come to a definitive break between me and my then-wife." "Vlastní hodnocení práce a jejích nedostatků," sent to Rudolf Slánský 24 April 1951, AČAV, Valouch Papers, correspondence.

CHAPTER 5

1. Marian Walczak writes that "it was due to conspiratorial teaching that all universities with all their faculties could be activated directly after liberation." *Szkolnictwo,* 101. See also the memoirs of Polonist Jerzy Pelc and historian Tadeusz Manteuffel on the self-reconstitution of Warsaw University's humanities. *Z dziejów,* 57–114, 222–23.

2. For the failure of any university to circumvent this "rigorous policy of dismissals," see Jessen, "Akademische Elite," 310. Between 40 and 60 percent of the teaching staff at German universities had belonged to the NSDAP. Ibid., 26. In Berlin the total was 47.2 percent in the winter semester 1942–43. Ibid., 549. In Halle the figure was 61 percent. Rupieper, "Wiederaufbau," 101. The figure in Leipzig too was close to 60 percent. Wartenberg, "Die Wiedereröffnung," 11.

3. The latter figure includes professors who switched their workplaces. Of the associate professors 13.9 percent continued, and of docents 9.4 percent. Jessen, "Akademische Elite," 319–20. Though it is true, as Jessen writes, that administrative denazification was numerically not the most significant cause of the diminishment of the professoriate, there is no reason to believe the Soviets would not have purged other former Nazis, had they remained. Denazification was therefore decisive in producing discontinuity.

4. Ibid., 123–28.

5. Lönnendonker, *Freie Universität,* 54, 57, 73–74. Lönnendonker speaks of the "legitimacy deficit" of the professorial councils that assembled in May–June 1945, ibid., 55.

6. Nikitin, "Die sowjetische Militäradministration," 409. The following year Spranger made his way to Tübingen. Most of Spranger's colleagues preferred to "wait inconspicuously" for what the occupiers would determine, rather than expose themselves. Spranger found one colleague willing to accompany him to the magistrate. Lönnendonker, *Freie Universität,* 54, 57, 73–74. As an example of Spranger's vague sense of the challenges of dealing with the legacy of the recent past, Lönnendonker cites his greeting at the founding of the official Culture Union (Kulturbund) in July 1945: "We shall start from the beginning! We shall again respect the law of the spirit as truth, beauty, and as reverence for the image of man. We shall demand everything from ourselves, mercilessly; but we shall also have faith that these earnest desires will succeed in making life livable once more." Ibid., 57.

7. Stroux, a prime example of a "progressive bourgeois scholar," made his first decision to keep the university in the eastern sector, putting to rest speculation that the level of destruction might necessitate a move to the West. He served as rector until 1948, and was also a vice-president in the Culture Union. From

1948 until his death in 1954 he was a member of the East German Parliament; Broszat and Weber, *SBZ-Handbuch,* 1039.

8. Müller and Müller, ". . . *stürmt die Festung,"* 65.

9. On the attempted self-purgation in Halle in 1945, see Rupieper, "Wiederaufbau," 98–103.

10. Borusiak, "Die Universität Leipzig," 368, 371; Hoyer, "Der Weg," 23.

11. Eighteen faculty members and 108 technicians and scientists from the Schott and Zeiss optical factories likewise left with the Americans. Schmidt, *Alma Mater Jenensis,* 302. The Americans took approximately 90 members of the University of Halle westward. Rupieper, "Wiederaufbau," 100.

12. Hoyer, "Der Weg," 25–26. On 26 October the government of Saxony-Anhalt ordered that officials be dismissed "regardless whether they were Nazi criminals, activists, holders of Party offices, members of the SA, SS, or any affiliates of the NSDAP." Rupieper, "Wiederaufbau," 103. On 27 October the Soviet Military Administration in Saxony ordered that all members of the NSDAP be removed from the civil service. Feige, "Zur Entnazifizierung," 800–801. On 9 November the Department of Education of the government of Saxony instructed educational institutions to "immediately dismiss all former members of the NSDAP still teaching in schools." Haritonow, "Entnazifizierung an der Bergakademie," 435.

13. These purges in Jena occurred after communications had taken place between Soviet agencies in Weimar and in Berlin; Protocol, Day 3, 85. On Leipzig: Hoyer, "Der Weg," 26.

14. This professor had joined the NSDAP in 1933, and was considered an informant for the Nazi Party's Security Service (SD). The Soviets also discovered many books that contradicted their order to remove "Nazi and militaristic literature." Hoyer, "Der Weg," 25.

15. Müller and Müller, ". . . *stürmt die Festung,"* 36; Richert, *"Sozialistische Universität,"* 26.

16. See the comments of Paul Wandel in a meeting at Leipzig University of 20 November 1946 in UAL, Rektorat 1. On the struggle of the first postwar rectorship in Halle to retain some former Nazis, see Rupieper, "Wiederaufbau," 103.

17. At the March 1947 meeting of the education ministers of the Soviet zone Paul Wandel admitted that two years earlier a decision was made on whether the new German intelligentsia would be formed "with or against the universities." He and the majority of those present had been opposed to granting universities the role of reshaping the German intelligentsia, and he now found that the experiences of the past two years had justified his hesitation. BAAP, R2/53, Bl. 23–24.

18. For example, this demand was communicated to Rostock University at the beginning of December 1945 by the Soviet Military Administration in Karlshorst, and on 15 December that university presented a faculty free of former NSDAP members to the Soviet Military Administration in the regional capital of Schwerin. Wachholder to Bergmann, 6 January 1946, UAR, RIII A 1/1. A significant number of former NSDAP members continued in the employ of their universities as researchers or as physicians in university clinics. Ernst, *"Die beste Prophylaxe,"* 168.

19. In August 1945 the government of Saxony-Anhalt appointed two professors for

pedagogy and Slavic languages for the university in Halle, despite the university's protests. Rupieper, "Wiederaufbau," 104.

20. Directive No. 24 of the Allied Control Council of 12 January 1946 had limited dismissals to those who joined the Nazi Party before 1937, were full-time NSDAP officials, or held high positions under the Nazi regime. Hoyer, "Der Weg," 27.

21. Jessen, "Akademische Elite," 325.

22. See Welsh, "Entnazifizierung," 349, 351.

23. On Soviet understandings of democracy, see Naimark, *The Russians*.

24. See the intervention in Jena in 1948, chapter 6 at n. 89.

25. These were Friedrich Elchlepp (SPD), Erich Schlesinger, and Franz Wohlgemuth (KPD). None of these men respected the principle of university autonomy. On Elchlepp, see Rupieper, "Wiederaufbau," 104–5.

26. Nikitin, "Die sowjetische Militäradministration," 409. On the "wish" of the "Russian administration" for a change of rectors in Rostock, see Neels to Grünberg, 24 October 1945, MLHA, MfVB 2258.

27. The case of Lohmeyer has never been solved. Robert Rompe recalled in an interview of 1991 going to Greifswald to attend the university's reopening and being told that Lohmeyer had been arrested. The Soviets supposedly claimed that photographs had been found of Lohmeyer's soldiers ostentatiously displaying executed Soviet partisans. Rompe was surprised to learn that Lohmeyer had never returned. Rompe then claimed to have received the task of convincing the physicist Seeliger, whom he knew from before the war, to take the job.

28. Havránek, "Studenti," 70. For a characteristic student demand based on the alleged fact that "no other stratum of the nation was exposed to such persecution as students," see Jan Kazimour, "Studenti nastupují," *Student*, 30 May 1945.

29. Zilynská, "Poválečná obnova," 236–37.

30. His supporter Professor Hobza cited Procházka's broad knowledge of "public administration in Soviet Russia." Matějka to Nejedlý, 14 November 1945, AČAV, Nejedlý Papers, č.k. 31; Pousta, "Právnická fakulta," 370; Matějka to AV České akademie věd a umění, 15 April 1948, AČAV, f. ČAVU, i.č. 243.

31. "Vysoké školy—universita," AČAV, Král Papers, i.č. 36. In July 1948, long after Polish Communists had sealed control of the state apparatus, senior philosophy professor Tadeusz Kotarbiński opposed granting a chair in philosophy at Warsaw University to Soviet-trained Adam Schaff, in many ways the Polish equivalent of Kolman. Kotarbiński insisted that Schaff first habilitate and spend at least two years in the West in order to become acquainted with formal logic. Kotarbiński did, however, believe that Schaff could immediately take up a chair "which would be specially dedicated to the cultivation of Marxism." AAN, MO 2917, k. 69.

32. A similar role was played in 1948 by V. Procházka of the law faculty.

33. Varíková, *Košický vládny program*, 120.

34. The professors of the law and philosophy faculties met to reject their would-be colleagues in February and March 1946, thus while the Communists still held the Education Ministry. SÚA, MŠK, č.k. 631E, sig. 5ID.

35. On 9 May the legions, comprising about 1,000 students, were charged with guarding property belonging to Charles University and the Technical Uni-

versity, altogether about ninety buildings. Kráčmarová, *Vysokoškoláci,* 30; Havránek, "Studenti," 77.

36. Havránek, "Studenti," 80.

37. Kavka, *Stručné dějiny,* 295.

38. "Filozofická fakulta," 33. Members of action committees were mostly well-known leftist students of the prewar period, who were commissioned by the Student National Committee on 15 May. Havránek, "Studenti," 83.

39. Havránek, "Studenti," 99.

40. Cf., for example, the resolution of several youth organizations in Kraków of 12 July 1945, which makes "appeals" to the government in several issues, including student admissions, stipends, and the expansion of studies in agriculture and technical sciences. AAN, MO 3160, k. 14–15.

41. Members of the students' club at the natural sciences faculty visited several professors and asked whether they would be willing to take up lectures. They disagreed with the professors' council on a position in organic chemistry, and approached their preferred candidates (Šorma, Wichterle) directly. Wichterle, *Vzpomínky,* 85.

42. Jordán, *Dějiny,* 266.

43. In fall 1947 elections, the KSČ won 28.1 percent of the vote among Prague's students, while the Czech National Socialists picked up 38.1 percent, and the Catholic Popular Democrats, 22.1 percent of the vote. In Brno the KSČ fared even worse, while the Catholics received almost 40 percent of the vote. Kráčmarová, *Vysokoškoláci,* 193. In the May 1946 general parliamentary elections, the KSČ had won 40.2 percent, the National Socialists 23.7 percent, and the Catholics 20.2 percent of the votes in the Czech lands. *Československé dějiny,* 632.

44. Krasiewicz, *Odbudowa,* 82–85.

45. Ibid., 65, 86.

46. Raabe served as Polish ambassador to the Soviet Union in 1945–46. Mołdawa, *Ludzie władzy,* 414–15.

47. Mauersberg, "Nauka," 415. The unpopularity of UMCS is partly explained, in the words of Hugo Steinhaus, by the absence in 1945 of "people or books." *Wspomnienia,* 342.

48. Polish historian Krasiewicz has described the city as a "market" for scholars. *Odbudowa,* 228. For an account of Łódź rector Kotarbiński fishing unsuccessfully for professors in Kraków, see Steinhaus, *Wspomnienia,* 330. Toruń's rector Kolankowski likewise came to Kraków in the fall of 1945 in search of faculty. Tomczak, *Wspomnienia pracowników,* 85.

49. Lewandowski, *Rodowód,* 23.

50. Krasiewicz, *Odbudowa,* 124–26. Of 116 prewar professors, 76 reported for work in 1945. Mauersberg, "Nauka," 420.

51. AAN, MO 2895, k. 1, 2, 5.

52. Mauersberg, "Nauka," 421.

53. For the 4 March 1945 letter of leading Warsaw professors, see Krasiewicz, *Odbudowa,* 137. See also the report of Warsaw University to Ministry of Education, 17 March 1945, AAN, MO 3043, k. 194.

54. Mołdawa, *Ludzie władzy,* 443; Kowalenko, *Tajny Uniwersytet,* 65.

55. Krasiewicz, *Odbudowa,* 138, 154.

56. Hübner, *Polityka naukowa,* 100–101.

57. Szarota, "Upowszechnienie," 425.

58. See the bitter account of J. Chałasiński, "O społeczny sens reformy uniwersytetów," *Kuźnica* 24 (17 June 1947): 3. The student-teacher (including assistants) ratios for the first four academic years were 20:1, 14:1, 12:1, 14.7:1. Krasiewicz, *Odbudowa,* 204–7.

59. Krasiewicz, *Odbudowa,* 200, 204.

60. Kenney, *Rebuilding Poland.*

61. Three of these were women, including historian Celina Bobińska, who subsequently went from Warsaw to Kraków. AAN, KC PPR 295/XVII/59, k. 238–39.

62. "Protokół z konferencji z Uniwersytetu Łódzkiego," 8 February 1951. AAN, MSW 163.

63. Hübner, *Nauka polska,* 26. Kulczyński had resigned from his post as rector of Lwów University in 1938 in protest of the introduction of ghetto benches for Jewish students. See the letter of Oskar Lange to the *New York Times,* 20 March 1938.

64. Krasiewicz, *Odbudowa,* 183, 186.

65. Ibid., 222–27. For the text of the 4 April 1945 letter from the Wilno professors, see AAN, MO 3048, k. 3.

66. Krasiewicz, *Odbudowa,* 228–30. Of 49 professors in December 1945 whose background can be identified 28 came from Wilno, 12 from Lwów, 5 from Poznań, 3 from Kraków, and 1 from Riga. The ratios of students to teachers in the first four postwar years were 12.6:1, 9.5:1, 11.7:1, 14.3:1.

67. Hübner, *Nauka polska,* 25.

68. AAN, KC PPR 295/XVII/57, k. 22.

69. AAN, MO 2876, k. 30.

CHAPTER 6

1. On the early Communist control of the levers of power throughout Eastern Europe, see Seton-Watson, *The East European Revolution,* 296–304.

2. For a selection of Esch's writings, see Kopke, *Mein Vaterland.*

3. Protocols of interrogations of three participants are contained in AUK, SVS B27; among the interrogators were Alex Urban and Joža Grohman, both leading Communist students.

4. *Slovo národa,* 12 December 1945.

5. Unanimous resolution of the workers of the iron mines at Krušná Hora of 17 December 1945, in AČAV, Nejedlý Papers, č.k. 24. The employees of an airplane factory near Prague demanded in a circular letter to universities "that government officials be merciless toward anyone who would disturb our work, and if it is necessary, we will help the government ourselves." AUK, právnická fakulta, i.č. 733. A trade-union committee of the Mautera Textile Factory in Náchod requested "expeditious legalization of factory militias." Letter of 18 December, AČAV, Nejedlý Papers, č.k. 24.

6. See his letter of 12 December 1945. AČAV, Nejedlý Papers, č.k. 31.

7. Most students in the mechanical and electrical engineering faculty were supporters of the Czech National Socialists. See the report from 1949, SÚA, AÚV KSČ, f. 19/7, a.j. 311, l. 327.

8. *Čin* (Brno), 23 May 1946. For a discussion of the lack of resistance to Nazi rule in the Czech working class, see Mastny, *The Czechs,* 37, 77, 80, 85.

9. The Ministry of Defense was held by fellow traveler General Ludvík Svoboda, later prominent in supporting and betraying the Prague Spring.

10. *Čin* (Brno), 10 February 1946; Kráčmarová, *Vysokoškoláci,* 151. *Práce* (Olomouc), 8 February 1946, claimed that the police detained forty-six students. For Hitler's views on Czech workers, see Picker, *Hitlers Tischgespräche,* 412.

11. AČAV, Nejedlý Papers, č.k. 24. Further resolutions can be found in the Gottwald Papers, SÚA, AÚV KSČ, f. 100/24, a.j. 980, l. 2–6.

12. Sládek, "Vliv," 535; Mastny, *The Czechs,* 65–85; Rhode, "The Protectorate," 318–19.

13. Estimates range from 500 to 1,400. Mazowiecki, *Pierwsze starcie,* 87–110.

14. Demonstrations also occurred in Gliwice, Łódź, Warsaw, Toruń, and Gdańsk. Walczak, *Ruch studencki,* 34–35. A complete list of the over fifty demonstrations is in Mazowiecki, *Pierwsze starcie,* 154. For reports from Łódź, where students shouted "down with the PPR" and "Long live Mikołajczyk," see letter of Wojewódzki Urząd Informacji i Propagandy, Łódź, to Miejski Urząd Informacji i Propagandy, 10 May 1946. Wojewódzkie Archiwum Państwowe, Łódź, MIiP no. 804, 80. Thanks to Padraic Kenney for this reference.

15. Mazowiecki, *Pierwsze starcie,* 215. Freedom and Independence (WiN) was a political resistance organization that grew out of the Home Army. Its leadership was broken in the autumn of 1946. Ciechanowski in Leslie, Polonsky, Ciechanowski, and Pełczyński, *History of Poland,* 290–91.

16. For use of this word by students in Chrzanów, Poznań, Gdańsk, Gdynia, and Toruń, see Mazowiecki, *Pierwsze starcie,* 173, 179–80, 190, 192.

17. Ibid., 184.

18. Some 250 such clubs existed throughout Poland in 1950. Yet little had been done by the state to influence their activities, which included running departmental libraries, organizing after-hours instruction, and publishing lecture notes. Some larger clubs were still in possession of property and could thus aid students materially. "Tezy do projektu nowej organizacji kół naukowych na Prezydium Rady Głównej," 2 December 1950, APAN-W, III-192, j. 74, k. 20; Walczak, *Ruch studencki,* 62.

19. For example, the ministry released a decree in November 1945 that permitted the state to transfer professors from one university to another, and to appoint tenured associate professors, so-called *docenci etatowi.* Lewandowski, *Rodowód,* 29. Yet these attempted infringements of university sovereignty caused alarm in the academic community. Though assured the decree would not be invoked, Jagiellonian University's senate nevertheless wrote Minister Wycech on 28 February 1946 demanding it be abrogated. AUJ, S III 18. For Jagiellonian University's protest against the ministry's attempted interference in student admissions, see Rector Lehr-Spławiński to the Ministry of Education, 28 July 1945, AAN, MO 2867, k. 16–17. For the rejection by leading Polish academics (Pieńkowski, Kotarbiński) of suggestions to increase prerogatives of ministry representatives in university cities, see the protocol of the first meeting of the ministry's scientific council (*rada naukowa*), 20 August 1945, AAN, MO 2801, k. 72. There were also coordinated protests against efforts to reduce universities to teaching institutions. Chodakowska, *Rozwój,* 100–101.

20. Mazowiecki, *Pierwsze starcie,* 226–37.

21. Maurycy Jaroszyński (1890–1974), a professor of law, had been vice-minister of internal affairs and parliamentary deputy for the interwar Sanacja regime. Jaczewski, "Organizacja," 149. As such, he was a proponent of a strong state in both the interwar and postwar periods. Jaroszyński came from a poor farming family and had to work to put himself through university, much in contrast, as he put it, to young people from the " 'better' spheres" of the intelligentsia, from whom he felt alienated. See his "Wspomnienia outsidera" (Memoirs of an outsider), APAN-W, III-212, j. 35, k. 220, 230.

22. Krasiewicz, *Odbudowa,* 327.

23. W. Sokorski, "Organizacja nauki i szkół wyższych," *Odrodzenie,* 18 May 1947.

24. The PPR-supported press accused Jagiellonian University students of participation in anti-Semitic excesses of August 1945 in Kraków, although, according to Rector Lehr-Spławiński, even the secret police admitted that students had not had a role. Lewandowski, *Rodowód,* 30–31. For the accusations, see "Oczyścić wyższe uczelnie z reakcji," *Głos Ludu,* 19 August 1945, and "Jak wychować młodzież akademicką w duchu demokratycznym," *Głos Ludu,* 29 August 1945.

25. Krasiewicz, *Odbudowa,* 323.

26. The educational establishment felt direct pressure to produce specialists for national reconstruction. See the demands from 1946 and 1947 by the Central Planning Board that universities train more experts in social medicine, town planning, and railway engineering in AAN, MO 2854, k. 47–48, 241–43.

27. For attempts by Jagiellonian University to draw up quickly programs of study for the introductory year, see the correspondence in AUJ, WP III 75 and S III 100. For a discussion of the general willingness of professors to help change the sociological makeup of universities, see Krasiewicz, *Odbudowa,* 99.

28. AAN, MO 2801, k. 40 (Kotarbiński); AUJ, S III 18 (Warcholski).

29. The Rectors' Council, for example, was not convinced that the solution to the low numbers of doctorates and habilitations was to place power over graduate studies in the hands of a single agency. Since the basic problem was financial, the proper response would be to give everyone in need a stipend. See discussions of the 16–17 October 1946 meeting, AUJ, S III 18.

30. AAN, MO 2847, k. 338. He wanted decisions in university admissions to be transferred to Ministry of Education representatives in university towns.

31. AAN, PPR 295/XVII/1, k. 131.

32. AAN, PPR 295/XVII/58, k. 6.

33. This response was drafted by the law faculty and bears the date 1 March 1947. AUJ, WP III 3.

34. Memorial of Warsaw University (undated), AUJ, S III 18. Here the professors were making a pun: a Russian general and plenipotentiary of that period, Novosiltsev, had personally investigated a conspiratorial movement at Wilno University in November 1823, exiled several students, and dismissed a number of professors. Davies, *God's Playground,* 314. "Nowosilny" suggests a reincarnation of the general, meaning "newly strong." Thanks to David Frick for pointing this out.

35. From the remarks of the senate of Nicolaus Copernicus University in Toruń to the preliminary project of Professor Jaroszyński in AUJ, S III 18. All of these resolutions were sent to Jagiellonian University, in whose archives they remain.

36. Krasiewicz, *Odbudowa,* 329–30.

37. Letter of 24 February 1947. APAN-W, III-212, j. 38, k. 11–13. Marchlewski, the nephew of leading Polish Socialist Julian Marchlewski, later became the rector of Jagiellonian University. He joined the PPR in 1945. AAN, KC PZPR 237/XVI/65, k. 18–20.

38. On 28 February the Ministry of Education's Department of Science and Higher Education put forth its own project, which was coordinated with the Central Committee of the PPS. Krasiewicz, *Odbudowa*, 327. Jaroszyński's proposal came to be seen as so controversial that plans for its publication were canceled. Hübner, *Polityka naukowa*, 215. A copy is located in AUJ, WP III 3.

39. AAN, KC PZPR 478/142, k. 4–5.

40. See the statements of J. Marowski, AAN, KC PZPR 478/142, k. 36–38; Krasiewicz, *Odbudowa*, 331; and of H. Raabe in *Naprzód*, 18 March 1947, AAN, KC PZPR 478/142, k. 39.

41. This provision was diluted by an emergency regulation toward the end of the decree that took away from the university the right to name candidates for a period of five years. Instead the Main Council, in consultation with local agencies of the Party, nominated rectors, deans, and their deputies. Hübner, *Nauka polska*, 54.

42. Polish historian Krasiewicz has written that "the creation of a Main Council for Science and Higher Education limited more the Ministry of Education than it did the prerogatives of the world of science." Krasiewicz, *Odbudowa*, 332.

43. *Svobodné noviny*, 7 June 1947.

44. *Tvorba*, 9 July 1947.

45. *Rudé právo*, 28 October 1947.

46. Compiled from reports in *Svobodné slovo*, 4 December 1947; *Národní osvobození*, 5 December 1947; and an undated flier of the Club of National Socialist Academics entitled "Ministerstvo Propagandy? Či snad nový Goebels [*sic*]?" in ANM, Engliš Papers, č.k. 778.

47. *Svobodné noviny*, 5 December 1947.

48. These are Czech versions of academic degrees. *Studentské noviny*, 21 January 1947.

49. *Národní osvobození*, 1 May 1947.

50. For example, Communist students demanded the arrest of National Socialist treasurer Karel Sešina, who had supposedly defiled the people's democratic system by stating: "the Republic is bound to fall, whether we do anything or not." *Rudé právo*, 25 October 1947; *Lidová demokracie*, 28 October 1947.

51. The compromise was motivated by a desire to make things easier for those who had been disadvantaged by the war. The normal procedure in law had been to take four sets of examinations on three days: church law, Roman law, medieval history, Czechoslovak history; civil law, civil process, trade law, penal law; economics, finance law; constitutional law, administrative law. Students who had taken part in the resistance movement felt that they should be allowed to skip examinations. Wichterle, *Vzpomínky*, 79. For a critique by President Beneš of students' "striving for all too great concessions," see *Svobodné slovo*, 8 March 1947.

52. *Mladá fronta*, 12 February 1947. Students' and professors' attitudes toward the issue of separate examinations were later noted in cadre materials. See, for example, the cadre report on Professor A. Wenig-Malovský in his personnel file, AUK.

53. *Mladá fronta,* 26 February 1947.

54. Quoted in Rupnik, "Intelektuálové," 540.

55. ANM, Engliš Papers, č.k. 778.

56. On 16 January Miloslav Valouch (KSČ), professor of physics at the Technical University in Prague, reported to the KSČ Central Committee that his senate had voted twelve to five (four abstained) merely to take cognizance of the Charles University protest supporting Engliš and "did not elect to join the protest." AČAV, Valouch Papers, č.k. 847.

57. The dean of the pedagogical faculty, Communist and later rector František Trávníček, would not support a resolution, because "Charles University had not requested one." Resolutions in support of Engliš were, however, transmitted by professors of Olomouc University, Brno's Technical University, and the mining school of Ostrava. Pousta, "Univerzita Karlova," 268-69.

58. *Lidová demokracie,* 11 December 1947.

59. *Svobodné noviny,* 18 December 1947; Minutes of the student union presidial meeting of 18 December 1947, AUK, SVS B14a.

60. Read at student union (Prague) presidial meeting, 17 December 1947, AUK, SVS B14a.

61. On the Czech intelligentsia's "historically embedded legitimacy to speak for the nation," see Abrams, "The Struggle," 432.

62. The number of participants in the first demonstration was estimated by contemporary observers between 6,000 and 9,000; in the second at 4,000. *Svobodné slovo,* 24 February 1948; Pousta, "Smuteční pochod." A reporter for Václav Kopecký estimated the number of students that reached the castle on 23 February at 1,500, and the total in the manifestation of 25 February between 4,000 and 5,000. SÚA, AÚV KSČ, f. 100/45, a.j. 106, l. 48, 67.

63. Increasingly, Soviet soldiers were made to live in fenced-off areas of towns and villages from which the German population had been expelled. Naimark, *The Russians,* 94-95. In the winter 1946-47 student council elections, the SED won 46 of 124 seats at the six East German universities. In the election of December 1947, it won 48 of 141 seats. Connelly, "East German Higher Education Policies," 275, 285.

64. BAAP, R2/1446, Bl. 271-74.

65. The German Communist Party may have had its origins with middle-class intellectuals, but the Party freed itself from their influence during its stalinization of the mid-1920s. Staritz, "Partei," 381; Epstein, "The Last Revolutionaries," 45. On the general susceptibility among intellectuals to a belief in a better "proletarian instinct," see Werblan, *Stalinizm,* 35; Słabek, *Intelektualistów,* 68-69.

66. Torhorst (1888-1989) was a teacher (*Studienrätin*) in the Karl-Marx-Schule in Berlin-Neukölln from 1929 until 1933, when she was fired for membership in the SPD. In 1943 she was incarcerated in the labor camp Hallendorf for having given accommodations to a Jewish Communist. After the war she joined the KPD. Broszat and Weber, *SBZ-Handbuch,* 1044.

67. Marie Torhorst, "Volksstudent und Universität," 22 March 1948. TLHA, MfVB 3123, Bl. 33. Paul Wandel also did not spare universities sharp words of criticism. In his view students had to give up the idea that they were "special citizens" (*Sonderbürger*). He addressed a letter to the five *Land* education minis-

tries in early 1948 that infuriated the professoriate: "If we compare . . . the honest and self-sacrificing work of the workers and peasants with what is taking place now at universities for the formation of a new democratic intelligentsia, then we cannot rest content with the results of the last two years' work. . . . The universities have first of all to fulfill the task of training highly qualified people who support the current constitution for our new democratic school, for the new health system, for the new justice system, and for the people's own enterprises." Ibid., 3115, Bl. 71. For similar complaints of student ingratitude, see the comments of Kurt Hager at the SED higher-education conference, 31 October 1953, SAPMO-BA, ZPA, IV 2/9.04/8, Bl. 35–36.

68. Grünberg, *Kumpel*, 248. This sort of anti-intellectualism was by no means limited to East Germany. For a similar exchange involving a functionary recruiting a candidate for philosophical studies in Poland ("Comrade, do you know anything about philosophy?" "No. . . ." "Good!" etc.), see Podgórecki, *Polish Society*, 165.

69. BAAP, R2/53, Bl. 23–24.

70. Letter in UAL, Rektorat 119.

71. "Wie lange noch . . .," *colloquium* 2 (March 1948): 14.

72. BAAP, R2/1446, Bl. 271–74.

73. See n. 100, and chapter 12 at n. 112.

74. See the report on the final meeting of the first Berlin Student Council, of 5 December 1947, in *colloquium* 1 (December 1947): 13. The SED representatives taunted their opponents with invectives like "fascist," "traitor," "reactionary." For examples of untranslated Latin, see Lönnendonker, *Freie Universität*, 229. The usage of Latin was also noted by Soviet observers: a 9 March 1948 report of Tiul'panov to Suslov mentions a poster made by the CDU referring to the SED: "Beware of Dog!" RTsKhIDNI, f. 17, op. 128, d. 566, l. 20.

75. In February 1947, 92 (2.1 percent) of Berlin's 4,312 students were officially classified as "victims of fascism." Of those, 53 were "racial," and 39 "political." BAAP, R2/644, Bl. 82. In December 1947, 1.6 percent of the students studying in Berlin, Halle, and Greifswald were recognized as "victims of fascism." BAAP, R2/1060, Bl. 22–28. In early 1948 the proportion of victims of fascism at the University in Jena was .5 percent. Though worker preparatory courses were supposed to make special efforts to attract "victims of fascism," in 1947–48 only 16 (.9 percent) of the 1,802 admitted could be counted in that category. The East German historian Kasper calculated that no more than 10 percent of the first four classes of the Berlin worker preparatory course were "victims of fascism." Kasper, "Der Kampf der SED," 162–63.

76. Wrazidlo had been liberated from Buchenwald by American troops. Lönnendonker, *Freie Universität*, 185.

77. On delimiting the category "victim of fascism," see Groehler, "Integration"; Tent, *The Free University*, 42.

78. MLHA, MfVB 2577, Bl. 198.

79. TLHA, MfVB 3325, Bl. 78–79.

80. See Connelly, "East German Higher Education Policies," 281–82.

81. BAAP, R2/1446, Bl. 296. The remarks were added in pencil by a DVV official to a letter dated 24 February 1947 that Wandel received listing the new student council leadership. Other notations included party membership and record

of military service. The official noted any factor that could be used to compromise the new representatives, or which might stiffen their resolve against the SED. Also preserved is a leaflet printed in West Berlin in December 1947 that lists candidates of the non-Communist parties for student council elections, upon which a DVV official has made notations of party membership, military service, and the appropriate Nazi racial categories (*Jude, Mischling*). There are also notations of students' fathers' experiences in the Third Reich. BAAP, R2/1446, Bl. 111. An additional list of candidates for Berlin student council elections dated December 1947 also indicates, besides party membership, whether a candidate had been a *Mischling*. BAAP, R2/1446, Bl. 29–41.

82. SAPMO-BA, ZPA, IV 2/9.04/6, Bl. 241.

83. "Stenographische Niederschrift über die Hochschulkonferenz der SED am 22. und 23. November 1947 im Hause des Kulturbundes," 80, SAPMO-BA, ZPA, IV 2/9.04/6.

84. Schulte, "Der Fall Natonek," 5.

85. Ibid., 6.

86. This allegation was printed in the East German student magazine *Forum* 2 (1949): 19. Cited in Müller and Müller, "... *stürmt die Festung*," 99–100.

87. Soviet officials made open threats. At a meeting of 15 March 1948 Zolotukhin told members of the student council in Berlin that they should not worry about arrested students; rather they should work better so that no further arrests were necessary. Despite these words, the council later voted 15 to 5 against an SED proposal that students take part in the official May Day celebration. Lönnendonker, *Freie Universität*, 227.

88. Müller and Müller, "... *stürmt die Festung*," 364–79.

89. Original (including commentary): "Für uns kommt nicht die in Ostzonesien gebräuchliche orientalische Volksdemokratie, sondern die Demokratie (damit meint er die westliche) in Frage." TLHA, MfVB 3325. *This* apparently Nazi usage bothered SED functionaries. In an article for the press entitled "Volksstudent und Universität" Torhorst wrote, "In Jena a student who had been elected as non-party candidate into the student council recently tried to ridicule our new people's state using the term 'oriental people's democracy' (the Nazis used to say 'Asian')." TLHA, MfVB 3123, Bl. 33.

90. TLHA, MfVB 3123, Bl. 37.

91. The shake-up occurred on the basis of Order No. 36 of the Thuringian SVA, of 15 March 1948, on the "Elimination of serious deficiencies that hamper the democratization of the University of Jena." Some seven students were arrested, mostly former SPD members; all were sentenced to twenty-five years' hard labor. TLHA, MfVB 3325, Bl. 78–79. Eleven students were expelled on the basis of evidence assembled by Soviet First Lieutenant Maltsev. For a record of the repressive measures taken in Jena, see TLHA, MfVB 3123.

92. Tent, *The Free University*, 92.

93. Ibid., 170–71.

94. *Tagesspiegel*, 25 May 1948 (cited in Lönnendonker, *Freie Universität*, 167).

95. Lönnendonker and Fichter, *Freie Universität Berlin 1948–1973*, 39; Lönnendonker, *Freie Universität*, 310. For fears of Professors Mellorowicz (economics) and Rörig (history) that the Free University would deepen the East-West divide,

see Tent, *The Free University*, 123, 156. Mellorowicz was not an SED supporter and later made his way westward.

96. Lönnendonker, *Freie Universität*, 247, 249.

97. Tent, *The Free University*, 122.

98. Lönnendonker, *Freie Universität*, 349. Rector Walter Hallstein of Frankfurt, later author of the Hallstein Doctrine, joined in the criticism of the Free University. Tent, *The Free University*, 156–57.

99. BAAP, R2/1446, Bl. 244, 257. Brugsch (1878–1963) was a left liberal who refused to separate from his Jewish wife and was therefore forced out of a professorship in Halle in 1935. After the war, he worked loyally in high positions in the DVV and the Culture Union (Kulturbund), throughout maintaining a lucrative private practice, which later included many prominent SED leaders. Anne-Sabine Ernst writes that "his life-style was hardly affected by the political changes after 1945. He retained villa, car with chauffeur, and servants, as well as theater subscription (*Premierenabonnement*). As a clinic director he thought in hierarchical terms, and conversed in Latin with his assistants at bedside as he always had." "*Die beste Prophylaxe*," 346–53.

100. See the senate's minutes from 1 August 1947 in UAL, Rektorat 1. Professor Litt protested that "political judgments had been customary for thirteen years." Plätzsch had said that if one needed to take a percentage of workers into university that was equal to their proportion of the population, then one should also take a number of imbeciles (*Schwachsinnige*) equal to their proportion of the population. No doubt Gadamer's and others' decisions to leave East Germany were strengthened by a desire to avoid participation in such "rationally necessary" measures.

101. Gadamer, *Philosophische Lehrjahre*, 128.

CHAPTER 7

1. Seton-Watson, *The East European Revolution*, 167–71.

2. For example, historian Tadeusz Manteuffel interrupted studies on feudalism, because this concept had become ideologically loaded "in a way inconsistent with previous scholarly understandings." He decided instead to work on the Cistercian Order in Poland. APAN-W, III-192, j. 119. His colleague Kazimierz Piwarski of Kraków "escaped" with many other historians into studies of Silesia, which were promoted by the Communist regime. Grodziski interview.

3. Communist student leader Jiří Pelikán wrote on 3 March: "progressive students have assumed the leadership of universities and progressive organizations." *Svobodné noviny*, 5 March 1948.

4. *Svobodné noviny*, 27 February 1948.

5. "Vysoké školy—universita," AČAV, Král Papers, i.č. 36.

6. *Mladá fronta*, 27 February 1948. According to Professor J. Král, Kozák had "wavered" between Kolman's supporters and the non-Communists, but finally decided to ingratiate himself with the former. "Vysoké školy—universita," AČAV, Král Papers, i.č. 36. See also Hruby, *Fools and Heroes*, 6.

7. *Mladá fronta*, 27 February 1948; Petráň, "Filozofická fakulta," 438.

8. Interview with Minister of Education Zdeněk Nejedlý, *Svobodné noviny*, 3 March 1948.

9. As was often the case, a number of these teachers later became caught in the wheels of injustice they helped establish. Fischl became a victim of the Slánský trial, and Rotter and Vlk were arrested in 1950 and 1952 respectively. Rotter and Kadlec were prominent supporters of the Prague Spring and removed from the KSČ in 1970; the latter became a signatory of Charter 77. Hávranek and Pousta, *Dějiny,* 376–77; *Československý biografický slovník,* 294.

10. Their major qualification was a favorable impression made upon Minister Nejedlý through work in Marxist publications. Husa and Charvát had worked in an archive, and Říha in the central trade-union council. Petráň, "Filozofická fakulta," 440.

11. Jordán, *Dějiny,* 273.

12. Ibid., 274. Similarly at the Higher Agricultural School in Brno the professorial leadership of the action committee had been hesitant to act decisively, and so the "purging action" was placed in the hands of "progressive elements of the students and employees." SÚA, AÚV KSČ, f. 19/7, a.j. 329, l. 14.

13. Jordán, *Dějiny,* 275; Weyr to Engliš, 10 April 1948, ANM, Engliš Papers, č.k. 399. The purge was considered extremely severe by Weyr, as it included not only unquestionable anti-Communists like himself, but also unobtrusive individuals like Professor Bohumil Kučera: "The Lord himself only knows why such a kindhearted and unassuming person as Prof. Kučera was expelled and is receiving only half pay."

14. Weyr to Engliš, 10 April 1948. ANM, Engliš Papers, č.k. 399.

15. Jordán, *Dějiny,* 275.

16. Ibid., 274; Kratochvil, *Kommunistische Hochschulpolitik,* 153.

17. The rector of Palacký University at Olomouc informed his deans on 29 April that "Neither the professors nor the deans can change anything that the action committees have done." Deans conference of 29 April 1948, SÚA, MŠK, č.k. 664.

18. J. Král claimed that Communist students, along with Professors Kozák and Rieger, had interceded for him. One of his assistants (Dědek) was dismissed immediately; another (Malý) was released some time later. "Vysoké školy — universita," AČAV, Král Papers, i.č. 36.

19. See, for example, the personnel files of Cyril Čechrák, Theodor Saturník, and Ladislav Vošta in AUK. In the case of Vošta, this justification for dismissal applied first from 11 July 1940, and then from 1 March 1948.

20. "Vysoké školy — universita." AČAV, Král Papers, i.č. 36.

21. This compromise was assiduously noted by informers. At the fifth KSČ district conference of higher schools in Prague, 14–15 April 1951, one student criticized the "fact" that "the Ministry of Education pays 12,000 Kčs [crowns] monthly to reactionary professors who no longer lecture." SÚA, AÚV KSČ, f. 19/7, a.j. 272/1, l. 39–41.

22. Their rights to teach, the "venia legendi," were revoked. AUK, SVS B2/1.

23. SÚA, AÚV KSČ, f. 19/7, a.j. 300, l. 11–21.

24. This formulation was used in other dismissals as well. See, for example, the personnel file of M. Boháček in AUK. Josef Král was kept from teaching and then had his apartment searched as an "inactive professor." Černý's bitter memoir is especially bitter on the subject of his former colleagues at the philosophical faculty, B. Havránek and J. Mukařovský, blaming the former for writing

a recommendation alleging Černý's sympathies for fascism, and the latter for rejecting a proposal (of A. Pražák) that Černý be employed at the Institute for Czech Literature in Prague. Both were supposedly complicit in removing other colleagues from the university as well. *Paměti*, 3:380–82.

25. See Procházka, "The Brno School."

26. Weyr to Engliš, 10 April 1948. ANM, Engliš Papers, č.k. 399; *Československý biografický slovník*, 130; Kratochvil, *Kommunistische Hochschulpolitik*, 180–81.

27. "Zpráva pro Pana Předsedu vlády o osnově vládního nařízení o některých změnách v organisaci vysokých škol," 30 June 1950; "Důvodová zpráva," 22 June 1950. SÚA, ÚPV, č.k. 833, sig. 812/30/10.

28. Central Committee to regional KSČ secretariats, 24 June 1950. SÚA, AÚV KSČ, f. 19/7, a.j. 104, l. 55.

29. Jaromír Blažke was permitted to teach for several years in Prague's law faculty. Third-year students from Brno were supposed to enroll in correspondence courses of the Prague law faculty while working in the socialist economy, yet several were sent to manual labor in mines and heavy industry. Jordán, *Dějiny*, 253.

30. For the additional faculty members, see the record of the faculty's protest of 19 May 1949 against the arrest of Gerhart Eisler in AUK, právnická fakulta, i.č. 736, and "Seznam pověřených přednáškami v zimním běhu 1950–51," in ibid., i.č. 201.

31. Kuhn and Böss, *Biographisches Handbuch*, 138.

32. Bláha published studies titled *Sociology of the Worker and Peasant* (Prague, 1925), *Child Sociology* (Prague, 1927), and *Sociology of the Intelligentsia* (Prague, 1937).

33. Letter of 14 March 1949. SÚA, MŠK, č.k. 309, sig. 3IIA. Their Prague colleague Josef Král also protested against the liquidation of sociology. Letter of 25 May 1949 to Ministry of Education, AČAV, Král Papers, i.č. 419.

34. Jordán, *Dějiny*, 255.

35. In the view of Roman Catholic critic N. Lobkowicz, writing in 1961, Král was the "most influential of Czech philosophers." *Marxismus-Leninismus*, 20.

36. Jordán, *Dějiny*, 244.

37. For their role in fostering causes of the left in the interwar period, see ibid., 181, 193, 202, 204.

38. *Filozofický časopis*, 1967, 559–60, cited in Kratochvil, *Kommunistische Hochschulpolitik*, 164–65.

39. Source: *Seznam přednášek*.

40. Svobodný, "Lékařské fakulty," 404.

41. Jordán, *Dějiny*, 276, 310.

42. SÚA, AÚV KSČ, f. 19/7, a.j. 300, l. 11–21.

43. Jordán, *Dějiny*, 259.

44. Nikitin, "Die sowjetische Militäradministration," 414.

45. "Die Philosophie," 250.

46. Among the losses were Leo Kofler and Max-Gustav Lange (Halle), and Hans Maus and Richard Thurnwald (Berlin). Staritz, "Partei," 393.

47. Zehm, "Repression," 455.

48. Because of its role in helping drain dissent from East German universities throughout the 1950s—most of its students in this period came from the

GDR — James Tent has called the Free University a "social safety valve" for the GDR. *The Free University,* 256.

49. Jessen, "Akademische Elite," 328–29. As professor at the German University in Prague during the war, Eduard Winter had been intimately connected to a group of anthropologists, geographers, and experts in racial hygiene at the Reinhard Heydrich Foundation, which worked with the Prague SD. Winter was decorated for his services to a lecture series that acquainted SS and German army officers with the geography and history of the occupied territories in Eastern Europe. Míšková, "Německá univerzita," 225, 228.

50. For the cases of other humanists who left the GDR to avoid spying and denunciations by junior colleagues, see Jessen, "Akademische Elite," 330–31.

51. This measurement does not include emeriti. For Rostock, see *Personal- und Vorlesungsverzeichnis,* Universität Rostock, SS 1945, WS 1947–48, Herbstsemester 1953–54; for Leipzig: *Personal- und Vorlesungsverzeichnis,* Universität Leipzig, SS 1945, WS 1947–48, Herbstsemester 1953–54; and for Jena: Schmidt, *Alma Mater Jenensis,* 519–51. In 1953–54, not even a docent taught history at Rostock. An institute of history was opened there in 1956, but its primary task was training high school teachers. Maeß, *Mögen viele Lehrmeinungen,* 123. In 1947–48 there were three docents, three lecturers, and two assistant professors among the historians in Leipzig. By 1953–54, two of the docents had left, and one was promoted to professor (W. Markov). He had been joined by Professors Ernst Engelberg (SED) in 1949 and (medievalist) Heinrich Sproemberg, from Rostock, in 1950. A new generation of historians was well in the making, however: there were twenty-two lecturers, nineteen of whom were either *Aspiranten* or assistant professors, and only one of whom was teaching in 1947–48 (the city archivist, Dr. Ernst Müller).

52. For Leipzig, see *Personal- und Vorlesungsverzeichnis,* Universität Leipzig, SS 1945, WS 1947–48, Herbstsemester 1953–54; for Jena: Schmidt, *Alma Mater Jenensis,* 519–51. One member of the 1953 faculty in Leipzig, E. Jacobi, had been a full professor there until 1933, when he was dismissed as a "half Jew." Jessen, "Akademische Elite," 352.

53. A third generation was waiting in the wings when the Berlin Wall fell. Kowalczuk identifies twenty-seven scholars as constituting the first generation of GDR historians, all of whom belonged to the SED, and less than half of whom had received doctorates before 1945. They trained over a hundred representatives of the second generation, who occupied practically all of the professorial chairs in GDR universities before 1989. Kowalczuk, *Legitimation,* 178–93.

54. Instructive in this regard is the volume *Wegbereiter der DDR-Geschichtswissenschaft* (Berlin, 1989), with short biographies of "bourgeois" historians who stayed in the GDR and helped train the East German historical profession: Karl Griewank, Friedrich Schneider (Jena); Martin Lintzel (Halle); Fritz Rörig, Eduard Winter (Berlin); Heinrich Sproemberg and Eberhard Wolfgram (Leipzig). Wolfgram (once NSDAP) was the only professor who came from the West. Only Griewank worked primarily in the modern period (revolutions of 1848). Griewank (1953), Lintzel (1955), and the gifted Rostock historian Johannes Nichtweiss (1958) committed suicide. In a report of 27 May 1950 Dr. W. Steinmetz of the Ministry of Education of the GDR had described Griewank as "openly reactionary" and an expert in "keeping to the rules of the

game." BAAP, R2/1899, Bl. 37. He was caught in a "two-front war between traditional academics and the new intelligentsia," which led to "existential crises." Jessen, "Vom Ordinarius," 96.

55. Kowalczuk, *Legitimation*, 206.

56. Jessen, "Vom Ordinarius," 94–97.

57. Jessen, "Akademische Elite," 350. One might have expected the replacement of professors lost to East German universities with professors of German universities lost to Poland, Russia, and Czechoslovakia, yet only 11 (5 percent) of 224 professors hired between 1945 and 1950 at the universities in Rostock, Leipzig, and Berlin had taught in Danzig, Breslau, Posen, Prague, or Königsberg. Ibid., 352.

58. The term "double labor market" has been employed by Ralph Jessen. He writes that "almost a quarter century was required to heal the deep break of the mid-1940s." Ibid., 338.

59. The prewar medical faculty at Charles University had consisted of 64 professors, and the faculty in 1948 had 56 professors in Prague, and a further 31 in new subsidiary faculties in Hradec Králové and Plzeň. The law faculty shrank by 1 professor to 23. Havránek and Pousta, *Dějiny*, 370, 404. The number of chair holders at Jagiellonian University increased from 125 in 1938–39 to 155 in 1947–48; the teaching staff in Poznań grew between 1939 and 1946 from 411 to 601. For further data on the recovery of Polish universities, and the formation of new universities in Lublin and Łódź, see Krasiewicz, *Odbudowa*, 82–85, 127–35, 138, 154, 161, 183, 186.

60. A draft of 18 September 1950 from the GDR Ministry of Education notes that the Higher-Education Department had "repeatedly attempted to get professors from the West. Yet almost every professor who was willing to come here then refused, because it took too long to reach a decision." BAAP, R2/1371, Bl. 29. See also the letter of Otto Halle to Fred Oelssner (Central Committee) of 2 November 1950 complaining that the Party's Cadre Department was delaying a number of appointments from the West. BAAP, R2/1421, Bl. 398. Though desired for technical abilities, professors were objects of intense suspicion. A draft from 29 June 1950 suggested that professors from the West be hired "only in exceptional circumstances, when they have been recommended in writing by democratic organizations in the West." BAAP, R2/1125, Bl. 110. Between October 1950 and June 1952, 55 university professors left East for West Germany, but only 9 went in the opposite direction. Jessen, "Akademische Elite," 353–54. For the failure to get professors from the West in 1953: "Jahresabschlussbericht der Abt. Hochschulbeziehungen zu Westdeutschland," 29 December 1953, BAAP, R3/149, Bl. 23.

61. "Bericht über Unterredung mit Prof. Thilo, Berlin, am 28.5.53 im Chemischen Institut, Hessische Str.," BAAP, R3/212, Bl. 137. The Barracked People's Police (KPV) formed the nucleus of the East German army, created in 1956. See Naimark, *The Russians*, 371. For letters of scholars who "fled the Republic" listing complaints similar to those voiced by Thilo, see Connelly, "Zur Republikflucht."

62. "Protokoll der Kontaktsitzung am 17. Februar 1953," 21 February 1953. BAAP, R3/212, Bl. 72.

63. Letter of 7 April 1953. BAAP, R3/212, Bl. 84.

64. Letter of 2 June 1953, cited in Jessen, "Akademische Elite," 355.
65. Ralph Jessen has counted 1,708 professors, docents, and assistant professors of the six universities and the Technical University in Dresden leaving East Germany from 1952 to 1961, excluding the years 1954 and 1957-58. In 1951 there were 2,360 professors, docents, lecturers, and assistant professors at all East German institutions of higher education; by 1960 that number had increased to 11,564. Ibid., 546, 557.
66. The process had begun in earnest with the new assistant professor ordinance (*Assistentenordnung*) of 1957, which gave state functionaries at universities (in Soviet-styled "prorectorates for academic recruitment") decisive say over entrance to academia across disciplines. Jessen, "Vom Ordinarius," 87-88, and "Zur Sozialgeschichte," 132-34.
67. "Protokół z posiedzenia Rady Głównej z dn. 14. VII. 1950r." AAN, MSW 597, k. 120-27.
68. Wolenski, "Philosophy inside Communism," 97-98. Logic, especially mathematical logic, was a strength of this school, which grew out of the seminars of Kazimierz Twardowski in Lwów and was united by an anti-irrationalistic attitude and a rigorously empirical method. Jordan, "Philosophy in Postwar Poland."
69. AAN, MSW 600, k. 178; Tatarkiewicz, "Roman Ingarden," 205.
70. In July 1951 Kotarbińska was transferred from the humanities faculty at Łódź to the faculty of social philosophy of Warsaw University. AAN, MSW 601, k. 133.
71. Spodenkiewicz, "Nowe widnokręgi," 28-29. Fabierkiewicz was dean of underground Warsaw University's economics-law faculty. Brodowska, "Freie polnische Hochschule," 392.
72. *Uniwersytet Mikołaja Kopernika*, 42, 55.
73. Słabek, *Intelektualistów*, 103. On Sinko: Hübner, "Last Flight." The following professors could resume full-time teaching at KUL only in 1956: Rev. Professors Stanisław Adamczyk, Józef Pastuczka, Stanisław Styś, Bogusław Waczyński, Jan Nowicki, and Dr. Czesław Strzeszewski. *Słowo Powszechne*, 29-30 December 1956.
74. *Uniwersytet Mikołaja Kopernika*, 48-49. He died in March 1956.
75. Werblan, *Stalinizm*, 34.
76. They were rehabilitated in January 1957. *Trybuna Ludu*, 13 January 1957.
77. *Trybuna Ludu*, 7 December 1956; Kłoskowska, *Uniwersytet Łódzki*, 70. On Heinrich: Śródka, *Uczeni polscy*, 2:26-27. Also retired in Łódź for "old age" were Professors Ludwik Domański and Bolesław Wilanowski. Spodenkiewicz, "Nowe widnokręgi," 28-29.
78. These two scholars were known as particularly uncompromising, and as docents were extremely vulnerable. Mycielski, formerly of Wilno University, had published a textbook in 1947 that compared the Soviet economy to that of Nazi Germany; another text—still used in Kraków in 1949—had depicted the Polish Parliament of the interwar period as "a reflection of the direct will of the people," in contrast to its postwar counterparts. Report of Zenon Wróblewski, 7 May 1949, AAN, BO KC PZPR, t. 8, k. 143; Kuta, "Moje wspomnienia," 251-52. Dąmbska worked in a library in Gdańsk during this period. Dąmbska and Mycielski returned to teaching in 1956. The lecturers Professor Stefan Schmidt and Dr. Kazimierz Majewski were kept from teaching at Kra-

ków's Agricultural University and returned only in 1956. *Słowo Powszechne,* 29–30 December 1956.

79. For example, in 1951 Kotarbiński and Czeżowski both switched from the departments of philosophy to the departments of logic at their respective universities. *Wielcy filozofowie,* 33; *Uniwersytet Mikołaja Kopernika,* 73.

80. Wolenski, "Philosophy inside Communism," 97–98. As rector, Ajdukiewicz did not perform the police functions expected of him by top PZPR functionaries. At a conference of 22 January 1952 in the Ministry of Higher Education a "Comrade Mach" asked Ajdukiewicz whether "people with non-Marxist worldviews among the academic staff were given special care." The rector answered simply that he did not know. Furthermore, he admitted frankly that he left it to the local PZPR cell to "research and react to expressions of hostile activity." "Protokół konferencji odbytej dnia 22 stycznia 1952 roku w Ministerstwie Szk. Wyższego," AAN, MSW 163. At a July 1950 meeting of the social sciences and humanities section of the First Congress of Polish Science, Adjukiewicz described the "scholarly production" of Marxist philosophy as "very slight." Hübner, *Polityka naukowa,* 799.

81. Łukaszewicz was a student of eminent Warsaw historian Marceli Handelsman, and had mixed loyalties. On the cohesion of the Handelsman milieu, see chapter 4 at n. 10 and chapter 8 at n. 46.

82. One of the docents, Wiktor Kornatowski, director of the Department of the Theory of State and Law, was transferred to Łódź University, but released from his new position in the fall of 1953 for political reasons. Kornatowski remained without an academic position until December 1958, when the law faculty re-emerged in Toruń. He supported himself in the interim with translations in the history of political doctrines. Biskup and Giziński, *Toruńscy twórcy,* 157–63.

83. Astronomy professor F. Pautsch took a position in Gdańsk in 1947, and mathematician Professor J. Rudnicki died in 1948. Only two professors (full or associate) joined the faculties in the natural sciences between 1947 and 1956: mathematician J. Łoś, who came from Wrocław in 1952, and W. Zabłocka, who had entered the faculty as docent in 1945 and was promoted to associate professor in 1954. *Uniwersytet Mikołaja Kopernika.*

84. Wolski interview.

85. Uniwersytet Wrocławski, *Skład osobowy;* Longchamps, *Uniwersytet Wrocławski.* On Wyszyński, see Tomczak, *Wspomnienia pracowników,* 296.

86. This was the highly regarded Władysław Konopczyński, who passed away isolated and disconsolate in 1952.

87. Grzybowski had been a legionist and supporter of Piłsudski, favored a strong state, and joined the PPS in 1946. Like many Polish professors, he was also a Mason. Bardach, "Pasje uczonego." In the early 1950s he encouraged students to circumvent the ministry's "overloaded" study programs by failing examinations and taking them again at their own pace, though in the eyes of state authorities, such disruption of plan discipline constituted a major form of "hostile activity" at universities. AAN, KC PZPR 237/XVI/24, k. 31. In a letter of 14 April 1953, Rektor Marchlewski asked Minister Rapacki to increase the pension of the eminent conservative economist Adam Krzyżanowski: "It has been made known to me that Professor Emeritus Adam Krzyżanowski,

who has just turned eighty, finds himself in extremely difficult material circumstances. Recently his wife went through a long and difficult sickness. Beyond this, he is compelled to assist his widowed daughter and her two sick young children. Considering the eminent didactic and scholarly contributions of Professor Adam Krzyżanowski, I request an increase in his pension." APAN-W, III-124, j. 11, k. 13.

88. APAN-W, III-192, j. 119, k. 118.
89. Of these, thirteen had been employed by the university in 1947–48. *Skład Uniwersytetu na rok akademicki 1947–48; Skład Uniwersytetu na rok akademicki 1955–56;* interviews with Kersten and Mączak.
90. Plans to do so were drawn up several times. UMCS rector Józef Parnas began demanding the transfer of the humanities faculty to his university almost as soon as he became rector. AAN, KC PZPR 237/XVI/87, k. 43–44.
91. In 1951 Central Committee functionary Zofia Zemankowa investigated a teacher at UMCS, who supposedly said that if the Vatican had good relations to Washington, that was because America protected religion, in contrast to the Polish government, which was violating a treaty signed with the Polish episcopate. For these remarks he was arrested. The PZPR cell at UMCS demanded the closing of KUL because it was supposedly the origin for such views, but Zemankowa called this a "false position." AAN, KC PZPR 237/XVI/24, k. 32– 35. For a similar reaction to "leftist" excesses in Toruń by the PZPR Voivodeship Committee in Bydgoszcz, see the report of 26 January 1953, in AAN, KC PZPR 237/XVI/71, k. 28.
92. Letter of 1 June 1952. Rkp BJ Przyb 277/76.
93. Letter to Edwin Jędrkiewicz, 21 December 1955. APAN-K, KIII-109.

CHAPTER 8

1. Steinhaus, *Wspomnienia,* 410.
2. Faculty councils spent thousands of hours filling out reports that had no analogue in the previous system. For examples, see Suleja, *Uniwersytet Wrocławski,* 39, 174; and the reminiscences of former Toruń rector Szarski in Tomczak, *Wspomnienia pracowników,* 334; also Steinhaus, *Wspomnienia,* 404.
3. A few of the many talented non-Party scholars held back from promotion in the 1950s include Henryk Wereszycki (Kraków); Edward Kuczyński, Ryszard Mienicki, and Bronisław Pawłowski (Toruń); Aleksander Kamiński and Mieczysław Siewierski (Łódź).
4. The number of academics arrested is unknown. Those who spent the war in the West were subjected to special scrutiny. Professor Jan Podoski, of Warsaw Polytechnic, had worked in Gen. Sokorski's staff in London and was arrested in 1949 under charges of espionage. In Gęsiówka prison in Warsaw, he joined a special "architectural-construction office," consisting of approximately 100 incarcerated engineers. Podoski was assigned to the electrical engineering section of this office, directed by Professor Andrzej Sowiński, also of the Polytechnic. After a general amnesty in 1956 the engineers were released, but reconstituted their "office" outside of prison, electing their former warden, Captain Góra of the Secret Police, as their business manager. In the view of the author, "this could happen only in Poland." Podoski, *Zbyt ciekawe czasy,* 232, 262–65.

5. Hübner, *I Kongres*. For a contemporary account of the intimidating effects of the Polonist conference, see the reminiscences of A. Hutnikiewicz in Tomczak, *Wspomnienia pracowników*, 99.

6. She spoke at the "Party group" in the Science Department of the PZPR Central Committee on 28 March 1950. AAN, KC PZPR 237/XVI/2, k. 42.

7. Ryszka, *Pamiętnik*, 2:129.

8. Steinhaus, *Wspomnienia*, 398. Her piece appeared in *Życie Nauki* 3–4 (1950): 147.

9. For examples of usage in Poland, see *Nauka i szkolnictwo wyższe*. Social scientists have retroactively applied the word "milieu" to intact communities of tradition in East Germany. See, for example, Jessen, "Vom Ordinarius."

10. Machonin was the director of the Organization Department of the Higher-Education Committee of the KSČ at Higher Schools in Prague (VV KSČ). "Zápis ze schůze Vysokoškolského Výboru," 16 March 1948, AUK, SVS B166.

11. The number of Brno professors in the KSČ went from 30 to 130 by May 1948. SÚA, AÚV KSČ, f. 19/7, a.j. 104, l. 26.

12. SÚA, AÚV KSČ, f. 19/7, a.j. 313, l. 373; a.j. 314, l. 17; a.j. 311, l. 214; a.j. 328, l. 14. An additional reason for the high number of KSČ members among teachers in the post-1948 era was the purges of non-Communist faculty in 1948–49. In Brno's law faculty, for example, seven of thirteen professors were dismissed for political reasons. Jordán, *Dějiny*, 274.

13. SÚA, AÚV KSČ, f. 19/7, a.j. 328, l. 18.

14. Jessen, "Professoren," 241. During the 1960s, the percentage of professors belonging to the SED went from thirty-five to sixty. Jessen, "Zur Sozialgeschichte," 121–43.

15. Jessen, "Vom Ordinarius," 94–97. For numbers of former NSDAP members per faculty, see chapter 7 at n. 56.

16. Kowalczuk, *Legitimation*, 245.

17. AAN, KC PPR 295/XVII/57, k. 175. In the 1950s, esteemed Polonist Henryk Markiewicz (PZPR) was charged with trying to talk his colleague Kazimierz Wyka into joining the PZPR. He failed. Markiewicz interview.

18. In the period before 1956, the Polish rate never rose above 6 percent, the Czech never sank beneath 13 percent. Membership in the Hungarian Party oscillated between 12.3 percent (1948) and 8.8 percent (1955). Grzymala-Busse, "Communist Party Strategies." The Czech and Hungarian figures dropped significantly because of purging in the early 1950s, whereas the SED total remained rather stable, between 7 and 9 percent. This had something to do with the gradual diminution of population in East Germany, from over 19.1 million in 1948, to 17.9 million in 1955, but also with the SED's determination to maintain a "mass cadre" base. The Polish total went from 4.3 percent (1948) to 5.5 percent (1950) to 4.9 percent (1955). On relative Party strengths, see also Brzezinski, *The Soviet Bloc*, 86; Foitzik, "Die stalinistischen Säuberungen."

19. Paczkowski, "Protokół rozbieżności."

20. These students were considered enemies of People's Poland because of membership in church youth organizations, wartime service with the Home Army, non-worker-peasant background, membership in Mikołajczyk's Peasant Party, hostile public statements, or family members in prison for political crimes. A letter from Parnas to Eugenia Krassowska complaining that no

more students could be expelled is contained in AAN, KC PZPR 237/XVI/87, k. 43–44. A proposal of 9 September 1949 by Colonel Brystygier of the Secret Police (UB) expressly advised against expelling more than sixty students from UMCS. AAN, BP KC PZPR, t. 7, p. 2, k. 219. Lists of students to be expelled are in AAN, KC PZPR 237/XVI/85, k. 37–56. In June 1950 four students were removed from Warsaw Polytechnic for disfiguring leaflets of the International Day of Solidarity with Youth of Colonial Countries, but unlike Czech victims of the 1949 purge, they could be readmitted if they "proved themselves with self-sacrificing professional work." AAN, KC PZPR 237/XVI/113, k. 1–5, 18–19. In 1953, the Central Committee intervened to overturn a number of student expulsions that had been ordered by the branch office of the UB in Białystok. AAN, KC PZPR 237/XVI/70.

21. There were also reports of weapons stolen from reserve officer training courses at institutions of higher education in Warsaw and Częstochowa. "Analiza sytuacji na odcinku młodzieży akademickiej," 1952, AAN, KC PZPR 237/XVI/15, k. 13.

22. BAAP, R3/211, Bl. 117–43. Recent memoir accounts by Professors Hans Mayer and Walter Markov, who both knew Harig in Leipzig, paint the picture of a man whom one can scarcely imagine directing such a purge. Mayer mistakenly recollects Harig's appointment to state secretary as a concession of the 1953 New Course: "The time of Kuba [writer Kurt Bartel] and the Bardach-enemy Wilhelm Girnus was temporarily over. With the physicist Gerhard Harig, who had survived Buchenwald, a careful and well-informed researcher came to the helm of the higher-education administration." *Der Turm von Babel*, 132. Actually, as we have seen, Harig was appointed state secretary in 1951 at the height of stalinism. Markov writes that "The physicist-philosopher Harig was a markedly quiet man, who thought things over three times before acting. In his capacity as minister [*sic*] he worked through a large quantity of dossiers in the 1950s, and made personnel decisions of frequently great consequence—or he put them on ice if he could be helpful that way. He adhered to his saying: 'whoever asks a lot of questions gets a lot of answers.' 'Letting things lie' was one of his tactics, because a lot of things adjust themselves, if one only gives them time and a fair chance. He considered settling things for the good a true art of governing, which of course presupposed the courage to take responsibility." *Zwiesprache*, 200–201.

23. For details, see chapter 13.

24. Gomułka, *Ku nowej Polsce*, 139.

25. On 19 October 1949, a meeting of leading PZPR higher-education functionaries determined that "a certain number of old experts are not suited for pedagogical work, but can be useful in helping complete the training of older students, who are already armed with a worldview." They agreed that "decided reactionaries and enemies" should be removed. AAN, KC PZPR 237/XVI/2, k. 2–3.

26. See Staszewski interview in Torańska, *Oni*, 105–65.

27. Letter of 4 October 1951. Rkp BJ Przyb 271/76.

28. Letter of late 1954 to Stefan Żółkiewski. Rkp BJ Przyb 465/73. Żółkiewski responded that such an institute would be formed, under Lehr's direction, as soon as a budget was approved.

29. The paper was entitled "A Turning Point in Soviet Studies of the Ethnogenesis of

Slavs." Letter to Polskie Towarzystwo Antropologiczne, 26 May 1952, Rkp BJ Przyb 463/73.

30. AAN, MO 2847, k. 104.

31. The term was coined in 1945 by Jerzy Borejsza. See "Rewolucja łagodna," *Odrodzenie* 10–12 (1945), cited in Hübner, *Polityka naukowa,* 67. For the view that "mild revolution" was abandoned in 1948, see Słabek, *Intelektualistów,* 73; or, in 1947, Suleja, *Uniwersytet Wrocławski,* 44.

32. AAN, KC PPR 295/XVII/57, k. 175.

33. Mołdawa, *Ludzie władzy,* 449. For a wealth of personal insights on Żółkiewski, see Kott, *Still Alive.*

34. *Polski słownik,* 34/1:88. For the plan, see Connelly and Suleja, "Projekt."

35. See, for example, protocols no. 80 and 89 of April and May 1951 detailing "distortions in collecting grain." AAN, BO KC PZPR, t. 19.

36. Żółkiewski founded the Institute for Literary Research in 1948 and directed it until 1952; from 1948 he was also acting professor at Warsaw University. He completed his doctorate in 1952 and advanced to full professor in 1954. Mołdawa, *Ludzie władzy,* 449.

37. Wyka based his Marxist interpretations in literature on the work of Polish writer Stanisław Brzozowski. Środka and Szczawiński, *Biogramy,* part 1, 3:553–57. On Brzozowski, see Miłosz, *Emperor of the Earth,* 186–253.

38. See the undated (1956–57) letter of Bielak to Wyka, APAN-K, KIII-47, j. 233: "Thank you very much for supporting my 'advance.' Perhaps at the 'highest places' this is not approved of, but I still most highly value human kindness—life's joy and embellishment" (*Po staremu najlepiej cenię życzliwość ludzką—rozkosz i ozdobę życia*). Bielak had completed a doctorate at Jagiellonian University in 1919 and taught Wyka in the 1930s, and together they had worked in Kraków's underground university during the war. He became docent at Jagiellonian University in 1959. Środka and Szczawiński, *Biogramy,* part 1, 1:106–7.

39. "While I am at it," Kleiner continued, "let me request that you concern yourself with the delayed appointments of Professor Irena Sławińska and Professor C. Zgorzelski [of KUL]. These are researchers of exceptional abilities and superb scholarly achievements.... Thank you very much for intervening for me with UNESCO. Perhaps as a result I will receive a contract, and not lose my author's honorarium." Sławińska became associate professor in 1956, and Zgorzelski in 1957. Letter of 27 March 1956, APAN-K, KIII-47, j. 187.

40. For a biography of Kołaczkowski, see *Polski słownik,* 13:328–29. Like his pupil, he was fascinated by the work of Brzozowski.

41. In March 1954 Żółkiewski became a full member of the Central Committee, and in April 1955 he assumed direction of that committee's Department of Science and Culture. Mołdawa, *Ludzie władzy,* 449. For Wyka's interventions in favor of returning Professors Wereszycki and Piwarski to Kraków, see chapter 9 at n. 23.

42. Żółkiewski to Wyka, 21 July 1955, APAN-K, KIII-47, j. 232. Żółkiewski wrote that "we in the Central Committee are most concerned about stagnancy in literature."

43. Connelly and Suleja, "Projekt," 106–7.

44. Markiewicz interview.

45. In the fall of 1949 Roman Pollak, professor of Polish literature in Poznań, re-

ceived a "slip of paper" (*papierek*) from the ministry refusing Zakrzewski's promotion to adjunct professor and demanding a break in his contract. Pollak to Pigoń, 8 November 1949, Rkp BJ Przyb 271/76. Zakrzewski wrote directly to Żółkiewski requesting assistance in continuing his scholarly career, and arrangements were made for his transfer to Wrocław. Zakrzewski interview. Despite the demands of the ministry, Zakrzewski was able to stay as adjunct in Poznań until transfer to Wrocław in 1953–54. He advanced to professor in 1958. *Kto jest Kim,* 1120. In his place the young Marxist Jerzy Ziomek went to Poznań, where he became professor.

46. Handelsman (1882–1945) was educated in Warsaw, Paris, Berlin, and Zurich and assumed the chair of modern history at Warsaw University in 1915. He organized decades of research on the political, social, and national ideology of the Polish emigration of the nineteenth century, as well as the socioeconomic transformations in modern Poland. Handelsman, a Jew and supporter of Piłsudski, was betrayed by nationalist extremists in the Polish underground in July 1944, and died in the camp Dora-Nordhausen in March 1945. Śródka and Szczawiński, *Biogramy,* part 1, 1:462–63. On the origins of the Warsaw school, see Gieysztor, "Środowisko historyczne," 88.

47. Gross, *Polish Society,* 235–36. Kula had been a student of N. Gąsiorowska, who taught in Warsaw during the 1930s but settled in Łódź after the war. He became professor in Warsaw after the war. Military historian S. Herbst, who became professor in Warsaw in 1954, had been a student of O. Halecki, H. Mościcki, and W. Tokarz at Warsaw University in the 1930s. Śródka and Szczawiński, *Biogramy,* part 1, 1:394, 461–63, 474–77. Arnold had taught both Gieysztor and Kieniewicz in the 1930s. Though a thorough "opportunist" in the postwar period (for example, as director of the Department of Universities and Science in the Ministry of Education from 1945 to 1947), he did not harm old colleagues. Henryk Jabłoński, later minister of higher education, and president of the State Council, had also been a student of Handelsman and felt loyalty to this circle. Kula helped rescue Małowist from the Warsaw ghetto. Kieniewicz interview; Jarocki, *Widzieć jasno,* 72. Other historians of the Warsaw school had worked with Manteuffel in organizing conspiratorial education: J. Woliński, W. Tomkiewicz, and E. Kipa. Zahorski, "Środowisko historyków," 169. Woliński and Tomkiewicz had studied in Warsaw before the war with Handelsman and Halecki, respectively. Kipa was a student of S. Askenazy, who taught in Warsaw in the early 1920s and is considered a cofounder of both the Lwów and Warsaw schools of history. Śródka and Szczawiński, *Biogramy,* part 1, 1:55, 454; 3:541.

48. He made possible the return of Kraków historian Karol Buczek to the historical profession after the latter's release from prison for antigovernment activities. Wyrozumski interview. On Arnold's "assistance for colleagues in difficult situations without regard to their opinions and convictions," see Keckowa, "Stanisław Arnold," 333.

49. Bardach interview. One Soviet historian, evidently gratified that a strong core of professionalism remained among Polish historians, wrote in an internal report that the Poles had learned from "our experience with vulgarization." Valkenier, "Stalinizing," 121, 129; Gorizontov, "Metodologicheskii perevorot." For the differences between Kula, Gieysztor, Manteuffel, and the Party histo-

rians at the First Congress of Polish Science in April 1951, see Hübner, *Polityka naukowa,* 800. See also Manteuffel's account of the "feeble" performance of the young IKKN historians, and the "kind disposition" of the Soviet guests, "whom we had to thank for the positive evaluation of the methodological standards of university history faculties," in APAN-W, III-142, j. 119.

50. Manteuffel, supported by Professors B. Leśnodorski (PZPR) and W. Kula, did much to uphold historical standards within the Polish Academy of Sciences, and also helped frustrate purges at Warsaw University. He was especially skilled in personnel policy and was prepared to engage in tactical compromises in order to achieve his goals. Kieniewicz interview. This Ketman of historical standards seemed a known quantity to authorities in Warsaw, who had worked with him in reorganizing history in higher education from the late 1940s. He was frequently called upon to write recommendations for scholarly promotion. In March 1951 Central Committee functionary Petrusewicz justified a proposal to make Manteuffel vice-director of the institute in the following words: "non-Party Professor Manteuffel is ideologically foreign to us, but he cooperates with us loyally, and is a very good organizer." AAN, KC PZPR 237/XVI/31, k. 6.

51. For years Manteuffel quietly assisted colleagues endangered by the new ideology, like the *środowisko* at KUL. Likewise important in supporting KUL historians were Warsovians Stefan Kieniewicz, Aleksander Gieysztor, and Stanisław Herbst. Gapski, *Historae peritus,* 42. Important for this connection to work was also Father Żywczyński, a student of Handelsman and friend of Manteuffel who taught at KUL. Żywczyński, a mediator reminiscent of Wyka, kept channels open to the co-opted Catholic organization PAX, including its director, former fascist Bolesław Piasecki, and thus managed to shield some of the young historians at KUL. Unpublished memoir of T. Manteuffel, APAN-W, III-142, j. 119; Kłoczowski interview. For more on PAX, see n. 67.

52. Małowist, "Uwagi," 488.

53. Kieniewicz interview.

54. For discussions held with Bobińska by Edward Ochab, see AAN, BP KC PZPR, t. 13, p. 3, k. 189. For the prohibition to hold Party posts in Kraków: Ochab to Bobińska, 6 September 1950, Bobińska Papers, Rkp BJ Przyb. Wolski (1901–76) had survived an eight-year (1933–41) stint in the gulags, and after 1945 occupied high posts in the Ministry of Public Administration, advancing to minister in January 1949. Mołdawa, *Ludzie władzy,* 442.

55. Bobińska was the chief of the Marxist Historical Society in Warsaw (including Ż. Kormanowa, Z. Cybylska, J. Sieradzki, P. Szulkin, and M. Turlejska) from 1948 to 1950. She received a *kandidat* degree at Moscow State University in 1945, was made acting professor in Kraków in 1950, advanced to associate professor in 1954, and full professor in 1962. *Kto jest kim,* 68; protocols in Bobińska correspondence, Rkp BJ Przyb.

56. Letter of 4 September 1950 in Bobińska correspondence, Rkp BJ Przyb.

57. Zgórniak and Grzybowski interviews. Owsińska had an unfavorable family background: her father had been in prison for political reasons, and her mother was part owner of a drugstore. Bobińska "overcame" political resistance to keeping Owsińska on the faculty. Lepszy to Ziembiński, 4 September 1955, Rkp BJ Przyb 785/73. For records of Bobińska's "intervention" (with minis-

try official Żurawicka) to secure Owsińska participation in a "methodological conference" in 1951, see the letters of Owsińska (31 July 1951) and Kazimierz Lepszy (17 July 1951) to Bobińska in Bobińska Papers, Rkp BJ Przyb. She had not been invited, and failure to attend would—in the view of Lepszy—have had an "unfavorable" effect on Owsińska's career.

58. Kędziorek to Central Committee, 18 January 1951, AAN, KC PZPR 237/XVI/80, k. 92; BPAN-K, sig. 9231; Podraza and Wyrozumski interviews. Not only was Grodecki not harmed, but in 1953 he was made an expert at the Central Qualification Commission for Scientific Workers—which made decisions on scholarly advancement—and received a state award worth 20,000 złotys for his work on the history of Silesia. A report written by the local personnel director (PZPR) gives some insight into the optimistic attitude of local Party functionaries toward "loyal" professors. Part of Grodecki's "political-social and professional report" read: "as an economic historian he naturally emphasizes research of economic and social relations and is thus close to Marxist positions, but in none of his works has he yet made clear statements in this spirit." An important component of Grodecki's value to the PZPR was his work on Silesia, which was seen to bolster Polish claims to that region. AUJ, Personnel file, R. Grodecki.

59. Gierowski interview. None of Bobińska's own protégés of the period (now Professors Buszko, Podraza, Zgórniak, and Francić) belonged to the Party. Wyrozumski interview.

60. For the general history of this institute, see Connelly, "Internal Bolshevization."

61. Schaff's connection at the Secret Police was Julia Brystygierowa. Kowalik interview. All of these erstwhile IKKN/INS students achieved national or international reputations. Bialer left Poland in the 1950s, and took a position at Columbia University, where he became a leading expert on Soviet politics. Kołakowski and Baczko taught philosophy and Brus political economy at Warsaw University until they were denied their professorships for defending students in March 1968. All three emigrated; Kołakowski and Brus took up posts at Oxford, and Baczko in Geneva. Tadeusz Kroński, a close friend of Czesław Miłosz, taught philosophy in Warsaw until his early death in 1958. See the sections on "Tiger" in Miłosz, *Native Realm*. Kersten, Turlejska, Madajczyk, and Holzer became top historians in Warsaw. Zimand (Polish literature) and Kowalik (economics) were both active in the dissident scene, and became important figures in Solidarity. Sociologist Henryk Holland committed a spectacular suicide in order to escape Secret Police harassment in 1961. His funeral was a crystallization point for independent intellectual milieus and inner-Party opposition.

62. Historian Maria Turlejska complained in a letter of 11 December 1950 to Celina Bobińska of the "ignoramuses" that taught her like the "great historian" Leon Grosfeld—who had nothing better to do than to ask how many hours a week she was reading Lenin's *Materialism and Empirocriticism;* in the "perfectly organized bureaucratic barracks system," students were not allowed to work at home "because then they could not supervise us," and had to appear at the institute every day at 8:00 A.M. Schaff "at first claimed that all scholarship is class-based and later that it was only partially class-based, and he continues

to juggle various truisms. He constantly changes his position, and though he does so intelligently, his exposition remains vague and schematic." Bobińska correspondence, Rkp BJ Przyb.

63. She proposed studies of the Polish struggle for independence, the PPS, and the hegemony of the working class. For this and other early voices of the Polish thaw in historiography, see Stobiecki, *Historia pod nadzorem,* 129–38.

64. AAN, ANS 5/12, k. 29. Among other things, this plenum underlined the need to strengthen the rule of law, that is, to return power to the Party that had been usurped by the Secret Police. Pełczyński in Leslie, Polonsky, Ciechanowski, and Pełczyński, *History of Poland,* 334–35.

65. AAN, BP KC PZPR, t. 33, k. 184.

66. One example of such reunification was the philosophical institute of the Polish Academy of Sciences, where in the early 1960s, former INS members Bronisław Baczko, Leszek Kołakowski, Henryk Hinz, and Anka Sładkowska-Hochfeldowa worked side by side with Andrzej Walicki, Barbara Skarga, Zygmunt Ogonowski, and Lech Szczucki. Walicki, *Spotkania,* 68.

67. Z. A. Pełczyński writes that the object of PAX was "to sow confusion and disunity among Polish Catholics." Headed by a former fascist, Bolesław Piasecki, it supported government policy, and maintained that there were no conflicts between Catholic doctrine and loyalty to the Polish Communist state. To the actual benefit of Polish Catholics, it also printed and sold considerable quantities of religious literature. Pełczyński in Leslie, Polonsky, Ciechanowski, and Pełczyński, *History of Poland,* 328.

68. Havemann, himself once a stalinist, knew what he was talking about. He told his Stasi interrogators in the late 1960s that the university rector, the state secretary of higher education, and the president of the Academy of Sciences who had ostracized him earlier in the decade were themselves all former NSDAP members. *Fragen,* 85.

69. Jessen mentions seven such cases. "Akademische Elite," 352.

70. On Lepszy's interwar political activities, see Tyrowicz, *W poszukiwaniu siebie,* 196. During the interwar period Konopczyński had authored provisions aimed at limiting the number of Jews in academia, and after the war was driven out of editorship of the *Polish Biographical Dictionary* he had founded, and forced into early retirement.

71. On this campaign, see Pełczyński, in Leslie, Polonsky, Ciechanowski, and Pełczyński, *History of Poland,* 389–92.

72. Letters of 4 January 1946 and 7 January 1947 from Professor E. Thilo, Berlin University, to Rector, Berlin University. UAG, Personalakte 2243. The National Committee for a Free Germany was a group of German prisoners of war who called upon fellow Germans—via radio and press—to liberate themselves from Nazi rule. Several—Rudolf Böhm, Franz Wohlgemuth, Ernst Hadermann—became prominent figures in the East German education administration. For a general discussion, see Weitz, *Creating,* 307–8.

73. Wohlgemuth to Grünberg, 4 July 1949. MLHA, MfVB 94, Bl. 49; UAG, Personalakte 2243.

74. Some 250 students were arrested when they attempted to organize a boycott in protest of the conversion. See Connelly, "Ulbricht," 340–41.

75. Approximately one-third of these rectors also belonged to the SED. Jessen, "Akademische Elite," 361.

CHAPTER 9

1. Tomczak, *Wspomnienia pracowników,* 100.
2. Ibid., 262. For a sober assessment of scholarship in People's Poland, see also Strzembosz, "Z historii najnowszej."
3. During the stalinist period, his was the best subscribed seminar in the History Department of Wrocław University. See the report of Wł. Czapliński of 25 June 1953 in personnel file Wereszycki, AUJ. In 1959, a docent made 3,000 złotys monthly, and a full professor 4,500 złotys. Hartmann, *Hochschulwesen,* 117.
4. *Kwartalnik Historyczny* 61:1 (1954): 137-49. Gwiazdomorski made his statement at a didactic conference of Polish law faculties in Wrocław on 20 April 1953. BPAN-K, sig. 9932. He also provided legal expertise for the drafting of a new constitution in the early 1950s. For further examples of historical research of this period, when numerous conservative scholars researched and taught the "class struggles" of their periods and regions, see Stobiecki, *Historia pod nadzorem.*
5. See the study plans submitted to the Ministry of Higher Education by Gwiazdomorski's colleagues Adam Chełmoński, Kamil Stefko, and Jerzy Falenciak on 7 July 1952, APAN-W, III-105, j. 45, k. 48-56.
6. See, for example, the drafts of Wrocław microbiologist Ludwik Hirszfeld in 1950-51 on planning in the field of medicine, or on his "impressions of the Second Congress of Peace in Warsaw in 1950." APAN-W, III-157, j. 94. In 1951 historian Tadeusz Manteuffel declared that "American aggressors were preparing to unleash a new war" and praised the efforts of the "heroic Chinese people to liberate completely the parts of their fatherland under imperialist occupation: Tibet and Taiwan." APAN-W, III-192, j. 110, k. 32-33.
7. Werblan, *Stalinizm,* 33-35.
8. Szwarcenberg-Czerny to Piasecki, 17 August 1953. Rkp BJ Przyb 464/73.
9. Thus the title of a symposium that took place in Warsaw on 7 November 1998 under the auspices of Towarzystwo im. Stanisława ze Skarbimierza with the participation of Professors Piotr Hübner, Janusz Gaćkowski, Wiesław Karel Szymański, Jarosław Marek Rymkiewicz, and Jacek Trznadel.
10. Schaff's "Library of the Classics of Philosophy" project was approved of by the Party leadership in January 1951, among other things, to employ philosophers who had lost their jobs. The statement of approval specified creation of an editorial board "from Marxist philosophical cadres, but with broad participation of non-Party professors." AAN, BP KC PZPR, t. 18, p. 4, k. 85.
11. Sociologist Maria Ossowska and philosophers Wiktor Wąsik (Łódź) and Henryk Elzenberg (Toruń), and Konrad Górski likewise found work in the "Library of the Classics." Andrzej Walicki was given a contract to edit two volumes of Belinsky for the "Library," and was so overworked that he unofficially subcontracted the poet Zbigniew Herbert to help him. *Spotkania,* 42.
12. Emphases in the original. Rkp BJ Przyb 277/76.
13. From memoirs of former rector Henryk Szarski, Tomczak, *Wspomnienia pracowników,* 339. Elzenberg is memorialized in Adam Michnik's *Z dziejów honoru w Polsce.*

14. *Polski słownik,* 34/1:89.

15. Much has been written about the closing of the Polish Academy of Arts in Kraków in 1952, and the transfer of its assets to the Soviet-style Academy of Sciences in Warsaw that emerged that same year. But many dozens of the members of the former organization entered the latter without protest, and in 1956 biologist Władysław Szafer, an elected member of the final Academy of Arts presidium, refused to support efforts to revitalize that organization, arguing that this was "unrealistic." Hübner, *Siła.*

16. Zofia Stefanowska to Stanisław Pigoń, 10 May 1957, Rkp BJ Przyb 280/76.

17. Grodziski interview.

18. Czesław Nowiński [Sawa Frydman] had attended Lande's seminar in Wilno in the 1920s. In 1947 he became minister of food supply (*aprowizacja*). In a letter of 26 February 1949 Lande apologized for writing nothing but "letters asking for favors" (*listy proteckcyjne*). Leon Kurowski was undersecretary of state in the Ministry of Finances, and in frequent contact with Nowiński as well as Lande. In 1947 he arranged for Lande's student K. Opałek to get leave of absence from his position in the public prosecutor's office: "since the prosecutor is 'under my authority' I will attempt to command him to give Dr. Opałek leave." Letter of Kurowski to Lande, 29 December 1947. Rkp BJ Przyb 109/74. That same year he pushed in both the Ministry and the faculty council for Lande's student J. Licki [Jerzy Finkelkraut] to be permitted to hold lectures on labor law at Toruń University. Letters of Kurowski, 27 August 1947, 21 November 1947, APAN-W, III-47, j. 43.

19. Lande was in touch with Piętka in order to secure a job at Warsaw University for Podgórecki, who for a mixture of professional, personal, and political reasons could not continue in Kraków. Rkp BJ Przyb 109/74. Podgórecki completed his training in Warsaw, and went on to succeed Maria Ossowska as chair in sociology at Warsaw University.

20. Letter of 13 January 1950. Rkp BJ Przyb 110/74.

21. APKr, KD PZPR, 62/XV/5, k. 13. For Opałek's tribute to Lande, a "noble personality," see his "Kierunek psychologiczny."

22. Piwarski was scheduled to contact Krauze in connection with his work on the history of the Vatican, but was advised to hurry, because Krauze was about to go on vacation. Manteuffel to Piwarski, 25 January 1955, APAN-K, KIII-24, j. 195.

23. APAN-K, KIII-47, j. 233.

24. Personnel files of Piwarski and Wereszycki, AUJ. Jan Gwiazdomorski returned from Wrocław's law faculty in April 1956. His request was supported by Professors Jan Wasilkowski and Stefan Rozmaryn, as well as several prominent officials in the justice administration, all of whom, as Gwiazdomorski noted in his request of 22 October 1955, were "members of the PZPR." Personnel file Gwiazdomorski, AUJ.

25. Decisions on promotion were supposed to be made by some fifteen "experts," yet as early as September 1948 a handful (three to five) of bureaucrats (the "Presidium") were making decisions on advancements in all of scholarship. The Presidium in the late 1940s and early 1950s variously included W. Sokorski (writer and minister of culture), H. Jabłoński (history), Eugenia Krassowska (ministry), Stanisław Leszczycki (economics/geography), Henryk Golański

(engineering), and Maurycy Jaroszyński (law). By early 1948 a tendency had emerged to place all important decisions in the Presidium. See the comments of H. Jabłoński in Hübner, "Formowanie."

26. This arrangement was made in the Kraków PZPR Voivodeship Committee. Lepszy to Ziembiński, 4 September 1955, Rkp BJ Przyb 785/73. Similar deals applied in the acceptance of non-Party assistant professors into the law faculty in the early 1950s.

27. AAN, KC PZPR 237/XVI/186, k. 5–6. Stomma is a legal scholar associated with the Catholic Kraków weekly *Tygodnik Powszechny.* See n. 64.

28. The positive opinions of two professors from Wrocław and Łódź were disqualified as too brief (only two pages) and not speaking to whether Falenciak possessed any work equal to an old-style doctorate. Falenciak had provoked the wrath of the older generation by publicly attacking his teacher, the esteemed papyrologist Rafał Taubenschlag, at a conference of historians of law in Toruń in 1950. Without academic guidance Falenciak then proved unable to achieve "mastery of a quite extensive and difficult subject, which is necessary to be a teacher of law students." In April 1956 Kraków professor Osuchowski had criticized Falenciak's use of the methods of historical materialism, which demand "an increase of knowledge on economic relations of a given epoch based on evidence." Yet the "author's slack platitudes on economics or on Roman trade turnover have no support in the sources and are an invention of the author himself." See the summary of Falenciak's case by Adam Vetulani, 24 May 1957, in APAN-K, KIII-58, j. 169. Falenciak was a leading stalinist functionary at Wrocław University. See Suleja, *Uniwersytet Wrocławski.*

29. See the opinion of Adam Vetulani, 17 May 1957. APAN-K, KIII-58, j. 169.

30. In 1948 PPR and PPS "cells of six" (*szóstki*) had begun producing opinions on "assistant professors (esp. at humanities faculties) who should be dismissed because of their ideological position." AAN, KC PPR 295/XVII/58, k. 161; Hübner, "Stalinowskie czystki," 215. For the creation of these cells, see chapter 2.

31. See the letter of 1 July 1948. AAN, KC PPR 295/XVII/58, k. 161. On 14 September Żółkiewski wrote a follow-up as a result of the decisions of the most recent Central Committee plenary session and requested names of "our comrades for advancement from lower positions to university chairs," and of "people who should be dismissed from professorial positions or transferred to other universities." Such recommendations would help bring about a "change in the atmosphere of teaching and scholarship at universities." AAN, KC PPR 295/XVII/58, k. 173.

32. "N" stood for *nauka* (science). See Hübner, *Nauka polska,* 98–101; Suleja, *Uniwersytet Wrocławski,* 45.

33. Tomczak, *Wspomnienia pracowników,* 72.

34. For examples of assistance of younger colleagues by older professors, see ibid., 111, 151, 199–200, 331.

35. Lande to Hanna Waśkiewicz, 1 May 1949. Rkp BJ Przyb 110/74.

36. Historian Kazimierz Hartleb of Toruń sent books and other materials to his colleague Władysław Pociecha of Jagiellonian University in 1948 by way of their mutual "colleague and friend Karol Koranyi. . . . He will certainly give you exact information about everything that may be of interest, although I have

no doubt that all the news about life and work in Toruń makes its way to you in any case." Letter of 6 April 1948, Rkp BJ Przyb 31/79.

37. Bardach belonged to the PZPR, but felt primary loyalty to old non-Party teachers like Vetulani, Koranyi, and Ludwik Ehrlich. Like many other Polish Communists, he had very mixed experiences with Soviet-style socialism. His brother had been a prisoner of the Gulag. See Bardach and Gleeson, *Man Is Wolf.*

38. Bardach interview. Koranyi and Vetulani were devout Roman Catholics. Presumably the purge in Toruń took place as a result of negative opinions produced by the PZPR cell at Toruń University. For the role of such cells, see Hübner, "Stalinowskie czystki," 215–17.

39. Voisé intervened in person with Żółkiewski. See the correspondence in Rkp BJ Przyb 174/73.

40. Professor Tadeusz Makowiecki, historian of literature and art, who had conducted seminars "which introduced students to the arcana of poetic art with unusual subtlety," was reduced to lecturing beginners' courses on bibliography and methodology, a situation that hastened the heart disease of which he died at age fifty-two. Biskup and Giziński, *Toruńscy twórcy,* 210–11.

41. Behind the offensive stood Hutnikiewicz's colleague mgr. Sławomir Rogowski as well as a university dropout, Mędelski, who worked in the provincial capital of Bydgoszcz.

42. He calls the sympathy of these students, who occasionally informed him of attacks planned against him, a "great moral support." Tomczak, *Wspomnienia pracowników,* 111.

43. Hutnikiewicz had hundreds of students' papers to grade and next to no assistance. In Warsaw the ideologically troublesome Maria Rzeuska was kept on until 1954 in Polish studies, and had over 900 students to teach. Characteristically, PZPR functionaries on the faculty, like Stefan Żółkiewski, were too busy with Party work to find time for teaching. Letter to Stanisław Pigoń, 24 February 1951, Rkp BJ Przyb 277/76. A similar case in Kraków involved Professor W. Kubacki, who was transferred from Poznań to Kraków to increase the Marxist presence there but did very little teaching.

44. Tomczak, *Wspomnienia pracowników,* 93–116; Hutnikiewicz interview.

45. Rogowski remained at the department, but did not complete his doctorate until 1961, and never defended the habilitation. Kalembka, *Pracownicy,* 586.

46. He, for example, explained and defended his ways of training graduate students to Pigoń. This is a task that by all accounts Mikulski achieved splendidly, training a large cohort in Renaissance studies, "with great consistency, independent of the fashions of the day." Suleja, *Uniwersytet Wrocławski,* 60. Mikulski remained loyal to his mentor; when in 1954 the ministry delegated him, as a "progressive," to inspect Kraków's program in Polish literature, he sent a blind carbon copy of his report back to Pigoń.

47. The Western Institute published *Review of Western Affairs* (*Przegląd Zachodni*). Pollak also recommended to Pigoń that he publish in the annual reports of the Polish Academy of Arts. Letter of 4 October 1951, Rkp BJ Przyb 271/76.

48. Both published in the proceedings of the international conference of philosophy (Brussels) in 1953; Czeżowski wrote on such things as "Certainty in Empirical Sciences," and Elzenberg on "Influences on One's Own World View." *Uniwersytet Mikołaja Kopernika,* 104–5.

49. See K. Ajdukiewicz, "W sprawie artykułu prof. A. Schaffa o moich poglądach filozoficznych," *Myśl Filozoficzna* 2:8 (1953): 292–334; "Logika, jej zadania i potrzeby w Polsce współczesnej," *Myśl Filozoficzna* 1:1–2 (1951): 50–67; T. Kotarbiński, "Humanistyka bez hipostaz," *Myśl Filozoficzna* 1:3 (1952): 257–70; T. Kotarbiński, "Odpowiedź," *Myśl Filozoficzna* 2:4 (1952): 315–30.

50. *Uniwersytet Mikołaja Kopernika*, 95, lists twenty-seven publications, from 1948 to 1956. Two scholars ostracized in Łódź, Wacław Fabierkiewicz and Bolesław Wilanowski, both also managed to publish during the stalinist period. Kita and Pytlas, *Profesorowie*, 40, 222.

51. In a letter of 4 July 1951 Dr. Maria Rzeuska of Warsaw University requested the help of Stanisław Pigoń in getting room at a sanatorium in Krynica for the persecuted philosopher T. Czeżowski, "a person very close to me, who for fifteen years patiently taught me to work as a scholar, and in particular . . . helped materially in difficult times." With her letter Rzeuska also sent Pigoń some sugar, because she heard there was a shortage in Kraków. Rkp BJ Przyb 277/76. The academic community paid attention to the plight of widows and of retired professors. See, for example, the efforts of Henryk Piętka and Jerzy Lande, students of Leon Petrażycki, to secure decent living conditions for Petrażycki's widow. Piętka to Lande, 30 August 1945, Rkp BJ Przyb 109/74. On 28 March 1956 Professor R. Grodecki (Kraków) received a letter from Stefan Inglot (Wrocław), asking support for a special pension for the widow of Professor Bujak, who taught in Kraków. BPAN-K, sig. 9231. On the intervention of Rector Marchlewski for the conservative economist A. Krzyżanowski, see chapter 7 at n. 87.

52. See, for example, the gratitude of R. Pollak for K. Wyka's "support of [his] candidacy for the autumn trip to Italy." Letter of 12 June 1955, APAN-K, KIII-47, j. 232. Wyka, on the other hand, used Stefan Żółkiewski's help to avoid being sent on foreign delegations that might waste his time. See the letter of 4 September 1955 in which Żółkiewski promised to "protect [Wyka] from all foreign trips. Warn me if you hear that they want to include you in any excursions." Ibid.

53. Letter of 24 January 1952. Rkp BJ Przyb 271/76. For Pigoń's securing of space at the Anna Maria, see the letter of Pollak, 20 November 1951, ibid.

54. Śródka and Szczawiński, *Biogramy*, part 1, 3:392.

55. Jordan, "Philosophy in Postwar Poland."

56. This is al. Mickiewicza 13. Other university apartment buildings are at al. Krasińskiego 22, Mickiewicza 15, 21, 22, 37, 39; Słowackiego 15, 66; ul. Czarnowiejska 101; ul. Kochanowskiego 11; ul. Łokietka 1; ul. Łobzowska 59, 61; ul. Podwale 1; pl. Inwalidów 4.

57. *Skład Uniwersytetu Jagiellońskiego w Krakowie. Rok akademicki 1948–49.*

58. Their cousin Antoni Mączak teaches history at Warsaw University.

59. Batowski, who duly became professor of history, had allegedly accused Lehr-Spławiński of "conscious partisanship and lack of competence." Letter to Dean Kazimierz Piwarski, 25 November 1949, Rkp BJ Przyb 463/73.

60. Pigoń had written a less than flattering review of a book by Górski. Letter of 13 April 1955, Rkp BJ Przyb 249/76. Górski and Pigoń did not break off relations and reached full reconciliation in 1958.

61. Letter of 22 November 1952. APAN-W, III-141, j. 138, k. 3.

62. Mączak interview. Leśnodorski was allied to the *środowiska* of Kraków and Warsaw through training and professional development. Likewise the denunciations that have become known in KUL emerged from ZMP activists, that is, from the younger generation.

63. During a moment of confidence he informed Soviet hosts of his "amazement" that Konorski had been included in the invitation to Moscow, for he knew of Konorski's intentions to publish a book in London [*sic*] critical of Pavlov. ARAN, f. 579, op. 1. dop., d. 3, ll. 155, 196. The Soviets began an investigation that culminated in the attacks mentioned in chapter 2 at n. 127.

64. For the cases of Bobińska and Marchlewski, see chapter 8 at n. 58 and chapter 7 at n. 87. As dean of the law faculty Grzybowski held on to Vetulani's student Stanisław Grodziski, who was threatened in the early 1950s, and he attempted to protect Catholic publicist Stanisław Stomma, who was released from his position as docent in 1950. Grodziski interview; Jarocki, *Czterdzieści pięć lat,* 160.

65. Kłoskowska, "Bunty i służebności," 14–15. In 1953–54, T. Szczurkiewicz, sociologist of Poznań University, was giving lectures on "selected questions of philosophy" to students of archaeology, psychology, and musicology. *Spis wykładów na rok akademicki 1953–54* (Poznań, 1953).

66. Rather, the seminar list includes works of H. Kelsen, E. Bierling, F.-S. Somlo, E. Westermarck, G. S. Seidler, L. Duguit, and G. Gurvitch. The third week considered the concept of "freedom" based on writings of C. Znamierowski and L. Petrażycki. APAN-W, III-47, j. 30, 35, 37.

67. The course was based on the work of Lassa Oppenheim, and made reference to the thought of Augustine, Gracjan, Thomas Aquinas, Innocence IV, Paweł Włodkowic, Jan Długosz, Andrzej Frycz Modrzewski, Piotr Skarga, Achilleis, Livius, F. de Vitoria, and F. Suarez. In a treatment of the question of just wars, Ehrlich cited the Polish thinker Konstanty Święcicki, who in 1763 had opposed alliances with "tyrants" as "collusion with injustice." Rkp BJ Przyb 93/73.

68. Report from 1951. AAN, KC PZPR 237/XVI/80, k. 36.

69. The author was Professor Estreicher. This was one of many examples of the problems in teaching law mentioned at a central PZPR meeting on higher education of 7 May 1949. AAN, BO KC PZPR, t. 8, k. 143.

70. Of Owsińska's inability to become passionate about the project of the institute to which she was attached—the socioeconomic history of the Polish Enlightenment—Lepszy wrote, "I am of the conviction that one has to take account of the individual interests of every historian." Letter to Ziembiński, 4 September 1955, Rkp BJ Przyb 785/73. Evaluations of doctoral and master's theses are in Rkp BJ Przyb 781–84/73.

71. From a recommendation for Dr. Adam Przyboś for a professorship at the Higher Pedagogical School in Kraków, 3 December 1951. Much in contrast to evaluations for such an advanced position in the Czech lands or East Germany, this letter contains not a mention of historical materialism, "social work," or the results of Soviet scholarship. Rkp BJ Przyb 784/73.

72. Evaluation of 4 October 1955. Rkp BJ Przyb 784/73.

73. If one excludes Marxism-Leninism and political economy, that figure rises to 75.3 percent. *Spis wykładów na rok akademicki 1953–54* (Kraków, 1953). Law students in Poznań had 58.8 percent of their lectures with associate and full

professors (73.2 percent when one excludes Marxism-Leninism and political economy). *Spis wykładów na rok akademicki 1953–54* (Poznań, 1953).

74. These were J. Feldman, W. Konopczyński, W. Sobieski, S. Kutrzeba, and S. Kot. *Spis wykładów na rok akademicki 1953–54* (Kraków, 1953). The total in Poznań was 37.3 percent. *Spis wykładów na rok akademicki 1953–54* (Poznań, 1953).

75. In November 1949 the law professors Tomsa, Valina, Čechrák, and Boháček were given leaves of absence in order to "deepen their knowledge of Marxism-Leninism." The following year Valina died, and the other three were discontinued.

76. This from lectures on nationalized enterprises given by Professor Arnošt Wenig-Malovský in the period 1948–53. He also said that workers would tell an enterprise director "where to go" if he bored them with the legal technicalities of their contract. Within such strictures Wenig did provide his students a wealth of logically organized materials on enterprise law, as he had in the pre-Communist period. AČAV, Wenig-Malovský Papers, i.č. 19–27.

77. See, for example, Brno professor Aleš Bláha's undated (1953) criticism of the work of the State Council for Higher Education, which had "functioned without representatives of industry and the working class" and therefore exhibited an "intellectualistic and academistic attitude toward the restructuring of higher education." SÚA, AÚV KSČ, f. 100/45, a.j. 106, l. 22.

78. Not included in the measurements are individuals who became professor without habilitation, like Oldřich Říha, who in the Polish case would be counted as acting professors. If one subtracts the lectures in Marxism-Leninism and political economy, the number of lectures given by professors increases to 21.6 percent. *Seznam přednášek.*

79. Letter of ministry to dean, law faculty, Charles University, 25 September 1950. AUK, právnická fakulta, i.č. 201.

80. See the lectures on the history of state and law given by V. Vaněček in 1952–53, which are organized entirely according to a scheme of historical materialism, with history divided into the stages of slavery, feudalism, capitalism. The lectures degenerate into factography within this rigid scheme, supposing a necessary relation between legal thought and socioeconomic base, and failing to problematize the relation between state and law. AČAV, Vaněček Papers, č.k. 44. For an example of mixed political-professional evaluation of a colleague, see Vaněček's letters on Professor Arnošt Wenig-Malovský of 10 October 1952, in ibid., č.k. 47.

CHAPTER 10

1. On one of the author's visits to East Germany in the early 1980s he learned that several high school students had gained a positive first impression of a new teacher. Why? Instead of with "Freundschaft!" she had opened the class with "Guten Tag."

2. See, for example, the lectures of Professor Václav Vaněček from the early 1950s, AČAV, Vaněček Papers, č.k. 44. On the use of the informal by students, see also Petráň, "Filozofická fakulta," 443; Knapp, *Proměny*, 130.

3. From "Zápis z aktivu, pořádaného pro posluchače, učitele a zaměstnance fakulty, konaného dne 30. března 1950." AUK, právnická fakulta, i.č. 204.

4. Jessen, "Akademische Elite," 213. The Party leadership was also loath to appoint individuals to positions at universities who had received qualifications only at Party institutes. Ibid., 168.

5. See, for example, the references to ministers Rapacki or Golański in protocols in AAN, MSW 25, k. 119–20.

6. For this reason a great deal of uncertainty remains among Polish professors as to who precisely belonged to the Party. For example, a number of interviewees and scholars claim that Konstanty Grzybowski, dean of Kraków's law faculty, must have been a Party member because of the influence he enjoyed in Warsaw. They assume that he was taken directly from the PPS—of which he was a member—into the PZPR, when PPR and PPS were merged in 1948. Actually he asked to be taken into the PZPR as a candidate member, and never became a full member. Bardach and Grzybowski interviews. Similarly, historian and prorector in the 1950s Kazimierz Lepszy is suspected of having been a member of the PZPR, though he was not. See the unrevised version of M. Tyrowicz's memoirs, vol. 2 in Tyrowicz Papers, APAN-K.

7. As a sign of protest, Celina Bobińska surrendered her PZPR Party card after the imposition of martial law in Poland in December 1981. She later told a colleague that she would never have surrendered a Party card of the Communist Party of the Soviet Union! Gierowski interview.

8. APAN-K, KIII-24, j. 169. Sieradzki's local Party rival Bolesław Drobner discovered that during the interwar years Sieradzki, known as Adolf Hirschberg, had written anti-Communist articles. Hirschberg was director of the Polish-language Jewish high school in Wilno. Tyrowicz, *W poszukiwaniu siebie*, 194–95.

9. APKr, KD PZPR, 62/XV/5, k. 9.

10. SAPMO-BA, ZPA, IV 2/9.04/458, Bl. 107–10.

11. A meeting of the Party leadership of Leipzig University on 16 January 1952 decided to obligate the university rector, SED member Georg Mayer, to admit only those students to doctoral studies who would write on topics "that emphasize the present societal problems of the GDR." SSA, IV 4.14/29, Bl. 15. For attention to political problems at natural sciences faculties, see minutes of the meeting of 26 February 1953. SSA, IV 4.14/29, Bl. 36.

12. Meeting of University Committee, 26 April 1952. APKr, KD PZPR, 62/XV/7, k. 22–27. Further examples of tasks taken on by the Party leadership at Leipzig University in 1954 that have no equivalent in Poland: signing up students for paramilitary training (*Kampfgruppen*, Gesellschaft für Sport und Technik camps); coordinating the fight against the church, for example by sending Communist students to observe student fellowships; controlling the work of the Cadre Department of the university and its hiring of administrators; attempting to place Party members in every university institute; "agitating" professors who were "problems"; organizing the visits of many hundreds of Communist students to private homes in Leipzig before elections. SSA, IV 4.14/30.

13. Meeting of 1 February 1955. APKr, KD PZPR, 62/XV/7, k. 56.

14. For examples, see chapter 11 at n. 56.

15. In 1950, the PZPR Voivodeship Committee in Warsaw had almost no role in di-

recting the work of basic Party organizations at institutions of higher education in that city. AAN, KC PZPR 237/XVI/25, k. 34–36. For similar complaints about Poznań, Kraków, and Łódź committees, see AAN, KC PZPR 237/XVI/26, k. 1–2.

16. APKr, KD PZPR, 62/XV/5, k. 28. On 11 February 1955 a Comrade Kogutek noted that much of the blame for poor results in the work of the university PZPR committee was shared by the Voivodeship Committee, "which gave insufficient assistance. During briefings at the Party Voivodeship Committee there was little of political substance, no understanding of the conditions in the university organization, and no atmosphere of criticism and self-criticism." APKr, KD PZPR, 62/XV/7.

17. Józef Kijowski had entered the PZPR in December 1948 at age twenty-five and received his diploma for completing the first stage of two-step studies on 30 June 1953. AUJ, S III 444, WFH 239.

18. For more on the "snooty behavior of the Polish women students," see the reports from March 1957. SAPMO-BA, ZPA, IV 2/9.04/640, Bl. 8–9.

19. SAPMO-BA, ZPA, IV 2/2/535.

20. In a meeting with foreign students during martial law in July 1982, the first secretary of the PZPR organization at Jagiellonian University used the supposed "poor organizational talents" of Poles to explain the state of the Polish economy.

21. He was rejected 79 to 1, with 9 abstentions. Meeting of 14 March 1951, APKr, KD PZPR, 62/XV/5, k. 13.

22. This meeting was called to elect delegates for the city and district Party conference. APKr, KD PZPR, 62/XV/5, k. 38–39. See also reports of information leaks at the meetings of 6 January 1951, ibid., 62/XV/5, k. 9; and 26 April 1952, ibid., 62/XV/7, k. 22–27.

23. A number of students of the Higher Pedagogical School in Kraków "could not control their laughter" at the news of Stalin's death. At the Medical Academy one student continued playing the piano while Stalin's funeral was transmitted over the public address system. A "rumor" made the rounds at Jagiellonian University that the pope had declared that "a person has died with a lot on his conscience." A commemoration of professors failed to take place because the delegated organizer failed to appear. AAN, KC PZPR 237/XVI/80, k. 23–25.

24. AAN, KC PZPR 237/XVI/31, k. 45. Ideological consistency was also not a hallmark of Czech communism. In 1950 an official in the KSČ Central Committee noted the cadre judgment of a professor of chemistry from Brno: "politically reactionary, professionally competent . . . a decent human being."

25. See chapter 8 at n. 20.

26. Reiss had only a master's degree and was acting professor of law. He admitted to having had the "incaution to speak out decisively in public against the activity of oppositional professors" at an academic conference the previous year. Central Committee functionaries decided not to extend his contract after this scandal, and to remove him from university teaching. See his letter of 2 June 1948 to the PPR Central Committee, with notations by Stefan Żółkiewski. AAN, KC PPR 295/XVII/60, k. 216. For reports of local Party officials habitually siding with non-Party and reactionary professors at the Silesian Medical Academy in Rokitnice: AAN, KC PZPR 237/XVI/77, k. 24; of cliques between

Party and non-Party members at the Medical Academy in Wrocław: AAN, KC PZPR 237/XVI/227, k. 18–24.

27. For examples of an abstract "enemy," see the report of Jarosław Ładosz, director of the youth department in the Central Council of the ZMP, 9 May 1952, AAN, KC PZPR 237/XVI/26, k. 5–6; minutes of the *collegium* meeting at the Ministry of Higher Education, 4 February 1954, AAN, MSW 21, k. 177; the report of the PZPR Voivodeship Committee in Katowice on the Medical Academy in Rokitnice, 23 November 1950, AAN, KC PZPR 237/XVI/77, k. 6; or the report of the basic Party organization of Toruń University, 15 January 1953, AAN, KC PZPR 237/XVI/71, k. 31.

28. Made anxious by such "hostile suggestions of the enemy" (*wrogich podszeptach wroga*), several students in Białystok abandoned plans to study in the Soviet Union. Report of 29 March 1952, AAN, KC PZPR 237/XVI/138, k. 37–38.

29. For a report of the removal of "hostile" (*feindlich*) students from Halle in 1952, see SAPMO-BA, ZPA, NL 182/934, Bl. 38; for reference to the "hostile machinations" of Western agent headquarters, see the report of Hannes Hörnig, Central Committee Science Department, 19 August 1955, SAPMO-BA, ZPA, IV 2/9.04/669; for the "hostile activity" of a theology student in Greifswald, see the letter of Lehmann, State Secretariat for Higher Education, 23 June 1958, SAPMO-BA, ZPA, IV 2/9.04/581; for the interpreting of a move to the West as a "hostile act," see the letter of Professor F. C. Althof, 18 May 1960, SAPMO-BA, ZPA, IV 2/9.04/668; for a report on the "enemies" and former functionaries Wohlgemuth and Mamat from 1960, see BAAP, R3/4211; or on the "enemy of the republic" Comrade Grimmling (1953), see SSA, IV 4.14/29, Bl. 140.

30. SAPMO-BA, ZPA, IV 2/2/569, Bl. 18; Klemperer, *So sitze ich*, 2:283. On the fear of Klemperer's colleagues in Halle that they would be denounced as "enemies of the state" in 1953, see SAPMO-BA, ZPA, IV 2/9.04/426, Bl. 33; on "activities hostile to the state" by the Protestant Church, see the report of Dr. Bonninger, State Secretariat for Higher Education, 28 January 1958, SAPMO-BA, ZPA, IV 2/9.04/581.

31. See the letter of Cardinals Sapieha and Wyszyński, introduction to part 2 at n. 32.

32. The meeting took place on 18 March 1949. AAN, KC PZPR 478/120, k. 156–59.

33. RTsKhIDNI, f. 17, op. 128, d. 1149, l. 260. Here are also reports on the dissatisfaction of Hungarian and Czech students with the material conditions in the Soviet Union; one Czech student "expressed doubt in the possibility of constructing socialism in the USSR."

34. AAN, KC PZPR 237/XVI/185, k. 76. The report also complained that "Polish students and *aspiranty* very rarely go to meetings of the CPSU or Komsomol, and very rarely and never in important matters go for advice to Party committees of the CPSU or Komsomol." Ibid., 237/XVI/185, k. 72.

35. A Central Committee report of May 1951 describes how Party organizations "almost exclusively led by students . . . in fact replaced the organs of educational administration" in February 1948. SÚA, AÚV KSČ, f. 100/1, a.j. 1155, l. 174.

36. Minutes of a meeting of the Action Committee of the National Front at Higher Schools in Prague, 8 March 1948. AUK, SVS B166.

37. Kavka, *Stručné Dějiny*, 304.

38. SÚA, AÚV KSČ, f. 19/9, a.j. 320.2/14/49.

39. The secretary at Olomouc University was thirty-seven years old.

40. Císař, born in 1920, finished studies in sociology in 1948, and in 1950 became responsible for questions of education — at all levels — in the Central Committee. See his *Člověk*, 165-71.

41. He argued that joining the Party was necessary, so that the philosophical faculty would not become "paralyzed," like the law faculty. Kratochvil, *Kommunistische Hochschulpolitik*, 154.

42. The deans of that university expressed "full confidence that their rector would do everything for Palacký University that he could." Protocol of sixth deans' conference of Palacký University, 27 February 1948, SÚA, MŠK, č.k. 664.

43. Speech to the eighth deans' conference of Palacký University, 29 April 1949. SÚA, MŠK, č.k. 664. Václav Černý recorded Fischer's remarks at the Congress of National Culture: "we must attempt to fashion our entire life-style in such a way, as, let us say, to accord with the spirit of the February days." Černý, *Paměti*, 3:206.

44. Letter of Weyr to Engliš, 10 April 1948. ANM, Engliš Papers, č.k. 399. In the end, Weyr was given a sabbatical and merit bonus by the ministry without his request. Letter of 16 December 1948 in ibid.

45. ANM, Engliš Papers, č.k. 53.

46. SÚA, AÚV KSČ, f. 100/1, a.j. 1159, l. 50-51.

47. Report of April 1952. SÚA, AÚV KSČ, f. 19/7, a.j. 314, l. 11.

48. SÚA, AÚV KSČ, f. 100/1, a.j. 1155, l. 174.

49. Report of April 1952. SÚA, AÚV KSČ, f. 19/7, a.j. 314, l. 11.

50. Jordán, *Dějiny*, 279.

51. SÚA, AÚV KSČ, f. 19/7, a.j. 272, l. 254.

52. See the recommendation of Václav Vaněček for Bohuslav Rouček of 4 September 1953, which makes reference to this "practice" in the faculty Party organization. AČAV, Vaněček Papers, č.k. 47. In these years tens of thousands of university-educated state bureaucrats were sent to work in industry. Kaplan, *Nekrvavá revoluce*, 209-20.

53. SÚA, AÚV KSČ, f. 19/7, a.j. 272, l. 110.

54. SÚA, AÚV KSČ, f. 19/7, a.j. 240, l. 88.

55. SÚA, AÚV KSČ, f. 19/7, a.j. 313, l. 85-86.

56. Lobkowicz, *Marxismus-Leninismus*, 30-31.

57. SÚA, AÚV KSČ, f. 19/7, a.j. 312, l. 12-14.

58. Report of April 1952. SÚA, AÚV KSČ, f. 19/7, a.j. 314, l. 11.

59. Report of 3 June 1952. AČAV, Valouch Papers, sig. IV, i.č. 852. Valouch related the experience of Professor Vrbenský, against whom a complaint had been raised for making wisecracks. Yet in Valouch's recollection this valuable expert — who now faced dismissal — was a "progressive man." The Soviets insisted that through "patient and tactful work" such a man must be gained for the regime. Reports from Prague's medical faculty of early 1954 talk of professors who had been "turned off" to scientific work because of the "harassment" of student Communists. Ever fewer doctors proved willing to join the Party; out of fifty-seven full professors, only seven now belonged to the Party. SÚA, AÚV KSČ, f. 19/7, a.j. 313, l. 84-86. See also ibid., a.j. 241, l. 8-9 (1954), for reports of "sectarian attitudes" among assistant professors, which had a "repugnant effect, especially on old professors."

60. SÚA, AÚV KSČ, f. 19/7, a.j. 272/2, l. 136-43.

61. GARF, f. 5283, op. 22, d. 462, ll. 73–74. For reminiscences of Soviet professors criticizing the KSČ for overeagerness in duplicating Soviet models in higher education, see Hájek, *Paměti,* 197–98.

62. For example, in 1949 the historian P. G. Sofinov had opined that a "serious battle awaits Czechoslovak universities," because of the "people with reactionary views among the professors." GARF, f. 9396, op. 30, d. 69, ll. 91–92.

63. See the reports in SÚA, AÚV KSČ, f. 19/7, a.j. 236, l. 13–14; a.j. 272/2, l. 144–50.

64. SÚA, AÚV KSČ, f. 19/7, a.j. 272/2, l. 136–43.

65. In 1951 Professor Josef Siblík and Docent Josef Klima were judged politically unfit for teaching by the law faculty in Prague. The latter supposedly attracted to his seminars "the politically worst students, who get along very well with Doc. Klima, and who have been trained by him to become lawyers for which people's democracy has no use." Tureček to the Ministry of Education, 18 July 1951, Personnel file Josef Klima, AUK. Siblík was found to be keeping contact with faculty members who had been dismissed, like Professor Jan Matějka, and suddenly evidence emerged—in 1951!—that he had "held lectures voluntarily for the League for Cooperation with the Germans" in World War II. His lectures continued to manifest "bourgeois character." Tureček to Ministry of Education, 20 July 1951, Personnel file Josef Siblík, AUK.

66. See, for example, the 1950 vote of the senate of Charles University against Professor Vratislav Bušek, who had been released by an action committee in March 1948, and thereafter escaped abroad. Personnel file, AUK.

67. See the protocols of meetings in AČAV, f. ČAVU, i.č. 241. Professors in this committee included historian Albert Pražák, mathematician Bohumil Bydžovský, philologist Jan Rypka, and linguist Karel Sochor. They excluded Professors Weyr, Křepelka, and Žáček from further meetings.

68. Letter to J. B. Kozák, 10 June 1948. AČAV, Král Papers, i.č. 662.

69. Letter of 15 November 1949. AČAV, Vaněček Papers, č.k. 20. By that point Saturník was dead and Bušek had emigrated, but Boháček and Čáda were still hoping to stay on the faculty.

70. Petráň, "Filozofická fakulta," 441–42. Charles University dean Mukařovský was also accused of helping professors who had been dismissed to find work, but who those professors were is not made clear.

71. Černý, *Paměti,* 3:197–98. Both taught aesthetics.

72. Ibid., 272. Trávníček and Havránek were members of the Prague linguistic circle.

73. Beer's funeral in 1950 was a last manifestation of the anti-Communist university opposition. It was celebrated by Brno's bishop Dr. Karel Skoupý. Kratochvil, *Kommunistische Hochschulpolitik,* 155, 165–66; Jordán, *Dějiny,* 385.

74. Kratochvil, *Kommunistische Hochschulpolitik,* 189.

75. Jessen, "Akademische Elite," 61.

76. UAL, Rektorat 122, Bl. 213.

77. For examples from Leipzig in the early 1950s, see UAL, Rektorat 120.

78. "Geschichte der FDJ. Schriftwechsel," UAR. In February 1950 the GDR Ministry of Education gave instructions to expel "reactionary elements" at universities who had "come out in the open" after the student council elections: "Of course, these measures should take place only with the approval of the newly elected student council." BAAP, R2/1897, Bl. 139. See also the report of an FDJ general assembly's demanding the expulsion of a student who had not taken

examinations on time in "Bericht über die Auswertung der 3. ZR-Tagung an der Universität Leipzig," March 1953, 2. SSA, IV 4.14/78.

79. See, for example, the discussions of the escape of two graduate students in the SED's Institute for Social Sciences of March 1956, SAPMO-BA, ZPA, IV 2/9.04/45, Bl. 13–15. The discussants recalled that one student had claimed that "for a writer it was inspiration and not consciousness that was decisive." The other had told a comrade during a party that "Moscow coughs and we act." The major problem was that this student was "not transparent" (*undurchsichtig*).

80. Stalinist-era rectors in Leipzig (G. Mayer), Greifswald (H. Beyer), Halle (L. Stern), Rostock (E. Schlesinger), and Jena (O. Schwarz) were recent imports into their academic environments, who had not even been professors before 1945.

81. See the correspondence in SAPMO-BA, ZPA, NL 90/559, Bl. 142–68. Characteristically, the other university senates soon thereafter voted against the resolution of their Rostock colleagues. For the discussion in Leipzig, see UAL, Rektorat 2. See also Victor Klemperer's vigorous condemnation of the "counterrevolutionary" Rostock initiative in *So sitze ich,* 2:283.

82. Pousta, "Universita Karlova," 280–81.

83. Letter to J. B. Kozák, 7 June 1948. AČAV, Král Papers, i.č. 662. Other dissenting opinions — though lacking such principled statements — were sent by psychologist V. Příhoda and pedagogue J. Hendrich.

84. *Bevormundung* means roughly to treat someone like a child. Letter of 11 November 1960, UAL, Rektorat 122, Bl. 215. Matzen's letters were the most daring expressions of open dissent I discovered in East German archives for the post-1949 period. For minutes of the faculty meeting, see the report of the SED organization at the Leipzig medical faculty, 12 February 1959. SSA, IV 4.14/88.

85. Polišenský interview; Urban and Hojda, "Velký historik." On postwar Czech historians, see Hanzal, "Čeští historici."

86. The organization in Halle had staged a conference for all East German university organizations. See chapter 2 at n. 22.

87. "Vierte Tagung des zentralen Hochschulausschusses der SED am 7. und 8. Februar 1948," 250. SAPMO-BA, ZPA, IV 2/9.04/6. The block parties were the official East German political spectrum beyond the SED, consisting at this time of the CDU and LDP.

88. Ibid., 162. Professor Heinrich Deiters, a former SPD member usually thought of as a cooler head, suggested during deliberations on how to increase numbers of SED professors that university senates and faculties be excluded from the process entirely: "One may refer to this simply as a temporary scientific dictatorship of the educational administrations." Ibid., 29.

89. Engelberg proved a loyal supporter of the Ulbricht line, condemning those who insisted upon "discussing mistakes," and calling for a renewed wave of repression against the Protestant student fellowships in early 1954. See Connelly, "Freie Meinungsäusserung." For painful reading of Engelberg's self-serving denunciations of colleagues and comrades like Kuczynski, Klein, Meusel, Schreiner, Stern — practically every potential rival — see Kowalczuk, *Legitimation,* 249–54.

90. Zwerenz, *Der Widerspruch,* 101. See also the reminiscences of writers Erich Loest, *Durch die Erde,* 304, 312; and Stefan Heym, *Nachruf,* 598.

91. Loest, *Durch die Erde,* 304.

92. Meeting of the SED Party leadership of Leipzig University, 29 April 1953. SSA, IV 4.14/29, Bl. 62.

93. *Neues Deutschland,* 20 April 1958, cited in Zwerenz, *Der Widerspruch,* 285–86. Bloch seemed to echo Brecht. On 17 June 1953 Bertolt Brecht had written Ulbricht: "At this moment, I feel a need to assure you of my solidarity [*Verbundenheit*] with the Socialist Unity Party of Germany." He was a "Marxist who stood loyally on the ground of the workers' and peasants' state." Cited in Mittenzwei, *Das Leben,* 493–94; Kantorowicz, *Etwas ist ausgeblieben,* 147, 214–15.

94. Letter of 22 January 1957. SAPMO-BA, ZPA, IV 2/9.04/163, Bl. 15–26.

95. In this case Bloch was referring to his students Zehm and Kleine. Interview of 25 January 1957, SAPMO-BA, ZPA, IV 2/9.04/163, Bl. 28. In December 1957 Bloch wrote the SED leadership: "if Zwerenz calls himself my student, then this is incorrect." Ibid., IV 2/2/2, Bl. 569. For the view that Bloch remained loyal to his students, see Grebing, *Der Revisionismus,* 165.

96. Just, *Zeuge,* 101–2.

97. Ibid., 108–9.

98. Gerhard Zwerenz has called Harich an "adventurer." *Der Widerspruch,* 212–13.

99. Kantorowicz, *Tagebuch,* 692.

100. Herzberg, "Ernst Bloch," 686.

101. Loest, *Durch die Erde,* 320–21.

102. Ibid., 309. For the failure of influential writers Anna Seghers, Willi Bredel, and Bodo Uhse and actor Helene Weigel to assist their friend Walter Janka, see Janka, *Schwierigkeiten,* 90–94; Just, *Zeuge,* 123–24.

103. The signatories included Emil Adler, Nina Assorodobraj, Bronisław Baczko, Zygmunt Bauman, Maria Bielińska, Julian Hochfeld, Leszek Kołakowski, Zdzisław Kochański, Władysław Krajewski, Tadeusz Kroński, Stefan Morawski, Jerzy Rudzki, Jadwiga Siekierska, Anna Sładkowska, Włodzimierz Wesołowski, Marian Dobrosielski, Helena Eilstein, Paweł Beylin, Irena Krońska, Jerzy Wiatr, Sabina Lewi, Jan Strzelecki, Jerzy Szacki, Jan Legowicz, and Janina Wojnar Sejecka. SAPMO-BA, ZPA, IV 2/10/158, Bl. 246–47.

104. Klein, "Dokumente," 43, 54.

105. Kuczynski, *Frost,* 64.

106. SAPMO-BA, ZPA, IV 2/9.04/148, Bl. 77.

107. Klein interview.

108. Aktennotiz, 18 March 1957. SAPMO-BA, ZPA, IV 2/9.04/148.

109. It was claimed, for example, that Kuczynski had denied the complicity of right-wing Social Democrats in Germany's entry into World War I. Kuczynski, *"Ein linientreuer,"* 104–29. For a discussion of revisionist ideas in the social sciences, see Jänicke, *Der dritte Weg,* 104–54.

110. Kuczynski, *Frost,* 76.

111. This conversation took place at Behrens's weekend house. SAPMO-BA, ZPA, IV 2/9.04/402, Bl. 123–28, 160.

112. SAPMO-BA, ZPA, IV 2/9.04/163, Bl. 110–11.

113. The SED leadership carefully cultivated a mythology of its antifascist past. Grunenberg, *Antifaschismus,* esp. 113–19. On the logic of antifascism within East German society, see also Meuschel, *Legitimation.*

114. On the French case, see Judt, *Past Imperfect,* 220–23.

115. Loest, *Durch die Erde,* 307. See also the sketches in Krüger, *Das Ende.*

116. SAPMO-BA, ZPA, IV 2/9.04/426, Bl. 97–99.

117. *So sitze ich,* 1:418, 425–26; 2:283, 296, 390.

118. Into the 1980s, the Western allies insisted on interviewing practically every East German who fled to West Berlin, though they had no technical right to do so.

119. "Notiz über das Auftreten des Gen. Havemann am 18. Juni 1957 in der Wahlversammlung bei Prof. Neunhöffer." SAPMO-BA, ZPA, IV 2/9.04/164, Bl. 105. Havemann lived in West Berlin until 1950.

120. Krüger, *Das Ende,* 44–46.

121. See the "individual discussions" with students who had applied to visit the West in the summer of 1956. SAPMO-BA, ZPA, IV 2/9.04/46, Bl. 19–21. For reports of students in Magdeburg comparing western and eastern living standards during vacation trips to West Germany, see the documentation from October 1955 in ibid., IV 2/9.04/83, Bl. 99.

122. In particular professors' wives, originally from West Germany, were suspected of luring their husbands out of the GDR. They were interested in better "social life." "Analyse der Republikflucht," 8 August 1959, SAPMO-BA, ZPA, IV 2/9.04/669. See also the letter of Harig to Ulbricht on the "negative influence of the young wife" of chemistry professor Thilo, 6 March 1953, BAAP, R3/212, Bl. 132; on the subject of wives, see also the letter of Walter Lindemann, Halle University, to the Central Committee, 13 June 1953, SAPMO-BA, ZPA, IV 2/9.04/426, Bl. 32–35; and the report of the Staatssekretariat für Hochschulwesen, 8 August 1960, SAPMO-BA, ZPA, IV 2/9.04/669. For the dangers of failing to denounce associates planning to leave the GDR, see the letter of Professor H. Staude (Chemistry, Leipzig) to Professor G. Mayer (Rector, Leipzig) of 18 September 1959 reporting the reasons for his "quick departure" from the GDR: an interrogation by the Stasi from 10:30 P.M. to 5:00 A.M. to discover whether he had known of the intention of one of his graduate students to "flee the republic." He admitted that he had. He was given the choice of two and one-half years' prison for failing to denounce her, or voluntary service for the Stasi in halting other escapes to West Germany. SSA, IV 4.14/88.

123. On professors' use of teaching offers in West Germany, see Jessen, "Zur Sozialgeschichte," 124–25, 134–37.

124. The majority of contracts were with members of the intelligentsia who were active in industry. Kowalczuk, "Die Durchsetzung," 53.

125. Jessen, "Zur Sozialgeschichte," 129.

126. Ibid., 134–35.

127. Full professors' salaries went from 3,100 to 4,350 złotys between September 1954 and September 1956, and those of docents from 2,200 to 3,000 złotys. A beginning (adjunct) professor earned just 2,030 złotys after September 1956. *Dziennik Ustaw,* Nr. 42, poz. 187 (1954); Nr. 41, poz. 192 (1956). In 1958 the ministry began placing limits on extra work, and in 1961–62 the government introduced a significant pay increase. Olszewski, *Politechnika,* 167.

128. AUJ, S III 161. On the problem of double workloads, see also Łuczak, *University of Poznań*, 255; Hartmann, *Hochschulwesen*, 117–18.

129. SÚA, AÚV KSČ, f. 19/7, a.j. 313, l. 81–82.

130. M. Valouch to L. Štoll, 16 April 1953. AČAV, Valouch Papers, correspondence. On lower salaries in higher education than in industry, see also SÚA, AÚV KSČ, f. 19/7, a.j. 241, l. 73.

131. SÚA, AÚV KSČ, f. 19/7, a.j. 241, l. 38.

132. Jessen, "Vom Ordinarius," 99.

133. Ibid.

134. *Statistická ročenka Republiky Československé 1957*, 232.

INTRODUCTION TO PART III

1. For the growth of the intelligentsia, see Maňák, "Početnost a struktura"; on numbers of workers' children at universities, Havránek, "Nineteenth Century," 17; Kavka, *Stručné dějiny*, 279.

CHAPTER 11

1. See chapter 6.

2. Of the students taking the examination, 9.5 percent failed. J. Sieradzki, "Pierwszy rok działalności Studium Nauki o Polsce i Świecie Współczesnym w UJ," AUJ, WP III 41.

3. Report of Professor J. Sieradzki to rector, Jagiellonian University, 22 August 1949. AUJ, S III 36.

4. AAN, MO 2856, k. 70–76. There was a system to the theologians learning Marxism-Leninism backward and forward. See also the report from Łódź in 1949, in which students of the Sodality of Our Lady were described as "intelligent and very well acquainted with Marxist philosophy." AAN, KC PZPR 237/XVI/128, k. 26. J. Sieradzki also reported in 1950 that students of the theological faculty in Kraków were either "very well or very poorly prepared." Report of 29 August 1950, AUJ, S III 37.

5. Announcement of Professor Patkaniowski, 14 May 1951. AUJ, WP III 103.

6. AAN, KC PZPR 237/XVI/219, k. 30.

7. Full lists of questions can be found in AUJ, WP III 41.

8. Letter of Ministry of Higher Education, 15 January 1952. AUJ, S III 251.

9. AAN, MSW 17, k. 142–46, 158.

10. AAN, KC PZPR 237/XVI/67, k. 69–70.

11. AAN, KC PZPR 237/XVI/67, k. 23. In a notation for the Politburo of December 1951, Adam Schaff wrote that the poor level of the teaching staff, who were chosen "by chance," could result in the danger that Marxism "is labeled by students 'science of religion.'" AAN, KC PZPR 237/XVI/67, k. 15.

12. AAN, KC PZPR 237/XVI/230, k. 25–29.

13. AAN, KC PZPR 237/XVI/224, k. 24–29.

14. AAN, KC PZPR 237/XVI/219, k. 29–33.

15. AAN, KC PZPR 237/XVI/224, k. 24–29.

16. AAN, KC PZPR 237/XVI/227, k. 12–16; AAN, KC PZPR 237/XVI/227, k. 17.

17. AAN, KC PZPR 237/XVI/186, k. 32. At the two other institutions of higher education in Upper Silesia, teaching staffs, though often competent, were too

overloaded to teach effectively, let alone concern themselves with their own education. The director of the Political Economy Department at the Medical Academy of Rokitnice, Comrade Figa, also worked at a Marxist-Leninist night school, was an employee of the voivodeship center for Party schooling, held lectures in the voivodeship Party school, and from time to time made inspection tours throughout the region for the Voivodeship Committee. His counterpart at the Higher Economics School in Stalinogród (Katowice) was simultaneously director of Marxism-Leninism at the Higher Music School and the Higher School for the Fine Arts. See the notes from 1954 in AAN, KC PZPR 237/XVI/219, k. 1–20.

18. AAN, KC PZPR 237/XVI/182, k. 161–66; AAN, KC PZPR 237/XVI/186, k. 68.

19. Sudakov discerned intrigue and sabotage everywhere in the alien Polish environment. For example, he could not reconcile himself to the Marxism-Leninism Department's location next to the Theology Department, and his daily encounters with priests in habits. Werblan interview.

20. Letter to DVV of 24 May 1947. BAAP, R2/1489, k. 81.

21. Letter to Paul Wandel, 6 January 1947. BAAP, R2/1453, Bl. 26–27. His colleague Theodor Litt protested the opening of a new faculty of political indoctrination in Leipzig—the social science faculty—because "certain leading people in this faculty are known not only as representatives of a political doctrine but also as people who quite openly want to reach some political end." "Protokoll der Senatsitzung," 5 March 1947, UAL, Rektorat 1, Bl. 113.

22. Philosophical faculties existed at all six East German universities, but as late as January 1948, philosophy had not been approved as a major subject. BAAP, R2/1422, Bl. 51–52, 54.

23. Alfred Meusel to Robert Rompe, 5 February 1947. BAAP, R2/1489, Bl. 46, 68.

24. BAAP, R2/1489, Bl. 106.

25. BAAP, R2/900, Bl. 25.

26. These were from Rostock and Greifswald. BAAP, R2/1898, Bl. 60. In the February 1950 elections, 22.8 percent of the ballots in Leipzig, and 28.4 percent in Jena were purposely invalidated. BAAP, R2/1258, Bl. 27; R2/1898, Bl. 40. Internal SED correspondence admits that the candidate lists were "prepared in a way that guaranteed that our candidates come through." "Stellungnahme des Sekretariats zu den Studentenratswahlen," 15 January 1950, SAPMO-BA, ZPA, IV 2/9.04/461.

27. BAAP, R2/1259, Bl. 222. See also the reports from Greifswald, Rostock, and Saxony; BAAP, R2/1897, Bl. 137; R2/1903, Bl. 4–7; R2/1897, Bl. 132. Halle was removed from his position by the Politburo in November 1950 for "backward behavior." He and his staff were accused of moving too slowly in higher-education reform. Müller and Müller, ". . . stürmt die Festung," 396. Halle was a waiter by profession, and had belonged to the KPD since the 1920s when he acted as district spokesperson in Halle-Merseburg. He spent the years 1935–45 in Buchenwald. From 1945 to 1949 he directed the Higher-Education Department of the Saxony-Anhalt Education Ministry. BAAP, R2/931.

28. BAAP, R2/1490, Bl. 58–59, 61.

29. Müller and Müller, ". . . stürmt die Festung," 239–40.

30. Ibid., 242–43.

31. SSA, IV 4.14/10.

32. SSA, IV 4.14/27, Bl. 73–84.

33. Müller and Müller, ". . . *stürmt die Festung*," 239–40.

34. BAAP, R3/150, Bl. 268.

35. Schmutzler, *Gegen den Strom*, 105.

36. UA der HUB, 359/2, Bl. 287, 291, 303, 309.

37. BAAP, R3/4159.

38. Meeting of 16 January 1952, SSA, IV 4.14/29.

39. In Greifswald between 80 and 90 percent of the first-year students attended lectures and seminars. Report of December 1951, "Vorlesungs- und Seminarbesuch," in BAAP, R3/4159.

40. This arrangement was changed in April 1953 to permit more "scientific" work by lecturers; they would prepare one weekly lecture, which could be held at two faculties of the same year of studies. BAAP, R3/223, Bl. 80.

41. BAAP, R3/146, Bl. 90–95, 104–7.

42. SÚA, AÚV KSČ, f. 02/4, a.j. 103, b. 5, l. 2.

43. Císař interview.

44. SÚA, AÚV KSČ, f. 19/7, a.j. 305, l. 12–13.

45. SÚA, AÚV KSČ, f. 19/7, a.j. 305, l. 44–45.

46. SÚA, AÚV KSČ, f. 19/7, a.j. 305, l. 14–15, 18–19.

47. SÚA, AÚV KSČ, f. 19/7, a.j. 305, l. 34–38.

48. SÚA, AÚV KSČ, f. 19/7, a.j. 292, l. 7.

49. SÚA, AÚV KSČ, f. 19/7, a.j. 293, l. 3–6.

50. SÚA, AÚV KSČ, f. 100/24, a.j. 975, l. 41, 44.

51. SÚA, AÚV KSČ, f. 02/5, a.j. 67, b. 13, l. 2–5; f. 19/7, a.j. 293, l. 8–10.

52. SÚA, AÚV KSČ, f. 19/7, a.j. 299, l. 107, 109, 112.

53. SÚA, AÚV KSČ, f. 19/7, a.j. 294, l. 10. For a similar report, see the letter of the Marxism-Leninism Department at Brno University to the Ministry of Education, 27 February 1954, SÚA, MŠK 5, č.k. 631E, sig. 5IJ.

54. SÚA, AÚV KSČ, f. 19/7, a.j. 294, l. 3.

55. SÚA, AÚV KSČ, f. 19/7, a.j. 294, l. 4, 8.

56. Meeting of 29 November 1954, SSA, IV 4.14/27.

57. "Parteiaktivenkonferenz der Parteiorganisation der Universität Leipzig," 24 September 1952. SSA, IV 4.14/10. "Friend" was short for "youth friend," which in FDJ circles had the same function as the word "comrade" in a Communist Party.

58. The functionary belonged to the SED District Committee of Leipzig. SSA, IV 2/9.02/522, Bl. 28.

59. Meeting of 25 November 1954, SSA, IV 4.14/27.

60. "Aktivistentagung vom Januar 1951." SSA, IV 4.14/10, Bl. 46.

61. SAPMO-BA, ZPA, IV 2/9.04/80, Bl. 8.

62. AAN, KC PZPR 237/XVI/221, k. 10. See also the complaint from April 1952 of Communist students in Warsaw about "comrades in high places [who] immediately detect the class enemy in people who criticize!" AAN, KC PZPR 237/XVI/102, k. 50–52. Copies of this complaint were circulated in the Central Committee.

63. SÚA, AÚV KSČ, f. 19/7, a.j. 313, l. 390.

64. AAN, KC PZPR 237/XVI/12, k. 57–60. On the persecution of the Polish Catholic Church in these years, which culminated in the arrest of Cardinal Wyszyński in September 1953, see Micewski, *Kościół*, 22–36.

65. AAN, KC PZPR 237/XVI/96, k. 93–95.

66. AAN, KC PZPR 237/XVI/71, k. 28; also: "Sprawozdanie wydziału nauki za okres od 1.II. do 10.II.1953 r.," AAN, KC PZPR 237/XVI/4, k. 53.

67. AAN, KC PZPR 237/XVI/15, k. 15.

68. Dozens of students abandoned plans to study in the Soviet Union. AAN, KC PZPR 237/XVI/138, k. 70–77. See also the case of a worker-course student who went back to his village and was asked whether he was permitted to attend church, and "whether lectures are in the Polish language." In another case, a student home on winter break was instructed in the confessional to abandon his worker course. Reports of 1951, AAN, KC PZPR 237/XVI/121, k. 115–16, 124.

69. Its first act was to organize an excursion to Zakopane. Teresa Birecka to Stanisław Pigoń, 27 January 1952, Rkp BJ Przyb 239/76.

70. Sławińska and Kłoczowski interviews. See also Irena Sławińska, *Szlakami*, and Gapski, *Historae peritus*. The Party was aware of these events. In a report of 9 May 1952, ZMP functionary Jarosław Ładosz speaks of "excursions and sporting activities organized by the clergy." AAN, KC PZPR 237/XVI/26, k. 5–6.

71. "Notatka w sprawie KUL," 25 May 1954. AAN, KC PZPR 237/XVI/182, k. 48–52. Neither state nor church took prisoners in Lublin: KUL's authorities let it be known that students attempting to transfer to the state university would not be let back if they failed, and local PZPR functionaries did their best to isolate members of KUL's community from the benefits of state social services. The child of KUL's janitor, suffering tuberculosis, was refused a place in a state sanitorium.

72. KUL, though a private university with control over its own admissions, did not accept fewer worker-peasant students than did state universities. AAN, KC PZPR 237/XVI/88, k. 2.

73. In Szczecin there were reports of "some Father Siwek," specially delegated by the curia, who "visits and agitates students, even on the grounds of state dormitories." "Analiza sytuacji na odcinku młodzieży akademickiej," 1952, AAN, KC PZPR 237/XVI/15, k. 13.

74. "Notatka w sprawie KUL," 25 May 1954, AAN, KC PZPR 237/XVI/182, k. 48–52.

75. AAN, KC PZPR 237/XVI/15, k. 14–15.

76. See the complaint of comrade Wätzold at a meeting of the SED Party executive of Leipzig University, 27 November 1952, SSA, IV 4.14/29.

77. "Bericht," 27 April 1953. SSA, IV 4.14/40. In September 1953 there were 5,966 students at Leipzig University. BAAP, E1/17050, Bl. 90. The student pastor in Leipzig, Georg-Siegfried Schmutzler, estimated the number of students in the fellowship during his tenure (1954–57) at 500 to 600. *Gegen den Strom*, 98.

78. "Protokoll über die Sitzung des Akademischen Senats der Karl-Marx-Universität," Leipzig, 16 May 1953. BAAP, R3/1538, Bl. 20. For a full description of this state-church conflict, see Besier, *Der SED-Staat*, 106–24.

79. BAAP, R3/1536. These expulsions contradict the recollections of Havemann in *Fragen*, 132. The remarks of Professor Elliger (theology) during this meeting

make clear that Havemann was involved in interrogating the students and had assembled "evidence" for a conspiracy on that basis. Elliger was the only member of the senate who did not support the resolution. In September 1953, there were 6,470 students at Humboldt University. BAAP, E1/17050, Bl. 90.

80. As a reflection of SED admissions policies, the young Christians were more often found in medical faculties than in history or the social sciences. On the historians, see the remarks of G. Benser at the meeting of the SED Party executive of Leipzig University, 27 November 1952, SSA, IV 4.14/29; and on students of medicine, see the executive meeting minutes of 28 January 1954, SSA, IV 4.14/30. In February 1954, about half the chemistry students in Leipzig were reported to be fellowship members. "Konferenz der Lehrkräfte des gesellschaftswissenschaftlichen Grundstudiums," 15 February 1954, BAAP, R3/4173.

81. On the breakthrough in the church's resistance to *Jugendweihe,* see Besier, *Der SED-Staat,* 255–56.

82. Schmutzler, *Gegen den Strom,* 72.

83. For the East German experience of 1956, see Mitter and Wolle, *Untergang;* Connelly, "Ulbricht."

84. Schmutzler, *Gegen den Strom,* 106–19.

85. "Aktennotiz Betr. Fürbittgottesdienst für Schmutzler," 28 December 1957. SAPMO-BA, ZPA, IV 2/9.04/581. Schmutzler later noted that "it was no surprise that the Leipzig faculty produced numerous conformist theologians." *Gegen den Strom,* 72. The situation was not much different elsewhere. On the development of GDR theological faculties in the 1950s, see also Besier, *Der SED-Staat,* 192–93, 216–17, 381–418.

86. See the excerpts from letters of GDR scholars who had fled westward detailing the harassment of their churchgoing children in East German schools: Letter of Zentralvorstand der Gewerkschaft Wissenschaft, 31 October 1960, SAPMO-BA, ZPA, IV 2/9.04/669; Report of Deimling, Staatssekretariat für Hochschulwesen, 8 August 1960, in ibid.

87. Secretariat meeting of 14 March 1950. SÚA, AÚV KSČ, f. 02/4, a.j. 110, b. 6, l. 4–6.

88. Seventeen of twenty students of a history study group (*kroužek*) in Brno were thought to be under religious influence. SÚA, AÚV KSČ, f. 19/7, a.j. 294, l. 1–22.

89. By this point, almost all students belonged to the ČSM. SÚA, AÚV KSČ, f. 02/2, a.j. 99, l. 18–19.

90. SÚA, AÚV KSČ, f. 19/7, a.j. 272/2, l. 164. For enrollment figures of Charles University, see Havránek and Pousta, *Dějiny,* 620.

91. In Poland in the early 1950s, there were far too many applicants for pharmaceutical, dental, and medical sciences, but often just enough for humanities and law. AAN, KC PZPR 237/XVI/78. In 1950 434 students applied for 450 places in the renowned law faculty at Kraków. By contrast, at the mathematics and natural sciences faculty there were 631 applications for 463 places, in agriculture 346 for 150 places, in forestry 291 for 100 places, and in theology 161 for 100 places (twice as many applicants as in the previous year). AUJ, DM 20. For a similar report from Łódź, see AAN, KC PZPR 237/XVI/28. In 1954 about 70 percent of the applications in East Germany went for the natural, medical, and technical sciences, but these disciplines made up only 40 percent of the

first-year slots. There were 10 applicants per place in chemistry and pharmacy, and 3 per place in journalism. BAAP, R3/151, Bl. 216–17. For the unwillingness of students to apply to social sciences in Leipzig, see the minutes of the meeting of the academic senate, UAL, Rektorat 2, Bl. 152. On East German students' avoiding philosophy, political economy, Slavic languages, pedagogy, and agricultural sciences in 1955–56, see SAPMO-BA, ZPA, IV 2/9.04/477, Bl. 17. In Prague, law and social sciences–economics faculties were undersubscribed. See the report from 1951, SÚA, AÚV KSČ, f. 19/7, a.j. 279, l. 170.

CHAPTER 12

1. Stallmann, *Hochschulzugang,* 430. The restrictions did not apply to those born after 1 January 1920, as long as they "gave the assurance, that they are of value for democratic reconstruction."
2. See Connelly, "East German Higher Education Policies."
3. Klein, *Humboldt-Universität,* 94, 96.
4. Professor Zolotukhin, for example, told an overeager German functionary that it was "impossible for reasons of propaganda toward the West to diverge from the international practice of preparatory education for university studies." See the notes of the representative of the Saxon *Land* administration, Helmut Häntzsche (SPD/SED), from Zolotukhin's visit to Leipzig in January 1946. SAPMO-BA, ZPA, IV 2/9.04/697.
5. Schneider, *Bildung,* 10–11.
6. Saxony had 40 to 48 percent of the Soviet zone's industry, and 60 percent of its working-class population. Broszat and Weber, *SBZ-Handbuch,* 126–28.
7. UAR, RIII I/2, Bd. 1.
8. Holtzhauer involved himself in university admissions beginning in late 1945, by suggesting members for the admissions boards in Leipzig to the personnel officer (KPD) in the State Administration in Dresden. See Holtzhauer's letter of 6 November 1945 to Träger, UAL, Rektorat 307a/4. In student admissions he worked closely with the State Administration's representative at Leipzig University, Jusek (SED), who was the university bursar and, as of October 1946, the organizational director of the SED central Party organization at the university.
9. This was a time when many former SPD members in public offices were being replaced by former KPD members. Broszat and Weber, *SBZ-Handbuch,* 135, 146.
10. Kasper, "Der Kampf," 105.
11. Ibid., 107.
12. Ibid., 110–13.
13. "Verordnung über die Errichtung von Vorbereitungskursen für das Studium an den Hochschulen vom 12. Februar 1946," in Lammel, *Dokumente,* 1:57.
14. Lammel, *Dokumente,* 1:69.
15. Kasper, "Der Kampf," 130.
16. BAAP, R2/900, Bl. 13–14.
17. The ministers adopted this formula in April 1948. BAAP, R2/900, Bl. 13–14.
18. The Leipzig preadmissions committee was headed by Communists Jusek (*Land* government) and Stiller (student council), and joined by local representatives of the LDP, the CDU, and two members without party affiliation. Four of the six were students, and none had an academic degree. Letter of Arbeitsgemein-

schaft demokratischer Studenten to Jusek, university bursary, 30 August 1946, in UAL, Rektorat 307a, Bl. 199. The main admissions committees in Leipzig consisted of the rector, a representative of the faculty concerned, a representative of the *Land* administration (Häntzsche), representatives of the city education office (Holtzhauer and Körting), and a representative of the SED (Dr. Ley), CDU (Dr. Köster), LDP (Dr. Zeissig), and student council (once more Stiller).

19. For the 22 July 1947 guidelines, see BAAP, R2/7432, Bl. 77. Soviet officer N. M. Voronov took part in the drafting of these guidelines.

20. Letter of 11 August 1947 from Dresden Education Ministry official Häntzsche (SED) to Rector Gadamer. UAL, Rektorat 307, Bl. 54.

21. Of these, half had started medical studies before 1945. In 1946–47, 465 students were studying medicine in Leipzig; in 1947–48 the number had increased to 609. BAAP, R2/1060, Bl. 24, 36.

22. Leipzig University objected that such an essay would be "beneficial to young people who have a weak character but a better ability to adapt themselves." See the minutes of the meetings of the academic senate of 31 July and 28 August 1946, UAL, Rektorat 1.

23. Minutes of the meeting of the academic senate of Leipzig University, 16 August 1947, UAL, Rektorat 1.

24. A subsequent letter of 8 February from the Agitation-Propaganda Department of the *Land* headquarters to the subordinate district [*Kreis*] headquarters announced as goals 1,000 "pupils" to be trained for university studies in all Saxony, of whom 400 were to be KPD members. Also in contrast to early Polish initiatives, it encouraged the recruitment of as many "girls and women" as possible. Committee of the KPD Saxony, Department for Agitation-Propaganda, to all Saxon *Kreis* committees, 8 February 1946, SAPMO-BA, ZPA, IV 2/9.04/697.

25. "Anweisung über die Durchführung der Prüfungen zur Aufnahme in die Vorstudienanstalt Berliner Hochschulen," in Lammel, *Dokumente,* 1:78–80. In Saxony-Anhalt applicants had to present certificates attesting to their "work achievements" as well as evidence of "social" activity. Kasper, *Der Kampf,* 151, 156. For a description of the early work of these organizations, see Broszat and Weber, *SBZ-Handbuch;* Pike, *Politics of Culture.*

26. In August 1946, for example, Captain Komarov of the Rostock Soviet Kommandantura requested from Rector Rienäcker of Rostock exact figures on party membership of professors and students. UAR, RIII I/2, Bd. 1.

27. The records of the meetings are contained in AUJ, S III 11. A press campaign of the fall of 1945 confirmed the PPR's determination to change the social composition of the student body. A PPR resolution alleged that "as a result of their social composition, most universities have become bases for activities of the National Armed Forces (NSZ) and other reactionary groups." Lewandowski, *Rodowód,* 29–31. The NSZ was a national extremist section of the Polish resistance in World War II. See Ciechanowski in Leslie, Polonsky, Ciechanowski, and Pełczyński, *History of Poland,* 233–34.

28. The university in Poznań accepted every applicant. Of 3,462 candidates, Warsaw University refused only 492, of whom 382 had applied for medicine. Only 8 candidates for the humanities were turned down. Similar figures were

recorded in Toruń and Lublin. Jagiellonian University allowed people with uncertain documentation to enroll as auditors, with the understanding that they could continue if they passed examinations. Lewandowski, *Rodowód*, 58–60. Universities were instructed to have understanding for candidates without proper documentation, assuming it may have been destroyed during the war. Letter from Education Undersecretary Bieńkowski, 10 July 1945, in AUJ, S III/254.

29. Rektorat UJ to Ministerstwo Oświaty, 27 October 1945. AUJ, WP III 75.

30. Inexplicably, the decree made no mention of social class. Its preamble read: "The six-year interruption in the normal functioning of our school system means that in the course of the next several years universities will be confronted with a catastrophic decrease in the influx of candidates who possess full preparation for higher education." "Dekret z dnia 24 maja 1945 o utworzeniu wstępnego roku studiów w szkołach wyższych," *Dziennik Ustaw* Nr. 21: Poz. 122 (1945).

31. For a frank contemporary account, see sociologist Nina Assorodobraj's "Kursy przygotowawcze." A report of the PPR Central Committee's education official of July 1946 explicitly recognized the "efforts" of ZWM Życie in "organizing preparatory courses in every university city." AAN, KC PPR 295/XVII/2, k. 1.

32. AAN, MO 2864, k. 75–76.

33. AAN, MO 2878, k. 131–33.

34. AAN, KC PPR 295/XVII/61, k. 84.

35. AAN, MO 2878, k. 130–40.

36. All the mentioned reports are in AAN, MO 2878.

37. In 1948, they were still not keeping records of this sort. See the letters of the law faculty dean to the rector, 23 June 1947, 2 June 1948, AUJ, WP III 75.

38. The category "intellectual workers" (*umysłowi pracownicy*) was quite flexible, better suited to assuaging the Party's fears of remaining isolated at universities than to analytical precision; the reporter of the Ministry of Education's "recruitment department" wrote for the 1947–48 admissions process that "under the category of intellectual workers is hidden undoubtedly an entire range of people who in essence are not intellectual workers." AAN, MO 2869, k. 10.

39. AAN, KC PPR 295/XVII/61, k. 590.

40. AAN, MO 2876, k. 28–31.

41. AAN, KC PPR 295/XVII/61, k. 41–43. The PPR voivodeship committees were to appoint the representatives of the Ministry of Education.

42. The "freeing from examinations was meant to bring about basic changes in the social structure of universities." Report of the "recruitment department" of the Ministry of Education for 1947–48, AAN, MO 2869, k. 10.

43. AAN, KC PPR 295/XVII/61, k. 41–43. Candidates supported by the PPR thus passed the entrance exam but failed to be admitted, because their relative performance was poor. In Wrocław 30 percent of the PPR candidates stumbled this way in 1947. AAN, MO 2869, k. 15.

44. The secret police (UB) was supposed to inform commissions about individuals who could not be accepted for reasons of political "hostility." See the reports of Toruń and Poznań in AAN, KC PPR 295/XVII/61, k. 334, 373.

45. AAN, KC PPR 295/XVII/61, k. 308, 308a.

46. See, for example, the reports from Poznań that veterans' associations had tried to "frustrate" the "recruiting action" by "bombarding" the commissions with

various certifications and petitions. AAN, KC PPR 295/XVII/61, k. 334, 335, 340.

47. AAN, MO 2869, k. 9–12.

48. AAN, KC PPR 295/XVII/61, k. 429, 429a. There were also students sympathetic to the PPR who did not join because of the underground "terror reigning in their regions." Report of 17 August 1948, AAN, MO 2869, k. 4–8.

49. AAN, KC PPR 295/XVII/61, k. 14–14a.

50. From entrance exams to the medical faculty, 20 September 1948. AAN, MO 2869, k. 21–26.

51. AAN, MO 2869, k. 47–50.

52. From "Sprawozdanie z akcji doboru kandydatów do szkół wyższych w r.szk. 1949–50." AAN, MO 2869, k. 76–77, 81–82.

53. The breakthrough achieved at this point in students' class background seemed clear to later observers. A report from 1951 on the state university in Lublin noted that "the growth of the ZMP organization at our university is very weak. This is caused by the fact that the percentage of organized students in the first years of studies is very high (sometimes above 90 percent), but in the older years students are mostly not organized and are often class-alien." AAN, KC PZPR 237/XVI/86, k. 68.

54. AAN, KC PZPR 237/XVI/134, k. 35–36.

55. No attempt was made to involve the PZPR in the appointment of these secretaries; their work was left entirely in the hands of the ZMP and ZAMP. See the "Instrukcja dla sekretarzy technicznych komisji dla doboru kandydatów na I-szy rok studiów państwowych szkół wyższych" (undated), in AAN, MO 2866, k. 13–15.

56. AAN, MO 2869, k. 33–46.

57. AAN, MO 2867, k. 71–72; AAN, KC PZPR 237/XVI/100, k. 5; AAN, KC PZPR 237/XVI/133, k. 1; "Wpisy na I rok studiów w Uniwersytet Jagielloński" (undated), in AUJ, S III 248.

58. AAN, KC PZPR 237/XVI/131, k. 50.

59. AAN, KC PZPR 237/XVI/100, k. 4.

60. See the statistical breakdowns in AAN, MSW 1174.

61. AAN, KC PZPR 237/XVI/131, k. 6, 20–21.

62. AAN, KC PZPR 237/XVI/131, k. 21–22, 32, 46.

63. AAN, KC PZPR 237/XVI/131, k. 48.

64. AAN, KC PZPR 237/XVI/134, k. 35–36.

65. AAN, MO 2869, k. 78. Of the 106,919 students of all five years of studies in Poland in November 1949, 70,112 (65.6 percent) belonged to Group I, 24,563 (23 percent) to Group II, and 12,244 (11.5 percent) to Group III. AAN, MO 2852, k. 206.

66. AAN, MO 2869, k. 79–81.

67. The commissions consisted of the cell's instructor (that is, propaganda expert), a Party activist, and a delegate of the region's ZMP. AAN, KC PZPR 237/XVI/131, k. 76.

68. AAN, KC PZPR 237/XVI/128, k. 17.

69. AAN, KC PZPR 237/XVI/127, k. 6.

70. AAN, KC PZPR 237/XVI/125, k. 36–38.

71. Report of 2 April 1952. AAN, KC PZPR 237/XVI/120, k. 131.

72. At the mechanical, electrical, and civil engineering faculties in Gliwice, the Party had three of five seats; at the chemical engineering faculty, five of five. In Szczecin 80 percent of commission members were PZPR members; they had been chosen by the Voivodeship Committee in agreement with the trade unions and ZAMP. In fact, the ZAMP functionaries represented the peasant union. AAN, KC PZPR 237/XVI/125, k. 10–11; 130, k. 26–27, 34–38.

73. See the report of 1950 from Kraków. AAN, MSW 1176, k. 94.

74. Petrusewicz to PZPR voivodeship committees, 18 September 1950. AAN, KC PZPR 237/XVI/20, k. 26. Officially, attention would be paid only to the "social work of the children." "Rozporządzenie Ministrów Oświaty i Zdrowia w sprawie trybu postępowania przy przymowaniu kandydatów na I rok studiów do szkół wyższych na rok szkolny 1950–51" (undated), in AUJ, S III 254; telegram from minister of higher education to rectors, 16 September 1950, AUJ, S III 254.

75. Meeting of the Organizational Bureau of the PZPR, 23 June 1952. AAN, BO KC PZPR, t. 25, p. 175.

76. Kolankiewicz, "Technical Intelligentsia," 189.

77. In 1954 the Ministry of Education, concerned about the high dropout rate of many students, ordered that only candidates be accepted who seemed likely to finish studies successfully and on time. This was to end the "mechanistic" discrimination against the "working intelligentsia." Ciesielski, "Rekrutacja," 160.

78. For SED functionaries' obsession with plan fulfillment, see the minutes of the meeting of Kurt Hager with functionaries in Saxony, 7 December 1951, SAPMO-BA, ZPA, IV 2/9.04/698.

79. Groups mentioned included parliamentary representatives, winners of the "National Prize," people who had been persecuted by the Nazi regime, heroes of labor, deserving physicians of the people, deserving teachers of the people, deserving inventors, deserving activists, deserving coal miners, and the best in the professional competition of German youth. The children of scientists returning from Soviet deportation were also given recognition. This did not, however, mean a surrendering of high quotas for worker-peasant applicants. Stallmann, *Hochschulzugang,* 321–27; Lammel, *Dokumente,* 2:87–89.

80. Richert, *"Sozialistische Universität,"* 112.

81. The Polish recruiting guidelines of April 1952 reflected a gradual evolution toward preference of political and economic usefulness over social background. They maintained three groups, the first of which would consist of "children of heroes of labor, production workers, members of collectives [*spółdzielni produkcyjnych*], the upwardly mobile intelligentsia, teachers, the creative and technical intelligentsia," the second of children of "small and medium peasants, workers for hire (blue- and white-collar), and the children of craftsmen who are members of collectives [*spółdzielni pracy*]." All other candidates would be admitted according to abilities. AAN, KC PZPR 237/XVI/34, k. 20–21. This signaled a decline in the position of peasants, who had once been accorded a position equivalent to that of workers. See "Rozporządzenie Ministra Oświaty," 19 May 1948, AUJ, S III 254. From 1951 there was greater emphasis on academic qualifications among worker-peasant youth in East Germany. Stallmann, *Hochschulzugang,* 326–27.

82. See, for example, "Analyse über die wissenschaftliche und politische Arbeit an

der Karl-Marx-Universität," 9 November 1954, SSA, IV 4.14/53, Bl. 14–16; "Bericht über die Immatrikulation für das Studienjahr 1955–56 an der Karl-Marx-Universität Leipzig," "Die Auswahl der Studienbewerber zum Studienjahr 1957–58 und Vorschläge zur Verbesserung der Zulassungsarbeit im Jahre 1958," 10 December 1957, SAPMO-BA, ZPA, IV 2/9.04/477, Bl. 38, 184.

83. Assorodobraj, "Kursy przygotowawcze," 132–33.

84. "Stenographische Niederschrift des Referats des Genossen Anton Ackermann auf der Arbeitstagung über die Frage der Auswahl und Zulassung zum Hochschulstudium; Freitag den 6.Mai 1949," 15. SAPMO-BA, ZPA, IV 2/9.04/464. In a speech of 1925 N. I. Bukharin had vowed to "process" intellectuals "as in a factory." Fitzpatrick, *The Cultural Front*, 61.

85. "Stenographische Niederschrift über die Konferenz von Angehörigen der Hochschulen am Sonnabend, dem 22. November 1947, und Sonntag, dem 23. November 1947 im Hause des Kulturbundes, Berlin," 42. SAPMO-BA, ZPA, IV 2/9.04/6.

86. In the words of Anton Ackermann: "We want to change not only the social composition of university students; more important is that this newly trained intelligentsia be educated and schooled in the spirit of a new ideology, in the spirit of scientific socialism." "Stenographische Niederschrift über die Hochschulkonferenz der SED am 13. und 14. September 1947 im Hause des Kulturbundes," 6, SAPMO-BA, ZPA, IV 2/9.04/6.

87. "Stenographische Niederschrift des Referats des Genossen Anton Ackermann auf der Arbeitstagung über die Frage der Auswahl und Zulassung zum Hochschulstudium; Freitag den 6. Mai 1949," 7–9. SAPMO-BA, ZPA, IV 2/9.04/464. In April 1949 the Small Secretariat of the SED Politburo had determined that "in order to arrive at a more precise description of the concept 'worker' the directives will indicate that all candidates count as 'workers' who have been professionally active as workers since 1945. All candidates whose parents have been professionally active as workers since 1942 will be counted as workers' children." SAPMO-BA, ZPA, JIV 2/3/018. For the application of these guidelines in Saxony, see the letter of the Saxon *Land* government to the education offices of the cities and counties of 26 May 1949, UAL, Rektorat 305, Bl. 22–25. The definition of worker was simplified for admissions in 1950 to both universities and worker-peasant faculties: "anyone who after finishing elementary school [*Volksschule*] worked as a worker." In other words, it was someone who had been a worker since birth, and never left that station. A peasant was someone who had no more than ten hectares of "good soil" or fifteen hectares of "poor soil." BAAP, R2/1224, Bl. 2, 6. In the mid-1950s, the definition of "worker child" was relaxed somewhat to include offspring of those who had worked at least five years as workers since 1945. Report of 4 September 1957, SAPMO-BA, ZPA, IV 2/9.02/477, Bl. 152–58.

88. In February 1950 the Ministry of Education in Weimar inquired whether petty officials (*kleine Angestellte*) such as messengers could be considered workers, because their "earnings and work are similar to those of workers." The GDR Ministry of Education responded that to begin accepting petty officials would "endanger the intended purpose" of the guidelines. BAAP, R2/1892, Bl. 37–39. Application of guidelines remained strict throughout the 1950s, giving frequent rise to complaints that insufficient attention was devoted to the "politi-

cal development of the applicant's family [*Elternhaus*]." Report of 4 September 1957, SAPMO-BA, ZPA, IV 2/9.02/477, Bl. 152–58. For complaints of the systematic privileging of worker students to the detriment of students from officials' or artisans' households who had greater "political clarity," see the report of 10 December 1957, SAPMO-BA, ZPA, IV 2/9.02/477, Bl. 183–87.

89. "Stenographische Niederschrift des Referats des Genossen Anton Ackermann auf der Arbeitstagung über die Frage der Auswahl und Zulassung zum Hochschulstudium; Freitag den 6. Mai 1949," 7–9. SAPMO-BA, ZPA, IV 2/9.04/464. Later, there was a strong tendency to review favorably the complaints from officials who were Party members. Report of 10 December 1957, SAPMO-BA, ZPA, IV 2/9.02/477, Bl. 187.

90. Workers who were identified as "enemies of German unity" or "saboteurs of the reconstruction of Germany" lost their preference in student admissions. BAAP, R2/1898, Bl. 1. The Party executive of Humboldt University reported in 1955 that "not all worker-peasant children could be admitted this year, because on the one hand not all can be considered worker-peasant children according to their behavior [*Haltung*], for example churchgoers, and on the other, some room has to remain for children of the intelligentsia." Beschlussprotokoll der Parteileitung der SED, Humboldt-Universität zu Berlin, 24 May 1955, SAPMO-BA, ZPA, IV 2/9.04/489, Bl. 30. There was also a complete unwillingness in the Party press to acknowledge that the strikers of 17 June 1953 had been workers.

91. From his speech of 6 May 1949, Kowalczuk, *Legitimation*, 96–97. On the insufficiency of information on social class alone, see the directive of State Secretary Harig at the *Collegium* meeting of 24 August 1954 to get "even more information from schools on students' family lives [*Elternhaus*]," and not "simply the father's profession," as was usually the case. BAAP, R3/151, Bl. 111.

92. "Stenographische Niederschrift des Referats des Genossen Anton Ackermann auf der Arbeitstagung über die Fragen der Auswahl und Zulassung zum Hochschulstudium," 6 May 1949. SAPMO-BA, ZPA, IV 2/9.04/464.

93. Ibid., 4. This was an echo of Stalin's dictum: "cadres decide everything."

94. Fijałkowska, *Polityka i twórcy*, 464.

95. They had to be delegated by their factory or the Peasants' Mutual Aid Society, and the act of delegation had to be approved by the local state education office. See the regulations of 20 March 1950, SAPMO-BA, ZPA, IV 2/9.04/465.

96. In 1952, 43 percent of the students at Warsaw University and 51 percent of the students at Wrocław University belonged to the ZMP. The figures at the medical academies in Warsaw and Wrocław and at the Academy of Mining and Metallurgy in Kraków were over 70 percent. AAN, KC PZPR 237/XVI/15, k. 9.

97. AAN, KC PZPR 237/XVI/126, k. 3–22.

98. "Stenographische Niederschrift über die Hochschulkonferenz der SED am 13. und 14. September 1947 im Hause des Kulturbundes," 5. SAPMO-BA, ZPA, IV 2/9.04/6.

99. AAN, KC PZPR 237/XVI/126, k. 3–22.

100. See the report of the voivodeship delegate for student recruitment in Kraków of 2 August 1952, which identifies *bikiniarzy* and others as enemies, quite independent of their social class. It is especially attentive to family history, and whether close relatives have been arrested for antiregime activity, for example,

in one case for the murder of PPR functionaries. AUJ, DM 20. In 1951, 751 persons were identified in Poland who "must not be admitted to universities." The list focused on the identities of the fathers. AAN, KC PZPR 237/XVI/135, k. 15–35.

101. Professor Horst Pätzold, then a student in Rostock, recalls how he and his "bourgeois" friends felt "threatened" by the new admissions regulations. *Nischen,* 170–74. For signs of resentment toward the new students, see chapter 6 at n. 72.

102. Brzezinski, *The Soviet Bloc,* 79.

103. For reference to the deadlines it set for registration, see the letter of 15 July 1946 of the *Land* government to Leipzig University, UAL, Rektorat 307a.

104. Minutes of the university senate, 31 July 1946. UAL, Rektorat 1.

105. Muller, *The Other God,* 220–21, 280–82.

106. Meeting of 16 August 1947, UAL, Rektorat 1.

107. Wójcik, "Przebieg," 165. Some worker students were called "double-zeros" because they had taken a succession of courses meant for beginners: the preparation courses and "introductory year"—both "zero years."

108. Letter to Ministry of Education, 28 November 1946. AAN, MO 2879.

109. Kolankiewicz, "Technical Intelligentsia," 184.

110. Of the worker students graduating from the Łódź course between 1947 and 1949, 21.6 percent belonged to the PPR/PZPR; of those graduating from 1950 to 1952, 7.0 percent were members of the Party. One reason suggested for the decline was the increasingly young age of participants. Olczak, "Skład," 133–34. At later workplaces graduates of worker courses were hesitant to reveal their educational background, for fear of discrimination. In general they were quite satisfied both with their professions and with the preparation the courses had given, however.

111. "Bericht über den Besuch der Leipziger Juristen-Fakultät am 15. und 16. Juli 1947." UAL, Rektorat 122, Bl. 82.

112. SSA, IV 4.14/27, Bl. 73–84.

113. Wójcik, "Przebieg," 170–73.

114. Ibid., 145–46.

115. A report from Leipzig of 1956 complained that graduates of the ABF had not presented their graduating certificates (equivalent of the *Abitur*), and might end up in subjects like medicine, physics, chemistry, and German, in which "too many" ABF graduates had failed in recent years. SAPMO-BA, ZPA, IV 2/9.04/477, Bl. 37.

116. Another eighty had tuberculosis. BAAP, R2/1371, Bl. 115. For a report of students contracting tuberculosis at Jagiellonian University's worker course, see the letter of Becki to Erdstein, 22 September 1953, AUJ, Sprzy 11.

117. AAN, KC PPR 295/XVII/61, k. 50, 53, 55.

118. AAN, MO 2878, k. 133a. In Łódź the difficulties in getting teachers and classroom space were so severe that the rector of the Polytechnic felt that holding a second introductory year was "a purpose impossible to realize." AAN, MO 2879, k. 15–16. For similar problems in Wrocław, see AAN, MO 2879, k. 8.

119. AAN, KC PPR 295/XVII/61, k. 334, 335, 340.

120. AAN, MSW 1176, k. 94. One might object that such cases existed in the other countries but were simply not found. This, however, would imply that a smaller Polish Party was better at detecting corruption than the far larger

Czech and East German apparatuses. The East German Party, moreover, was reinforced by Soviet military authorities, which had their own police and justice arms. For failed attempts by rejected students at bribing the prorector for student affairs in Leipzig in 1955, see SAPMO-BA, ZPA, IV 2/9.04/477, Bl. 39. In a *Collegium* meeting of 24 August 1954, State Secretary Harig noted that there had been no reports from the provinces whatsoever on "personal contacts playing a role in admissions committees, or of bribery." BAAP, R3/151, Bl. 111.

121. For accounts of this submilieu, see Walczak, *Ruch studencki;* Kuroń, *Wiara i wina;* Słabek, *Intelektualistów,* 54-80. For a critical discussion of ZAMP work at Wrocław University, see Suleja, *Uniwersytet Wrocławski,* 270-94. Neither the archival materials that I have reviewed nor these works give much sense of the sociocultural backgrounds of these young enthusiasts.

122. See Schneider, *Bildung;* Lewandowski, *Rodowód.*

123. See, for example, Szczepański, *Ze studiów;* Jerschina, *Osobowość społeczna,* 17-18.

CHAPTER 13

1. Fitzpatrick, *Education,* 118; Somr, *Dějiny,* 305.

2. Speech to the Central Committee of 17 November 1948. SÚA, AÚV KSČ, f. 19/7, a.j. 359, l. 4.

3. Pelikán, *Ein Frühling,* 76. Pelikán resided in Rome from 1970 to his death in 1999, and in 1979 was elected by the Italian Socialist Party as its representative at the European Parliament. Pelikán also judges that this democratization largely succeeded. Also Čestmír Císař, who had a leading role in the Party's cultural and educational bureaucracy of that time, believed that policies of affirmative action for workers largely succeeded. Císař interview.

4. SÚA, AÚV KSČ, f. 19/7, a.j. 308, l. 28-30.

5. SÚA, AÚV KSČ, f. 19/7, a.j. 260, l. 2.

6. SÚA, AÚV KSČ, f. 100/1, a.j. 1155, l. 17.

7. SÚA, AÚV KSČ, f. 19/7, a.j. 308, l. 28-30. Functionaries in the Central Action Committee recognized that there had been cases of "bureaucratic interrogations and police tactics" in the purging that they could not control. They had supposedly intended "a positive, friendly, persuasive character of the screening." SÚA, AÚV KSČ, f. 100/1, a.j. 1155, l. 17. For complaints of expulsions of KSČ members, see SÚA, AÚV KSČ, f. 19/7, a.j. 308, l. 28-30.

8. SÚA, AÚV KSČ, f. 02/4, a.j. 113, b. 19, l. 1-8.

9. SÚA, AÚV KSČ, f. 19/7, a.j. 288, l. 21-22.

10. SÚA, AÚV KSČ, f. 100/1, a.j. 1155, l. 15.

11. Circular No. 16, Ministerstvo sociální péče, 1 February 1949. SÚA, ÚPV, č.k. 1259, i.č. 1477.

12. Pelikán, *Ein Frühling,* 77.

13. See the extensive reports: SÚA, AÚV KSČ, f. 19/7, a.j. 260, l. 2-7; a.j. 288, l. 21-22; a.j. 308, l. 28-30; f. 100/1, a.j. 1155, l. 12, 16-19; f. 02/4, a.j. 174/27, l. 3-6.

14. Malý interview. Over 10,000 students were expelled by March 1949, almost three times the number who had indicated interest in studying in Germany in 1942. SÚA, AÚV KSČ, f. 02/4, a.j. 113/19, l. 1-8.

15. SÚA, AÚV KSČ, f. 02/4, a.j. 174/27, l. 3-6.

16. See the report on a campaign launched by the KSČ newspaper in Jihlava in

July 1951 against "enemies" studying at Prague's Higher School of Economics. "Chats" were arranged for each senior on "life, work, and political views." Twenty-five students were not permitted to continue. SÚA, AÚV KSČ, f. 19/7, a.j. 299, l. 57.

17. See chapter 8 at nn. 20–22.

18. Václav Pavlíček, "Čísla která nutí k zamyšlení," *Tvorba* 15 (1957): 3. In the 1953–54 school year, 26.6 percent of all Charles University students, and 36.8 percent of its law students, were of worker or peasant background. "Statistika škol a zařízení spravovaných ministrem škol za školní rok 1953–54," SÚA, ÚPV, i.č. 2481. Education Minister František Kahuda likewise pointed to the low number of students of working-class origin to account for the student demonstrations. *Neue Zürcher Zeitung*, 7 July 1956.

19. McClelland, "Proletarianizing," 142. On the continuing importance of social background in determining access to higher education in and beyond East Central Europe, see Shavit and Blossfeld, *Persistent Inequality*.

20. SÚA, AÚV KSČ, f. 19/7, a.j. 358, l. 17–18. For students per age cohort, see introduction, n. 18.

21. "Zákon ze dne 21. dubna 1948 o základní úpravě jednotného školství (školský zákon)," *Sbírka zákonů*, č. 95/1948, 831–33.

22. SÚA, AÚV KSČ, f. 19/7, a.j. 358, l. 11–15.

23. The rest were divided among small businessmen (9.7 percent), pensioners (5.7 percent), and large farmers (3.9 percent). SÚA, AÚV KSČ, f. 19/7, a.j. 260, l. 37.

24. SÚA, AÚV KSČ, f. 19/7, a.j. 359, l. 109–11.

25. SÚA, AÚV KSČ, f. 19/7, a.j. 260, l. 39.

26. In 1949, of 33,869 applicants in Poland, 22,438 were accepted. AAN, KC PZPR 237/XVI/134, k. 35–36. For the 1951–52 class of 23,588, 9,126 students were rejected. AAN, MSW 1191, k. 17, 80, 91–92. In East Germany, the plan was difficult to fulfill in 1951, but "thereafter there was always considerably more demand for university studies than supply." In the Halle region, for example, over half the high school graduates (*Abiturienten*) were rejected in 1952. Stallmann, *Hochschulzugang*, 330–31. Throughout the GDR, over 8,000 young people applied for fewer than 4,000 places in technical subjects that year. BAAP, E1/17049, Bl. 84. There were 27,000 applications for 17,000 spots in the 1955–56 school year. SAPMO-BA, ZPA, IV 2/9.04/477, Bl. 17. In 1956, the Technical University in Dresden accepted 1,000 of 3,000 applicants. SAPMO-BA, ZPA, IV 2/9.04/477, Bl. 80.

27. In the 1951–52 school year, 36 percent of first-year *gimnazjum* students in Poland were of working-class, and 31.4 percent of peasant origin. Pęcherski, "Das Schulwesen," 293. By 1954, the percentage of worker-peasant children had risen to 49.0 percent at East German high schools (*Oberschulen*). Stallmann, *Hochschulzugang*, 150.

28. The additional places at higher schools would be filled by about 1,700 graduates of special preparatory schools for worker-peasants, the ADKs (*absolventy dělnických kursů*, or graduates of worker courses).

29. SÚA, AÚV KSČ, f. 19/7, a.j. 278, l. 287. Only slightly more than 1,300 ADKs would enter higher schools in 1950, however. SÚA, AÚV KSČ, f. 19/7, a.j. 290, l. 2.

30. SÚA, AÚV KSČ, f. 19/7, a.j. 316, l. 22.

31. SÚA, AÚV KSČ, f. 19/7, a.j. 300, l. 11–12.

32. SÚA, AÚV KSČ, f. 19/7, a.j. 300, l. 85–86.

33. SÚA, AÚV KSČ, f. 19/7, a.j. 359, l. 121.

34. SÚA, AÚV KSČ, f. 19/7, a.j. 302, l. 20.

35. SÚA, AÚV KSČ, f. 19/7, a.j. 279, l. 170.

36. See chapter 11 at n. 91.

37. This was an improvement over the 38.6 percent of the previous year. SÚA, AÚV KSČ, f. 19/7, a.j. 279, l. 170.

38. SÚA, AÚV KSČ, f. 19/7, a.j. 302, l. 118.

39. The figures are from October 1948. SÚA, AÚV KSČ, f. 19/7, a.j. 358, l. 11–15.

40. SÚA, AÚV KSČ, f. 19/7, a.j. 359, l. 123. In December 1952 a member of the planning staff explained the drop-off in high school graduates by the fact that in 1945 there had been a return to five-class primary schools in the Czech lands in place of the four-class schools the Nazi occupiers had decreed. This meant a decrease by 46 percent in numbers of students who had started the then eight-class high school (gymnázium). "Informace pro soudruha Ministra," 6 December 1952, SÚA, SÚP, č.k. 435. Yet other evidence makes clear that this shortfall was foreseeable from the moment Communists seized power in 1948, but that planners preferred to bolster other kinds of secondary education for immediate needs. In the years 1948–53 numbers of students in vocational high schools went from 92,610 to 115,088, and in industrial high schools from 28,440 to 49,457. Numbers of students in gymnázia decreased from 70,440 to 40,289. Dąbrowska-Zembrzuska, Szkolnictwo, 73–74.

41. The general idea was to approximate the Soviet school, which prepared students for a five-year university in ten years. In a speech before the Czechoslovak National Assembly of 24 April 1953 Minister of Education E. Sýkora made explicit reference to the decisions of the CPSU Nineteenth Party Congress to create a general ten-year high school within the current Five-Year Plan. Dąbrowska-Zembrzuska, Szkolnictwo, 85–87. Soviet visitors had urged the shortening of Czech university preparation in order to enable the lengthening of university studies to five years. They warned that otherwise graduates of Czech universities might fall behind graduates of Soviet universities in the quality of their knowledge. Minister Nejedlý, and the majority of education experts, favored cutting only the gymnázium by a year. The Political Secretariat of the Central Committee chose the more radical solution. SÚA, AÚV KSČ, f. 19/7, a.j. 283, l. 38–57. Yet because of the inability of graduates of eleven-year high schools to function well at university, a reform of 1960 introduced a nine-year basic school, followed by a three-year high school for those choosing to apply for university. Dąbrowska-Zembrzuska, Szkolnictwo, 96–106.

42. "Zákon ze dne 24. dubna 1953 o školské soustavě a vzdělávání učitelů (školský zákon)," 23 April 1953, Sbírka zákonů, č. 31/1953, 193–95. Urban, Die Organisation, 211.

43. Letter of State Planning Commission to Minister of Education Ernest Sýkora, 15 July 1953. SÚA, SÚP, č.k. 435. In order to meet the plan for university freshmen in 1954–55, the planners suggested keeping juniors in high school.

44. Letter from Štoll to Široký, 18 February 1954. SÚA, ÚPV, i.č. 2474, sig. 12/3.83.3.

45. See, for example, the extensive reports in SÚA, SÚP, č.k. 435, which fail to project the numbers of worker students to be accepted into university freshmen classes.

46. SÚA, AÚV KSČ, f. 19/7, a.j. 349, l. 63.

47. SÚA, AÚV KSČ, f. 19/7, a.j. 265, l. 55; f. 02/4, a.j. 176, l. 10.

48. SÚA, AÚV KSČ, f. 19/7, a.j. 349, l. 47-48.

49. SÚA, AÚV KSČ, f. 19/7, a.j. 347, l. 180.

50. In another case, a number of middle-class children were recommended for high school, but the regional commission revoked their acceptance. This left the town with one class of high school students instead of the two that were planned. SÚA, AÚV KSČ, f. 19/7, a.j. 347, l. 180. In general, the report said, teachers did not even know the social origin of their students.

51. Still *gymnázia* had the poorest worker representation of any type of post–middle school form (44.5 percent). SÚA, AÚV KSČ, f. 19/7, a.j. 347, l. 223. For similar reports on the resistance of workers to sending children to higher education, see SÚA, AÚV KSČ, f. 19/7, a.j. 349, l. 54-55 (Hradec Králové); and SÚA, AÚV KSČ, f. 19/7, a.j. 252/2, l. 99-100 (Ostrava).

52. SÚA, AÚV KSČ, f. 19/7, a.j. 347, l. 234.

53. SÚA, AÚV KSČ, f. 19/7, a.j. 349, l. 8.

54. SÚA, AÚV KSČ, f. 19/7, a.j. 349, l. 16-17. For similar reports from Prague see SÚA, AÚV KSČ, f. 19/7, a.j. 349, l. 26.

55. A colleague in Humpolce likewise attested bourgeois children unfit for physical labor. SÚA, AÚV KSČ, f. 19/7, a.j. 349, l. 8-9.

56. SÚA, AÚV KSČ, f. 02/5, a.j. 79, b. 4, l. 2.

57. Stipends might have been especially useful for families who took their children out of school because of distance. SÚA, AÚV KSČ, f. 19/7, a.j. 347, l. 72-73.

58. SÚA, AÚV KSČ, f. 19/7, a.j. 347, l. 72-73.

59. SÚA, AÚV KSČ, f. 19/7, a.j. 359, l. 4.

60. SÚA, AÚV KSČ, f. 19/7, a.j. 260, l. 2-7.

61. AUK, SVS B166.

62. SÚA, AÚV KSČ, f. 19/7, a.j. 290, l. 8.

63. SÚA, AÚV KSČ, f. 19/7, a.j. 290, l. 17.

64. SÚA, AÚV KSČ, f. 19/7, a.j. 290, l. 10. A concern that students might want to better their material situation plagued Communists throughout the region. See, for example, the April 1951 communication of the PZPR committee at the Higher Engineering School in Poznań, where students were still burdened with "petty bourgeois residues," and had come to study in order to "earn good money." AAN, KC PZPR 237/XVI/95, k. 61.

65. SÚA, AÚV KSČ, f. 19/7, a.j. 290, l. 77-78.

66. SÚA, AÚV KSČ, f. 19/7, a.j. 290, l. 31.

67. See the 1951 suggestion for extending the courses to two years in order to get more candidates in SÚA, AÚV KSČ, f. 19/7, a.j. 290, l. 133.

68. SÚA, AÚV KSČ, f. 02/4, a.j. 113/21, l. 3.

69. SÚA, AÚV KSČ, f. 19/7, a.j. 290, l. 90, 92.

70. A total of 1,012 entered technical sciences, 62 studied law, 42 science, 58 the arts, 133 education, and 56 medicine; 30 went on to the military medical academy. SÚA, AÚV KSČ, f. 19/7, a.j. 290, l. 29-30.

71. SÚA, AÚV KSČ, f. 19/7, a.j. 290, l. 78.

72. SÚA, AÚV KSČ, f. 02/4, a.j. 107, b. 29, l. 1–2. The breakdown was coordinated with several ministries.

73. SÚA, AÚV KSČ, f. 02/4, a.j. 113, b. 21, l. 3–4. East German Communists issued more precise definitions, aiming at workers involved in production from before the war. See chapter 12 at n. 87.

74. See, for example, records of trip taken by ministry officials to the provinces in March 1950. SÚA, AÚV KSČ, f. 19/7, a.j. 260, l. 19.

75. SÚA, AÚV KSČ, f. 19/7, a.j. 290, l. 78.

76. SÚA, AÚV KSČ, f. 19/7, a.j. 260, l. 175.

77. SÚA, AÚV KSČ, f. 19/7, a.j. 290, l. 121.

78. SÚA, AÚV KSČ, f. 19/7, a.j. 290, l. 78–79.

79. SÚA, AÚV KSČ, f. 100/1, a.j. 1154, l. 34.

80. During the entrance examinations ministry representatives took special pains to make sure that "academic" criteria not prevail: "At the beginning, the method of testing was sometimes a bit academic (Hradec, Ostrava), although in the course of the examinations a correction was made." SÚA, AÚV KSČ, f. 19/7, a.j. 290, l. 107–10, 120–21.

81. Emphasis in original. SÚA, AÚV KSČ, f. 19/7, a.j. 290, l. 107.

82. SÚA, AÚV KSČ, f. 19/7, a.j. 260, l. 178.

83. A report from early 1951 speaks of a very strenuous schedule, with "escalating competition," "daily inspections," "exhausting student meetings," "collective kinds of study in so-called shock-worker groups." SÚA, AÚV KSČ, f. 19/7, a.j. 290, l. 1.

84. SÚA, AÚV KSČ, f. 19/7, a.j. 290, l. 83, 90–92.

85. Course members worked as political agitators and took part in labor "brigades," for example, at mines or construction sites. SÚA, AÚV KSČ, f. 19/7, a.j. 290, l. 115–16.

86. This point was introduced by cadre department chief Bruno Köhler at the meeting of 5 June 1951. SÚA, AÚV KSČ, f. 02/4, a.j. 188, b. 18, l. 3–4.

87. SÚA, AÚV KSČ, f. 19/7, a.j. 260, l. 175.

88. SÚA, AÚV KSČ, f. 19/7, a.j. 260, l. 244.

89. SÚA, AÚV KSČ, f. 19/7, a.j. 265, l. 59.

90. SÚA, AÚV KSČ, f. 19/7, a.j. 265, l. 59; a.j. 260, l. 129, 244.

91. SÚA, AÚV KSČ, f. 19/7, a.j. 290, l. 11–12.

92. SÚA, AÚV KSČ, f. 19/7, a.j. 331, l. 27–29.

93. SÚA, AÚV KSČ, f. 19/7, a.j. 283, l. 25–26.

94. SÚA, AÚV KSČ, f. 19/7, a.j. 283, l. 43.

95. SÚA, AÚV KSČ, f. 19/7, a.j. 290, l. 32.

96. SÚA, AÚV KSČ, f. 19/7, a.j. 290, l. 33–34. See also the report of 27 July 1951, which shows that ADKs did better in agricultural and social sciences, yet worse in mathematics and chemistry. SÚA, AÚV KSČ, f. 19/7, a.j. 287, l. 8.

97. The quality of ADKs fell in successive classes at the Technical University's mechanical engineering faculty, the faculty that had enrolled the greatest numbers of worker-course graduates. In 1951, 27.7 percent of the freshmen and 34 percent of the sophomores there were graduates of worker courses. Their performance was testimony to the weakness of the selection process, and to the inadequacy of one year's preparation, especially in mathematics and descrip-

tive geometry. An increase in instruction of one-half to one year was strongly advised. SÚA, AÚV KSČ, f. 19/7, a.j. 311, l. 28, 34.

98. SÚA, AÚV KSČ, f. 19/7, a.j. 290, l. 32–34; f. 100/1, a.j. 1155, l. 171–72.

99. SÚA, AÚV KSČ, f. 02/4, a.j. 87, l. 2–4.

100. "Stížnosti na s. Valoucha z Brna" (undated). AČAV, Valouch Papers, i.č. 852.

101. Letter to Nejedlý from "Skupina ADK," 12 June 1954, AČAV, Nejedlý Papers, č.k. 24.

102. On the Party's resistance to permitting expelled students to return to universities, see the 8 November 1951 report of Miloslav Valouch, AČAV, Valouch Papers, i.č. 833; also SÚA, AÚV KSČ, f. 19/7, a.j. 288, l. 24.

103. The figure in Poland was about 15 percent. Bauman, "Social Dissent," 124.

104. Somr, *Dějiny,* 301–3.

105. A resolution by "progressive" students of the summer of 1945 included a point demanding "planned admission of students to universities, which guarantees the future intelligentsia a right to work and a decent existence." Havránek, "Studenti," 87–88. Like this, most of the demands aimed at gaining students better conditions of study and work, rather than changing the social constitution of the student body.

106. Zdeněk Nejedlý caused some embarrassment to his Party by proposing in February 1946 that tuition be used to reduce numbers of students. This of course would have prejudiced the poor. SÚA, AÚV KSČ, f. 19/7, a.j. 272, l. 291. In the end the Communists elected not to participate in a bill that introduced entrance examinations as a way of lessening total numbers of students. A copy of the bill can be found in AUK, SVS B14a. Instead, Communist writers now criticized the other parties for allegedly frightening students with the specter of unemployment. SÚA, AÚV KSČ, f. 19/7, a.j. 338, l. 40–41.

107. Letter of 8 February 1946 from the District Committee of the KPD Saxony, Department for Agitation-Propaganda, to all Saxon *Kreis* committees. SAPMO-BA, ZPA, IV 2/9.04/697.

108. For example, see Tent, *The Free University,* 43–45.

109. SAPMO-BA, ZPA, NL 182/933, Bl. 197. A note from Ulbricht's files suggests that "petty-bourgeois" ideology regarding women's studies had yet to be overcome in the Central Committee apparatus, however. In June 1950 a functionary there told an Ulbricht assistant who requested statistics on women that the "question was not so urgent." He was told to go to the Education Ministry himself and get them—although the ministry itself had not yet made these calculations. SAPMO-BA, ZPA, NL 182/933, Bl. 222.

110. B. Skrzeszowska's report to the Central Committee of 31 January 1950 noted that "on the basis of information received up to now the interest of women in recruitment is very weak." AAN, KC PZPR 237/XVI/121, k. 27. For the ministry's efforts to attract women to worker courses by lowering age restrictions, see the letter of Erdstein to ZMP Opole, 8 March 1952, AUJ, Sprzy 31.

111. See "Richtlinien für die Auswahl und Zulassung zu den Arbeiter- und Bauern-fakultäten," early 1950, SAPMO-BA, ZPA, IV 2/9.04/464; "Richtlinien für die Aufnahmen in die Arbeiter-und-Bauern-Fakultäten," 20 March 1950, SAPMO-BA, ZPA, IV 2/9.04/465. The percentage of women at ABFs increased from 27.8 percent in 1951 to 42.8 percent in 1952. BAAP, R3/145, Bl.

29–32. In 1953–54 slightly more than one-quarter of those accepted to worker-peasant faculties were females. BAAP, R3/148, Bl. 132. In July 1954, 3,500 of 12,500 ABF graduates at higher schools were women. Lammel, *Dokumente,* 2:130–43. The 1950–51 recruiting campaign for worker courses in Poland attempted to recruit 40 percent women, but succeeded in enrolling only 24 percent. AAN, KC PZPR 237/XVI/121, k. 11–12; AAN, KC PZPR 237/XVI/121, k. 33, 47.

112. These were, respectively, Z. Zemankowa, E. Krassowska, and B. Skrzeszowska. Mathematician Hugo Steinhaus even accused Eugenia Krassowska, vice-minister of education from 1947 to 1964, of purposely employing female subordinates. He claimed that the "Ministry of Education has a feminine psyche." *Wspomnienia,* 411. Also remarkable is the prominent place of women among Party social scientists, for example, historians N. Gąsiorowska, Ż. Kormanowa, C. Bobińska, M. Turlejska, and Z. Cybulska and sociologist N. Assorodobraj.

113. Report of 3 June 1952. AČAV, Valouch Papers, sig. IV, i.č. 852.

114. Kopecký also alleged that the Central Committee apparatus had been stacked with functionaries "who for the most part do not know the Czech language, and do not know or understand the Czech people." From notes of the provisional Soviet chargé d'affaires in Prague, P. G. Krekoten', 18 September 1951. Murashko, "Delo," 3 (1997): 12–13.

115. See, for example, his communication to Klement Gottwald of 24 November 1952: "Although I submitted myself in my work in the Central Committee apparatus to the directions of Slánský, often accepted his opinions uncritically, adopted his methods and fulfilled his orders and popularized his person, although I was of Jewish origin, he never even in allusions confided in me his intentions, either in whole or in part." SÚA, AÚV KSČ, f. 100/24, a.j. 1168, l. 19–27. Bareš and his wife thanked Gottwald for the "faith" he had in them. For Bareš's "self-criticism" at the December 1951 Central Committee plenary session, as reported by Czech Communist Antonín Novotný to the Soviet embassy, see Murashko, "Delo," 3 (1997): 17.

116. Before he took leave, Nejedlý's declining health had greatly limited his ability to manage educational affairs. SÚA, AÚV KSČ, f. 100/24, a.j. 975, l. 49. Resistance to the radical duplication of Soviet norms was already making Nejedlý an outsider in educational affairs.

117. SÚA, AÚV KSČ, f. 100/24, a.j. 975, l. 35–38.

118. Fitzpatrick, *Education,* 16, 182, 242.

119. For example, the 1948–49 recruiting drive for students in Poland "obligated" Party, youth, trade-union, and peasant organizations to direct to universities "the most gifted and socialized [*uspołeczniona*] worker-peasant youth." AAN, KC PPR 295/XVII/61, k. 14–14a. By February 1950 education authorities in Thuringia had begun delegating workers from factories and machine tractor stations, and no longer recruited for the courses. BAAP, R2/1903, Bl. 52. See also the reports from Mecklenburg of May and December 1950 on instructions to factories to prepare "young activists," that is, the best young workers, for the ABF, BAAP, R2/1903, Bl. 44; R2/1903, Bl. 14. In March 1954 the GDR State Secretariat for Higher Education ordered that high school directors observe the 60 percent quota for worker-peasant students in the admission of

students "in all subjects." SAPMO-BA, ZPA, IV 2/9.04/477, Bl. 11. See also the discussion at nn. 162–66 on the involvement of Walter Ulbricht and Anton Ackermann in worker studies.

120. Authorities in Saxony had begun attracting large classes of worker and peasant students to secondary education through stipends beginning in 1948. BAAP, R2/1893, Bl. 3–4. Numbers of dormitories for high school students dropped in the Czech lands from 157 in 1953–54 to 145 in 1958–59. Dąbrowska-Zembrzuska, *Szkolnictwo,* 190.

121. According to guidelines used in 1952–53, if there were too many applicants for a given discipline "the least able" were to be rejected. "Směrnice pro přijímání studentů na vysoké školy ve studijním roce 1952–53," SÚA, AÚV KSČ, f. 02/5, sv. 27, a.j. 98, l. 1–5. The 1949–50 guidelines had given priority among "able applicants" to the children of "a/ workers [*dělníků*], b/ small farmers, c/ remaining laborers [*pracujících*]." No definition was made of these categories, and no provisions were made for university admissions commissions to investigate the accuracy of candidates' statements. "Směrnice k výnosu MŠVU ze dne 18. května 1949, č. 72.200/49-III/1, o přijímání do I. ročníku vysokých škol universitního a technického směru ve studijním roce 1948–49," SÚA, MŠK, č.k. 309, sig. 3II/A.

122. "Richtlinien für die Zulassung zum Studium an den Universitäten und Hochschulen der Deutschen Demokratischen Republik für das Jahr 1950," 12 April 1950, BAAP, R2/1224, Bl. 1–3; Stallmann, *Hochschulzugang,* 326–37.

123. "Richtlinien für die Auswahl und Zulassung von Abiturienten" (undated [1950]), BAAP, R2/1371, Bl. 213. For provisions in the Czech case see "Směrnice k výnosu MŠVU ze dne 18. května 1949, č. 72.200/49-III/1, o přijímání do I. ročníku vysokých škol universitního a technického směru ve studijním roce 1948–49," SÚA, MŠK, č.k. 309, sig. 3II/A.

124. SÚA, AÚV KSČ, f. 19/7, a.j. 321, l. 124–25.

125. Brabec, "Životní úroveň," 1072. This trend worsened. From the 1970s to the 1980s the average pay in the cultural sphere dropped from 89.1 percent of the national average to 65.5 percent. Korovitsyna, "Novaia intelligentsiia," 132.

126. Krejčí, *Social Change,* 71–72.

127. SÚA, AÚV KSČ, f. 100/3, a.j. 25, l. 1.

128. Underlining in original in pencil. GARF, f. 5283, op. 22, d. 462, l. 81.

129. Cited in Connor, *Socialism,* 220. The KSČ was indeed a heavily working-class Party. About 15 percent of the population were members of the KSČ in the pre-1948 period, but among workers the total was close to 25 percent, and among intellectuals about 13 percent. Maňák, "Sociální aspekty," 679. In 1946, 68 percent of KSČ members were blue-collar workers, compared with 64.5 percent of Polish and 42.6 percent of Hungarian Communists. That percentage in the KSČ would drop continually, however, to 40.7 percent in 1955, and 32.9 percent in 1965. Grzymala-Busse, "Communist Party Strategies."

130. The proportion of industrial workers was greater in rural communes with under 2,000 inhabitants than it was in urban areas of more than 50,000. Otherwise, the development of industry in Bohemia approximated the "classical" patterns of Western Europe, with similar distribution of sectors, relation between producer and consumer industries, etc. Heumos, "Die Arbeiterschaft," 50–54.

131. On the relatively recent emergence of the Czech intelligentsia from the labor-

ing classes of rural and small-town milieus, see Maňák, "Početnost a struktura," 409.

132. Krejčí, *Social Change,* 104.

133. In 1959 a reporter at the Ministry of Foreign Affairs recommended against attempting to improve the crash courses because "we strive to get our employees from the universities." SÚA, AÚV KSČ, f. 100/3, a.j. 25, l. 62. I am grateful to Igor Lukes for this reference.

134. Schöpflin, *Politics,* 153.

135. Several of its leading figures were among the few worker cadres who had finished university. Foreign policy expert Václav Kotyk and professor of aesthetics Miloš Jůzl were both ADKs. Havránek interview, 11 July 1996; and Kotášek interview, 12 July 1996.

136. In 1964 and 1970 respectively, the top decile in Czechoslovakia and East Germany was receiving 17 percent of the personal income. *Compendium,* 616.

137. The Czech Communists' solution to this "onslaught" was ultimately to purge the student body.

138. BAAP, R2/1060, Bl. 46; Kasper, "Der Kampf," 272.

139. In a report of January 1951, Leipzig dean of students (later state secretary) Gerhard Harig, noted the intense desire of the "petty bourgeois" to attain some "sound position" (*festen Halt*) after the losses of property and other wealth during World War II. "Grundsätzliche Bemerkungen zu einem kommenden Stipendien-Gesetz," BAAP, R2/1893, Bl. 3.

140. "Verordnung über die Regelung des Stipendienwesens an Hoch- und Fachschulen vom 19. Januar 1950," *Gesetzblatt,* no. 4, 24 January 1950, 17–20; "Verordnung über die Gewährung von Stipendien an Studierende der Universitäten und Hochschulen," approved by SED Politburo on 8 February 1955; SAPMO-BA, ZPA, IV 2/2/404, Bl. 48–49.

141. "Instrukcja w sprawie przyznawania stypendiów zwyczajnych studentom pierwszego roku studiów," 25 September 1950. AUJ, DM 14.

142. The lowest stipends were given to those studying medicine, law, economics, and the humanities, the highest to those studying technical subjects like shipbuilding, mining, and metallurgy. See the "Nowe zasady systemu stypendiów," AAN, KC PZPR 237/XVI/149, k. 78–83.

143. "Směrnice pro přiznávání státního studijního stipendia vysokoškolským studentům ve stud. roce 1951–52." SÚA, AÚV KSČ, f. 19/7, a.j. 302/1, l. 35–36.

144. On the unredeemable debt of students to "the people," see the comments of Marie Torhorst, chapter 6 at n. 67.

145. Even in the 1950s, old *Gymnasien* in East Germany managed to reproduce traditional *bildungsbürgerliche* milieus. Worse—in the eyes of the SED—they produced some of the most serious youthful opposition. The longest-lasting and best-organized elaboration of dissent during the GDR's first decade emerged from a high school in the Thuringian town of Eisenberg. See Mühlen, *Der "Eisenberger Kreis."*

146. Haritonow, *Sowjetische Hochschulpolitik,* 235. The Soviets claimed that two years were sufficient.

147. Not until 1951 were Polish worker courses placed at universities. See the decision of the PZPR Politburo, 19 January 1951, AAN, BP KC PZPR, t. 18, p. 4, k. 87–88. The impetus for placing East German worker faculties at universities

seems to have been the success of non-Communist parties in student council elections in late 1947. The SED hoped that the worker students would increase its share of the vote. Schneider, *Bildung,* 17–18.

148. Text in BAAP, R2/900, Bl. 14–15.

149. BAAP, R3/145, Bl. 29–32.

150. BAAP, R3/148, Bl. 132.

151. Speech of Gerhard Harig, 5 July 1954, in Lammel, *Dokumente,* 2:130–43. For the "courageous" behavior of the ABF in Görlitz, which supposedly hindered the destruction of its instructional materials by 1,500 demonstrators, see "Beschlussprotokoll der 23/53. Sitzung des Kollegiums im Staatssekretariat für Hochschulwesen," 23 June 1953, BAAP, R3/147, Bl. 63.

152. Jessen, " 'Entbürgerlichung,' " 68–70; "Zur Sozialgeschichte," 122, 137.

153. Participants at this meeting dwelt at length on numbers of students at various faculties who had failed out, numbers of hours lost due to students missing exercises, and numbers of permissions granted by the rector for students to take time off. "Protokół konferencji odbytej dnia 22 stycznia 1952 roku w Ministerstwie Szk. Wyższego z udziałem Obyw. Min. Krassowskiej, przedstawicieli Uniw. Poznańskiego," 22 January 1952, AAN, MSW 163. On students taking advantage of the central bureaucracy's obsession with numbers, see also AAN, KC PZPR 237/XVI/15, k. 25.

154. For the attributing of problems in plan fulfillment to a characteristically anonymous enemy, see the 1950 report from the Higher School of Economics in Łódź, where the Party's "unremitting struggle to reduce the dropout rate mobilized the enemy." AAN, KC PZPR 237/XVI/91, k. 53–54. See also the minutes of the meeting of the ministry *collegium* of 12 December 1951, AAN, MSW 18; or the minutes of the meeting of the basic PZPR organization of Jagiellonian University, 20 December 1951, APKr, KD PZPR, 62/XV/5, k. 56.

155. Fitzpatrick, *Education.*

156. For the failure in Poland to plan graduate studies or the replacement of professors in philosophical-historical faculties, see the report from Poznań University of 22 June 1954, Rkp BJ Przyb 785/73. For the Czech case, see the ministry order introducing *aspirantura,* MŠVU č. 129 708/50-III/1, 28 September 1950, SÚA, MŠK, č.k. 312.

157. For such cases in Poland, see chapter 12 at n. 118.

158. Using West German information, the East German education authorities estimated that one-ninth (2,500 of 22,000) of the high school graduating class left the GDR in 1957 to pursue studies in the West. Of this number about half were children of academics, and the rest divided among officials, independent artisans, entrepreneurs, and wealthy farmers. Report of 10 December 1957, SAPMO-BA, ZPA, IV 2/9.04/477, Bl. 189. In 1961, 3.4 percent of the male population of West Germany was university-educated. Of the male refugees from East Germany, the percentage was 7.2 percent. Heidemeyer, *Flucht,* 50.

159. Tent, *The Free University,* 256.

160. Rühle, *Idee,* 170, 174.

161. In Prague, see the Gottwald Papers, esp. SÚA, AÚV KSČ, f. 100/24, a.j. 956, 975, 978; and f. 19/7, a.j. 1–346. In Warsaw, see the Party collections AAN, KC PPR 295/XVII; KC PZPR 237/XVI; and the state collections of Ministerstwo Oświaty and Ministerstwo Szkolnictwa Wyższego.

162. In June 1950 Ulbricht demanded that the entering class for worker-peasant faculties that year be increased from 1,500 to 4,500. Ulbricht to Halle, 5 June 1950, BAAP, C20/1019, Bl. 82–85. For other records of Ulbricht's extraordinary activism, see BAAP, C20/16, C20/1011; R2/1892, Bl. 76; R2/1154, Bl. 1; R2/1125, Bl. 115; R2/1478, Bl. 252; R3/223, Bl. 5; E1/17085, Bl. 60–92; E1/17514, Bl. 6; SAPMO-BA, ZPA, NL 182/933; IV 2/9.04/465.

163. BAAP, R2/1892, Bl. 59; BAAP, E1/17050, Bl. 6.

164. They were to complete a first round of visits by 14 June 1950—that is, within ten days of Ulbricht's letter—and then undertake a second round the following week "to inspect the realization of the directives and immediately eliminate any mistakes or shortcomings." The group included Siegfried Wagner of the SED Party Executive (*Parteivorstand*), Peter Heilmann of the FDJ, and Willy Laudien of the Free German Trade Union. O. Halle to Dr. Ludwig, 9 June 1950, BAAP, R2/1371, Bl. 97–99.

165. Kasper, "Der Kampf," 177–78.

166. "Stenographische Niederschrift des Referats des Genossen Anton Ackermann auf der Arbeitstagung über die Frage der Auswahl und Zulassung zum Hochschulstudium; Freitag den 6. Mai 1949," 10–12. SAPMO-BA, ZPA, IV 2/9.04/464.

167. On the decline of rural industry and concentration of the German population in cities as a result of industrialization, see Kiesewetter, *Industrielle Revolution*, 132–37; Hochstadt, *Mobility and Modernity*, 119–201. As a whole the German population was more urban. In 1930, 12.7 percent of the population of the Czech lands lived in cities of more than 100,000 people. In 1935 that same figure for the German population was 30.4 percent. *Annuaire statistique*, 5; *Statistisches Jahrbuch für das deutsche Reich*, 16.

168. As early as 1955, a number of high schools were permitting male students to advance to university only after they had signed up for the East German proto-army, the barracked people's police (*Kasernierte Volkspolizei*). The State Secretariat was directed by the Central Committee to give preference to applicants for university who had served in these units. SAPMO-BA, ZPA, IV 2/9.02/477, Bl. 31, 42. People with relatives in West Germany were systematically disadvantaged. They were considered implicitly disloyal. Report of 4 September 1957, SAPMO-BA, ZPA, IV 2/9.02/477, Bl. 152–58.

169. See Helwig, *Schule*, esp. 90–110; Klier, *Lüg Vaterland*.

170. GARF, f. 9396, op. 30, d. 968, l. 8.

171. GARF, f. 9396, op. 30, d. 968, l. 54.

172. This was a one-of-a-kind award presented for Pigoń's aid during the political struggles of the early postwar period. *Polski słownik*, 26:210. For Pigoń's role in defending students of Jagiellonian University in his position as *kurator*, see Mazowiecki, *Pierwsze starcie*, 107–9, 240.

173. Letter of Zofia Bażantówna, 30 December 1953. Rkp BJ Przyb 238/76.

174. *Słownik historyków polskich*, 165.

175. Letter of 8 July 1951 by Kazimierz Piwarski. APAN-K, KIII-24, j. 109. The Party's personnel officer at the Silesian Medical Academy had falsified his own high school diploma. AAN, KC PZPR 237/XVI/77, k. 12.

176. AAN, KC PZPR 237/XVI/25, k. 98. In early 1956 the Party's two leading assistant professors at Toruń University's faculty of fine arts had to be fired because

of incompetence. Both had been Party secretaries of the faculty, as well as political appointees. "Błędy, ktore się mszczą," *Trybuna Ludu,* 5 May 1956.

177. Cited in Feige, "Die Gesellschaftswissenschaftliche Fakultät." Feige writes that the actual social composition of the faculty made Brecht's words wishful thinking.

178. Cited in Epstein, "The Last Revolutionaries," 2.

179. Kant's mythologized memoir of a worker-peasant collective at Greifswald University, *Die Aula,* was among the most printed books in the GDR. For Brecht's poem, see Lammel, *Dokumente,* 2:149.

180. Krüger, *Das Ende,* 179–80.

181. The relatively critical social scientists within the Party who have been mentioned—Behrens, Hans Mayer, Bloch, and Kuczynski—were maneuvered out of teaching positions by the early 1960s. Those who remained were utterly loyal; Ilko-Sascha Kowalczuk calls GDR historians "the most important intellectual pioneers and the ideological engineers of the Wall." See his exhaustively researched and passionately argued *Legitimation,* here, 331.

182. Zygmunt Bauman has spoken in general terms about the propensity for peasant students to repay East European regimes with political loyalty. "Social Dissent," 129. For description of the general logic of recruiting an elite from "young people of working-class origin," see also Miłosz, *Captive Mind,* 197.

CONCLUSION

1. Benda et al., *Studenti,* 60.

2. Huschner, "Der 17. Juni," 681–92; Sieber and Freytag, *Kinder.*

3. See Schaff's *Moje spotkania.*

4. See ibid., 9–10; Hübner, *Polityka naukowa,* 433; Connelly and Suleja, "Projekt"; as well as the exchanges between A. Podgórecki, J. Jasiński, and Z. Grabowski in *Zeszyty Towarzystwa Popierania i Krzewienia Nauk* 17–19 (1995).

5. For a compelling argument on the relation between economic scarcity and political development in East Central Europe, see Janos, "The Politics of Backwardness."

6. Lepsius, *Demokratie,* 38.

7. In analogous samples of close to 1,000 files from the central committee science and education departments in Warsaw and Berlin, the East German documents use the word *unbedingt* (unconditional) eighteen times. In Polish documents the equivalent *bezwarunkowo* appears not at all. The East German documents make reference to the need to "train and educate" (*erziehen*) not only students, but also professors. See, for example, the letter of Dr. Osburg of the State Secretariat for Higher Education of 1 November 1958 on further uses for the pedagogue Professor Fritz Müller, who had played important roles in making Rostock University socialist but, like many activists of the early postwar years, had fallen afoul of the Party during the antirevisionist campaign of 1957–58: Müller was given work at the Institute for Pedagogy in Rostock, so that the "collective of the institute can help train him [*erzieherisch auf ihn einwirken*]." Personnel file Fritz Müller, UAR. On the need to "train" bourgeois professors, see also the remarks of Schleifstein at the meeting of the SED leadership of Leipzig University, 16 January 1952, SSA, IV 4.14/29; or the need to "train" a Professor Teichmann (SED), meeting of 10 August 1953, SSA,

IV 4.14/29; or the need to "train" scientists, meeting of 11 May 1953, SSA, IV 4.14/29. The Polish and Czech equivalents *vychovat* and *wychować* are used almost exclusively in relation to young people or Party cadres, not professors.

8. See my review of Bessel and Jessen, *Grenzen,* in *Central European History* 32:1 (1999): 133-37.

9. Meeting of 18 January 1954. SSA, IV 4.14/30. For numbers of former NSDAP members in the SED during the 1950s, see Foitzik, "Die stalinistischen 'Säuberungen.'"

10. SSA, IV 4.14/29/158.

11. See the comments of Anton Ackermann, introduction to part 2 at n. 2.

12. Tent, *The Free University,* 256.

13. Note, for example, the absence of any reference to Pelikán's leading role in the Communist student movement in his obituary in the *New York Times,* 29 June 1999.

14. See chapter 6 at n. 46.

15. This was the conclusion of state and Party functionaries who met in June 1951 to discuss allocating space. SÚA, AÚV KSČ, f. 19/7, a.j. 260, l. 220.

16. Kenneth Jowitt distinguishes between elite, regime, and community political culture. Jowitt, *New World Disorder,* 55-56.

17. See, for example, Milena Jesenská's reports of the enthusiastic mobilization of soldiers in Bohemia in May 1938, cited in Buber-Neumann, *Milena,* 104-6.

18. In both Poland and Serbia the elites were possessed of peculiar notions of "national honor," which were strengthened by the respective populations' condemnation of any appearance of concessions to Germany. Olshausen, *Zwischenspiel,* 48-49; Wolff, *The Balkans,* 199-200; Rothschild, *East Central Europe,* 72, and *Return,* 46.

19. Miłosz, *Native Realm,* 167. For the case of Professor Stiebitz, see chapter 10 at n. 41, and for the letter from Weyr to Engliš, chapter 10 at n. 44.

BOOKS, ARTICLES, AND DISSERTATIONS

Abrams, Bradley F. " 'The Struggle for the Soul of the Nation': Czech Culture and Socialism, 1945–1948." Ph.D. diss., Stanford University, 1997.

Aland, Kurt, ed. *Glanz und Niedergang der deutschen Universität. 50 Jahre deutscher Wissenschaftsgeschichte in Briefen an und von Hans Lietzmann 1892–1942.* Berlin, 1979.

Annuaire statistique de la République Tchéchoslovaque. Prague, 1935.

Anweiler, Oskar, and Klaus Meyer, eds. *Die sowjetische Bildungspolitik seit 1917. Dokumente und Texte.* Heidelberg, 1961.

Ash, Mitchell G. "Common and Disparate Dilemmas of German and American Universities." In *Universities in the Twenty-first Century,* edited by Steven Muller, 37–46. Providence, R.I., 1996.

————. "Verordnete Umbrüche—konstruierte Kontinuitäten. Zur Entnazifizierung von Wissenschaftlern und Wissenschaften nach 1945." *Zeitschrift für Geschichtswissenschaft* 43:10 (1995): 903–23.

Assorodobraj, Nina. "Kursy przygotowawcze a zagadnienie społecznej selekcji młodzieży akademickiej." *Przegląd Sociologiczny* 9:2 (1947): 125–43.

August, Jochen. *"Sonderaktion Krakau." Die Verhaftung der Krakauer Wissenschaftler am 6. November 1939.* Hamburg, 1997.

Bardach, Janusz, and Kathleen Gleeson. *Man Is Wolf to Man: Surviving the Gulag.* Berkeley and Los Angeles, 1999.

Bardach, Juliusz. "Pasje uczonego. Rzecz o Konstantym Grzybowskim." *Czasopismo Prawno-Historyczne* 48:1–2 (1996): 119–46.

Batowski, Henryk. "Nazi Germany and the Jagiellonian University." In Buszko and Paczyńska, *Universities,* 211–18.

Bauman, Zygmunt. "Social Dissent in the East European Political System." In *The Social Structure of Eastern Europe,* edited by Bernard L. Faber. New York, 1976.

Benda, Marek, et al. *Studenti psali revoluci.* Prague, 1990.

Bender, Peter. *East Europe in Search of Security.* London, 1972.

Berend, Ivan T. *Central and Eastern Europe, 1944–1993: Detour from the Periphery to the Periphery.* Cambridge, 1998.

Besier, Gerhard. *Der SED-Staat und die Kirche: Der Weg in die Anpassung.* Munich, 1993.

Bessel, Richard, and Ralph Jessen, eds. *Die Grenzen der Diktatur. Staat und Gesellschaft in der DDR.* Göttingen, 1996.

Bialer, Seweryn. *Wybrałem prawdę.* New York, 1956.

Birke, Ernst, and Rudolf Neumann, eds. *Die Sowjetisierung Ost-Mitteleuropas. Untersuchungen zu ihrem Ablauf in den einzelnen Ländern.* Frankfurt am Main and Berlin, 1959.

Biskup, Marian, and Andrzej Giziński, eds. *Toruńscy twórcy nauki i kultury. 1945–1985.* Warsaw, 1989.

Bonwetsch, Bernd. "Sowjetische Politik in der SBZ 1945–1949." In *Sowjetische*

Politik in der SBZ 1945–1949. Dokumente zur Tätigkeit der Propaganda-
verwaltung der SMAD unter Sergej Tjul'panov, edited by B. Bonwetsch,
G. Bordjugov, and N. Naimark, xix–lv. Bonn, 1998.

Borusiak, Horst. "Die Universität Leipzig nach der Zerschlagung des
faschistischen Staates und ihre Neueröffnung am 5. Februar 1946." In
Karl-Marx-Universität Leipzig 1409–1959, 340–89. Leipzig, 1959.

Bourdieu, Pierre. *Homo Academicus.* Stanford, Calif., 1988.

Brabec, Václav. "Životní úroveň a některé stránky diferenciace čs. společnosti v
padesátých letech." *Revue dějin socialismu,* special number, 1968, 1072.

Bresch, Ulrike, and Gert Noack. " 'Freiheit im Sozialismus': Ein Streitgespräch an
der Humboldt-Universität zu Berlin 1963." *Zeitschrift für
Geschichtswissenschaft* 41:7 (1993): 605–21.

Brodowska, Helena. "Freie polnische Hochschule zu Warszawa." In Buszko and
Paczyńska, *Universities,* 391–95.

Broszat, Martin, and Hermann Weber, eds. *SBZ-Handbuch. Staatliche Ver-*
*waltungen, Parteien, gesellschaftliche Organisationen und ihre Führungskräfte
in der Sowjetischen Besatzungszone Deutschlands 1945–1949.* Munich, 1990.

Brown, Archie, ed. *Political Culture and Communist Studies.* New York, 1984.

Bruch, Rüdiger vom. "A Slow Farewell to Humboldt? Stages in the History of
German Universities, 1810–1945." In *German Universities Past and Future:
Crisis or Renewal,* edited by Mitchell G. Ash, 3–27. Providence, R.I., and
Oxford, 1997.

Brus, Włodzimierz. "Stalinism and the People's Democracies." In *Stalinism: Essays
in Historical Interpretation,* edited by Robert C. Tucker, 239–56. New York,
1977.

Brzezinski, Zbigniew K. *The Soviet Bloc: Unity and Conflict.* Cambridge, Mass.,
1960.

Buber-Neumann, Margarete. *Milena: The Story of a Remarkable Friendship.*
Translated by Ralph Manheim. New York, 1988.

Buszko, Józef. "Solidaritätsaktionen mit den in der 'Sonderaktion Krakau'
verhafteten Krakauer Professoren." In Buszko and Paczyńska, *Universities,*
67–97.

Buszko, Józef, and Irena Paczyńska, eds. *Universities during World War II.* Kraków,
1984.

Butiagin, A., and J. Saltanow. "30 lat wyższego szkolnictwa w ZSRR." *Myśl
Współczesna* 2 (November 1947): 369–89.

Černý, Jochen, ed. *Wer war wer—DDR. Ein biographisches Lexikon.* Berlin, 1992.

Černý, Václav. *Paměti.* 3 vols. Prague, 1992–94.

Československé dějiny v datech. Prague, 1986.

Československý biografický slovník. Prague, 1992.

Chałasiński, Józef. *Przeszłość i przyszłość inteligencji polskiej.* Warsaw, 1997.

———. *Społeczna genealogia inteligencji polskiej.* Warsaw, 1946.

Chanbarisov, Sh. Kh. *Formirovanie sovetskoi universitetskoi sistemy.* Moscow, 1988.

Chodakowska, Janina. *Rozwój szkolnictwa wyższego w Polsce Ludowej w latach
1944–1951.* Wrocław, 1981.

Churaň, Milan, et al. *Kdo byl kdo v našich dějinách ve 20. století.* Prague, 1994.

Ciesielski, Stanisław. "Rekrutacja młodzieży na studia dzienne w Uniwersytecie

Wrocławskim w latach 1945–1985." *Studia i Materiały z Dziejów Uniwersytetu Wrocławskiego* 2 (1993): 153–74.

Císař, Čestmír. *Člověk a politik. Kniha vzpomínek a úvah.* Prague, 1998.

Cohen, Stephen F. *Rethinking the Soviet Experience: Politics and History since 1917.* New York, 1985.

Compendium of Social Statistics and Indicators, 1988. New York, 1991.

Connelly, John. "East German Higher Education Policies and Student Resistance, 1945–1948." *Central European History* 28:3 (1995): 259–98.

———. "Freie Meinungsäußerung auch außerhalb der Partei?" *Deutschland Archiv* 29:5 (1996): 772–73.

———. "Internal Bolshevization? Elite Social Science Training in Stalinist Poland." *Minerva* 34:4 (1996): 323–46.

———. "Ulbricht and the Intellectuals." *Contemporary European History* 6:3 (1997): 329–59.

———. "Zur 'Republikflucht' von DDR-Wissenschaftlern in den fünfziger Jahren." *Zeitschrift für Geschichtswissenschaft* 42:4 (1994): 331–52.

Connelly, John, and Teresa Suleja. " 'Projekt reformy personalnej polonistyki uniwersyteckiej' Stefana Żółkiewskiego z 1950 roku." *Arcana* 2 (1997): 93–113.

Connor, Walter D. *Socialism, Politics, and Equality: Hierarchy and Change in Eastern Europe and the USSR.* New York, 1979.

Crampton, R. J. *Eastern Europe in the Twentieth Century.* London and New York, 1994.

Crew, David F., ed. *Nazism and German Society.* London, 1994.

Cywiński, Bohdan. *Rodowody niepokornych.* Warsaw, 1971.

Dąbrowska-Zembrzuska, Eugenia. *Szkolnictwo w Czechosłowacji.* Wrocław, 1963.

David-Fox, Michael. "The Assault on the Universities and the Dynamics of the Great Break, 1928–1932." Paper presented at a seminar on Academia in Upheaval: The Origins and Demise of the Communist Academic Regime in Russia and East Central Europe, Trondheim, Norway, 3–7 April 1997.

———. *Revolution of the Mind: Higher Learning among the Bolsheviks, 1918–1929.* Ithaca, N.Y., 1997.

Davies, Norman. *God's Playground: A History of Poland.* 2 vols. New York, 1981.

Denzler, Georg, and Volker Fabricius. *Die Kirchen im Dritten Reich.* Vol. 1. Frankfurt am Main, 1984.

Dietrich, Gerd. *Politik und Kultur in der Sowjetischen Besatzungszone Deutschlands 1945–1949.* Bern, 1993.

Dobroszycki, Lucjan. *Reptile Journalism: The Official Polish-Language Press under the Nazis, 1939–1945.* New Haven, 1994.

Doležal, Jiří. *Česká kultura za protektorátu: Školství, písemnictví, kinematografie.* Prague, 1996.

Dubček, Alexander. *Hope Dies Last: The Autobiography of Alexander Dubček.* Translated by Jiří Hochman. New York, 1993.

Dunin-Wąsowicz, Krzysztof. "On the Scholarly and Educational Activity Undertaken by the Poles Interned at Concentration and War-Prisoners' Camps." In Buszko and Paczyńska, *Universities,* 379–90.

Ekiert, Grzegorz. *The State against Society: Political Crises and Their Aftermath in East Central Europe.* Princeton, 1996.

Epstein, Catherine. "The Last Revolutionaries: The Old Communists of East Germany, 1945–1989." Ph.D. diss., Harvard University, 1998.

Ernst, Anne-Sabine. *"Die beste Prophylaxe ist der Sozialismus": Ärzte und medizinische Hochschullehrer in der SBZ/DDR 1945–1961*. Berlin, 1997.

Feige, Hans-Uwe. "Der Aufbau der SED Betriebsgruppe an der Universität Leipzig 1945–1948." *Beiträge zur Geschichte der Arbeiterbewegung* 26:2 (1984): 247–56.

———. "Die Gesellschaftswissenschaftliche Fakultät der Universität Leipzig." *Deutschland Archiv* 26:5 (1993): 572–83.

———. "Zur Entnazifizierung des Lehrkörpers an der Universität Leipzig." *Zeitschrift für Geschichtswissenschaft* 42:9 (1994): 795–808.

Féjtö, François. *A History of the People's Democracies: Eastern Europe since Stalin*. Translated by Daniel Weissbort. London, 1971.

Fijałkowska, Barbara. *Polityka i twórcy. 1948–1959*. Warsaw, 1985.

Fischer, Alexander, and Günther Heydemann, eds. *Geschichtswissenschaft in der DDR*. Vol. 1. Berlin, 1988.

Fitzpatrick, Sheila. *The Commissariat of Enlightenment: Soviet Organization of Education and the Arts under Lunacharsky, October 1917–1921*. Cambridge, 1970.

———. *The Cultural Front: Power and Culture in Revolutionary Russia*. Ithaca, N.Y., and London, 1992.

———. *Education and Social Mobility in the Soviet Union, 1921–1934*. London and New York, 1979.

———, ed. *Cultural Revolution in Russia, 1928–1931*. Bloomington, Ind., 1978.

Foitzik, Jan. "Die stalinistischen 'Säuberungen' in den ostmitteleuropäischen kommunistischen Parteien. Ein vergleichender Überblick." *Zeitschrift für Geschichtswissenschaft* 40:8 (1992): 737–49.

Fricke, Karl Wilhelm. *Opposition und Widerstand in der DDR*. Cologne, 1984.

Friszke, Andrzej. *Opozycja polityczna w PRL 1945–1980*. London, 1994.

Gadamer, Hans-Georg. *Philosophische Lehrjahre: Eine Rückschau*. Frankfurt am Main, 1977.

Gapski, Henryk, ed. *Historae peritus. Księga jubileuszowa Profesora Jerzego Kłoczowskiego*. Part 2. Lublin, 1998.

Garlicki, Andrzej. *Stalinizm*. Warsaw, 1993.

Gella, Aleksander. *Development of Class Structure in Eastern Europe: Poland and Her Southern Neighbors*. Albany, N.Y., 1989.

Gellner, Ernest. "The Pluralist Anti-Levellers of Prague." *Government and Opposition* 7:1 (Winter 1972): 20–37.

Gieysztor, Aleksander. "Środowisko historyczne Warszawy w okresie międzywojennym." In *Nauka i szkolnictwo wyższe w Warszawie*, 88–106.

Giles, Geoffrey J. "Professor und Partei: Der Hamburger Lehrkörper und der Nationalsozialismus." In Krause et al., *Hochschulalltag im "Dritten Reich": Die Hamburger Universität 1933–1945*, part 1, 113–24.

———. *The Structure of Higher Education in the German Democratic Republic*. Yale Higher Education Program Working Paper, YHEP-12. New Haven, 1976.

Gładysz, Antoni. *Oświata—kultura—nauka w latach 1947–1959. Węzłowe problemy polityczne*. Warsaw and Kraków, 1981.

Gomułka, Władysław. *Ku nowej Polsce: sprawozdanie polityczne i przemówienia wygłoszone na I Zjeździe PPR*. Łódź, 1946.

Gorizontov, L. E. "Metodologicheskii perevorot v pol'skoi istoriografii na rubezhe 1940–1950-kh godov i sovetskie istoriki." *Slavianovedenie* 6 (1993): 50–66.

Grant, Nigel. *Schools and Progress in Eastern Europe*. Oxford, 1969.

Grebing, Helga. *Der Revisionismus: Von Bernstein bis zum Prager Frühling*. Munich, 1977.

Groehler, Olaf. "Integration und Ausgrenzung von NS-Opfern. Zur Anerkennungs- und Entschädigungsdebatte in der Sowjetischen Besatzungszone Deutschlands." In *Historische DDR-Forschung: Aufsätze und Studien*, edited by Jürgen Kocka, 105–27. Berlin, 1993.

Gross, Jan T. *Polish Society under German Occupation: The Generalgouvernement, 1939–1944*. Princeton, 1979.

———. "Social Consequences of War: Preliminaries to the Study of Imposition of Communist Regimes in East Central Europe." *East European Politics and Societies* 3:2 (Spring 1989): 198–214.

Grünberg, Gottfried. *Kumpel, Kämpfer, Kommunist*. Berlin, 1977.

Grunenberg, Antonia. *Antifaschismus—ein deutscher Mythos*. Reinbek, 1993.

Grzymala-Busse, Anna. "Communist Party Strategies in the Era of State Socialism: Saturation, Negotiation, and Change." Paper presented at a workshop on New Directions in the Study of East European State Socialism, Minda de Gunzburg Center for European Studies, Harvard University, Cambridge, Mass., 7–9 November 1997.

Hacker, Jens. *Der Ostblock: Entstehung, Entwicklung und Struktur 1939–1980*. Baden-Baden, 1983.

Hájek, Jiří. *Paměti*. Prague, 1997.

Handel, Gottfried. *Chronik der Gesellschaftswissenschaftlichen Fakultät Leipzig*. Leipzig, 1973.

Handel, Gottfried, and Roland Köhler, eds. *Dokumente der Sowjetischen Militäradministration in Deutschland zum Hoch- und Fachschulwesen 1945–1949*. Berlin, 1974.

Hanzal, Josef. "Čeští historici před únorem 1948." *Český časopis historický* 91:2 (1993): 268–85.

———. "Studijní prověrky na vysokých školách." *Dějiny a současnost* 11:6 (1969): 28–30.

Haritonow, Alexandr. "Entnazifizierung an der Bergakademie Freiberg 1945–1948." *Bildung und Erziehung* 45:4 (1992): 433–41.

———. *Sowjetische Hochschulpolitik in Sachsen 1945–1949*. Weimar, 1995.

Hartmann, Karl. *Hochschulwesen und Wissenschaft in Polen. Entwicklung, Organisation und Stand, 1918–1960*. Frankfurt am Main, 1962.

Havemann, Robert. *Fragen-Antworten-Fragen: Aus der Biographie eines deutschen Marxisten*. Munich, 1970.

———. *Warum ich Stalinist war und Antistalinist wurde*. Berlin, 1990.

Havránek, Jan. "Der 17. November 1939—die Schliessung der tschechischen Hochschulen." In Buszko and Paczyńska, *Universities*, 187–202.

———. "Nineteenth Century Universities in Central Europe: Their Dominant Position in the Sciences and Humanities." In *Bildungswesen und*

Sozialstruktur in Mitteleuropa im 19. und 20. Jahrhundert, edited by Victor Karady and Wolfgang Mitter, 9–26. Cologne, 1990.

———. "Studenti Univerzity Karlovy na jaře a v létě roku pětačtyřicátého." *Zprávy archivu Univerzity Karlovy* 7 (1985): 70–134.

———. "Univerzita Karlova v letech 1953–1969." In Havránek and Pousta, *Dějiny Univerzity Karlovy,* 307–24.

Havránek, Jan, and Zdeněk Pousta, eds. *Dějiny Univerzity Karlovy 1918–1990.* Vol. 4. Prague, 1998.

Heidemeyer, Helge. *Flucht und Zuwanderung aus der SBZ/DDR 1945/1949–1961.* Düsseldorf, 1994.

Hejl, Vilém. *Zpráva o organisovaném násilí.* Prague, 1990.

Helwig, Gisela, ed. *Schule in der DDR.* Cologne, 1988.

Herf, Jeffrey. *Divided Memory: The Nazi Past in the Two Germanys.* Cambridge, Mass., 1997.

Hertwig, Manfred. "Der Umgang des Staates mit oppositionellem und widerständigem Verhalten. Die Opposition von Intellektuellen in der SED/DDR in den fünfziger Jahren, insbesondere 1953, 1956/57, ihre Unterdrückung und Ausschaltung." In *Materialien der Enquete-Kommission "Aufarbeitung von Geschichte und Folgen der SED-Diktatur in Deutschland,"* edited by Deutscher Bundestag, 7:873–95. Baden-Baden, 1995.

Herzberg, Guntolf. "Ernst Bloch in Leipzig: Der operative Vorgang 'Wild.'" *Zeitschrift für Geschichtswissenschaft* 42:8 (1994): 677–93.

Heumos, Peter. "Die Arbeiterschaft in der ersten Tschechoslowakischen Republik." *Bohemia* 29:1 (1988): 50–72.

Heym, Stefan. *Nachruf.* Berlin, 1990.

Historická statistická ročenka ČSSR. Prague, 1985.

Hochstadt, Steve. *Mobility and Modernity: Migration in Germany, 1820–1989.* Ann Arbor, Mich., 1999.

Hoensch, Jörg K. *Sowjetische Osteuropa-Politik 1945–1975.* Kronberg/Ts., 1977.

Hoffmann, Dieter. "Robert Havemann: Antifascist, Communist, Dissident." In *Science under Socialism: East Germany in Comparative Perspective,* edited by Kristie Macrakis and Dieter Hoffmann, 269–85. Cambridge, Mass., 1999.

Hoffmann, Dieter, and Kristie Macrakis, eds. *Naturwissenschaft und Technik in der DDR.* Berlin, 1997.

Hoyer, Siegfried. "Der Weg zur Wiedereröffnung der Universität Leipzig 1946." *Universität Leipzig* 1 (1996): 23–28.

Hruby, Peter. *Fools and Heroes: The Changing Role of Communist Intellectuals in Czechoslovakia.* Oxford, 1980.

Hübner, Piotr. "Formowanie systemu polityki naukowej 1944–1951." In *Historia nauki polskiej,* edited by Bogdan Suchodolski, 5.1:529–41. Wrocław, 1992.

———. *I Kongres Nauki Polskiej jako forma realizacji założeń polityki naukowej państwa ludowego.* Wrocław, 1983.

———. "The Last Flight of Pegasus: The Story of the Polish Academy of Science and Letters and the Warsaw Scientific Society, 1945–52." *East European Politics and Societies* 13:1 (1999): 71–116.

———. *Nauka polska po II wojnie światowej—idee i instytucje.* Warsaw, 1987.

———. *Polityka naukowa w Polsce w latach 1944–1953. Geneza systemu.* Warsaw, 1992.

————. *Siła przeciw rozumowi: Losy Polskiej Akademii Umiejętności w latach 1939–1989.* Kraków, 1994.

————. "Stalinowskie 'czystki' w nauce polskiej." In *Skryte oblicze systemu komunistycznego,* edited by Roman Bäcker, 211–24. Warsaw, 1997.

Huschner, Anke. "Der 17. Juni 1953 an Universitäten und Hochschulen der DDR." *Beiträge zur Geschichte der Arbeiterbewegung* 5 (1991): 681–92.

Jaczewski, Bohdan. "Organizacja i instytucje życia naukowego w Polsce. Listopad 1918–1939." In *Historia nauki polskiej,* edited by Bogdan Suchodolski, 5.1:36–315. Wrocław, 1992.

Jagiełło, Michał. *Tygodnik Powszechny i komunizm. 1945–1953.* Warsaw, 1988.

Jänicke, Martin. *Der dritte Weg: Die antistalinistische Opposition gegen Ulbricht seit 1953.* Cologne, 1964.

Janka, Walter. *Schwierigkeiten mit der Wahrheit.* Reinbek, 1989.

Janos, Andrew C. "The Politics of Backwardness in Continental Europe, 1780–1945." *World Politics* 41:3 (1989): 325–58.

Jansen, Christian. *Professoren und Politik: Politisches Denken und Handeln der Heidelberger Hochschullehrer 1914–1935.* Göttingen, 1992.

————. *Vom Gelehrten zum Beamten. Karriereverläufe und soziale Lage der Heidelberger Hochschullehrer 1914–1933.* Heidelberg, 1992.

Jarausch, Konrad H., ed. *Zwischen Parteilichkeit und Professionalität. Bilanz der Geschichtswissenschaft der DDR.* Berlin, 1991.

Jarocki, Robert. *Czterdzieści pięć lat w opozycji.* Kraków, 1990.

————. *Widzieć jasno bez zachwytu.* Warsaw, 1982.

Jędruszczak, Hanna. "Miasta i przemysł w okresie odbudowy." In *Polska Ludowa 1944–1950. Przemiany społeczne,* edited by Franciszek Ryszka, 279–407. Wrocław, 1974.

Jerschina, Jan. *Osobowość społeczna studentów Uniwersytetu Jagiellońskiego chłopskiego pochodzenia.* Wrocław, 1972.

Jessen, Ralph. "Akademische Elite und kommunistische Diktatur. Studien zur Geschichte der Hochschullehrerschaft in der Ulbricht-Ära." Habilitation, Free University of Berlin, 1997.

————. "Die 'Entbürgerlichung' der Hochschullehrer in der DDR — Elitenwechsel mit Hindernissen." *Hochschule Ost* 3 (1995): 61–71.

————. "Professoren im Sozialismus. Aspekte des Strukturwandels der Hochschullehrerschaft in der Ulbricht-Ära." In Kaelble et al., *Sozialgeschichte der DDR,* 217–53.

————. "Vom Ordinarius zum sozialistischen Professor." In *Die Grenzen der Diktatur. Staat und Gesellschaft in der DDR,* edited by Richard Bessel and Ralph Jessen, 76–107. Göttingen, 1996.

————. "Zur Sozialgeschichte der ostdeutschen Gelehrtenschaft. 1945–1970." In *Historische Forschung und sozialistische Diktatur. Beiträge zur Geschichtswissenschaft der DDR,* edited by Martin Sabrow and Peter Th. Walter, 121–43. Leipzig, 1995.

John, Jürgen. "Die Jenaer Universität im Jahre 1945." In *Die Wiedereröffnung der Friedrich-Schiller-Universität,* edited by J. John, V. Wahl, and L. Arnold, 12–74. Rudolstadt, 1998.

Jordán, František, ed. *Dějiny University v Brně.* Brno, 1969.

Jordan, Z. A. "Philosophy in Postwar Poland." Russian Research Center Seminar Notes, Harvard University, Cambridge, Mass., 3 May 1963.

Jowitt, Kenneth. *New World Disorder: The Leninist Extinction.* Berkeley and Los Angeles, 1992.

Judt, Tony. *Past Imperfect: French Intellectuals, 1944–1956.* Berkeley and Los Angeles, 1992.

Just, Gustav. *Zeuge in eigener Sache. Die fünfziger Jahre.* Berlin, 1990.

Kádner, Otakar. *Vývoj a dnešní soustava školství.* Parts 2–4. Prague, 1931–38.

Kaelble, Hartmut, Jürgen Kocka, and Hartmut Zwahr, eds. *Sozialgeschichte der DDR.* Stuttgart, 1994.

Kalembka, Sławomir, ed. *Pracownicy nauki i dydaktyki Uniwersytetu Mikołaja Kopernika.* Toruń, 1995.

Kantorowicz, Alfred. *Deutsches Tagebuch.* Vol. 2. Munich, 1961.

————. *Etwas ist ausgeblieben: Zur geistigen Einheit der deutschen Literatur nach 1945.* Hamburg, 1985.

Kaplan, Karel. *Nekrvavá revoluce.* Prague, 1993.

————. *Sovětští poradci v Československu 1949–1956.* Prague, 1993.

Karpiński, Jakub. *Nie być w myśleniu posłusznym. Ossowscy, socjologia, filozofia.* London, 1989.

Kasper, Hans-Hendrik. "Der Kampf der SED um die Heranbildung einer Intelligenz aus der Arbeiterklasse und der werktätigen Bauernschaft über die Vorstudienanstalten an den Universitäten und Hochschulen der sowjetischen Besatzungszone Deutschlands 1945/46–1949." Ph.D. diss., Bergbau Akademie Freiberg, 1979.

Kavka, František. *Univerzita Karlova a padesát let Československa.* Prague, 1968.

————, ed. *Stručné dějiny Univerzity Karlovy.* Prague, 1964.

Keckowa, Antonina. "Stanisław Arnold, 1895–1973." In *Historycy warszawscy ostatnich dwóch stuleci.* Warsaw, 1986.

Kenney, Padraic. *Rebuilding Poland: Workers and Communists, 1945–1950.* Ithaca, N.Y., and London, 1997.

Kersten, Krystyna. *Między wyzwoleniem a zniewoleniem. Polska 1944–1956.* London, 1993.

————. *Narodziny systemu władzy. Polska 1943–1948.* Poznań, 1990.

Kiesewetter, Hubert. *Industrielle Revolution in Deutschland 1815–1914.* Frankfurt am Main, 1989.

Kita, Jarosław, and Stefan Pytlas. *Profesorowie Uniwersytetu Łódzkiego w latach 1945–1994.* Łódź, 1995.

Klein, Fritz. "Dokumente aus den Anfangsjahren der ZfG." *Zeitschrift für Geschichtswissenschaft* 42:1 (1994): 39–55.

Klein, Helmut, ed. *Humboldt-Universität zu Berlin, Überblick 1810–1985.* Berlin, 1985.

Klemperer, Victor. *So sitze ich denn zwischen allen Stühlen. Tagebücher 1950–1959.* 2 vols. Berlin, 1999.

Klessmann, Christoph. "Die Zerstörung des Schulwesens als Bestandteil deutscher Okkupationspolitik im Osten am Beispiel Polens." In *Erziehung und Schulung im Dritten Reich,* edited by Manfred Heinemann, part 1, 176–92. Stuttgart, 1980.

Klier, Freya. *Lüg Vaterland. Erziehung in der DDR.* Munich, 1990.

Kłoskowska, Antonina. "Bunty i służebności uczonego." In *Bunty i służebności uczonego. Profesor Józef Chałasiński,* 7–21. Łódź, 1992.

———, ed. *Uniwersytet Łódzki 1945–1970.* Łódź, 1970.

Knapp, Viktor. *Proměny času.* Prague, 1998.

Kocka, Jürgen. "Zur jüngeren marxistischen Sozialgeschichte. Eine kritische Analyse unter besonderer Berücksichtigung sozialgeschichtlicher Ansätze in der DDR." In Fischer and Heydemann, *Geschichtswissenschaft in der DDR,* 1:395–422.

Kolankiewicz, George. "The Technical Intelligentsia." In Lane and Kolankiewicz, *Social Groups,* 180–232.

Kolman, Arnošt. *Die verirrte Generation. So hätten wir nicht leben sollen. Eine Biographie.* Frankfurt am Main, 1979.

Konecny, Peter. "Chaos on Campus: The 1924 Student *Proverka* in Leningrad." *Europe-Asia Studies* 46:4 (1994): 617–35.

Kopke, Horst. *Mein Vaterland ist die Freiheit.* Rostock, 1990.

Kopstein, Jeffrey. *The Politics of Economic Decline in East Germany.* Chapel Hill, N.C., and London, 1997.

Korbonski, Andrzej. "Poland: 1918–1990." In *The Columbia History of Eastern Europe in the Twentieth Century,* edited by Joseph Held, 229–76. New York, 1992.

Korovitsyna, N. V. "Novaia intelligentsiia v istorii sotsialisticheeskogo Eksperimenta na materialakh Chekhii i Slovakii." In *Vlast' i intelligentsiia. Iz opyta poslevoennogo razvitiia stran vostochnoi evropy,* edited by Iu. S. Novopashin, 128–54. Moscow, 1993.

Kotarbiński, Tadeusz. *Myśli o ludziach i ludzkich sprawach.* Wrocław, 1986.

Kott, Jan. *Still Alive.* New Haven, 1993.

Kovály, Heda Margolius. *Under a Cruel Star: A Life in Prague, 1941–1968.* Cambridge, Mass., 1986.

Kowalczuk, Ilko-Sascha. "Anfänge und Grundlinien der Universitätspolitik der SED." *German Studies Review* 17 (Fall 1994): 113–30.

———. "Die Durchsetzung des Marxismus-Leninismus in der Geschichtswissenschaft der DDR 1945–1961." In Sabrow and Walter, *Historische Forschung und sozialistische Diktatur,* 31–58.

———. *Legitimation eines neuen Staates. Parteiarbeiter an der historischen Front. Geschichtswissenschaft in der SBZ/DDR 1945 bis 1961.* Berlin, 1997.

———. "Volkserhebung ohne 'Geistesarbeiter'? Die Intelligenz in der DDR." In *Der Tag X 17. Juni 1953,* edited by Ilko-Sascha Kowalczuk, Armin Mitter, and Stefan Wolle, 129–69. Berlin, 1996.

———. " 'Wo gehobelt wird, da fallen Späne.' Zur Entwicklung der DDR-Geschichtswissenschaft bis in die späten fünfziger Jahre." *Zeitschrift für Geschichtswissenschaft* 42:4 (1994): 302–18.

Kowalenko, Władysław. *Tajny Uniwersytet Ziem Zachodnich. Uniwersytet Poznański 1940–1945.* Poznań, 1961.

Kráčmarová, Hana. "Působení KSČ na pražských vysokých školách před Únorem 1948." *Acta Universitatis Carolinae* 7:1 (1966): 7–48.

———. *Vysokoškoláci v revolučních letech 1945–48.* Prague, 1976.

Krajina, Vladímir. *Vysoká hra. Vzpomínky.* Prague, 1994.

Krasiewicz, Bolesław. *Odbudowa szkolnictwa wyższego w Polsce Ludowej w latach 1944–1948.* Wrocław, 1976.

Krasucki, Józef. *Tajne szkolnictwo polskie w okresie okupacji hitlerowskiej 1939–1945.* Warsaw, 1977.

Kratochvil, Antonín. *Die kommunistische Hochschulpolitik in der Tschechoslowakei.* Munich, 1968.

———. *Žaluji. Cesta k Sionu.* Vol. 3. Prague, 1990.

Krause, Eckart, Ludwig Huber, and Holger Fischer, eds. *Hochschulalltag im "Dritten Reich": Die Hamburger Universität 1933–1945.* Part 1. Berlin, 1991.

Krejčí, Jaroslav. *Social Change and Stratification in Postwar Czechoslovakia.* New York, 1972.

Krofta, Kamil. *A Short History of Czechoslovakia.* New York, 1934.

Krönig, Waldemar, and Klaus-Dieter Müller. *Anpassung, Widerstand, Verfolgung: Hochschule und Studenten in der SBZ und DDR 1945–1961.* Cologne, 1994.

Krüger, Horst, ed. *Das Ende einer Utopie: Hingabe und Selbstbefreiung früherer Kommunisten.* Olten and Freiburg im Breisgau, 1963.

Kto jest Kim w Polsce 1984. Warsaw, 1984.

Kuczynski, Jürgen. *Frost nach dem Tauwetter. Mein Historikerstreit.* Berlin, 1993.

———. *"Ein linientreuer Dissident." Memoiren 1945–1989.* Berlin, 1992.

Kuhn, Heinrich, and Otto Böss, eds. *Biographisches Handbuch der Tschechoslowakei.* Munich, 1969.

Kuroń, Jacek. *Wiara i wina. Do i od komunizmu.* Warsaw, 1990.

Kuroń, Jacek, and Jacek Żakowski. *PRL dla początkujących.* Wrocław, 1996.

Kusin, Vladimir. *The Intellectual Origins of the Prague Spring: The Development of Reformist Ideas in Czechoslovakia.* Cambridge, 1971.

Kuta, Tadeusz. "Moje wspomnienia jako studenta, a następnie pomocniczego pracownika nauki w początkach drogi rozwojowej Uniwersytetu Wrocław-skiego." *Studia i Materiały z Dziejów Uniwersytetu Wrocławskiego* 2 (1993): 235–62.

Lammel, Hans-Joachim, ed. *Dokumente zur Geschichte der Arbeiter-und-Bauern-Fakultäten der Universitäten und Hochschulen der DDR.* 2 vols. Berlin, 1987–88.

Lane, David. "Structural and Social Change in Poland." In Lane and Kolankiewicz, *Social Groups,* 1–28.

Lane, David, and George Kolankiewicz, eds. *Social Groups in Polish Society.* London and Basingstoke, 1973.

Lange, M. G., E. Richert, and O. Stammer. "Das Problem der 'neuen Intelligenz' in der sowjetischen Besatzungszone. Ein Beitrag zur politischen Soziologie der kommunistischen Herrschaftsordnung." In *Veritas-Iustitia-Libertas. Festschrift zur 200-Jahrfeier der Columbia University New York,* 191–246. Berlin, 1954.

Lapidus, Gail. "Educational Strategies and Cultural Revolution: The Politics of Soviet Development." In Fitzpatrick, *Cultural Revolution in Russia, 1928–1931,* 78–104.

Lemberg, Hans, ed. *Sowjetisches Modell und nationale Prägung. Kontinuität und Wandel in Ostmitteleuropa nach dem Zweiten Weltkrieg.* Marburg, 1991.

Lentze, Hans. *Die Universitätsreform des Ministers Graf Leo Thun-Hohenstein.* Vienna, 1962.

Leonhard, Wolfgang. *Die Revolution entlässt ihre Kinder.* Vol. 1. Leipzig, 1990.

Lepsius, M. Rainer. *Demokratie in Deutschland: Soziologisch-historische Konstellationsanalysen. Ausgewählte Aufsätze.* Göttingen, 1993.

Leslie, R. F., Antony Polonsky, Jan M. Ciechanowski, and Z. A. Pełczyński. *The History of Poland since 1863.* Cambridge, 1983.

Lewandowski, Czesław. *Kierunki tak zwanej ofensywy ideologicznej w polskiej oświecie, nauce i szkołach wyższych w latach 1944–1948.* Wrocław, 1993.

Lewandowski, Jan. *Rodowód społeczny powojennej inteligencji polskiej. 1944–1949.* Szczecin, 1991.

Lewy, Guenter. *The Catholic Church and Nazi Germany.* New York, 1964.

Litsch, Karel. "17. listopad 1939." *Zprávy archivu Univerzity Karlovy* 7 (1985): 46–62.

Lobkowicz, N. *Marxismus-Leninismus in der ČSR. Die tschechoslowakische Philosophie seit 1945.* Dordrecht, 1961.

Loest, Erich. *Durch die Erde ein Riss.* Leipzig, 1990.

Longchamps, Franciszek, ed. *Uniwersytet Wrocławski w latach 1945–1955.* Wrocław, 1959.

Longworth, Philip. *The Making of Eastern Europe: From Prehistory to Postcommunism.* New York, 1997.

Lönnendonker, Siegward. *Freie Universität Berlin: Gründung einer politischen Universität.* Berlin, 1988.

Lönnendonker, Siegward, and Tilman Fichter, eds. *Freie Universität Berlin 1948–1973—Hochschule im Umbruch, 1945–1949, "Gegengründung wozu?"* Vol. 1. Berlin, 1973.

Lovenduski, Joni, and Jean Woodall. *Politics and Society in Eastern Europe.* London, 1987.

Łuczak, Czesław. "Polnische Wissenschaft und polnisches Hochschulwesen während der Hitlerokkupation." In Buszko and Paczyńska, *Universities,* 37–46.

———, ed. *University of Poznań 1919–1969.* Poznań, 1971.

McClellan, Woodford. "Postwar Political Evolution." In *Contemporary Yugoslavia: Twenty Years of Socialist Experiment,* edited by Wayne S. Vucinich, 119–53. Berkeley and Los Angeles, 1969.

McClelland, James C. *Autocrats and Academics: Education, Culture, and Society in Tsarist Russia.* Chicago, 1979.

———. "Proletarianizing the Student Body: The Soviet Experience during the New Economic Policy." *Past and Present* 80 (August 1978): 122–46.

Machonin, Pavel, ed. *Československá společnost.* Bratislava, 1969.

Maeß, Gerhard. *Mögen viele Lehrmeinungen um die eine Wahrheit ringen.* Rostock, 1994.

Maier, Charles S. *Dissolution: The Crisis of Communism and the End of East Germany.* Princeton, 1997.

Małowist, Marian. "Uwagi do artykułu Piotra Hübnera." *Przegląd Historyczny* 78:3 (1987): 483–90.

Maňák, Jiří. "Početnost a struktura české inteligence v letech 1945–1948." *Sociologický časopis* 4 (1967): 398–409.

———. "Problematika odměnovaní české inteligence v letech 1945–1948. Příspěvek k objasnění nivelizace." *Sociologický časopis* 5 (1967): 529–40.

———. "Sociální aspekty politiky KSČ vůči inteligenci v letech 1947–1953." *Revue dějin socialismu* 5 (1969): 675–706.

Markov, Walter. *Zwiesprache mit dem Jahrhundert.* Cologne, 1990.

Mason, Timothy W. *Nazism, Fascism and the Working Class.* Edited by Jane Caplan. Cambridge, 1995.

Mastny, Vojtech. *The Czechs under Nazi Rule.* New York, 1971.

Mates, Pavel, Petr Průcha, and Jan Svatoš. *Vývoj organizace a řízení česko-slovenských vysokých škol v letech 1918–1983.* Prague, 1984.

Matthews, Mervyn. *Education in the Soviet Union: Policies and Institutions since Stalin.* London, 1982.

Mauersberg, Stanisław. "Nauka i szkolnictwo wyższe w latach 1939–1951." In *Historia nauki polskiej,* edited by Bogdan Suchodolski, 5.1:316–468. Wrocław, 1992.

Mayer, Hans. *Der Turm von Babel: Erinnerung an eine Deutsche Demokratische Republik.* Frankfurt am Main, 1991.

Mazowiecki, Wojciech. *Pierwsze starcie: Wydarzenia 3 maja 1946.* Warsaw, 1998.

Merker, Wolfgang. "Die Deutschen Zentralverwaltungen in der Sowjetischen Besatzungszone Deutschlands 1945–1947." Ph.D. diss., Berlin, 1980.

Merquior, J. G. *Rousseau and Weber: Two Studies in the Theory of Legitimacy.* London, 1980.

Meuschel, Sigrid. *Legitimation und Parteiherrschaft: Zum Paradox von Stabilität und Revolution in der DDR, 1945–1989.* Frankfurt am Main, 1992.

Meyer, Alfred G. "Communist Revolutions and Cultural Change." *Studies in Comparative Communism* 5:4 (1972): 345–70.

Micewski, Andrzej. *Kościół—państwo 1945–1949.* Warsaw, 1995.

Michałowski, Kazimierz. *Wspomnienia.* Warsaw, 1986.

Michnik, Adam. *Z dziejów honoru w Polsce.* Paris, 1985.

Milczarek, W. "Sytuacja zawodowa i pozycja społeczna absolwentów Kursów Przygotowawczych." In Szczepański, *Ze studiów,* 189–223.

Miłosz, Czesław. *The Captive Mind.* Translated by Jane Zielonko. New York, 1990.

———. *Emperor of the Earth: Modes of Eccentric Vision.* Berkeley, 1977.

———. *Native Realm: A Search for Self-Definition.* Berkeley, 1968.

Míšková, Alena. "Německá univerzita za druhé světové války." In Havránek and Pousta, *Dějiny Univerzity Karlovy,* 213–31.

Mittenzwei, Werner. *Das Leben des Bertolt Brecht oder der Umgang mit den Welträtseln.* Vol. 2. Berlin and Weimar, 1988.

Mitter, Armin, and Stefan Wolle. *Untergang auf Raten: Unbekannte Kapitel der DDR-Geschichte.* Munich, 1993.

Mlynář, Zdeněk. *Nightfrost in Prague: The End of Humane Socialism.* Translated by Paul Wilson. New York, 1980.

Mołdawa, Tadeusz. *Ludzie władzy 1944–1991.* Warsaw, 1991.

Mühle, Eduard. *Die "Entsowjetisierung" der russischen Hochschule.* Bonn, 1995.

Mühlen, Patrik von zur. *Der "Eisenberger Kreis." Jugendwiderstand und Verfolgung in der DDR 1953–1958.* Bonn, 1995.

Muller, Jerry Z. *The Other God That Failed: Hans Freyer and the Deradicalization of German Conservatism.* Princeton, 1987.

Müller, Marianne, and Egon Erwin Müller. ". . . stürmt die Festung Wissenschaft!" Die Sowjetisierung der mitteldeutschen Universitäten seit 1945. Berlin, 1953.

Murashko, G. P. "Delo Slanskogo." Voprosy Istorii 3 (1997): 3-20; 4 (1990): 3-18.

Myant, M. R. Socialism and Democracy in Czechoslovakia, 1945-1948. Cambridge, 1981.

Mycielska, Dorota. "Postawy polityczne profesorów wyższych uczelni w dwudziestoleciu międzywojennym." In Inteligencja polska XIX i XX Wieku, edited by Ryszarda Czepulis-Rastenis, 4:293-335. Warsaw, 1985.

Naimark, Norman M. "Politik und Geschichtswissenschaft im osteuropäischen Kontext." In Jarausch, Zwischen Parteilichkeit und Professionalität, 125-38.

———. The Russians in Germany: A History of the Soviet Zone of Occupation, 1945-1949. Cambridge, Mass., 1995.

Nauka i szkolnictwo wyższe w Warszawie. Warsaw, 1987.

Neubert, Ehrhart. Geschichte der Opposition in der DDR 1949-1989. Berlin, 1997.

Neuhäusser-Wespy, Ulrich. "Der Parteiapparat als zentrale Lenkungsinstanz der Geschichtswissenschaft der DDR in den fünfziger und sechziger Jahren." In Sabrow and Walther, Historische Forschung, 145-79.

Niethammer, Lutz, ed. Der gesäuberte Antifaschismus. Die SED und die roten Kapos von Buchenwald. Berlin, 1994.

Nikitin, A. P. "Die sowjetische Militäradministration und die Sowjetisierung des Bildungssystems in Ostdeutschland 1945-1949." Bildung und Erziehung 45:4 (1992): 405-16.

Nikitin, P. I. Zwischen Dogma und gesundem Menschenverstand. Berlin, 1997.

Noskova, A. F. "Moskovskie sovetniki v stranakh Vostochnoi Evropy. 1945-1953 gg." Voprosy Istorii 1 (1998): 104-13.

Novikov, M. M. "Moskovskii Universitet v pervyi period Bolshevitskago rezhima." In Moskovskii Universitet 1755-1930, edited by V. B. Eliashevich, A. A. Kizevetter, and M. M. Novikov, 156-92. Paris, 1930.

Okey, Robin. Eastern Europe, 1740-1980: Feudalism to Communism. Minneapolis, 1982.

Olczak, M. "Skład społeczny i wyniki nauki uczestników Kursów w okresie ich pobytu na Kursach Przygotowawczych." In Szczepański, Ze studiów, 122-59.

Olshausen, Klaus. Zwischenspiel auf dem Balkan. Die deutsche Politik gegenüber Jugoslawien und Griechenland von März bis Juli 1941. Stuttgart, 1973.

Olszewski, Eugeniusz, ed. Politechnika Warszawska 1915-1965. Warsaw, 1965.

Opałek, Kazimierz. "Kierunek psychologiczny w teorii prawa. Jerzy Lande (1886-1954)." In Studia z dziejów wydziału prawa Uniwersytetu Jagiellońskiego, edited by Michał Patkaniowski, 117-26. Kraków, 1964.

Osa, Maryjane. "Resistance, Persistence, and Change: The Transformation of the Catholic Church in Poland." Eastern European Politics and Societies 3:2 (Spring 1989): 268-99.

Paczkowski, Andrzej. Pół wieku dziejów Polski 1939-1989. Warsaw, 1998.

———. "Protokół rozbieżności w sprawie wesołego baraku." Gazeta Wyborcza 17-18 (October 1998): 26-27.

Paczkowski, Andrzej, and Jakub Karpiński. "Czy PRL byla państwem polskim." Mowią Wieki 10-11 (1994): 64-69.

Pasák, Tomáš. Soupis legálních novin, časopisů a úředních věstníků v českých zemích 1939-1945. Prague, 1980.

Pätzold, Horst. *Nischen im Gras. Ein Leben in zwei Diktaturen.* Hamburg, 1997.

Pęcherski, Mieczysław. "Das Schulwesen in Volkspolen." In *Das Schulwesen sozialistischer Länder in Europa,* edited by Deutsches Pädagogisches Zentralinstitut, 285–369. Berlin, 1962.

Pelikán, Jiří. *Ein Frühling, der nie zu Ende geht. Erinnerungen eines Prager Kommunisten.* Frankfurt am Main, 1976.

Perkowska, Urszula. *Kształtowanie się zespołu naukowego w Uniwersytecie Jagiellońskim. 1860–1920.* Wrocław, 1975.

Pernes, Jiří. "Dělnické demonstrace v Brně v roce 1951." *Soudobé dějiny* 1 (1996): 23–41.

Personal- und Vorlesungsverzeichnis, Universität Leipzig, SS 1945; WS 1947–48; Herbstsemester 1953–54.

Personal- und Vorlesungsverzeichnis, Universität Rostock, SS 1945; WS 1947–48; Herbstsemester 1953–54.

Péteri, György. *Academia and State Socialism: Essays on the Political History of Academic Life in Post-1945 Hungary and Eastern Europe.* New York, 1998.

Petráň, Josef. "Filozofická fakulta." In Havránek and Pousta, *Dějiny Univerzity Karlovy,* 431–72.

"Die Philosophie in der Sowjetzone." *Der Monat* 2:21 (1950): 250–57.

Picker, Henry. *Hitlers Tischgespräche im Führerhauptquartier.* Stuttgart, 1976.

Pike, David. *The Politics of Culture in Soviet-Occupied Germany, 1945–1949.* Stanford, Calif., 1992.

Pilch, Andrzej. *Studencki ruch polityczny w Polsce w latach 1932–1939.* Warsaw and Kraków, 1972.

Podgórecki, Adam. *Polish Society.* Westport, Conn., 1994.

———. *A Story of a Polish Thinker.* Cologne, 1986.

Podoski, Jan. *Zbyt ciekawe czasy.* Warsaw, 1991.

Podradisz, Jan. "Bemühungen der Familien verhafteter Professoren um ihre Befreiung." In Buszko and Paczyńska, *Universities,* 223–28.

Polišenský, Josef. "Filozofická fakulta UK na jaře památného roku 1945." *Zprávy archivu Univerzity Karlovy* 7 (1985): 30–34.

Polski słownik biograficzny. Kraków, 1935–.

Poppe, Ulrike, Rainer Eckert, and Ilko-Sascha Kowalczuk. *Zwischen Selbstbehauptung und Anpassung: Formen des Widerstandes und der Opposition in der DDR.* Berlin, 1995.

Port, Andrew. "When Workers Rumbled: The Wismut Upheaval of August 1951 in East Germany." *Social History* 22:2 (1997): 145–73.

Pousta, Zdeněk. "Právnická fakulta." In Havránek and Pousta, *Dějiny Univerzity Karlovy,* 369–88.

———. "Smuteční pochod za demokracii." In *Stránkami soudobých dějin. Sborník statií k pětašedesátinám historika Karla Kaplana,* edited by Karel Jech, 198–207. Prague, 1993.

———. "Univerzita Karlova v letech 1947–1953." In Havránek and Pousta, *Dějiny Univerzity Karlovy,* 263–306.

Praszałowicz, Dorota. "Inteligencja polska." In *Zbiorowy portret Polaków,* edited by Grzegorz Babiński and Tadeusz Paleczny, 117–38. Kraków, 1997.

Procházka, Adolf. "The Brno School of Jurisprudence." In *The Czechoslovak*

Contribution to World Culture, edited by Miloslav Rechcigl, 405–13. The Hague, 1964.

Protocol of meeting with former Soviet cultural officers, organized by Prof. Manfred Heinemann, Hannover, September 1992 in Gosen bei Berlin. Unpublished manuscript.

Rabehl, Bernd. *Am Ende der Utopie: Die politische Geschichte der Freien Universität Berlin.* Berlin, 1988.

Raina, Peter, ed. *Kościół w PRL: Kościół katolicki a państwo w świetle dokumentów.* Vol. 1. Poznań, 1994.

Reich, Jens. *Abschied von den Lebenslügen. Die Intelligenz und die Macht.* Berlin, 1992.

Rektor der FSU, ed. *Vergangenheitserklärung an der FSU Jena: Beiträge zur Tagung "Unrecht und Aufarbeitung" am 19. und 20.6.1992.* Leipzig, 1994.

Rhode, Gotthold. "The Protectorate of Bohemia and Moravia, 1939–1945." In *A History of the Czechoslovak Republic, 1918–1948,* edited by Victor S. Mamatey and Radomir Luža, 296–322. Princeton, 1973.

Richert, Ernst. *"Sozialistische Universität": Die Hochschulpolitik der SED.* Berlin, 1967.

Ringer, Fritz K. *The Decline of the German Mandarins: The German Academic Community, 1890–1933.* Hanover, N.H., and London, 1990.

———. *Fields of Knowledge: French Academic Culture in Comparative Perspective, 1890–1920.* Cambridge, 1992.

Rocznik statystyczny 1949. Warsaw, 1950.

Rocznik statystyczny 1950. Warsaw, 1951.

Rocznik statystyczny 1958. Warsaw, 1958.

Rocznik statystyczny 1959. Warsaw, 1959.

Rocznik statystyczny 1960. Warsaw, 1960.

Rocznik statystyczny 1970. Warsaw, 1970.

Rothschild, Joseph. *East Central Europe between the Two World Wars.* Seattle, 1974.

———. *Return to Diversity: A Political History of East Central Europe since World War II.* 3rd ed. New York, 2000.

Rühle, Otto. *Idee und Gestalt der deutschen Universität. Tradition und Aufgabe.* Berlin, 1966.

Rupieper, Hermann-Josef. "Wiederaufbau und Umstrukturierung der Universität 1945–1949." In *Martin-Luther-Universität. Von der Gründung bis zur Neugestaltung nach zwei Diktaturen,* edited by Gunnar Berg and Hans-Hermann Hartwich, 97–116. Opladen, 1994.

Rupnik, Jacques. "Intelektuálové a moc v Československu." *Soudobé dějiny* 1:4–5 (1994): 540–50.

———. *The Other Europe: The Rise and Fall of Communism in East-Central Europe.* New York, 1989.

———. "Promeškané setkání: Rok 1956 v pohledu z Prahy." *Soudobé dějiny* 3:4 (1996): 535–39.

Ryszka, Franciszek. *Pamiętnik inteligenta.* Vol. 2. Łódź, 1996.

Sabrow, Martin, and Peter Th. Walter, eds. *Historische Forschung und sozialistische Diktatur. Beiträge zur Geschichtswissenschaft der DDR.* Leipzig, 1995.

Schaff, Adam. *Moje spotkania z nauką polską.* Warsaw, 1997.

————. *Pora na spowiedź.* Warsaw, 1993.

Schmidt, Siegfried, ed. *Alma Mater Jenensis: Geschichte der Universität Jena.* Weimar, 1983.

Schmutzler, Georg-Siegfried. *Gegen den Strom: Erlebtes aus Leipzig unter Hitler und der Stasi.* Göttingen, 1992.

Schneider, Michael C. *Bildung für neue Eliten. Die Gründung der Arbeiter- und Bauernfakultäten in der SBZ/DDR.* Dresden, 1998.

Schöpflin, George. *Politics in Eastern Europe, 1945–1992.* Oxford, 1993.

Schulte, Volker. "Der Fall Natonek—ein Fall der SED." *Universität Leipzig* 4 (June–July 1992): 5–7.

Seton-Watson, Hugh. *The East European Revolution.* New York, 1966.

————. *Eastern Europe between the Wars, 1918–1941.* Hamden, Conn., 1962.

Seznam osob a ústavů university Karlovy v Praze jakož i státních zkušebních komisí 1948. Prague, 1948.

Seznam přednášek na filologické fakultě v studijním roce 1953–54. Prague, 1953.

Shavit, Yossi, and Hans-Peter Blossfeld. *Persistent Inequality: Changing Educational Attainment in Thirteen Countries.* Boulder, Colo., 1993.

Shumilin, I. N. *Soviet Higher Education.* Munich, 1962.

Sieber, Malte, and Ronald Freytag. *Kinder des Systems. DDR-Studenten vor, im und nach dem Herbst '89.* Berlin, 1993.

Simons, Thomas W. *Eastern Europe in the Postwar World.* New York, 1991.

Skład Uniwersytetu Jagiellońskiego w Krakówie. Rok akademicki 1948/49. Kraków, 1948.

Skład Uniwersytetu na rok akademicki 1947–48. Warsaw, 1947.

Skład Uniwersytetu na rok akademicki 1955–56. Warsaw, 1956.

Sládek, Zdeněk. "Vliv nacistické nadvlády na politický vývoj v Čechách a na Moravě." *Soudobé dějiny* 1:4–5 (1994): 532–35.

Słabek, Henryk. *Intelektualistów obraz własny 1944–1989.* Warsaw, 1997.

Sławińska, Irena. *Szlakami moich wód.* Lublin, 1998.

Słownik historyków polskich. Warsaw, 1994.

Somr, Miroslav, et al. *Dějiny školství a pedagogiky.* Prague, 1987.

Sovětizace východní evropy. Země střední a jihovýchodní evropy v letech 1944–1948. Prague, 1995.

Spis wykładów na rok akademicki 1953–54. Kraków, 1953.

Spis wykładów na rok akademicki 1953–54. Poznań, 1953.

Spodenkiewicz, Paweł. "Nowe widnokręgi." In *Bunty i służebności uczonego. Profesor Józef Chałasiński,* 22–37. Łódź, 1992.

Spór o PRL. Kraków, 1996.

Śródka, Andrzej. *Uczeni polscy.* Vol. 2. Warsaw, 1995.

Śródka, Andrzej, and Paweł Szczawiński. *Biogramy uczonych polskich.* Part 1, vols. 1–3. Warsaw, 1983–85.

Stallmann, Herbert. *Hochschulzugang in der SBZ/DDR 1945–1959.* St. Augustin, 1980.

Staritz, Dietrich. "Partei, Intellektuelle, Parteiintellektuelle: Die Intellektuellen im Kalkül der frühen SED." In *Sozialismus und Kommunismus im Wandel, Hermann Weber zum 65. Geburtstag,* edited by Klaus Schönhoven and Dietrich Staritz, 378–98. Cologne, 1993.

Statistická ročenka Československé Socialistické Republiky 1960. Prague, 1960.

Statistická ročenka Československé Socialistické Republiky 1962. Prague, 1962.

Statistická ročenka Republiky Československé 1957. Prague, 1957.

Statistisches Jahrbuch der Deutschen Demokratischen Republik 1955. Berlin, 1956.

Statistisches Jahrbuch der Deutschen Demokratischen Republik 1960–61. Berlin, 1961.

Statistisches Jahrbuch der Deutschen Demokratischen Republik 1970. Berlin, 1970.

Statistisches Jahrbuch für das Deutsche Reich 1935. Berlin, 1935.

Steinhaus, Hugo. *Wspomnienia i zapiski.* London, 1992.

Stobiecki, Rafał. *Historia pod nadzorem: Spory o nowy model historii w Polsce.* Łódź, 1993.

Stokes, Gale. *From Stalinism to Pluralism: A Documentary History of Eastern Europe since 1945.* New York and Oxford, 1991.

Stratonov, V. "Poteria Moskovskim Universitetom svobody." In *Moskovskii Universitet 1755–1930,* edited by V. B. Eliashevich, A. A. Kizevetter, and M. M. Novikov, 193–244. Paris, 1930.

Strzembosz, Tomasz. "Z historii najnowszej." *Arca* 48 (1993): 61–63.

Stykalin, A. S. "Ideologicheskaia i kul'turnaia ekspansiia stalinizma v Vengrii." *Slavianovedenie* 6 (1992): 15–26.

———. "Nauchnaia intelligentsiia stran Tsentral'noi i Iugo-Vostochnoi Evropy i ee otnoshenie k SSSR i sovetskoi nauke." In *Intelligentsiia v usloviiakh obshchestvennoi nestabil'nosti,* edited by A. I. Studenikin, 92–104. Moscow, 1996.

———. "Politika SSSR po formirovaniiu obshchestvennogo mneniia v stranakh Tsentral'noi Evropy i nastroeniia intelligentsii." *Slavianovedenie* 3 (1997): 50–62.

———. "Propaganda SSSR na zarubezhnuiu auditoriiu i obshchestvennoe mnenie stran zapada v pervye poslevoennye gody." *Vestnik Mosk. Un-ta,* ser. 10 (Zhurnalistika) 1 (1997): 57–70.

Suleja, Teresa. *Uniwersytet Wrocławski w okresie centralizmu stalinowskiego 1950–1955.* Wrocław, 1995.

Suny, Ronald G., and Lewis H. Siegelbaum, eds. *Making Workers Soviet: Power, Class, and Identity.* Ithaca, N.Y., 1994.

Svobodný, Petr. "Lékařské fakulty." In Havránek and Pousta, *Dějiny Univerzity Karlovy,* 389–418.

Szarota, Tomasz. "Upowszechnienie kultury." In *Polska Ludowa 1944–1950. Przemiany społeczne,* edited by Franciszek Ryszka, 408–70. Wrocław, 1974.

Szczepański, Jan, ed. *Ze studiów nad kursami przygotowawczymi.* Wrocław, 1962.

Taborsky, Edward. *Communism in Czechoslovakia, 1948–60.* Princeton, 1961.

Tatarkiewicz, Władysław. "Roman Ingarden 1893–1970." In *Portrety uczonych polskich,* edited by Andrzej Biernacki, 204–6. Kraków, 1974.

Tent, James F. *The Free University of Berlin: A Political History.* Bloomington, Ind., 1988.

Tismaneanu, Vladimir. *Reinventing Politics: Eastern Europe from Stalin to Havel.* New York, 1992.

Tomaszewski, Jerzy. *The Socialist Regimes of East Central Europe: Their Establishment and Consolidation, 1944–67.* Translated by Jolanta Krauze. London and New York, 1989.

Tomczak, Andrzej, ed. *Uniwersytet Mikołaja Kopernika. Wspomnienia pracowników.* Toruń, 1995.

Topolski, Jerzy. "Polish Historians and Marxism after World War II." *Studies in Soviet Thought* 43 (1992): 169–83.

Torańska, Teresa. *Oni.* London, 1985.

Torpey, John C. *Intellectuals, Socialism, and Dissent: The East German Opposition and Its Legacy.* Minneapolis, 1995.

Trznadel, Jacek. *Hańba domowa: rozmowy z pisarzami.* Lublin, 1990.

———. "An Interview with Zbigniew Herbert." *Partisan Review* 54:4 (1987): 557–75.

Tucker, Robert C. "Culture, Political Culture, and Communist Society." *Political Science Quarterly* 88:2 (1973): 173–90.

Tyrowicz, Marian. *W poszukiwaniu siebie: wspomnienia i refleksje.* Vol. 2. Lublin, 1988.

Uniwersytet Mikołaja Kopernika 1945–1955. Warsaw, 1957.

Uniwersytet Wrocławski imienia Bolesława Bieruta. *Skład osobowy wdłg. stanu z dnia 1 sierpnia 1955 roku.* Wrocław, 1955.

Urban, Jan, and Zdeněk Hojda. "Velký historik ztracené generace." *Dějiny a současnost* 15:4 (1993): 41–46.

Urban, Rudolf. *Die Organisation der Wissenschaft in der Tschechoslowakei.* Marburg, 1958.

Usko, Marianne. *Hochschulen in der DDR.* Berlin, 1974.

Valkenier, Elizabeth Kridl. "Stalinizing Polish Historiography: What Soviet Archives Disclose." *East European Politics and Societies* 7:1 (Winter 1993): 109–34.

Varíková, Marta, ed. *Košický vládny program.* Bratislava, 1978.

Verband Ehemaliger Rostocker Studenten. *Namen und Schicksale der von 1945 bis 1962 in der SBZ/DDR verhafteten und verschleppten Professoren und Studenten.* Rostock, 1994.

Vogel, Barbara. "Anpassung und Widerstand: Das Verhältnis Hamburger Hochschullehrer zum Staat 1919 bis 1945." In Krause et al., *Hochschulalltag im "Dritten Reich": Die Hamburger Universität 1933–1945,* part 1, 3–84.

Vollnhals, Clemens, ed. *Entnazifizierung: Politische Säuberung und Rehabilitierung in den vier Besatzungszonen 1945–1949.* Munich, 1991.

Vývoj společnosti ČSSR v číslech. Prague, 1965.

Walczak, Jan. *Ruch studencki w Polsce 1944–1984.* Wrocław, 1990.

Walczak, Marian. *Szkolnictwo wyższe i nauka polska w latach wojny i okupacji 1939–1945.* Wrocław, 1978.

Walicki, Andrzej. *Spotkania z Miłoszem.* London, 1985.

Wandycz, Piotr. "The Poles in the Habsburg Monarchy." *Austrian History Yearbook* 3:2 (1967): 261–86.

———. *The Price of Freedom: A History of East Central Europe from the Middle Ages to the Present.* London and New York, 1993.

Wartenberg, Günther. "Die Wiedereröffnung der Universität Leipzig am 5. Februar 1946." *Universität Leipzig* 2 (1996): 9–12.

Weitz, Eric D. *Creating German Communism, 1890–1990: From Popular Protests to Socialist State.* Princeton, 1997.

Welsh, Helga A. "Deutsche Zentralverwaltung für Volksbildung. DVV." In Broszat and Weber, *SBZ-Handbuch,* 229–38.

———. "Entnazifizierung und Wiedereröffnung der Universität Leipzig 1945–

1946. Ein Bericht des damaligen Rektors Professor Bernhard Schweitzer." *Vierteljahrshefte für Zeitgeschichte* 33 (1987): 339–72.

———. *Revolutionärer Wandel auf Befehl? Entnazifizierungs- und Personalpolitik in Thüringen und Sachsen. 1945–1948.* Munich, 1989.

Werblan, Andrzej. *Stalinizm w Polsce.* Warsaw, 1991.

———. *Władysław Gomułka. Sekretarz Generalny PPR.* Warsaw, 1988.

Wichterle, Otto. *Vzpomínky.* Prague, 1992.

Wielcy filozofowie polscy, sześć studiów. Warsaw, 1997.

Wójcik, Z. "Przebieg studiów absolwentów Kursów Przygotowawczych w wyższych uczelniach." In Szczepański, *Ze studiów,* 160–88.

Wolenski, Jan. "Philosophy inside Communism: The Case of Poland." *Studies in Soviet Thought* 43 (1992): 93–100.

Wolff, Robert. *The Balkans in Our Time.* Cambridge, Mass., 1956.

Wyka, Kazimierz. *Życie na niby.* Warsaw, 1957.

Zahorski, Andrzej. "Środowisko historyków warszawskich w Polsce Ludowej." In *Nauka i szkolnictwo wyższe w Warszawie,* 168–81.

Zank, Wolfgang, and Helga Welsh. "Zentralverwaltungen: Einleitung." In Broszat and Weber, *SBZ-Handbuch,* 201–7.

Zaręba, Maria, and Alfred Zaręba, eds. *Ne Cedat Academia. Kartki z dziejów tajnego nauczania w Uniwersytecie Jagiellońskim 1939–1945.* Kraków, 1975.

Żarnowski, Janusz. "Społeczeństwo polskie." In *Historia Nauki Polskiej,* edited by Bogdan Suchodolski, 5.1:11–35. Wrocław, 1992.

———. *Struktura społeczna inteligencji w Polsce w latach 1918–1939.* Warsaw, 1964.

Z dziejów podziemnego Uniwersytetu Warszawskiego. Warsaw, 1961.

Zehm, Günter. "Repression und Widerstand an der Universität Jena 1949–1989." *Bildung und Erziehung* 45:4 (1992): 453–66.

Zilynská, Blanka. "Poválečná obnova a zápas o charakter univerzity." In Havránek and Pousta, *Dějiny Univerzity Karlovy,* 235–61.

Ziółek, Jan. "The Imprisonment of the Professors of the Catholic University of Lublin." In Buszko and Paczyńska, *Universities,* 247–49.

Zwerenz, Gerhard. *Der Widerspruch. Autobiografischer Bericht.* Berlin, 1991.

Żyndul, Jolanta. *Zajścia antyżydowskie w Polsce w latach 1935–1937.* Warsaw, 1994.

INTERVIEWS

All interviews were conducted by the author.

Juliusz Bardach, May 1998

Karol Maria Bartel, November 1991

Celina Bobińska, July 1992

Čestmír Císař, July 1993

Miloslav Doležal, November 1991

Koloman Gajan, September 1991

Józef Gierowski, October 1998

Stanisław Grodziski, November 1998

Stanisław Grzybowski, October 1998

Jan Havránek, July 1993, July 1996

Artur Hutnikiewicz, November 1998 (by telephone)

Eva Jonas, May 1993

František Kavka, September 1991

Krystyna Kersten, November 1998

Stefan Kieniewicz, June 1986

Fritz Klein, September 1996

Jerzy Kłoczowski, November 1998

Antonina Kłoskowska, May 1998

Jiří Kotášek, July 1996

Tadeusz Kowalik, February 1996

Jürgen Kuczynski, September 1996

Pavel Machonin, July 1996

Antoni Mączak, November 1998

Karel Malý, August 1993

Henryk Markiewicz, October 1998

Jiří Navrátil, July 1993
Kazimierz Opałek, November 1998
Horst Pätzold, July 1990
Jiří Pelikán, October 1991
Antoni Podraza, June 1986
Josef Polišenský, September 1991,
    November 1998
Gerhard Roger, July 1989
Robert Rompe, March 1991
Adam Schaff, June 1992
Johannes Schmidt, June 1991

Irena Sławińska, November 1998
Stanisław Stomma, November 1998
H. J. Vormelker, July 1990
Paul Wandel, October 1990
Andrzej Werblan, May 1992
Henryk Wereszycki, June 1986
Józef Wolski, October 1998
Jerzy Wyrozumski, October 1998
Bogdan Zakrzewski, November 1998
    (by telephone)
Marian Zgórniak, October 1998

OFFICIAL COLLECTIONS OF LAWS, STATUTES, ORDINANCES, ETC.
Dziennik Ustaw Polskiej Rzeczypospolitej Ludowej
Gesetzblatt der Deutschen Demokratischen Republik
Sbírka zákonů a nařízení republiky Československé

NEWSPAPERS AND JOURNALS
Czech
  Čin
  Dnešek
  Lidová demokracie
  Lidové noviny
  Mladá fronta
  Národní osvobození
  Obzory
  Práce
  Předvoj
  Revue dějin socialismu
  Rovnost
  Ruch filozofický
  Rudé právo
  Slovo národa
  Student
  Studentské noviny
  Studentské slovo
  Svobodné noviny
  Svobodné slovo
  Tvorba

German
  colloquium
  Forum
  Frankfurter Allgemeine Zeitung
  Neue Zürcher Zeitung
  Neues Deutschland
  Tagesspiegel

Polish
  Arca
  Głos Ludu
  Głos Pracy
  Kuźnica
  Kwartalnik Historyczny
  Myśl Filozoficzna
  Naprzód
  Odrodzenie
  Robotnik
  Słowo Powszechne
  Statystyka Szkolnictwa
  Trybuna Ludu
  Tygodnik Powszechny
  Zeszyty Towarzystwa Popierania i Krzewienia Nauk
  Życie Nauki

Soviet
  Voprosy filosofii

U.S.
  New York Times